Stanley Sadie's

Brief Guide to Music

Stanley Sadie's

Brief Guide to Music

edited by Stanley Sadie
with Alison Latham

Third Edition

Prentice Hall
Upper Saddle River, NJ 07458

1993 North and South American editions
published by Prentice Hall, Inc.
Upper Saddle River, NJ 07458

10 9 8 7 6 5 4 3 2

A shorter edition of
Stanley Sadie's Music Guide (1986)

ISBN 0-13 086851 5 (without cassette)
ISBN 0-13 086869 8 (with cassette)

This book was designed and produced by
CALMANN AND KING LTD, LONDON

Cover: Joseph Marius Avy, *The White Ball* (detail), 1903
Oil on canvas, 4ft 7ins × 7ft 2ins (1.39 × 2.19m).
Giraudon/Bridgeman Art Library

Frontispiece: Leonard Bernstein conducting.
Archive photos, New York.

Designed by Bridgewater Design
Printed in Spain

Abbreviations in music examples:
bn., bassoon; cl., clarinet; cont., basso continuo;
db., double bass; fl., flute; hn., horn; m. (mm.) measure(s);
ob., oboe; orch., orchestra; pf., pianoforte;
str., strings; tpt., trumpet; trbn., trombone; va., viola;
vc., cello; vn., violin; ww., woodwind.

In the Listening Guides and lists of works, capital letters
denote major keys, lower-case ones minor keys.
Square-bracketed times in the Listening Guides signify
timings in repeated sections.

Contents

Part V The Classical Era

Part VI The Romantic Era

Part VII   The Turn of the Century

Part VIII   The Modern Age

Part IX Popular Music Traditions

Preface

The principal aim of this book, a much-revised shortened version of the original *Music Guide*, remains to enhance people's pleasure and understanding in listening to music. Although it is designed for those with little experience or musical knowledge, I hope that its mixture of musical description and background information may also prove attractive and helpful to the general music-lover. This new edition sees a number of modifications, particularly towards the simplification of the discussion of the technical aspects of music and in a presentation of the historical material in a way that focuses more sharply on the works treated in detail.

The approach here to the repertory of music is perhaps slightly different from those commonly found in introductory books. Description and elucidation remain the first considerations; but some emphasis is also placed on history and context. I do not find myself especially sympathetic to a philosophy in which every work of art is regarded as an independent entity that can profitably be discussed simply for what it is: "what it is" – and thus the understanding of it – depends on when it was created, how people were thinking at the time, and the purpose for which it was created, as well as the techniques used in its creation.

The book begins with a section on the "elements" of music, treating pitch, rhythm, harmony, key, etc, chiefly for the benefit of those not familiar or not fully familiar with them. It is designed to equip the reader for what is to come, introducing concepts one at a time and assuming no prior knowledge. This section, which also deals with the structure of music, is followed by one on musical instruments.

The main part of the book, sections III to VIII, discusses the music of six different eras in Western culture, from the Middle Ages to the present day, in chronological order. The first and last of these incorporate material originally supplied by Judith Nagley and Paul Griffiths. In the introductions to these sections, I have attempted to draw attention to features of contemporary social, cultural, and political history that bear on the music discussed, and to outline the new stylistic weapons that composers forged to enable them to rise to the challenges of a changing world. The aim is to give the reader a sense of music as a part of the fabric of life, as something that changes as the world does, and so to heighten his or her understanding of it through this broader human context. The changes in content and emphasis that we have made for this revised edition are indicative of the way that, as time has moved on, perspectives have shifted: we have increased the coverage of music composed by women across the ages, and have made new choices of several twentieth-century items in particular in the light of changing taste and recent developments.

In line with this general approach, we have laid more stress on biography than is usual in introductory books. Without biographical discussion it is rarely possible to explain the purpose for which a piece of music was composed, on which its structure may acutely depend. Except in the earliest historical section, where the material scarcely exists, and the latest, where the familiarity of the modern world renders it progressively less necessary, biographical information is included for important composers; we also give, in tabular form, summary lists of works. I believe that biography can be inherently interesting, can cast light on the society to which a composer belongs, and that, taken with the music itself, it may serve to stimulate the reader's interest and increase his or her involvement. I hope that the enthusiasm and the love of music that I and my co-authors feel, and have made no special effort to hide, may also infect the reader.

Many people come to music first of all through popular music. Parts of our final section, IX, originally contributed by Alyn Shipton, have been revised or, in the case of the material on rock, written afresh in expanded form for this edition by Andrew Clements. The objective remains: the tradition of popular music is treated in a similar way to that pursued in the other, historical chapters. I hope that this chapter may provide a valuable way into music for students and others more familiar with popular music than with other kinds.

The absence of any substantial discussion of non-Western music ought not to be regarded as a symptom of ethnocentricity. The Western musical tradition (with its relatively recent African-American infusion, as treated in Part IX) is quite big enough, rich enough, and complex enough to be the subject of an entire volume. There are other, non-Western traditions of richness and complexity, too, and to treat them cursorily or perfunctorily would be patronizing.

A set of seven compact discs is available as a listening companion. For students, a single cassette or a three-cassette set of a selection from the featured music is also available. Details of the music are listed on the Contents pages. The recorded items are described in the Listening Guides, printed at appropriate points, with Listening Outlines through which the music may be followed in some detail. These Outlines follow no fixed scheme, since different music needs to be listened to in different ways, though they all follow the same principles, with timings and descriptions of the main events in each piece. The Guides and Outlines have been redesigned to make them easier to use. The Outlines are designed to be read, with help and guidance from an instructor where appropriate, while the music is being heard. Suggestions for further listening, based on representative works, are offered on pp. 427–8.

It is never possible in the discussion of music to avoid technical vocabulary. Much of this is explained as it is introduced, but all of it is covered in the Glossary (pp. 432–40). There is also a general index, principally of names.

Lastly, I should like to acknowledge the collaboration, at every stage in the preparation of the book, of my close colleague and helper Alison Latham, who, as well as working on the main text, prepared the tabular matter and the Glossary; I am grateful, too, to the panel of advisers to Prentice Hall Inc, whose various suggestions have done much to make this edition easier to use.

Stanley Sadie

Part I The Elements

1 *Introduction*

In every society, in every period of history, men and women have made music. They have sung it and danced to it. They have used it in solemn rituals and in light-hearted entertainments. They have listened to it in fields and forests, in temples, in bars, in concert halls and opera houses. They have made it not only with their voices but by adapting natural objects and banging them, scraping them, and blowing through them. They have used it to generate collective emotion – to excite, to calm, to inspire action, to draw tears. Music is not a fringe activity or a luxury one. It is a central and necessary part of human existence.

Every culture has found a musical style, and a means of expressing it, that arise from its needs, its history, and its environment. In Black Africa, for example, where there has been a crucial need for quick communication over large distances, the musical culture is more closely concerned with drums and drumming than any other culture in the world. The "gong-chime culture" of Indonesia (the most important instruments are in effect sets of gongs) owes its existence to the fact that the region found its musical character during the late Bronze Age. The ancient courtly cultures of the East – such countries as China and Japan, India and Vietnam

1 Opposite *Map of Europe showing the principal centers of musical importance.*

2 *Blind harpist: scene in sunk relief from the offering chapel of the tomb of Paatenemheb, originally from Saqqara (Egypt), c1340–1320 BC. Rijksmuseum van Oudheden, Leiden.*

– developed musical traditions of high elaboration and refinement; the rural populations used much simpler music.

In the West (Europe and America), the chief concern of this book, musical traditions arose mainly from chant used in the early church, from the sophisticated art forms developed at the courts of kings and nobles, from the needs of the wider audiences that industrialization created, and from the technologies of the electronic age. The rural population, and in more recent times the urban industrial one, has developed a more popular tradition of its own (see **Part IX**).

What, then, *is* music? It has been defined as "organized sound". A musical tone is the product of regular vibration, and is perceived when an inner part of the listener's ear is made to vibrate in sympathy. A noise, by contrast, is the product of *irregular* vibration. Of the banging, scraping, and blowing we mentioned above, the first may produce music or noise, according to the object banged and the ways in which it vibrates. Normally, scraping or striking a taut string, or causing a column of air to vibrate, will produce a musical tone. Any musical composition, or piece of music, will be made up of a large number of musical tones, intended to be heard in a carefully ordered pattern.

There are three basic systems of ordering: *rhythm*, which governs the movement of music in time; *melody*, which means the linear arrangement of tones; and *harmony*, which deals with the simultaneous sounding of different tones. There are other important elements, too, including *texture* (about the strands that go to make up the sound of a piece and their arrangement) and *structure* (the design of the time-plan of a piece). We shall discuss these in turn; to supplement and clarify this discussion there are boxes to explain how music is notated.

2 *Rhythm*

The most basic element in music is *rhythm*. Some musical systems, in fact, in culture areas where drumming is important, use rhythm alone. While painting and architecture exist in space, music exists in time. Our perception of time in traditional music of the kind we are discussing in this book is dependent on two factors. First, music needs a regular pulse (for which there are models in nature and everyday life, like a person's heartbeat, breathing, or walking, or the ticking of a clock). Secondly, we can perceive rhythmic groupings where there are regular stresses or accents.

PULSE, TEMPO

The most usual way for a composer to show rhythmic structure in music – that is, the timing of the notes – is indicating the *pulse*: this is done with a conventional word (see p. 18), to suggest the speed or tempo (Italian terms are chiefly used, as Italian composers dominated European music when tempo marks came into use).

A composer may be more precise and state exactly how many beats are required per minute, using a metronome marking (a metronome is a clockwork pendulum, calibrated so that it can be set at different speeds). Then the composer will indicate how the beats are to be grouped, normally in twos, threes, or fours:

ONE two ONE two ONE two ONE two . . .
ONE two three ONE two three ONE two three . . .
ONE two THREE four ONE two THREE four ONE two THREE . . .

(Capital letters denote the accented beats; in groups of four, a secondary, lighter accent falls on the third beat.)

METER

Counting in this manner shows the *meter* of a piece of music – that is, the beats and their groupings. The rhythms are heard with the meter as an understood background. In some kinds of music, for example music for dancing, communal singing, or above all in pop music, the meter or beat will tend to be strongly emphasized. Marches provide a good example of a meter in twos, or duple. Familiar instances of duple meter are *She'll be comin' round the mountain* and *Greensleeves* (this is an example of compound duple meter; see below). Waltzes are always in triple meter; so is *The Star-Spangled Banner*. In quadruple meter are *O come, all ye faithful* and *Way down upon the Swanee river*. (It is worth trying to hum through some of these, thinking about the meter and the accents. Try other songs you know, too, to increase your awareness of meter.) Some music is without meter at all: early church chant is often performed without meter, taking its rhythm from the words (see **Listening Guide 2**), and there are types of non-Western and experimental Western music that have no meter.

The notation of rhythm

If the pitch of a note is the "vertical" element when we look at musical notation, then the horizontal element is rhythm. The height of a note on the staff shows its pitch (see p. 19). Its placing in horizontal distance along the staff – reading from left to right, as one reads words in Western languages – shows when it is to be sounded.

In modern rhythmic notation, the shape of a note, its color (whether it is hollow or solid), and the stem attached to it (and the flags attached to the stem) signify its duration. Nowadays the longest note in normal use is the "whole-note". Below are shown the standard note values. Musical notation has to provide not only for notes but also for silences of exact length: so there exists a system of *rests*, equivalent in length to each of the note values.

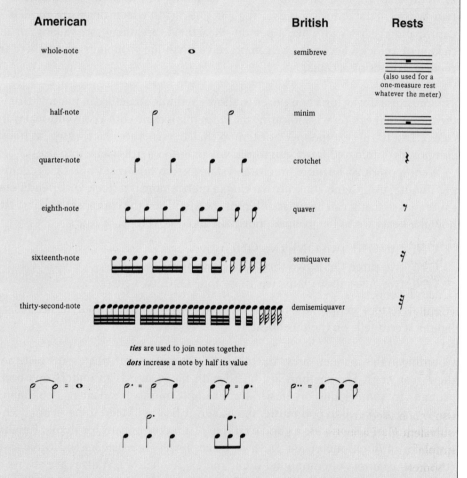

American		British	Rests
whole-note		semibreve	(also used for a one-measure rest whatever the meter)
half-note		minim	
quarter-note		crotchet	
eighth-note		quaver	
sixteenth-note		semiquaver	
thirty-second-note		demisemiquaver	

ties are used to join notes together

dots increase a note by half its value

The American note names work on a mathematical basis of proportional lengths (as do the German): the British (like most other European) preserve something of the original Latin names.

Eighth-notes and shorter ones may be written with "beams" (as shown on the left) to improve legibility and to indicate metrical groupings; the grouping with beams may be shorter (as shown just right of center) as long as it conforms to the metrical divisions, or the notes may be shown separated (as on the right). Note the "flags": none on a quarter-note, one on an eighth, two on a sixteenth, and so on.

The notation of meter

Regular meter is conveyed in notation by means of a *time signature* or *meter signature*. This, consisting of one number above another, is placed at the beginning of each piece to tell the performer how the beats are grouped and what the duration of each of them is. The lower number indicates the unit: 4 (the most common) represents a quarter-note, 2 a half-note, 8 an eighth-note. The upper number shows how many of this unit are in each *measure* or *bar*; the measures are ruled off by vertical bar-lines. The first note of each measure has a natural metrical accent.

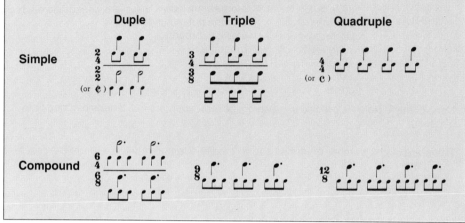

The length of a tone is a feature that has to be conveyed by notation (see p. 16). Musical notation also has to allow for silence, or *rests*, to be of a specified length.

Regular meter is conveyed in notation by means of a *time signature* or *meter signature* (see above). The most common time signature is 4/4 (often indicated by a C, a relic of early systems, sometimes taken to stand for "common time"): some typical groupings of note values in measures of 4/4 are shown in **ex. 1**.

ex. 1

Also much used among duple and quadruple signatures are 2/4 and 2/2 (or its equivalent ₵). Easily the most common triple-time signature is 3/4. All these are "simple" time signatures, meaning that their unit beats are divisible by 2.

Sometimes, however, the unit beats need to be divisible by 3, and have to be dotted notes; a dot following a note adds half again to its length. These are "compound" time signatures; the commonest of them is 6/8. In 6/8 there are six eighth-notes in each measure, divided into two groups of three; 6/8 is a duple meter, but a *compound* duple one. The most common time signatures are given in the box at the top of this page.

Tempo markings

prestissimo	very fast indeed
presto	very fast
allegro	fast, cheerful
vivace	vivacious
allegretto	moderately fast
moderato	moderate
andantino	moderately slow
andante	slowish but moving along
larghetto	slowish, broadly
largo	broadly
adagio	slow
lento	slow
grave	gravely

None of these terms is precise in meaning: several are more indications of mood than of speed.

There are also a number of terms used to modify a tempo mark; these are the most important:

assai	enough
molto	very
poco	a little
più	more
meno	less
ma non troppo	but not too much

The following indicate a gradual change in tempo:

rit. (= *ritenuto, ritardando*) } becoming slower
rall. (= *rallentando*)
accel. (= *acccelerando*)   becoming faster

3 *Melody*

We described a tone as sounding high or low, and this description conveys that tone's *pitch*. A bass voice, for example, is pitched lower than a soprano. The pitch of a tone is one of the facts that notation has to specify (see below).

The notation of pitch

The standard Western system of notation shows pitch by the positioning of the symbol or note, representing each tone, on a *staff* (or *stave*) consisting of five lines. The pitch at which the staff is to be read is conveyed by a sign at the beginning of each line; this sign is called a *clef*, which provides the key – *clef* is the French word for key – to where the pitch is fixed.

On the staff below, the sign at the left, an adaptation of a traditional script for the letter G, indicates that a note on the second line from the bottom represents the tone called by that letter (in modern use, one produced by a vibration of about 390 cycles per second, or, as generally given nowadays, 390 Hertz or Hz). This, the G clef, also called the *treble clef*, is used for music for women's voices, for the pianist's right hand, and for high-pitched instruments such as the violin. The first note shown on the staff signifies the tone G; those that follow move up in sequence to form a scale. They are placed alternately on the lines and the spaces between them. Where the music needs to run off the top or the bottom of the staff, small extra lines (*leger* or *ledger* lines) are added, as we see for the last three notes.

Music that is lower pitched is written in the F clef or *bass clef*, where the symbol on the fourth line up signifies an F, the note nine steps below the treble-clef G; this is used for lower men's voices and lower-pitched instruments. The C clef, fixing the note halfway between these, is used for instruments of intermediate pitch. Below are shown the notes on and close to the treble and bass clefs. The notes are labeled alphabetically, in upward sequence, with the letters from A to G, which are then repeated.

Intervals

An *interval* is the distance between two pitches. The simplest interval is the octave, the interval at which pitches sound "duplicated". If you sing or play a simple scale (see **ex. 3a**), the eighth note seems in some clear but indefinable way to be "the same" as the first, only higher. When women and men sing together, the men automatically sing an octave lower than the women.

There is a natural 2:1 ratio between tones an octave apart. A string two feet long, set in vibration, will produce a particular tone; halve the length to one foot (and keep the tension the same), and the resulting tone will be an octave higher; or double the tension (and keep the length the same), and the sound will also be an octave higher. This applies equally to a column of air: a tube two feet long will produce a tone an octave lower than a tube one foot long.

This is a matter of vibration: the longer string or the longer tube creates vibrations at half the speed of the shorter. The note to which most symphony orchestras tune their instruments is A, a vibration speed of 440Hz. The note an octave lower is 220Hz, an octave higher 880. On a full-size modern piano, the lowest note is an A, 27.5Hz, and the highest A – seven octaves higher – is 3520Hz. The human ear can cope with musical sounds almost an octave below the lowest A before they degenerate into mere rumble, and more than two octaves above the highest.

No relationship among the notes is as close as that between two an octave apart, but some of the intervals are closer in feeling than others. As well as the 2:1 octave relationship, there is a 3:2 relationship for notes a 5th apart, and 4:3 for a 4th (see **ex. 2**). There are simple number ratios for all the basic intervals between notes of the scale.

Intervals are defined by the number of notes they include, counting both the bottom one and the top one. The octave is eight notes, from one A to the next, the 5th five notes (A–E), the 2nd two (A–B). Some intervals – 2nds, 3rds, 6ths, and 7ths – need to be identified as "major" or "minor" as they may include different numbers of semitones: C–E, for example, is a major 3rd, made up of four semitones, while D–F, of three, is a minor 3rd. Intervals of 4ths and 5ths are described as "perfect" when made up of five and seven semitones respectively. In the white-note diatonic scale there is one 4th (F–B) and one 5th (B–F) of six semitones, called (respectively) "augmented" and "diminished". **Ex. 2a** shows the intervals in semitones up from C; **ex. 2b** shows them with their inversions (that is, the intervals that complement them in the octave).

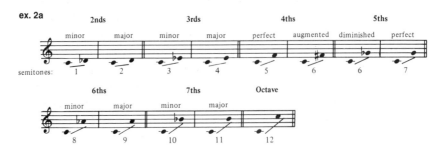

ex. 2b

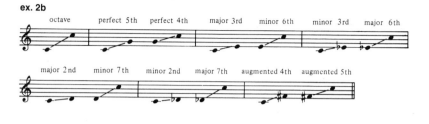

ex. 3a

(half-steps are shown ⌐)

ex. 3b

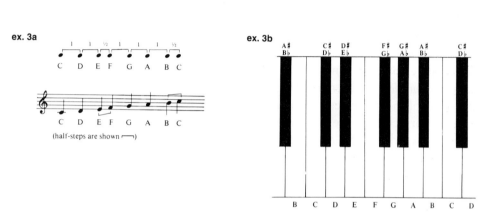

On a piano keyboard, the white notes form a *diatonic scale*. The seven intervals between its eight notes are made up of five full steps (a whole tone or two semitones) and two half steps (one semitone); the half steps fall at E–F and B–C as shown in **ex. 3**. This kind of scale was used well into the Middle Ages. Intermediate steps began to be used; as the diagram of the piano keyboard in **ex. 3b** shows, the five larger steps of the diatonic scale were filled in, with black notes. The note midway between C and D is called C sharp (notated C♯) or D flat (D♭). This shows how the octave is divided into 12 equal steps (or semitones), forming the *chromatic scale* (**ex. 4**). The sharp and flat signs are called *accidentals*; they can be contradicted by the natural sign (♮).

SCALES

ex. 4

The Western division of the octave into seven and 12, though it has some basis in natural, scientific fact, is not universal. Many folk cultures use a five-note division (called *pentatonic*). A familiar example of a pentatonic melody is *Auld lang syne* (see p. 23). Pentatonic scales are widely used, for example in China, parts of Africa and South-east Asia, and in much European folksong. More complex divisions of the octave are also found, for example in India, where there are 22-note scales. Intervals smaller than a semitone have also been used in Western music, especially by eastern Europeans ("microtones" are found in some of their folk music) and modern experimental composers.

THE NATURE OF MELODY

Melody has been defined as a "succession of tones in a musically expressive order". To most people's minds, melody is the heart of music. No aspect of musical skill is as much prized as the ability to compose melodies that are shapely, expressive, and memorable.

Anything that involves a perceptible sequence of tones may be regarded as a melody – from a nursery song to a phrase of church chant, from a folk dance to the angular music of some twentieth-century composers, from a Bach fugue subject to a current pop song.

Generally we think of melody in terms of tunefulness, in the capacity of a line of music to impress itself quickly and clearly on the memory. **Ex. 5** shows four melodies: *The Star-Spangled Banner*, of which the tune was composed by J. S. Smith in the late eighteenth century; the traditional *Auld lang syne*; Schubert's German song *Heidenröslein*, written in 1815; and *Corinne Corinna*. Each of these is built out of a series of short phrases, planned sometimes to answer one another, sometimes to repeat or echo. All are vocal melodies, so that there is a relationship between music and words. Mostly, a phrase in the music corresponds with a line in the poem.

The Star-Spangled Banner consists of two-measure and four-measure phrases, in a 2+2+4 pattern, so that each pair of short phrases is answered by a longer one. The first group of this kind is immediately repeated, then comes a *sequence* (a phrase repeated at higher or – as here – lower pitch) of two measures, followed by a phrase which echoes as its close one heard earlier. Finally, the concluding phrase takes the music to a clear climax with the ascent to the high note just before the end. The use of upward-leaping phrases and dotted rhythms is typical of music intended to be stirring (they are a feature, for example, of the French national anthem, the *Marseillaise*).

The phrase structure of *Auld lang syne* is much simpler: 4+4+4+4. Also the last four measures match almost exactly the second four, while the third four follow the first quite closely. The rhythms, also very consistent, are largely determined by the meter of the verse. Here again there is a high note near the end to provide a sense of climax.

In the Schubert song, *Heidenröslein* ("Wild rose on the heath"; see **Listening Guide 30**), the opening four-measure phrase is answered by another – beginning the same way, then taking a new twist in the second measure by changing the C to C♯, and a further new twist by adding two further measures before reaching a point of rest. Then two further two-measure phrases, the first of them a clear echo of measures 3 and 4, carry the music away from the resting-point of D to G. Note the point of climax on the high note (with a pause sign over it, showing that the singer may linger there) close to the end; note too the smooth movement of the whole melodic line, which tends to go by stepping from one note to another rather than skipping. Writing of this kind, called *conjunct*, is normally used in gentle, lyrical contexts, while more *disjunct* melodies, with many skips, are used to make a stronger, more energetic effect.

ex. 5a

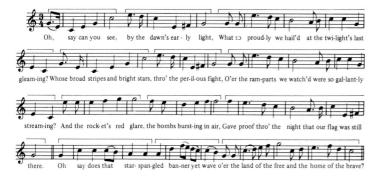

Oh, say can you see, by the dawn's ear-ly light, What so proud-ly we hail'd at the twi-light's last

gleam-ing? Whose broad stripes and bright stars, thro' the per-il-ous fight, O'er the ram-parts we watch'd were so gal-lant-ly

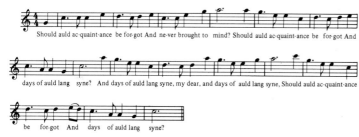

stream-ing? And the rock-et's red glare, the bombs burst-ing in air, Gave proof thro' the night that our flag was still

there. Oh say does that star-span-gled ban-ner yet wave o'er the land of the free and the home of the brave?

ex. 5b

Should auld ac-quaint-ance be for-got And ne-ver brought to mind? Should auld ac-quaint-ance be for-got And

days of auld lang syne? And days of auld lang syne, my dear, and days of auld lang syne, Should auld ac-quaint-ance

be for-got And days of auld lang syne?

ex. 5c

Sah ein Knab ein Rös-lein stehn, Rös-lein auf der Hei - den, war so jung und mor-gen-schön,

lief er schnell, es nah zu sehn sah's mit vie-len Freu - den. Rös-lein, Rös-lein, Rös-lein rot,

Rös-lein auf der Hei - den.

A boy saw a wild rose growing on the heath; it was so young and morning-fresh that he ran quickly to it, with great delight: wild red rose in the heather. (In the succeeding verses he goes to pick it; it refuses to be picked, threatening to prick him so that he will not forget it; he does pick it, and although he is pricked its protests are in vain.)

ex. 5d

Cor-inne Cor - inn - a, where you stay last night? Cor-inne Cor - inn - a,

where you stay last night? Your hair's all messed up and your clothes don't fit you right.

We have seen in these melodies how the shape and length of phrases and the way they are put together can convey a special flavor, mood, or character. The same principles apply to the melodies of jazz and of folk and rock music. Folktunes, which for centuries were passed on aurally, are generally simple in design and direct in their emotional appeal, for example the English folktune *Greensleeves*.

The traditional tune *Corinne Corinna* (**ex. 5d**) opens with a simple, four-measure phrase, ending on B♭; it is answered by another of similar shape, ending on F; a four-measure phrase concludes the melody back on B♭. It has been used by numerous jazz musicians, and the singer-songwriter Joni Mitchell has made it well known in her arrangement *A Bird that Whistles*. *Corinne Corinna*, in fact, follows the pattern of 12-bar blues.

Blues tunes (see p. 399) are usually constructed 4+4+4, and are generally of a doleful nature in keeping with the words they are expressing. However, in many types of jazz (as we shall see in Part IX) the melodic line is improvised to some degree by a solo performer, while an accompanying instrument or group repeats a progression of chords. Certain melodies have lent themselves to numerous jazz treatments, for example "Summertime" from George Gershwin's *Porgy and Bess* its haunting, melancholy opening four-measure phrase is "answered" by another, then repeated and answered differently, in a 4+4+4+4 pattern.

In pop music, melody is often not an important element. We can sing the tunes of all the melodies we have cited. But in many pop and rock pieces, driving rhythms and colorful instrumentation give a piece its character, not a well-defined melody. However, there are pop melodies which have become very widely known, for instance Paul Simon's *Bridge over Troubled Water*, and many of the songs John Lennon and Paul McCartney wrote for the Beatles. Among these last is *Yesterday*, an evocative, nostalgic ballad with an irregular phrase structure (7+7+8+7+8+7) and a melody that moves smoothly by step over a wide range.

A number of general points can be made about melodies.

(1) They are made up of individual phrases, usually of two or four measures. Often the composer aims at some variety in phrase length and at balancing shorter and longer phrases.

(2) The music heard at the beginning may recur later, as an immediate repeat or as a recall after other music.

Cadence (3) There are likely to be resting-points, or *cadences*, in the course of the melody; some are momentary, some more strongly defined; there is virtually always a decisive cadence at the end. (The word "cadence" is derived from a Latin word meaning "fall".)

(4) There may be patterns, of line or of rhythms or both, that recur to give the melody a clear sense of unity.

(5) There is often some kind of climax point, with a rising phrase and a high note, close to the end.

One matter of particular importance in musical form – that is, the way elements are arranged in a musical work to make it coherent – is *tonality*. If you hear or play any of the melodies we have been considering, and break off shortly before the end, you will find that you instinctively and unmistakably know what the final tone should be. The music is drawn to a particular tone as if with a gravitational pull. If, as with the first two melodies, that tone is C, the music is said to be "in C". Had we written *The Star-Spangled Banner* beginning one note higher, on A rather than G, and kept all the same relationships between notes, it would have ended on D and been "in D"; we would have *transposed* it (or changed its key) from C into D.

It is not, however, simply a matter of the last tone. The fact that the melody is in C affects the role each tone plays in it. C is the central tone, the *tonic*, but G is almost as important: note how the music comes to rest on G at "light" and "fight", and later (more decisively) at "there" – and it is a G that provides the climax (on "free") at the end. When music is in C, G (the note five steps above) is called the *dominant*, and is almost always treated as the obvious alternative tonic – for in all but very short pieces the composer will generally change the tonal center or *key* from time to time. Of course, all this applies equally at different pitches: for music in A, the dominant is E, and for music in E♭ it is B♭. Any piece of music may be transposed from one pitch to another without changing its internal tone relationships; it will merely sound higher or lower.

We saw earlier (p. 21) that the diatonic scale consists of a sequence of notes equivalent to the white notes on the piano keyboard. This group of seven different pitches (the octave duplication does not count), which provided the basic material of music well into the Middle Ages, can still provide all that is necessary for music that does not change key (*Auld lang syne*, for example, has no notes with *accidentals* (extra sharps or flats that temporarily alter the pitch of a note) and *The Star-Spangled Banner* adds only sharps to the note F when it leans towards the key of G).

The white notes on the piano make up the scale of C major. Make all the F's into F sharps, and the notes make up G major; sharpen the C's as well, and it is D major. Or flatten the B's, and a scale of F major results. The process of adding sharps and flats may be continued up to six of each – six sharps is F♯ major, six flats G♭ major (different ways of saying the same thing, because on the piano F♯ and G♭ are the same). Each key has its own *key signature* (see p. 26).

Major, minor

So far we have discussed only *major* keys. The white notes on a piano make up a major scale of C. Music using them normally gravitates towards C and is said to be "in C major".

Some music, however, works differently: when the same tones are used, the music gravitates not towards C but towards A. This is music in a *minor* key and is said to be "in A minor". The tonal center in a minor-key piece is a minor 3rd (three semitones) below that of its major equivalent; A minor is called the *relative minor* of C major, and C major the *relative major* of A minor. In practice, the scales used are not identical, even though the key signatures are; in A minor, for example, the note

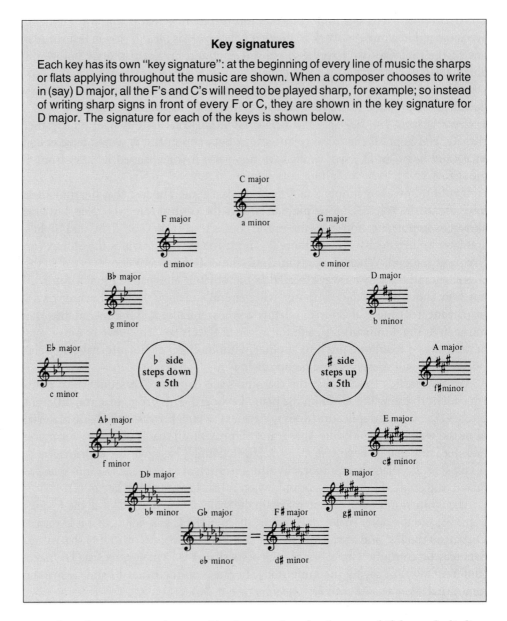

Key signatures

Each key has its own "key signature": at the beginning of every line of music the sharps or flats applying throughout the music are shown. When a composer chooses to write in (say) D major, all the F's and C's will need to be played sharp, for example; so instead of writing sharp signs in front of every F or C, they are shown in the key signature for D major. The signature for each of the keys is shown below.

G (and to a lesser extent the note F) often needs to be sharpened if the melodic line is to sound smooth. The parallel minor of C major would be C minor, in which the major 3rd, 6th, and 7th are reduced by a semitone to become minor intervals. It is generally felt that music in minor keys is more sad, more serious, perhaps more threatening in character than that in major keys (though of course there is plenty of sad major-key and cheerful minor-key music).

Modulation

It will be clear from the special relationship we have seen between a key and its dominant that some keys are more closely related than others. When C is the tonic, G, we saw, is the chief complementary key. But F is also close – one step in the flat direction, while G is one step in the sharp direction (and C, of course, is the dominant of F: which is why we call F the *subdominant* of C). A piece of music in C major is likely to change key first of all to G, but it may well change, too, to A minor, and to other nearby keys.

Composers use such key changes for contrast and to help establish the form of a piece – for the changes are perceptible to the listener and create natural divisions between its sections. In a longer piece, or one where the composer is aiming for dramatic effects, changes to more distant keys are usual. The process of changing key is called *modulation*.

Tonality came to be an important element in musical composition around the year 1600. But well before then the pull of a tonic, or a home tone, was an important factor in composition. The home tone was not, however, always C or A when the diatonic scale A–B–C–D–E–F–G was used.

Medieval theorists, borrowing an idea from the ancient Greeks, devised a series of six *modes* (to which they gave Greek names), with the whole steps and half steps differently related to the final tone. The Dorian mode, for example, had D as the final tone when the white notes were used. Medieval and Renaissance composers were keenly aware of the different expressive character of each mode.

4 *Harmony and Texture*

So far, we have been discussing music as if it were a single line of sound. In fact, for about the last thousand years almost all Western art music has involved two or more simultaneous sounds. The term used for the combination of sounds into organized groups of notes is *harmony*.

HARMONY

The earliest forms of harmony in Western music – harmony is primarily a Western phenomenon – arose when church chant was sung not by all the monks or nuns together but by only some of them while others sang something different, usually either a fixed tone or tones moving parallel with the chant (see **ex. 6**). This was regarded as adding a "clothing" to the melody and depth to the music. Harmony still has that function, as we hear when, for example, a hymn is sung with organ accompaniment, or a guitar plays in support of a voice, or a pianist adds a left-hand part below a right-hand melody. The organ, the guitar, or the pianist's left hand will normally play combinations of tones, or *chords*.

Chords   Ideas have varied a great deal as to what tone combinations make "good" harmony. **Ex. 6** shows that in the tenth century the interval of a 4th was much used. Other types of early harmony move mainly in 5ths; movement in parallel 5ths is also used in some folk singing.

ex. 6

(chant in white notes, added part in black notes)

te   hu - mi - les   fa - mu - li   mo - du - lis   ve - ne - ran - do   pi - is

By the Renaissance, the main unit of harmony was the *triad*, a three-tone chord built up in 3rds, or by filling in the central gap in the interval of a 5th. The triad remained the basic element in Western harmony until well into the present century; it is used not only with the notes in their basic order, 1–3–5, as shown in **ex. 7a**, but also in *inversions* – that is, with the same notes but in a different vertical order, as shown in **ex. 7b**.

Anyone who has tried picking out a melody on the piano and adding chords knows that a harmony can be made for many melodies just by using two or three triads. **Ex. 8** shows the opening of *Auld lang syne* harmonized with three triads, those on the tonic, the dominant, and the subdominant. *The Star-Spangled Banner* is a more developed melody, and though it too could be very simply harmonized it sounds much better with a wider range of harmonies, as **ex. 9**, with its opening measures, shows; two chords there (marked*) are inversions. The full stirring effect of the melody can be made only with its proper, rich harmony.

The way a note is harmonized often changes its sense. **Ex. 10a** shows the same note with several different harmonies, and if you listen to these you will realize that your expectation of what (if anything) is likely to follow differs from one to another.

ex. 10a   ex. 10b

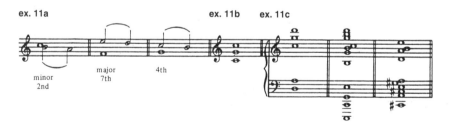

Ex. 10b shows two of these chords with others that naturally succeed them. The first of each of those pairs is a *dissonance*: it conveys a feeling of clashing or of tension, which needs to be resolved. The chord that resolves a dissonance is normally a *consonance* or a smoother-sounding chord. The tension generated by dissonances can impart a sense of movement and energy to a piece of music. Sometimes a composer resolves one dissonance on to another, and then a third, and so on, holding the listener in a state of tension until the moment of resolution.

CONSONANCE,
DISSONANCE

Ideas have differed a great deal from time to time about which intervals are consonant and which are dissonant. In traditional Western triadic harmony, two tones a semitone (or minor 2nd) apart, or the inversion of that (a major 7th), form the strongest dissonance; also quite dissonant is the 4th. These are shown, with their usual resolutions, in **ex. 11a**. In the fifteenth century, even a full major triad was felt inappropriate for the final chord of a piece and an "open 5th" was preferred (**ex. 11b**); full triads were usual for concluding chords in the period 1600–1900, but in the twentieth century, composers have tended to treat dissonance more freely – **ex. 11c** shows the final chords of three works by Stravinsky.

ex. 11a   ex. 11b   ex. 11c

minor   major   4th
2nd   7th

If harmony can give a sense of forward movement in music, it can also do the opposite and provide a musical equivalent of punctuation marks. We saw, in the melodies of **ex. 5**, that there are natural stopping places or cadences. When they have a clear air of finality they are called "perfect cadences" or "full cadences". These, the primary type of cadence, generally lead from the dominant to the tonic. The most important secondary kind, called "imperfect cadences" or "half cadences", lead to the dominant. There are examples of both in **ex. 12** (see p. 30), a partial harmonization of a line of *Auld lang syne*.

ex. 12

Cadences of these kinds are the most basic material of harmony, for harmony is not simply single chords but progressions of chords, and it derives its characters from the way they relate.

COUNTERPOINT

Much music, as we have seen, consists of melody with accompanying harmony. But much, too, consists of melodic lines heard against one another, woven together so that their individual notes harmonize. The word for this kind of writing, *counterpoint*, derives from the idea of note-against-note, or point-against-point – for which the medieval Latin is *punctus contra punctum*. Music that uses counterpoint is called *contrapuntal*.

A more general term for music made up of several strands is *polyphony* (Greek for "many sounds"). Terms related to it are *monophony* ("one sound", or a single line of melody) and *homophony* ("like sounds", when the voices move in the same rhythm, like a melody with each note harmonized, or a melody with accompanying chords).

Techniques of counterpoint, or composing one line against another, were particularly important in the late Middle Ages and the Renaissance, when it was usual for church music to incorporate traditional chants – sequences of notes, to be chanted by a priest or members of a choir. Ways were devised of composing melodies to be sung against these chants, or of weaving the chants into the musical texture of a piece (*texture* is a useful term for distinguishing between music that is mainly harmonic, or homophonic, and music that is mainly polyphonic or contrapuntal).

The late Renaissance period was a "golden age" of polyphony, when these techniques were brought to the highest refinement. Central to this kind of polyphony was the idea of *imitation* – that is, of one voice (or instrument) imitating the music sung (or played) by another. **Ex. 13a** shows a brief passage in simple counterpoint, where the two lines have some melodic character but "go" together (the lower is not simply a harmonization of the upper); **ex. 13b** shows a brief passage in imitative counterpoint, where two phrases (*x* and *y*) are heard first in one voice and then imitated in the other.

Imitation

ex. 13a

ex. 13b

The concept of imitative counterpoint is not unfamiliar to anyone who has tried to sing *Three Blind Mice* or *Frère Jacques*; these are *rounds*, and the music is in *canon*, a kind of imitation that is continuous and very exact. In most imitative counterpoint the imitation continues for only a few notes and it is usually at a different pitch.

There was another golden age of counterpoint in the early eighteenth century, with J. S. Bach as its greatest figure. This is a more elaborate, faster-moving type of counterpoint than that of the sixteenth century, more instrumental than vocal. Composers have continued to use counterpoint to enrich and add variety to the texture of their music, and to give it greater depth and intellectual weight – for music in which all the interest lies on the surface is apt to seem thinner than music where, sometimes at least, it runs through the entire texture.

COLOR, DYNAMICS

A composer can create variety in music by several different means: by its texture, its rhythmic character, its speed, its key structure. Two other means at a composer's disposal are tone color and dynamic level. A tone sounds quite different when played on different instruments or sung by the human voice: in Part II we will look more closely at the instruments a composer can use. With most instruments, the player can produce sounds at various levels of volume. Like speeds, these are indicated by a series of Italian terms (see below).

Dynamic markings

ff	*fortissimo*	very loud
f	*forte*	loud
mf	*mezzo forte*	moderately loud
mp	*mezzo piano*	moderately quiet
p	*piano*	quiet
pp	*pianissimo*	very quiet

Some composers wanting extreme effects have gone further, in each direction; in a few scores *fff* and *ffff* are to be found, as are *ppp* and *pppp* – Tchaikovsky even asked for *pppppp* at one point in a symphony. There are also terms for other effects that involve dynamic levels:

cresc.	*crescendo*	growing (louder)
dim.	*diminuendo*	diminishing, getting quieter
sf		
sfz	*sforzando, sforzato*	forced, accented
fz	*forzando, forzato*	

5 *Structure*

Every piece of music, from the simplest song to the most elaborate symphony, needs to have some kind of organization, or form, if it is to be coherent to the listener. In music – as in the other arts – form has to do with the arrangement of the various elements. For the listener, it has chiefly to do with recognition. By hearing something you have heard before, and recognizing it, you can perceive a piece as something more than a blurred series of unrelated sounds.

In this chapter we shall consider some of the ways in which composers have organized their music, which elements they have used, and how they have used them.

PHRASE, MOTIF, THEME

The basic elements in the organization of Western music are melody and key. The easiest thing to recognize is a *melody* that one has recently heard, so composers repeat melodies to give shape and unity to a composition.

A structural unit in music, however, may be smaller than a melody. It may be a *phrase*, of perhaps six or seven notes, or even a *motif* (or a *figure*), of two or three, which the composer uses persistently so that it imprints itself firmly on the hearer's mind and gives the piece a sense of unity. The term *theme* is often used for a musical idea on which a work is based; it means something longer than a motif, forming a unit in itself but capable, like a motif, of giving rise to some kind of musical "argument" or working-out.

These various structural units are used by composers to clarify, or articulate, the design of their work at different levels. For example, a movement lasting 15 minutes may have three main sections, each about five minutes long, the last of them beginning like the first and the middle one beginning with an altered version of the same material.

Sometimes a rhythm may be at least as important as a melodic line: Beethoven, for example, takes the "short–short–short–long" figure that opens his famous Fifth Symphony and uses it in different melody patterns, but it remains instantly recognizable (see **Listening Guide 28**).

KEY, HARMONY

Second in importance to melody is *key*. As we have seen, most Western music has a strong gravitational pull towards a tonal center: we talk of a Symphony in D, or a Concerto in B♭ minor, when the music feels as though it has a natural tendency to end on a chord of D major or one of B♭ minor. We have seen, too, that composers cause their music to change key during a movement, usually to one or more of the keys nearly related to the principal one of the movement. A piece in C major normally modulates first of all to G major, which as we saw on p. 25 uses the same tones as C major except one (F♯ instead of F). Examples of this can be seen in two of the melodies discussed on p. 22, *The Star-Spangled Banner* and *Heidenröslein*; one modulates from the key of C to the key of G, the other from G to D. A listener soon comes to recognize that particular modulation and what it signifies in the design of a piece. He or she also soon recognizes the points at which a piece returns to its home key, which similarly have a structural meaning.

Composers developed subtle ways of handling key to convey structural meaning – for example, by moving to remote keys to create a sense of distance from the home key, or by changing key rapidly. They could, further, couple key and melody to powerful effect. In the main Classical form-type, known as "sonata form" (see p. 35), composers generally – at a point about two-thirds or three-quarters through a movement – moved to the home key and at the same time reintroduced the opening theme. This "double return" creates a moment of particular force in the structure.

There are other ways in which *harmony* is used in the structure of a movement. Composers of the Baroque period, for example, often based an entire movement on a recurring pattern of harmonies (much as in jazz). Movements were often constructed over a repeating bass-line, called a "ground bass" (because the bass serves as the ground on which the piece is built). These are not the only kinds of compositional device by which a composer can manipulate the structure of a movement.

Most of these devices belong to the Baroque, Classical, and Romantic periods, and to a lesser extent to the twentieth century. In the Middle Ages and the Renaissance (that is, up to about 1600), one of the chief organizational devices was the *cantus firmus* (Latin for "fixed song" or "fixed melody"). Here the composer chooses a particular melody, which might be sung or played in long notes by one voice or instrument while the others sing free, faster-moving parts around it; or the melody might be worked into the music in another way, or might be sung in elaborated form. The fixed melody might be repeated several times, in a recurring rhythmic pattern: this gave the piece a certain unity.

Cantus firmus, plainsong, chorale

The fixed melody would normally be taken from the traditional repertory of chant, or *plainsong*, drawn up by the church (see p. 68), in which each melody is associated with a particular part of the liturgy (the prescribed form of church service); the music would thus contain an element familiar to the congregation.

Later, after the Reformation, the Lutheran church in Germany built up a similar repertory of familiar hymn-tunes, called *chorales*, which composers used as a basis for cantatas and organ pieces (chorale preludes). Some were adapted from popular songs, just as were some of the melodies that Catholic composers of the Renaissance had used in Mass settings or motets. Sacred or secular, from chant or popular song, the purpose was the same: to provide something familiar to the listener, and to give the composer a foundation for the piece.

There is an analogy to this in twentieth-century music. In the early years of the century, many composers felt a need for a new method of formal control. One of

12-tone row

the most important of these is the 12-tone system established by Arnold Schoenberg, in which a "series", consisting of the 12 tones of the chromatic scale arranged in a specific, fixed order, which remains unchanged for the entire movement or work, is used as the basic organizing unit.

The series can be used harmonically as well as melodically (that is, with the tones heard simultaneously, in chords, as well as successively, as a melody); each tone can be used at any level of pitch, high or low; the whole series can be transposed (that is, it can start on any tone, as long as its interval structure is kept the same); and it can be played not only in its basic form but also upside-down, backwards, or both. This kind of principle of serial organization of pitch was later applied also to elements other than pitch, such as rhythmic values and dynamic levels.

It is, of course, very hard to recognize a melody that is played backwards (even upside-down is difficult, and both upside-down and backwards is virtually impossible). Schoenberg's aim was not principally to provide something that the listener could readily grasp but to give the composer a disciplined basis for composition.

THE MAIN FORMS

Here our concern is perceptible musical form, the structure of a piece of music as it can be grasped by the listener and can aid understanding. In the chapters that follow, where we shall be looking at composers and their music in a historical context, and examining a selection of their music, the ways in which the music is organized will frequently be discussed. This will often involve the use of special terms to describe particular procedures; we shall now look at these terms and outline their meaning.

Binary

Binary form means simply two-part form. The term can be applied to anything from a short melody (a folksong, a hymn-tune) to an extended movement, as long as it consists of two sections that in some sense balance each other. Among the simplest examples are songs in which each verse ends with a chorus, such as the *Battle Hymn of the Republic*. In the Renaissance and Baroque periods, dances were often written in binary form. The dance-rhythm pieces in the suites of Bach are also binary. They tend to follow a regular pattern:

melody	A	B	:	:	A	B
key	T	D	:	:	D	T

A – opening theme   B – cadence material
T – tonic (or home) key   D – dominant (or complementary) key

Each half of such a movement is repeated, and the listener is always aware of the fresh beginning – with the opening theme heard in a new key at the start of the second half. In some examples, the closing theme (*B*) consists of merely a few notes leading to the cadence; in others it can be several measures long. The second part of the movement is often rather longer than the first and might touch on a number of nearby keys.

Ternary form means three-part form, on the pattern *A–B–A* (that is, the third part is identical with, or very similar to, the first). This is again a form found in folksongs and hymns, even in children's songs like *Twinkle, twinkle, little star*. The idea of repeating the first part of a piece after a different section has been heard is, of course, an obvious one, and ternary form has a long history. Composers in the Baroque period wrote many ternary songs or arias: this form is known as the "da capo aria" ("da capo" means "from the head", indicating that the performer should go back to the beginning). The minuet-and-trio movements – usually the third – of Classical symphonies and chamber works are ternary, in that the minuet is repeated after the trio.

Ternary

Rondo form is an extension of ternary. It is a form in which the main section recurs two or more times; its plan, at its simplest, is *A–B–A–C–A*. Longer examples can be shown *A–B–A–C–A–D–A* or *A–B–A–C–A–B′–A* (where *B′* is a variant of *B*). This form goes back to the seventeenth century and was particularly favored by the harpsichord composers working in France, such as François Couperin, early in the eighteenth. Composers of the Classical period – Haydn, Mozart, and Beethoven – used rondo form on a larger scale, usually as the last movement in a sonata, chamber work, or orchestral piece. A feature of rondo form is that the recurrences of the *A* section are in the home key; the episodes, the *B*, *C*, or *D* sections, are normally in nearby keys, such as the dominant or the relative minor/major. Here are typical rondo-type movements:

Rondo

1	*melody*	*A*	*B*	*A*	*C*	*A*
	key	T	D	T	M	T

2	*melody*	*A*	*B*	*A*	*C*	*A*	*B′*	*A*
	key	T	D	T	S	T	T	T

3	*melody*	*A*	*B*	*A*	*C*	*A*	*D*	*A*
	key	T	D	T	M	T	S	T

4	*melody*	*A*	*B*	*A*	*C*	*B′*	*A*
	key	T	D	T	V	T	T

T – tonic D – dominant M – relative minor S – subdominant V – various

Sonata form is the most important form of the Classical and Romantic periods. It came into being soon after the middle of the eighteenth century and remained in use at least to the middle of the twentieth, with various modifications. What we call "sonata form" is more a style, or a way of thinking, than a structure. It evolved to accommodate the musical idioms of its time; its ground-plan is not a mold but a natural outcome of the ideas themselves.

A sonata-form movement falls into three main sections: Exposition, Development, and Recapitulation. This is the ground-plan:

Sonata form

		Exposition		Development		Recapitulation	
material	:	*A B*	:	*A/B*	:	*A B*	:
key		T D		various		T T	

The *exposition* "exposes", or lays out, the thematic material of the movement. This divides into two *groups* of themes, *A* and *B* (or two *subjects*, as they are sometimes called). Depending upon the length of the movement – and movements in sonata form can last anything between one minute and half-an-hour – each group may be anything from one melody to a succession of melodies, or an assemblage of motifs with little melodic character. The one thing common to all of them is that the first-group material is in the main key of the work and the second is in a complementary key, normally the dominant (in a major-key work; the relative major in a minor-key one). There may be contrast between the themes themselves (some composers tended to use brisk, "masculine" themes in the first subject and gentler, more lyrical, "feminine" ones in the second); but there is always contrast between the keys of the two groups.

The exposition normally ends in the secondary key, and the *development* follows. This generally uses material from the exposition and "develops" it. Themes may be broken up into fragments, and used in dialog; they may be treated contrapuntally; phrases from them may be repeated at different pitches; they may be used as starting-points for new ideas. The music is likely to range into different keys, perhaps even quite distant ones. Often the development section provides a climax of activity and excitement.

It may, however, be the arrival of the *recapitulation* that forms the principal climax, with the "double return" to the home key and the music that began the movement. The essential feature of the recapitulation is that, when the second-group material returns, it is now in the home key. The experienced listener is made aware of the sense of homecoming that this conveys, and realizes that the end of the movement cannot be far off. In an extended movement – the first one of Beethoven's Fifth Symphony is a good example – there is often a substantial coda, which helps provide a proper feeling of finality.

The principle behind sonata form – the presentation of material in two keys, and its later re-presentation all in the home key – runs through many musical forms in the Classical and Romantic periods. An important example is sonata-rondo form, of which the plans shown as (2) and (4) on p. 35 are examples. There the *B* material is presented first in the dominant, second in the home key.

Ritornello

A standard form of the Baroque period is *ritornello* form, used in Baroque concerto first movements. Like rondo, it is based on a recurring theme, but here the theme is not always in the home key. Here is a typical plan of a concerto-type movement:

orchestra or solo	O	S	O'	S	O'	S	O
key	T	T–D	D	D–M	M	M–T	T

O – orchestra
S – solo

T – tonic
D – dominant
M – relative minor or other key

The orchestra opens and closes the movement with complete statements of its main material, the "ritornello" (O); parts of the ritornello (O′) appear during the movement. In the soloist's three main sections, the music is likely to change key. The solo material often calls for virtuoso skills. This design is also used in arias. During the Classical period, ritornello form was enlarged with second-group material, as in sonata form.

Variation form has been used in all periods. The principle is simple: state a theme, then embellish it and elaborate it in various ways. Variation methods were applied to plainsong, as we have seen (p. 33), in the Middle Ages and the Renaissance. In the Baroque era, the Lutheran composers of northern Europe varied chorale melodies for organ; Bach contributed notably to that repertory (see p. 119). A type of variation movement used at this period was the *ground bass*, where a bass pattern is repeated with different music heard above it. Purcell and Bach were the two greatest masters of the ground-bass form.

Variation,
ground bass

In the Classical period, composers preferred the purely melodic type of variation. Mozart wrote several sets for the piano, which gave scope for his virtuosity both as composer and pianist. Usually the first two or three variations are quite simple and stay close to the theme, which the listener can readily follow; later ones become increasingly complex and increasingly distant from the original melody. Beethoven's variations become more like miniature developments of motifs in the theme than mere melodic elaborations. He wrote most of his variations for piano, but there are many large-scale sets of variations in chamber works and in orchestral music.

A particularly interesting set of orchestral variations written at the end of the nineteenth century is Elgar's *Enigma Variations* in which each variation is designed to portray the character of one of Elgar's friends. Composers often wrote their own themes for treatment in variation form, but sometimes used well-known, existing ones or borrowed them from other composers. In the twentieth century, variation form was used in fairly traditional ways by such composers as Britten (see **Listening Guide 1**) and Copland, while Schoenberg and Webern adapted its techniques to their less traditional idioms.

The *fugue* of Bach's time represents a late flowering of the techniques used by the composers of the sixteenth century, the first golden age of polyphony. It may be useful to outline these techniques and the repertory to which they gave rise.

Fugue

The basic principle of sixteenth-century polyphony is that the voices sing, in succession, the same music to the same words. As they sing at different pitch, one hears each musical phrase several times over, at various levels. The voices seem to imitate one another. This style, as we have seen (p. 30), is often called "imitative counterpoint". The same style was used in music of this period and the early Baroque for instrumental ensemble (under such titles as canzona, fantasy or ricercare). The word fugue – from the Latin *fuga*, meaning "flight" or "pursuit" – was applied to movements of this kind.

LISTENING GUIDE 1

Britten: *Young Person's Guide to the Orchestra*, op. 34 (1946)

The English composer Benjamin Britten (1913–76) composed his *Young Person's Guide to the Orchestra* as music for a film about the instruments of the orchestra. It is in the form of a theme and variations, the theme being a dance by Henry Purcell written in 1695 for use in a play called *Abdelazer*, and is a fine example of Britten's craftsmanship.

The theme (ex. 1) is presented in six brief opening sections, the first and last of them identical and for full orchestra; of the sections in between, one is for woodwind, one for brass, one for strings (including harp), and one for percussion. 13 variations follow, each highlighting a different instrument and reflecting that instrument's character in mood, speed, and dynamics. Then comes a fugue, in which the composer 'reassembles' the orchestra by having each instrument enter in turn in the order in which we first heard them.

 Listening Outline

Time			
0.00	**theme**		full orchestra, ex. 1
0.22			woodwinds
0.44			brass
1.03			strings
1.20			percussion
1.36			full orchestra
1.55	**variations**		flutes; the piccolo joins with high trills
2.28		woodwinds	oboes
3.31			clarinets
4.08			bassoons
5.01			violins; in the rhythm of the *polacca*, a Polish dance
5.33			violas (entry on long note)
6.35		strings	cellos
7.52			double basses
8.51			harp
9.39			horns
10.25		brass	trumpets
10.57			trombones and tuba (11.10)
11.58		percussion	timpani, bass drum followed by cymbals (12.11), tambourine – triangle (12.21), side drum (12.32), Chinese woodblock (12.36), xylophone (12.42), castanets (12.52), gong or tam-tam (12.58), whip (13.05)
13.41	**fugue**		piccolo plays the fugue subject (ex. 2), then other woodwinds
14.23			violins, then other strings
14.54			harp
15.06			horns, then other brass
15.26			percussion
15.36			original theme returns
16.23			(end)

ex. 1

ex. 2

(fugue subject: given here in its main key, D major)

Many keyboard composers of the seventeenth century wrote fugues, for harpsichord or organ. The most inventive and most original of fugues are those by Bach. He wrote many for organ and even more for harpsichord, including two books with preludes, one in each of the major and minor keys (24 in each book: the set is often known as the "48"), called *The Well-Tempered Keyboard*.

Fugues by Bach and other composers usually begin with an exposition, in which the *subject* – the theme on which the entire piece is based – is heard, successively, in all the voices. (The term *voice* is used, in instrumental music as well as vocal, for the contrapuntal strands of a composition. Bach's harpsichord fugues are mostly in three or four voices.) As each voice enters, the texture grows fuller. In the remainder of the fugue, the subject is likely to be heard several more times. In between the appearances of the subject there will be passages called *episodes*, which are usually related to the subject in some way.

Bach used fugue not only in his keyboard music but also in his chamber and orchestral music. He also wrote fugal choruses in his vocal works, such as his cantatas and, notably, in his Mass in B minor. But the most famous exponent of the choral fugue was his contemporary, Handel.

After the time of Bach and Handel, fugue was less a part of the standard musical language. But composers long continued to use it in church music and in other contexts for special effect – for example, to round off a set of variations (as in Britten's *Young Person's Guide to the Orchestra*; see **Listening Guide 1**).

Part II The Making of Music

1 *Strings*

The term "string instrument" (or "stringed") refers not only to those played with a bow, like the violin but also to many plucked instruments, like the guitar or the harp. It also covers keyboard instruments like the piano (where the strings are struck) and the harpsichord (where they are plucked).

BOWED INSTRUMENTS

Chief among the bowed instruments are the violin and the other instruments like it – the viola, a large violin of lower pitch, and the cello (its full name is violoncello), a much larger instrument pitched an octave below the viola. To these we may add the double bass, which is larger still but structurally rather different.

Violin

The violin (see **fig. 3**) is basically a resonating box with a neck attached, across which, with a system of pegs and bridges, four strings are attached. The strings are made of gut, often with silver wire wound round them, or of steel. They are held taut and stretched across a piece of wood (the fingerboard) in such a way that the player can press them down with the fingers of the left hand and so shorten their vibrating length. With the right hand the bow is drawn across the strings, bringing its horsehair (made sticky with rosin) into contact with one of them and causing

---

The origins of instruments

In the opening chapter we saw that musical sounds are produced by regular vibration in the air. Humans have devised numerous ways of creating this vibration in addition to using their own voices. The simplest, most primitive kinds of instruments are lumps of wood or stone, fashioned so that the player can strike them. Lumps of different sizes were found to produce sounds of different pitches, and hollow objects to produce a fuller sound than solid ones (because the air in the cavity takes up the vibration in resonance). A skin stretched across a hollowed-out object gives a still better sound: this creates a drum.

The simplest wind instruments came into being when someone blew across a leaf or a straw, through a hollow bone or horn, or into a reedpipe. Anthropologists have found animal bones with holes made in them which would enable a player to produce sounds of different pitch. The earliest string instruments probably grew out of the discovery that a taut string, when plucked, could produce a musical sound, and that the sound could be magnified by the attachment of a resonating box to the object bearing the string.

---

it to vibrate. The vibration passes through the bridge and into the hollow body of the instrument (the soundbox), which amplifies it and transmits the vibration to the air and to the listener as a musical tone.

Violins have existed since the sixteenth century. The great age of violin making was the seventeenth century and the early eighteenth, the time of such men as Stradivari and Amati, who built instruments of incomparable sweetness, richness, and power of tone. It was at this time too that the violin became the basic instrument in the orchestra and in chamber music, a position in which it is still unchallenged because of the beauty and the expressiveness of its sound and its unrivalled agility. Its capacity to draw a silvery line of tone and to play with great brilliance and rapidity make it specially prized as a solo instrument. Many composers (Bach, Beethoven, Mendelssohn, Brahms) have written concertos for it.

The four strings of the violin are tuned as shown in **ex. 14a**. Since the player can modify the length of the string only by shortening it, by pressing it against the fingerboard, all he or she can do is raise the pitch from these four "open notes", so the first note shown (G) is the lowest of which the instrument is capable. The highest is more than three octaves higher, produced by pressing the E string at the end of the fingerboard. The violin offers an almost infinite range of possibilities for varying the sound: among the most important are *vibrato* (when the player's left hand has a controlled wobble, greatly enriching the tone), double stopping (playing on two strings at once), and plucking.

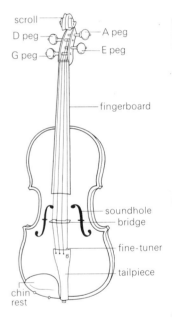

3 *Diagram of a modern violin showing principal features.*

ex. 14

Viola

The viola is tuned a 5th lower than the violin (**ex. 14b**); the instrument is itself some six inches longer. Its tone is rather darker and less sweet, less brilliant than the violin's. The viola is only quite rarely used as a solo instrument, its main role being to play a middle, accompanying voice. In England it was once called the "tenor", and in France it is still called the "alto" – which makes clear the kind of part it is usually asked to play (see p. 63).

Cello

By the rules of acoustics the viola, since its pitch is a 5th below the violin's, ought to be half as big again as the violin. But then it would be impossible, when the player tucked it under the chin to play, to reach the other end or to support its weight. So the viola has to be made smaller than its acoustical ideal. The cello, however, is built rather closer to its proper acoustical size, since it is played not under the chin but held between the player's knees (see **fig. 26** and **Color Plate 12**). Its tuning is shown in **ex. 14c**. Otherwise its technique is exactly like that of the violin or viola, except in left-hand fingering: because of the longer strings, the points at which the player has to press them down, or "stop" them, are much further apart. The cello is an instrument of outstanding eloquence and warmth, with a rich middle register and an intensely expressive top register. Many composers have written for it music of a specially personal quality, such as Dvořák and Elgar, in their concertos.

Double bass

In the modern orchestra, a deeper foundation is needed than the cellos can provide; this is supplied by the double bass. Its most usual tuning is shown in **ex. 14d**; note that the strings are set not a 5th apart, as with the upper instruments, but a 4th, for the distances that the player's hands have to travel between notes would otherwise be too great. The instrument's tone is somewhat gruff when it is heard alone, but coupled with the cello an octave higher it sounds firm and clear.

Viols

The way that the shoulders of the double bass slope gently up to the neck mark it out as closely related to the viol family. The viols developed about the same time as the violins, and were much used for chamber music in the sixteenth and seventeenth centuries (see **Color Plate 6**): their gentle, slightly reedy tone makes them ideal for the contrapuntal music popular at that time. Viols are made in several sizes, of which the main three are the treble, the tenor, and the bass; they have six (occasionally seven) strings. All of them, even the smallest, are played with the instrument held vertically, between the knees like a cello. Unlike violins, viols have frets (strips of gut, wood, or metal) on the fingerboard against which the strings are stopped.

PLUCKED INSTRUMENTS

Most of the plucked string instruments work on the same principle as the bowed ones: they have a resonating body, and a neck along which the strings are stretched with a system of pegs and bridges; the player stops the strings against a fingerboard (with frets) attached to the neck to shorten the strings' sounding length and so produce the full range of notes.

Types of instruments

Virtually all instruments belong to one of four categories. The simplest are *idiophones* ("own-sounding"), where the body of the instrument is set in vibration by the player and is itself the sound-producing object. Examples are bells, cymbals, xylophones, and rattles. When a skin or membrane – rather than the instrument's actual vibrating body – is struck, the instruments are *membranophones*; this group includes little other than drums, though kazoos also belong to it (so does the comb-and-paper). Wind instruments are called *aerophones*; this category includes trumpets, flutes, clarinets, and organs. String instruments, or *chordophones*, range from the piano and the harp to the violin and the guitar. To these four classes a fifth has lately been added, *electrophones*, instruments that produce their sound by electric or electronic means, like the electric organ or the synthesizer.

The best known of these is the guitar. The modern guitar (see **fig. 4**) has six strings (earlier ones had four or five), tuned as shown in **ex. 15a**. Its body has a flat back with incurved sidewalls. The strings are nowadays of nylon, with the lower ones wound in metal. The instrument is specially associated with Spanish and Latin American music, but it is used in folk and popular music in many countries. The guitar can be plucked or strummed, either with the fingers or, if a sharper sound is wanted, with a plectrum (made of hard material). The electric guitar, an instrument amplified electronically, is the one chiefly used in pop music.

Guitar

ex. 15

(a) Guitar

4 *The most important instruments in the lute family.*

Lute

ex. 15

(b) Lute

Historically, the most important plucked instrument is the lute (see **figs. 4** and **6**, and **Color Plate 4**). In the sixteenth century it was the most popular domestic instrument, like the piano later or the guitar today, and was used for solo music and for accompanying songs or ensembles. The classical lute generally has a flat soundboard and a bowl-shaped or pear-shaped body; there are several sizes with necks of various lengths and shapes but typically lutes have six strings tuned as shown in **ex. 15b**.

There are numerous other instruments of the lute type (see **fig. 4**). Among them are the mandolin, a small instrument with four or five double wire strings, whose thrumming adds a special color to Italian (particularly Neapolitan) folk music; the banjo, a favorite instrument among black American minstrel groups, much used in parlor music, with a round body and usually five wire strings; and the ukelele, a Hawaiian instrument like a small, four-string guitar.

The most important non-Western instrument of this kind is the *sitar*, the best-known of all Indian instruments. It has a long neck, a bowl-shaped body, five playing strings, two "drone" strings (lower-pitched ones that sound constantly), and a dozen or more strings that vibrate in sympathy with the plucked ones, adding a kind of halo to the sound. The Japanese *shamisen*, a three-string instrument with a square soundbox, is used in both folk and art music.

Harp

The harp (see **fig. 5**) is of an altogether different type. Unlike the other plucked instruments, it has a place in the modern orchestra. The harp is an ancient instrument, known in biblical times and in many cultures, notably in Africa and South America. The orchestral harp is a highly developed instrument with about 45 strings, tuned to a diatonic scale. At its base is a set of seven pedals with which the player can shorten the strings and raise their pitch by one or two semitones; one pedal controls all the C strings, one the D strings, and so on. The harp has always had an important place in folk music, especially in Ireland and Wales; in art music it can add color and atmosphere to orchestral music with its delicacy and its gentle washes of sound.

KEYBOARD INSTRUMENTS

Piano, harpsichord

The piano is a struck string instrument; here the striking is done at one remove, through a complex mechanism operated by a keyboard (see **fig. 8**). It was invented just before 1700 by an Italian, Bartolomeo Cristofori, who wanted to build an instrument that – unlike the harpsichord, the most important keyboard instrument of the day – could be played soft and loud, or *piano* and *forte*: hence its full name, pianoforte (or fortepiano).

Both the piano and the harpsichord consist of a set of tuned strings held taut in a wooden case, with a sounding-board underneath; both possess keyboards in which the keys for the diatonic notes are at the front (usually of white ivory) and the keys for the other five notes, the sharps and flats (usually of black ebony), are set a little further from the player. The harpsichord, however, is a plucked instrument (see **fig. 7** and **Color Plate 7**). When a key is depressed by the player, a strip of wood (the jack) is thrown up and a piece of quill (or plastic in modern instru-

5 Above *Pedal harp by Salvi, 1974.*

6 Girl with a lute: *painting by Bartolommeo Veneto, early 16th century. Isabella Stewart Gardner Museum, Boston.*

ments) attached to it plucks the string. The player has no control over the speed at which the jack is projected, and therefore cannot affect the force with which the string is plucked. So each tone on the harpsichord sounds at the same volume. By the eighteenth century harpsichords often had two keyboards ("manuals"), which gave the player opportunities for creating a wider range of tone quality.

The harpsichord went out of fashion in the late eighteenth century, when composers increasingly felt that variation in volume was important for the kind of expressiveness they wanted. It was revived in the present century, because performers began to realize that, if we wanted to hear music in the sense intended by its composers, it was necessary to use the kinds of instrument they had in mind.

The action of the piano, unlike the harpsichord's, allows the pianist to control, by the force he or she applies, the speed at which the hammer strikes the strings and, accordingly, the volume of each tone. The piano became the principal domestic instrument during the nineteenth century; virtually every cultured home in

7 Man playing the harpsichord: *painting by Gonzales Coques (1614–84). Private collection.*

Europe and the USA had one. It also became the instrument that many composers of the time played and used for much of their most original and most personal music (Beethoven and Chopin, for example). It has a huge repertory, most of it solo music, some of it music with strings, some of it accompanying the voice; conventionally the piano has no place within the orchestra, but it is sometimes used in modern orchestral works and there are many piano concertos, in which the piano adopts a solo role with an orchestra.

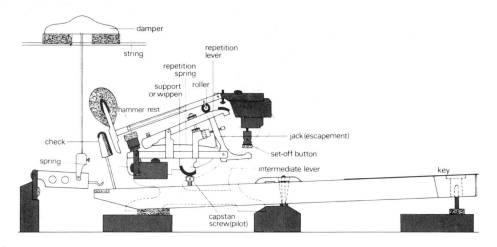

8 *Action of a modern grand piano: on pressing the key the movement is transmitted via the pilot to the intermediate lever; the jack then acts on the roller of the hammer which rises toward the string. The moment the backward projection of the jack contacts the set-off button the jack moves back, permitting the hammer to escape and to continue in free flight to strike the string and then begin its descent; it is then caught and retained by the check and repetition lever as long as the key remains depressed. If the key is partly released the hammer is freed from the check, and the roller is acted on directly by the repetition lever; it is thus possible to strike the string again by depressing the key a second time (the jack will re-engage with the roller only when the key has been fully released so that a full hammer stroke may be made).*

9 *Beethoven's last piano, by Conrad Graf, a gift from the maker. Beethovenhaus, Bonn.*

In the late eighteenth century, the tone of the piano was crisper and lighter, less warm and less "singing". Its sustaining power and volume have greatly increased, not only because of changes in musical style but also with the rise of public concerts in large halls, where the music has to be loud enough to carry to a substantial audience. To support the extra string tension needed for this extra volume, wooden frames gave way to iron ones in the early nineteenth century. The traditional "wing" shape, derived from the harpsichord and convenient for accommodating strings long in the bass and short in the treble, has remained in use for concert grands and large domestic pianos. The upright piano, in which the frame and strings are mounted vertically, has long been normal for use in the home, occupying much less space and producing an ample volume for an ordinary parlor (a further variety of early piano, the "square", is shown in **Color Plate 12**).

The harpsichord too has smaller domestic equivalents, the virginal or the spinet. Another domestic keyboard instrument is the clavichord, whose delicate tone is produced by the impact of a brass tongue on the string.

₂*Wind Instruments*

The basic principle of any wind instrument is that an air column in a tube is made to vibrate to produce a musical tone. There are three main ways in which this can be done: first, by blowing across a sharp edge on the tube; second, by attaching to it a reed that will vibrate; and third, by the player using the lips in the role of a reed. The choice of method affects the sound. Other factors too influence the sound – the nature of the reed, the materials of which the instrument is made, and the bore of the tube (whether it is wide or narrow, and is uniform or widens towards the far end). Wind instruments are usually divided between so-called woodwind and brass. This usage helps clarify the role of each in the orchestra, though it is inexact – some "woodwind" instruments are made of metal, and the category "brass" includes some made of wood.

WOODWIND

The simplest wind instruments are the flute type, in which the player directs the breath at an edge, creating eddies of air that set the column in vibration. (The principle is the one that enables someone blowing across the top of a glass bottle to produce a faint sound; pour water into the bottle, reducing the effective size of the tube, and the tone will rise in pitch.) Flutes divide into two main types, the end-blown (like the recorder) and the side-blown (like the standard flute).

Recorder

The recorder (see **fig. 10**) has a long history in Western music, probably dating back to the fourteenth century. It is built in various sizes, to play at different pitch levels: the four main ones are the soprano (or descant), the alto (or treble), the tenor, and the bass (the lowest tone of each is shown in **ex. 16**). Recorders have traditionally been made of wood, or occasionally of ivory, until recent times when their massive use in schools has led to the manufacture of smaller types in plastic. The instrument has a beak-shaped mouthpiece, with a whistle-like aperture a little below it to provide the edge that sets up the vibration. Its main body, which is cylindrical, has holes which are covered or uncovered by seven fingers and one thumb to produce different tones. With all the holes covered, the tube sounds at its full length and gives its lowest tone, but by blowing in a more tightly focused way the player forces the tube to vibrate in two halves and produce a tone an octave higher.

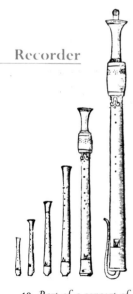

10 *Part of a consort of recorders: woodcut from* Syntagma musicum *(1619) by Michael Praetorius.*

ex. 16

Recorders
Soprano   Alto   Tenor   Bass

lowest tones

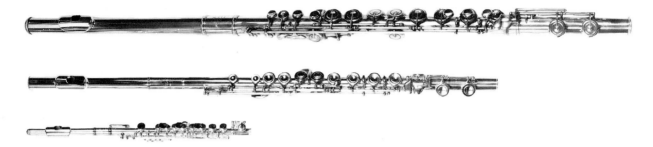

The recorder's chief repertory comes from the Renaissance and Baroque periods; around 1700, particularly, many composers wrote sonatas for it. Bach and Handel included it in many of their works. Its clear, piping sound was less well suited to later music and it fell out of use. But it has been revived, partly to answer the need of music educators for an instrument suitable for children.

Flute

The flute (see **figs. 11** and **12** and **Color Plate 4**), at first a simple cylindrical tube with six finger-holes, came into prominence in the late seventeenth century when a group of French makers devised improvements. The flute was more difficult than the recorder to play in tune; attempts were made to improve it by adding more keys, but the first fully successful one came only in the 1840s with the work of Theobald Boehm, who devised an ingenious system (soon adapted for other instruments) using rings as well as keys.

Early flutes were normally made of wood, or occasionally ivory; nowadays metal ones – of silver or alloy, occasionally gold or platinum – are much more common. The sound of the instrument, when gently played, is cool and limpid; its lowest register can achieve a soft, almost sensuous expressiveness, but its extreme top can add sharpness and brilliance to an ensemble. Besides the normal flute, there is a half-size instrument, the piccolo, and the larger alto flute. The compasses of these are shown in **ex. 17**.

The flute has a large repertory of sonatas from the beginning of the eighteenth century. When the recorder fell into disuse, the flute remained, being particularly well suited to the character of mid- and late eighteenth-century music and popular among amateurs. Two flutes became the standard in the orchestra by 1800. In the present century its flexibility and its delicate, unassuming sound have won it much favor, especially among French composers.

Every culture uses flutes, such as the Arab *nay* and the Indonesian *suling*. Other varieties include the ocarina and the nose-blown flutes of Polynesia.

11 *Modern flutes: alto (top), concert, piccolo, by Rudall Carte & Co.*

12 *Playing a one-key flute: engraving from* Principes de la flûte traversière *(1707) by Jacques Hotteterre.*

ex. 17

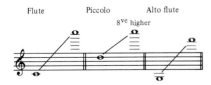

Oboes, bassoons

All the other orchestral woodwind instruments are reed-operated. There are two types of reed: the single reed, a blade of cane tied to the mouthpiece and made to vibrate against it when the player blows, and the double reed, consisting of a pair of blades which vibrate against each other.

The oboe (see **fig. 13**) is the principal double-reed instrument of soprano pitch. The word "oboe" comes from the French *hautbois*, meaning "high wood", a loud wooden instrument. Its precursor was the shawm, which made a loud, shrill sound and was much used in court ceremonial music and town bands.

Like the flute, the oboe was refined in the late seventeenth century, with the addition of keys to improve its tuning. By the middle of the eighteenth century it was the first woodwind instrument firmly established in the orchestra. Two oboes have been a basic part of the orchestra ever since.

Oboes have been built in various sizes. The most important is the english horn (or *cor anglais*), curiously named since it is neither English nor a horn – it is a tenor oboe, pitched a 5th lower than the ordinary instrument and having a richer, more throaty sound. It is called for in many scores of the nineteenth and twentieth centuries. There was also the oboe d'amore (the gentle-toned "love oboe"), much used in Bach's time. The compasses of these instruments are shown in **ex. 18**.

Double-reed instruments of the oboe type are used in many cultures, for example the North African *zurna* and the Indian *shahnai*.

Various attempts have been made to build a satisfactory bass oboe, but the existence of the bassoon (see **fig. 13** and **Color Plate 10**), a double-reed instrument and the true bass of the woodwind group, makes it unnecessary. The bassoon has a warmer, smoother, less reedy sound than the oboe and its immediate relatives. The size of a bass instrument poses special problems: the long tube (nine feet) of the bassoon needs to be doubled back on itself and the finger-holes have to be bored obliquely through the wood if the player is to reach them.

The bassoon came into the orchestra during the eighteenth century as the bass to the oboes. It has had something of a reputation as "clown of the orchestra" because of its capacity for comic effects, but bassoonists resent this since it can also be eloquent or somber. An octave lower than the bassoon is the double bassoon, whose 18-foot tube is twice doubled back on itself: this instrument provides a deep and resonant bass to the woodwind section. The compasses are shown in **ex. 18**.

13 Above *Modern oboe and english horn, by Howarth of London;* Above right *Modern German bassoon by Wilhelm Heckel.*

ex. 18

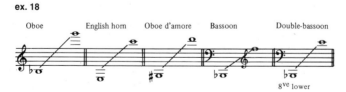

Clarinet

The clarinet (see **figs. 14** and **15**) has a shorter history than the other orchestral woodwinds, beginning in the early eighteenth century. It has a single reed, fastened to the mouthpiece against which it vibrates. The tube, normally of African blackwood, is cylindrical. Because of the acoustical properties of a cylindrical tube with a single reed, when a player blows more acutely the sound does not rise an octave (as with the other instruments we have been considering) but an octave and a 5th. Since players have only sufficient fingers to uncover enough holes for an octave, the clarinetist has to use special keys to fill the gap between the basic tones produced by the full tube length and the next series an octave and a 5th higher. This makes the clarinet's timbre rather different from one register to another – rich and oily in the lowest, a little pale in the middle, clear and singing in the medium-high, quite shrill at the top.

The strength of its upper registers quickly secured the clarinet a place in military bands. It was slower to find its way into the orchestra and was not regularly used until close on 1800. Mozart contributed notably to its repertory. Nineteenth-century

14 Young man holding a clarinet: *painting, 1813, by Johannes Reekers. Frans Halsmuseum, Haarlem.*

15 *Modern clarinets:*
sopranino, soprano in B♭
(Schmidt-Kolbe system, by
Fritz Wurlitzer), soprano
in A, basset horn in F,
bass in B♭, by Leblanc.

composers found its romantic tone appealing and made much use of it for poetic effects. In the twentieth century it has had an important role in jazz.

Clarinets are made in a variety of sizes. All are transposing instruments; this means that the tone that is heard differs from the one the player sees notated in the music and plays. This curious system enables a player to change from one size of instrument to another without altering fingering technique. The standard clarinet is said to be "in B♭", which means that when the player plays C the tone that sounds is B♭. There is also a clarinet in A, more convenient for music in certain keys. Smaller, shriller instruments in D and E♭ are used for special effects and in bands. A larger tenor clarinet usually pitched in F and called the basset horn was used by Mozart and others. But more important is the bass clarinet, pitched an octave below the standard one. The compasses of all these are shown in **ex. 19a**.

ex. 19a

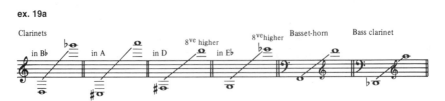

ex. 19b

Another single-reed instrument is the saxophone, invented by Adolphe Sax in the mid-nineteenth century. The saxophone is made of metal, with a conical tube (its compass is shown in **ex. 19b**). Sax built it in seven sizes. The saxophones have never found a regular place in the orchestra, but are used in military bands and above all in jazz, where their smoothness and flexibility find a natural place.

Saxophone

The so-called brass instruments – they may be of other metals, or even wood or horn – work on a principle similar to that of reed instruments; but here the player's lips act as the reed. The player presses them to a cup-shaped (or funnel-shaped) mouthpiece against which they vibrate, setting the air in the tube in vibration. Anyone who has tried blowing in this way into a simple piece of tubing, like a garden hose, knows that a musical (or fairly musical) sound can be made but that only a limited number of tones can be sounded because the length of the air column cannot be varied. But it can be made to vibrate in sections – halves, thirds, quarters, and so on. These tones form what is called the *harmonic series*; **ex. 20** shows the tones that can be obtained from a tube about eight feet in length (in theory: physical reasons sometimes limit the number). The lowest tones are produced with the lips relaxed, the highest with them very tight.

BRASS

ex. 20

(the notes shown in black are imperfectly tuned)

Instruments of this type were used in ancient civilizations, commonly for ceremonial or ritual purposes, because the sound produced is generally loud and noble. Animal horns were often used, for example the original Roman *buccina* and the Jewish *shofar*; the alphorn, used in mountainous countries for long-distance signaling, is of wood. An early metal example is the Scandinavian *lur*, a long, conical instrument in the shape of a bent S.

   The impossibility of playing even a simple scale on a brass instrument (except at the top of its compass, which is insecure and difficult) long kept such instruments out of ordinary music-making. The only one that found a place was the cornett – not to be confused with the modern cornet – which was wooden and had finger-holes that enabled the player to alter the sounding length. It was prominent in the sixteenth and seventeenth centuries, and much used for ceremonial church music, including the playing of hymns from church towers in harmony with trombones. But it fell out of use as soon as there were other instruments to replace it early in the eighteenth century.

Cornett

Horn

16 *Triple horn in F/Bb/F alto, with five rotary valves, by Paxman (first manufactured in 1965).*

17 Below *Hand-horn player: lithograph, c1835, by C. Tellier.*

The first true brass instrument to establish itself in the orchestra was the horn (usually called "French horn", but in fact many are nowadays German in origin; see **figs. 16** and **17**). In the early eighteenth century it was mainly used in outdoor music or pieces referring to the hunt. By the middle of the century there were normally two horns in an orchestra. The style of music then being written could accommodate the instrument's limited range of tones, and horns added warmth and fullness to the orchestral sound. At the end of the century it was occasionally used as a solo instrument (notably in Mozart's concertos). In the nineteenth century the horn's romantic qualities brought it into special favor; it was also useful for supplying unobtrusive inner harmony. Four horns were often used, sometimes six or even eight. The instrument's compass is shown in **ex. 21**.

ex. 21

By that time the horn could play more than just the tones of the harmonic series. Structurally, it had originally been simply a coiled, slightly conical brass tube, with a flared opening (or bell). But in the eighteenth century, so that it could play its limited tones in the prevailing key, the player would use a "crook" – an extra coil of tubing – to supplement its basic length. Early in the nineteenth century a system of valves was devised which made crooks unnecessary: the valves enabled the player to switch extra lengths of tubing into action by pressing pistons and so alter the series of available tones. The horn could now manage a full range of tones. Since then, the bore of the tube has been widened to give a smoother sound and make it easier to play. The horn, the least "brassy" of the brass instruments, blends readily with the woodwinds and even the strings.

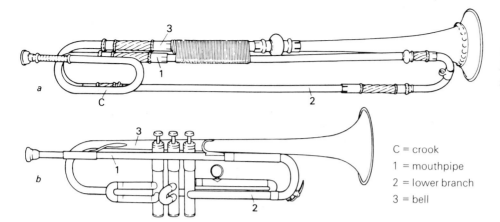

18 *Diagram comparing a Baroque and a modern trumpet.*

C = crook
1 = mouthpipe
2 = lower branch
3 = bell

Trumpet

The highest-pitched of the brass instruments (their compasses are shown in **ex. 21**) is the trumpet (see **fig. 18**). A simple cylindrical tube, either straight or twice doubled back on itself, it began to be used in orchestral music during the Baroque period, when the fanfare-like phrases it could play – like the horn, it could manage only the tones of the harmonic series – fitted well with the cut of the melodies. During the late eighteenth century a pair of trumpets came to be used regularly in larger orchestras, especially in music of a formal or ceremonial kind. As with the horn, crooks were used to adapt it to the key of the music.

Valves were applied to the trumpet, too, early in the nineteenth century, enabling it to play a full range of tones. Since then composers have taken advantage of its brilliant and forthright sound and its ability to penetrate, or ride over, the full orchestral ensemble. The trumpet, of course, is much used in jazz. There, and occasionally in orchestral music, its sound is modified by the insertion of a mute – a kind of large plug – in its bell. Mutes of various shapes and materials affect its tone quality, enabling it to do anything from moaning to snarling. Also sometimes found is the cornet, a gentler-toned instrument looking like a short, stubby trumpet, less noble in sound but easier to play; it is more common in bands.

Trombone

The "heavy brass" instruments are the trombones (see **fig. 19**) and the tuba (see **fig. 20**). A trombone has no need for valves as it has a movable slide; by altering the

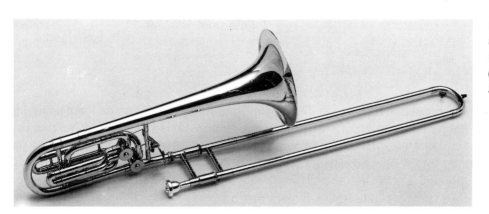

19 *Modern American bass trombone in B♭/F/E♭, with two thumb valves (Vincent Bach model), by Selmer.*

length of the tube and (as with the horn or trumpet) varying the lip pressure, the trombonist can play any tone in the instrument's compass. Trombones are made in two sizes, though nowadays a single instrument fitted with a valve so that it can play the music of both the tenor and the bass is widely used. In earlier periods trombones (an early form was the sackbut) were much used in church music, and their noble, solemn sound is now often called upon when an effect of grandeur or ritual is wanted. They are heard too in noisy, brilliant climaxes. Three trombones are usually found in the orchestra today.

Tuba   At the bass of the brass ensemble comes the tuba (see **fig. 20**), a large instrument of the horn type with a wide bore and three or four valves. Tubas are made in numerous sizes; the most usual orchestral one has about 16 feet of tubing (not including the lengths controlled by valves). They are made in a variety of shapes, some of them (like the sousaphone – named after the composer – and the helicon) winding round the player so that he can support it when marching. Its tone is deep, sonorous, and well rounded, lacking the bite and edge of the trombones.

20   *A modern tuba.*

ORGAN   The organ (see **figs. 21** and **22**) is a wind instrument, but the player fortunately does not have to blow it; the air is supplied by pumps and bellows. An organ may have hundreds, even thousands, of pipes: one (sometimes more) for every tone in every stop. "Stop" is the term used for the group of pipes that produce a particular quality of sound. The player can pull out a series of buttons to engage each of them (hence the expression "pulling out all the stops"). The pipes may be of wood, tin, or other metals; they may be flue pipes (on the edge principle) or reed ones; they may be narrow or wide, open or closed, round or rectangular in shape. Each type produces a different sound. Every country, and in some of them every locality, has its own tradition of organ building and its own preferences over tone quality.

A large instrument may have three keyboards, or even more, operated by the hands, and a further one (a pedalboard, laid out like a keyboard but larger) for the feet. Traditionally, the action of an organ – the series of links between the keyboard and the air supply – was purely mechanical, but nowadays electrical systems are widely used. And electronic organs, without pipes at all, have reached a point of development where almost any sound can be accurately and cheaply reproduced – a threat to the traditional pipe organ despite the latter's beauty, variety, and grandeur of sound.

The organ's repertory reached a peak in the early eighteenth century, with the incomparable music of Bach, and includes several masterpieces from the nineteenth and twentieth centuries. A few composers have written organ concertos, notably Handel, but the organ has never had a regular place within the orchestra; its natural home is of course the church, and its natural repertory sacred music.

Organs, old and new:
21 Below left Organ by
Christian Müller
(built 1735–8), Groote
Kerk, Haarlem.
22 Below right Organ by
the Holtkamp Organ Co.
(inaugurated 1967).
University of New Mexico,
Albuquerque.

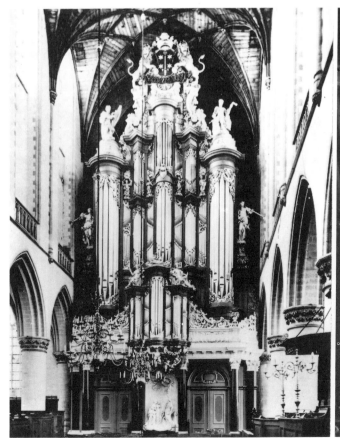

3 *Percussion and Electronic Instruments*

PERCUSSION

Percussion instruments (see **fig. 23**) are those that are sounded by being struck or, in a few cases, shaken. Most are made of wood or metal. Some, *untuned percussion*, produce on impact a noise rather than a definite musical tone; others, *tuned percussion*, sound a recognizable pitch. Percussion instruments are used more for rhythmic than melodic purposes.

Drums

The most important percussion instrument in Western music is the drum, in particular the kettledrums, or timpani. Pairs of kettledrums have been used in orchestral music since the early eighteenth century, often with trumpets to add pomp and brilliance. The kettledrum is a large bowl-shaped vessel, usually of copper, with a skin held taut across the top. It sounds a tone of definite pitch, determined by the instrument's size and the tension of the skin, which is adjustable either with hand-screws or with a foot-operated mechanism.

23 Modern percussion instruments.

bass drum

cymbals

timpani

side drum

tam tam

xylophone

glockenspiel

tubular bells

Other types of drum include the bass drum, much used in bands, which provides a deep, unpitched thump, and the side drum (or snare drum), a small instrument with strings (snares) that rattle against the head when it is struck, producing a sizzling sound. These are basic to the rhythm sections of jazz and dance bands. So is the cymbal, a resonant brass plate that can be played either with a drumstick or – as in dramatic climaxes in orchestral music – clashed one against another.

Another instrument often heard at climactic moments is the large gong or tam-tam: struck with a soft, heavy beater, it can produce a solemn, awesome noise that menacingly grows in volume for a few moments after the impact. Gongs play a large role in the music of Indonesia, where the gong-based orchestra is known as the *gamelan*; the type of gong used there, unlike the tam-tam, sounds a definite pitch.

Untuned percussion

Tuned percussion instruments include the bells, or chimes, a series of metal tubes suspended in a frame; they are often called upon to imitate church bells. Smaller bells are represented on the glockenspiel, a series of metal bars struck with small hammers. A similar instrument operated from a keyboard is called the celesta because of its sweet, "celestial" sound. Wooden instruments of these types produce a harder, drier tone. Chief among them is the xylophone, a series of wooden (or synthetic resin) bars laid out like a piano keyboard with metal resonators underneath; it is struck with small mallets. A larger version is the marimba – the name comes from Africa, where (as in parts of Latin America) such instrument types are common. A metal instrument of this kind, with disk resonators made to revolve by a motor and so producing an effect of vibration, is known as the vibraphone or vibraharp (or simply "vibes"); it is much used in jazz.

Tuned percussion

Almost any sound can be analyzed by electronic means and then re-created. The people who have experimented during the present century with electric methods of creating sound have added enormously to the range of sound and the means of organizing it. Electronics may be used to amplify the sound of conventional instruments, for example the electric guitar. But they are also used in the creation of sound.

ELECTRONIC INSTRUMENTS

There are instruments like the *ondes martenot*, operated from a keyboard and a control panel and sounding like a depersonalized human voice. More recent is the electric piano, which can sustain notes in a way that the real piano cannot. There is also the tape recorder, with which an ingenious and imaginative musician may devise new ways of making and shaping musical sounds; and ultimately the synthesizer, which has an almost unlimited capacity for the generation of sounds or the modification of existing ones.

4 *Orchestras, Bands, and Ensembles*

The orchestra

The orchestra as we know it dates back to the late seventeenth and early eighteenth centuries, when groups of musicians began to be employed to play in opera houses and at courts. As early as 1626 a royal band of 24 string players had been assembled by King Louis XIII of France. Later, wind players were added. Orchestras varied in size, depending on the wealth of their patron or employing organization, the kind of music to be played, and the size of the building in which they performed. Generally, an orchestra of the mid-eighteenth century might be expected to have a dozen violins, eight other string players, a flute, two each of oboes, bassoons, and horns, an accompanying (or "continuo") harpsichord, and for important occasions a pair of trumpets and kettledrums.

By the beginning of the next century, when larger halls were in use and music of a grander kind was being composed, an orchestra could well have 24 violins, ten violas, six each of cellos and double basses, and pairs of flutes, oboes, clarinets, bassoons, horns, trumpets, and kettledrums, with a few extra instruments – a piccolo, an extra horn or two, two or three trombones – as required. A modern symphony orchestra at full size might typically have 32 violins (divided into 16 firsts and 16 seconds), 14 violas, 12 cellos, and ten double basses, with a piccolo and three flutes, three oboes and an english horn, three clarinets and a bass clarinet, three bassoons and a double bassoon, six horns, three trumpets, three trombones and a tuba, two harps, and four to six percussion players. A typical arrangement of a modern orchestra on a concert platform is shown in **fig. 25**.

Bands

In early times, many towns had their own wind bands using such instruments as shawms and sackbuts. There were also military bands. In the modern wind or military band the clarinets play a central role, akin to that of the violins in the orchestra. A large band may include ten or 12 clarinets, along with other woodwinds (piccolo, flutes, oboes, high-pitched clarinets, bassoons, saxophones) and a substantial body of brass (cornets, trumpets, horns, euphonium, trombones, and tubas) as well as percussion and sometimes bass strings (cellos, double basses). One of the more famous bands was that of the American conductor and composer John Philip Sousa, who became known as the "March King". Brass bands, popular in industrial societies in the nineteenth and twentieth centuries, are largely based on cornets and various sizes of tuba.

24 *Daniel Barenboim conducting the Chicago Symphony Orchestra, Orchestra Hall, Chicago 1991.*

25 *Typical layout of a modern orchestra.*

Another important large ensemble is the jazz band. Jazz is commonly played by small groups, for example a clarinet, a trumpet, a trombone, a saxophone, and a rhythm section with piano, string bass (double bass), and percussion including drums. In the big-band days, however, there might be as many as four or five each of saxophones (with the same players doubling clarinets if needed), trumpets, and trombones, with piano, guitar, string bass, and drums (see **Part IX**).

**Chamber
ensembles**

Composers have written music for numerous different combinations of instruments. But there are some standard groups for which large and attractive repertories have been created. These are itemized in the table below. Chamber music was originally intended for performance not in concert halls but in "chambers", or rooms in a house; works of this kind are written in such a way that they are to be played with just one player to each part.

Chamber ensembles	
Trio sonata	2 violins (or recorders, flutes, oboes, or 1 violin and 1 flute etc.) and continuo
String trio	violin, viola, cello
String quartet	2 violins, viola, cello
String quintet	string quartet + an extra viola or cello
Piano trio	piano, violin, cello
Piano quartet	piano, violin, viola, cello
Piano quintet	piano, 2 violins, viola, cello
Violin sonata	violin, piano
Cello sonata	cello, piano
Wind quintet	flute, oboe, clarinet, bassoon, horn

26 *Amadeus Quartet: (left to right) Norbert Brainin, Siegmund Nissel, Peter Schidlof, and Martin Lovett.*

5 *Voices*

The human voice is the oldest means of music-making, and it remains the most natural and the most expressive. Unlike the other sources of sound already discussed, the voice is actually a part of the performer's body; he or she is thus more dependent on natural gifts. The "vocal cords", which vibrate when we sing, are folds of skin in the throat. We make their vibrations resonate in the cavities of the chest or head, and can adjust the shape and size of those cavities by muscular control according to the tone we want to sing and the syllable we sing to it.

Female

We saw in Part I that the pitch of a woman's voice is normally in the range notated in the treble clef and a man's in that of the bass. But there is a good deal of variation. A high-pitched woman's voice is called *soprano*, a low one *contralto* or simply *alto*, and an intermediate one *mezzo-soprano* (meaning "half-soprano" and sometimes called just *mezzo*). The normal pitch ranges of these voices are shown in **ex. 22**. Voices vary greatly, however, and many singers can range wider.

ex. 22

The soprano voice is probably the most prized of all. The vast majority of the great women's roles in opera are for sopranos; a significant exception is Carmen, Bizet's sultry gypsy, which is a mezzo part. Sopranos may be gentle and lyrical, or bright and bell-like with a capacity for rapid, high singing, or grand and brilliant. In a large modern choir the sopranos are usually the largest group, not only because it is the commonest voice among women but because the soprano voice is generally the lightest and more are needed if the sopranos are to hold their own against the other groups.

Male

The highest normal male voice is the *tenor*, the lowest the *bass*; between them lies the *baritone*. The pitch ranges are shown in **ex. 23**. For the last two hundred years the tenor has been regarded as the main voice for heroic singing and for expressing ardent love. Opera composers tend to have tenor heroes and bass villains, though the richness and masculinity of the bass voice have frequently led to its use for kings or warriors, or sympathetic fathers; there is also a tradition of comic bass parts. The strong, warm sound of the baritone voice is often used for dramatic and heroic roles.

All these different voice types are used in large choirs; most of the repertory of choral music is composed for "SATB" (soprano, alto, tenor, and bass). Often, boys (known as trebles) are used in preference to sopranos, especially in European church music, much of which was composed at a time when women were prohibited from singing in church. Boys tend to produce a strong and firm, sometimes even raucous, sound, less soft and sweet than that of girls or women. In earlier times, too, the alto part was regularly sung by men, as it still is in some church choirs; good male altos produced a light, sharply defined sound that is well suited to contrapuntal music. Some men singing these parts use what is called "falsetto" (meaning an unnatural, "put on" high voice), but with others this type of singing is more like a natural extension of the top of the tenor voice; it is generally called *countertenor*.

ex. 23

Tenor   Baritone   Bass

Castrato

There is another type of high voice of historical importance. In the sixteenth century the custom developed in southern Europe of castrating boys who had musical gifts and particularly fine voices, to prevent their voices from breaking. Italian church choirs began to use these *castrato* voices, and in the seventeenth and eighteenth centuries *castrato* singers dominated serious opera. The combination of a boy's vocal quality and a man's lungs evidently produced a sound of extraordinary beauty, power, and flexibility. *Castrato* singers took the roles of heroes, warriors, and lovers for two centuries (for example Handel's Julius Caesar and Gluck's Orpheus). Most had roughly the same range as a mezzo-soprano; the roles they took are nowadays best sung by a woman. The practice of castration began to be regarded as abhorrent in the eighteenth century and was abandoned during the nineteenth.

Plate 1 Opposite
*15th-century fresco of a
musician following his
score while playing a
portative organ and hand
chimes. Palazzo Trinci,
Foligno.*

Part III Music before 1600

1 *The Middle Ages*

The history of the music of Western culture – which we should remember is only one of many, by no means the oldest, and only in recent times the most various and complex – may reasonably be regarded as beginning with the cultures in which it has roots, such as the Jewish, the Greek, and the Roman. We know, from (for example) the Bible or classical Greek drama, with their numerous references to instruments and singing, and from pottery, sculpture, and painting, that music played an important part in the life of these peoples. But we have very little idea of what it sounded like. We know something about their instruments but almost nothing certain about what was played on them. There are no musical notations that we can read and fully understand; and, with the so-called Dark Ages intervening, there is no historical continuity between ancient Greece or Rome and the Europe of the Middle Ages in which present Western culture has its true beginnings.

Western musical history, then, must begin around the sixth or seventh century AD, when the traditional repertory of church chant, normally passed on orally from one generation to the next, began to be set down and codified. It would be misleading if, through the limitations of our knowledge, the impression were to be given that all music was church music. Rather, all *notated* music at this time was

Composers of the Middle Ages

	1100	1150	1200	1250	1300	1350	1400	1450

Hildegard of Bingen

Marcabru

Bernart de Ventadorn

Léonin

Gace Brulé

Pérotin

Guiot de Dijon

Adam de la Halle

Philippe de Vitry

Guillaume de Machaut

Francesco Landini

Johannes Ciconia

John Dunstable

church music: monks were almost the only people who could read or write.

Even at this date there was certainly music at courts and in the homes of noble families. Royal courts were soon to be central to musical culture outside the church, for example the brilliant court in the twelfth century of Eleanor of Aquitaine, queen first of France and then of England. Humbler people, too, must have sung in their homes, at work and convivially. But it is with the music of the church that this survey must begin: music that emanates from the great Gothic and Romanesque cathedrals and the ancient monasteries, and was read from the hand-copied books used at their religious services, or, more rarely, from the superb illuminated manuscripts prepared as records or as lavish gifts to kings, popes, or princes.

2 *Church Music*

By the beginning of the eleventh century, the form of the church service – celebrating the feasts of the church year, the saints' days, and other liturgical occasions – had become more or less standardized in western Europe, though there was regional and local variation. Throughout the Christian world the centerpiece of the liturgy was (and remains) the Mass. This ritual re-enactment of the Last Supper was designed to inspire people with the certainty that the spiritual world offered, in contrast to the less certain circumstances of everyday life. Although most people could not understand the Latin text of the Mass, those without sufficient education to follow it would be familiar with the ritual and, if they attended a large church, would be affected by the pomp and ceremony of the liturgical celebration and the splendor of its music.

27 *Drawings contrasting "holy" and "worldly" music from a Psalter, possibly from Rheims, 12th century. St John's College, Cambridge.*

The earliest music in the medieval church was plainsong, or plainchant, sometimes known as "Gregorian" chant because of its association with Pope Gregory I (590–604). During his reign chants used in the Western churches were collected and categorized. For High Mass much of the text would be chanted to music. Some sections, forming the "Ordinary", always had the same words on every occasion.

Structure of the Mass

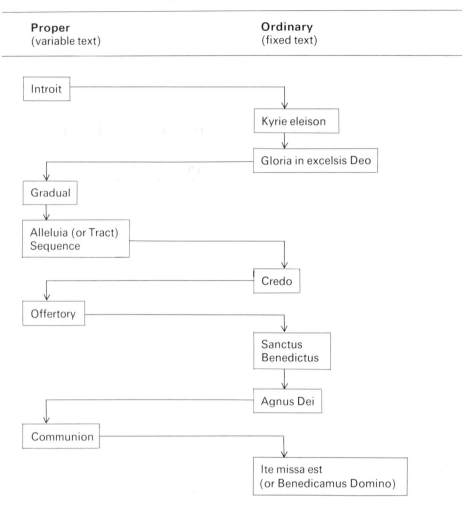

Proper (variable text)	Ordinary (fixed text)
Introit	
	Kyrie eleison
	Gloria in excelsis Deo
Gradual	
Alleluia (or Tract) Sequence	
	Credo
Offertory	
	Sanctus Benedictus
	Agnus Dei
Communion	
	Ite missa est (or Benedicamus Domino)

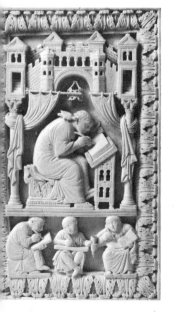

28 *St Gregory, the pope responsible for the categorizing of plainchant, and scribes: ivory book cover, 10th century. Kunsthistorisches Museum, Vienna.*

Others, the "Proper", used different texts according to the feasts of the church year and the demands of the local liturgy. The table above shows how some of these sections might relate in a typical celebration of the Mass (spoken text would intervene between these chanted sections).

Plainsong is a single line of text and melody, sung either by the priest or by several voices of the choir in unison, or by priest and choir in alternation. It has a smoothly flowing, undulating line, often following the rhythm of the text, and falls naturally into separate phrases, with breaks for "punctuation", rather like spoken prose. Some chants have only one note for each text syllable ("syllabic chant"). Others have more than one note, and sometimes extended groups, to each syllable ("melismatic chant") (see **Listening Guide 2**).

A mood of calm assurance, common to much plainsong, reflects the unquestioning confidence that medieval people had in their religion. Plainsong melodies are

Gregorian Chant
Ave Maria from the *Graduale Romanum*, Proper Chants

The body of chant, or plainsong, that serves as the central music of the Roman Catholic liturgy is generally supposed to have been set down and codified under Pope Gregory I in about the year 600. Recent research, however, has suggested that the codification took place rather later, and that it was in fact Gregory II who was responsible. The chants now in use, set out in the *Graduale Romanum* (1974), remain essentially the same, although early notation was not specific about rhythm and we do not know precisely how chant was sung in early times.

The *Ave Maria* recorded here comes from the Mass Propers (those parts that vary according to the church calendar). The chant is of the melismatic type, having several notes to each syllable; its mode is Dorian.

 Listening Outline

Time
0.00	'Ave Maria'
0.39	'Dominus tecum'
1.10	'benedicta tu'
1.36	'et benedictus'
2.08	(end)

Ave Maria, gratia plena, Dominus tecum, benedicta tu in mulieribus, et benedictus fructus ventris tui.	Hail Mary, full of grace, the Lord is with thee, Blessed art thou among women, And blessed is the fruit of thy womb.

classified according to mode (the particular pattern of tones and semitones used within an octave; see p. 27). The church modes were of fundamental importance to medieval composers.

The plainsong melodies used in medieval churches and monasteries, as they were transmitted orally, differed in detail from one community to another. But they gradually took on a more or less standard, traditional form that could be notated. Early plainsong notation is known as "neumatic" – each note or group of notes was indicated by a "neume", or sloping sign, written above the appropriate text syllable. There was no music staff; only the direction of the neume and its position relative to its neighbors showed the shape of the melody. At the beginning of the thirteenth century a more precise staff notation, using square note-shapes, was developed. This could convey different rhythmic values within the melody; it is still used in the liturgical books of the Catholic church.

A vast body of plainsong survives – over 3000 melodies, each with its own significance in the liturgy – and it has long played an important part in church music. Chant, moreover, has been so greatly revered as a fixed point of reference that, besides being sung in its own right, it has formed the basis of much of the religious music composed during the medieval and Renaissance periods in Europe.

3 *Secular Song*

From the end of the eleventh century secular music enjoyed something of a golden age, of around two hundred years, among minstrels who traveled between the feudal courts of Europe. At different times and places they were referred to by different names – goliards, jongleurs, scops, gleemen, troubadours, trouvères, minnesinger. There was a common aim: the expression through words and music of the ideal of "courtly love". Their love lyrics, which often idolized women as beautiful and unattainable, illustrate a side of medieval life very different from the austere spirituality of the chanting monks who were their contemporaries.

Among the exponents of this great flowering of secular song, the best known today are the troubadours, virtuoso poet-musicians who were active mainly in Provence, in southern France. They wrote their own poetry, not in Latin but in the vernacular (known in Provence as *langue d'oc*), set it to music, and performed it as entertainment at all levels of society, either unaccompanied or accompanying themselves on instruments such as the harp, lute, or fiddle.

Given the ravages of time and war, and the fact that the transmission of their music must have been mainly oral, it is remarkable that we have not only the names of many of these musicians – among the most famous are Bernart de Ventadorn (*d. c*1195) and Adam de la Halle (*c*1250–*c*1290) – but also some of their compositions. These are among the earliest composers known by name. Although they came from a variety of social backgrounds, trouvères (from northern France) and troubadours in particular were often men of high birth – esquires, knights, even kings (for example Thibaut IV, King of Navarre). The musical forms they used take their names from contemporary poetic forms. The most important are the *lai*, *ballade*, *rondeau*, and *virelai*. In these last three, the fixed patterns of meter and rhyme of the verse dictated the form of the music; they are sometimes known as *formes fixes* ("fixed forms"). These and the secular motet became the principal secular vocal forms of fourteenth- and fifteenth-century music.

The songs of the troubadours and trouvères range widely in style and mood: some delicate and restrained, some unadorned and syllabic, some rhythmic and dance-like (these often in triple time). They are usually easy to listen to and direct in appeal; and they are highly evocative of the age of chivalry and courtly love (see **Listening Guide 3**).

LISTENING GUIDE 3

Guiot de Dijon: *Chanterai por mon corage* (*c*1220)

Guiot de Dijon was a French trouvère; he came from Burgundy. Nothing is known of his life, except that he probably received the patronage of Erard II de Chassenay, who took part in the fifth crusade and returned to France in 1220. Guiot is named as the author of some 17 songs but it is impossible to be sure how many of these are truly his.

Chanterai por mon corage ('I shall sing to cheer my spirit') is a crusade song, presumably connected with the fifth crusade and so written in about 1220. It has three verses; we hear the first and the repeated refrain. The words express the grief and anxiety of a woman whose lover has gone on a crusade to the land of the Saracen, from which few men return. In this interpretation the solo soprano voice is shadowed – not supported by harmony – by a group of instruments (flute, lute, bass rebec, a small violin-like instrument, and harp). The flute plays the melody given in ex. 1; the voice then enters and sings the simple tune, altered slightly from line to line. It is decorated in different ways in successive verses, which are separated by the refrain reiterating the singer's fears.

 Listening Outline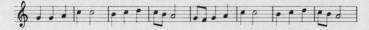

Time

0.00   flute plays the refrain (ex. 1) accompanied by the lute and
       rebec
0.11   the singer starts the first verse which repeats the melody
       stated by the flute
1.22   the flute plays the refrain again
1.34   (end)

Chanterai por mon corage	I shall sing to cheer my spirit
Que je vueil reconforter,	which I want to comfort,
Qu'avecques mon grant domage	so that with my great grief
Ne quier morir ne foler.	I may not die or go mad.
Quant de la terre sauvage	From the cruel land
Ne voi mes nul retorner	I see no one returning.
Qu cil est qui rassoage	Where is he who soothes
Mes maus quant g'en oi parler.	my heart when I hear him spoken of.
Dex, quant crïeront 'Outree'.	God! when they cry 'Outree'.
Sire, aid és au pelerin	Lord, help the pilgrim
Par cui sui espaventee,	for whom I am so afraid,
Car felon sont Sarazin.	for the Saracens are evil.

ex. 1

4 *Polyphony and the Motet*

So far, the music we have looked at has been "monophonic" (from the Greek, meaning "single-sounded"): that is, consisting of a single line of melody. The late Middle Ages saw a development that now seems to have been the most far-reaching in the history of Western music. At a time when the visual arts were beginning to be concerned with depth and perspective, the more learned of musicians – generally the highly educated clerics and the scholars attached to the more sophisticated ecclesiastical centers of Europe – began to have analogous ideas. They combined two or more melodic lines simultaneously to give "depth" to the music.

This style of composition became known as "polyphonic" (from the Greek, "many-sounded"). At first there were only two melodic lines, both based on plainsong, moving in exactly the same rhythm and in parallel, one a 4th or a 5th below the other. Later, a third or fourth voice was introduced, an octave below or above the first or second. This rather severe style of early polyphony was known as *organum*.

In the late eleventh century and the twelfth, musicians began to elaborate on this simple style of *organum* by giving the plainsong melody (or *cantus firmus*) to the lower voice in long, held notes while a second voice above had a freely flowing line in shorter ones. The lower, principal voice was called the tenor (from the Latin *tenere*, "to hold"). The church apparently encouraged the use of *organum* as long as elaboration did not obscure the meaning of the text.

It was natural that the cathedral of Notre Dame in Paris, one of the leading ecclesiastical centers of northern Europe, should be in the forefront of musical development. In the late twelfth century a large group of musicians gathered there. This group of early polyphonists is generally called the "Notre Dame school".

Organum illustrated the twofold importance of plainsong in medieval composition: structural and spiritual. The long tenor notes of the chant, though usually too drawn out to be easily heard as a melody, provide a structural foundation allowing the composer to devise more inventive upper parts. Spiritually, the plainsong served as a symbolic reminder of the music's liturgical meaning. These two functions can be observed to some degree in most of the sacred music of the medieval and Renaissance periods that relies on chant.

The most effective music that emanated from Notre Dame, as from Europe's other great cathedrals and monasteries, was well matched to the Gothic architec-

29 Procession of the Blessed (with a positive organ): detail from a Last Judgement scene over the west door of León Cathedral, Spain, 13th century.

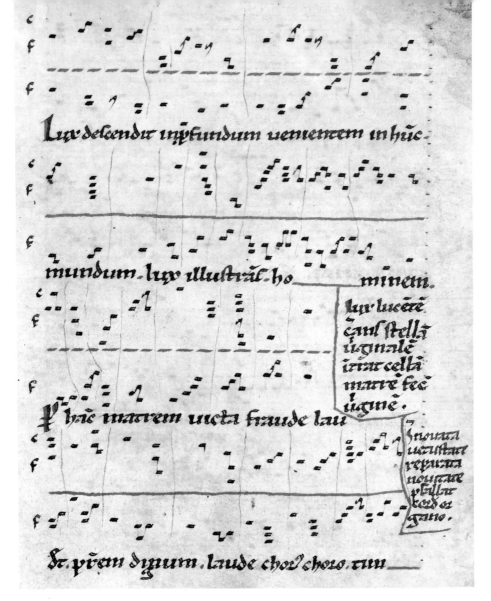

Lux descendit in profundum venientem in huc

mundum lux illustrat ho— minem.

lur lucere
caul stella
ugmale
irtar cella
matre fec
ugine.

hic matrem victa fraude lau

snouata
uetustate
reputata
nouitate
pbillar
tecs ot
gano.

Se. piem dignum laude choa choa cum

30 *Organum "Lux descendit" from a 12th-century manuscript from St Martial. British Library, London.*

ture that surrounded it — soaring, magnificent, and resonant — and it laid the foundation of a polyphonic style that flourished for some 400 years.

Much medieval music is characterized by the same combination of "fixity" and "freedom" as appears in *organum*. Fixity is often present in the form of plainsong, usually in the tenor, which determines the structure and acts as a reference point for the other voices. Freedom is reflected in the parts that are freshly composed and which may even have a different text (or texts) from the liturgical tenor chant.

During the thirteenth century the most important new form, distinguished by this joint reliance on fixity and freedom, was the motet. It came to be used not only in the church, but as a secular form; sacred and secular texts could even be used in the same piece. For example, a traditional Latin liturgical text in one voice might be combined with a French secular poem in another, while the tenor retained the notes and Latin text of a plainsong melody (the *cantus firmus*, or "fixed song"; see p. 33). The term "motet" itself probably derives from the French *mot*, "word", which may refer to the added texts in the upper parts. By the end of the thirteenth century the *cantus firmus* motet had become a sophisticated and complex form, testing the skills and inventiveness of composers to the full. Most of the pieces that survive from this period are for three voices and are by anonymous composers of the Notre Dame school.

Music theorists of the early fourteenth century described this thirteenth-century music as "Ars Antiqua" ("the old art"), for early in the century a new style, which they called "Ars Nova" ("the new art"), was gaining currency.

5 *Machaut and Landini*

MACHAUT

The representative figure of this new style is Guillaume de Machaut (*d.*1377), statesman, cleric, and poet as well as composer. Born around 1300, he was secretary to the King of Bohemia for nearly 20 years. Later he was a canon of several major French churches and served members of the nobility. Machaut was highly regarded by his patrons as both poet and musician, and for them he supervised the preparation of his works in several beautifully illuminated manuscripts, which present a broad selection of his music unique for a composer of the Middle Ages.

Machaut's music looks both backwards to the thirteenth century and the age of chivalry, and forwards to the fifteenth century and the early Renaissance. He was one of the first to produce polyphonic settings of secular poetry in traditional *formes fixes* and to write polyphony for four voices as well as the more usual three. In addition, Machaut was the earliest composer by whom there survives a complete polyphonic setting of the Mass Ordinary. Previously, as we have seen, the texts of the Mass were changed monophonically; the polyphonic Mass was a form that was to be central to liturgical music in the fifteenth century (see **Listening Guide 4**).

Machaut's music hints at a smoothness and sweetness, brought about by his use of consonant intervals between the voices, that is lacking in earlier medieval music. It shows a glimmer of the same ideals that inspired the works of fourteenth-century Italian painters like Giotto – religious symbolism gradually giving place to a more worldly expression of human feelings. This secularization of the arts may have been related to the series of disasters that rocked Europe in the fourteenth century: the battle over papal authority that led to the papal schism; the terrible suffering caused by the plague of 1348; the growing discord between church and state; and the

31 Guillaume de Machaut: *miniature from a French manuscript, 14th century. Bibliothèque Nationale, Paris.*

LISTENING GUIDE 4

Machaut: *Messe de Nostre Dame* (?1364), Kyrie 1

Machaut's *Messe de Nostre Dame*, his only surviving setting of the Mass text, is a work of great sophistication and skill. It is for four voices. Of its six movements, four (Kyrie, Sanctus, Agnus Dei, and Ite missa est) use *isorhythm* and have a plainsong *cantus firmus* in the tenor voice; this serves as a framework and as a unifying element. The movements also have melodic links. Before each, one voice gives out the plainsong phrase on which the *cantus firmus* is based; then the others enter with the composed polyphony. While the Kyrie uses flowing contrapuntal lines, against which the *cantus firmus* is barely audible, the Gloria and Credo are in a simpler, note-against-note style, which helps clarify the words of these longer, more involved texts. Audibility of the words was a particular concern of the church authorities.

Like other settings of the Mass Ordinary, Machaut's Mass was intended to play a part in the celebration of the liturgy. It was performed, and can best be appreciated, not as a succession of six movements but with the polyphonic Ordinary movements interspersed with the chants of the Mass Proper appropriate to a specific feast in the church year (see table, p. 70). If we can imagine listening to the Mass beneath the lofty echoing arches of a great Gothic cathedral, like Rheims, it is easy to see how this contrast between the modesty of plainsong and the grandeur of four-part polyphony can make a powerful impression.

The Kyrie's three sections symbolize the Holy Trinity and follow the structure of the plainsong on which it is based. This melody (ex. 1) is in a middle voice; against it the upper voices – sung by tenors, in the modern sense of the word – weave a polyphonic texture in free rhythm, often with momentary breaks. The original notation of a work such as this does not give precise instructions to the performers and needs to be interpreted. In the present performance, the high tenor voice at the top of the texture is supported by a recorder and a fiddle, the second voice by a harp and a reed organ, the third (singing the plainsong) by a small organ and a large fiddle, the lowest by a lute and a dulzian (a double-reed instrument of low pitch, like a soft-toned bassoon).

 Listening Outline . . . .

Time	
0.00	Kyrie begins
0.59	Kyrie, second time
1.59	Kyrie, third time
2.56	(end)

Kyrie eleison.　　　Lord, have mercy upon us.

ex. 1

squabbles between the states themselves, particularly in Italy. Yet at the same time in secular Italy there was great artistic activity. It was the era of such great poets and writers as Petrarch, Boccaccio, and Dante, and as secular literature flourished, so did secular music.

LANDINI

The greatest Italian composer of this period was Francesco Landini (*c*1325–97). Blind from childhood, he learned to play several instruments, to sing and to write poetry. He spent most of his life in Florence and took part in the main philosophical and religious disputations of his day. He was renowned both as an organist and organ builder and as an intellectual. Most of his compositions are *ballate* for two or three voices. Many are simple, one-note-to-a-syllable, dance-like settings (see **Listening Guide 5**). Others are more complex, but all show his great melodic gift.

Italian polyphony of this period is vigorous and lively. Much of it reflects the pastoral, often lighthearted mood of its texts; favorite forms were the madrigal, the *ballata*, and the *caccia*, all based on poetic forms. Unlike sacred music based on chant, this type of secular composition gives the important melodic material to the upper voice or voices, while the lower adopts a subsidiary role.

32 Below *Tombstone of Francesco Landini. S Lorenzo, Florence.*

33 Below *Minstrels at a wedding feast, with nakers, two shawms, bagpipes, two trumpets, fiddle, and portative organ: miniature from the* Thebiad of Statius, *Italian, c1380–90. Chester Beatty Library, Dublin.*

LISTENING GUIDE 5

Landini: *Ecco la primavera* (mid–late fourteenth century)

Most of Landini's compositions are songs in the *ballata* form; he wrote about a hundred altogether. The *ballata* was a dance-song, usually with a text about love; it originated in the late thirteenth century and remained in use into the fifteenth. This example is for two voices and was probably written fairly early in Landini's life, perhaps soon after the middle of the fourteenth century. The text is a joyful welcoming of the spring.

It begins, in this performance, with percussion instruments setting the rhythm; then wind instruments give out the melody, which is taken up by the two voices (ex. 1) while the percussion continue to give rhythmic support. Typically, the song is in triple meter. There are three verses, the first of them repeated at the end; each has the same music.

 Listening Outline

Time

0.00	instruments play the song through as introduction
0.20	voices sing first verse (ex. 1)
0.32	second verse
0.46	third verse
0.57	first verse repeated
1.10	(end)

Ecco la primavera	Spring is here
Che'l cor fa rallegrare.	And it fills the heart with joy.
Temp'è d'annamorare	Now is the time to fall in love
E star con lieta cera.	And to be happy.
No'vegiam l'aria e'l tempo	We see the air and the fine weather
Che pul chiam' allegrezza.	Which also call us to be happy.
In questo vago tempo	In this sweet time
Ogni cosa ha vaghezza.	Everything is so beautiful.
L'erbe con gran freschezza	Fresh green grass
E tior' copron i prati,	And flowers cover the meadows,
E gli alberi adornati	And the trees are adorned
Sono in simil manera.	In the same way.
Ecco la primavera . . .	Spring is here . . .

ex. 1

6 *The Renaissance*

The period traditionally known as the Renaissance (the term means "rebirth") extends from about the middle of the fifteenth century until the last years of the sixteenth. Artists, thinkers, writers, and musicians of the time all felt that some kind of corner had been turned, that the darkness and the dogmatisms of the Middle Ages were passing, and that a new era was dawning. This new era found much of its inspiration in the ancient classics and their values: hence the idea of rebirth. Such values were particularly focused on human beings, their individuality, and their emotions, as opposed to the medieval preoccupation with the mystical and the divine; the concept of "humanism" and its link with the study of ancient Greece and Rome is central to Renaissance thought. "Academies" began to be founded at which intellectual noblemen gathered to discuss the classics and their implications for the arts of the time. The first was in Florence in 1470; 80 years later, there were some 200 across the whole of Italy.

Composers before 1600

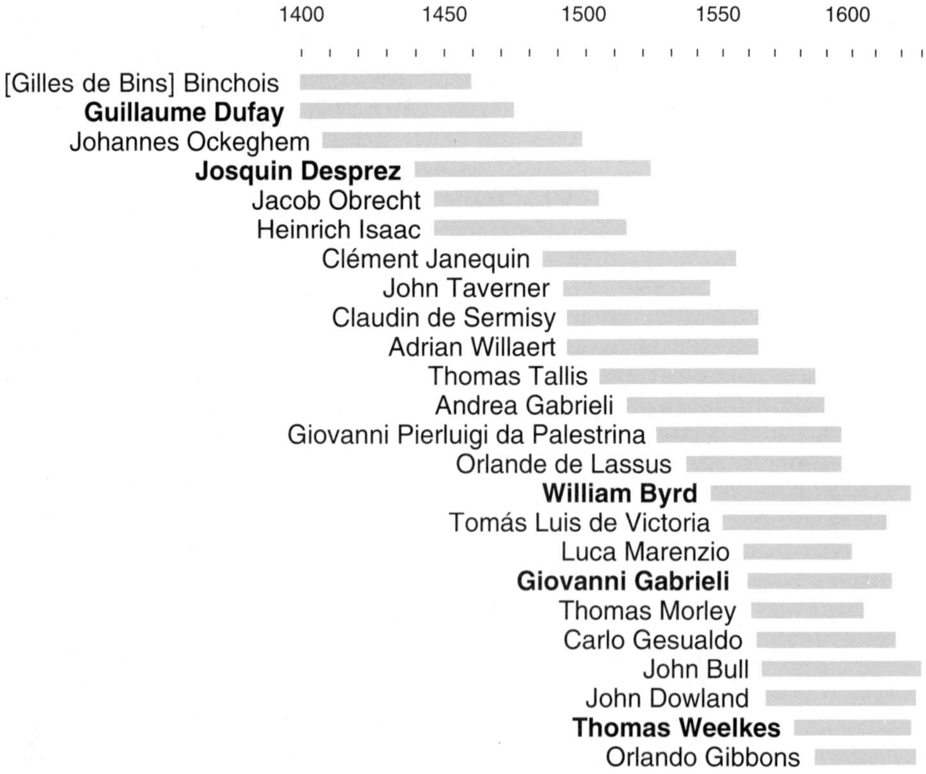

	1400	1450	1500	1550	1600

[Gilles de Bins] Binchois
Guillaume Dufay
Johannes Ockeghem
Josquin Desprez
Jacob Obrecht
Heinrich Isaac
Clément Janequin
John Taverner
Claudin de Sermisy
Adrian Willaert
Thomas Tallis
Andrea Gabrieli
Giovanni Pierluigi da Palestrina
Orlande de Lassus
William Byrd
Tomás Luis de Victoria
Luca Marenzio
Giovanni Gabrieli
Thomas Morley
Carlo Gesualdo
John Bull
John Dowland
Thomas Weelkes
Orlando Gibbons

34 Emperor Maximilian I surrounded by musicians and instruments: *woodcut, 1505–16, by Hans Burgkmair.*

The visual arts

The Renaissance was essentially an Italian movement, at least in its origins. It produced a uniquely marvelous crop of painters and sculptors in that country – Piero della Francesca, Bellini, Mantegna, Perugino, Botticelli, Leonardo da Vinci, Michelangelo, Giorgione, Raphael, Titian, Tintoretto. In music there is nothing of that order; there were few significant Italian composers until Palestrina. But the Italian courts, centers of artistic patronage, drew an immensely talented collection of composers from the north (mainly from northeast France and from Flanders, present-day Belgium). Their music shows a change of approach, as compared with the previous generation's, analogous to that of Renaissance art. There, the stiff, mystical, abstract, and highly stylized postures of the Middle Ages began to be superseded by natural, flowing ones, which allow human beings to be seen feeling ordinary human emotions; a man or a woman can be an object of interest in himself or herself, not merely in relation to the divine.

Such a change was not sudden; in painting, it is already hinted at in the work of Giotto (*c*1266–1337) and his contemporaries, as it is in the writings of Dante (1265–1321) and, in the next generation, Petrarch and Boccaccio. But the change was not consistent or universal at that early date, and in music (although parallels might be seen in the work of such men as Landini or Machaut) it is only with the generation of composers active in the late fifteenth century that such a "humanistic" element is regularly found.

In painting, part of this quality is related to the development of the art of perspective. Renaissance pictures generally have a sense of depth – only the tentative beginnings of this can be seen in medieval ones – and thus a realistic way of relating people to their context. At just the same time, a way of giving music an audible depth was developing. The medieval composer depended upon such rigid devices as isorhythm – a system of repeated rhythmic patterns which provides a convenient framework but has little meaning for the listener. The Renaissance composer worked in a different way, composing the voice-parts in careful relation to one another, and with newly supple lines providing a succession of harmonies. This quickly led to the lowest voice having a slightly different status (and accordingly a slightly different style) from the others: here are the very beginnings of Western harmony, or sense of perspective in music. (It is, by the way, intriguing to note that some 450 years later composers abandoned the traditional ways of handling harmony just as artists were abandoning perspective.) Further, to give their pieces some degree of internal unity, they tended to assign the same musical phrases to each voice, normally in such a way that each sang the same phrase to a particular group of words. The voices enter successively with the same phrase, so that the polyphony becomes increasingly rich and interwoven: this "imitative" technique is the classical style of the Renaissance – and eventually it was to lead to the fugues of Bach.

Humanism

The new emphasis on the human being was part of a general move towards the secular as opposed to the sacred, which had dominated life for so long. Power moved in the same direction, away from the church towards kings and princes. These, notably in the city-states of north Italy, were often men of high education and enlightenment, for example in Florence, where the Medici family held sway, or Ferrara, ruled by the Este family. Such people were eager to display their power, wealth, and taste, in lavish entertainments. At their courts secular forms like the madrigal especially flourished, and at Florence in particular the *intermedio*, a mixed entertainment of dance, music of various kinds, and poetry, was cultivated. At Rome, under the pope, church music remained central, as it also did at Venice, under civic rule. North of the Alps too there was a strong move towards the secular, notably in England where Henry VIII threw off papal influence; he, and later Elizabeth I, were important patrons of music, as was Francis I in France. Burgundy, now a part of France but then an independent country which included areas of what are now the Low Countries, had one of the most brilliant of all the courts of the fifteenth century, but its separate history came to an end in 1477.

The Reformation

The biggest change during this period, however, originated in Germany. This was the Reformation. It began as an attempt to rid the Catholic church of corruption and abuse and to "rationalize" religious practice by allowing every man and woman the right to worship in his or her own language. It caused bloodshed and destruction on a vast scale, over many decades, though in the light of history we can see it as an inevitable development of the Renaissance and its modes of thought. Its leader was Martin Luther (1483–1546). To him music was a vital part of worship, and although he greatly admired the Latin works of such composers as Josquin he realized that ordinary people's involvement in religion would be deepened were they allowed to participate in services rather than listen passively to Latin chant from the clergy and, in the larger churches, Latin polyphony from the choir.

Luther established a repertory of hymns, or "chorales" (so called because they were to be sung chorally), sometimes drawing on well-known songs, which would be familiar to his congregations, and sometimes composing new melodies himself: among his own compositions is *Ein feste Burg* ("A stronghold sure"), often called the battle-song of the Reformation. In the reformed church the chorale largely came to take the place that plainsong had traditionally occupied in the Catholic church, as a basis for newly composed works.

The Lutheran reforms had great influence in Germany, especially the northern and eastern parts, and in Scandinavia. Another reformer, Jean Calvin (1509–64), was more influential in his native France, Switzerland, the Low Countries, and Scotland; he was less interested in music than was Luther and advocated the use of psalms in austere, unaccompanied versions. In England too the church was reformed, under Henry VIII, and an Anglican church established with congregational participation and use of the English language.

The Counter-Reformation

The Catholic church was bound to react to the spread of the Reformation, which by the middle of the sixteenth century had created a huge schism. What is called the Counter-Reformation began in the 1540s: a move by the Catholic church to rid itself of malpractices and to encourage greater piety among the people, involving a revival of Catholic principles and their application in a carefully monitored, disciplined way. Music and its use in the church were among the topics discussed in the series of meetings held at Trent, in northern Italy, between 1545 and 1563. The Council of Trent expressed concern over the use of secular melodies in church (for example as *cantus firmi* in Mass settings: see p. 85) and the weakening of the traditions of plainsong, and objected to over-elaborate polyphony that might obscure the liturgical words; virtuoso singing in particular was deplored, and so was the use of instruments other than the organ. In countering Luther and his reforms, the Council was in fact compelled to tread a similar path.

The new result was not only music of a new simplicity: the music of the Counter-Reformation is marked by its fervor, its emotional content, and its feeling of mysticism. Its greatest composer was Palestrina, but the colorful polychoral and ensemble music of the two Gabrielis, Andrea and Giovanni, from Venice, is imbued with the Counter-Reformation spirit, and so is much music from Spain. The staunch Catholicism of that powerful country, whose empire included most of what is now Belgium, put it in the forefront of the fight against the Reformation.

35 *Frontispiece to Antico's collection* Frottole intabulate da sonar organi (1517).

Printing

It is difficult to imagine how the Reformation could have made any real progress without the invention of printing. Printing was invented (in the West) in the mid-fifteenth century; music printing began in about 1473 and in the last quarter of the century many liturgical music books, for the singing of chant, were produced from woodblocks, carved and inked. It was in 1501 that the first polyphonic music was printed, by Ottaviano Petrucci of Venice, using movable type; this was an anthology mainly of *chansons* by French and Flemish composers. It must have been a success, to judge by his reprints and his further publications. His methods were quickly copied elsewhere – in Germany, France, and England, and in other Italian cities. Until this time, music had circulated only in manuscript, a laborious and costly process; now it became available to a much wider public. The international exchange of ideas that was now possible was important to the dissemination of Renaissance culture.

Petrucci and his followers printed music of all sorts: polyphony, both sacred and secular, instrumental music (including tablatures for the lute – that is, music that tells you not what notes to sound but where to put your fingers for the ones that should be played), and, in the "reformed" countries, hymn books and psalm collections.

This new spread of music and ideas – supported by the idea of "Renaissance man", interested and skilled in all the arts and sciences – made it possible for music-making to become popular among the higher social classes in the sixteenth century. People learned to read music, to sing, and to play instruments, and a new demand arose for any kind of music that could be performed in the home by a small number of modestly capable musicians. This demand was chiefly met by the new forms of secular song: the madrigal in Italy, and later in England and other parts of northern Europe, in France the *chanson*, in Germany the polyphonic *Lied*. The singing of madrigals and similar works came to be regarded as a pleasant domestic pastime. With one voice to a part, it offered an intimate form of music-making – primarily to entertain the performers themselves, and perhaps a few guests, but not a formal audience. The time of the public concert was still a long way off; and we understand music of the Renaissance best if we listen to it with an awareness of the role in society that it was originally intended to play.

7 *The Genres of Renaissance Music*

MASS

As we have seen, the central ritual of Christian worship in the Middle Ages was the *Mass* (see p. 68). With the Renaissance it came to assume a central musical importance too. With the coming of polyphony, composers could bring a unity to their settings of the Mass in one of two ways. They could either use similar openings to each of the five movements (Kyrie, Gloria, Credo, Sanctus with Benedictus, and Agnus Dei); or they could base the work on an existing melody or *cantus firmus*, which might be a piece of plainsong but could equally be a secular song, perhaps a popular one that would be familiar to listeners and so would add to the music's appeal. This technique began to be used regularly in the late fifteenth century. Some tunes became particular favorites, for example *L'homme armé*, set by all the leading composers and many lesser ones. In the early sixteenth century the borrowing technique was carried further and many "parody masses" were written in which an entire existing work (usually a motet) was used as a model. All the great composers of the polyphonic era – such as Dufay, Josquin, Lassus, Palestrina, and Byrd – wrote Masses, usually for four, five, or six voices in imitative counterpoint.

MOTET

Of almost equal importance with the Mass is the *motet*. Its history begins in the thirteenth century, when words were added to musical phrases previously performed without text. These developed into independent compositions in which two or three voices took part, often singing different though related texts (sometimes in different languages; see p. 75–6). By the fifteenth century the motet had become a polyphonic setting of a Latin religious text, at first often for three voices, later usually for four or more. Sometimes a *cantus firmus* was used as a basis. The style was usually imitative: indeed imitative writing is sometimes called "the motet style".

With the Reformation, the motet was superseded in England by the English-language anthem, used by such composers as Byrd and Gibbons; it has a continuing history in Britain and America.

CHANSON

Of the polyphonic secular vocal forms, the oldest is the *chanson*, which goes back to the Middle Ages. There is a large and varied repertory of *chansons* from the fifteenth and sixteenth centuries, settings of French words mostly for three voices (probably they were sometimes performed with combinations of voices and instruments). Leading composers include Dufay, Ockeghem, Josquin, and Lassus.

MADRIGAL

The Italian counterpart of this French and Netherlandish form was the *madrigal*. The term was first used for a fourteenth-century form, normally for two voices, of which Landini was a leading exponent. It applies more importantly to a large repertory of the sixteenth and early seventeenth centuries, covering music for any number of voices from one to eight or even ten, but most commonly four or five. It found its poetic inspiration in the verse of the fourteenth-century poet Petrarch; musically it took as its starting-point a slightly earlier form, the *frottola*, a light-weight type of four-voice song.

 The madrigal at its height, in the middle and late sixteenth century, embodied imitative counterpoint but also a great variety of texture, with sensitive and often intense expression of the words. Leading composers of this time were Palestrina, Lassus, and Andrea Gabrieli. At the end of the century the style became more

36 *Wind band with treble and two tenor shawms, cornett, trombone, and curtal: detail of the painting* Procession of the Religious Orders of Antwerp on the Feast Day of the Rosary, *1616, by Denis van Aisloot. Museo del Prado, Madrid.*

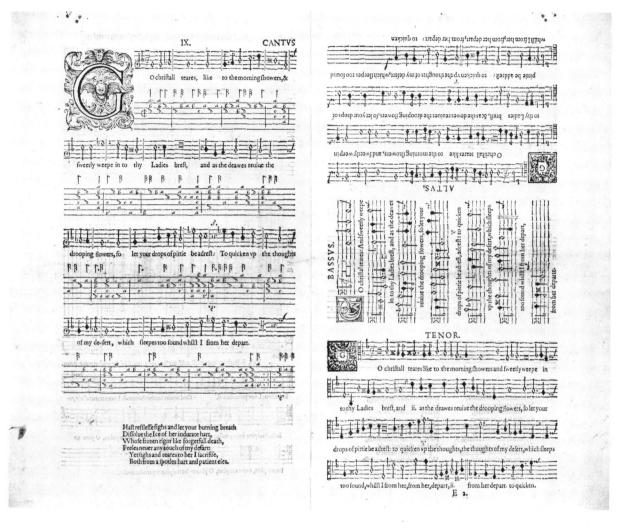

elaborate and dramatic, with much stress on color; Marenzio, Monteverdi, and Gesualdo are the most important composers of this late period in the madrigal's history. The form traveled abroad, most notably to England, where it found exponents in Byrd, Morley, and (of the later generation) Weelkes. The dance-type madrigal, the *balletto* or ballett, was particularly favored in England.

Another form of song, for one voice with lute or viols, was popular in England: the *ayre* (or air), cultivated particularly by John Dowland. The French had an equivalent to this in their *air de cour*, or "courtly air". The Italian equivalent is "aria", which is the standard term in Italy for song. Unlike the madrigal, with its equal and usually imitative voices, the ayre had its chief melodic interest in the top line. But it could be performed by several voices (accompanied or unaccompanied) or, more commonly, as a lute-song with a solo voice taking the top line and a lute supplying the lower parts, possibly with a viol reinforcing the bass.

37 *"Go christall teares" by John Dowland from his* First Book of Songes or Ayres *(1597). It can be sung by four singers round a table, or by one with lute.*

AYRE

ENSEMBLES

As in the Middle Ages, instruments during the Renaissance took various roles. They were originally used functionally, to accompany voices or, in domestic music-making, to take a voice part; some madrigal publications were issued as "for voyces or violls". Many instrumental adaptations exist of *chansons* and madrigals. The instruments used would normally be viols or recorders, of various sizes, grouped in "consorts" or families. The commonest viols, for example, were the treble, the tenor, and bass (held between the knees, like a cello). At first, such ensembles rarely played anything other than arrangements of vocal pieces; later, instrumental consort music was composed, by Byrd and his successors, notably Orlando Gibbons (1583–1625); these were often contrapuntal pieces entitled "fantasia" in England, "canzona" or "ricercar" in Italy and Germany. There was also much dance music for ensemble. Such pieces might be for "whole consort" (all viols, or all recorders) or "broken consort" (a mixture of string and wind instruments).

The relatively soft-toned instruments, and the lute, were sometimes described as *bas* ("low" or "soft"), while the strident ones were classified as *haut* ("high" or "loud"). The latter included wind instruments such as the cornett, trumpet, shawm, and sackbut, as well as percussion. They were suitable for playing outdoors, to accompany dancing or in processions or in elaborate church ceremonial, as practiced by the Gabrielis in Venice, for example; these roles helped instrumental music gain independence from vocal. Dance music was soon being composed specifically for instruments, both solo and ensemble. Popular dances were the pavan (a slow, stately dance in duple time), which was often followed by a galliard (in a livelier triple time) and a passamezzo (an Italian duple-time dance, slightly faster than the pavan). There are many pictures of ensemble music in performance; see, for example, **Color Plate 4**.

KEYBOARD

In the earlier Renaissance there was little distinction between music for keyboard instruments with plucked strings, such as the harpsichord or spinet, and that written for the organ, in spite of their differing capabilities. For example, a note played on the organ can be sustained for as long as the air is supplied to the pipe; but plucked string instruments have virtually no sustaining power. It may be easier to play faster music more satisfactorily on a plucked string instrument than on the organ, and on the clavichord (where the strings are struck) some variation in volume can be achieved by touch.

Much of the music for keyboard players and lutenists in this period was transcribed from vocal works, *chansons*, madrigals, and motets. But these instruments could not sustain the sound as voices can, so composers tended to avoid long-held notes, dividing them up into a number of shorter ones, almost in a decorative fashion. This device was similar to the technique of writing variations on an existing theme, as practiced by, for example, Byrd. These factors helped establish idiomatic styles of writing for the keyboard and for the lute. For instrumental ensembles – of viols, of wind instruments such as recorders, shawms, or cornetts, or combinations of strings and winds – the polyphonic style used in vocal music still soon prevailed, though a more rhythmically decisive style soon developed for dance music.

8 Dufay and Josquin

At the court of Burgundy, a rich and splendid cultural environment was nurtured under the patronage of a succession of four dukes. By the time of the last duke's death in 1477 the Burgundian ruling family was famed for both its political successes and the artistic brilliance of its court, and it attracted some of the greatest artists and musicians of the period.

Among the composers of the "Burgundian school" was Guillaume Dufay (*c*1400– 1474), the most significant figure of the period. Born in northern France, he spent several years in Italy, where he sang in the papal chapel and traveled extensively between the region, in northern France, where he was born and the great centers of church and courtly patronage in Italy. So he was well placed to fuse the late medieval style of his native France and the early Italian Renaissance style, with its literary and humanist associations.

DUFAY

One of the striking features of Dufay's music is its relative straightforwardness as compared with the complexities of some of the late Gothic music that preceded it. Many of his works impress the listener first for their predominantly melodic character.

38 *Dufay (with a portative organ) with another song composer, Binchois (with a harp): miniature from* Champion des Dames *by Martin le Franc, French, 15th century. Bibliothèque Nationale, Paris.*

Dufay: Mass *'Se la face ay pale'*, Sanctus (part)

Guillaume Dufay's *chanson, Se la face ay pale*, is thought to have been composed in the 1430s, when he was employed at the court of the dukes of Savoy. The Mass he based on it was probably written about 20 years later; it may have been intended for use in connection with some celebration in the ruling Savoy family (it could have been in 1452, on the consummation of a marriage contracted many years earlier between infants, the Savoy heir and a French princess).

In composing the Mass, Dufay took the tenor line – not the top part – from the *chanson* and used it in the tenor of the Mass (ex. 1). It appears three times over in each of the long movements (the Gloria and the Credo), first three times slower, then twice, and lastly at normal speed. In each of the other three movements, including the Sanctus, it appears once, moving twice as slowly as the other voices. It is present only in the movements in full, four-voice texture.

 Listening Outline

Time

0.00 'Sanctus': begins with two-voice writing (ex. 2); the falling phrase at the beginning (*a*) is used at the start of each section of the Mass

0.34 full texture, with larger choir and doubling by cornetts and trombones; the *cantus firmus* (ex. 1) is in the tenor

1.39 'Pleni sunt caeli': two-voice texture, solo, alto, and tenor; bass voice enters and tenor pauses (2.22), tenor resumes and alto pauses (2.46), all three together (3.03)

3.35 'Osanna in excelsis': four-voice texture, *cantus firmus* in tenor

4.33 (end)

Sanctus, Sanctus, Sanctus, Dominus Deus Sabaoth,	Holy, holy, holy, Lord God of hosts,
Pleni sunt caeli et terra gloria tua,	Heaven and earth are full of thy glory
Osanna in excelsis.	Hosanna in the highest.

ex. 1

ex. 2

Guillaume Dufay	Works

born c1400; *died* Cambrai, 1474

Sacred vocal music 8 Masses – Se la face ay pale; Ave regina caelorum; Mass movements; over 20 motets; hymns

Secular vocal music over 80 chansons (rondeaux, ballades, virelais) for 3 voices – Ce moys de may

The *cantus firmus* of his Mass *Se la face ay pale*, for example, is not a piece of plainsong but derives from a song Dufay had composed some 20 years earlier. The use of a secular *cantus firmus* in a sacred work became common in the fifteenth century and gives an idea of the degree of "secularization" of liturgical music at this period (see **Listening Guide 6**).

Dufay was also one of the greatest composers of polyphonic *chansons* in the fifteenth century. His 80 or so surviving songs show a new, flexible attitude to the standard medieval song forms like the *rondeau* and the *ballade*. Most of his *chansons* are early works; some are linked with political or social events. His range of expression was wide, and his techniques varied according to the words of each song and the purpose for which it was composed. For example, in a *ballade* written in 1423 for the marriage of Carlo Malatesta to a niece of the pope the style is florid and the text is designed to glorify Malatesta. In a different style is *Adieu ces bons vins de Lannoys*, a nostalgic *rondeau* that reflects Dufay's sorrow on leaving the area (and the wines) of Laon, in northern France, in 1426. *Ce moys de may* ("This month of May"), also a *rondeau*, shows Dufay in a more energetic and carefree vein. The instruments used in *chansons* might have included wind (recorders, shawms, sackbuts), plucked and bowed strings (viols, fiddles, lutes), and percussion (drums, tambourines).

Dufay's greatness lies in the scope and consistent high quality of his output, which sums up the compositional styles of his time and reflects the increasing flexibility with which medieval forms were being handled. Related to this flexibility, and perhaps also to a growing secularization, is the personal stamp found on some of his music, a feature rare in the medieval period but commoner in the years to come.

The greatest composer of the central years of the Renaissance was Josquin Desprez (c1440–1521). Josquin was another north Frenchman who spent most of his adult life in Italy. First he was a singer at Milan Cathedral and in the service of the powerful Sforza family, rulers of Milan. Later he sang in the papal choir in Rome, and served the Este family in Ferrara, in northern Italy, before returning as a canon of a collegiate church in northern France, where he died.

JOSQUIN

Before he had left the north, Josquin composed in a reserved, sober style, like his old teacher, the composer Johannes Ockeghem, and his predecessors. But his experiences in Italy brought him into contact with a more fluent and flexible style, influenced by lighter secular forms; the music from these middle and later periods

Josquin Desprez: *Nymphes des bois* (1497)

This *chanson* is a lament on the death of the composer Ockeghem. Josquin made its funerary nature clear to both performers and listeners: to performers, by writing it in a black notation that had fallen out of use; to listeners, by using a plainsong *cantus firmus* which would instantly be recognized as the 'Requiem aeternam' from the Mass for the Dead (ex. 1 shows the melody line above the plainsong). The original is reproduced on p. 94.

Using a *cantus firmus* in a *chanson* was a reversion to an older manner, but Josquin seems here to be using this older manner in deference to Ockeghem: in the first part of the *chanson* the range of the lines is narrow, there are long melismas, and the cadences are merged into the musical fabric rather than (as in most of Josquin's music) helping to clarify its structure. The second section is more what one would expect from Josquin, with its shorter phrases and more clearly marked cadences. The sadness that pervades the piece comes from the choice of mode, with its 'minor-key' feeling; but the shape of the lines – the way they arch upward and fall back – also plays a part. This is typical of the expressive quality of Josquin's music.

 Listening Outline

Time	
0.00	'Nymphes des bois': rich, dense, and expressive four-voice texture
0.59	'Car d'Atropos': note the falling phrase in the lower voices, in 3rds, at 'molestations' and 'par sa rigueur attrappe'
1.32	'Le vray trésoir': note the gentle, expressive cadence at 'que la terre coeuvre'
2.30	'Acoutrez vous': the texture is lighter, less sustained; each of the composer's names is set to a falling 3rd
2.56	'Et plorez': the falling 3rds reappear, as if falling tears ('grosses larmes de oeil')
3.26	'Requiescat in pace. Amen': note the extended cadence
4.01	(end)

Nymphes des bois, déesses des fontaines,	Nymphs of the woods, goddesses of the fountains,
Chantres expers de toutes nations,	fine singers of all the nations,
Changez voz voix fort clères et haultaines	change your strong, clear, high voices
En cris tranchantz et lamentations.	into searing cries and lamentations.
Car d'Atropos les molestations	For the ravages of Atropos
Vostre Okeghem par sa rigueur attrappe	have cruelly ensnared your Ockeghem,
Le vray trésoir de musicque et chef d'oeuvre,	the true treasure and supreme master of music,
Qui de trépas désormais plus n'eschappe,	who can no longer escape death,
Dont grant doumaige est que la terre coeuvre.	and who, alas, is covered by the earth.
Acoutrez vous d'abitz de deuil:	Dress yourselves in clothes of mourning:
Josquin, Brumel, Pirchon, Compère	Josquin, Brumel, Pierchon, Compère
Et plorez grosses larmes de oeil:	And let your eyes weep copious tears:
Perdu avez vostre bon père.	for you have lost a good father.
Requiescat in pace. Amen.	May he rest in peace. Amen.

(one voice sings the following throughout)

Requiem aeternam dona ei Domine	Eternal rest give to him, O Lord:
et lux perpetua luceat ei.	and let perpetual light shine upon him.

ex. 1

of his life is regarded as his finest. He was extremely prolific and very wide-ranging. Though Masses form a large part of his output, he also wrote over 80 polyphonic motets and about 70 secular songs (mostly in French).

There are several reasons why Josquin's music sounds so different from that of the fourteenth century. His melodies are more flowing and wider-ranging, free of the formulaic patterns of plainsong. His rhythms are more varied, less restricted by meter and by such devices as isorhythm. His harmony is richer, his intervals are more sonorous, and his chord progressions move more naturally. Imitation has become an important structural feature and its smooth progress is often arrested by chordal sections where the voices move together. Dissonance has now gained an expressive value of its own and contributes greatly to the effect.

The most significant difference between Josquin's music and that of the Middle Ages is in general approach. Josquin is the first great composer to attempt to express emotion in music in any consistent way. In all but the richest churches and chapels of his time, sacred music still meant monophonic music; polyphony was relatively new. The harnessing of the technical complexities of counterpoint preoccupied late medieval composers – an objective that went hand in hand with the intellectual spirit of the period. If we listen to almost any medieval motet without reading the text, we are hard pressed to tell from the music alone whether the piece is narrative or reflective, whether its subject is penitence or rejoicing, where the significant points in the text occur, whether it closes optimistically or gloomily. Josquin was among the first to explore the new humanistic Renaissance attitudes – not only to

39 Josquin Desprez: *woodcut from* Opus chronographicum *(1611) by Petrus Opmeer.*

Josquin Desprez	Works
*born c*1440; *died* Condé, 1521	

Sacred vocal music 20 Masses – Missa pange lingua; Mass movements; over 80 motets – Ave Maria . . . virgo serena

*Secular vocal music c*70 chansons – Nymphes des bois

40 *Opening of Josquin's* Nymphes des bois *("La déploration de Johan. Ockeghem"), showing the superius and contratenor parts, with the Requiem text in the tenor. Biblioteca Medicea Laurenziana, Florence.*

religious expression but to peoples' whole approach to their relationship with the outside world. This is typified by his *chanson Nymphes des bois*, a deeply felt lament on the death of Ockeghem (see **Listening Guide 7**). It is this expressive quality in Josquin's music that places him unchallenged at the pinnacle of the period. (For the original notation of *Nymphes des bois* see **fig. 40**.)

9 *Lassus, Palestrina, and Gabrieli*

The greatest composer that northern Europe produced in the generation after Josquin's spent most of his adult life in southern Europe. Orlande (or Roland) de Lassus, or Orlando di Lasso as he was known in Italy, was born in 1532 in the Franco-Flemish town of Mons in Hainaut, an area that had produced a number of famous musicians. He is thought to have been a fine singer as a boy; there is even a tale that he was three times kidnapped for the sake of his beautiful voice. From about the age of 12 he was in Italy, at several of the most important courts and finally in Rome, where he was in charge of the music at the large, papal church of St John Lateran when he was only 21. In 1556 he joined the musical establishment of Duke Albrecht V of Bavaria in Munich and soon took over the ducal chapel, where he remained for more than 30 years. He died in 1594.

Lassus continued to visit Italy, and his fame as a composer spread rapidly, not least because his output was immense (over 2000 works). Most of his music was published during his lifetime, and he was widely regarded as the leading composer of his time. He was a true Renaissance man. As well as spiritual and devotional madrigals, he set lighthearted pastorals and racy ditties in several languages, including rumbustious German drinking-songs, which show yet another side of his personality.

Lassus's music combines features of several national styles: the beauty and expressiveness of Italian melody, the charm and elegance of French text-setting, and the solidity and richness of Flemish and German polyphony. But like all the best composers he had something of his own to add – a vivid imagination, with which he made dramatic and emotional musical responses to the words. That is particularly evident in his motets (see **Listening Guide 8**).

41 Orlande de Lassus: *engraving, 16th century.*

Orlande de Lassus	Works
born Mons, 1532; *died* Munich, 1594	

Sacred vocal music c70 Masses; 4 Passions; c100 Magnificat settings; over 500 motets – Alma redemptoris mater, Prophetiae sibyllarum; Magnus opus musicum; Penitential psalms; Lamentations; hymns

Secular vocal music c200 Italian madrigals and villanellas for 4–6 voices; c140 chansons for 4–8 voices; c90 lieder for 3–8 voices

LISTENING GUIDE 8

Lassus: *Alma redemptoris mater*

This brief motet, composed during Lassus's period at Munich and published in the large collection of his works issued by his sons after his death, is in eight voices – two four-part choirs, singing on this recording (as originally intended) from opposite sides, to give a spatial (or antiphonal) effect. A prayer to the Virgin Mary, it is typical of Lassus's fervent style, with its rich sound, its stately harmonic movement, the sense of the inner voices intertwining and echoing one another, the occasional highlighting of important words with dissonances, and the quiet, rapt moment as a tenor sings the words 'Virgo prius et posterius' ('Virgin, first and last'): all these demonstrate the intensely devotional, almost mystical atmosphere of the church music of the Counter-Reformation. One needs to imagine such a piece sung by a small but skilled choir in a side-chapel of a dark Catholic church, the air heavy with incense, the walls lavishly ornamented with Renaissance works of art and images dedicated to the Virgin.

 Listening Outline

Time	
0.00	'Alma redemptoris mater': rich, full textures, interplay between the choirs on opposite sides
0.40	'Et stella maris': note the downward phrase at 'cadenti' ('falling') and the ascending one at 'surgere' ('to rise')
1.26	'Tu quae genuisti'
2.09	'Virgo prius': momentary tenor solo, with a more intimate tone to the ensuing passage
2.26	'Gabrielis ab ore': textures fill out again
2.46	'Ave, peccatorum miserere': fervent music for the final pleas
3.47	(end)

Alma redemptoris mater,
quae pervia coeli porta manes,
Et stella maris, succurre cadenti
surgere qui curat populo:

Tu quae genuisti, natura mirante,
tuum sanctum genitorem,
Virgo prius et posterius,
Gabrielis ab ore sumens illud:

Ave, peccatorum miserere.

Gracious mother of the redeemer,
who stands at the doors of heaven,
star of the sea, aid the falling,
the people who struggle to rise:

You who gave birth, by wonder of nature,
to the Lord almighty,
eternal virgin,
who received from the lips of Gabriel that greeting:

have mercy on our sins.

PALESTRINA

Among other composers of church music working at the time of the Council of Trent was Giovanni Pierluigi da Palestrina (c1525–94). He was well attuned to the spirit of the Counter-Reformation and his music has traditionally been revered as the summit of sixteenth-century polyphony. He took his name from his birthplace, Palestrina, near Rome, and his entire life was devoted to the service of the greatest churches of the city – S. Maria Maggiore, St John Lateran, and St Peter's.

Palestrina owed his early success to the Bishop of Palestrina, who on his election in 1550 as Pope Julius III asked the composer to accompany him to Rome. Palestrina never enjoyed quite the same favor under subsequent popes, but always seems to have been comfortably placed, at the head of a division of the papal chapel. By his mid-30s he had earned a remarkable reputation as a composer and music director. Though attempts were made to entice him elsewhere, he never left Rome.

LISTENING GUIDE 9

Palestrina: *Missa brevis* (1570), Kyrie

Among Palestrina's Masses, the *Missa brevis*, composed in 1570, is of a special type, by virtue of its brevity. Most are longer, and many are based on plainsong or other pre-existing melodies. This Mass is nevertheless a classical example of Renaissance polyphony. Each of its three sections is built on a single phrase, treated in imitation; as can be seen in ex. 1, the imitation between voices may be as much as 12 notes long, though often it is shorter.

 Listening Outline . . . .

Time

0.00   Kyrie eleison, ex. 1: the alto enters first, imitated in turn by bass, soprano, and tenor (imitations are indicated in ex. 1 by *a*). Sometimes the theme is sung in 'diminution', that is, with shorter note-lengths – see for example the alto voice at m. 10 (the phrase is marked *a*)

1.10   Christe eleison, ex. 2: the imitation is closer, the second voice (soprano) entering only one beat after the alto

2.16   Kyrie eleison, ex. 3: the voices enter in ascending order, bass–tenor–alto–soprano; once all have begun, the bass has the opening two-measure phrase five times over, each time one step lower

3.16   (end)

Kyrie eleison.	Lord have mercy.
Christe eleison.	Christ have mercy.
Kyrie eleison.	Lord have mercy.

ex. 1

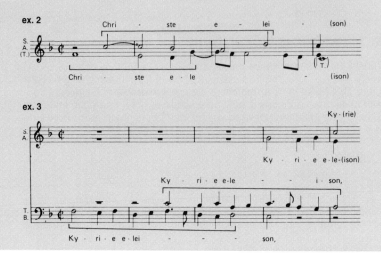

Like his great contemporary Lassus, Palestrina was extremely prolific. He wrote many secular pieces, but his ecclesiastical appointments concentrated his main energies on church music and he produced over 100 Masses (more than any other composer of the period), nearly 400 motets, and many other sacred works. The almost legendary reverence in which Palestrina has been held began during his lifetime. Much of his music was published and widely diffused during the second half of the century, and so great was his reputation within the church that in 1577 he was asked to revise the standard texts of plainsong in accordance with the guidelines laid down by the Council of Trent – a task he never in fact finished. One of his most famous Masses, the *Missa Papae Marcelli* ("Mass for Pope Marcellus"), may have been written to show that the Council of Trent requirements were not necessarily incompatible with beautiful polyphony in the traditional mold.

Palestrina's Masses embrace all the current types of Mass composition. Many are "parody Masses", which use existing pieces by other composers (or by himself), usually motets, interpolated into the structure of the Mass – at that period a standard method. Other Masses are based on a *cantus firmus*, usually plainsong (as had been common in the early Renaissance), though there are a few examples of secular tunes. Still others are freely composed, without reference to pre-existing music; it is in that category that the four-voice *Missa brevis* ("Short Mass") of 1570 belongs (see **Listening Guide 9**).

Plate 3 Opposite *A detail from a* cassone *or marriage chest showing Florentine court musicians playing shawms and a slide-trumpet at the wedding of Boccaccio Adimari and Lisa Ricasoli, c1450. Accademia, Florence.*

Giovanni Pierluigi da Palestrina	Works

born c1525; *died* Rome, 1594

Sacred vocal music over 100 Masses – Missa Papae Marcelli; Missa brevis; 375 motets – Stabat mater; 35 Magnificat settings; 68 offertories; Lamentations, litanies, sacred madrigals, hymns

Secular vocal music c140 madrigals

IOANNIS PETRI Loysij Praenestini in basilica S. Petri de vrbe capellae Magistri. MISSARVM LIBER PRIMVS.

Plate 4 Opposite *Musicians playing the flute and the lute in a polyphonic chanson (see p. 86): detail from the painting* The Prodigal Son among the Courtesans, *16th century, artist unknown. Musée Carnavalet, Paris.*

42 *Title-page of Palestrina's* Missarum liber primus *("First book of Masses", 1554), showing the composer handing his work to Pope Julius III.*

Unlike Lassus, Palestrina was basically conservative in his musical outlook. His constant presence in Rome, at the center of the Counter-Reformation, meant that he was more restricted in the music he wrote and less free to experiment. But this seems to have suited him well. Rather than attempt new methods he refined the existing ones, and in doing so produced some of the most glorious sacred music of the period.

Palestrina was the ultimate master of the "imitative style", the backbone of sixteenth-century polyphony and probably the single most characteristic feature of Renaissance music. At the same time, stepwise melody is essential to Palestrina's style: his lines have no awkward leaps, no feeling of imbalance. Every dissonance is prepared and resolved according to the rules governing smooth harmonic progression. There are few full cadences; instead, the phrases tend to overlap to form a "seamless" texture, in which the equality of voices gives the music a sense of perfect proportion. It is through this beautifully restrained yet expressive style that Palestrina's music has come to be regarded as the classic model of Renaissance polyphony.

GIOVANNI GABRIELI

Venice, a trading city under an elected ruler rather than a princely family, reached the height of its prosperity in the sixteenth century. It acquired a musical tradition of a sumptuousness to match its wealth, artistic richness, and love of pomp. The city's basilica, St Mark's, was the center of its ceremonial life and its musical life too. Among the first Italians to hold important posts at St Mark's at this time were Andrea Gabrieli (c1533–85) and his nephew Giovanni Gabrieli (c1555–1612).

Andrea, in his sacred works, developed an individual style to suit the needs of St Mark's for ceremonial music. He was quick to see the special possibilities offered by the cathedral's architecture and sometimes divided up his players and singers into groups so that the listener would hear music from different directions. This *cori spezzati* ("spaced choirs") technique was not exclusive to St Mark's or to Venice, but developed there in response to the cathedral's design and the Venetian love of the grandiose.

Giovanni Gabrieli followed up his uncle's work. In 1587 he published a volume called *Concerti*, "Containing church music, madrigals, and other works" by himself and Andrea, mainly for opposing groups of singers and players. This is the earliest use of the word "concerto". Giovanni used dialog techniques with great freedom and variety and with specific and colorful instrumental writing (see **Listening Guide 10**). In some respects he belongs – as we shall see in the next chapter – as much to the Baroque era as to the Renaissance, with his emphasis, especially in the works of his last years, on contrast of various sorts and his development of the concerto-like (or *concertato*) style.

Giovanni Gabrieli   **Works**

born Venice, c1555; *died* Venice, 1612

Sacred vocal music Symphoniae sacrae (1597, 1615): Mass movements; c100 motets – In ecclesiis

Instrumental music Canzoni e sonate (1615); Sonata pian e forte (1597); canzonas, ricercares, fugues, toccatas for wind ensemble

Secular vocal music c30 madrigals

Giovanni Gabrieli: *Canzon XIII* (1597), *septimi e octavi toni*

This canzona was included in Gabrieli's 1597 publication, *Sacrae symphoniae*. The 'septimi e octavi toni' of the title refers to the mode in which it is written. It is typical of the antiphonal music favored in Venice, with separate 'choirs' of instruments. Here there are choirs of cornetts and sackbuts (trombones) to the left and right, while in the center is a softer-toned group consisting of string instruments and dulzian (akin to a bassoon).

The piece begins with a short passage for all the instruments together; but most of it is in the form of a three-way dialog, between the two 'brass' groups and the third. Sometimes one choir simply echoes another (though the time-span between original and echo varies), but often one answers another in true dialog, carrying the music forward as if in discussion; and sometimes all join together for a rich-sounding passage, in which imitative writing within the texture can be heard. Some of the musical ideas are brief, others are much longer. Towards the end the music heard in the first solo sections recurs. There is some brilliant ornamental writing, principally for the leaders of each group.

 Listening Outline . . . .

Time

0.00	full ensemble opens the canzona with the traditional rhythm, long–short–short
0.15	small brass ensemble enters
0.18	'soft-toned' group of strings and dulzian
0.23	brass ensemble enters
0.29	soft group
0.33	brass enters – an antiphonal passage follows
0.49	full ensemble
0.53	small brass group takes over
0.59	brass group features cornett solo (1.02)
1.07	soft group heard again, alternately with small brass group with many antiphonal passages between groups
1.40	string solo
1.44	cornett solo answers, followed by a great deal of antiphonal activity
2.05	full ensemble; then antiphonal passages
2.25	small brass ensemble as in the beginning
2.53	(end)

10 *English Music*

The greatest English composer of the sixteenth century was William Byrd (1543–1623). The range, versatility, and outstanding quality of his work set him above his English contemporaries and successors; he is often referred to as the English counterpart of Palestrina and Lassus. He was the last great English composer of Catholic church music and the first of the "golden" Elizabethan age of secular and instrumental music.

Byrd was appointed organist of Lincoln Cathedral at the age of 19 or 20, and remained there for about ten years. In 1570 he joined the Chapel Royal in London as a singer and soon afterwards became its organist, a post he at first shared with his predecessor Thomas Tallis (c1505–85). Tallis and Byrd worked closely together; in 1575 they were granted a valuable royal monopoly on music printing in England and on the issue of printed manuscript paper.

Byrd remained in court service all his life. After the Catholicism that prevailed during the reign of Mary Tudor (1553–8, the period of Byrd's upbringing), England returned to Protestantism under Elizabeth and many Catholics feared persecution. The queen seems to have tolerated Byrd's Catholic sympathies, however, for he is not known to have suffered for them. He was able to write music for both churches, including three Latin Masses and a large number of motets. For the Anglican church he wrote Services (that is, polyphonic settings of the *Magnificat* and *Nunc dimittis*, *Venite*, *Te Deum*, *Jubilate* etc) and anthems (the English equivalent of motets), usually accompanied by the organ or other instruments, sometimes with solo vocal parts.

Byrd's restraint and expressiveness as a composer of sacred music are shown at their finest in his short four-part motet *Ave verum corpus*, published in the first volume of his motet collection of 1605 entitled *Gradualia* (see **Listening Guide 11**). Byrd excelled in elegiac music, but not all his works are somber. As he grew

---

William Byrd   Works

born 1543; *died* Massey, 1623

Sacred choral music Cantiones (with Tallis, 1575); Cantiones sacrae (1589, 1591); Gradualia (1605, 1607); 3 Masses; Mass movements; Services – Short Service, Great Service; anthems; motets – Ave verum corpus; Anglican liturgical settings

Vocal chamber music Psalmes, Sonets and Songs (1588); Songs of Sundrie Natures (1589); Psalmes, Songs and Sonnets (1611)

Instrumental music fantasias and In Nomines for viol consort

Keyboard music fantasias, variations, dances, grounds for virginals

LISTENING GUIDE 11

Byrd: *Ave verum corpus* (1605)

This motet, published in a collection of 1605, has always been one of Byrd's most popular and admired works. For four voices, it shows his expressive technique used fully (though without the freedom or extravagance that might be applied in a madrigal) to treat a text about which Byrd, as a staunch Catholic, must have had strong emotional feelings. His style is very free compared with the orthodox imitative polyphony of, for example, the Palestrina *Missa brevis*. Rather, he makes his effects with telling harmony – at the very opening, for example, and again at 'O dulcis, o pie'. This harmonic device ('false relation') was especially favored by the English composers. There is, later, a little imitative writing, but even this is often unorthodox; Palestrina's imitation is almost always at simple intervals, like the octave, the 4th, or the 5th, while Byrd's, at any pitch, may lend the imitated phrase different color and meaning.

 Listening Outline . . . .

Time

0.00 'Ave verum': ex. 1 – note the G and G♯ in different voices (marked *x*), a 'false relation', producing an arresting and poignant effect

0.34 'Vere passum': some imitation at 'immolatum'

1.03 'Cuius latus': note the downward phrase in imitation (high voices leading) at 'unda fluxit'

1.30 'Esto nobis': a somber tone at 'in mortis examine'

1.54 'O dulcis, o pie': ex. 2 – more false relations, and an increase of intensity towards 'o Iesu'

2.24 'Miserere mei': a phrase treated imitatively here, but with characteristically unorthodox intervals of imitation (ex. 3)

2.57 repeat of music from 'O dulcis' (1.54–2.57 = 2.57–4.01)

4.01 'Amen'

4.23 (end)

Ave verum corpus natum	Hail, true body, born
de Maria vergine:	of the Virgin Mary:
Vere passum, immolatum	who truly suffered and died
in cruce pro homine:	on the cross for mankind:
Cuius latus perforatum	from whose pierced side
unda fluxit sanguine:	water flowed with blood:
Esto nobis praegustatum	be a consolation to us
in mortis examine.	at our last hour.
O dulcis, o pie, o Iesu fili Mariae	O sweet one, O pious one, O Jesus, son of Mary,
miserere mei. Amen.	have mercy upon me. Amen.

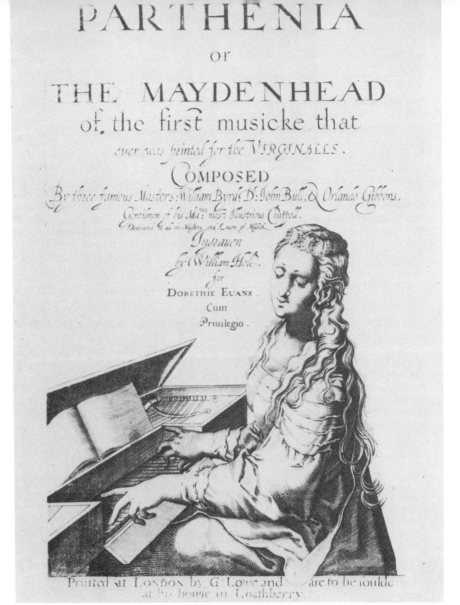

PARTHENIA
or
THE MAYDENHEAD
of the first musicke that
ever was printed for the VIRGINALLS.
COMPOSED
By three famous Masters: William Byrd Dr: John Bull, & Orlando Gibbons,
Gentlemen of his Maᵗⁱᵉ most Illustrious Chappell.
Dedicated to all the Maisters and Louers of Musick
Ingrauen
by William Hole.
for
DORETHIE EVANS
Cum
Priuilegio.

Printed at LONDON by G. Lowe and ____ are to be soulde
at his howse in Loathberry.

43 *Title-page of
Parthenia (1612/13), a
collection of English
virginal music containing
works by Byrd, Bull, and
Gibbons.*

older he seems to have become more cheerful; both his Latin and his Anglican music
include joyful pieces, such as an exuberant six-part anthem *Sing joyfully*, where the
overlapping voice parts ring out like peals of bells.

In his secular music too Byrd encompassed a wide range of texts and moods.
Though he issued no volumes of madrigals he did publish two volumes of *Psalmes,
Songs and Sonnets* (1588 and 1611) and one of *Songs of Sundrie Natures* (1589), whose
titles convey the miscellany of their contents. Some of the polyphonic songs here are
madrigalian in their subject matter, but few approach the text imagery of Byrd's
Italian contemporaries, or, indeed, of his English successors such as Thomas
Weelkes. Byrd's most productive years came before the Italian madrigal had taken
a hold in England. Instead, he cultivated intricate, flowing counterpoint in his
songs, as in some of his church music, in a style that he had inherited from earlier
English composers such as Tallis.

Byrd was also a distinguished composer of instrumental music, both for solo keyboard instruments and for ensemble. Many of the keyboard pieces, intended for harpsichord, virginals, spinet, or organ, are dance movements (e.g. pairings of pavan and galliard; see p. 88) or arrangements of popular tunes or vocal pieces. Their main interest lies in the imaginative way Byrd developed sets of "variations" on each tune, by dividing long notes into shorter ones, by changing the meter or the rhythmic detail, or by moving the tune from one level in the contrapuntal texture to another. His unending inventiveness in keyboard variations and pieces for five-part instrumental "consort" shows how a composer can use his imagination even within the strict framework of a pre-existing melody.

Many of Byrd's keyboard pieces are in the line music manuscripts of the period: *My Ladye Nevells Booke*, devoted exclusively to Byrd and written in an exquisitely beautiful hand by the singer and composer John Baldwin in about 1591; and the enormous Fitzwilliam Virginal Book, an anthology copied by Francis Tregian, a Catholic imprisoned for his beliefs in the early 1600s. Others were published in *Parthenia* (1612–13), a famous engraved anthology of keyboard music, the first to be printed in England. His reputation during his lifetime was remarkable: he was described as "Father of British Music", a title justified by his fertile imagination and by the consistently high quality of his music.

The madrigal

In Italy, the end of the sixteenth century witnessed the decline of the madrigal (see p. 86–7) in favor of a new style of song composition which properly belongs to the period we call "Baroque". But the madrigal was not dead. By about 1570, individual pieces had reached England, where the genre was taken up enthusiastically by both professionals and amateurs. Printed anthologies of Italian madrigals were circulated with translated texts (*Musica transalpina*, 1588; *Italian Madrigalls Englished*, 1590), and soon English composers began to write their own, for there was a wealth of English poetry to draw on. The Elizabethan age set great store by literary and musical accomplishment, and in an environment where domestic music-making flourished (as in Italy) the madrigal was bound to thrive.

It was left to Byrd's successors to carry the English madrigal to its peak. There was no shortage of composers able and willing to do so: by the end of the sixteenth century there was a whole school of English madrigalists, amateurs and professionals, talented and not so talented. While the public demand was there, new pieces continued to appear in a veritable fever of production.

WEELKES

Among the related forms was the "ballett", also of Italian origin – a light, dance-like piece, less sophisticated than the madrigal proper, in repeating verses and often with a "fa-la" refrain. Thomas Weelkes (c1575–1623) was one of its chief exponents. Weelkes, who was organist of Winchester College and then of Chichester Cathedral in the south of England, until he was dismissed for his habitual drunkenness and swearing, later worked at the Chapel Royal. He wrote some bold and original madrigals, very Italianate in their approach to word-painting: *As Vesta was from Latmos hill descending* is a good example (see **Listening Guide 12**).

Thomas Weelkes   Works

born Sussex, *c*1575; *died* London, 1623

Secular vocal music four books of madrigals (1597, 1958, 1600, 1608) – As Vesta was from Latmos hill descending; Thule, the period of cosmographie; O care thou wilt dispatch mee; On the plaines fairie traines

Sacred vocal music *c*50 anthems – When David heard; 9 services

LISTENING GUIDE 12   CD 1 TRACK 31

Weelkes: *As Vesta was from Latmos hill descending* (1601)

The Triumphes of Oriana was a collection of madrigals by English composers, edited by the composer and publisher Thomas Morley in honor of Queen Elizabeth I of England. It was assembled in 1601. Each of the madrigals in it ends with a refrain, 'Long live fair Oriana!' – Oriana referring, of course, to the maiden queen herself. The set was modeled on a similar collection, called *Trionfo di Dori*, issued some ten years earlier by a publisher in Venice.

Weelkes's contribution, a madrigal for six voices, is particularly notable for its 'word-painting', the use of pictorial devices to illustrate the words. It may seem naive to have, for example, a downward phrase for 'descending', but (as a writer at the time pointed out) it would be unnatural to use a rising phrase for such a word. The result here is colorful and entertaining, as well as highly ingenious. And the effect of the ending, where the literal, picturesque manner gives way to a rich texture for the climax, where all six voices interweave in praise of Oriana, is strengthened by the holding back of full polyphony for this moment.

 Listening Outline . . . .

Time
0.00   'As Vesta was': the word 'hill' is treated in a series of upward phrases, then neatly turned downward for a cadence on 'descending'
0.33   'attended on by all': a straightforward harmonic passage, sung by all the voices
0.50   'to whom Diana': rapid downward phrases for 'came running down amain'
1.13   'First two by two, then three by three': phrases sung by voices first in pairs, then in threes
1.22   'leaving their goddess all alone': a momentary solo voice here, while 'and mingling' has overlapping counterpoints
1.57   'Then sang the shepherds': full, six-voice counterpoint
3.05   (end)

As Vesta was from Latmos hill descending,
she spied a maiden queen the same ascending,
attended on by all the shepherds swain,
to whom Diana's darlings came running down amain.

First two by two, then three by three together,
leaving their goddess all alone, hasted thither,
and mingling with the shepherds of her train
with mirthful tunes her presence entertain.
    Then sang the shepherds and nymphs of Diana,
    Long live fair Oriana!

Part IV The Baroque Era

1 *Music of a New Age*

By the "Baroque" era, musicians generally understand the period from roughly 1600 to 1750 – beginning with Monteverdi, ending with Bach and Handel. The word is in fact little more than a convenient label for a period that has a certain degree of underlying unity because of its techniques and its approach to musical expression.

"Baroque" comes from the French, and, further back, from a Portuguese term (*barroco*) for a misshapen pearl. It seems to have been used at first in the discussion of art and architecture, mainly by writers at the end of the period itself and usually in a negative, critical way, implying something that was clumsy, strange, and overblown. Musicians adopted it, generally in the sense of confused, over-elaborate, and harsh; the generation that followed the Baroque era, as we shall see in the next section, was eager to simplify and regularize the language of music and regarded the style of their immediate forebears as extravagant and irregular. Thus the word "Baroque" came into use, both in art and music criticism, for the products of the seventeenth century and the early eighteenth. Nowadays, with the broader historical view that we have gained through the lapse of time, we apply the term to this period without any of its original disapproving implications

Composers of the Baroque Era

	1550	1600	1650	1700	1750

Claudio Monteverdi
Girolamo Frescobaldi
Heinrich Schütz
Francesco Cavalli
Giacomo Carissimi
Barbara Strozzi
Louis Couperin
Jean-Baptiste Lully
Dietrich Buxtehude
Arcangelo Corelli
Henry Purcell
Alessandro Scarlatti
Elisabeth-Claude Jacquet de la Guerre
François Couperin
Antonio Vivaldi
Georg Philipp Telemann
Jean-Philippe Rameau
Johann Sebastian Bach
Domenico Scarlatti
George Frideric Handel
Giovanni Battista Pergolesi

of the clumsy or the rough: though the notions of extravagance and some kinds of irregularity, at least as compared with the music of the periods just before and just after, still have meaning.

The Renaissance, in its arts, emphasized clarity, unity, and proportion. But as the sixteenth century moved towards its close, the representation of human emotion came to be seen as increasingly important. Serenity and perfection of form were now overtaken by the urgency of the expression of feeling. In the visual arts this is seen in the forceful, dramatically colored paintings of Caravaggio (1573–1619). We have already noted its beginnings in music, for example in the late sixteenth-century madrigal (see pp. 86-7); the next generation was to carry it much further.

To create these strong effects, it was necessary to develop a new musical style. The smooth polyphony of the Renaissance was not, generally speaking, adaptable to a set of priorities so different from those of the era in which it had arisen. One of the most important creations of the Baroque was the concept of contrast. Renaissance music is typified by its flowing, interweaving lines, most commonly four or five in number, each of them singing (or playing) music that moved at roughly the same pace. Textures of that kind became increasingly rare in the years after 1600, and when they were used it was almost exclusively in the realm of church music – naturally the most conservative area because it was tied to traditional, unchanging liturgical patterns.

Contrast could exist on various planes: loud and soft; one color and another; solo

Contrast

and tutti; high and low; fast and slow (this could occur in two main ways, either a fast-moving part against a slow-moving one, or a fast section next to a slow one). All these, and others, had their place in the musical schemes of the new Baroque era. Many of them are represented in the music of the important transitional composer, the Venetian Giovanni Gabrieli, whose interest in contrast we noted on p. 102. Numerous composers used the *concerto* or *concertante* style (meaning a style with a marked contrasting element), the essence of which was a texture that varied, sometimes with solo voice or voices, sometimes with larger groups; it was mostly applied to sacred music, particularly motets.

The most striking, most violent contrasts, however, were those in the new genre that we call "monody". This means a kind of solo song, with a vocal line that may be very florid and a slow-moving accompaniment for an instrument of the lute type or a harpsichord. The most important exponent of this genre (and to some extent its creator, in his epoch-making publication *Le nuove musiche* – "The new music" – of 1602) was the composer and singer Giulio Caccini (c1545–1618). The vocal line, taking its cue from the meaning of the words, could vary greatly in pace and in texture, from the simple to the highly embellished; this further contrasted with the static line played by the accompanying instrument. Caccini had been a member of the group of musicians, intellectuals, and noblemen of Florence (the "Camerata") who had met during the 1570s and 80s with the idea of re-creating what they took to be the ancient Greek ideal of expressing in music the "affect" (or emotional character) of the words; the style of monody follows up the thinking of that group. Writers of the time called the new style the "Seconda Prattica" ("second practice"), a new style with contrasts, as opposed to the "Prima Prattica".

The word "accompany", used above, does not appear in the discussion of mainstream Renaissance music: as a concept, it belongs to the Baroque – it implies, of course, a difference in status between instrumental parts. And in fact the most important unifying feature of all Baroque music is the characteristic accompanying part, the *basso continuo* (or simply *continuo*). The continuo player, at a keyboard instrument (like the harpsichord or the organ) or a plucked string instrument (like the lute or guitar), was given a bass line, above which figures were usually written to indicate what additional notes should be played to fill in the harmony. Often there were two continuo players, one playing the written line on a sustaining instrument, like the cello, viol, or bassoon, the other also supplying the harmony.

Continuo

The kind of texture that the use of continuo implies – a top, melodic line for a voice or instrument, a bottom line for a bass instrument, and a harmonic filling to the sandwich – is typical of the Baroque; often, just as typically, there might be two upper lines, perhaps for a pair of singers or (in a trio sonata) a pair of violins. The use of this kind of pattern, and especially the almost invariable presence of the continuo line, shows how important and how central to the idiom of Baroque music was the idea of a bass line that generated harmony. This was not a sudden development; throughout the sixteenth century there had been a tendency for the bottom line of the music to become distinct from the other strands of the polyphony. Only with the new Baroque idioms was this distinction fully recognized.

Harmony, cadence, rhythm

Along with these changes came other, related ones. With the abandonment of polyphony (or, more exactly, its relegation to the status of an old-fashioned method, to be used almost exclusively in certain types of church music), a new way of constructing movements was needed; and the emphasis on harmony led naturally towards the use of harmonic goals as stopping-points in a piece of music. These stopping-points, or cadences, would be arrived at by a sequence of harmonies of some standardized kind. Linked with these harmonic developments are rhythmic ones. In vocal music, the need to reflect the sense of the words meant that the music was obliged to follow, or even exaggerate, natural speech rhythms. In instrumental music (and some kinds of vocal piece, choral ones especially), dance rhythms came to be used. The bass patterns associated with the regular rhythms of dance music hastened the development of a sense of key, of the music's gravitational pull towards particular notes.

At the same time, new instruments were developing that accelerated these processes, the most important being the violin family. The viol had a tone-quality well adapted to polyphonic clarity but it was weak in rhythmic impetus; the violin, however, with its clearly defined attack and its capacity for brilliant effect was suited to music in dance rhythms and to sonatas of a virtuosity comparable with the new generation of singer, whose trills and flourishes were arousing a new range of emotions in the world of monody. The interchange of vocal and instrumental idioms was a typical Baroque device; it may seem strange that the Baroque should have created these different idioms only to exchange them in its search for novelty and effect.

Passion and grandeur

It is the pursuit of striking effect, above all, that marks out the Baroque era from those immediately before and after. Composers aimed to move the passions (or the "affections", to use the word favored at the time), and not just instantaneously: they tried to sustain the "affect" of a movement – that is, the prevailing emotion that it expressed – throughout its length. The idea of exciting appropriate emotion was, moreover, closely attuned to the spirit of the Counter-Reformation.

There are parallels to be seen between music and the other arts. The Baroque emotional extravagance that we find in the grandiose motets of Italy and the other Catholic countries in the early seventeenth century, some of them with multiple choirs and bold harmonic effects, may be seen as analogous to, for example, the new architecture of Rome: this was the period when the huge, overwhelming square and cathedral of St Peter's were built, and also the main part of the cathedral of St John Lateran. Like the giant Salzburg Cathedral across the Alps, these are designed – in a sense that no Renaissance one was – to make the mere human being who entered them feel puny beside these grand creations that embodied divine mysteries. Similarly, the decorated lines of the music have much in common with the florid ornament found in such buildings with their elaborate statuary – in Rome particularly, where the sculptor Gianlorenzo Bernini (1598–1680) enriched the new churches and public buildings.

Further north, it was rather different, for this exuberant spirit was alien to Protestantism: the churches and the music alike are more sober. But the new mercantile spirit encouraged by the reformed faiths found musical outlets too, in the civic musical patronage of the north German cities like Hamburg and Leipzig, for example. It was mainly in the northern lands that a middle-class concert life arose towards the end of the seventeenth century – and in the eighteenth it was the middle classes who lent support to Bach's concerts in Leipzig, where his concertos were first heard, and to Handel's oratorio performances in London.

Patronage

Courts, however, remained important centers of musical patronage, along with the church. In Italy, it was the Gonzaga family, the rulers of Mantua, who employed Monteverdi before he worked for the church in Venice; and it was the great Venetian noble families who opened the earliest opera house to a wider public. Composers like Alessandro Scarlatti, Arcangelo Corelli (1653-1719, the leading violinist of his day, who worked in Rome), and Handel were supported by the princely families around Rome. Germany suffered the Thirty Years War in the early seventeenth century; after it, in 1648, the country was divided into numerous dukedoms, marquisates, and the like, as well as some "free cities" (governed by city fathers) and church lands (governed by bishops). Many of them had their own courts, with musical establishments headed by a *Kapellmeister* ("chapelmaster") whose duties included the organization of a choir and instrumental ensemble to provide music for worship and for entertainment. In France and England, with a central court, musical patronage was based firmly in Paris and London and there was relatively little musical activity elsewhere, except in the large noble and ecclesiastical establishments, until the rise of the bourgeois groups towards the end of the seventeenth century.

2 *The Genres of Baroque Music*

OPERA

One of the first creations of the Baroque era was *opera*. It arose partly out of the interest of the Florentine Camerata in re-creating the ancient Greek drama with music (see p. 111). But it has other ancestors, for example the lavish court entertainments of the time (called *intermedi*) that mingled music, dance, mime, drama, and speech, along with fine scenery and costumes. The earliest operas were given at court – or at learned academies – but by 1637 the first public opera house was opened, in Venice. Leading composers in this period were Monteverdi and Francesco Cavalli, in whose operas musically heightened speech is used for the dialog while the characters express their emotions in music of a more lyrical kind.

44 *Stage design by Francesco Galli-Bibiena (1659–1737) for an unknown* opera seria. *Museo Nacional de Arte Antiga, Lisbon.*

Other leading opera centers in the seventeenth century were Rome, where operas on sacred topics were given, under papal influence, and Naples. Alessandro Scarlatti was a leading figure in both cities. Italian opera was exported to other parts of Europe, notably Paris and Vienna. But in the 1670s Lully established opera in French, influenced by the traditions of French theater and literature as well as the national love of dance and the fondness of the king, Louis XIV, for lavish spectacle. The first German opera house was opened in Hamburg in 1678, under civic patronage, and with a leaning towards operas on moral, often religious, topics. In London, some opera was given in English, but Italian opera was dominant there (Handel composed some 30 operas in Italian for English audiences) as it was across Europe, from Spain to Russia, during much of the eighteenth century.

Most Baroque opera is based on plots drawn from classical mythology or history, reinterpreted in line with the spirit of the time – and in particular stressing that virtue has its proper rewards and that kings and princes were just and benevolent.

Opera developed a number of clear-cut patterns in the early eighteenth century. In Italy, *opera seria* (serious opera) became standardized as a succession of arias linked by the simple form of musical narrative known as *recitative*; it always dealt with heroic topics, with a castrato hero (see p. 64) and a soprano *prima donna* (first lady). Earlier, serious operas had often included comic scenes for the everyday characters; now a type of opera that was purely comic (*opera buffa*) began to be composed, in a faster-moving, less exalted style, treating ordinary people and their doings rather than godly or heroic ones. The Italians continued to use recitative for the dialog, but that did not work well with other languages. In Germany, the standard comic form was the *Singspiel*, rather like a play with songs; a similar type grew in England, with spoken dialog. England also had ballad opera, in which popular tunes of the day were given new words and sung by actors. France alone maintained a serious tradition in the native tongue alongside a more popular type, *opéra comique*, which developed at the lively, open-air street theaters and included spoken dialog.

ORATORIO

The sacred counterpart to opera was *oratorio*. It arose at the time of the Counter-Reformation. The word itself means "prayer hall" and oratorios were designed to be performed in such rooms – not as part of the liturgy but as a "spiritual exercise". The early examples, from around 1600, tell of the story in a speech-like musical setting (or recitative), with songs from the principal characters in the drama and short choruses (the "characters" may be abstract, like "Goodness" or "Temptation", for many of these are moral tales in which evil is overcome by religious virtue). Oratorios were only rarely given in acted form, though they used the same musical means as operas, including recitative narration and lyrical music for emotional expression; they also made more use of choral music.

The oratorio originated in Rome, and its earliest master was Carissimi, in the mid-seventeenth century, who wrote works based on biblical stories with important parts for the chorus. His style was carried to France by Charpentier, but it was through Handel – who visited Italy as a young man and came into contact with Italian traditions – that the oratorio truly flowered. In England, during the 1730s and 40s, he devised a new style of dramatic oratorio with arias, recitatives, and choruses that drew on English traditions of choral singing, and created a set of masterpieces (such as *Saul*, *Messiah*, and *Judas Maccabaeus*).

PASSION

A particular type of oratorio that became prominent in the Baroque period is the *Passion*. The telling of the story of the Passion of Christ had long been an important part of the liturgy each Easter, and musical settings were often used. In some early settings, the words of the narrator or "Evangelist" and the secondary characters were chanted, and those of Christ and the people sung in polyphony; other settings treated the whole polyphonically. In the seventeenth century, the great German composer Heinrich Schütz wrote Passions in which the narration and the words of the characters are sung to an unaccompanied line, and the words of groups are sung by choruses.

There are fine settings of the Passion from the early eighteenth century, by Bach and his German contemporaries such as Handel and Telemann. Bach's are the supreme examples.

45 *Massed choirs performing Handel's* Messiah *in Westminster Abbey, London, for his commemoration in 1784.*

OTHER SACRED MUSIC

The tradition of the polyphonic Mass setting came to an end at the beginning of the Baroque era; settings continued to be composed, but now using instruments and solo as well as choral singing. Similar changes affected the motet. Italian composers, especially, applied to it the new styles used in dramatic music, embodying contrasts – again, involving the use of instruments and both solo and choral singing. Prominent in these developments were Monteverdi, in Venice, his colleague there Giovanni Gabrieli, and in Germany their pupil and follower Heinrich Schütz.

There were similar developments in the English anthem, with the "verse anthem", involving both solo and choral singing, of which Purcell was the leading exponent. Bach, in the early eighteenth century, wrote six motets in a rich, elaborate style, for voices with only an instrumental bass. More important, however, are his sacred cantatas.

The word "cantata" does not strictly mean a sacred work but is always used in that sense for the Lutheran church works of which Bach's – some 200 have survived – represent the highest achievement. Intended for devotional use at Sunday and festival services, though not actually settings of the day's prescribed liturgical texts (more often they were a free commentary on a theme in them), they typically consists of an opening chorus, two or three arias (or a duet in place of one), and a closing chorale, all linked by recitative (see p. 155f for a fuller discussion). In France, a special tradition of ceremonial motet developed in the late seventeenth century at the court of Louis XIV, where Lully and his followers wrote works with large-scale choruses and expressive solos.

CANTATA

In the Baroque period, the madrigal, a polyphonic form, was replaced as the principal genre of secular music by the *cantata*. This term meant, in the seventeenth century and the early eighteenth, a composition for one or two voices and continuo, possibly with another instrument (usually violin or sometimes flute), or two instruments, or even a larger group. Typically, an Italian cantata of this time – such as those written by Alessandro Scarlatti or Handel – would consist of two or three arias each preceded by a recitative. There are also longer examples where, for example, two singers have alternate arias and finally join in a duet. The theme of almost all these works is love, and particularly its betrayal, which allows the composer an opportunity for the expression of strong emotion.

Aria, recitative

The *aria*, the main unit in larger vocal compositions such as opera, oratorio, or cantata, took various forms in the seventeenth century. There were arias on ground basses, arias in strophic form (that is, with the same music repeated to different verses of the text), arias in an *A–B–B* pattern, and by the end of the century *A–B–A*. This last, the *da capo* aria, was of special importance in the early eighteenth century as the chief type used by Bach in his cantatas and Passions and Handel in his operas, oratorios, and cantatas.

While arias, usually lyrical and flowing in style, served for the expression of feeling, recitative was generally used for the narrative or dialog sections in such works. Here the words are sung in a manner best described as conversational, which can be rapid (especially in comic opera) and lightly accompanied, or can be heightened by a musical setting that exaggerates the inflections of speech, to convey strong feeling. Recitative, an Italian invention, works most effectively in Italian, but it has been adapted to fit the needs of other languages.

CONCERTO

We have seen (p. 110) that one of the chief characteristics of Baroque art was the exploitation of contrast. The idea of setting two groups of players, a small group and a larger one, in contrast had a natural appeal to the Baroque sense of drama. The term *concerto* was applied to pieces of this type from the early seventeenth century. At first it was used chiefly in vocal music, particularly of a kind of motet involving contrasts (the "sacred concerto"); later the term came to stand for an instrumental work, in which a few players or even a single player was set against a larger group. It developed, particularly at such Italian centers as Venice, Bologna, and Rome, into the solo concerto and the multiple concerto, or concerto grosso (meaning "large concerto"), of the early eighteenth century.

The Italian composer Vivaldi was one of its leading figures; he composed several hundred concertos, many for a solo instrument (usually violin) and orchestra. Bach wrote early examples of the keyboard concerto, for harpsichord and orchestra; both he and Handel (who wrote organ concertos) also composed fine sets of works of the concerto grosso type. Some are in three movements (fast–slow–fast), Vivaldi's usual pattern, but Handel's often have four or five. Ritornello form is normal for the fast movements (see p. 37).

OTHER INSTRUMENTAL MUSIC

Another orchestral genre of this period was the *overture* or sinfonia (the Italian form of the word "symphony"). The traditional Italian opera overture generally had three movements, in a fast–slow–fast sequence. Pieces of this type soon began to be drawn out of the opera house into the concert room, when, around 1700, the era of public concerts began; the overture's development is specially associated with Alessandro Scarlatti. The French had a different kind of opera overture, beginning in a vigorous, rather jerky yet ceremonial style, then continuing with a lively fugue. This form was devised by Lully in the late seventeenth century, but was widely copied, by (among others) Bach in Germany and Handel in England. The French type of overture was

46 *Rehearsal for a sacred cantata: gouache, c1775, artist unknown. Germanisches Nationalmuseuem, Nuremberg.*

often followed by one or more movements in dance rhythm, to form a "suite". The idea of collecting groups of dances together, however, belongs primarily to music for small ensemble or solo harpsichord.

The *suite* was one of four main types of keyboard work in the seventeenth century and the early eighteenth. Dances had often been performed in pairs (usually slow–fast); in this period it became usual to group them in sets of four or five, often Allemande–Courante–Sarabande–Gigue (in effect, moderate–fast–slow–fast), with an extra one or two (minuet, gavotte, or bourrée, for example) after the sarabande (for particulars of these dances, see **Glossary**). Bach, Handel, and Couperin are among those who wrote suites for the harpsichord.

The other types were, first, the contrapuntal piece – called capriccio, canzona, or ricercare, most commonly – often preceded by an introduction in a brilliant style, which might be called toccata or prelude (to reach its height in the preludes and fugues of J. S. Bach). Such pieces were normally for organ or harpsichord. Secondly, there was the "genre" piece, designed to describe a person or emotion, which became a French specialty, and was handled with particular refinement by Bach's contemporary François Couperin. Lastly, there was the chorale prelude. This was a genre for church use in Lutheran Germany in which, as we saw on pp. 32–3, a well-known hymn melody is used as the basis of a piece for organ: it might be decorated, or worked into the texture of the music, or heard in slow notes against other music, or used as the basis for a fugue. (For a different usage of chorales, see p. 158.)

CHAMBER MUSIC

Chamber music, though nowadays played at many concerts and recitals, and much recorded, was originally not intended to be listened to at all (the term means "room music"). It was composed simply for the pleasure of those who played it. In the early seventeenth century, the chief chamber music genres were for groups, or consorts, often of viols or recorders. The repertory consisted of *fantasias* and *canzonas* (or similarly titled works) and arrangements of songs, usually in a contrapuntal style or using dance rhythms. Another term often used was *sonata*, which means simply a piece to be sounded (that is, "played" – as opposed to a cantata, one to be sung). We have already met this term in the context of sonata form (see p. 36) – which acquired its name as this structure was the one commonly used in sonatas of the late eighteenth century, the Classical period. Taken by itself, the term signifies an instrumental composition, either for keyboard alone (the piano sonata) or for an ensemble.

The word "sonata" was first regularly used for the trio sonata, a genre that came into existence in the early seventeenth century, at the advent of the violin. Generally for two melody instruments (such as violins, recorders, flutes, oboes, even cornetts) and continuo, it had two streams of development: the church sonata, primarily contrapuntal and in four movements, slow–fast–slow–fast, and the chamber sonata, which consisted of a group of movements in dance rhythm. The leading composer here was Corelli; Handel and Bach wrote some too. These composers also wrote sonatas for one instrument and continuo, a type particularly cultivated by virtuoso performers as it allowed them to display their technical brilliance.

3 *Monteverdi*

Claudio Monteverdi, born in 1567 in Cremona, the main Italian center of violin making, has been described as a revolutionary and as "the creator of modern music". In that he represented human emotion in music with a new force and richness there is some truth in it. He was only 17 when his first musical publication was issued. By the early 1590s he had an appointment at Mantua, playing the violin or viol in the duke's group of musicians, and was a leading madrigal composer. He succeeded to the post of *maestro di cappella* ("master of the chapel") in 1601.

Claudio Monteverdi   Life and Works

1567	born in Cremona, 15 May
1587	first book of madrigals published
*c***1591**	string player at the Gonzaga court in Mantua
1600	reputation as a composer firmly established
1601	appointed *maestro di cappella* at Mantua
1607	*Orfeo* produced in Mantua; his wife, Claudia, died
1608	*Arianna*; returned to Cremona in a depressed state and tried to leave service of the Gonzagas
1610	*Vespers* published; began writing sacred music
1613	*maestro di cappella* of St Mark's, Venice; began reorganizing musical establishment there
1619	seventh book of madrigals published, including works in more modern style
1620–25	period of opera composition
1630–31	plague in Venice
1632	took holy orders
1638	*Madrigals of Love and War* (eighth book) published
1640	*The Return of Ulysses to his Country*
1642	*The Coronation of Poppaea*
1643	died in Venice, 29 November

Operas Orfeo (1607), Arianna (1608, music lost except for lament), Il ritorno d'Ulisse in patria (The Return of Ulysses to his Country, 1640), L'incoronazione di Poppea (The Coronation of Poppaea, 1642)

Madrigals Books 1–4 for 5 voices (1587–1603); Book 5 for 5 voices and continuo (1605); Book 6 for 7 voices and continuo (1614); Book 7 for 1–6 voices and instruments (1619); Book 8, 'Madrigals of Love and War', for 1–8 voices and instruments (1638); Book 9 for 2–3 voices and continuo (1651); 2 books of scherzi musicali for 3 voices (1607, 1632)

Sacred vocal music Vespers (1610); Masses, psalms

47 *Claudio Monteverdi: portrait by the court painter Bernardo Strozzi. Tiroler Landesmuseum Ferdinandeum, Innsbruck.*

In 1607 Monteverdi's opera *Orfeo* was given as a court entertainment in Mantua. Another opera, *Arianna*, followed the next year, adding further to his reputation particularly because of its famous Lament (the only part of the opera that now survives). His later years at Mantua, however, were unhappy: his wife, his daughters, and his favorite pupil had died and he wanted to move to a larger city with greater opportunities. His publication in 1610 of an original and highly dramatic collection of church music, under the title *Vespers*, was planned to impress prospective employers (it was dedicated to the pope). In 1613 Monteverdi was appointed head of music at one of the most famous churches in Italy, St Mark's, Venice.

There his first task was to reorganize what had become an inefficient musical establishment. Monteverdi engaged new, younger singers and instrumentalists, improved the pay, and brought the library up to date. He continued composing church music, madrigals, and operas, and when, in 1637, the first public opera houses opened in Venice he soon began to compose for them. He died in 1643.

Monteverdi: *Orfeo* (1607), excerpt from Act 2

Monteverdi's *Orfeo*, the earliest opera regularly performed in opera houses today, combines several features of the music of its time. The choruses draw on the new madrigal style. The main action is carried out in expressive dialog, not unlike monody, but treated with a freedom that enabled Monteverdi to mirror in the music the sense of the words (for example by using harsh harmonies or unexpected melodic leaps to heighten an expression of grief, or by varying the pace to convey a sense of urgency). An instance of such writing occurs in the scene here. Orpheus is singing joyfully of the prospect of marriage when the tragic news comes of Eurydice's death: flowing dance-like rhythms and lyrical lines give way to a halting recitative accompanied by jarring dissonances.

Monteverdi also aimed at something new in his use of instruments. At the front of his score he listed the instruments required – two harpsichords, two small wooden organs and a reed organ, a harp, two large lutes, three bass viols, ten violins and two small violins, two instruments like small double basses, four each of trumpets and trombones, two cornetts, and two recorders. At various points in the score, he indicated which should play, choosing the color to suit the dramatic meaning.

48 Title-page of Monteverdi's Orfeo.

The music we hear is from Act 2, where Orpheus (tenor), with his friends the shepherds, is celebrating his forthcoming union with Eurydice, whom he has long loved.

 Listening Outline

Time

Time	
0.00	dance for string instruments, the ritornello to Orpheus's song
0.13	Orpheus: 'Vi ricorda' (ex. 1)
0.40	ritornello 2
0.53	Orpheus: 'Dite all'hor'
1.19	ritornello 3
1.33	Orpheus: 'Vissi già mesto'
2.00	ritornello 4
2.14	Orpheus: 'Sol per te bella Euridice': the music slows as a shepherd greets Orpheus
2.46	Shepherd: 'Mira, Orfeo'
3.25	The serene, cheerful, major-key music ceases, and a harshly foreign note is heard in the orchestra as the Messenger enters: 'Ahi! caso acerbo!' ('Oh, bitter event!', ex. 2); the music turns to a, with strange dissonances, and goes into recitative style
3.54	Shepherd: 'Qual suon dolente', in C
4.02	Messenger: 'Lassa dunque debb'io': back to a
4.39	Shepherd: 'Questa è Silvia'
5.18	Messenger: 'Pastor, lasciate il canto'
5.44	Orpheus: 'D'onde vieni?'
5.55	Messenger: 'A te ne vengo' (ex. 3)
6.25	Orpheus: 'Ohimè'; note abrupt changes of key
6.31	Messenger: 'La tua diletta sposa è morta'
6.52	Orpheus: 'Ohimè'
7.00	(end)

ex. 1

Vi ri - cor - da, o boschi omb - ro - si, Vi ri - cor - da, o boschi omb -
- ro - si, de' miei lungh' as - pri tor - men - ti quan-do i sa - ssi ai miei la -
- men - ti ris-pon-dean fat - ti pie - to - si?

ex. 2

ex. 3

ORPHEUS

Vi ricorda, o boschi ombrosi,
De' miei lungh' aspri tormenti
quando i sassi ai miei lamenti
rispondean fatti pietosi?

Dite all'hor non vi sembrai
più d'ogn'altro sconsolato?
Hor fortuna ha stil cangiato
et ha volto in festa i guai.

Vissi già mesto e dolente,
hor gioisco e quegli affanni
che sofferti ho per tant'anni
fan più caro il ben presente.

Sol per te bella Euridice,
benedico il mio tormento,
dopo il duol si è più contento
dopo il mal si è più felice.

Mira, Orfeo, che d'ogni intorno
ride il bosco e ride il prato.
Segui pur col plettr'aurato
d'addolcir l'aria in si beato giorno.

Ahi! caso acerbo!
Ahi! fat'empio e crudele!
Ahi! stelle ingiuriose!
Ahi! ciel'avaro!

Qual suon dolente il lieto di perturba?

Lassa dunque debb'io
mentre Orfeo con sue note il ciel
consola
con le parole mie passargli il core.

ORPHEUS
Do you remember, O shady woods,
my long and bitter torments
when the rocks to my laments
took pity and responded?

Tell me, did I not then seem
more inconsolable than any other?
Now fortune has changed
and has turned my woes into joys.

I have lived with sadness and grief;
Now I rejoice, and those sorrows
that I suffered for so many years
make my present joy the more dear.

For you alone, fair Eurydice,
I bless my former torments;
after grief one is the more content,
after suffering one is the more happy.

SHEPHERD
Wonder, Orpheus, that all around you
the woods and the meadows join in laughter.
Continue with your golden plectrum
to sweeten the air on so blessed a day.

MESSENGER
Oh, bitter event!
Oh, impious and cruel fate!
Oh, unjust stars!
Oh, avaricious heaven!

SHEPHERD
What mournful sound disturbs our happiness?

MESSENGER
I am wretched, for now I must,
while Orpheus with his tones consoles the
heavens,
pierce his heart with my words.

	SHEPHERD
Questa è Silvia gentile, dolcissima compagna della bell'Euridice. O quanto e in vista dolorosa; hor che sia? Deh, sommi dei non torcete da noi benigno il guardo.	This is the lovely Sylvia, the sweetest companion of the beautiful Eurydice. Oh, how her face is sad; what has befallen? O mighty gods, do not turn your kindly glances away from us.

	MESSENGER
Pastor, lasciate il canto, ch'ogni nostra allegrezza in doglia è volta.	Shepherd, cease your singing, all our happiness is turned to grief.

	ORPHEUS
D'onde vieni? ove vai? Ninfa, che porti?	Where do you come from? where are you going? Nymph, what do you bear?

	MESSENGER
A te ne vengo Orfeo messagera infelice di caso più infelice e più funesto. La tua belle Euridice	To you I come, Orpheus, unhappy messenger, of a matter most unhappy and most terrible. Your lovely Eurydice

	ORPHEUS
Ohimè, che odo?	Alas! what do I hear?

	MESSENGER
La tua diletta sposa è morta.	Your beloved wife is dead.

	ORPHEUS
Ohimè.	Alas!

MUSIC

In his early madrigals, Monteverdi followed the current trends. He moved away from smooth Renaissance polyphony and laid increasing stress on expressing the text. He particularly liked to match extravagant words – about pain, love, or death – with a musical device that highlighted them, usually a harsh discord or an abrupt leap. He carried this further in his fourth and fifth books of madrigals, working towards a new freedom of style that was related, in its treatment of words, to the new types of monody. And he continued to make increasing use of dissonance, so much so that he became involved in an angry dispute about what was proper to the art of music.

He used all these techniques in his dramatic music, including *Orfeo* (see **Listening Guide 13**), and even in his *Vespers*, producing church music of a vividness and drama that must have seemed revolutionary to his contemporaries, although he continued, in the more solemn movements (such as the Mass setting), to use old-fashioned Renaissance polyphony. In his late madrigals, he added instruments to the vocal ensemble and invented some new styles of writing for them. In particular, he wrote in what he called the "agitated style", with rapid repeated notes to produce a vigorous, aggressive effect. This was strongly expressive of war-like emotions, and also of the emotions aroused by the battles of amorous conquest.

Monteverdi's insight into human emotion, so poignantly expressed in the tragic scenes of *Orfeo*, comes out again in these madrigals of his last years, and, particularly in his final opera *The Coronation of Poppaea*, which tells the story of how the all-powerful love of Poppaea and the Roman emperor Nero overcomes all obstacles, whatever suffering it causes for others. His music depicts both the force of the love and the pain of the suffering with a new power.

4 *Women Composers: Barbara Strozzi*

WOMEN IN THE EARLY MUSICAL WORLD

Literacy, in particular musical literacy, was for many centuries acquired only by members of the secular and religious aristocracies. The rise of female monasticism in the year 512 formalized the education of women, which right from the Middle Ages included instruction in singing and composing music. Hildegard of Bingen (1098–1179), the daughter of a knight, became a Benedictine abbess. She won unrivaled papal approval for her mystical and scientific writings as well as for her liturgical music and is therefore today the best known among early women composers. Because of the nature and tradition of monastic institutions, many of their music manuscripts have survived. Only a small amount of the secular music composed and improvised by noble troubadours and trouvères has come down to us, however; most is attributed to men, though not all of it, and it is very likely that a substantial proportion of the surviving anonymous secular monophonic music may in fact have been composed by noble women.

With the growth of commerce and cities during the Renaissance, women of the artisan class – especially the daughters of the greatest artists, writers, and musicians – acquired skills not otherwise open to members of their sex. Marietta Robusti (1560–90), working alongside her father, the Venetian painter Tintoretto, and her brothers, produced paintings of sufficient merit for them to have been confused with those of her famous father. Recognition of her talent led Emperor Maximilian II and Philip II of Spain to offer her court appointments, which her father refused so that she might remain in his household as long as he lived.

STROZZI

The extraordinary Venetian composer, Barbara Strozzi (1619–after 1664), seems to have suffered a similar fate. As the illegitimate daughter of the poet and librettist Giulio Strozzi, she was both well educated and highly trained as a musician. Her singing was renowned and her music appeared between 1644 and 1664 in nine printed volumes and in anthologies, alongside that of the most famous male composers of the day. Strozzi was not, however, the first woman to publish secular music: that distinction belongs to her Venetian predecessor, Maddalena Casulana (d. c1590).

In view of the fact that Strozzi had studied composition with the eminent Venetian opera composer Francesco Cavalli, it is surprising that she wrote no operas, as Francesca Caccini (1587–c1640), the daughter of Giulio Caccini, had done in Florence in 1625. Strozzi's role as the muse of her father's libertine Accademia degli

Strozzi: *Tradimento, tradimento* (1659)

Barbara Strozzi composed and published nine collections of her music, mostly songs, duets, or madrigals. Her seventh collection, issued in 1659, had the fanciful title *Diporti di Euterpe, overo Cantate e ariette a voce sola* ('Disportings of Euterpe, or Cantatas and little arias for solo voice'; Euterpe was one of the 'muses' of classical times).

This collection includes 'Tradimento, tradimento', an arietta (or 'little song') with continuo accompaniment (which would normally be played on a lute). There are three verses, with cries of 'Tradimento' ('Betrayal!') intervening. The music has a dramatic flavor which she learned from her teacher, the eminent Venetian opera composer Francesco Cavalli. It uses the 'concitato' ('agitated') style, which Monteverdi favored for music about war, whether real or allegorical; as often in Monteverdi's music, war is used as a metaphor for love.

Each of the verses has a rhythm of its own, to suit the sense of the words, and the character of the melodic line portrays some of the words individually.

 Listening Outline

Time			
0.00	a fanfare-like figure in D (ex. 1)	Tradimento, tradimento.	Betrayal, betrayal!
0.14	verse 1: in 6/4 meter, typical of flowing Italian melody of this period	Amore e la speranza voglion farmi prigioniero e à tal segno il male s'avanza ch'hò scoperto ch'il pensiero dice d'esserne contento.	Love and hope want to make me their prisoner and so far advanced is the malady I have realized that the thought only makes me happy.
1.25	(ex. 1)	Tradimento, tradimento.	Betrayal, betrayal!
1.35	verse 2: in 4/4 meter, with florid runs on appropriate words ('legarmi', 'bind me'; 'lusinga', 'deceive'; and especially 'incatenarmi', 'enchain me' – note the chromatic, minor-key inflection here, 1.59)	La speranza per legarmi è gran cose mi lusinga s'io le credo avvien che stringa lacci sol da incatenarmi.	Hope, to bind me, deceives me with great things and the more I believe what she says the more tightly she ties my chains.
2.22	verse 3: in triple meter; note the falling line at 's'uccida', 'kill her', and the increase of pace and change of meter to 4/4 at 'è periglioso', 'is dangerous' (2.49)	Mi mio core all'armi so contra l'infida si prenda s'uccida sù presto è periglioso ogni momento.	To arms, my heart, against the unfaithful one, to capture and kill her, Every moment of delay is dangerous.
3.06	(ex. 1)	Tradimento, tradimento.	Betrayal, betrayal!
3.13	(end)		

ex. 1

Unisoni (a musical offshoot of the more famous Accademia degli Incogniti), a learned society devoted to discourses on love in poetry and music, may have compromised her opportunities, for she was apparently a courtesan of the most exalted kind. In the 1630s and 40s she was the subject and dedicatee of the works of the academicians; she is known to have performed her music at their meetings, though her later collections were dedicated to various royal and noble personages, from whom she presumably hoped to gain patronage. For unlike her contemporary in Novara, Isabella Leonarda (1620–1704), an Ursuline nun of noble birth who published sonatas, Masses, motets, and sacred concertos, Strozzi was forced to support herself – whether by her publications or her other skills – after her father's death in 1652. Her portrait, painted by Bernardo Strozzi about 1637, captures the seriousness and sensuousness reflected in her music.

Strozzi's compositions are mostly secular songs, madrigals, and cantatas, setting texts about unrequited love by the greatest poets of the day. Her music reveals a composer of passionate eloquence, showing a wide range of vocal writing (see **Listening Guide 14**).

49 Henry Purcell: *portrait, 1695, attributed to John Clostermann. National Portrait Gallery, London.*

5 *Purcell*

LIFE

Henry Purcell is one of that small group of enormously talented composers, including Mozart and Schubert, who developed rapidly and died young. He was trained as a choirboy in the Chapel Royal (the king's musical establishment) in London; a song was published as his when he was eight. At 15 he was appointed to tune the organ at Westminster Abbey; at 18 he was named a composer to the royal band; and at 20 he became organist of Westminster Abbey – his former teacher, a leading English church composer of the time, seems to have stood down in his favor. In 1682 he also became a Chapel Royal organist. He had begun in 1680 supplying music for use in the London theaters. He died at 36, in 1695, recognized and mourned as a great composer.

MUSIC

Purcell was a highly original composer. His command of melody was exceptional for its freedom and its readiness to take its rhythm and shape from the sense and the sounds of the words he was setting. He was also exceptionally bold in his use of harmony, especially to give force and color to his texts.

His instrumental music includes a set of sonatas for two violins and continuo, written, he said, "in imitation of the most fam'd Italian masters". He was eager to bring new, up-to-date styles into the conservative world of English music. He did the same in his sacred works, particularly his verse anthems, which are also Italian-influenced and widen the expressive resources of English church music.

Purcell: *Dido and Aeneas* (1689), excerpt from Act 3

Purcell's *Dido and Aeneas*, written for performance at a girls' school, tells the story of Prince Aeneas of Troy who, while fleeing from the destruction of his native city, falls in love with Queen Dido of Carthage; he is forced to leave her after a single night, at the gods' command – for it is his destiny to found a new Troy, which is to be Rome, in Italy. This colorful work depicts Dido's court at Carthage, a hunt, a covey of malicious witches, and a sailors' scene. There are choruses, dances, recitatives, songs, duets, and other ensembles, and several of them use ground bass, a favorite device of Purcell's and one he handled with particular skill and subtlety.

The climax of the opera comes in the third act. Queen Dido (soprano), deeply offended at Aeneas's obedience to the gods' command, proudly dismisses him, and looks forward to death in her famous lament. Like many laments in the Baroque period, this one is constructed on a ground bass (see p. 37), which in this chromatic falling pattern is a traditional elegiac device.

 Listening Outline . . . .

Time	
0.00	recitative, 'Thy hand, Belinda': note the expressively falling vocal line
1.02	orchestra plays the ground, ex. 1, a chromatic descending line
1.19	'When I am laid in earth'
2.01	'When I am . . .', second time
2.41	'Remember me'
4.08	instrumental conclusion
4.56	(end)

Thy hand, Belinda; darkness shades me
On thy bosom let me rest;
More I would, but Death invades me:
Death is now a welcome guest.

When I am laid in earth,
May my wrongs create
No trouble in thy breast;
Remember me, but ah! forget my fate.

(*words by Nahum Tate*)

ex. 1

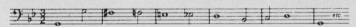

Purcell divided his time between the organ loft and the theater, and his contributions to theatrical music are perhaps his highest achievement. Had he lived beyond the age of 36, he might have created a tradition of English opera. As it was, he wrote a great many songs and dances to be given in plays, one true opera (*Dido and Aeneas*; see **Listening Guide 15**), and a handful of "semi-operas", extended musical sections for performance within theatrical plays.

Purcell's range was wide. He composed everything from bawdy catches to impassioned prayers, intimate chamber music to ceremonial court odes, spirited dances to elegiac laments. It is perhaps in the expression of the darker moods, grief, pathos, and despair, that he proved himself even in so brief a life the greatest English composer of the Baroque and perhaps of any era.

Henry Purcell — Life and Works

1659	born in southern England
1660s	chorister in the Chapel Royal
1674–8	organ tuner at Westminster Abbey, London
1677	composer to the royal band
1679	organist of Westminster Abbey
1680	fantasias for strings published; composed first 'welcome' song and first music for the theater
1682	organist of the Chapel Royal
1683	organ maker and master of the king's instruments
1685	anthem *My heart is inditing* composed for James II's coronation
1689	*Dido and Aeneas* performed in Chelsea
1695	died in London, 21 November

Dramatic music Dido and Aeneas (1689); semi-operas – King Arthur (1691), The Fairy Queen (1692), The Indian Queen (1695); incidental music and songs for plays

Secular choral music 24 odes and welcome songs – Sound the trumpet (1687); Hail, bright Cecilia (1692); Come, ye sons of art, away; songs, duets

Sacred choral music c55 verse anthems, c16 full anthems; Te Deum and Jubilate (1694); services

Instrumental music fantasias for strings; sonatas, suites for harpsichord, organ voluntaries

6 *Vivaldi*

Antonio Vivaldi was born in Venice in 1678, the son of a violinist. He was trained for the priesthood and ordained in 1703, though on grounds of health he was soon granted dispensation from saying Mass. Meanwhile he had become a skilled violinist and sometimes deputized for his father in the orchestra at St Mark's. In 1703 he was appointed master of the violin at one of the Venetian orphanages, the Ospedale della Pietà (the Hospital of Piety). This institution, one of four for which Venice was famous, took in orphaned, abandoned, or poor girls and educated them, and in particular trained them in music if they showed any aptitude. The Pietà orchestra was well known for its virtuosity; several visitors to Venice reported on its concerts, during which the girls were discreetly shielded from the audience's view to avoid any impropriety. Vivaldi worked at the Pietà for some 15 years, during which time he wrote many of his concertos and some sacred music for the Pietà girls; the wide range of instruments for which he composed reflects the girls' abilities.

LIFE

Vivaldi: Violin Concerto in a, op. 3 no. 6 (1712), first movement

Vivaldi wrote close on 500 concertos; of these, more than 200 were for his own instrument, the violin. Several times he made collections of what he thought to be his best concertos, or the ones most likely to be suitable for public sale, and sent them from Italy to a publisher in Amsterdam, an important commercial center where some of the best music engraving was done. The A minor violin concerto comes from the set of 12 published, in 1712, as his op. 3, under the title *L'estro armonico* (meaning 'Musical Fancy'); he had earlier published collections of sonatas, but op. 3 was his first set of concertos to become known outside his native Venice. Each of the concertos is in three movements.

The present one is typical; after the first movement, in ritornello form, there is a slow movement in which the violin plays a floridly decorated melodic line with an accompaniment only for violins and violas, and the last movement is a lively quick piece, in ritornello form again but more direct in style than the first movement. As in many of Vivaldi's ritornello movements, the opening material of the first movement returns in full only at the end, though extracts from it appear regularly throughout it; also typical of Vivaldi are the 'interruptions' by the soloist of the closing appearance of the ritornello theme. The vigorous, pounding rhythms of the orchestral music and the athletic style of the solo part, with its mixture of rapid movement and large leaps (especially in the solo immediately following the main central ritornello), are found in many Italian Baroque concertos and Vivaldi's in particular; the sequences – passages repeated identically at a different pitch – are also a hallmark of Vivaldi's style.

 Listening Outline . . . .

First movement (Allegro): ritornello form, a
solo violin, strings (1st and 2nd violins, viola, cello, violone), continuo

Time		
0.00	**ritornello 1, a**	two principal ideas: ex. 1, based on repeated notes, and ex. 2, on an arpeggio figure (0.13)
0.26	**solo 1, a–c**	begins as ex. 1
0.45	**ritornello 2, a**	based on ex. 1, fig. *a*
0.50	**solo 2, a–e**	violin passage-work and scales
1.16	**ritornello 3, e**	main central ritornello, in the dominant, a shortened version of mm. 1–12 of ritornello 1
1.36	**solo 3, e–a**	mainly built on ex. 1 material
2.04	**ritornello 4, a**	final ritornello, first part
2.09	**solo 4, a**	first interruption, for virtuoso passage-work
2.28	**ritornello 5, a**	final ritornello, second part
2.34	**solo 5, a**	a second, shorter interruption
2.42	**ritornello 6, a**	final ritornello, third and last part
2.56		(end)

ex. 1

ex. 2

Later he turned to the world of opera – both its composition and its management. He wrote some 40 operas, several for performance in Venice but also for other cities in north Italy, Rome, and Prague. This involved him in lengthy spells away, during which he kept in contact with the Pietà and even sent concertos by post. But after about 1718, because of his continual absences, he was employed there only in the period 1735–8. In 1740 Vivaldi went to Austria; he died in Vienna, apparently in poverty, in the summer of 1741. He was little mourned, even in Venice: he had been a difficult man, vain and avaricious – but he left a deep mark on the history of music.

It is as an instrumental composer, particularly of concertos, that Vivaldi was – and is today – chiefly famous. Of his 500 concertos, close on half are for solo violin; over 100 are for solo bassoon, cello, oboe, or flute, and about 150 have multiple soloists or are "orchestral concertos".

The music itself is marked by its sheer energy, its driving momentum, and its strongly rhythmic character; it is clearly the work of a violinist, drawing its style from what is possible and effective on a violin. His opening themes are nearly always

MUSIC

Antonio Vivaldi — Life and Works

1678	born in Venice, 4 March
1693	began training for the priesthood and learned to play the violin, deputizing for his father, a violinist at St Mark's; suffered chronic ill-health
1703	ordained priest
1703–9	master of the violin at the Ospedale della Pietà; began composing
1711	*L'estro armonico*, a collection of 12 concertos, published
1711–16	returned to post at the Pietà
1713	started composing opera and working in opera houses
1718	beginning of years of travel
1725	*Il cimento dell'armonia e dell'inventione*, containing *The Four Seasons*, published
1726–8	composer and impresario at the Teatro S Angelo, Venice
1729–33	further wide travels, including to Vienna and Prague
1738	Amsterdam
1740	Austria
1741	died in Vienna, 28 July

Concertos c230 violin concertos – The Four Seasons, op. 8 nos. 1–4; c70 orchestral concertos, c80 double and triple concertos – L'estro armonico, op. 3 (1711); c100 bassoon, cello, oboe, and flute concertos

Chamber music c40 violin sonatas, 9 cello sonatas; 27 trio sonatas; chamber concertos

Operas (over 45) Orlando finto pazzo (1714), Giustino (1724), Griselda (1735)

Sacred choral music Gloria, D; Magnificat, g; Juditha triumphans, oratorio (1716); Mass movements, psalms, motets

direct and memorable, and their memorability is important because their recur-rences need to be instantly recognized if the form of the movement is to be grasped. He also made much use of sequences – that is, repeating the same pattern at different pitches (see **Listening Guide 16**).

Vivaldi wrote a number of "programmatic" concertos – works that tell a story in their music, or at least carry some meaning outside the music itself. There is for example *La notte* ("The Night"), with dark and sinister effects (this is a bassoon concerto), and *La tempesta di mare* ("The Storm at Sea"). The most famous of his concertos of this type is the group *The Four Seasons*, which Vivaldi included in a set he published in about 1725 as op. 8, with the fanciful title *Il cimento dell'armonia e dell'inventione* ("The Contest of Harmony and Invention").

The Four Seasons go further than the others in that their music represents phenomena associated with each season – birdsong in the spring, for example, summer thunderstorms, harvesting in the fall, shivering and skating in winter. Yet the basis of the concerto form remains unchanged for it is in the solo music (these are violin concertos) that Vivaldi generally depicts the changing events in the story he is telling, using music for full orchestra either not at all or to depict a recurring element, for example the torpor created by the heat of summer. The same applies to the slow movements, which as in most of Vivaldi's concertos are generally a simple melody with light orchestral accompaniment; though in the Summer concerto distant thunder is heard and in Spring the soloist represents a sleeping goatherd, the viola the barks of his dog, and the orchestral violins presumably the rustling leaves. Vivaldi published with the concertos a set of sonnets outlining the events they portray.

Vivaldi's gifts had a certain brilliance and waywardness. But he brought to the concerto a new tone of passion, a new vigor, a new awareness of instrumental color and of how to exploit it. The freshness and clarity of his invention made his concertos attractive and influential: many other composers imitated and learned from them, the greatest of them being Bach.

7 *Handel*

The two great composers of the later Baroque period, George Frideric Handel and Johann Sebastian Bach, were born in neighboring provinces of Germany within four weeks, into the same religious faith and a similar social background. But while Bach remained in central Germany, and continued composing in the manner traditional to his background, Handel traveled widely and made his career far away from his homeland. His music reflects his cosmopolitan life and the taste of the wider public for whom he composed.

Handel was born in the Saxon town of Halle in 1685. His father, a barber-surgeon, discouraged his musical leanings and directed him towards the law. As a boy, Handel pursued music surreptitiously; he is said to have sneaked a clavichord into an attic where he could practice unheard. When the family visited the nearby court at Weissenfels, where his father was court surgeon, the duke heard Handel playing the organ and advised his father to let him study music. Handel's house stood close by the city's main Lutheran church, and the boy studied with the organist there, under whom he made rapid progress both as composer and as player (of the violin as well as keyboard instruments). When he was 17 he entered the university, and he also took a temporary post as organist of the Calvinist cathedral.

A year later he went to Hamburg, a busy commercial center with a lively musical life and an opera house. It was at the opera house that he found employment, as a second violinist and later as harpsichordist; and he made friends with Johann Mattheson (1681–1764), later an eminent composer and theorist. He and Mattheson went to Lübeck in 1703 to hear Buxtehude (as Bach did later: see p. 143) and evidently considered applying to succeed him, but were put off by the obligation the post carried to marry Buxtehude's daughter. Handel, it seems, was already wedded to an operatic career. His first opera, *Almira*, was given at the beginning of 1705 (he was still not quite 20), his second (a failure) a few weeks later.

Handel composed two further operas for Hamburg, but by the time they were given, in 1708, he had left the city. There was only one place that an ambitious young composer keen on opera could study: Italy. He spent more than three years there, dividing his time between Florence, Rome, and Venice. Opera was now forbidden at Rome, by papal decree; but the cardinals and princes in or near the city were noted patrons and at least four of them commissioned music from Handel or employed him.

Handel wrote two oratorios in Rome, one a moral tale about abstract virtues, the other a setting of the Resurrection story, and numerous cantatas, mostly pieces some ten minutes long for solo voice and continuo consisting of two songs (usually about unrequited love), each preceded by a recitative. Handel quickly developed a

GERMANY, ITALY

50 *Handel: marble statue, 1738, by Louis François Roubiliac, commissioned for Vauxhall Gardens. Victoria and Albert Museum, London.*

George Frideric Handel

Life and Works

1685	born in Halle, 23 February
1694	pupil of Zachow at the Church of Our Lady, Halle
1702	law student at Halle University; organist of the Calvinist cathedral
1703	violinist and harpsichordist in Hamburg opera orchestra
1705	*Almira* (Hamburg)
1706–9	Italy: Florence, Rome, and Venice; contact with the Scarlattis and Corelli; oratorios, operas, many cantatas
1710	*Kapellmeister* to the Elector of Hanover; first visit to London
1711	*Rinaldo* (London); Hanover
1712	settled in London
1717	*Water Music*; director of music to Earl of Carnarvon (later Duke of Chandos) at Cannons, near London
1718	*Acis and Galatea*
1719	visit to Germany to recruit singers for the Royal Academy of Music, of which he was musical director
1723	composer to the Chapel Royal
1724	*Julius Caesar*
1727	naturalized English; anthems for George II's coronation, including *Zadok the Priest*
1729	second Royal Academy established after collapse of first; to Italy to recruit singers
1733	first organ concertos
1735	first Lent series of oratorios in London; *Alcina*
1737	collapse of Handel's opera company (and its rival, the Opera of the Nobility); Handel ill
1739	*Saul, Israel in Egypt*; composed 12 Grand Concertos, op. 6
1742	*Messiah* (Dublin)
1752	*Jephtha*; deterioration of eyesight leading to virtual blindness in two years
1759	died in London, 13 April

Operas (over 40) Almira (1705), Rinaldo (1711), Giulio Cesare (1724), Rodelinda (1725), Orlando (1732), Ariodante (1735), Alcina (1735), Serse (1738)

Oratorios (over 30) Acis and Galatea (1718), Athalia (1733), Alexander's Feast (1736), Saul (1739), Israel in Egypt (1739), Messiah (1742), Samson (1743), Semele (1744), Belshazzar (1745), Judas Maccabaeus (1747), Solomon (1749), Jephtha (1752)

Other sacred vocal music 11 Chandos anthems; 4 coronation anthems; Utrecht Te Deum and Jubilate (1713); Latin church music – Dixit Dominus (1707)

Secular vocal music over 100 Italian cantatas; trios, duets, songs

Orchestral music Water Music (1717); 6 Concerti grossi, op. 3 (1734); 12 Grand Concertos, op. 6 (1740); Music for Royal Fireworks (1749); organ concertos; suites, overtures, dance movements

Chamber music trio sonatas; sonatas for recorder, flute, oboe, violin

Keyboard music harpsichord suites, dance movements, chaconnes, airs, preludes, fugues

new vein of melody suited to the Italian language, thus acquiring the experience he needed to be a success in the opera house. These fluent, graceful pieces offer the earliest evidence of the great melodist that Handel was to be. It was in Rome, too, that he composed a group of works for the church, writing in Latin for the Roman Catholic liturgy. Their choral effects and vigorous, punched-out rhythms show that he was already a masterly composer for chorus.

As an opera composer, he had two notable successes: in Florence, probably at the end of 1707, and in Venice, in winter 1709–10, when his *Agrippina* was so well received that it was given 27 times, an exceptionally high number.

In Italy Handel met many of the leading composers of the day, among them the violinist-composer Corelli, who organized most of the music-making in Rome, and Vivaldi. He is said to have engaged in competition with the brilliant young harpsichordist and composer, Domenico Scarlatti, whom he far surpassed on the organ though on the harpsichord they were judged equals. He was much influenced in his composition by Scarlatti's father, Alessandro, the leading Italian opera composer of the time, whose warm, flowing melodic style was to be his model. He also met potential patrons, among them several Englishmen who pressed him to go to London. But the invitation he accepted was from the Elector of Hanover, and when in 1710 he left Italy it was to go to the north German city of Hanover, as *Kapellmeister* at the electoral court.

LONDON: THE EARLY YEARS

One of Handel's conditions of acceptance of the Hanover post was that he should immediately take a year's leave to visit England. The Elector was heir to the English throne, then occupied by the aging Queen Anne; possibly there was an understanding that Handel would eventually work for him in London.

Handel spent his first visit to the English capital establishing a position for himself. London had a flourishing theatrical life, but opera was not yet a part of it; a few English operas had been given, and some in Italian, with mixed success. English connoisseurs were realizing that if they wanted to hear the kinds of singing that they had heard in Italy and in some German cities there would have to be an Italian opera house in London. So they set about founding one. It still exists: the Royal Opera House, Covent Garden, is its direct descendant.

At the beginning of 1711, then, Handel composed the first Italian opera written for London, *Rinaldo*. It was a success, but it also started a controversy. The audiences were delighted with the singing, the music itself, and the theatrical effects (which included ingenious machinery for scene transformations and the release of live sparrows for a woodland episode), but some literary intellectuals were contemptuous of the effects and scorned the idea of opera in Italian, sung by castratos before an English-speaking audience.

Handel went back to Hanover in the summer, and remained there for more than a year. By the fall of 1712 he was back in London, having been allowed leave "for a reasonable time". He stayed for the rest of his life. He lived first at the house of Lord Burlington, a noted patron of the arts, where he met many leading literary figures. He began to establish himself at the English court, composing ceremonial music and

Handel: *Acis and Galatea* (1718), excerpt from Act 2

Handel wrote *Acis and Galatea* when he was working just outside London as resident composer to the Earl of Carnarvon. It is a setting of a well-known mythological, pastoral tale, and it was probably designed not for stage performance but for some kind of semi-dramatic representation – possibly in the open air, on the attractive terraces (which still exist, although the house, Cannons, has been much rebuilt) that looked over the earl's spaciously landscaped garden, with its garden statues and distant lake.

The work was probably intended for performance by just five singers and a small group of players; Handel later rearranged it for a larger body of musicians when he gave it in London. In the story, the shepherd Acis and the nymph Galatea (who is part-goddess) are in love; the first half of the work is largely given over to their love-music. In the second half, the grotesque giant Polyphemus, overcome by Galatea's beauty, is consumed with jealousy; he threatens to kill Acis, and does so at the end of the trio 'The flocks shall leave the mountains' (in which the lovers swear undying devotion). Later, Galatea exercises her divine powers to turn the dead Acis into a fountain, in whose 'crystal flood' she can bathe.

The sturdy, resolute music of the opening C minor section contrasts with the softer music, initially in E♭, for the second stanza sung by the lovers. This will have made the audience of Handel's time expect a *da capo*, a return in the usual way to the music of the opening – and its failure to come, because of Acis's death, reinforces musically the sense of shock that his death causes. The mixture in this work of light, ironic comedy with tragic feeling, of gently amorous music with real depth of expression, is typical of the pastoral tradition – going back to Renaissance Italy – to which *Acis and Galatea* belongs.

 Listening Outline

'The flocks shall leave the mountains' (*Andante*), 4/4, c
Galatea (soprano), Acis (tenor), Polyphemus (bass), with oboes, strings, and continuo

Time
0.00 instrumental introduction
0.15 Acis: 'The flocks . . .', c, ex. 1
0.29 Galatea answers, g; the two sing together, leading to cadence, c
0.58 Polyphemus joins in with exclamations – 'Torture! fury!'
1.14 Acis and Galatea reiterate, 'The flocks . . .' as Polyphemus continues to rage; cadence in g (Polyphemus's rage seems to overflow beyond the cadence; his is a little later)
1.39 more lyrical section, 'Not show'rs to larks more pleasing', ex. 2, E♭ – c, but Polyphemus has seized a rock – 'Fly swift, thou massy ruin, fly!' – to hurl at Acis
2.13 the lovers reach a cadence in c; but again Polyphemus's angry music overflows ('Die, presumptuous Acis, die!') – he has the last word, and Acis falls, dying
2.30 (end)

ACIS, GALATEA	The flocks shall leave the mountains
	    The woods the turtle dove,
	The nymphs forsake the fountains,
	    Ere I forsake my love!
		ACIS, GALATEA	Not show'rs to larks so pleasing,
			    Not sunshine to the bee,
			Not sleep to toil so easing,
			    As these dear smiles to me.

POLYPHEMUS	Torture! fury! rage! despair! I cannot, cannot bear!	POLYPHEMUS	Fly swift, thou massy ruin, fly! Die, presumptuous Acis, die!

an ode in honor of Queen Anne's birthday. That was in 1713, the year the queen awarded him a generous salary. The following year she died, and the Elector of Hanover went to London as the new king, George I. Stories have been told of how Handel, embarrassed at having overstayed his leave, sought to restore his favor with George I by arranging a serenade for him at a water-party on the Thames. The tale is unlikely, for probably Handel was never truly out of royal favor; George had soon doubled his salary. But the music for a water-party – one took place in 1717 – survives, and the *Water Music* is among his most popular works.

About 1717 Handel took a position as resident composer at the country house, just outside London, of the Earl of Carnarvon (later the Duke of Chandos), a newly rich nobleman with a small musical establishment. Handel remained at this house, Cannons, until about 1720, and composed both sacred and dramatic music there. One of the dramatic works was a setting of the biblical story of Esther, in effect Handel's first English oratorio. The other was *Acis and Galatea*, a miniature opera (see **Listening Guide 17**).

THE OPERA VENTURES

Up to this time, operatic life in London had been haphazard. A group of noblemen now founded an organization to finance and regularize the hiring of theaters, players, singers, scene designers, composers, and so on, and to raise money by selling subscriptions for seats. It was called the Royal Academy of Music (the king's patronage meant that "Royal" could be used). Handel, appointed musical director, went off in 1719 to the main courts and opera centers of Europe to hear singers and engage those he wanted. In 1720 the Academy opened; Handel's *Radamisto* was its second opera, performed at the King's Theatre to great applause.

The main triumphs of the Academy were still to come. For the second season, some of the singers Handel had hired arrived, notably the superb castrato Senesino; his powerful alto voice made him the ideal singer of the big heroic roles. Another composer, Giovanni Bononcini (1670–1747), was enlisted to help supply new operas, which he did at least as successfully as Handel himself. Then in 1723 a new soprano, Francesca Cuzzoni, arrived; her brilliant singing created a sensation. In 1724 and 1725 Handel composed some of his finest operatic music, particularly in *Giulio Cesare* and *Rodelinda*.

LISTENING GUIDE 18

Handel: Organ Concerto in B♭, op. 4 no. 2 (1735), first movement

In an early oratorio composed in Italy, Handel had written an instrumental interlude in which he included a solo part for the organ – which he would certainly have played himself at the original performances. This must have been in his mind when, in 1735 after he had been established in London for some time, he decided to give seasons of oratorios. The oratorio singers were English, some of them church musicians, lacking the element of vocal virtuosity that had made the performances of his operas – by Italian theater singers – exciting and attractive to audiences. Handel may have felt that he could supply this missing element as organ soloist.

In 1735, in a performance of *Esther*, he played organ concertos probably for the first time in London. Two were given, one of them almost certainly op. 4 no. 2. Three years later he published it, in a collection of six such works. This one has three movements: after the one recorded here comes a short and highly florid, improvisatory slow movement, followed by a minuet-like Allegro. Improvisation was always a part of his performances, and often the scores of these concertos carry such an indication as 'ad libitum', to mark the point at which a soloist may feel at liberty to add a suitably brilliant passage.

 Listening Outline . . . .

First movement (A tempo ordinario – Allegro), 4/4, B♭; introduction, then ritornello form

Time		
0.00	**introduction, B♭**	in dotted rhythms, akin to a French overture; ends with cadence on F
0.57	**ritornello 1, B♭**	orchestra states main theme, 14 mm., ex. 1
1.27	**solo 1, B♭–F**	organ takes up ex. 1, then goes into virtuoso figuration
2.08	**ritornello 2, F**	freely based on ex. 1
2.23	**solo 2, F–g**	organ passage-work, with orchestra marking cadences; then dialog between organ and orchestra, using figure (ex. 2) based on opening of ex. 1
3.04	**ritornello 3**	brief, with cadence in g
3.14	**solo 3, g–c**	organ passage-work
3.35	**ritornello 4, c**	short assertion of c, with another variant (ex. 3) of opening figure of ex. 1
3.44	**solo 4, c–B♭**	organ writing of increasing virtuosity
4.18	**ritornello 5, B♭**	a full statement, as if to close the movement
4.46	**solo 5, B♭**	an extra solo: it is marked 'ad libitum' at the end to allow the soloist to improvise freely if desired
5.04	**ritornello 6, B♭**	short final ritornello
5.21		(end)

ex. 1

ex. 2

ex. 3

The Royal Academy continued putting on Handel's operas, but it steadily lost money and in 1728 it collapsed. Meanwhile, Handel had been active in other spheres: in 1723 he was appointed composer of the Chapel Royal, and he wrote four anthems for the coronation of George II in Westminster Abbey in 1727 (one, *Zadok the Priest*, has been performed at every British coronation since). That year he became a naturalized English subject.

In 1729, Handel and the Academy theater manager decided to put on operas themselves. But their success was limited, and soon a rival opera organization was set up. Not surprisingly, both collapsed, in 1737; by then Handel had composed no fewer than 13 operas since the closing of the Academy, including some of his finest. Handel's interest in opera – or perhaps his confidence in the possibility of pursuing it successfully – seems to have faded, and after four more operas he abandoned the form in 1741. By then he had a good idea of the new directions his creative career was taking.

ORATORIO

Back in 1718, as we saw, Handel had written two dramatic works to English words. The occasion for them had passed, and they had been put aside. But in 1732 *Esther* was privately performed, by friends of Handel's, at a London tavern. Then another group, unconnected with Handel, advertised a performance. There was no law of copyright, and Handel could not prevent it. But he retaliated, giving a performance himself, with extra music, so that his version would seem to be the most up-to-date and authoritative. The Bishop of London, however, forbade him to have a biblical story acted on the stage. A little later, the same happened with *Acis and Galatea* – a performance by rivals, a retaliation by Handel with extra music but no stage action.

The success of these works gave Handel new ideas. In 1733 he performed a new biblical oratorio, *Deborah*, during Lent, when opera was not allowed. That summer, in Oxford, he gave *Acis and Galatea* and another new oratorio, *Athalia*. In Lent 1735 he held an oratorio season in London, and during the intermissions he played organ concertos – an entirely new genre in which, during the 1730s and 40s, Handel (and then a few other composers in England) created a repertory. Handel's own concertos are notable for their brilliance and grandeur, and his performances helped attract audiences (see **Listening Guide 18**).

During the late 1730s, as Handel's interest in opera waned, he turned to other large-scale vocal forms. He also wrote a quantity of instrumental works around this time, including his finest ones, a set of 12 concertos for strings, written in the first place for use at his oratorio concerts. These and Bach's Brandenburg Concertos (see pp. 146–8) stand as twin peaks of the Baroque concerto repertory.

In 1741, Handel was invited to visit Dublin and give concerts in aid of charities there. He accepted, and set about preparing two new works. One was what he called a "Sacred Oratorio", better known as *Messiah*; the other was *Samson*, based on verse by Milton. He arrived there in November and gave a concert series with great success. The climax was the first performance, on 13 April 1742, of *Messiah* (see **Listening Guide 19**). The hall was full; the ladies had been asked to wear dresses without hoops, and the gentlemen to abandon their swords, so that more people could be admitted. A reporter wrote that "words are wanting to express the exquisite delight it afforded to the admiring crouded audience. The sublime, the grand, and the tender, adapted to the most elevated, majestick and moving words, conspired to transport and charm the ravished heart and ear".

Back in London, Handel gave seasons of oratorios and similar works at the new Covent Garden theater. He was composing now not primarily for the small, aristocratic class with inherited wealth, land, and titles, but for a more broadly based middle-class public as well. Created by the new commercial and industrial activity that had already made London the biggest, busiest, and most prosperous city in the world, this new public was keen to share the cultural pleasures of the upper classes but was also touched by the religious spirit of the times and thus wanted "improvement" from their pleasures as well as diversion.

LISTENING GUIDE 19

CD 2 TRACK 6; CASS. 1 EX. 5

Handel: *Messiah* (1742), Hallelujah Chorus

Messiah is not only the most famous and most loved of Handel's works, but also the most famous and most loved of choral works in the English-speaking world. Most of Handel's oratorios are based on biblical stories, dramatically related; although they are not for performance on the stage, they are almost, in effect, sacred operas.

Messiah is different: it does have some narrative element, in that it is concerned with the Christmas and Easter stories, but it is primarily a contemplation on these stories using words directly drawn from the Bible. Handel composed it during six weeks of intensive work in the summer of 1741. Its music draws on Handel's background in the traditions of German Passion music, but also on his Italian melodic writing (in fact in some of the choruses he used music he had originally composed as Italian love duets) and on the grand choral effects inherited from the English tradition through Henry Purcell. Handel's theatrical sense is in evidence too: in the music announcing the birth of Christ (with distant trumpets and the effect of a choir of angels), in the drama of the Passion music, and in the grandeur of the most famous number, the Hallelujah chorus. Handel said that, while composing it, he saw 'the great God himself upon his throne, and all his company of angels'.

The Hallelujah chorus concludes the second of the three parts of *Messiah*. It is typical of his triumphal choral style, though there are contrapuntal sections and a fugal exposition; the music is less consistently contrapuntal than Bach's, and at climaxes Handel tends to move back to the powerful block harmony and vigorous rhythms that can make so grand an effect.

Listening Outline . . . .

Allegro, 4/4, D

Time

0.00	orchestral introduction
0.07	chorus enters: 'Hallelujah', ex. 1
0.26	'For the Lord God', ex. 2, chorus in unison
0.49	ex. 2 worked contrapuntally against rhythm of 'Hallelujah', ex. 1, fig. *a*; cadence in D
1.17	'The Kingdom of this world': choir in block harmony
1.35	'And he shall reign', ex. 3: fugal exposition, voices entering in the order bass–tenor–alto–treble
1.58	'King of Kings': upper voices sustain, 'Hallelujah' rhythm in lower; trumpet entry (2.09), after which trebles move upwards by step each three measures
2.40	further contrapuntal development of ex. 3; then sustained notes in lower voices, 'Hallelujah' in upper
3.07	final section ('King of Kings'), with increasing emphasis, with ringing trumpets and more 'Hallelujahs'
3.44	(end)

Hallelujah! Hallelujah!
For the Lord God omnipotent reigneth
The Kingdom of this world is become
   the Kingdom of Our Lord
And of his Christ.
And he shall reign for ever and ever
King of Kings and Lord of Lords
And he shall reign for ever and ever
Hallelujah! Hallelujah!

ex. 1

ex. 2

ex. 3

Handel gave his new *Samson* (he had not performed it in Dublin) in Lent 1743, with great success. *Messiah*, which followed, was a failure – the singing of biblical words in a theater offended many people and the work became popular in London only when, in 1750, Handel performed it in a chapel for charity. The oratorio seasons continued. At some, Handel experimented: in 1744 he gave *Semele*, not an oratorio but more like an opera, based on an erotic story from classical mythology, set in English with oratorio-like choruses and with no acting. It was a failure; the new audiences found none of the moral uplift they were seeking. The same happened the following season with *Hercules*, another classical drama. These two are among Handel's finest works, the former for its portrayal of sensual love (the well-known "Where'er you walk" comes from it), the latter for its powerful treatment of jealousy. Neither was liked in Handel's time and only recently have they come to be appreciated.

So Handel turned back to biblical oratorios, each of them relating, in musical-dramatic terms, a story, usually a well-known one. Each singer plays a particular character: in *Saul*, for example, the Jewish king himself is a bass, his son Jonathan a tenor, and David an alto. The chorus may assume different roles: sometimes they represent an army or a populace, sometimes they simply provide an external observer's commentary on events.

The last of Handel's biblical oratorios was *Jephtha*, written in 1751. As he composed it his eyesight began to fail; at one point in the score, at the chorus "How dark, O Lord, are thy decrees, All hid from mortal sight", he noted in the margin that he had to pause owing to the failure of his left eye. By 1753 he was virtually blind; he continued to attend performances, and even managed to play organ concertos – at first relying on his memory, later improvising the solo sections.

There are a number of enigmas surrounding Handel. One concerns his "borrowings". He often re-used music from an early work in a later one; *Rinaldo*, for example, hastily written when he first went to London, incorporates items from his Italian compositions. But he also used other composers' music. Usually he adapted and rewrote what he used, nearly always improving it and stamping his own character upon it. He "borrowed" music frequently, extensively, and throughout his life. Sometimes he bought music from abroad and within months was using ideas from it in his own works. That there was some deception in all this is clear. Yet the individuality, the grandeur, and the honesty that shine through his music provide their own answer.

Handel was much esteemed by those who knew him. He was a quick-tempered man, but keenly witty. He had a gluttonous appetite. In his young days he played in private concerts, at the homes of patrons, but he gradually withdrew into a life of more privacy. He practiced the harpsichord a great deal; it is said that the keys of his instrument were worn hollow. He attended church regularly in his later years, going to St George's, Hanover Square, from his house nearby (which still stands). He died in April 1759, aged 74. Three thousand Londoners attended his funeral; he was buried in Westminster Abbey.

8 *Bach*

Between the middle of the sixteenth century and the middle of the nineteenth there were more than 80 musicians in Germany who bore the name Bach. The area in which they chiefly lived was Thuringia, a rural part of central Germany, firmly Lutheran in faith, governed in small regions by dukes. Musical life flourished at the courts of the local noblemen and in civic institutions – the churches, first, but also the local town bands. The greatest member of the family, Johann Sebastian Bach, was born in 1685, the son of a town musician of Eisenach (trumpeter and director of the band) who himself was the son of a town musician.

EARLY LIFE

J. S. Bach began his schooling in Eisenach, but when he was nine his parents died and he went to Ohrdruf, where his elder brother was organist, attending school there until he was 15. Then he went north to Lüneburg to a boarding school, free to needy boys with good voices.

In 1702 Bach left Lüneburg. Appointments as organist were normally open to competition: Bach applied for one, won it, and was offered the post, but the local duke intervened and appointed an older man. Bach soon found a position at Weimar, as "lackey-musician" (servant with musical duties). After a few months he became organist of the New Church in Arnstadt. He did not stay long: he was once told that his work was unsatisfactory. Soon after that he was granted leave to go to Lübeck – some 250 miles away, a journey he made on foot – to hear the eminent organist Buxtehude play; he overstayed by almost three months. Again he was in trouble on his return, not only for his long absence but also for his work; the authorities now complained that he introduced strange notes and elaborations into the hymns, making them difficult for the congregation to follow. And he was in trouble for bringing a young woman into the church.

Bach was soon looking elsewhere for a post, and in 1707 he successfully undertook a trial for the organistship of the St Blasius Church at Mühlhausen, about 35 miles away. That year he married his second cousin Maria Barbara Bach. His stay at Mühlhausen was short: the pastor was a strict Pietist who objected to any but the simplest music in church. The congregation too was conservative. Again, this was no place for a young musician whose brain and fingers teemed with new and imaginative ideas. So when he received an invitation to become court organist at Weimar, the following summer, he at once accepted. By now he was an authority on organs and he was asked to see through the rebuilding of the instrument at his old church.

WEIMAR, CÖTHEN

Bach's post at Weimar was his most important yet. The duke admired his organ playing, and seems to have encouraged him in composition. Many of his organ works

Johann Sebastian Bach — Life and Works

1685	born in Eisenach, 21 March
1700	chorister at St Michael, Lüneburg
1703	organist at the New Church, Arnstadt
1705–6	visited Lübeck to hear Buxtehude playing the organ
1707	organist at St Blasius, Mühlhausen; married Maria Barbara Bach
1708	court organist in Weimar; prolific output of organ works
1713	*Konzertmeister* at Weimar court, responsible for providing a new cantata every four weeks
1717	*Kapellmeister* to Prince Leopold in Cöthen; many instrumental works, including Brandenburg Concertos, violin concertos, sonatas and keyboard music
1720	Maria Barbara Bach died
1721	married Anna Magdalena Wilcken
1723	*Kantor* of St Thomas's School, Leipzig, supplying cantatas for the main city churches each Sunday
1727	*St Matthew Passion*
1729	director of the *collegium musicum* in Leipzig
1741	Berlin and Dresden; *Goldberg Variations*
*c*1745	*The Art of Fugue*
1747	visited Frederick the Great's court in Berlin; *Musical Offering*
1749	B minor Mass
1750	died in Leipzig, 28 July

Sacred choral music St John Passion (1724); St Matthew Passion (1727); Christmas Oratorio (1734); Mass, b (1749); Magnificat, D (1723); over 200 church cantatas – no. 80, Ein' feste Burg ist unser Gott (*c*1744), no. 140, Wachet auf (1731); motets – Singet dem Herrn (1727), Jesu meine Freude (?1723); chorales, sacred songs, arias

Secular vocal music over 30 cantatas – no. 211, 'Coffee Cantata' (*c*1735); no. 212, 'Peasant Cantata' (1742)

Orchestral music Brandenburg Concertos nos. 1–6 (1721); 4 orchestral suites – C (*c*1725), b (*c*1731), D (*c*1731), D (1725); harpsichord concertos; sinfonias

Chamber music 6 sonatas and partitas for solo violin (1720); 6 sonatas for violin and harpsichord (1723); 6 suites for solo cello (*c*1720); Musical Offering (1747); flute sonatas, trio sonatas

Keyboard music Chromatic fantasia and fugue, d (*c*1720); The Well-Tempered Keyboard, '48' (1722, 1742); 6 English Suites (*c*1724); 6 French Suites (*c*1724); 6 Partitas (1731); Italian Concerto (1735); French Overture (1735); Goldberg Variations (1741); The Art of Fugue (*c*1745); inventions, suites, dances, toccatas, fugues, capriccios

Organ music over 600 chorale preludes; concertos, preludes, fugues, toccatas, fantasias, sonatas

were written there. He was there until 1717. Six children were born to him and his wife, including two who were to become composers, Wilhelm Friedemann (born in 1712) and Carl Philipp Emanuel (born in 1714). Professionally, he was active in teaching and in organ and harpsichord construction and repairs. In 1713 he was offered a position elsewhere, but the duke gave Bach a salary increase and promoted him to *Konzertmeister*, with the task of providing a new cantata every four weeks.

Soon, however, something went wrong. From 1716 there are few cantatas, and none from 1717. At the end of 1716 the old *Kapellmeister* died, and perhaps Bach expected to be promoted again to the senior post; but he heard that the duke was looking elsewhere. So Bach sought a similar position, and was offered one by Prince Leopold of Cöthen. He applied in such strong terms for his release that the duke sent him to prison for four weeks and then dismissed him.

Bach must have been glad to move. Prince Leopold, a younger man, was a keen music-lover, a good amateur player, and a kind employer and good friend to Bach. By faith he was Calvinist, which meant that music was little used in his chapel. Bach wrote a few cantatas for special occasions, but his chief duty was to provide music for his employer's entertainment and perhaps participation. Bach's life was active and varied: he was in demand for testing new organs, he had trips to Berlin to buy a harpsichord, and he was one of the small group of musicians who accompanied Prince Leopold when he went to take the waters at a fashionable spa. It was during the second such visit, in 1720, that tragedy struck the Bach family: he came back to find his wife, Maria Barbara, dead and buried. She was only 36, and left a family of four (two had died in infancy). At the end of 1721, Bach remarried: his new wife, Anna Magdalena, was a singer at the court, and like his first wife came from local musical stock. She was 20; Bach was 36. She bore him no fewer than 13 children, of whom six grew to maturity and two achieved fame as composers, Johann Christoph Friedrich (born in 1732), and Johann Christian (born in 1735).

In the month of Bach's marriage, his employer also married. Leopold's new wife did not share his love for music, and from this time on Bach found his position at the court decreasing in importance. Bach had earlier considered leaving Cöthen: in 1720 he had applied for an important post as organist in Hamburg, had played there, and had been offered the position; but he declined, possibly because a hefty donation to the church funds seems to have been expected of him.

A new opportunity came up in 1723, in Leipzig, the largest city near Bach's home. This was the post of *Kantor* of the school at the church of St Thomas, which carried with it the city directorship of music. The duties were heavy, but the prestige was high and the salary good. The *Kantor* had responsibility for music in the city's four principal churches, in two of which regular performances with orchestra and choir were the rule. He also had to supervise the other civic musical activities, compose for weddings and funerals as well as Sunday services, select the choirs and train the senior one, and teach music at the school. Other distinguished musicians applied, but then withdrew: the third choice was Bach.

51 *Portrait of J. S. Bach aged 61 by E. G. Hausmann, painted in 1746 for presentation to the Mizler Society for Musical Sciences; he holds his entry manuscript, a "Canon Triplex".*

INSTRUMENTAL MUSIC

Most of Bach's chamber and orchestral works belong to the Cöthen years, as well as much of his harpsichord music. Of all these the best known are the Brandenburg Concertos, so called because Bach presented a manuscript of these six works to the Margrave of Brandenburg, who heard him play and asked to have some of his music. It is unlikely that Bach composed them specially; probably he had written them for the Cöthen players.

Bach: Brandenburg Concerto no. 4 in G (1721)

In late 1718 or early 1719, Bach paid a visit to Berlin in the course of negotiations for the purchase, by his employer the Prince of Anhalt-Cöthen, of a new harpsichord. There he played before the Margrave of Brandenburg, who said afterwards that he would like to have some of Bach's music. This was a normal form of patronage at the time: it was a request that Bach send him some music, in response to which he would send a sum of money – if he liked the music.

Bach did him proud: he put together a set of six concertos, probably mainly drawn from the repertory he was performing at Cöthen, and in 1721 sent the collection, in a fair copy, to the Margrave. The Margrave had only a modest musical establishment and could not have the concertos played; probably the score was put in his library and never used. There is no record that Bach was ever thanked or paid for sending the Margrave the greatest collection of Baroque concertos of their kind – and through them immortalizing the Brandenburg name.

As a young man at Weimar, Bach had copied out many concertos by his contemporaries, arranging them for solo keyboard (a harpsichord with two manuals could effectively imitate the difference between tutti and solo sections). Several of those he copied and arranged were by Vivaldi. He follows Vivaldi's style of ritornello form (see pp. 36–7, 130) in his own concertos. But Bach favored the much fuller and richer textures generally preferred by German composers of the time, and he also used the ritornello material more rigorously and economically, employing motifs from it in the solo music and within the textures, and so providing a strong force towards unity and logic in the music. Further, the clear-cut divisions between sections characteristic of Vivaldi are lacking in Bach, whose method of thematic working tends to produce solo sections that build up gradually into the tuttis.

 Listening Outline ·

solo violin, two recorders
1st and 2nd violins, viola, cello, violone, continuo

First movement (Allegro), 3/8, G: ritornello form

Time		
0.00	**ritornello 1, G**	an unusually long ritornello (83 mm.); the main idea (ex. 1) appears three times, the second in D: between the first and second there is passage-work on ex. 2 (0.11), between the second and third, on ex. 3 (0.32)
1.19	**solo 1, G–D**	violin solo, with reminders of ex. 1 from recorders; then exx. 2 and 3 material, in D, b, and e (1.57)
2.08	**ritornello 2, e**	exx. 1 and 2, cadence in e
2.27	**solo 2, e–C**	recorders, ex. 4, linked with ex. 3 material; then rapid, brilliant violin passage, a–C (2.56)
3.17	**ritornello 3, C**	exx. 1 and 2
3.42	**solo 3, C–G**	violin in constant 16ths, with recorders
4.08	**ritornello 4, G**	on exx. 2 and 3
4.28	**solo 4, G–b**	recorders; then ex. 4 with violin
4.53	**ritornello 5, b**	violins, ex. 3; tutti, ex. 1; cadence in b
5.26	**ritornello 6, G**	identical with ritornello 1 (5.26–6.50 = 0.00–1.19)
6.50		(end)

ex. 1

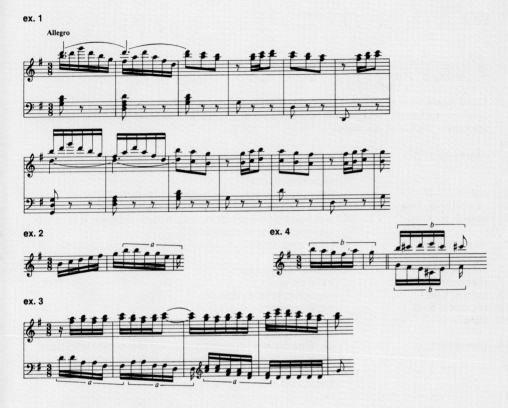

ex. 2

ex. 4

ex. 3

Second movement (Andante), 3/4, e; free form, based on echo principle

Time	
0.00	opening, ex. 5: solo group echoes phrases first heard on full orchestra
0.52	cadence in e; after it, short phrases on solo group answered by orchestra
1.22	cadence in a; faster-moving recorder phrases
1.56	cadence on dominant of b
2.14	cadence in b; solo phrases answered by orchestra
2.45	cadence in e; lower instruments have material based on ex. 5
3.05	passage for soloists, with cadence in e, a recorder flourish, and a close on the dominant of e, leading to third movement
3.45	(end)

ex. 5

ex. 6

Third movement (Presto), 2/2, G; ritornello/fugue (in ritornello form, but fugal: ritornello sections correspond roughly with the sections of a fugue in which the subject is heard, the solos with the fugue episodes)

Time		
0.00	**ritornello 1, G**	subject (ex. 6) in viola, then violin 2 (0.04), violin 1 (0.11), bass (0.15), recorders (0.24), with extra statement in recorders (0.39)
0.45	**solo 1, G–D**	8th-notes in violin while recorders have dialog on ex. 5
1.14	**ritornello 2, D–e**	ex. 6 in bass, later in violin 1, G; cadence in e
1.37	**solo 2, e**	violin passage-work of increasing brilliance; ex. 6 in background on violins 1 and 2
2.22	**ritornello 3, e**	ex. 6 successively in violin 1, recorders, and basses; cadence in b
2.51	**solo 3, e–C**	mainly for recorders
3.17	**ritornello 4, C**	ex. 6 on violin 1
3.22	**solo 4, C–G**	recorders resume episode
3.33	**ritornello 5, G**	ex. 6 on violins
3.38	**solo 5, G**	again solo group resumes, but violins enter to introduce final ritornello
3.54	**ritornello 6, G**	ex. 6 on basses; sustained textures (especially held bass note) and dramatic gestures give an air of finality, and after a rhetorical passage two last appearances of ex. 6 (basses, recorders) round the movement off
4.41		(end)

In Weimar, Bach had become interested in the current styles of Italian instrumental music, though he liked – in accordance with German tradition – textures rather fuller and more contrapuntal than the Italian ones. He also followed German tradition in another way; Vivaldi's published concertos (the only ones Bach had access to) were for strings, but Bach liked to use wind instruments. He obviously enjoyed experimenting with instrumental combinations, for example in the Brandenburg Concertos. The schemes for all the concertos are unusual. The first two are the most colorful, with their wind groups. No. 3 departs in another way, by treating the groups of three (violins, violas, cellos) as soloists, each with different music to play in the solo sections, but having them play the same music, in unison, in the tutti ones; the contrast in texture is thus between emphatic tuttis and gentle, multi-strand music in the solo episodes. No. 6 works on a similar principle, and in the absence of violins its colors are dusky and veiled. No. 5 represents another important departure, with a solo part for the harpsichord: this is one of the very earliest keyboard concertos. No. 4 is almost a violin concerto: the two recorders have solo parts though less prominent and less virtuoso than the violin's. As in Vivaldi's concertos, there are divisions between solo and tutti sections; but the textures are much fuller, and the material is used more economically and more rigorously to provide stronger unity and logic (see **Listening Guide 20**).

Plate 5 The Death of Dido: *painting by Guercino (1591–1666; see p. 128). Galleria Spada, Rome.*

Plate 7 Florentine Court Musicians: *painting by Anton Domenico Gabbiani (1652–1726). Palazzo Pitti, Florence. A cantata with violin and harpsichord.*

Plate 6 Opposite *Consort of viols at the court of Duke August the Younger: detail of the portrait* Duke August and Family, *c1645, by Albert Freyse. Landesmuseum, Brunswick.*

Plate 8 Jupiter and Semele: *painting, 1722–3, by William Kent (see p. 142). Ceiling of the King's Drawing Room, Kensington Palace, London.*

Bach also wrote music in the French style, a set of orchestral suites, with overtures in the jerky rhythms that the French favoured in their theater music, then a fugal movement, and after that a series of dances (minuets, gavottes, bourrées etc.). These are among Bach's most cheerful and tuneful works; one has a solo part for flute, and two gain a touch of ceremonial splendor from the use of three trumpets and a pair of drums.

Bach wrote much keyboard music at this period. There are notebooks of simple pieces for his eldest son and his new wife; there are what he called "inventions" and "sinfonias" (exercises, in composition and performance, in the interchange of material between the hands, to help the player to gain independence of hand action); and two fine books of dance suites, known as the English Suites (which have long, concerto-like preludes as well as dances) and the French Suites. Each suite has the four basic dances (Allemande, Courante, Sarabande, Gigue) with an extra one between the last pair.

Much of his keyboard music was intended for teaching. The most important of his teaching works of the Cöthen years was the series of preludes and fugues for the harpsichord or clavichord, one in each of the 24 keys, major and minor, which he began writing around 1722. He called this *The Well-Tempered Keyboard*: it was partly designed to demonstrate that an instrument could be tuned to play effectively in every key. These 24 preludes and fugues eventually, by 1742, became the first half of the work known by musicians as the "48", for Bach later wrote a second set. The preludes are of various kinds; the fugues (see p. 39) form a rich compendium of fugal techniques (see **Listening Guide 21**).

LIFE AT LEIPZIG

In May 1723 Bach moved to Leipzig. In this thriving commercial city he would be the employee not of a private patron, who could act on whim, but of the civic and church authorities; his sons could attend St Thomas's School and be sure of obtaining a sound education. And the musical duties offered more of a challenge than he had faced in his earlier posts.

Bach had to supply cantatas for performance each Sunday, and decided to build up a new repertory. Starting within weeks of his arrival, he composed in his first year a complete cycle of cantatas (one for each Sunday of the church year: about 60 allowing for feast days as well); in his second year he produced another complete cycle. He embarked on a third, which he took two years to complete. Then followed a fourth, in 1728–9 – though we cannot be certain about this as only a handful of the cantatas composed after 1727 have survived. Probably he wrote a fifth cycle during the 1730s and 1740s.

Bach was, then, astonishingly industrious. Soon after he arrived in Leipzig he applied to the university for the restitution of a traditional right of the holder of his post to direct the music at certain services there; a dispute ensued, and a compromise was reached. This was one of numerous quarrels in which Bach was involved. He was constantly alert for any infringements of his rights or privileges. Later, he was often at odds with the headmaster of St Thomas's School, for example over his neglect of teaching or his absence without permission (he still made many

Bach: *Prelude and Fugue in c*, from 48 Preludes and Fugues, Book I (1721)

In about 1722, Bach began to compose a series of preludes and fugues in all the keys – 24 of them – for the harpsichord or clavichord (the favorite domestic instrument). He called this *The Well-Tempered Keyboard*, for it was partly designed to demonstrate that an instrument could be tuned to play effectively in all the keys, given a good choice of temperament. (Physical factors make it impossible to tune an instrument with all the intervals smooth and sweet; new forms of compromise were being devised in Bach's time to accommodate a wider range of keys. Nowadays we use equal temperament, in which no interval is perfect but each is equally compromised, so that all keys sound the same.)

These 24 preludes and fugues eventually became the first half of the '48', for Bach later wrote a second set. Some of the preludes are brilliant display pieces, others are lyrical, and some are contrapuntal or involve the working-out of some pattern of figuration. The fugues embody the richest array of fugal techniques ever assembled; in them Bach shows that in spite of the disciplines it requires, fugue is not a mechanical process but a live artistic creation. No. 2 in C minor, from Book I of the '48', is an example of direct and logical handling of fugal writing.

The prelude is of the type designed to show the brilliance of the player and the capacities of the instrument; Bach takes a pattern of notes and uses it with changing harmonies. The fugue is in three voices (that is, clearly defined contrapuntal lines), which for convenience we may call soprano, alto, and bass. In this particular fugue, when any voice has the subject, the other two have countersubjects: for example, when the bass enters with the subject, the soprano has the first countersubject and the alto the second (see ex. 3). The chart below shows the assignment of these three lines at each appearance of the subject. In between the entries of the subject are episodes, in which figures from the subject are treated, usually in dialog.

 Listening Outline . . . .

Prelude

Time	
0.00	begins as shown in ex. 1; the same pattern is followed: ex. 2 shows the harmonic scheme of the first few measures
0.55	pattern changes
1.04	a free Presto passage
1.17	a brief Adagio, the climax of the piece, followed by a short Allegro with arpeggio figuration
1.41	(end)

ex. 1   ex. 2

Fugue

Time		
1.44	**exposition, c, g, c**	alto alone, with subject; then soprano has subject (modified, as answer) and alto countersubject 1; then (after an episode, with syncopated figure against fig. *a*), bass has subject and soprano and alto countersubjects 1 and 2: see ex. 3

2.09	**episode, c–E♭**	16ths in bass, dialog in soprano and alto
2.15	**entry 1, E♭**	subject in soprano
2.22	**episode 2, E♭–c**	16ths in soprano, fig. *a* in other voices
2.28	**entry 2, g**	subject in alto
2.34	**episode 2, g–c**	syncopated theme from the short episode within the exposition appears, first in alto, then bass, against figure *a*
2.44	**entry 3, c**	subject in soprano
2.50	**episode 3, c**	16ths in bass, as in episode 1 but extended
3.04	**entry 4, c**	subject in bass
3.14	**coda**	final appearance of subject, in soprano, over a bass pedal (held C)
3.27		(end)

ex. 3

Diagram of subject entries

Time	1.44	1.49	2.03	2.15	2.28	2.44	3.04	3.14
Soprano		S	C_1	S	C_1	S	C_2	S
Alto	S	C_1	C_2	C_2	S	C_1	C_1	–
Bass			S	C_1	C_2	C_2	S	–
Key	c	g	c	E♭	g	c	c	c

S – Subject C_1 – Countersubject 1 C_2 – Countersubject 2

52 *Opening of the Fugue in C minor by J. S. Bach from* The Well-Tempered Keyboard, *book 1, 1772, autograph manuscript. Deutsche Staatsbibliothek, Berlin.*

journeys to report on organs, and paid visits to nearby courts on special occasions).

Bach still found time to pursue other musical activities. Music was his preoccupation at home as well as at work: there were musical evenings (he noted, in 1730, that his family could provide a vocal and instrumental ensemble) and he must have expended time on his sons' musical education. He did much other private teaching, especially in the 1740s; several of the best German organists and composers of the next generation were his pupils.

He wrote more works with an eye to their usefulness for instruction, among them the second set of 24 preludes and fugues in all the keys and four books entitled *Clavier-Übung* ("Keyboard Exercise"), including organ chorale preludes and dance suites and variations for the harpsichord. One especially interesting collection forms the third book: here Bach contrasts the Italian and the French styles, publishing side by side an "Overture in the French Manner" and "Concerto in the Italian Style", to make their differences clear to the student. In all this, his music never merely imitates that of composers from other countries; it always sounds his own, and in its seriousness and careful, detailed working sounds German.

Another important side activity of Bach's was his organization of the local *collegium musicum* (musical society). He took up the directorship in 1729, when his

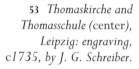

53 Thomaskirche and Thomasschule (center), Leipzig: engraving, c1735, by J. G. Schreiber.

period of intensive cantata composition was finishing. The society gave concerts weekly during its seasons – in a coffee-house in the winter, a coffee-garden in the summer. Bach revived his Cöthen repertory of instrumental music and supplemented it with new harpsichord concertos and other music for small orchestra.

The concerto for harpsichord was a novel idea; never before had the solo role in a concerto been given to a keyboard instrument (remarkably, at just the same time Handel, far away in London, was beginning to compose concertos for organ: see pp. 138–9). Most of Bach's harpsichord concertos are adaptations of works originally written as violin concertos: Bach ingeniously rewrote passages that were designed to be effective on a string instrument to make them sound well on the harpsichord. He also wrote multiple concertos – two for two harpsichords, two for three, and one (arranged from a Vivaldi four-violin concerto) for four. It must have been difficult to get four harpsichords and four harpsichordists together in a coffee-house music room, with an orchestra, but Bach's delight in rich textures and unusual instrumental effects justified it. He also performed other composers' music at these concerts – suites by his cousin Johann Ludwig Bach, for example, and pieces by the many musicians who visited Leipzig. He remained with the *collegium musicum* up to 1741, when the owner of the coffee-house died; it ceased activities soon after.

Among Bach's travels was a journey in 1741, to Dresden (where he held a title as Court Composer). He went to present one of his patrons with a new work, the *Goldberg Variations* (named after the young harpsichordist, probably a pupil of Bach's, whom the patron is said to have employed). This, which Bach later published as the fourth and last book in his *Clavier-Übung*, is his longest and most demanding harpsichord work. It uses traditional variation form but in a new way, similar to a ground bass; the 30 variations in turn dazzle by their virtuosity, move by their depth of expression, and fascinate by their contrapuntal elaboration. The set is like a summation of the musical forms that Bach had used in his harpsichord music – French overture, fugue, invention, dance movements, and so on.

Another journey Bach made in 1741 was to Berlin, probably to his son Carl Philipp Emanuel, now court harpsichordist there. A visit to Berlin six years later proved particularly important. His son's employer, King Frederick the Great of Prussia, admired his learned art and invited him to improvise at the piano a fugue on a theme by Frederick himself (he was a skilled flutist and a composer). Bach did so, and promised to publish the fugue. But when he got home to Leipzig he decided to go further and offer the king a musical collection built around his theme. This he called *Musical Offering*. It includes not only a written-out version of this improvised fugue but also a larger one for six voices (playable on the organ), a series of canons of different kinds, and a trio sonata for flute, violin, and continuo – this sonata, some of it in a distinctly more modern style than the rest, was clearly intended to please the flute-playing king, the more so because he worked the royal theme into it. Here again we see Bach, in his last years, anxious to enshrine his art.

Bach's central work, for the rest of his life, was in the church, and especially in the provision of music for St Thomas's. One of the first works he had performed on his arrival in Leipzig was the *St John Passion*, a musical setting of the Passion story as related by St John. He followed this up a few years later with the *St Matthew Passion*, a longer work (it takes around three hours to perform) and one of his greatest achievements. By Bach's time, a full-length Passion setting involved a narrator (or Evangelist), singers to take the roles of Christ, Pilate, Peter, and the other participants, and a chorus to represent the crowd; the Evangelist would tell the story, in lightly accompanied recitative, and the other characters would play their own parts. The story was frequently interrupted, for hymns (chorales) to be sung by the congregation at appropriate reflective moments, in highly expressive harmonizations, and for arias of meditation on the religious message of the events described. Bach also framed the entire work with large-scale, contemplative choruses.

Bach wrote three Passion settings (St Matthew, St John, and St Mark, the last of which is mostly lost) for Good Friday performances. His basic work for St Thomas's was the production of a weekly cantata, as we have seen. Probably he wrote about 300, for soloists and orchestra. The congregation would normally join in singing the closing chorale. The unity of the text was often supported by a musical one, derived from the chorale melody linked with the text; in the cantatas of 1724–5, particularly, Bach wove the chorale melodies into his music – since these, and the words that belonged with them, were familiar to his congregation, this helped hold their interest and remind them of the religious message. We may look at this process in one of the finest of his cantatas, *Wachet auf*, no. 140 (see **Listening Guide 22**).

In fugue composition, too, Bach left a monument. He wrote, probably in the early 1740s, a work that he called *The Art of Fugue*. It has fugues of all sorts: simple, inverted, double, triple, and quadruple, in the French style, and "mirror-wise" – this last meaning a fugue in which all the music could be played inverted (high notes for low ones, upward-moving phrases for downward, etc), a tremendous *tour de force* of technique for a composer. For this work Bach provided his own theme, not unlike the king's, but more flexible and better adapted to the smooth textures used here. In this rather austere, abstract work it could well be that Bach was setting down models of his fugal art, for a generation that no longer cherished it.

The work we call the B minor Mass may belong to the same category. Bach wrote a "Missa" (the shorter, Lutheran Mass) in 1733, dedicating it to the Dresden court. This consists of a Kyrie and Gloria, the first two movements of the traditional Roman Catholic Mass. It was not until the late 1740s that he enlarged the work into a full Roman Catholic Mass, which he did by composing two new movements and adapting a number of others from cantatas and similar works. The B minor Mass was never performed by Bach, nor indeed intended for performance; it again seems that in putting it together he was satisfying his desire to create a model example of this ancient and traditional form. In this work, as in the other late compositions of the same sort, he used a wide variety of forms and techniques, some of them belonging to earlier eras. Sometimes he worked old plainsong melodies into the texture as was done in medieval and Renaissance music; there are also plain fugal movements without independent orchestra accompaniment, of a kind outdated by the 1740s.

Bach: Cantata no. 140: Wachet auf! ruft uns die Stimme (1731), excerpt

Central to the work of any musician in charge of the music of a large Lutheran church in Germany was the provision of cantatas for worship each Sunday. The words would be supplied by a poet, using the text for the day in the church year as a starting-point; this would normally feature in a chorale (hymn-tune) setting, and the other numbers might be meditations on it, so producing a work that is a religious entity. By using the chorale in several of the items, the composer could reinforce that unity with a musical one. Cantatas were usually about 20 or 25 minutes long, composed for a small choir (Bach liked to have about 12 singers, but often had to manage with fewer), with solo arias or duets for two or three of the choir members, and an orchestra of strings and organ with up to half a dozen wind instruments. The congregation would normally join in the singing of the final chorale; typically, there might be an opening chorus and two arias, each preceded by a short recitative.

Cantata no. 140 was composed in 1731 for the 27th Sunday after Trinity, and first performed in November that year. It is one of Bach's latest surviving cantatas (most were written in the mid- to late 1720s), and is based on the chorale 'Wachet auf! ruft uns die Stimme' (ex. 1). We hear the first and fourth of the seven movements.

 Listening Outline . . . .

First movement, 3/4, E♭

Time		
0.00	**ritornello**	fanfare-like figure on the orchestra, then dialog (violin/oboe) on phrases based on the opening notes of the chorale, ex. 2 (see notes marked *)
0.28	**chorale, first part, 1**	ex. 3: chorale melody in top voice, imitative counterpoint in others; each line of the chorale is treated the same way, while the orchestra continues with fanfare figures and material from ex. 2
1.33	**ritornello**	as first time
2.02	**chorale, first part, 2**	music as before, to continuation of words
3.08	**ritornello**	now modulates to B♭
3.27	**chorale, second part**	the next two lines are identical, to different words; again the melody is in the top voice with counterpoint below; at 'Alleluja' there is a fugal passage begun by the alto (4.00: ex. 4, based on ex. 2), in g, later B♭ and (when top voice completes 'Alleluja'), c (4.37) and for the next line A♭ (4.55); then the last lines (5.01) affirm the home key, E♭
5.35	**repeat of introduction**	
6.06		(end)

Fourth movement, 4/4, E♭: tenor solo, with chorale as *cantus firmus*

0.00	**introduction, E♭**	string melody stated (ex. 5)
0.38	**chorale, first part**	sung by tenor, with string melody continuing (but note the changed sequence of its phrases) and leading to B♭
1.42	**chorale, first part repeated**	as in first movement, same music but different text; but the string melody is slightly shortened, and moves to B♭
2.31	**chorale, second part**	string melody moves to c and then g as tenor sings the second part; full, final statement of string melody, beginning at 'Wir folgén all' (3.09), now adjusted to end in E♭
3.45		(end)

no. 1

0.28	Wachet auf! ruft uns die Stimme der Wächter sehr hoch auf der Zinne: wach auf du Stadt Jerusalem!	Wake up, cries the voice of the watchman very high on the battlements: wake up, city of Jerusalem!
2.02	Mitternacht heisst dieser Stunde; sie rufen uns mit hellem Munde: wo seid ihr klugen Jungfrauen?	Midnight is now the hour; they call to us with clear voices: where are you, wise virgins?
3.27	Wohl' auf! der Bräut'gam kommt, steht auf! die Lampen nehmt Alleluja!	Be up! the bridegroom comes, arise; take your lamps, Alleluia.
5.01	Macht euch bereit zu der Hochzeit, ihr müsset ihm entgegen gehn.	Prepare yourselves for the wedding, you must go forth to meet him.

no. 4

0.38	Zion hört die Wächter singen, das Herz thut ihr vor Freuden springen, sie wachet, und steht eiland auf.	Zion hears the watchmen singing; her heart bounds with joy, she wakes and quickly rises.
1.42	Ihr Freund kommt vom Himmel prächtig, von Gnaden stark, von Wahrheit mächtig, ihr Licht wird hell, ihr Stern geht auf.	Her friend comes splendidly from heaven, in mercy strong, in truth mighty; her light shines bright, her star rises.
2.31	Nun komm, du werthe Kron, Herr Jesu, Gottes Sohn, Hosanna!	Now come, thou valued crown, Lord Jesus, God's son, Hosanna!
3.09	Wir folgen all' zum Freudensaal, und halten mit das Abendmahl.	We all follow to the joyful hall and partake of the evening meal.

ex. 1

ex. 2

ex. 3

ex. 4

ex. 5

Bach was in fact regarded in his day as an old-fashioned composer. He was not "old-fashioned" because he was out of touch with new currents of musical thought; on the contrary, he was familiar with the works of younger men; he simply chose a more conservative path. He was criticized for his methods – for example, writing music too intricate in line and counterpoint to be "natural" (which to the new thinkers of the mid-eighteenth century meant tuneful and lightly accompanied), and asking voices to sing lines as complicated as those he could play on the keyboard. When he died in the summer of 1750, after a year of uncertain health and finally blindness, he could reflect on the music he had created and see in it a comprehensive summary of the musical art of the Baroque period, drawn together with an unparalleled inventiveness and intellectual concentration.

Part V The Classical Era

1 *Music of the Enlightenment*

"Classical" is a misused word. Even when it is used properly, it has several different though related meanings. Its chief misuse, these days, is when "classical music" is opposed to "popular music"; there it is intended to include all kinds of "serious" music, irrespective of when or for what purpose they were composed. Here we use the term mainly to denote the music of the period that runs roughly from 1750 to the death of Beethoven in 1827.

Classicism

Why *classical*? That word, strictly, applies to the ancient Greeks and Romans, to "classical antiquity", the two great Western civilizations of early times. Many eras since then have looked back at "the ancients" and tried to borrow what is best about their cultures. They did so, as we have seen, in the Renaissance, and then again at the beginning of the Baroque period. But it was the mid-eighteenth century that truly began to rediscover classical antiquity, especially through archeology, and to build

Composers of the Classical Era

	1700	1750	1800	1850

Thomas Augustine Arne
Christoph Willibald Gluck
Carl Philipp Emanuel Bach
Johann Stamitz
Niccolò Piccinni
Franz Joseph Haydn
Johann Christian Bach
Carl Ditters von Dittersdorf
André-Ernest-Modeste Grétry
Luigi Boccherini
Domenico Cimarosa
Antonio Salieri
Muzio Clementi
Wolfgang Amadeus Mozart
Luigi Cherubini
Ludwig van Beethoven

up a new picture of its simplicity, its grandeur, its serenity, its strength, its grace, all typified in the newly found and excavated temples of Greece and southern Italy. The remains of Pompeii, for example, were found in 1748: artists drew them; engravers copied them, for wider circulation; theorists worked out the principles along which they were designed.

Historians and estheticians – the most famous was the German J. J. Winckelmann (1717–68) – studied and praised the works of classical antiquity and put them forward as models for their own times. Creative artists quickly followed: Sir Joshua Reynolds (1723–92), for example, stressed that the highest achievement in painting depended on the use of Greek or Roman subjects and their representation of heroic or suffering humanity, a principle also followed notably by Jacques-Louis David (1748–1825), the official artist of the French Revolution, in his heroic paintings. Sculptors too, like Antonio Canova (1757–1822), used classical statues as the basis for their figures of modern men and women. Classical history, mythology, and philosophy came to be increasingly influential, as the opera plots favored at this time show with their settings in ancient times and their identification with the ancient virtues.

Borrowing from the association of merit with the ancient civilizations, people have always regarded the word "classical" as implying a standard of excellence. To say that something is "a classic" suggests, whether it be a poem or an automobile, that it is a superior example of its kind, still praised, admired, and suitable to be considered a model. We also tend to use the word to imply something about design, for example in the expression "classical proportions", which means proportions that possess a natural balance, without extravagance or special originality, but following an accepted principle of rightness. It is the acceptance of such principles of "just proportion" and natural balance that marks out an important distinguishing feature of music of the Classical period. This was a time when virtually all composers pursued the same basic ideas as to how music should be constructed: the idea of balance between keys, to give the listener a clear sense of where the music was going, and between sections, so that the listener was always correctly oriented within a piece and had a good idea of what to expect of it. Composers could be original less by varying the systems of composition or the outlines within which they worked than by the ingenuity and the enterprise they could exercise to charm or surprise the listener.

It may be said that there was no "Classical period" in music, only a "Classical style", the one in which Haydn, Mozart, and Beethoven wrote their masterpieces. In terms of "models of excellence", that is partly true. Yet the styles used by those three men were not created by them alone: others writing at the same time composed in basically the same manner, and all drew on the same traditions. We shall now examine some of the ways in which the Classical style differs from that of the late Baroque, that used by Bach and Handel.

There are a number of intermediate stages between the Baroque and the Classical. As with the term "Baroque" itself, music historians have drawn on other disciplines for words to describe them. One such is "Rococo", a term that art historians have used particularly of French decorative work of the late seventeenth and early eighteenth centuries. In French architecture of that time, the strong, severe lines came to be broken or softened by shell-work (*rocaille* in French), and there developed a newly picturesque, elegant, fanciful style. Like all aspects of French culture and taste, this style traveled rapidly across Europe; it was particularly favored in southern Germany and Austria. It is always dangerous to try to draw close parallels between music and other arts, but there was in music a similar breaking down of larger lines and a growing interest in graceful, detailed elaboration; it also manifested itself, though differently and somewhat later, in Germany, Austria, and Italy (where the gentle melodies of the Neapolitan composers are typical of it). The *Rococo*, though not a central development in music history, represents a symptom of the breakdown of the severe grandeur of the Baroque, a breakdown that was essential if a new style was to replace it.

Another term from France, *galant*, has wider implications in the growth of the Classical style. It means "gallant", at its simplest; but its meaning in the arts was richer than that. It implied, first, the idea of pleasure, of a fairly straightforward, undemanding kind: sensuous pleasure, quite apart from moral uplift or deeper artistic satisfaction. It also implied a certain elegance and worldliness. Musically it carried a range of meanings. First, it meant a flowing melodic style, free of the complexities of counterpoint; for a *galant* melody to be heard to maximum advantage it would normally be lightly accompanied, generally by a continuo instrument (like the harpsichord) with a static or slow-moving bass line that did nothing to draw attention away from the melody.

The ideal medium for *galant* melody was the singing voice, in a cantata or an operatic song (preferably on an amorous text); the composer would construct it in

Rococo, galant

simple, regular phrases, answering one another in an agreeably predictable fashion, and the singer would shade the line expressively. Another popular medium was the flute (as opposed to the more old-fashioned and austere recorder), which was specially esteemed for its capacity for elegant and tender shading. The term *galant* could also imply the use of dance rhythms (the extra dance movements that Bach and others included in their keyboard suites were known as "galanteries"); it often signified the use of a number of stereotyped melodic phrases, akin to graceful bows and curtseys.

The term was applied to music soon after 1700. The style it described began to gain currency in the 1720s but came to be the prevalent one only around the middle of the century, as the generation of Bach and Handel and their contemporaries

54 *St Michael's Square, Vienna, with the Burgtheater* (right foreground) *and Spanish Riding School behind it: engraving, 1783, by C. Schütz.*

disappeared and a new one assumed importance. By then, the driving bass lines of the Baroque masters, which could impart so much vitality to a piece, were giving way to ones that moved more slowly and merely served to support what went on above them. The Baroque preference for fugal texture was superseded by one in which the top line came an easy first, with the bass second and the middle ones nowhere. The long and generally quite irregular phrases of Baroque music were replaced by shorter ones, usually in two- or four-measure patterns, in which the listener could sense the outcome as he or she heard the beginning.

The Enlightenment

What were the reasons for these changes in the language of music? A major one is that the climate of thought was changing, with what is called the Enlightenment. The early part of the eighteenth century saw important changes in philosophy, in the wake of the scientific discoveries of Isaac Newton in England and René Descartes in France: rationalism and humanitarian ideals came to the fore, mysticism and superstition faded. The idea of extending culture to the ordinary man and woman – that is, to the middle classes as well as the nobility to whom it had exclusively belonged in the past – was one of the goals of the Enlightenment: human life should be enriched by the arts.

Thus we find, in the early eighteenth century, forms of opera arising that were given not only in foreign languages and private theaters but in native languages and in public. In France, the genre known as "opéra comique", in which songs were interspersed with spoken dialog in simple stories about common folk, got decisively under way in the mid-1720s at the Paris "fair theaters", appealing to a public far wider than could ever have ventured into the court Opéra. In England, while Italian opera entertained the London aristocratic audiences, a middle-class public

55 *Wind band of the Prince of Oettingen-Wallerstein: silhouette on gold ground, 1791. Schloss Harburg.*

enjoyed, especially from the 1730s, lightweight operas with spoken dialog, composed in a simple and tuneful style; these were performed not just in London but all over the country. In Germany, English operas of this kind, translated and given in Berlin and Hamburg around the middle of the century, provoked the development of the native German form, the *Singspiel*. In Italy, new forms of comic opera appeared in the early part of the century, often in local dialects, in Naples, Venice, and other centers, appealing with their popular subject matter and their catchy melodies to a public that found the behavior of the classical and mythological figures of serious opera incomprehensible and their music boring. And even serious opera, written for the aristocratic courts, began to change – as we shall see.

Opera was only one of the media that showed this spread of culture. It was in these years that music publishing became a substantial industry, enabling ordinary people to buy music and sing or play it at home – on the instruments which, with the development of new manufacturing techniques, they could now afford. It became an important social accomplishment for a young woman, especially, to play the harpsichord or the piano; the flute and the violin, the other favored amateur instruments, remained on the whole male preserves. Numerous home tutors were published for these instruments in the eighteenth century. Composers, writing music for home consumption, were eager to make it easy enough to play yet interesting enough to play with taste and elegance; this was a factor in the shift, discussed above, towards a more regular melodic style. The amateur was also much encouraged to sing the music he or she might have heard at public entertainments: books of "favorite songs" from the newest operas (in London also those sung at the famous outdoor pleasure gardens) were printed and sold while they were fresh in the audience's memories.

It was not only opera that was attracting new listeners. It was in the eighteenth century that concert life began as we know it. In earlier times instrumental music was chiefly intended for performance at court or for groups of gentleman amateurs to play in their homes. Now a new phenomenon arose. Groups of people, often of both amateurs and professionals, got together to give concerts for their own pleasure (or for their living) and for the pleasure of others who came to hear them. In large cities, where more professionals were to be found, orchestral concerts were regularly given. London and Paris led, and others were quick to follow. The concerts of court orchestras were often opened to a paying public. During the late eighteenth century in particular, concert life developed rapidly; traveling virtuosos went from city to city, organizing concerts in each, while local musicians of repute often gave annual "benefit concerts" (from which they retained the takings). The orchestra as an entity began to take firm shape. The concept of a public that came to concerts to listen was a novel one, demanding a novel approach to composition; it was more than ever necessary for a piece of music to have a logical and clearly perceptible shape, so that it would grasp and hold the listener's attention and interest. Composers rose to this challenge: above all, the three great men of the era, Haydn, Mozart, and Beethoven.

₂ *The Genres of Classical Music*

SYMPHONY

The central type of orchestral music, from the middle of the eighteenth century onwards, has been the *symphony*. The word itself means simply "sounding together". In the Baroque period the term was used for an orchestral interlude in a vocal piece, and in the early eighteenth century (as we saw, p. 118) it meant the same as "overture" – an orchestral work designed to be played before an opera, and usually in three movements, fast ones to begin and end with, a slow one in the middle. That is the form of the earliest orchestral pieces used as concert music in the middle of the eighteenth century; later, composers from Germany and Austria, and then from other parts of Europe too, came to add an extra movement – a minuet (in triple meter, based on a popular dance of the time), between the slow movement and the final one.

The Austrian composer Joseph Haydn is often called the father of the symphony. He wrote more than 100 during the second half of the eighteenth century. Many others were also composing such works, but the body of symphonies that he created, especially those written at the end of his life for performance in Paris and London, represents a foundation for the genre. During the same period, Mozart wrote some 50 symphonies (the traditional numbering, which excludes some of his early works, ends at 41). The mature symphonies of these two men take some 25 to 30 minutes in performance.

The next generation is represented by Beethoven, who expanded the form, producing works up to 45 minutes in length; his last symphony, his ninth, calls for a chorus as well as an orchestra and is more than an hour long. In these Classical symphonies, the first movement – which sometimes has a slow introductory section – is normally in sonata form, and is the intellectual core of the work. Usually the slow movement too is in sonata form, though Haydn often favored variations (see p. 182). The minuet, as we have seen, is normally ternary. The finale is usually in sonata or sonata-rondo form; in early examples, it is often a short and lightweight movement, but composers later came to feel the need of something that could better balance the first movement and supplied music of more substance. They also replaced the courtly minuet with the much livelier scherzo.

CONCERTO

Virtually all music of the Classical period has sonata form as its basis. The *concerto*, the main orchestral form of the Baroque, became modified and expanded in the Classical era, with its ritornello structure now accommodating material stated first in a contrasting key (normally the dominant) and recapitulated in the tonic. It did, however, remain a three-movement form. Haydn wrote a few concertos, including some with solo cello and a fine one for trumpet. But the greatest concerto composer of the time was Mozart, who wrote for a variety of instruments, including five for violin, four for horn, and – his supreme achievement in the form – 21 for piano (again the traditional numbering is a muddle: some arrangements he made as a child and two concertos for two or three pianos are included, so that the last, actually the 21st, is called No. 27). Beethoven, like Mozart a concert pianist, wrote five piano concertos, culminating in the grand and majestic "Emperor".

STRING QUARTET

The central chamber music form of the Classical period was the *string quartet*, for two violins, viola, and cello. It developed in Austria, above all in the hands of Joseph Haydn, who occupies the same central position here as he does in the rise of the symphony. He wrote his first string quartets in the 1750s, his last in 1802–3; there are about 70 in all, containing much of his most subtle and refined music. He had great influence on Mozart (24 years his junior), who composed 26 string quartets and indeed dedicated six of the finest of them to Haydn. All these are four-movement works, usually fast–slow–minuet–fast, though sometimes the minuet is placed second and the slow movement third. Sonata form is virtually always used in the first movement, and often in the slow movement and the finale (the latter is often a sonata-rondo). Variation form works well for the string quartet combination and composers often used it, generally for slow movements or finales. It was more rarely used in a first movement, where the intellectual "arguing" nature of sonata form seems to be needed in this genre, which is always regarded as a serious and intimate one designed for a knowledgeable audience.

Beethoven wrote 17 string quartets, much expanding the form – from the 25-minute scale of the Haydn-Mozart era to 40 minutes or more. The searching, profoundly original quartets of his last years mostly abandon the four-movement pattern; one has as many as seven, played without a break.

OTHER CHAMBER MUSIC

Works for string trio (violin, viola, cello) and string quintet (two violins, viola, and cello, with an extra viola or cello) were also composed in some abundance in the Classical period. Beethoven wrote trios as a young man, and Mozart wrote six quintets, two of them among his finest works.

Less central to the repertory are the miscellaneous works written for string and wind instruments together, like the numerous flute quartets (flute, violin, viola, and cello) written in the eighteenth century – Mozart's quintet with clarinet, which blends particularly well with strings, has always been one of his most loved works. For wind instruments alone there is a considerable eighteenth-century repertory of serenade-type music for the band ensembles of the time, for example two each of oboes, clarinets, bassoons, and horns; Mozart, Haydn, and Beethoven wrote for such groups.

PIANO SONATA

The chief keyboard genre of the period was the *piano sonata*. Central figures in its establishment were Bach's sons, Carl Philipp Emanuel, working in Germany, and Johann Christian, in London. Haydn wrote more than 50 piano sonatas, Mozart nearly 20, Beethoven 32. The large majority of these are in the usual three-movement form, fast–slow–fast, the first movement in sonata form, the slow usually in some kind of ternary (it may also be in sonata form, though often a shorter version of it with the development curtailed or omitted), and the finale in rondo or sonata-rondo. Variation form is sometimes used, too, more often for the slow movement or finale than for the first movement.

As we saw (p. 167), the piano became a favorite domestic instrument during the late eighteenth century, and particularly the instrument preferred by women. Men more often played the violin or the flute. A large repertory came into existence, dictated by the manners of the time, in which the piano was accompanied by the violin or flute: the pianist nearly always had the main melody, her accompanist a retiring role (and usually a rather easy one). This so-called "accompanied sonata" flourished from the 1770s to the end of the eighteenth century, as the chief form of domestic music. By then, a more natural balance between instruments had asserted itself, and the sonata for violin and piano arose out of it.

Mozart's sonatas of this type show a steady progression from the accompanied type to the true violin and piano sonata, in which the instruments have an equal partnership, as they do in Beethoven's ten sonatas for these instruments. Similarly, Mozart saw the accompanied sonata with additional cello develop into the true piano trio, as did Haydn, who composed 32 piano trios; Beethoven wrote half-a-dozen. There are a few examples of chamber works for piano and four or five string instruments.

SACRED MUSIC

The church's patronage of music and musicians declined somewhat in the later eighteenth century, as one would expect during the secular Enlightenment period. Since religion occupied a less important place in people's lives, it is not surprising that the sacred music of the time is historically less important than is that of the Renaissance or the Baroque. But the Mass for ceremonial use flourished to some degree in Italy and in the staunchly Catholic Austria; so it is not surprising that the Viennese Classical composers contributed to this repertory. Haydn wrote Masses for his employers, the Esterházy family, notably six substantial works at the end of his life, and Mozart composed several for his employer the Prince-Archbishop of Salzburg. These are all for soloists, chorus, and orchestra, in a symphonic style. Beethoven wrote two, the second of them (known as the *Missa solemnis*) on a huge scale that makes it impossible to use as part of a church service but provides a profoundly moving evening in the concert hall.

OPERA

In this secular age, the most prestigious of all musical forms was Italian *opera*, as we have seen (pp. 166–7). It was performed not only in Italy but also in Vienna, at most of the courts in Germany, and at any of the great European capitals that had a public or a rich patron to support the most fashionable form of entertainment – from

Lisbon in the west to St Petersburg in the north, as well as in such centers as Stockholm and London. Only the French, who had a distinct opera tradition of their own, struggled to hold out against it. Everywhere else, composers from Naples and Venice were frequent visitors, and they often brought singers (especially castratos) along with them.

At first, the operas they performed were usually serious, on mythological or historical subjects, consisting mainly of arias linked by recitatives. The action took place in the recitatives; in the arias, the characters gave expression to their emotions. But fashions began to change soon after the middle of the eighteenth century, as society changed. This began to affect the ways in which composers worked. One of the most admired composers of Italian opera at the time was Christoph Willibald Gluck (German-Bohemian by birth). A leading figure in the "reform" of opera, he was eager to simplify the tortuous plots, to get rid of the exhibitionistic singing of the castratos, to avoid the discontinuity of the breaks between recitatives and arias, and to provide a simpler and more natural, and more

56 Orpheus in the Underworld before Pluto and Persephone: *pen and ink drawing with wash by John Michael Rysbrack (1694–1770). Private collection. The Orpheus legend was a popular subject for opera composers.*

57 *Group portrait,*
c1750, by Jacopo
Amigoni, showing the
great castrato Farinelli
(center) with the
soprano Teresa Castellini
and the librettist
Pietro Metastasio.
National Gallery of
Victoria, Melbourne.
Felton bequest 1949–50.

immediately moving, form of drama. His opera on the story of Orpheus and Eurydice, given in Vienna in 1762 and revised and translated for Paris in 1774, was a landmark, and it greatly influenced operas over the next hundred years.

Reform of this kind was not necessary in comic opera, which already aimed at a greater degree of naturalism. As we have seen, it was given not only in Italian but also in the audience's own language – German in Germany, English in England, etc. In comic opera the rigid division between aria and recitative had never been so marked; there were more ensembles – items for two, three, or more singers – in which the action of the opera is carried forward. One of the most important developments in the later eighteenth century was the growth of the ensemble finale and the merging, to some extent, of the comic and the serious. This is found at its finest in the late comic operas of Mozart, which achieve a Shakespearean balance: some of the characters are serious, some of them comic, and the situations in which they find themselves deal with human issues in which real emotion is involved in a manner that can be both amusing and moving.

One of Haydn's duties, during much of his life, was the musical management of his employer's opera house. This involved composing new operas and conducting old ones. But opera was never the center of Haydn's output as it was Mozart's. Mozart wrote operas of several different kinds, German and Italian, comic and serious. Beethoven composed only a single opera, which embodies some comic elements but is essentially heroic and political.

3 *Haydn*

When Joseph Haydn was born, in 1732, J. S. Bach had just composed his *St Matthew Passion*; Handel's *Messiah* was still ten years off. When he died, in 1809, Beethoven had written his Fifth Symphony. His long life thus covers a vast series of changes in musical style. What is more, he himself was central to those changes and was recognized as such by his contemporaries. It would be wrong to regard Haydn as a revolutionary, certainly as an intentional one; the changes he instituted arose not from a conscious desire for change but from a wish to supply the kinds of music society demanded of him – whether it be the princely family, the Esterházys, who employed him during most of his working life, or the public, in Vienna, London, and elsewhere, who bought his music and went to his concerts. In exercising his skill and his ingenuity to answer these needs, he devised many new ways of putting music together and delighting his hearers.

Haydn was born in a village in Lower Austria; his father, a cartwright, was fond of music. At the age of eight he joined the choir of St Stephen's Cathedral in Vienna. He remained there some nine years, acquiring sufficient musical skills to scrape a modest living when he left by giving lessons, playing the violin or the organ in church or serenade orchestras, and accompanying. It was through accompanying for the Italian composer Nicola Porpora that he learned much about singing and the Italian language, and came into contact with some of the leading figures in Viennese musical life; Porpora also gave him instruction in composition.

His first appointment, around 1759, was as music director to a local nobleman. During these early years he composed a few sacred works, keyboard pieces, and many divertimentos – pieces for various combinations of instruments, usually intended to provide more or less easygoing pleasure for listeners and performers. Probably his earliest string quartets date from this period.

In 1761 Haydn was appointed to the service of the aristocratic Esterházy family. The Esterházys were Hungarians with long traditions of artistic patronage. They owned a castle in Eisenstadt, not far from Vienna, and in the 1760s built a new palace on the Neusiedler lake (just within present-day Hungary), called Eszterháza, in which there was an opera house. In 1766 Haydn assumed full charge of the prince's musical establishment, with some 15 musicians. He had to compose exclusively for his employer and to take charge of the music library and the instruments.

Haydn's post was a demanding one. He was expected to compose in a wide range of media, and in large quantity. His music in the late 1760s and early 1770s includes symphonies, divertimentos, chamber music, pieces for the baryton (the viol-like instrument which Prince Nikolaus Esterházy himself played), operas, and church music. He later said of his music of this time: "I was away from the world, there was

LIFE

Early years

58 Joseph Haydn: *portrait, 1791, by John Hoppner. Royal Collection, London.*

Franz Joseph Haydn | Life and Works

1732	born in Rohrau, Lower Austria, 31 March
1740–49	choirboy at St Stephen's Cathedral, Vienna
1750–55	freelance teacher and musician in Vienna
1755–9	study with Nicola Porpora; period of great musical development and contact with prominent musicians and patrons
1759	*Kapellmeister* to Count Morzin; instrumental and keyboard works
1760	married Maria Keller
1761	appointed to the service of Prince Paul Anton Esterházy at Eisenstadt
1766	*Kapellmeister* of Prince Nikolaus Esterházy's musical establishment at the new palace at Eszterháza; beginning of prolific output of church music, opera, symphonies, baryton music, string quartets, piano sonatas
1768–72	'Sturm und Drang' ('Storm and Stress') period of expressive, passionate minor-key instrumental works
1775–85	concentration on operas
1781	commissions from publishers; String Quartets op. 33 composed 'in a new and original manner'
1785	Paris symphonies; beginning of friendship with Mozart
1791	returned to Vienna after Prince Nikolaus Esterházy's death
1791–2	first visit to London, with the concert manager J. P. Salomon; Symphonies nos. 93–8 performed
1792	took Beethoven as pupil in Vienna; String Quartets opp. 71 and 74
1794–5	second visit to London; Symphonies nos. 99–104 performed
1795	*Kapellmeister* to the younger Prince Nikolaus Esterházy, composing a Mass each year for Eisenstadt
1798	*The Creation*
1801	*The Seasons*
1803	last public appearance
1809	died in Vienna, 31 May

Symphonies   no. 6, 'Le matin', D (?1761); no. 7, 'Le midi', C (1761); no. 8, 'Le soir', G (?1761); no. 22, 'The Philosopher', E♭ (1764); no. 45, 'Farewell', f♯ (1772); no. 49, 'La passione', f (1786); no. 73, 'La chasse', D (?1781); nos. 82–7, Paris Symphonies; no. 92, 'Oxford', G (1789); nos. 93–104, London Symphonies: no. 94, 'Surprise', G (1791), no. 100, 'Military', G (1794), no. 101, 'Clock', D (1794), no. 103, 'Drum Roll', E♭ (1795), no. 104, 'London', D (1795)

Other orchestral music   violin and cello concertos; divertimentos, dances, marches

Chamber music   *c*70 string quartets – op. 20 nos. 1–6 (1772); op. 33 nos. 1–6 (1781); op. 50 nos. 1–6 (1787); op. 54 nos. 1–3 (1788); op. 55 nos. 1–3 (1788); op. 64 nos. 1–6 (1790); op. 71 nos. 1–3 (1793); op. 74 nos. 1–3 (1793); op. 76 nos. 1–6 (1797); op. 77 nos. 1–2 (1799); op. 103 (1803, unfinished); 32 piano trios; string trios, baryton trios

Operas   (*c*11) Il mondo della luna (1777), L'isola disabitata (1799), La fedeltà premiata (1780)

Oratorios   The Seven Last Words (1796), The Creation (1798), The Seasons (1801)

Choral music   14 Masses; sacred and secular works

Keyboard music   52 sonatas; variations

Vocal music   solo cantatas, canzonettas, arrangements of British folksongs

no one nearby to confuse or disturb me, and I was forced to become original".

Haydn reserved his most striking and original ideas for his chamber works, especially his string quartets, and his symphonies. The string quartet was regarded as the form for the connoisseur; it was designed for the groups of music-lovers who gathered regularly to savor this repertory. Haydn's quartets were not written exclusively for Prince Esterházy but (with the prince's permission) for printing and publication in Vienna, where they could, and did, enlarge his reputation.

International figure

Haydn's reputation steadily widened. His music had been carried by the activities of international music publishers – who in the days before copyright laws could "pirate" and print any foreign publication they thought they could sell, without payment to its composer. From Spain came a request for a church work, for Passion week; from Italy, the King of Naples commissioned concertos for a kind of hurdy-gurdy, like a street organ; from Paris, one of the greatest musical centers, came an invitation to compose six symphonies – to which Haydn responded with nos. 82–7.

But the most important contact was with London. He had earlier declined an invitation to the English capital, but had sold music to publishers there. This time a leading violinist and concert promoter from the city, J. P. Salomon, on hearing of Nikolaus Esterházy's death in 1790 and realizing that Haydn would be free, went to Vienna and took him back.

This was a great adventure for Haydn, now approaching 60. London was a famous center for commerce, industry, and the arts, and was the largest city in the world,

59 Garden front of the Esterházy palace, where Haydn was employed. On the left is the Opera House, where many of his works were first performed.

offering rewards like no other. He was well treated during his two long visits: received at court, rapturously applauded at his concerts, richly entertained, greeted with warmth by his fellow-musicians, honored with an Oxford doctorate of music, taken to choral performances on a scale he had never imagined. And he fell in love with Rebecca Schroeter, the widow of a musician (his wife, a shrewish woman with whom he had never been happy, had stayed in Austria).

Haydn returned to Vienna a contented man – and a rich one. For his London concerts he had composed 12 symphonies, his greatest achievement in orchestral music. After a career as a provincial *Kapellmeister*, he had become an international celebrity, applauded by connoisseurs and fêted by royalty. He was a simple enough man to take enormous pleasure in his new status as the greatest living composer, at a time when social change had not only raised the standing of the creative artist but also ensured that he could reap the proper financial rewards. The London visits also profoundly influenced the music he was still to write.

The final years

Between his two journeys to London, Haydn spent a year and a half in Vienna (1792–3). His new reputation had as yet made little impact on the Viennese, and he spent much of his time preparing new works for the second visit. Among them are six string quartets; Salomon's concert programs were not purely orchestral, as orchestral concerts are today, but also included songs, concertos, sometimes keyboard music, and usually chamber works. String quartets, formerly exclusive to the connoisseur's salon, were now given in the concert room. This affected Haydn's style. Most of his earlier quartets begin quietly, with the statement of a theme; but the quartets of this group and most of his later ones start with a loud, arresting gesture – essential to quieten the hubbub of a talkative audience.

The last years of Haydn's creative life, however, were spent primarily on vocal music rather than instrumental. Hearing large choirs in London singing the music of Handel had filled him with awe, and had inspired him, as a deeply religious man, with a desire to write sacred music. The opportunities came. The new Esterházy prince, Nikolaus the younger, asked Haydn to resume charge of his musical establishment, but with lighter responsibilities. Haydn agreed. His chief duty was to write a new Mass to celebrate the princess's name-day: he wrote six such works in the seven years 1796–1802. He carried the Austrian Mass tradition to a noble climax by integrating its conservative manner with a symphonic concentration and unity. Most of the movements have the clear, strong structure that Haydn, with his experience of composing symphonies, had at his command.

Haydn also wrote two extended choral works more directly related to his experience in England. These were oratorios, composed not for church perform- ance or private patrons but for large-scale concert performance before a wide public. Haydn had composed oratorios before, but these were quite different, emphasizing the chorus rather than the soloists and thus turning the work towards the character of a collective religious celebration. One was *The Creation* (1798), based on *Genesis*, the first book of the Bible; the other was *The Seasons* (1801), in which the bounties of Nature as provided by God are praised.

If there is a single work that summarizes Haydn the man and Haydn the composer, it is *The Creation*. Musically, it embraces his mature symphonic style, but it draws too on Viennese traditions and on English, Handelian ones. And the music wonderfully reflects Haydn's grandeur and simplicity of spirit. *The Creation* treats of many topics close to Haydn's heart. Appropriately, it was the last work he heard, at a concert in March 1808. Little more than a year later, Napoleon's armies were bombarding Vienna, and indeed Napoleon had posted a guard of honor outside Haydn's house by the time the aged composer died, on 31 May 1809. After his death he was rightly honored as the principal creator of the Classical style.

As we have seen, one of the forms that Haydn took particularly seriously was the string quartet. He wrote his earliest sets about 1760. Then he wrote three sets each of six works, the standard publisher's package and a convenient quantity of music for an evening's music-making in the early 1770s. These established the four-movement pattern, with quick outer movements, and a slow movement and a minuet in between. They also show a remarkable series of changes in Haydn's musical thinking. The first set radiates the confidence of a composer full of strong, new ideas about how to make a piece interesting – there are ingenious accompaniments, sudden changes of pace in the melodic first violin part, spacious first movements, much fire, many strokes of wit. In the next set this vitality is disciplined; each work is more purposefully organized and holds better together.

The process is carried further in the third set (numbered op. 20 by his publisher); the ideas are more fully worked, the moods are more strongly defined and sustained, the scale of imagination is larger, and each quartet has a marked character. Several of the last movements are fugues. Haydn revived this Baroque form to provide a new

60 *Fanfare to the performance of Haydn's* The Creation *given in the Old University, Vienna, on 27 March 1808 to mark his 76th birthday (he is seated center foreground). Historisches Museum der Stadt Wien.*

String quartets

Haydn: *String Quartet in D*, op. 76 no. 5 (1797), excerpt

Haydn's String Quartet in D comes from the last complete set of six quartets (the traditional number for a set) that he composed. They were commissioned in 1796 by a Hungarian patron, Count Joseph Erdődy, and composed within the next few months.

All Haydn's string quartets after the very early ones follow the same four-movement pattern: a first movement (almost always in sonata form), then a slow movement (sometimes sonata form, sometimes ternary or variation), a minuet and trio, and a finale (often a rondo, but here too variations or sonata form sometimes appear). Occasionally the minuet is the second movement, preceding the slow one. Haydn never followed routines; in treating his themes and motifs in the ways he wanted to, he often departed from the conventional patterns that the lesser men of his time followed simply out of habit. He was more original and more inventive, and this often led him into startling departures – for example, using remote keys for slow movements or trio sections of his minuets, or springing surprises in his sonata-form movements by deceiving the listener with what seems like a recapitulation that in the event turns out to be just another phase of development.

The minuets of Haydn's string quartets, although they all follow the same scheme, vary greatly in character and treatment. The opening section (or 'strain', as it is sometimes called) is usually eight measures long, giving out the main idea of the movement; it is then repeated. Then, typically, Haydn takes up an idea from it and develops it in some way – here it is the three-note figure (*a* in ex. 1) that ends each phrase, and particularly the final phrase, that is used. This is two beats in a three-beat meter, and Haydn's repetition of it cuts across the triple rhythm. The opening music returns, with a new extension. The trio, in D minor, is begun by the cello, its theme taken up and counterpointed with itself by the upper instruments.

The finale is a very brilliant and witty movement in sonata form, based on a single theme that is used in several different ways – first as a simple four-measure statement (ex. 3a), then turned upside-down and extended (ex. 3b), and next, still upside-down, to produce a new, more orderly theme for two instruments (ex. 3c) which brings the exposition to an end.

 Listening Outline . . . .

Third movement (Menuetto: Allegro), 3/4, D; minuet and trio

Time	main section	
0.00	first part, D–A	made up of phrases of 4, 2, and 2 mm., ending in A (ex. 1) (repeated)
0.16 [0.41]	second part, A–D	fig. *a* (ex. 1) is echoed and developed; ex. 1 returns (0.25 [0.50]) and is extended with further treatment of fig. *a* to end in D
	trio	
1.08	first part, d–a	12-m. theme on cello, based on scale patterns (ex. 2), ending in a (repeated)
1.33 [1.56]	second part, a–d	first violin takes up ex. 2, with viola and then second violin; then cello returns, remaining in d, and upper strings add coda (repeated)
	repeat of main section	
2.18		first part
2.26		second part
2.52		(end)

ex. 1

ex. 2

Fourth movement (Presto), 2/4, D; sonata form

0.00	**exposition**	
	first group, D	a phrase built on a two-note figure (*b*) precedes the main theme (*c*) (ex. 3a), which is heard on first violin, then cello; after reiteration of fig. *b*, ex. 3a is heard in A; more development of fig. *b* leads to a cadence on the dominant of A
0.31	second group, A	after a passage based on repeated tones, ex. 3b is played, at first in b, then in A, leading to a unison passage in the rhythm of ex. 3; then violins play ex. 3c (note the cello entry, based on ex. 3b); this is repeated with a different division of the material between instruments, and with virtuoso first-violin writing
1.23	**development**	music shifts to B♭ (1.29), then, with development of ex. 3, to c (1.40) and d (1.44); repeated-note passages return as the music changes key swiftly, and then in dialog before further development of ex. 3
	recapitulation	
2.14	first group, D	the opening material returns, but with the second violin in busy, rushing sixteenths below; the recapitulation is condensed, with no formal appearance of ex. 3a
2.34	second group, D	ex. 3b (2.34), ex. 3c (2.48); opening two-note figure (*b*) appears at the end
3.26		(end)

ex. 3a

ex. 3b

ex. 3c

Haydn: Symphony no. 104 in D (1795), first movement

This is the last of the 12 symphonies that Haydn wrote for performance during his two visits to London. It was given in April 1795 at a series called the 'Opera Concerts', with great success; he never had occasion to write another symphony and this is the last of the long and distinguished series which had begun almost half a century before – and in which Haydn had set the pattern for what was to be the central form of orchestral music for over two hundred years.

The symphony is in the four movements usual at the time. Increasingly over the preceding ten or 15 years, composers had been writing slow introductions to their symphonies, recognizing the new seriousness that music was assuming at this period. Haydn was also making his music more concentrated in style than it had previously been, partly with his economical use of themes and his way of thoroughly developing them. This applies especially to the first movement, always the most intellectual part of a symphony. Here, Haydn uses a typical theme; it sounds direct enough but is full of the kind of easily recognized tone-patterns that provide ideal material for development. The first eight measures of the second group, typically again, are the same as those of the first: by minimizing contrast in this way, Haydn could create a tight, unified structure.

After this, the slow movement is more lyrical in style, though typically it uses one of Haydn's favorite devices, variation, when its opening section is repeated. The main rhythmic figure uses the jerky rhythm characteristic of the French overture. The traditional minuet comes third, with a contrasting 'trio' section. The finale is again in sonata form but in a more direct and even boisterous style and making use of a folk theme that Haydn may have known as a child.

 Listening Outline

First movement (Adagio: Allegretto), 4/4, D; sonata form
2 flutes, 2 oboes, 2 clarinets, 2 bassoons
2 horns, 2 trumpets; timpani
1st and 2nd violins, violas, cellos, double basses

Time		
0.00	**slow introduction,** d	a fanfare-like figure, using dotted rhythms; full orchestra alternates with strings
1.55	**exposition**	
[3.35]	first group, D	consists of two phrases, each 8 mm. (ex. 1), heard on the violins; an energetic tutti follows (2.09 [3.50], using fig. *a* from ex. 1) and leads to the dominant key, A
2.40	second group, A	the second group begins like the first but then moves off in
[4.21]		a different direction; after a busy tutti comes a quieter section with a theme of its own (ex. 2, related to *a*; 3.12 [4.53]), and a short tutti ends the exposition
3.35	**exposition repeated**	3.35–5.16 = (1.55–3.35)
5.16	**development**	main material is figure *b* from ex. 1, first for strings, then with flutes and oboes, then in a tutti where *z* from ex. 2 reappears (5.28); the music ranges through various keys, among which e is persistent
	recapitulation	
6.21	first group, D	ex. 1, D: the music follows the exposition up to halfway through the first tutti, but now it remains in the home key, D (note the emphatic tutti based on *b*)
7.11	second group, D	now treated more briefly, with dialog in orchestra
7.29		ex. 2, changed in orchestration; final tutti reaffirms home key, D
7.57		(end)

ex. 1

ex. 2

kind of finale, exploiting the string quartet as four equal voices and offering a way of writing a fairly weighty movement in a different style.

His next set of string quartets, op. 33 (1781), Haydn said were composed "in a new and special manner". This may concern the dialog-like style of the instrumental writing, but more likely the works' lighter, more polished character. These and the next set, op. 50 (1787), became increasingly concentrated in style, with fewer actual themes but more of musical argument, or development. With the later sets his writing for quartet became increasingly free and adventurous.

The opp. 71 and 74 group, composed between Haydn's last two visits to London, include virtuoso writing for Salomon's violin as well as richer, more orchestral textures. This more "public" quartet style remained with him in the op. 76 set (see **Listening Guide 23**). A new self-confidence can be seen in their sheer variety: some are serious and tightly argued, some lyrical, some playful.

Symphonies   A large proportion – some 95% – of works from the third quarter of the eighteenth century were in major keys; the minor was used exceptionally, generally for music of a passionate, angry, or sometimes sad character. Haydn composed many symphonies, probably 30 or 40, for the entertainment of the Esterházy family during the 1760s; only one or two are in minor keys. But of those of the early 1770s, almost half are minor. Much German art – literature, drama, painting – was affected during the 1760s and 1770s by what is called the "Storm and Stress" movement, and the Haydn symphonies numbered from 39 to 52 show him departing from elegant, tasteful entertainment music, written to charm his patrons, in favor of music that embodied urgency and strong feeling. The slow movements are slower and more intense, the rhythms less regular, the lines less smooth, and there are sudden changes of pace.

From the mid-1770s Haydn seems to have drawn away from this style. Perhaps his employer found it uncongenial; perhaps it was a passing phase. In any case, it was opera that chiefly occupied him in the ten years from 1775 – not only composing but also arranging, planning the repertory, and directing the performances. He wrote several comic operas, but also serious ones. For all the beauty of their music, stage performances show that they lack some essential ingredient as regards dramatic vitality and feeling for character. The symphonies of this period are traditional, expansive, cheerful works, less personal than his earlier ones.

In the mid-1780s Haydn composed a set of symphonies (nos. 82–7) for a musical organization in Paris, spirited works in the vigorous and brilliant manner favored in the French capital. But his finest work came at the very end, in those he wrote for his London concerts (nos. 92–104). They include works that have since earned themselves nicknames – the "Surprise", with its loud chord to arouse anyone who might doze; the "Clock", with its ticking figure in the slow movement; the "Drum Roll", called after its unusual opening; and the "Miracle", so called because miraculously no one was hurt when at its première a chandelier fell on the audience seats, as all the audience had rushed forward to applaud. The last of the symphonies, No. 104 in D, is, for no special reason, known as the "London"; it has features that show the directions in which Haydn's music had moved (see **Listening Guide 24**). One of its most striking features is the tight, unified structure of its sonata-form movements. Such tautness of design enabled composers – Haydn himself, but especially the next generation and most of all Beethoven – to write more extended works which nevertheless retained their structural wholeness.

Another design Haydn particularly liked was variation form, because it lent itself to the kinds of continuous development process that appealed to him. Many of his slow movements are in some sort of variation pattern, often double, with two ideas alternately varied: *A–B–A′–B′–A″* is a scheme he favored. The London Symphony Andante is similar, *A–B–A′*, but made the more concentrated by the *B* section itself being something between a variation and a development of *A*. The finale is another elaborately worked structure, for all its carefree air and its themes hinting at folk music (complete with a bagpipe-like drone bass).

4 *Mozart*

Haydn's greatest contemporary, and the other master of the mature Classical style, was Wolfgang Amadeus Mozart, born at Salzburg in 1756. Both were Austrians; yet their careers were quite dissimilar, and their music is remarkably different in character. Born 24 years after Haydn, and dying 18 years before him, Mozart composed a lesser quantity of music, but he excelled in every sphere – opera, sacred music, the concerto, the symphony, chamber music.

Wolfgang's father, Leopold Mozart, was a composer and violinist, and author of an important book about violin playing. By the time Wolfgang was four he could play the harpsichord; when he was five he was composing. Before his sixth birthday his father took him from their home city of Salzburg to play at the Elector of Bavaria's court in Munich. Soon Leopold devoted himself exclusively to fostering "the miracle that God let be born in Salzburg". The next years were spent traveling Europe to exhibit the boy's genius. Leopold saw it as his ordained task to show his child to the world, and was not averse to any financial rewards for doing so. Mozart was put to various tests, like playing the harpsichord with a cloth covering his hands or improvising on themes supplied to him. In 1770 he went on the first of three journeys to Italy, the home of opera; he heard operas by leading composers, took lessons from the most famous teacher of the day, played at concerts, and wrote operas for production at Milan, the first when he was only 14.

When Mozart came back to Salzburg from his last Italian journey, early in 1773, he was 17. His compositions were already voluminous. There was sacred music, and also dramatic works, among them two full-scale operas for Italy and shorter ones composed in Salzburg. There were more than 30 symphonies, mostly about ten minutes long, and about a dozen lighter orchestral works (serenades or divertimentos, intended as background music for festivities). Mozart's father had given him composition lessons, but the quick, impressionable boy had learned mainly by listening to other composers' music and imitating the things he liked. Later in 1773, Mozart spent ten weeks in Vienna; there he came into contact with Haydn's latest music, and the string quartets and symphonies of the following months show him adopting some of Haydn's techniques.

61 Wolfgang Amadeus Mozart: *silverpoint drawing, 1789, by Doris Stock. Private collection.*

By this time, Leopold Mozart was seeking a post for his son. He himself was an employee of the Prince-Archbishop of Salzburg, who ruled the region and employed a "chapel" of instrumentalists and singers to supply music, for worship in the cathedral and entertainment at his palace. Wolfgang, when he was only 13, had been taken on as concertmaster, at first unpaid. But provincial Salzburg, Leopold felt, was no place for his son. He could earn a decent living in a court post, but there were

Wolfgang Amadeus Mozart   Life and Works

1756	born in Salzburg, 27 January
1761	first public appearance; taken by his father, Leopold, to Munich; beginning of career as child prodigy touring European musical centers (Paris 1763, 1765; London 1764–5) playing the harpsichord
1770–73	three journeys to Italy; *Lucio Silla* (Milan 1772)
1773	Vienna; contact with Haydn's music; composed first works that hold a place in the repertory, instrumental music and sacred works for Prince-Archbishop of Salzburg
1775–7	concertmaster in Salzburg; first piano sonatas and concertos
1777–8	visits to Munich, Mannheim, Paris, seeking a post; Symphony no. 31 for Concert Spirituel, Paris
1779	court organist in Salzburg; cosmopolitan orchestral works
1781	*Idomeneo* (Munich); resigned from Salzburg court service; beginning of career in Vienna, playing, teaching, and composing for piano
1782	*The Abduction from the Harem* (Vienna); married Constanze Weber
1783	concentration on vocal, contrapuntal, and wind music; six string quartets dedicated to Haydn
1784–6	highpoint of acclaim in Vienna; 12 mature piano concertos; became a freemason
1786	*The Marriage of Figaro* (Vienna)
1787	Leopold Mozart died; *Don Giovanni* (Prague)
1788	court chamber musician in Vienna; Symphonies nos. 39, 40, and 41 ('Jupiter')
1790	*Così fan tutte* (Vienna)
1791	*The Magic Flute* (Vienna), *La clemenza di Tito* (Prague); died in Vienna, 5 December

Operas Idomeneo (1781), Die Entführung aus dem Serail (The Abduction from the Harem, 1782), Le nozze di Figaro (The Marriage of Figaro, 1786), Don Giovanni (1787), Così fan tutte (1790), Die Zauberflöte (The Magic Flute, 1791), La clemenza di Tito (1791)

Symphonies no. 31, 'Paris', D (1778); no. 35, 'Haffner', D (1782); no. 36, 'Linz', C (1783); no. 38, 'Prague', D (1786); no. 39, E♭ (1788); no. 40, g (1788); no. 41, 'Jupiter', C (1788)

Concertos piano concertos – no. 9, E♭, K271 (1777); no. 14, E♭, K449 (1784); no. 15, B♭, K450 (1784); no. 17, G, K453 (1784); no. 18, B♭, K456 (1784); no. 19, F, K459 (1784); no. 20, d, K466 (1785); no. 21, C, K467 (1785); no. 22, E♭, K482 (1785); no. 23, A, K488 (1786); no. 24, c, K491 (1786); no. 25, C, K503 (1786); no. 26, 'Coronation', D, K537 (1788); no. 27, B♭, K595 (1791); 5 violin concertos; Sinfonia concertante for violin and viola, K364 (1779); concertos for bassoon, clarinet, flute, flute and harp, oboe, horn

Other orchestral music serenades – Serenata notturna, K239 (1776), 'Haffner', K250 (1776); Eine kleine Nachtmusik, K525 (1787); divertimentos, cassations, dances

Sacred music 18 Masses – 'Coronation' (1779), c (1783, unfinished); Requiem (1791, unfinished); Exsultate jubilate (1773); oratorios, short sacred works

Chamber music 23 string quartets – 'Haydn Quartets' (1783–5) – G, K387, d, K421; 'Dissonance', C, K465; 'Prussian Quartets' (1789–90); 6 string quintets – C, K515 (1787), g, K516 (1787); clarinet quintet, 4 flute quartets, 2 piano quartets, piano trios, string trios, piano and violin sonatas, piano and wind quintet

Piano music 17 sonatas; rondos, variations, fantasias, works for piano duet and 2 pianos

Vocal music concert arias for voice and orchestra; songs for voice and piano

Plate 9 *A scene in an 18th-century opera house; it may well represent a performance at Eszterháza, with Haydn conducting from the piano, (bottom left). Theatre Museum, Munich.*

Plate 10 Opposite *The bassoonist Felix Reiner, a court musician, and instruments: detail of a painting, 1774, by Peter Jakob Horemans. Bayerische Staatsgemaldesammlungen, Munich.*

Plate 11 *Anonymous painting of the mid-1780s, showing an initiation ceremony at a masonic lodge. Mozart was a keen Freemason (it has been suggested that he is depicted, on the extreme right, in this picture), and he introduced Haydn to Freemasonry; Prince Nikolaus I Esterházy was Master of Ceremonies at the local lodge.*

Plate 12 *Musicians
playing the cello and
square piano: detail of the
painting* George, Third
Earl of Cowper and the
Gore Family *by Johann
Zoffany (1733–1810).
Yale Center for
British Art.*

slender opportunities to prosper through writing operas or playing before noble patrons. Moreover, with the recent death of the old archbishop and the appointment of a less easygoing successor, Leopold recognized that leave to compose or perform elsewhere was likely to be restricted.

However, none of Leopold's approaches bore fruit. Wolfgang was too young for a senior post, too accomplished for a junior one, and likely to disturb the smooth running of a musical establishment because of his superior abilities and his likely need for long periods of leave. So he had to remain at Salzburg and to produce the kinds of music required – church music and lighter orchestral music. There were also concertos, among them several for violin (Mozart may have played some of these himself: he was a capable violinist as well as a superb pianist) and four for piano, of which the last, in E♭, was written for a visiting virtuoso and hints at the great things he was later to do in this genre.

In 1777 the Mozarts' patience with Salzburg ran out. Leopold sent his son to Munich, where he was refused a post; to Mannheim, where he was told there was no vacancy; and to Paris, where he met tragedy as well as failure, when his mother, who had traveled with him, died. Mozart disliked the French, and his music made no strong impression. It is fascinating to see, in the symphony he wrote for the leading Paris concert organization, how he adapted his style to the local taste. The orchestra, probably the finest in Europe, prided itself on its violins' vigorous and precise attack. Mozart, knowing his symphony would make a good effect if he exploited that, began it with a brilliant, dashing scale. Throughout, he used a showy orchestral style of a kind he had not attempted before.

While Mozart was in Paris his father, seeing the hopelessness of his quest for a better job, arranged for him to return to Salzburg with a more senior concertmaster's position. This he accepted, but with little pleasure; he disliked Salzburg's provincialism, felt he was undervalued there, and was frustrated by the limited opportunities. So for most of 1779–80 he was back in his native city writing church music as well as orchestral works that reflected what he had learned in Mannheim and Paris. In 1780 he was invited to Munich to compose an opera for the court theater. The archbishop let him go and he enjoyed a great success with one of his noblest works, *Idomeneo*, a serious opera on a theme from Greek mythology. He was still in Munich when an instruction arrived from Salzburg: the archbishop was about to visit Vienna, and Mozart should go there to attend on him. This was a turning-point. After consorting with noblemen in Munich and playing in Vienna before the emperor, he found himself placed among the valets and cooks at the archbishop's table. Moreover, the archbishop refused him permission to play elsewhere. Angry and insulted, Mozart complained and asked for his discharge; at first it was refused, but eventually he was released, as he wrote, "with a kick on my arse . . . by order of our worthy Prince-Archbishop".

Mozart: Piano Concerto in G K453 (1784), first movement

Of the six piano concertos Mozart composed in 1784, three were written for him to play himself at his concerts (of two of them, he said, in a letter to his father, 'these are concertos to make you sweat', and they are technically among his most difficult). One of the other three was composed for a visiting pianist of renown, and two were for his own very gifted pupil Barbara Ployer. The work in G K453 was for Ployer, though Mozart undoubtedly played it too – the time at which he wrote it, in April 1784, coincides with his busiest-ever spell as a concert pianist.

The first movement is a good example of Mozart's concerto form. His actual organization of themes varied from one concerto to another, according to the character of the material. But almost all follow the scheme described below with a secondary theme in the opening ritornello and a further secondary theme exclusive to the soloist. Sometimes this form is described as having a 'double exposition'. Mozart's second movements vary greatly in form: some (such as this same concerto) show a sonata-ritornello pattern, while others are akin to rondo and some are in variation form. The finales almost all use some variety of sonata-rondo but this concerto, like a handful of others, has a variation finale.

 ## Listening Outline · · · · · · · · · · · · · · · · · · ·

First movement (Allegro), 4/4, G; sonata-ritornello form
solo piano
flute, 2 oboes, 2 bassoons, 2 horns
1st and 2nd violins, violas, cellos, double basses

Time			
0.00	**opening ritornello**	first theme, G	strings with answering woodwinds, ex. 1
0.26		tutti, G	ex. 2
0.59		second theme, G	strings, repeated by woodwinds, ex. 3; followed by a short tutti with modulation to E♭ (1.24), then closing theme and short tutti, ex. 4 (1.59)
2.08	**solo exposition**, G–D	first theme, G	piano version of ex. 1; followed by a brief tutti (ex. 2, 2.43) and bravura
3.10		third theme, D	ex. 5, leading to woodwind dialog and piano bravura
4.00		second theme, D	ex. 3, now in D and presented by soloist and then woodwinds; then further bravura
4.55	**central section**, D etc	tutti, D	exx. 2 and 4
5.14		free passage	there is rarely 'development' at this point in a Mozart concerto; here the piano has arpeggio writing against woodwinds, then material on fig. *a* from ex. 5: main keys B♭, a, e (5.51), c (6.05), g
6.33	**recapitulation**	first theme, G	now piano takes over from orchestra
6.59		tutti, G	as in opening ritornello
7.30		third theme, G	soloist's theme, as before
8.20		second theme, G	as in exposition
9.08		tutti, E♭	earlier modulation to E♭ echoed here, leading to . . .
9.25		cadenza	opportunity for soloist, alone, to show his/her skill in improvised music, mixing themes and bravura [Mozart in fact wrote out two sets of cadenzas for this concerto]
10.40		final tutti, G	uses earlier closing theme, from opening ritornello, and ex. 4, ending as opening ritornello did but with extra emphasis
11.20		(end)	

ex. 1

ex. 2

ex. 3
(echoes, 2nd time only)

ex. 4
etc.

ex. 5 (piano)
a
etc.

During these weeks in Vienna, Mozart had investigated the possibility of earning a living there, by teaching, playing, and composing and perhaps later with a court appointment. Vienna, Mozart once wrote, was "the land of the piano", and he quickly set about establishing himself as a pianist. He wrote and published piano sonatas, following these with three concertos. He took on several pupils and so was assured of a regular income. In 1782 he had a new German opera, *Die Entführung aus dem Serail* ("The Abduction from the Harem"), performed. During that year he was married, to Constanze Weber, with whose elder sister, a singer, he had fallen in love five years before.

But the new compositions about which Mozart cared most were six string quartets. They would make him little money, but quartets were for connoisseurs, and he was eager to show a mastery of the genre akin to that of Haydn – to whom, as supreme master of the string quartet, he gracefully dedicated them on publication (rather than to a rich patron who would pay him for it).

Mozart's middle years in Vienna reached a climax with the piano concertos of 1784–6. This was the time when the Viennese public recognized and admired his genius as composer and pianist and flocked to his concerts, which he gave during Lent when the theaters were closed. In the 12 piano concertos of these years he greatly enlarged the concept of the concerto (see **Listening Guide 25**).

Six of the piano concertos were written in 1784; three more followed in 1785 and a further three in 1786. After that he wrote only another two. These figures are significant: they show all too plainly that the famously fickle Viennese public were losing interest in him as a pianist-composer.

In 1786, however, he had an opera given at the court theater, *The Marriage of Figaro*, based on the revolutionary comedy by the French playwright Beaumarchais (see **Listening Guide 26**). It met with reasonable success in Vienna, but was particularly admired in the nearby Bohemian capital, Prague; and it was the Prague opera company that commissioned his next opera, *Don Giovanni*. It is said that the

Mozart: *The Marriage of Figaro* (1786), excerpt from Act 1

Mozart wrote his comic opera *The Marriage of Figaro* in 1785–6; it had its first performance at the Vienna court theater on 1 May 1786 and was very successful, although it was never, because of its more complicated style, as popular as some of the operas by Italian composers. A common theater plot at this period concerned the aristocrat who tried to seduce every pretty girl he met, feeling that his rank and the customs of the time entitled him to do so; but times were changing, and in all such plots he ends up frustrated and embarrassed. In the French play on which this opera was based, the Spanish Count Almaviva, although recently married, has his eye on Susanna, his wife's maidservant and the promised bride of his personal valet, Figaro; in the end he fails to win her, and having quite mistakenly charged his wife with infidelity, he is forced to apologize to her publicly.

Act 1: terzet, 'Cosa sento!'
The Count (baritone), Don Basilio (tenor), Susanna (soprano)

The Count had come to Susanna's room to arrange an assignation with her. When he arrived, she was (innocently) with the page Cherubino (a page is a young man of aristocratic background, sent to live with another family to acquire more social polish). Cherubino's adolescent amorousness had already got him into trouble with the Count; so at the Count's approach he hid behind a chair – hearing the Count's remarks to Susanna, of course. When the Count heard Don Basilio (a cleric and music-master) nearby, he concealed himself behind the same chair, while Cherubino slipped round and sat on it, covering himself with a dress that was draped over it. But in conversation with Susanna Basilio makes remarks about Cherubino's adoration of the Countess, and that – for the Count is a fiercely jealous man – provokes him into revealing himself.

This terzet (a word used for a trio of voices) shows how the sonata-form type of structure could be used in vocal music. The arrangement of thematic material and keys is exactly like that of an instrumental sonata-form movement, with ex. 1 as the first subject and ex. 3 as the second; the opening up to 1.06 corresponds to an exposition, the passage up to 2.58 to a development and from then to the end to a recapitulation. But the nature of the material, and the ways in which it recurs, are so managed as to give extra force and subtlety to the drama. Note, for example, how ex. 1 comes at each assertion of authoritarian anger from the Count; how ex. 3's appearance at 1.19 is in the same sense as its original one; and how ex. 2 is used with irony – the hint is there first time (0.17), comes again at his hypocritical disavowal of malice (1.36), and finally, after the Count has used the same music while discovering Cherubino, with the sharpest irony (3.34).

Listening Outline . . . .

		Time	key	
COUNT				
Cosa sento! tosto andate, E scacciate il seduttor.	What do I hear? Go at once and send the seducer away.	0.03	B♭	ex. 1: the Count expresses his anger
BASILIO				
In mal punto son qui giunto, Perdonate, o mio signor.	I have come at a bad moment, Forgive me, my lord.	0.17	B♭	ex. 2; Basilio (with a hint of irony and malice)
SUSANNA *(almost fainting)*				
Che ruina, me meschina! Son oppressa dal dolor.	Unfortunate me, I'm ruined! I am cast down with misery.	0.25	b♭–f	shift to minor at Susanna's anxiety
COUNT, BASILIO *(supporting her)*				
Ah già svien la poverina! Come oh dio! le batte il cor!	Ah, the poor girl is fainting! Good heavens, how her heart beats!	0.48	F	ex. 3: expression of sympathy
BASILIO				
Pian pianin su questo seggio.	Gently to this chair.	1.07	F	close of section; modulating section begins
SUSANNA *(reviving)*				
Dove sono! cosa veggio! Che insolenza, andate fuor.	Where am I? what is happening? How dare you! let me go!	1.10	g	Susanna's anger at being handled – and guided to the chair on which Cherubino is hiding
COUNT				
Siamo qui per aiutarti, Non turbati, oh mio tesor.	We are only helping you; Do not be disturbed, my treasure	1.19	E♭	ex. 3: note expression similar to 0.48
BASILIO				
Siamo qui per aiutarti, È sicuro il vostro onor.	We are only helping you; Your honor is safe.			

Italian	English	Time	Key	Notes
Ah del paggio qual che ho detto Era solo un mio sospetto!	What I said about the page was no more than my suspicion!	1.36	E♭– B♭	ex. 2
SUSANNA È un'insidia, una perfidia, Non credete all'impostor.	It's a trap and a falsehood; Don't believe this deceiver.	1.45	B♭	
COUNT Parta, parta il damerino!	This little beau must go away!	1.54	B♭	ex. 1: the Count's anger
SUSANNA, BASILIO Poverino!	Poor boy!	1.58		
COUNT *(ironically)* Poverino! Ma da me sorpreso ancor.	Poor boy! But I've found him out again.	2.05		
SUSANNA, BASILIO Come! Che!	How so? what?	2.11		
COUNT Da tua cugina L'uscio ier trovai rinchiuso, Picchio, m'apre Barbarina Paurosa fuor dell'uso. Io dal muso insospettito, Guardo, cerco in ogni sito,	At your cousin's place I found the door locked: I knocked, and Barbarina let me in, looking unusually flustered. My suspicions aroused, I looked, I searched everywhere,	2.18	B♭	recitative-like section for the narrative
Ed alzando pian pianino Il tappetto al tavolino Vedo il paggio . . .	And lifting very gently the cloth from the table there I saw the page! . . .	2.38	B♭	ex. 2
(he illustrates this with the dress on the chair, discovering the page)		2.50		note how ex. 2 turns upward as the page is discovered
Ah! cosa veggio!	Ah, what do I see!	2.53		
SUSANNA Ah! crude stelle!	Oh, cruel heavens!	2.55		
BASILIO *(laughing)* Ah! meglio ancora!	Oh, better still!	2.58		
COUNT *(ironically)* Onestissima signora! Or capisco come va!	You most virtuous lady! Now I understand how things are!	3.01	B♭	ex. 1: the Count's anger again, now quiet and menacing
SUSANNA Accader non può di peggio; Giusti dei! che mai sarà!	Nothing worse could happen; Great heavens! whatever next?			
BASILIO Così fan tutte le belle; Non c'è alcuna novità!	All the women are the same; There's nothing new about it!	3.11	B♭	part of ex. 3
Ah del paggio quel che ho detto Era solo un mio sospetto!	What I said about the page was no more than my suspicion!	3.34	B♭	ex. 2, reflecting Basilio's irony
(same words)		3.52 4.03 4.26		ex. 3, second part coda (end)

ex. 1

ex. 2

ex. 3

Viennese emperor, Joseph II, called the opera "tough meat for the teeth of my Viennese" when it was given the next year (1788). And certainly this complex work was less successful with the Viennese public than were the much lighter operas of Mozart's Italian contemporaries. His chamber music, too, some of which he published in those years, was generally found difficult, both to play and to understand.

Mozart's last years were difficult ones. He was constantly in debt – not because he was underpaid (he now had a salary as a junior court composer, an undemanding job, and he earned money too by teaching). Mozart and his family never starved, and could always afford a servant and a carriage of their own. But it seems that he always wanted to live a little more lavishly than he could afford.

Mozart was under considerable stress during 1788 when he wrote his last three symphonies. Probably they were intended for a concert series, in Vienna, which however never took place; the three works are often seen as showing three aspects of his art – the lyrical (no. 39 in E♭), the tragic (no. 40: see **Listening Guide 27**), and the majestic (no. 41, the "Jupiter"). He must have spent much of the last months of 1789 working on the new opera that was given in Vienna at the beginning of 1790.

62　*Opening of Bartolo's aria in Act 1 scene iii from the autograph of Mozart's opera* The Marriage of Figaro, *completed 29 April 1786. Deutsche Staatsbibliothek, Berlin.*

Mozart's last year, 1791, was particularly active. In the summer he wrote two operas, one for a popular Viennese theater, the other for performance at Prague during coronation celebrations for the new emperor. Although his operas had always been warmly received there, the new work, *La clemenza di Tito*, was only moderately successful in September 1791. Mozart returned to Vienna, where at the end of the month *The Magic Flute* was first given – to increasing applause during October. Meanwhile, he worked on a *Requiem*, which had been requested from him in mysterious circumstances (it was commissioned by a nobleman who wanted to pass it off as his own); later it was said that Mozart thought he was composing it for himself. For in November he became unwell, and after a three-week feverish illness that defied the doctors, and still defies diagnosis (it was not poisoning, as has been suggested), he died on 5 December.

63 *Stage design by G. Fuentes for the 1799 Frankfurt production of Mozart's opera* La clemenza di Tito. *Institut für Theaterwissenschaft, University of Cologne.*

Most of the music Mozart wrote during his boyhood, though astonishing for its fluency and inventiveness, is relatively conventional. His earliest pieces regularly played today belong to 1773–4, when he was 18. Outstanding are two symphonies, one in G minor, K183 (Mozart's works are always identified with "K" numbers, indicating their place in the chronological catalog compiled by Köchel), and one in A, K201. The G minor work, departing sharply from the traditional pattern of graceful, entertaining music, has an urgent and agitated tone. Even the last movement – most symphonies of this time end with cheerful, high-spirited music – remains taut and impassioned. The work in A major stands out in other ways, combining a gentle and refined manner with real passion. Mozart was turning from a gifted child into a composer of high originality.

These qualities are particularly clear in his piano concertos. The concerto, as we have seen, was originally a Baroque form, in which solo episodes alternated with orchestral ritornellos. In tune with the thinking of his time, Mozart added to this a Classical-style, sonata-form contrast of keys and themes and achieved a uniquely satisfying balance of elements, including the soloist's virtuosity. He did this, at least at first, less by using the kinds of detailed working of themes that Haydn (and Mozart himself to some degree) had applied to the string quartet than by allowing them to multiply. Ideas are linked either by brilliant passage-work (scales, arpeggios etc) or by orchestral tuttis. The relationship between piano and orchestra is subtle. The orchestra states some of the themes, and provides accompaniment and punctuation; the piano re-interprets some of these, ventures some of its own, occasionally accompanies the orchestra's leading wind players, has opportunities to show its brilliance, and brings the movement to a climax in a solo cadenza.

Typical of the concertos of 1784 is K453 in G, composed for one of Mozart's pupils, with its lyrical themes, its clear-cut form, its attractive writing for wind instruments, and its fluent virtuoso passages (see **Listening Guide 25**). For the slow movement the piano has music that is florid, dramatic, and rich in expression, often elaborating ideas already heard in the orchestra; in the finale piano and orchestra share the interest evenly in a witty set of variations. No two of Mozart's concertos follow the same scheme. In the later ones he tended to move away from the multiplicity of lyrical themes towards shorter, more motif-like ideas, and this led to music more strongly unified.

In the later group are Mozart's two minor-key concertos, which are among his supreme achievements. Both begin with material that is essentially orchestral in style which the pianist cannot take up – so in each case the solo entry begins with a new, lyrical theme of particular pathos and gentle beauty, a way of establishing a different kind of relationship between piano and orchestra. The C minor work is outstanding for the elaborate and colorful wind writing in its slow movement and for its inventive variation finale.

There is an analogy between the piano soloist in a concerto and the singer of an operatic aria. It is no coincidence that Mozart excelled in writing for both. From this time date Mozart's most famous operas: *The Marriage of Figaro* and *Don Giovanni*.

Like Shakespeare's comedies, Mozart's comic operas (as these are) are not simply funny. We saw (p. 171) what Gluck did for serious opera; Mozart did something parallel for comic opera by infusing it with a new humanity and depth of feeling.

There were numerous operas in the middle and late eighteenth century about noblemen with too eager an eye for country girls, and in all of them the nobleman is frustrated and virtue triumphs. That happens, too, in *The Marriage of Figaro* (*Le nozze di Figaro* – it was composed in Italian), but with a difference (see **Listening Guide 26**). *Don Giovanni* too deals with the tensions of class and sex: Giovanni is a Spanish nobleman with an insatiable desire for sexual conquest. When, at the end,

Operas

64 *Mozart's opera* The Marriage of Figaro*: Kathleen Battle (Susanna), Thomas Allen (Count), and Frederica von Stade (Cherubino) in the Metropolitan Opera, New York, 1988.*

Mozart: Symphony no. 40 in g (1788)

Mozart's Symphony no. 40 in G minor was written in the summer of 1788, the second of a group of three symphonies that were to be his last. All three are differently scored: no. 39 in E♭ includes a pair of clarinets – then still quite a new instrument, not regularly used in the orchestra – in place of the usual oboes, and both this work and no. 41 in C call for trumpets and timpani. No. 40 was written in the first place with a flute and two each of oboes, bassoons, and horns, along with strings. Later, Mozart added clarinets, assigning to them some of the music that he had originally given to the oboes. This may have been for a concert in which a pair of clarinetists played, given in aid of the Viennese musicians' charity in the spring of 1791.

No. 40 has always been one of the most loved of Mozart's symphonies. It has usually been regarded as a serious, even tragic work, as the use of a minor key suggests. But Schumann talked of its Grecian grace, and some writers have drawn attention to rhythms in it that reflect Italian comic opera. When Mozart was working on the symphony he was in a deeply troubled state of mind (he wrote to a friend 'black thoughts come to me often, thoughts that I banish with tremendous effort'). The symphony is not simply an expression of Mozart's suffering: his art rises above such matters. But the cut of its themes, which so often seem to aspire upward and then curve down, do seem to support the prevailing view of the symphony as a work, in the words of the American writer and pianist Charles Rosen, 'of passion, violence, and grief'.

 Listening Outline . . . .

First movement (Allegro molto), 2/2, g; sonata form

Time		
	exposition	
0.00 [1.45]	first group, g	the main theme (ex. 1) is of 8 mm., first heard with a 20 mm. responding phrase, then leading to an energetic tutti (ex. 2) in B♭ (0.28 [2.12]). Note fig. *a* (basic to the movement), the unusual viola accompaniment, the slower falling semitone, fig. *b*, and fig. *c*.
0.45 [2.29]	second group, B♭	in dialog, with winds answering strings (ex. 3; note fig. *b*); first phrase 8 mm., with response (now strings answering winds), interrupted to lead into a tutti
1.15 [2.59]	closing section	note use of figs. *a* and *b* (ex. 4)
1.45	**exposition repeated**	(0.00–1.44 = 1.45–3.27)
3.28	**development**	the music turns sharply to a distant key, f♯, with ex. 1, and then to e. There a vigorous tutti breaks out (3.43), with ex. 1 in alternation between the bass instruments and the violins, ending with the violins, in d. A quieter dialog follows, for violins and upper woodwinds, on fig. *a* (4.07), leading to a loud outburst in g (violins against lower strings, 4.22) before the winds gently lead the music back for the recapitulation
	recapitulation	
4.35	first group, g	as the exposition (except in scoring details), but the music takes a new turn towards the tutti, which is prolonged, with development of fig. *c*; it begins in E♭ and passes through f and c before settling decisively in g
5.39	second group, g	now different in feeling, as what was earlier major-key music is now in the minor
6.14	closing section	as before, but adjusted to include a last appearance of the opening of ex. 1 (6.41)
6.56		(end)

Second movement (Andante), 6/8, E♭; sonata form

exposition

0.00 [3.02]	first group, E♭	the main 'theme' begins with the instruments in imitation (ex. 5; note figs. *d* and *e*), with an expressive bass, 8 mm.; it then appears with the 'bass' (slightly varied) in the violins (0.29 [3.31]) and continues to a cadence (note fig. *f*). A bridge section, on *f*, follows (1.08 [4.10])
1.39 [4.41]	second group, D♭, B♭	the first part, on *d*, is in the remote key of D♭, against a variant of *f* on woodwinds; the second, in the orthodox key of B♭, is a 4-mm. phrase, repeated with woodwinds and leading to a chromatic tutti (2.07 [5.09]); there is a brief coda
3.02	**exposition repeated**	(0.00–3.01 = 3.02–6.03)
6.04	**development**	starts with a powerful chromatic tutti using figs. *d* and *f*, alternately, between woodwinds and upper strings. The music settles in c; *d* is heard on the bassoons (6.58 [10.58]), to which the upper woodwinds add a variant of *e* and the strings *f*
7.14 [11.14]	**recapitulation**	follows the exposition, except that bridge section material intervenes in the first group (7.56 [4.56]) Second group material now begins in G♭ (8.43 [12.43])
	development and recapitulation repeated	(6.04–10.03 = 10.04–14.05)
14.05		(end)

ex. 5

Third movement (Menuetto: Allegretto), 3/4, g; ternary form

main section

0.00 [0.18]	first part, g–d	a vigorous idea (ex. 6), with syncopated rhythms: the main theme of the minuet. Repeat
0.35 [1.10]	second part, B♭–g	begins in B♭, with ex. 6 in upper woodwinds and bass strings; ex. 6 returns in g in violins (0.51 [1.26]), with imitations, and forms basis of coda. Repeat

trio

1.46 [2.09]	first part, G–D	begins with strings, continues with woodwinds; ends (strings again) in D. Repeat
2.31 [3.03]	second part, D–G	dialog, bass strings and woodwinds; then first part returns, with horns and woodwinds, ending in G. Repeat
3.34	**main section returns**	(0.00–1.45 = 3.34–5.22) [both repeats observed here]
5.22		(end)

ex. 6

Fourth movement (Allegro assai), 2/2, g; sonata form

exposition

0.00 [1.49]	first group, g	lively, springing theme in violins, with tutti response (ex. 7; note figs. *g* and *h*), 8+8 mm.; continuation (8+8 mm.), then a tutti (using fig. *h*), leading to B♭ (0.27 [2.15])
1.00 [2.49]	second group, B♭	new theme on strings, repeated (with differences) by woodwinds; a further tutti (again with *h*) ends the section (1.27 [3.16])
1.49	**exposition repeated**	(0.00–1.48 = 1.49–3.36)
3.37 [6.18]	**development**	a violent outburst takes the music to d where, after a dialog passage (on fig. *g*) a fugal passage in *f* begins (3.57 [6.38]), eventually turning to complex dialogs on *g* and a tutti in the remote key of c♯ (4.21 [7.02]); a further violent, chromatic passage twists the music back to g (4.35 [7.16])
4.49 [7.30]	**recapitulation,** g	as before, but the first tutti takes different directions and the music remains in g for the second group (5.23 [8.04])
6.18	**development and recapitulation repeated** (3.37–6.18 = 6.18–9.02)	
9.02		(end)

ex. 7

he is consigned to eternal damnation, in a great scene where the statue drags him, unrepenting, down to the flames, Mozart provides a noble, inexorable setting in D minor. Giovanni's victims (or intended ones) are carefully differentiated: the peasant girl Zerlina, with her simple, pretty tunefulness; Donna Elvira, whom he has betrayed, and whose venom towards him is faintly flavored with the comic since a scorned woman pursuing her former lover could not escape concealed laughter; and Donna Anna, the proud young woman whose father he killed and whose passion for vengeance underlies the opera. The contrasting character sketches of Giovanni and his servant Leporello again show Mozart's musical representation of social class. Though still a comic opera, *Don Giovanni* deals with serious issues; but Leporello's presence, and his common-man's comments, wry or facetious, distinguish it from true tragedy.

Italian was the language preferred for operas at the Vienna court theater. Outside court circles, however, German was spoken. An opera for middle-class audiences had to be in that language. Mozart, happy to write in his native tongue, accepted in 1791 an invitation to collaborate with the theater manager and actor, Emanuel Schikaneder, on a pantomime-like German opera. Since 1784 Mozart had been a freemason, and the text and music of *The Magic Flute* incorporate masonic symbolism. It starts like a traditional fairy-tale with a heroic prince (Tamino) attempting to rescue a beautiful princess (Pamina) from the clutches of a wicked magician (Sarastro); but soon it becomes clear that Sarastro represents the forces of light and Pamina's mother, the Queen of Night, those of darkness.

The Magic Flute has a jokey libretto. But it is artfully designed to provide many different kinds of music: the Queen of Night's angrily glittering, spiky, high singing; Sarastro's and his priests' noble utterances; the popular ditties for the birdcatcher Papageno (sung by Schikaneder) who accompanies Tamino on his quest; the tense trios for the Queen's Ladies and the serene ones for the three Boys or Genii who support Tamino; and the music for Tamino and Pamina themselves, which is direct and intimate as the music of Mozart's Italian operas is not. This is a philosophical opera, about two people's lofty quest for realization and ideal union; with this is contrasted Papageno and his role as a child of nature. The sublimity of the music with which Mozart clothed *The Magic Flute* shows him unmistakably as a true man of the Age of Enlightenment.

5 *Beethoven*

It was with the explosion of the genius of Ludwig van Beethoven, at the turn of the century, that the Classical era reached both a climax and a dissolution. "Explosion" is the word: for Beethoven's music embodied a new dynamism and power which not only demanded that it be listened to in different ways but also symbolized the changing role of the composer in society – no longer its servant, required meekly to meet its needs, but its visionary, its hero-figure.

LIFE

Early years

Beethoven was born in Bonn, in western Germany. At the Bonn court of the Electors of Cologne, his grandfather had briefly been in charge of the musical establishment and his father was a tenor singer when, at the end of 1770, Ludwig was born. Discovering his exceptional musical talent, his father wanted him to be a child prodigy, a second Mozart, and compelled him to practice long hours. He played in public when he was eight, but his precocity was not of the order of Mozart's. He had instruction on the piano, the organ, and the violin, and when he was about ten he began more serious studies, including composition with the Bonn court organist. At 13 he was assistant organist, and four years later he was sent to Vienna to study; but the trip was brief as Beethoven was summoned home to see his dying mother. In 1789 he had to manage the family: his father was a heavy drinker. His main court duty was to play the viola in the chapel and theater orchestras. But Bonn was too small a town for a developing composer, and in 1792, soon after Haydn passed through on his journey back to Vienna from London, Beethoven was sent there to study under him.

The lessons were not successful; Beethoven afterwards said that Haydn took little trouble over him, and though Haydn admired the younger man he seems to have been unsympathetic to his musical ideas. When Haydn went back to England, Beethoven turned to another teacher. Meanwhile, he was establishing himself as a pianist, playing in the salon concerts organized by noblemen in their houses and making his Viennese public début early in 1795. About this time his first important publications were issued: three piano trios op. 1 and three piano sonatas op. 2 (see **Listening Guide 29**). As a pianist Beethoven, according to reports of the time, had immense fire, brilliance, and fantasy, as well as depth of feeling. In no other musical medium could he be so bold or so wholly himself.

In his early Viennese days, Beethoven lived on a salary from his Bonn employer and was given lodgings by various noble patrons, such as Prince Lichnowsky. It was with him that in 1796 Beethoven embarked on his first concert tour, to Prague, Dresden, and Berlin. Lichnowsky was the dedicatee of one of Beethoven's most striking works, the Piano Sonata in C minor op. 13, known as the *Pathétique*. One of his op. 1 trios was also in C minor. Haydn, on seeing it, had advised Beethoven

65 Ludwig van Beethoven: *cartoon*.

Ludwig van Beethoven   Life and Works

1770	born in Bonn, baptized 17 December
1792	studied with Haydn in Vienna
1795	public début as pianist and composer in Vienna
1799	publication of Piano Sonata no. 8 in c, op. 13 ('Pathétique')
1800–2	deterioration of hearing and period of depression
1802	Heiligenstadt Testament, October
1803	beginning of heroic 'middle period'; 'Eroica' Symphony
1805	*Fidelio*
1806–8	prolific composition, mostly large-scale instrumental works, including Symphonies nos. 5 and 6 ('Pastoral') and 'Razumovsky' Quartets
1812	letter to the 'Eternal Beloved'; beginning of 'silent period'
1813	beginning of 'final period'
1814	highpoint of popular acclaim in Vienna; last public appearance as a pianist; revision of *Fidelio*
1815	appointed guardian of nephew Karl
1818	Piano Sonata no. 29 in B♭ op. 106 ('Hammerklavier') completed
1820–23	compositional activity; late piano sonatas, 'Diabelli' Variations
1823	*Missa solemnis* completed, Symphony no. 9 ('Choral') begun
1825–6	concentration on string quartets
1827	died in Vienna, 26 March

Symphonies   no. 1, C (1800); no. 2, D (1802); no. 3, 'Eroica', E♭ (1803); no. 4, B♭ (1806); no. 5, c (1808); no. 6, 'Pastoral', F (1808); no. 7, A (1812); no. 8, F (1812); no. 9, 'Choral', d (1824)

Concertos   5 piano concertos – no. 4, G (1806), no. 5, 'Emperor', E♭ (1809); Violin Concerto, D (1806); Triple Concerto for piano, violin, and cello, C (1804)

Overtures and incidental music   Coriolan (1807); Leonore Overtures nos. 1, 2, and 3 (1805–6); Egmont (1810)

Opera   Fidelio (1805, rev. 1806, 1814)

Choral music   Mass, D (Missa solemnis, 1819–23)

Piano music   32 sonatas – no. 8, 'Pathétique', c, op. 13 (1799), no. 14, 'Moonlight', c♯, op. 27 no. 2 (1801), no. 21, 'Waldstein', C, op. 53 (1804), no. 23, 'Appassionata', f (1805), no. 26, 'Les adieux', E♭, op. 81a (1810), no. 29, 'Hammerklavier', B♭, op. 106 (1818); 33 Variations on a Waltz by Diabelli, op. 120 (1823); variations, bagatelles

String quartets   op. 18 nos. 1–6 (1798–1800); op. 59 nos. 1–3, 'Razumovsky Quartets' (1806); op. 74, 'Harp' (1809); op. 95 (1810); op. 127 (1824); op. 132 (1825); op. 130 (1826); op. 133, 'Grosse Fuge' (1826); op. 131 (1826); op. 135 (1826)

Other chamber music   piano trios – op. 97, 'Archduke' (1811); string quintets; piano quintet; sonatas for piano and violin – op. 24, 'Spring' (1801), op. 47, 'Kreutzer' (1803); Octet for wind instruments (1793)

Songs   An die ferne Geliebte ('To the distant beloved'), song cycle for tenor and piano (1816); Scottish songs

not to publish it. Beethoven ignored the advice. In 1800 and 1802 he wrote his first two symphonies; by that time he had also composed three piano concertos (the third is in C minor again), the ideal music for him to play in public.

Beethoven's creative life has traditionally been divided into three periods: his youth and early manhood, with his establishment as a major composer (1770–1802); his middle life (1803–12), in which he handled all musical forms with full command and produced many of his most famous works; and his final period (1813–27), when the personal stresses he underwent are reflected first in the small number of works he produced and secondly in their intensely serious, often very intimate character. This division makes good sense and relates convincingly with the times of change, or of personal crisis, in Beethoven's life.

The "heroic" period

During 1802 Beethoven went through some kind of profound depression. It was probably in 1796 that he first became aware that his hearing had become less acute: by 1800 he was aware not only that it was impaired but also that the condition was worsening and was unlikely to be arrested, still less cured. To Beethoven the composer, it was not a catastrophe. As a gifted and trained musician, with a perfect "inner ear", he could hear music, however complicated, by looking at it, and could write down the ideas that came into his head. (He had never composed at the piano, but rather at his desk, jotting down his ideas in sketchy form, then working at them to give them shape and meaning.) But to Beethoven the pianist, it was a disaster. His ideas of a career as a virtuoso, traveling Europe to great applause, would have to be abandoned. So would teaching (an important source of income); so would conducting his own music. And to Beethoven the man, deafness was a tragedy.

He wrote to a friend in 1801 that he was "living a miserable life. For almost two years I have ceased attending social functions, simply because I cannot say to people 'I am deaf'". His ability to communicate freely was appallingly damaged; he could never hope for a normal social life. As time went on, he became more turned in on himself, growing steadily more odd, more eccentric, probably more aggressive.

This was a gradual process. In 1802 he still had several years of concert-giving ahead of him and his social life was not yet a void. But in October, when he was in a village called Heiligenstadt outside Vienna, he wrote a strange "Testament" – a kind of will, addressed to his two younger brothers. It describes his bitter unhappiness over his affliction in terms suggesting that he thought death was near.

Beethoven, however, came through this depression with his determination strengthened. He wrote of "seizing Fate by the throat" and of the impossibility "of leaving this world before I have produced all the works that I feel the urge to write". This new readiness to fight against adversity is echoed in the "heroic" character of his music of the ensuing years. Nearly all Beethoven's music so far had been "absolute" (that is, with no content outside music). But now he wrote large works that carry implications about his attitudes to life: in his oratorio *Christ on the Mount of Olives* there is clearly some identification between Christ's suffering and his own; in the opera *Fidelio* (or *Leonore*, as it was at first called) other aspects of Beethoven's suffering and aspirations are dealt with.

Beethoven: Symphony no. 5 in c, op. 67 (1808)

Beethoven's Fifth Symphony was composed in the early years of the nineteenth century, during his 'heroic' phase. It had its first performance in a concert on a heroic scale; it included the premières of two of his symphonies and the first Viennese hearings of a piano concerto, parts of a Mass and a large-scale song, and finally a work for piano, chorus, and orchestra – not quite finished when Beethoven sat down to play, and not properly rehearsed. It was in an unheated theater on a bitter December night, in 1808, and was at best a mixed success.

But the grandeur of the Fifth must have been clear even in those circumstances. With the famous motif that runs through it, and is said to represent 'Fate knocking at the door', it demands to be interpreted as a triumph over adversity. C minor was a key for some of Beethoven's darkest and most serious works. The menace of the first movement and the darkness and sinister qualities of the scherzo give way to the confident, blazing C major of the finale, where the four-note motif changes from threatening to jubilant. And the 'meaning' of the symphony is the more obvious by the way the finale follows without a break from the scherzo – and is further emphasized by the return of the scherzo music during the finale and the 'defeat' once more of C minor by C major.

 Listening Outline . . . .

First movement (Allegro con brio), 2/4, c; sonata form
2 flutes (and piccolo in finale), 2 oboes, 2 clarinets, 2 bassoons (and double bassoon in finale)
2 horns, 2 trumpets, 3 trombones (in finale only); timpani
1st and 2nd violins, violas, cellos, double basses

Time		
	exposition	
0.00 [1.20]	first group, c	the main idea is a four-note motif, ex. 1 fig. *a*, rather than a 'theme'; the rhythm of this motif is used throughout the movement (and the whole symphony). Here it is worked up towards a dramatic pause, then runs down through the orchestra and propels a powerful tutti (0.31 [1.52])
0.41 [2.02]	second group, E♭	ex. 2; note the continued presence of fig. *a* in this gentler music and the following tutti (1.02 [2.23])
1.20	**exposition repeat**	(0.00–1.20 = 1.20–2.40)
2.40	**development**	again fig. *a*, stated forcefully at the start, is the main subject matter. The music passes through f, c, and g, where the two-note fig. *b* becomes (3.24) the central topic of development with pairs of chords, then single ones, alternately on strings and woodwinds; but fig. *a* returns, to make the arrival of the recapitulation a climax
	recapitulation	
3.55	first group, c	as the exposition (but note the oboe cadenza at the pause, 4.12); the music remains in c
4.42	second group, C/c	as before, though differences in scoring and other detail; section ends in C
5.24	**coda**	carries the music back to c; in its use of fig. *a* and its extension of ideas from fig. *b* it is like a further development, and it culminates in a restatement of ex. 1 and its continuation (6.25)
6.43		(end)

ex. 1

ex. 2

Second movement (Andante con moto), 3/8, A♭; double variation form

0.00	**first theme, A♭**	on violas and cellos, ex. 3; last phrase echoed on violins, then woodwinds, and continued to cadence
0.58	**second theme, A♭, C**	on clarinets and bassoons (ex. 4; note fig. *a* and the relationship with ex. 3, fig. *c*); oboes and brasses take over when key changes to C (1.20)
2.07	**first theme varied, *1***	now in a smoother rhythm; Beethoven's variation process is always like one of development
3.02	**second theme varied, *1***	now with more active accompaniment
4.10	**first theme varied, *2***	in faster movement: lower strings, then violins, then tutti (4,47); a woodwind variant leads to an episode for woodwinds (5.23)
6.09	**second theme varied, *2***	a brief tutti, in C; then the music returns to A♭ and a♭ (6.57)
7.41	**first theme varied, *3***	a tutti, powerful and eloquent
8.36	**coda**	begins with a recall on bassoon of the earlier woodwind variant; phrases from ex. 4 are used
10.26		(end)

ex. 3

ex. 4

(continuation)

Third movement (Allegro), 3/4, c; ternary form

0.00 [3.12]	**first section, c**	a phrase on bass strings (ex. 5) is answered by upper strings; then horns announce a theme (ex. 6) using the rhythms of fig. *a* (0.20 [3.34]). These ideas alternate and are combined. Note the extension downward of the bass theme (after 1.38 [4.50])
1.48 [5.02]	**second section, C**	ex. 7, on cellos and double basses, is developed as a brief fugue, ending in G, then repeated; it restarts, at first hesitantly (2.17 [5.32]), then more fully developed, in C, but when this is repeated (2.43 [5.58]) the texture of the music softens and it breaks off
3.12	**repeat of first and second sections**	(0.00–3.12 = 3.12–6.26) [in some performances this repeat is not observed; scholars have recently found evidence that Beethoven did intend it to be given as it is here]

6.27	**extra repeat of first section**	a close repeat of the first section, but with the original full, sustained orchestral writing replaced by a thin, ghostly sound using plucked strings and solo, staccato woodwinds. At the end the ghostly atmosphere continues, with hushed timpani (7.39), sustained low notes and stray violin phrases gradually working up to a grand climax – beginning of next movement
8.17		(end/beginning of finale)

ex. 5

ex. 6

ex. 7

Fourth movement (Allegro), 4/4, C; sonata form
exposition

0.00 [2.10]	first group, C	a brilliant, exultant fanfare-like array of themes for full orchestra (ex. 8); a new theme (ex. 9, 0.38 [2.48]) heralds the change of key
1.07 [3.17]	second group, G	a smoother but still energetic theme (ex. 10), on violins, with contrasting phrases (loud/soft, upward/downward). Note again the use of the fig. *a* rhythm, which is almost always present (in ex. 8 and ex. 10), as it is again in the secondary theme (ex. 11, 1.37 [3.47]) that leads to the close of the section
	exposition repeat	(0.00–2.10 = 2.10–4.20)
4.21	**development**	mainly based on ex. 10 and its bass (fig. *d*); it moves through several keys, notably A, F, Bb, Db, and f, to C, where after a long, loud tutti (mainly on fig. *d*), music from the end of the third movement returns (6.02); this leads into the recapitulation (just as previously it led into the exposition, though here in shortened form)
	recapitulation	
6.41	first group, C	as before until ex. 9 (7.18), which takes a different direction
7.52	second group, C	as before
8.53	**coda**	material from ex. 10 leads to a dramatic break; a new idea (actually from ex. 9) is heard on bassoons (9.29), horns and throughout the orchestra, leading to a climax, a quickening of pace (10.18–10.30), with material based on ex. 11 and a final reminder of the movement's first theme, ex. 8 (10.49)
11.35		(end)

ex. 8

ex. 9

ex. 10

ex. 11

The most obvious product of Beethoven's "heroic" phase is the *Eroica* Symphony (his third), of 1803. He first called it "Bonaparte", as a tribute to Napoleon, the hero of revolutionary France. But the following spring news arrived that Napoleon had proclaimed himself emperor; Beethoven, angry and disillusioned at what he saw as a betrayal, ripped the title-page bearing the dedication off the score, tore it in half, and wrote on the symphony "Heroic Symphony, composed to celebrate the memory of a great man".

Like the *Eroica* the Fifth (see **Listening Guide 28**) is a large-scale symphony. So is the *Pastoral*, no. 6. This is about the countryside – or, rather, about Beethoven's reactions to the countryside, which he loved. He lived in a large city, but went each spring and summer to stay in some nearby spa or small town and to take country walks. In his time, natural rural beauty was only just beginning to be admired; the previous generation, the age of landscape gardening, had held that unruly nature could be bettered by human art.

By the early years of the new century, Beethoven was widely recognized – not only in his home city of Vienna – as a leading composer, a highly original one whose latest works were eagerly awaited by connoisseurs and the public and were competed for by music publishers. With an annuity guaranteed by Prince Lichnowsky he could live in reasonable comfort. He was now anxious to prove himself in a new sphere: opera, which offered a composer the richest rewards, both financial and in reputation. An opportunity came in 1803, and Beethoven started work; but the opera-house manager lost his job and plans were abandoned.

The next year he had an invitation to write an opera for Vienna. Only a topic close to his heart, he felt, could draw from him music that embodied his deepest feelings. He did not have to look far for a plot. Since the French Revolution, many operas had been written that appealed to love of freedom and hatred of tyranny; many were "rescue operas", having as their climax the last-minute rescue from death of the hero or heroine. A literary friend of Beethoven's prepared for him a libretto using a French story allegedly based on an actual incident: it was called *Leonore, or Married Love*. Beethoven worked at the opera, to be called *Fidelio*, during much of 1804 and 1805. He had immense trouble composing it and when it was first per- formed, late in 1805, it was a failure – though that was partly because it was given

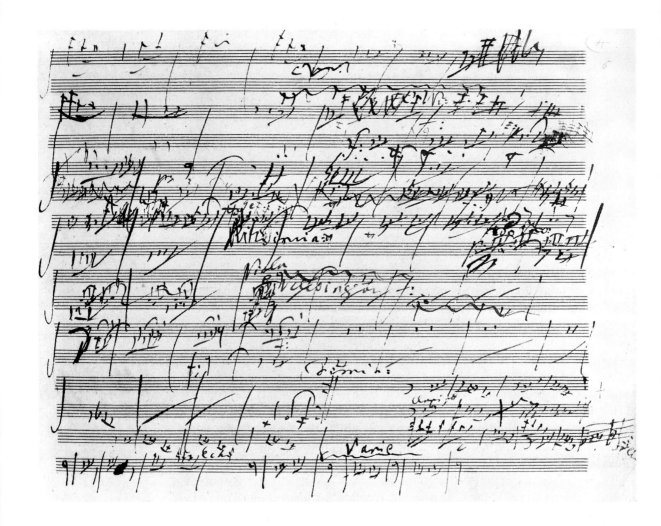

66 *Autograph sketches for Beethoven's Symphony no. 6 in F ("Pastoral"), 1808. British Library, London.*

before an audience largely of French officers (Napoleon's army had conquered Vienna a week before). Beethoven's friends told him that it was too long and began too slowly; he shortened it, and it had two performances, but then Beethoven quarreled with the theater authorities and withdrew it. He did not revive it again until 1814, when he had made extensive further changes, directed towards making it less the story of two particular people and more a generalized tale of good and evil.

One reason why Beethoven found the subject of *Fidelio* so attractive is that it dealt with freedom and justice. Another is that it dealt with a heroic theme and triumph over adversity. A third is that it dealt with marriage. Beethoven longed to marry; at the time he was composing *Fidelio* he was in love with Josephine von Brunsvik. Like his earlier love, in 1801, for a countess, it came to nothing. In both cases the women were Beethoven's pupils; in both, the barriers of social class proved insurmountable. In any case, we cannot know whether they reciprocated Beethoven's passion.

Possibly Beethoven never found a woman who could match his lofty image; and we may doubt whether a man so violent in his feelings, so absorbed in his art, so unruly and quarrelsome, was capable of a stable relationship.

But he continued, it seems, to hope. A strange letter, written in 1812 and addressed to the "Eternally Beloved", has survived; it is a passionate love letter, expressing a desire for total union yet also expressing resignation at its impossibility; it speaks of fidelity, of the pain of separation, of hopes for a life together. It is hard to know what it means. The weight of evidence points to its having been addressed to Antonie Brentano, a Viennese aristocrat married to a Frankfurt businessman – they and their ten-year-old daughter had known Beethoven for two years, and we know that she admired him. But there is little reason to think that she and Beethoven had a love affair or even contemplated living together; we do not even know whether the letter was sent. It could have been the product of an intense private fantasy about marriage to an ideal, but unattainable, woman.

The last period

The year 1812 – critical in European history, with Napoleon's defeat in Russia – was a turning-point in Beethoven's life. In the preceding years he had composed much of the music by which he is chiefly remembered: the fourth to eighth symphonies, the fourth and fifth piano concertos (no. 5, the "Emperor", one of his grandest conceptions, with the piano's heroic strivings and commanding assertions), the supremely lyrical Violin Concerto, a Mass, songs, chamber music, and piano sonatas including the great *Appassionata*.

In 1808 Beethoven had considered becoming musical director at the King of Westphalia's court in Kassel; but he was not eager to leave a busy capital city for a small, provincial one, and when three Viennese noblemen banded together to provide him with a guaranteed income he was glad to be able to stay. His career as a pianist was finished. He played his last public concerto in 1808; when he appeared at a charity concert in 1814 he could not hear himself, and banged in the loud passages while in the quiet ones he played so delicately that the notes did not sound.

The years following 1812 have been called Beethoven's silent years: he composed relatively little and he was more than ever cut off from the world by his deafness becoming increasingly morose, suspicious, and quarrelsome. He drove away all but his most tolerant friends with his aggressive behavior, was unable to keep servants, and lived in perpetual confusion and squalor. From 1815 he had another great worry: his nephew Karl, son of his brother Carl Caspar (who died that year). Beethoven thought the boy's mother a bad influence and fought with her in the courts to be appointed guardian – he succeeded, but as guardian was a failure, and Karl grew up an unhappy and wild young man who felt little of the gratitude or affection his uncle demanded.

The trials that Beethoven underwent, social and personal, have a clear reflection in his music. Deafness prevented his hearing new works by other composers, and his own idiom, instead of altering as the years passed, stayed basically the same, only growing more refined and concentrated.

The climaxes to his life's work were a group of string quartets and two choral works. One was a Mass, begun for performance at the ceremony in which one of his oldest and most trusted friends and patrons, the Archduke Rudolph of Austria, was to be enthroned as an archbishop. Unfortunately it was not finished in time. The other was a choral symphony. In 1817, Beethoven had agreed to write two symphonies for the Philharmonic Society of London and to go there to direct them. He did not do so but the invitation drew him back to symphonic composition. The result was the Choral Symphony, no. 9, a work an hour in length culminating in a setting for solo singers and chorus of words from Schiller's *Ode to Joy*.

Beethoven finished work on the Choral Symphony early in 1824; in May it had its first performance – he was too deaf to conduct (two years earlier he had had to give up an attempt to conduct *Fidelio*) and, at the end, sat in total absorption until a friend tugged his sleeve and told him that the audience were applauding wildly. A dinner party he gave afterwards for the conductor, the concertmaster Schuppanzigh, and his own assistant Schindler ended in disaster as Beethoven virtually accused them all of cheating him of money due from the performance. He was as difficult and quarrelsome as ever.

In 1823 Beethoven had accepted a commission from Prince Golitsïn, of St Petersburg, for some string quartets, a form he had not considered since 1810. With the Choral Symphony premières behind him, he set to work, designing them for the quartet led by Schuppanzigh. They occupied him for the rest of his creative life and form a personal, intimate counterpart to the public statements of the Choral Symphony and the Mass for Archduke Rudolph. Golitsïn had asked for three works, but Beethoven had more to say and produced another two.

He finished his last quartet in the fall of 1826. During the preceding summer he had been profoundly disturbed when his nephew Karl tried to commit suicide. Beethoven and his nephew went to spend some weeks at the country home of Beethoven's second brother. He returned, in haste (after a quarrel, apparently), in December, and was taken ill. The doctors could do little but relieve the symptoms. Everyone knew he was dying, and he was sent gifts, among them money from the London Philharmonic Society and wine from one of his publishers. On 26 March 1827, he died, during a thunderstorm; his last action was to raise a clenched fist. Some 10,000 came to mourn at his funeral: he had lived into the age – indeed had helped create it – when the artist was the property of mankind at large.

MUSIC

Piano sonatas

It was as a pianist that Beethoven made his reputation as a young man, and it was naturally through the piano that he could express himself most characteristically. The piano is a dynamic instrument, capable of dramatic and even violent effects, as his earliest sonatas show (see **Listening Guide 29**). But it was not only through fiery writing, such as that in his first piano sonata, that he startled his listeners. The slow movements are often very slow, intense in feeling, and highly original in the shape of their melodic lines and the force of their harmonies. Key changes that to Mozart or Haydn would have seemed too alarming, because they are unexpected and damaging to the music's flow, were often used by Beethoven, who was more ready, even eager, to shock the listener. This is at the root of Haydn's doubts about

67 Ludwig van Beethoven: *pencil drawing, c1818, by Carl Friedrich August von Kloeber. Beethovenhaus, Bonn.*

such a work as the C minor Piano Trio that Beethoven published in his op. 1: it uses extremes of speed and volume and arresting textures and dynamics in a way that a composer of Haydn's generation was bound to regard as rough, uncivilized, and disturbing to the musical equilibrium.

By the year 1802, Beethoven had written 20 of his 32 piano sonatas. They include some of the most famous, such as the ones called *Pathétique* and *Moonlight*, both outstandingly original. The former, in C minor, a key Beethoven was inclined to use for some of his most powerful thoughts, has a brief slow introduction, an arresting phrase that Beethoven brings back in the course of the movement, to strikingly novel effect; the restless and fiery mood of the first movement returns in the last. The

Beethoven: Piano Sonata in f, op. 2 no. 1 (1793–5), first movement

Beethoven's first significant published works – the first issued with an opus number – were the three piano trios op. 1; a few months later three piano sonatas followed, as his op. 2, bearing a dedication to Haydn. Vienna had little concert life at this period, but Beethoven played a great deal at the musical evenings given by members of the nobility at their houses; and these sonatas must have been among the music he performed.

Of these first three sonatas, the most characteristic, and the one that most foreshadows the intensity of the mature Beethoven, is no. 1 in F minor. It is in four movements – already a departure from the standard three-movement scheme of Haydn and Mozart. After the fiery first movement, where the motivic nature of all the themes is typical of Beethoven's way of concentrating his material, there is an Adagio, in an elaborate melodic style, a minuet and trio, and a fiercely stormy final movement, marked Prestissimo ('Very fast') with a busy, rapidly-moving left-hand part that lends unusual urgency to the music, combined with large right-hand chords and broadly sweeping melodic lines.

 . Listening Outline . . . .

First movement (Allegro), 2/2, f; sonata form

Time		
	exposition	
0.00 [1.01]	first group, f	main theme, ex. 1, simply an arpeggio and a flourish (fig. *a*)
0.12 [1.13]	bridge passage	starting with ex. 1 in the left hand, and using fig. *a*
0.26 [1.27]	second group, A♭	the main idea is simply a downward curving phrase, ex. 2: note the rhythmic similarity to ex. 1; ex. 3 shows a secondary one (0.40 [1.41])
0.50 [1.51]	closing section	
2.00	**exposition repeat**	(0.00–1.00 = 1.01–2.01)
[4.03]	**development**	ex. 1, A♭; then ex. 2, passing through b♭ and c, and (now in left hand) c, b♭, and A♭ (2.29 [4.33]) leading to c and f, where after a spell of static harmony fig. *a* is introduced (2.55 [4.59]) to herald the . . .
	recapitulation	
3.02 [5.06]	first group, f	as in exposition
3.13 [5.17]	bridge	adjusted to remain in f
3.25 [5.30]	second group, f	as in exposition
3.48 [5.54]	closing section	slightly extended
	development and recapitulation repeat	(2.01–4.05 = 4.06–6.13)
6.13		(end)

ex. 1

ex. 2

ex. 3

Moonlight, with its poetic figuration above slow-changing harmony, is in an alto-gether new vein. From the same time comes another piano sonata, with a slow movement entitled "Funeral March on the Death of a Hero", a somber movement that recalls the sound of a military funeral with its dark sound, its march-like rhythms and its imitation of flourishes of trumpets and muffled drums. All these brought new elements into the piano sonata, taking it further from the urbane drawing-room entertainment for well-educated young ladies, which is what it had essentially been in the eighteenth century.

Orchestral music was not immune from Beethoven's boldness: when his First Symphony had its première, in 1801, audiences were astonished that it began not only with a dissonance but one in a foreign key. There was scarcely a work of Beethoven's early years that did not cause shock; and in this Beethoven was not simply defying convention or trying to alarm his listeners – rather, he was trying to enlarge the vocabulary of music and to make it say new things.

Middle period

In his early years, Beethoven sometimes did this clumsily, so that we are more aware of the departure itself than of its significance. In his second creative period, 1803–12, he extended the scope of his music to accommodate the big effects at which he was aiming. This is the time of his *Eroica* Symphony, no. 3. A symphony by Haydn takes some 25 minutes to perform; the *Eroica* takes about 45. Yet it does not have long themes. It is built up of motifs of a new notes, particularly its first movement, held together by the intricate weaving of its ideas and the powerful momentum Beethoven develops. Although the *Eroica* has no specific program, it does include a heroic funeral march and clearly embodies Beethoven's early thoughts about Napoleon. The Fifth Symphony is less specific but more clear: it begins with a threat, in C minor, and ends with a triumph, in C major (see **Listening Guide 28**). This is a typical product of Beethoven's "heroic phase"; it is impossible to doubt that he saw the work as symbolizing his personal struggles and his eventual conquest of the adverse forces surrounding him. From this period too comes his oratorio *Christ on the Mount of Olives*, where he depicts poignantly Christ's suffering and his over-coming of it, clearly with some sense of identification. The heroic theme comes up again in the opera *Fidelio*.

The expansion that we have seen in the *Eroica* Symphony affects most of the music of this period; a large canvas is needed for the treatment of large-scale ideas. Beethoven's chamber music of this time also reflects his expansive ways of thinking. He wrote three string quartets in 1806; the first, op. 59 no. 1, proclaims its character in its opening measures, with their lengthy melodic lines and their slow-moving harmony (its first change is after no fewer than six and a half measures, its second after another eleven and a half). The second movement of this quartet is another of Beethoven's very slow and very intense pieces, full of dissonances of the kind traditionally expressive of grief; he wrote in the margin of his sketches here a note about "a willow or acacia tree over my brother's grave" – his brothers were in fact both alive and well, but clearly he was thinking in elegiac terms.

Late style

The compositions of his late years saw a further intensification of Beethoven's musical style. The music becomes denser and more closely argued, and Beethoven came to prefer forms, or elements of forms, that enabled him to compose music of an increasingly concentrated kind.

One of these was variation form. He used it in several of the piano sonatas of the 1820s, not in the traditional Classical way of elaborating a theme but rather by taking a motif from the theme and developing it, as if probing into the deepest nature of an idea rather than simply embellishing it. One of the most striking of his piano variations is the set he wrote for the publisher Diabelli, who had sent a trivial waltz theme to several Austrian composers, asking each to write a variation on it. Beethoven sent 33 variations, of intense complexity and technical difficulty.

The finale of the Choral Symphony is another example of variation form, on a massive scale. This movement sees Beethoven for once making the meaning of an instrumental work articulate. Many earlier finales, as we have seen, carried strong hints of extra-musical meaning, like the triumph of the Fifth; but here Beethoven provides a verbal text and introduces a chorus and soloists to join in the expression of feelings about humanity and universal brotherhood. In this he echoed the composers of post-Revolution France. The words are from Schiller's *Ode to Joy*, which Beethoven had long admired and considered setting.

The theme associated with *Ode to Joy* is presented first by the cellos and double basses, then woven into a rich contrapuntal texture, before it is presented by the voices: later it appears as the basis of a military march (to words about marching to victory over sorrow or tyranny), and blended with another theme in a double fugue for the chorus. This long movement is one of the most difficult and strenuous ever written – intentionally so, for the sense of striving and effort are essential to the message of the work.

The use of fugue in the Choral Symphony may seem surprising: fugue is after all a form of the Baroque era, long past. But Beethoven saw in it another means of intensification. He wrote fugues in several of his late piano sonatas, some of them on arresting, dramatic themes, some on plain, even bland ones: the kind of close argument he could use in a fugue could produce a very dense musical texture. He used it too in his string quartets, one of which begins with a slow fugue, almost like Renaissance polyphony in the way it slowly unfolds, and another of which ends with a long, harsh, and immensely demanding one – so difficult, in fact, for both player and listener that Beethoven's publisher persuaded him to replace it with a shorter and simpler movement. Yet in these later works, along with this dynamic inner energy that seems to drive Beethoven into music ever more complex and more tortuous, there is also a vein of deep lyricism: in the slow movements particularly, his melodies show a new intensity and often poignancy.

Part VI The Romantic Era

1 *Music in a Changing Society*

Unlike the terms "Baroque" and "Classical", which have little use in ordinary conversation or writing, "Romantic" is a word full of everyday meanings. Dictionaries define it as to do with romance, imagination, the strange, the picturesque, the fantastic. In the arts, it is similarly applied – to literature, painting, or music in which fantasy and imagination are in their own right more important than such classical features as balance, symmetry, and wholeness. Because the Romantic era succeeded the Classical one, roughly at the turn of the eighteenth century, it is usual, and convenient, to define the characteristics of Romantic art and especially music by comparison with that of the Classical period.

    The most obvious difference between Classical music and Romantic music is usually expressed as one of precedence: in the Classical world, form and order come first; in the Romantic era, expressive content does. A Classical piece of music, broadly speaking, has a clear-cut structure which the hearer is intended to perceive

Romantic art

Composers of the Romantic Era

Composer	1750 — 1800 — 1850 — 1900
Johann Nepomuk Hummel	
Nicolò Paganini	
Louis Spohr	
Carl Maria Weber	
Giacomo Meyerbeer	
Gioachino Rossini	
Franz Schubert	
Gaetano Donizetti	
Vincenzo Bellini	
Hector Berlioz	
Fanny Mendelssohn	
Felix Mendelssohn	
Fryderyk Chopin	
Robert Schumann	
Franz Liszt	
Richard Wagner	
Giuseppe Verdi	
Charles Gounod	
Jacques Offenbach	
Clara Schumann	
César Franck	
Bedřich Smetana	
Anton Bruckner	
Johann Strauss jr	
Stephen Foster	
Louis-Moreau Gottschalk	
Johannes Brahms	

(at some level of awareness) as an important part of the musical experience, indeed as its basis, within which the emotion generated by any incident takes its place. By contrast, a Romantic piece depends on strong emotional expression, which may be generated by some subtlety or richness of harmony or color, by some dramatic juncture, or by a variety of other means; and this is more important to the work's impact than is its form. While the form of the Classical work was a natural outcome of the material of which it was composed, a way of giving it logic and order and balance, Romantic artists tended to accept the form as an entity in itself and to fill out the traditional Classical patterns with ideas ever more arresting, attractive, and laden with emotion, or to vary them as the spirit moved.

The Classical age, then, was one – as we have seen – of orderliness, of serenity, taking its models from the ancient cultures of Greece and Rome; it is no coincidence that the plots of serious operas were taken from classical mythology and history, which stressed the virtues admired in the eighteenth century. That period was called the Age of Reason, or the Enlightenment. In *The Magic Flute*, the three temples that lead to a symbolic heaven are labeled "Wisdom", "Nature", and

68 Walpurgis Night: *scene from Delacroix's illustrated edition (1828) of Goethe's* Faust.

"Reason"; there is no worshiping Fantasy or Imagination. Yet even during the eighteenth century some disquieted figures had rebelled against the prevalence of the rational and the well-proportioned: this disquiet manifested itself in the German "Storm and Stress" movement, in England in "gothick" architecture which attempted to re-create medieval styles (and along with them a sense of mystery), and in all Europe in an interest in the Orient, with its fascinating remoteness.

By the turn of the century the lure of the Middle Ages, and things associated with that period, was rapidly gaining ground. New opera plots were often drawn from medieval history or legend, or from such works as the Waverley novels of Sir Walter Scott (1771–1832), which aimed to recapture an age of chivalry and high romance. Mysticism, the demonic, the supernatural: all these, which had no place in the rationalist schemes of the eighteenth century, began to reassert themselves as a part of human experience.

The most famous and most influential manifestation of these interests is in the *Faust* of the great German writer Johann Wolfgang von Goethe (1749–1832) – in Faust's compact with the devil in his search for immortality and for sensual experience with an idealized woman. Numerous composers wrote works around Faust, Mephistopheles, and Gretchen; some also treated the more philosophical second part of Goethe's great work. In the graphic arts similar interest in the dark, nightmarish side of human experience is seen in the works of such painters as Francisco Goya (1746–1828), John Henry Fuseli (1741–1825), and William Blake (1757–1827); in music, examples of their strong expression are Schubert's song *The Erlking*, where a boy's soul is snatched by an evil spirit during a ride through a forest, or the Wolf's Glen scene in Weber's opera *Der Freischütz*, where magic bullets are cast with the devil's aid, or the Witches' Sabbath in Berlioz's *Fantastic Symphony* with its shrieks and its ominous sounding of the "Dies irae" ("Day of Wrath") plainsong.

Religion and politics, too, form a part of this picture. Catholicism, as the faith of the Middle Ages, underwent a new revival: its music, departing from the decorative Rococo that in effect Mozart and Haydn had been content with, acquired a new solemnity and plainness – the restoration of polyphony and plainsong were widely encouraged, and Renaissance church music began to be seriously studied and even used as a model.

Social change

Socially, this was a time of rapid change. With the American Revolution of 1776, a colony for the first time proclaimed its independence from its rulers: this was the first of a series of momentous events. The French Revolution, in 1789, had seen the near-extinction of the ruling classes in France; all the other crowned and noble heads of Europe were trembling. The Napoleonic Wars which raged from the late 1790s to 1815 created confusion and poverty; meanwhile, the Industrial Revolution was fast gaining momentum and the shape of society was undergoing fundamental and permanent changes, with great cities growing up (often with appalling living and working conditions) and the countryside becoming depopulated. Political or social oppression became a subject susceptible to treatment through artistic protest; obvious examples are found in the poetry of William Blake (who writes of the "dark, satanic mills") and in his paintings of industrial desolation.

In music, as we have seen, Beethoven could hymn the brotherhood of man in his Choral Symphony (a type of work which owes its existence to the massive choral "revolutionary hymns" created in the wake of the French Revolution), and for his only opera could set a plot concerned with freeing an innocent man from politically motivated oppression. Other composers had earlier set the *Fidelio* story, which is only one (if the greatest by far) in the tradition of "rescue operas", coming in the first place from France but traversing much of Europe – except where a conservative monarchy could still suppress such subversive ideas. Other political themes, often of an epic, historical character involving the oppression of national or religious groups, gained favor, especially in France, where massive spectacles, made possible by advances in theater design and lighting, were especially admired.

Escapism and Nature

Another aspect of Romanticism involved the use of art to escape from the increasingly unpleasant realities of life. One of the precursors of Romanticism, the German writer W. H. Wackenroder (1773–98), talked of the "wonder of music" as the "land of faith . . . where all our doubts and sufferings are lost in a resounding ocean". Nature offered one escape route. The eighteenth century had paid homage to Nature, but chiefly packaged into beautifully laid-out landscapes, artificially created from a crude and imperfect original, where idyllic scenes could be relished. Raw Nature was admired rather less: when Dr Samuel Johnson traveled to the Scottish Highlands he drew the carriage blinds, as he was disturbed by the prospect of the hills. The nineteenth century however saw Nature as a huge and mysterious force, beside which people shrank into insignificance. The paintings of Caspar David Friedrich (1774–1840) illustrate powerfully the impact of Nature, often portraying a solitary figure standing in awe or fascination at some wild scene of

69 Winter: *oil painting, 1808, by Caspar David Friedrich (original destroyed). Neue Pinakothek, Munich.*

mists, rocks, turbulent waves, or gaunt trees (which sometimes look as if struck by lightning). A musical analogy might be the storm movement in Beethoven's *Pastoral Symphony* or the country scene in Berlioz's *Fantastic Symphony*. The poetry of William Wordsworth (1770–1850) also talks of Nature and its ability to exalt or fill with awe.

Haydn and Mozart did not, of course, portray Nature in their music (except in Haydn's direct imitations, in his late oratorios, *The Creation* and *The Seasons*). Beethoven did; so did Mendelssohn, for example in his *Hebrides* Overture (where the music unmistakably symbolizes the waves of the Scottish coastal waters) and in his *Italian Symphony*; so did Schumann in his *Spring Symphony* and Liszt in his symphonic poems, to cite only a few. Here we find music used to draw pictures, sometimes to depict events. Or, it may be argued, music does not draw or depict but conveys the same emotion as do the pictures or the events themselves. The same kinds of analogy came to exist between music and the literary arts; no longer is a song simply a poem set to music but, in the hands of a Schubert or a Schumann, a distillation of the emotion referred to in the words. This alliance between the arts is particularly characteristic of the Romantic era, and it found its ultimate expression in the "total art work" (*Gesamtkunstwerk*) conception of Richard Wagner's mature operas, in which music, words, scenery, and stage movement combine in a single whole – or at least that was Wagner's objective. This represented the highest ideal of the Romantics, the all-embracing, transcendent artistic experience: its culmination in acts of love and of death, in *Tristan und Isolde*, carries Romanticism to its farthest point, indeed to the farthest points of life itself.

Yet the huge scale of Wagner's operas represents only one side of the Romantic spirit. In the early days of Romanticism, especially, the emphasis is not on the large but the small. Beethoven, the last great Classicist and a "pre-Romantic", wrote large-scale music; but the next generation were essentially miniaturists. Schubert's spirit is conveyed more essentially in his short songs or piano pieces rather than his large works. The greatest poet of the piano, Fryderyk Chopin, created miniatures – waltzes, Polish mazurkas, atmospheric night-pieces that he called "nocturnes" – which catch a fleeting series of emotions in a brief time-span. The nature of the music written by these composers, and others, rules out extended works; the expression of the moment is too pungent to be viable in an extended structure.

The music of Chopin and Liszt raises another issue central to the Romantics: technical virtuosity. Virtuosos had of course long been admired; Bach and Mozart, and many earlier players, were performers of dazzling skill. But now virtuosity attained new dimensions; what in an earlier age might have been thought tasteless and lacking in musical substance became attractive to audiences. Players technically as accomplished as Chopin or Liszt, but not their equals as musicians, toured Europe and America and filled the concert halls. One of particular fame was the Italian violinist, Nicolò Paganini (1782–1840), whose cadaverous appearance and phenomenal technical skill led those who heard him to suspect some sinister alliance with the devil. Audiences were larger, and drawn from a wider social range, than those of the eighteenth century; larger concert rooms – necessary economically – had to accommodate performances less intimate, less refined, more arresting, and more immediately appealing than those that had satisfied the previous generation, when art was the preserve of the connoisseur.

Naturally enough, it is to this age that the concept of "artist as hero" belongs. We have already seen the beginnings of it with Beethoven. While a man like Haydn was content to accept the status of a servant – he would not have thought of questioning it – the Romantic composer took a quite different view. The composer was not simply supplying a commodity to an employer but was a creator of something valuable and permanent. Haydn would not have expected his symphonies to outlive him; he wrote them by the hundred and regarded them as expendable, to be surpassed and superseded by those of the next generation. During Haydn's lifetime, however, the idea of preserving and even performing the music of the past began to gain currency, and to Beethoven and the Romantics composition was for posterity.

The creative artist was now the visionary – compare any eighteenth-century composer portrait with the famous one of Chopin by Eugène Delacroix (1798–1863) (**Plate 13**), expressing his agonized, Romantic genius – and the equal of anyone. When, in the middle of the nineteenth century, Liszt went to Weimar, in central Germany, to work for the duke, it was as a friend and an honored guest, not as an employee to write music to order. In this new context, it is not surprising that the Romantic composer set a great deal more store than the Classical on originality. The Classicist was generally content to conform with existing standards and models; the Romantic was always under pressure to assert individuality.

2 *The Genres of Romantic Music*

As we look in more detail at the main Romantic composers and their music, we shall see the emergence of a series of patterns. Among the musical genres they used, most come from the Classical era, now adapted to meet different needs.

SYMPHONY

The days when composers wrote 100, or even 20, symphonies had passed with the eighteenth century. The weightier works of the nineteenth were not of a kind that could be turned out by the dozen; each was an individual utterance, not an evening's disposable entertainment for a princeling, as Haydn's were. Beethoven's nine came to be regarded as a magic number that no one dared exceed. Schubert completed seven; Schumann wrote four, one of them called the "Spring", another the "Rhenish", because of their sources of inspiration. Beethoven's "Pastoral" had already suggested that a symphony could be other than "absolute music" – that is, music without reference to anything outside itself. Berlioz, in France, went further; his best-known symphony, the *Fantastic*, is sub-titled "Episodes in the Life of an Artist" and has a theme running through its five movements that represents his beloved and what happens to her. Traditional symphonies were still composed in the nineteenth century, by Brahms. Almost all are in four movements.

SYMPHONIC POEM

The line to which Berlioz's *Fantastic Symphony* belongs turned into a separate outgrowth, the *symphonic poem* or tone-poem. Liszt wrote several such pieces, expressing in most of them his reactions to literary or artistic works: *Hamlet*, for example, is an evocation of the Shakespeare character, though one passage describes Ophelia; his *Faust Symphony* is sub-titled "three character studies after Goethe". Several Czech and Russian composers towards the end of the century were also to use the genre, for example Smetana, who depicted in music scenes and legends of his native Bohemia, and Mussorgsky, in his ghostly *St John's Night on the Bare Mountain*; its final leading exponent was Richard Strauss, who wrote several of a vivid kind, sometimes telling stories in music that can be brilliantly descriptive.

OVERTURE

Closely related to the symphonic poem in the nineteenth century is the *overture*, which after about 1800 composers tended to write for concert use. These are usually like miniature symphonic poems. A good example is Mendelssohn's over-ture to *A Midsummer Night's Dream*, which clearly depicts elements in Shakespeare's play but was not designed to be performed with it. His *Hebrides* overture was

70 *The Salle Pleyel, Paris, where Chopin often played: engraving from* L'illustration *(9 June 1855).*

inspired by the island scenery off the west coast of Scotland. Many other composers, like Brahms (*Tragic Overture*) and Tchaikovsky (*Romeo and Juliet*), have written concert overtures, usually in one movement (often in sonata form); these and overtures from operas are performed in the concert hall.

CONCERTO

With the Romantic era, the *concerto* became increasingly a vehicle for the virtuoso, in which a "heroic" soloist may battle, symbolically, against the world (the orchestra) – and, of course, triumph. This was foreshadowed in the piano concertos of Beethoven, but it is still more obvious in those of Liszt, Schumann, Brahms, and Tchaikovsky. The violin concerto flourished too, with such composers as Mendelssohn, Brahms, and Tchaikovsky again taking Beethoven's violin concerto as their starting-point in pitting the gentle and poetic solo voice against the orchestra. Almost all concertos retain the traditional three-movement form.

PIANO MUSIC

Piano music in the Romantic era moves away from the abstract sonata towards the genre piece (designed to capture a particular mood, emotion, or atmosphere) and the idealized dance. Schubert wrote several sonatas for the piano, and so did Chopin and Brahms. But Schubert also wrote pieces that he called "impromptu" or "moment musical". Mendelssohn called his pieces "Songs without Words". Schumann used literary titles or ones that made some allusion outside music for most of his – "Butterflies", for example, or "Carnival Jest in Vienna". Chopin wrote many in the dance forms of his native Poland, like the mazurka or polonaise, and he also used the waltz, the study (or *étude*: these are designed to highlight some aspect of piano technique), and the nocturne or night-piece, in which he created a dreamy, romantic atmosphere. Liszt covered everything: there are dances, abstract pieces, atmospheric ones, literary ones (based on Petrarch sonnets, for example), and a huge, one-movement sonata. Brahms, more austere and traditional, used titles like intermezzo or capriccio: he also wrote sonatas and large-scale sets of variations, in the Beethoven tradition.

Chamber music, moving out of the drawing-room and into the concert hall, changes its character radically. The accomplished amateur could no longer meet the composers' technical demands and even the string quartet, in the hands of Schubert, Mendelssohn, or Brahms, becomes more public a medium. The heavier textured genres like the string quintet and sextet, and those for strings and piano, naturally flourished, but they retained their abstract character as well as the four-movement form of the previous era.

CHAMBER MUSIC

Few major nineteenth-century composers wrote music for church use – a commentary on the church, society, and music of the time. But one ecclesiastical genre did come into some prominence, the *Requiem*, the Catholic Mass for the dead, which had a special appeal in the Romantic era. That Mozart had left a *Requiem* unfinished at his own death only added to the fascination. A highly dramatic view of death, typical of the nineteenth century, is shown in the colossal scale of Berlioz's *Requiem* and the passion and fire-and-brimstone of Verdi's; others of their contemporaries (Liszt, Dvořák) produced notable settings, as especially did Fauré, who wrote a touching, gentle work. Brahms's *German Requiem* is not a true Requiem but a setting of German biblical texts relating to death and consolation.

REQUIEM

Opera took markedly different directions in different countries during the nineteenth century. Germany moved into a central role, with Weber as the most important early Romantic composer; Wagner was at the climax of the era. In Wagner's large-scale works all the arts come together; his operas have a continuous texture, without the traditional breaks between aria (for expression of emotion) and recitative (for narrative or conversation). In Italy, the early part of the century was dominated by the comic genius of Rossini; later, Verdi, with his powerful handling of drama and his appealing use of the human voice, emerged as a figure comparable in stature with Wagner – and more widely admired because of the directness of his music.

OPERA

In all the rivalries that run through the history of opera, like that between Wagner and Verdi, there is an element of words vs. music, or dramatic integrity vs. music. It need not be a real conflict, as Mozart for one proved; but opera reformers like Gluck and Wagner have always wanted to get away from what has seemed to them its artificial aspects, with clearly defined arias in which musical considerations seem to override dramatic ones. But in fact any approach may succeed if executed with sufficient genius.

France, in the post-Revolution era, produced a type of "grand opera" on national, political, or religious themes; Rossini and Verdi contributed to this repertory, in French, and in some respects the greatest exponent of its spectacular aspects was the German composer Giacomo Meyerbeer. But the only native French-man of true importance was Berlioz. Later in the century the other, spoken-dialog tradition gave rise to Bizet's *Carmen* (perhaps the most popular opera ever) and also successful, somewhat sentimental works by Gounod and Massenet. A Russian school arose, too, producing the grandly epic works of Mussorgsky as well as the more conventionally Romantic operas of Tchaikovsky.

Italian opera was led into the twentieth century by Puccini, who added more naturalism and sentimentality to the Verdian tradition. Newer ideas came from France, with Debussy's sole but highly influential opera, *Pelléas et Mélisande*, a symbolist work in which the characters scarcely express their emotions but the orchestral music constantly hints at them. By contrast, the early operas of Richard Strauss favor a powerful, even violent, emotional expression.

OPERETTA

An important development in the later nineteenth century was the growth of *operetta* – light opera, intended for a large, less intellectual audience. With Johann Strauss in Vienna, Jacques Offenbach in Paris, and Arthur Sullivan in London (to name only three leading figures), this soon became a popular genre, treating amorous and sentimental topics, often with a touch of satire and parody. (There was a local counterpart in Spain and Latin America, the *zarzuela*.) It led to the musical comedy (or "musical"), which flourished chiefly on Broadway in New York and in the West End of London in its early days and became in the early twentieth century a vigorous expression of American popular culture (see **Part IX**).

SONG

71 *Bizet's* Carmen: *Agnes Baltsa and José Carreras, Metropolitan Opera, New York.*

The nineteenth century was a great age for *song*. With the great flowering of German literature in the Classical and Romantic eras, composers found high inspiration in poetry and created the genre known as the *Lied* (German for "song"; plural *Lieder*). There were parallels elsewhere, such as France (with the *mélodies* of Debussy and Fauré) and Russia (with Mussorgsky's songs in particular). The *Lied* tradition had its beginnings in the time of Mozart and Beethoven, but it was with Schubert that a new balance was found between words and music, a new absorption into the music of the words' meaning. Some of Schubert's songs, which number more than 600, are in sequences or cycles that relate a story – an adventure of the soul rather than the body. The tradition was continued by Schumann, Brahms, and Wolf, and on into the present century by Strauss and Mahler. The repertory created in the *Lied* tradition, like that of the Italian madrigal three centuries before, represents one of the richest products of human sensibility.

3 *Schubert*

If, as the saying goes, "those whom the gods love die young", Schubert was even more divinely beloved than Mozart; Mozart died at 35, Schubert at 31. Like the elder master, Schubert, with his prodigious natural gift and his wide range of feeling, seems to have reached even at that modest age a kind of maturity that escapes many who live far longer.

Franz Peter Schubert was a Viennese by birth, unlike the other three "Viennese Classicists" (Haydn, Mozart, and Beethoven); he is often counted as a fourth but he more properly belongs to the Romantic age. Schubert's parents moved to the capital, Vienna, from the nearby countryside. He was born in 1797. His father, a schoolmaster, taught him the violin, his eldest brother the piano, but he soon overtook them both. When he was 11 he became a choirboy in the imperial chapel, which involved attending a leading boarding school where music was important. Schubert soon became concertmaster of the orchestra and came under the tuition of the court music director, Antonio Salieri, a former colleague of Mozart's who had given lessons to the young Beethoven.

Schubert did well in all subjects, but in music he shone brilliantly. Already he was composing songs and instrumental pieces, including string quartets which he played with his father and brothers. He produced numerous composition exercises, and also his First Symphony and an attempt at an opera. Most important were his songs, which he poured out in abundance.

In 1815, Schubert became a schoolmaster. He continued to compose, and at great speed. That year saw the composition of almost 150 songs, as well as two symphonies, piano music, and other pieces. Several of the songs are to texts by Goethe, by the great classical poet Friedrich von Schiller (1759–1805), and by the pseudo-medieval Scottish poet known as Ossian whose mock-ancient tales of the romantic north fascinated musicians. One of the songs of 1815 was the Goethe setting *The Erlking*. Schubert composed it at great speed and his friends immediately gathered to hear it – which they did with astonishment and enthusiasm.

Schubert had always enjoyed music-making in the family home. Now, by 1816, he was building up a circle of friends who took part in "Schubertiads", evenings of performing Schubert's newest music. It was partly for these gatherings of middle-class, artistically aware, enthusiastic young people that Schubert composed. But gradually his reputation widened: a well-known opera baritone began to sing his songs, with the composer accompanying, in drawing-room recitals during 1817 and the next year one of his songs was published. In the summer of 1818 he gave up teaching and accepted a post as music master in the family of Count Johann Esterházy (relatives of Haydn's former patrons).

72 *Franz Schubert: pencil drawing by Moritz von Schwind (1804–71). Private collection.*

Franz Schubert — Life and Works

1797	born in Vienna, 31 January
1808	choirboy in the imperial chapel, Vienna
1810	studied with Antonio Salieri
1814	*Gretchen at the Spinning Wheel*
1815	schoolmaster; prolific output, especially of songs; *The Erlking*
1816	abandoned teaching; organized first 'Schubertiads', evenings with close friends to perform his music
1818	music master to the children of Count Johann Esterházy, Zseliz
1821	Vienna; reputation increased and circle of friends widened; *Erlking* published
1822	*Wanderer* Fantasia, 'Unfinished' Symphony
1823	first period of serious illness; *The Beautiful Maid of the Mill*
1824	Octet, *Death and the Maiden* Quartet, A minor Quartet
1825	'Schubertiads' resumed; 'Great C major' Symphony
1827	*Winter's Journey*; torchbearer at Beethoven's funeral
1828	three piano sonatas, string quintet; died in Vienna, 19 November

Songs song cycles – Die schöne Müllerin (The Beautiful Maid of the Mill, 1823), Winterreise (Winter's Journey, 1827), Schwanengesang (Swansong, 1828); *c* 600 others – Gretchen at the Spinning Wheel (1814), Heidenröslein (Little Rose on the Heath, 1815), The Erlking (1815), The Wanderer (1816), Death and the Maiden (1817), To Music (1817), The Trout (*c*1817), The Shepherd on the Rock (1828), with clarinet

Orchestral music symphonies – no. 5, B♭ (1816), no. 8, 'Unfinished', b (1822), no. 9, 'Great', C (*c*1825); overtures

Chamber music 15 string quartets – a (1824), 'Death and the Maiden', d (1824); String quintet, C (1828); Piano quintet, 'The Trout', A (1819); Octet for clarinet, bassoon, horn, 2 violins, viola, cello, and double bass (1824); piano trios, violin sonatas and sonatinas

Piano music 21 sonatas – c (1828), A (1828), B♭ (1828); Wanderer Fantasia, C (1822); Moments musicaux (1828); impromptus, dances; piano duets – Sonata, 'Grand Duo', C (1824), Fantasia, f (1828), variations, marches

Operas Alfonso und Estrella (1822), Fierabras (1823)

Incidental music Rosamunde (1823)

Sacred choral music 7 Masses; *c*30 other works

Partsongs

Back in Vienna at the end of 1818, Schubert took rooms with his friend the poet Johann Mayrhofer. This began a period that was happy and productive and saw his reputation steadily increase. In the summer he was commissioned to write a piano quintet – the "Trout" quintet, of which the fourth movement is a happy set of variations on a song he had written the previous year.

Schubert's circle of friends now came to include poets, court officials, singers, and the painter Moritz von Schwind, who left us a famous depiction of a Schubertiad (see **fig. 73**). Some of Schubert's friends got together to have *The Erlking* and others of his songs published; curiously, the Viennese publishers were slow to take up Schubert's music, probably because he had no real reputation as a concert performer. In late 1821 he worked on an opera, *Alfonso und Estrella*, which was unperformed during his lifetime.

The great outpouring of songs of 1815, 1816, and 1817 had now slowed to a trickle. Only about 15 date from 1818; in 1819 he wrote about double that number, and each of the next three years saw the composition of around 15 to 20. He was now concentrating on instrumental music and from this period dates the Unfinished Symphony. Schubert started to sketch a third movement for it, but got no further. We do not know why he did not finish what was potentially so great a work; perhaps he put it aside because he had no need of a symphony at that moment, then later could not recapture its expressive world. In fact, he probably gave the manuscript to his friends the Hüttenbrenner brothers in 1823 (possibly to discharge some sort of obligation to them) – it remained in Anselm Hüttenbrenner's possession until 1865 and had its first hearing 37 years after Schubert's death. He never heard it himself.

There may be other, more tragic factors, for at the end of 1822 a catastrophe occurred in Schubert's life. He contracted syphilis. For the rest of his life he suffered uncomfortable and often distressing symptoms. The disease moved fast, and it was of this (not typhus or typhoid fever, as some books say) that he died. The compositions of his remaining years, 1823–8, have to be seen in the light of his

Maturity

73 Schubert evening at the home of Joseph von Spaun: *sepia drawing by Moritz von Schwind (1804–71). Historisches Museum der Stadt Wien. Schubert is at the piano, with the singer Vogl on his right, and von Spaun on his left.*

awareness of his illness and of his suffering, and it may be that it was some mental association between the composition of the Unfinished Symphony and the contraction of this illness that made it impossible for a man of such sensitive temperament to return to the work.

The year 1823 began with Schubert's return to the family home. The *Wanderer Fantasia* was published early in the year, and Schubert sold several collections of songs to Viennese publishing firms; his reputation was now sufficient to attract publishers' interest. He turned again to dramatic music, writing a short operetta and a more ambitious serious opera, *Fierabras* (both remained unheard, again, until after his death).

During the fall he was ill again but able to work, and the chief product of the late part of the year was the song cycle *Die schöne Müllerin* ("The Beautiful Maid of the Mill"). The choice of topic, with its resignation and bitterness, seems appropriate to Schubert's state of mind, though this kind of expression – love and despair, mirrored through Nature – is typical of early Romantic art. The next year was virtually blank as far as song is concerned, but it saw Schubert return to chamber music after a gap of several years.

For the spring and summer of 1824 Schubert went again to the Esterházy family in Hungary. His circle of friends in Vienna had dwindled, and for more than one reason he was inclined to sigh for happier, more innocent days. Back in Vienna, he went early in 1825 to live near to Schwind, now his closest friend; a new group formed, and Schubertiads resumed. Meanwhile, more of his music was being performed elsewhere and more was reaching print.

Schubert spent much of the 1825 summer in Upper Austria. It was probably at this time that he composed his last and greatest symphony, known as the "Great C major". It is another work that Schubert never heard. Probably he had intended it for the Vienna Philharmonic Society, but it lay unknown in the possession of his brother Ferdinand until 1837, when Schumann found it; the first performance, in which passages were omitted because of the work's length, was conducted by Mendelssohn two years later.

Schubert was back in Vienna by October 1825. More publications appeared, particularly of piano music, in 1826, and his name was gradually becoming better known – though his application for a post in the emperor's musical establishment was turned down. It was not a prolific time for composition, but he wrote nearly 20 songs and a fine string quartet; there is almost a sense of personal pain and anger behind the remarkable, deeply original music of this work.

A similar pain runs through Schubert's main composition of 1827, the song cycle *Winterreise* ("Winter's Journey"). It is not surprising that Schubert's friends were disturbed at the gloom and desolation of this work; they feared for his state of mind – it is hard to imagine anyone's composing such music unless it arose from personal experience of the emotions depicted.

Although his illness continued to trouble him a good deal, composition continued, sometimes at a rapid pace. To late 1827 and early 1828 belong the two fine piano trios and several short, attractive piano pieces, published under the titles

Impromptu and *Moment musical*. Schubert must have been heartened when, in March, a concert exclusively of his music – the only one he gave – took place in an inn owned by the Philharmonic Society and brought him some useful income. His publishing plans went forward. He composed a new Mass and a group of songs (later to be gathered together under the title "Swansong"); he also worked on a new symphony. In September he moved to lodgings with his brother, and within a few weeks produced four major instrumental works – three piano sonatas and a string quintet.

Schubert's piano music achieved a climax of greatness in these last three sonatas of the late summer of 1828. The Piano Sonata in B♭ of September 1828, the last and grandest of these three, shows a powerful and spacious structure. It is not comparable with Beethoven's partly because Schubert's objectives were quite different from the elder composer's. His gifts, his musical personality, were of another kind – gentler, more lyrical, more concerned with harmonic effect and the quality of piano texture. His chamber music too reached new heights with the String Quintet in C, written at much the same time, a work dark in mood.

There was reason for darkness, and Schubert probably knew it. He went for a brief walking tour in October 1828, about the time he was working on the quintet, but was weak and exhausted. Curiously, he arranged to take counterpoint lessons from a well-known Viennese music theorist during November, and even wrote some exercises. It seems that he never took the lessons; during November he was increasingly weak, often unable to eat, barely able to correct the proofs of the second part of *Winterreise*. Schubert's own wintry journey was ending: he died on 19 November 1828. The poet Grillparzer's famous epitaph – "The Art of Music here entombs a rich possession but even finer hopes" – is appropriate enough for a genius who died at 31; but it is typical of its times in failing to recognize that this man's genius did in fact reach full maturity, and that the legacy of his last few years places him among the very greatest of masters.

MUSIC

The songs

Schubert wrote more than 600 songs, and it is as a song composer that he was first famous and is still unrivaled. Written at 17, *Gretchen at the Spinning Wheel* already shows his special qualities – the ability to depict poetically in his music something non-musical, the spinning of the wheel, and to couple with this the expression of the words, so that the wheel itself seems to express Gretchen's unhappiness.

To the next year belong several Goethe songs, including the simple, folksong-like *Heidenröslein* (see **Listening Guide 30**). But the greatest song of 1815 was another Goethe setting, *The Erlking*. It is of the ballad type, telling a story rather than portraying a mood: a father is carrying his son on horseback through a forest, trying to ward off the evil spirit (the Elf King) who appears to the fevered child and eventually kills him. The pounding piano accompaniment symbolizes first the horse's hooves, but also the intense agitation felt by father and son, while the fiercely dissonant harmony depicts the tragic events and the boy's terror. Its vivid, passionate expression, its feeling of alarm and horror at the confrontation of the innocent child with death and the supernatural, sound a new note in music, different from anything of Mozart or even Beethoven. This is music of the new, Romantic age.

Schubert: *Heidenröslein* (1815)

A German folksong on the subject of the wild rose on the heath dates back to the sixteenth century. In 1771 two German poets rewrote its text, Johann Gottfried Herder and Johann Wolfgang von Goethe. It was Goethe's version of the words (with their sexual implications) that Schubert chose when, on 19 August 1815, he wrote five songs – all to Goethe poems.

The style of Schubert's setting is simple, appropriate to words of folk origins; and in fact a variant of Schubert's melody, as arranged by a slightly later composer, is still sung as a folksong in Germany. Schubert's setting was published in 1821. (For the song melody, see p. 23.) It is in three verses, with identical music; often Schubert modified his music for a final verse, where there might be an emotional twist, but here the effect is made by irony.

The first two lines remain in the home key, G; the third moves towards the dominant, D, with an interrupted cadence at the end of the fourth and a perfect cadence to end the fifth. The refrain carries the music back to the home key of G.

 Listening Outline

Time

0.00 Sah ein Knab ein Röslein stehn,
Röslein auf der Heiden,
War so jung und morgenschön,
Lief er schnell, es nah zu sehn,
Sah's mit vielen Freuden.
  Röslein, Röslein, Röslein rot,
  Röslein auf der Heiden.

A boy saw a wild rose growing on the heath; it was so young and morning-fresh that he ran quickly to it, with great delight. Wild red rose on the heath.

0.34 Knabe sprach: Ich breche dich,
Röslein auf der Heiden!
Röslein sprach: Ich steche dich,
Dass du ewig denkst an mich,
Und ich will's nicht leiden.
  Röslein, *etc.*

The boy said, 'I shall pluck you, wild rose on the heath!' The wild rose said, 'I shall prick you so that you will never forget me, and I shall not permit it'. Wild red rose *etc.*

1.09 Und der wilde knabe brach
's Röslein auf der Heiden;
Röslein wehrte sich und stach,
Half ihm doch kein Weh und Ach,
musst es eben leiden.
  Röslein, *etc.*

And the wilful boy picked the wild rose on the heath; the wild rose resisted and pricked him, but her cries were in vain and she had to suffer. Wild red rose, *etc.*

1.50 (end)

1816 was another amazingly prolific year, again with song at the forefront of his output; so was 1817, with a sudden burst of interest in the piano sonata and many songs. Among these are three favorites: the gently grave *To Music*, a setting of words by Schubert's friend Franz von Schober in praise of the art of music, lovingly and subtly composed in such a way that the "art of music" – a graceful melody and some characteristically expressive harmony – makes the point on its own behalf; the somber *Death and the Maiden*, akin in topic to *The Erlking* but making its effect more simply and darkly as Death invites the Maiden to sleep in his arms; and *The Trout*, where, against a lyrical voice melody, a piano figure represents the glittering fish darting in the stream.

The Trout uses one of Schubert's typical methods in making its point. It is a "modified strophic" song (a strophic one being in several verses to the same music). Schubert often set out as if to write a simple strophic one, then, coming to its emotional climax in the final verse, changed the music to arrest to listener's attention by its unexpectedness and to color the crucial words more sharply. The potential of a verse for this treatment was one of the factors that dictated Schubert's choice of poetry. He read a great deal, seeking suitable material; he set many fine poets, but also some indifferent ones, for a good song – as he proved – can be made out of quite ordinary verse if its images and structure lend themselves to musical treatment.

Two works from the end of 1822 show that Schubert was now putting more of his personality and intellectual and emotional concentration into instrumental music: the *Wanderer* Fantasia for piano and the Unfinished Symphony. Schubert already had behind him about a dozen piano sonatas, numerous dances, and other shorter pieces, as well as piano duets (well suited to his convivial musical evenings). This Fantasia however attempts something that composers had scarcely done before, nor even thought of the need or desirability for doing. Virtually the whole four-movement work is organized around the same theme, stated emphatically at the opening. The slow movement, which gives the work its name, is based on a song, *The Wanderer* (1816). But even this seems to be based on the same theme, or at least the same rhythm. The scherzo is more distantly derived from it, but the finale sounds almost like a fugal continuation of the first movement. This transformation of themes, where the same musical idea is made to acquire a range of different expressive senses, was later to be pursued by such men as Liszt, Berlioz, and Wagner. Schubert's idea was chiefly to find a way of bringing unity to an extended work.

The later works

The other remarkable work of late 1822 was the famous Unfinished Symphony. It is unlike any other earlier symphony in its profoundly poetic manner, its mystery, and its pathos, as the dark-colored opening shows with its hushed cellos and basses, then throbbing strings over which oboe and clarinet in a strange unison float their theme (see **Listening Guide 31**). Later there is symphonic "argument" of a more usual, Beethovenian kind, but the atmosphere of the work is that of its opening measures, and the slow movement that follows does nothing to contradict that.

In 1823, as we have seen, came the song cycle *Die schöne Müllerin*. This collection of 20 songs tells a story in which the poet (and thus the singer) is protagonist: he arrives at the mill, falls in love with the mill-girl, enjoys happiness with her, feels anger and jealousy when she turns to another man, and dies. The bubbling of the brook is heard in the piano accompaniment to many of the songs and there is much Nature imagery in the music, designed to reflect the emotion expressed in the words.

Schubert's last and greatest symphony, known as the "Great C major" (usually called no. 9, sometimes no. 7; counting only the complete symphonies and the Unfinished, it should really be no. 8), probably from 1825, is on a large scale; all its

Schubert: Symphony no. 8 in b, Unfinished (1822), first movement

No one knows why Schubert's 'Unfinished Symphony' is unfinished. He began writing it in the fall of 1822 and two movements were complete by the end of October. He started writing a third movement, a scherzo, but although he sketched about three-quarters of it fairly fully the relatively routine work of orchestrating it remained to be done; he apparently never touched the work again. Several explanations have been offered: that he lost interest in the work; that he could not manage to write a conclusion worthy of the first two movements; that he forgot about it; that he noticed marked resemblances to one of Beethoven's symphonies and did not want to be charged with borrowing another composer's ideas; and that it had melancholy associations for him that he could not bear to recall (it was written soon after his syphilis was diagnosed). None of these sounds very convincing.

The fact remains that Schubert set it aside and made no effort to secure a performance of it (as he did for the next symphony he was to write). He did however send the score to his old friend Anselm Hüttenbrenner, in Graz, where he was connected with the Styrian Music Association; that society had offered Schubert honorary membership, but it is unlikely that he would have responded by sending them an incomplete work. Hüttenbrenner made an arrangement of the music for two pianos, but kept the score to himself; it was not until 1860 that attention was drawn to it, and not until 1865 that it had its first performance. Schubert had been dead for 37 years when what is probably his best-loved work was first heard.

 Listening Outline

First movement (Allegro moderato), 3/4, b; sonata form
2 flutes, 2 oboes, 2 clarinets, 2 bassoons
2 horns, 2 trumpets, 3 trombones; timpani
1st and 2nd violins, violas, cellos, double basses

Time		
	exposition	
0.00 [3.24]	first group, b	consists of a combination of ideas (exx. 1, 2, 3) with similar features (note fig. *a*). A crescendo leads to a cadence in b (1.07 [4.31]) and a 4-m. link (horns, bassoons)
1.16 [4.40]	second group, G	cellos (later violins) play a lyrical theme (ex. 4) against a throbbing accompaniment (fig. *b*) with clarinets. This leads to a break (1.55 [5.19]) and dialog on fig. *c*, then a cadence in G
2.52 [6.16]	closing section, G	dialog on ex. 4
3.24	**exposition repeat**	(0.00–3.24 = 3.24–6.48)
6.56	**development**	ex. 1 provides main material and fig. *b* is also prominent; the music passes through e, b, c♯, e. A vigorous tutti (8.54) brings the section to a climax, in D (9.41), but the music quickly turns back to b
	recapitulation	
10.07	first group, b	begins with ex. 2 and ex. 3; adjusted to have cadence in f♯
11.15	second group, D	ex. 4, ending differently to bring music back to b
12.59	closing section	as before
13.29	**coda**	begins with ex. 1 (not heard in its original form since the opening); the music at first recalls the start of the development
14.54		(end)

ex. 1

ex. 2

ex. 3

ex. 4

ideas are extended and fully worked out. The Andante introduction, with its solitary horn melody, sounds a Romantic voice; a distant horn conjures up favorite Romantic images. But the main part of the movement is more Classical – much more so than the Unfinished – in its orderly statements and repetitions, and in the expressive blandness of the material itself, better designed for symphonic argument than most of Schubert's ideas. There are moments of Romantic mystery, too. In the first-movement exposition the music, where it might be expected to settle into the dominant key, G major, dips into remote E♭. The sound of soft trombones – instruments used mainly for their effectiveness in loud music – playing a broad melody that gradually seems to guide the music back where it ought to be, is one of the most imaginative strokes in symphonic music. The rest of the symphony is on a correspondingly large scale.

The words of the second song cycle, *Winterreise*, which followed in 1827, are like those of *Die schöne Müllerin*, the work of Wilhelm Müller, whose flowing words, attractive imagery, and shapely structures made them ideal for Schubert. Again the poems tell, largely through analogies with Nature, of desolation and longing; sometimes they refer to rejection in love, to bitter loneliness, to happy memories that have grown sad in recollection, to solitude and misery in a world where everyone else is joyous, to aimless wandering through cold and dark, and ultimately to death. The music is austere; most of the songs are in minor keys, many are slow, and the old warmth and harmonic richness are rare.

The last flowering of chamber music saw the creation of three string quartets and two piano trios and, in 1828, the String Quintet in C. For this work Schubert specified an ensemble consisting of string quartet plus an extra cello; this allows for greater enrichment of the sound and for the possibility of a low-pitched bass line continuing even when the first cello is playing in its high, tenor register. The music is full of lyrical expansive melodies, subtle and emotionally suggestive turns of harmony, and original effects of musical texture. The equally remarkable slow movement contains perhaps the stormiest, blackest music that Schubert wrote, full of angry, dissonant harmonies, supported by tremolos and dislocated rhythms, and in the distant key of F minor. Then, in the middle of the hectic Scherzo comes a trio section which, instead of the conventional lyrical contrast, offers slow, bleak music, again in remote F minor. The finale is outwardly happier, but (typically) makes much of major/minor alternation, tingeing the music with darkness.

4 *Berlioz*

LIFE

Among the early Romantic masters the solitary Frenchman Hector Berlioz stands a little apart. He was no pianist, and no purveyor of piano miniatures, but a man with flair, grand ideas, and a formidable sense of drama.

Berlioz was born in 1803, not far from Lyons. His father expected his son to follow him into the medical profession. But Hector, who played the flute and the guitar, and had jotted down a few compositions in his youth – a Paris publisher had even printed a song he had sent in – was bent on a musical career. In 1821 he went to medical school in Paris, but found dissections and operations hateful. More to his taste were the opera performances he heard, especially those of works by Gluck. He continued medical studies up to 1824, half-heartedly, but also studied music and wrote an opera, a Mass, and other works. The Mass, after an abortive attempt that only reinforced his father's opposition to a musical career, was performed, and he was encouraged to pursue music. He did. He scraped a living by writing, singing, teaching, and anything else he could manage. He enrolled in 1826 at the Paris Conservatoire, and was now finding his voice as a composer – from this period an overture and part of an opera survive.

In 1827 Berlioz went to the theater to hear *Hamlet*, in English (which he did not understand); he was profoundly impressed by the play – Shakespeare was to be a lifelong influence – and still more by the Irish actress playing Ophelia, Harriet Smithson, for whom he conceived a romantic passion. He pursued her unremittingly, and the unruly love he felt for her stands behind his first great work, the *Symphonie fantastique* ("Fantastic Symphony"). In fact, a rather more immediate love affair with a lively young piano teacher, Camille Moke, whom he nearly married, provided him with the perspective on his passion for Harriet Smithson which he needed to be able to write the symphony. Although Beethoven, whom Berlioz worshiped, was the model, little about the symphony is Beethovenian (see **Listening Guide 32**).

Shortly before the première of the *Fantastic Symphony*, Berlioz had been awarded the Prix de Rome, a scholarship to Rome for a Conservatoire student (he had

Hector Berlioz   Life and Works

1803	born in La Côte-St-André, Isère, 11 December
1821–4	medical student in Paris; composition lessons with Jean Le Sueur
1826	entered Paris Conservatoire; first noteworthy compositions
1827	saw *Hamlet* in Paris and developed passion for Shakespeare and Harriet Smithson, the actress who played Ophelia
1830	*Fantastic Symphony*
1831	to Rome after winning the Prix de Rome at the Conservatoire
1833	married Harriet Smithson
1834–40	period of greatest works, including *Requiem, Romeo and Juliet, Les nuits d'été*; active as a musical journalist
1841	beginning of decline in popularity in France
1842	first concert tour of Europe as a conductor
1844	separated from Harriet Smithson; beginning of increased concert-giving in Europe and of literary activity
1846	*The Damnation of Faust* performed in Paris and poorly received
1848	beginning of period of further tours and less concentrated composing
1852	Weimar with Liszt, who put on a Berlioz Festival
1854	married Marie Recio, with whom he had been for 12 years
1856–8	work on *The Trojans*
1863	second part of *The Trojans* performed in Paris with limited success
1862	*Beatrice and Benedict*
1864	health deteriorating
1869	died in Paris, 8 March

Operas Benvenuto Cellini (1838), Les troyens (1858), Béatrice et Bénédict (1862)

Orchestral symphonies – Symphonie fantastique (1830), Harold en Italie (1834), Roméo et Juliette (1839); Grande symphonie funèbre et triomphale (1840); overtures – Waverley (1828), Le roi Lear (1831); Le carnaval romain (1844)

Choral music Lélio (1832); Grande messe des morts (Requiem) (1837); La damnation de Faust (1846); Te Deum (1849); L'enfance du Christ (1854); motets

Vocal music (solo voice with orchestra) La mort de Cléopâtre (1829); Les nuits d'été (Summer Nights, 1841)

---

entered four times, had failed the previous year because his work was "too original", so wrote a conventional piece that the examiners would be sure to like). But he was unsettled in Rome and almost returned to Paris, particularly as he heard nothing from Camille, to whom he was betrothed; then he heard that she was to marry someone else, and set off to kill her, her fiancé, her mother, and himself – but thought better of it and went back. This inspired in him a sequel to the *Fantastic Symphony*, called *Lélio, or The Return to Life*; that work, and one song, were the sole products of 15 months in Italy during which he concentrated more on absorbing atmosphere than on work.

Back in Paris late in 1832, Berlioz gave a concert with the *Fantastic Symphony* and its new sequel; he arranged for Harriet Smithson to attend, and they were introduced. She could hardly fail to be impressed by the composer who had put his passion for her into this music; she reciprocated, and they were soon married – contrary to the advice of friends and both families. By about 1840 they had drifted apart. Meanwhile Berlioz was busy both with composition and, to earn a living, journalism; he was a brilliant, witty, opinionated, and colorful writer for the Parisian periodicals. Several important works belong to this period: the symphony *Harold in Italy*, based on Byron's epic poem *Childe Harold*, commissioned by the famous Italian virtuoso Paganini and including a solo viola part for him (1834); the opera *Benvenuto Cellini*, at first rejected but given at the Paris Opéra in 1838 – a highly original if patchy score, full of spirited ideas, which the orchestra and singers could barely cope with and which was taken off after a mere three performances;

74 A concert in the year 1846: *engraving by Cajetan after Geiger, based on Grandville's popular view of Berlioz's flamboyant conducting, with a vast orchestra and deafened audience.*

and the *Grande messe des morts* (or *Requiem*), written to a government commission for performance in the large Invalides church and performed in 1837.

From *Benvenuto Cellini* Berlioz extracted one of his finest concert pieces, the overture *Roman Carnival*. The *Grande symphonie funèbre et triomphale* ("Great Funereal and Triumphant Symphony"), commissioned by the government to commemorate the tenth anniversary of the 1830 revolution, represents Berlioz's ceremonial side; the solemn martial tone and the "funeral oration" for solo trombone are like nothing else in his output. Between these he wrote a "dramatic symphony" on the story of *Romeo and Juliet*; the Shakespeare play had always moved him intensely, especially because of its association with Harriet, and he treated it as a kind of choral symphony. Among the audience at the first performance, in 1839, was the young Richard Wagner, who was deeply impressed by the work and the artistic ideals behind it.

Berlioz had composed a number of concert overtures; most are brilliant, effective orchestral pieces, usually inspired by some literary work, for example Shakespeare's *King Lear*. Partly through these, his reputation had begun to travel abroad. In the early 1840s, he wanted to travel abroad himself, the more so as his marriage was showing signs of strain. His position in Parisian musical life was acknowledged, but he still felt cynical towards the conservative musical establishment. So in 1842 he embarked on the first of a series of concert journeys across Europe, taking with him a singer, Marie Recio; he and Harriet were to separate in 1844 and he married Marie ten years later, after Harriet's death.

Berlioz's early concert tours were to Germany, Belgium, and the French provinces. Later he went as far afield as Russia, and several times to London. He was better appreciated abroad; he was a celebrity and his new ideas were welcomed as they never had been in Paris. The point was driven home in 1846. He had composed a major new work based on Goethe's *Faust*, a "dramatic legend" called *La damnation de Faust*, for chorus, soloists, and orchestra. When he gave it in Paris in 1846 he was deeply hurt by the public indifference towards one of his most original and spectacular creations.

In 1848, the year that Europe (Paris included) was torn by revolution, Berlioz was in London, conducting operas and concerts of his own music. In 1852 he was in Weimar, where Liszt put on a revised version of his *Benvenuto Cellini* and a Berlioz festival; the two composers exchanged dedications of their Faust works. *Cellini* failed in London the next year, but Berlioz had the satisfaction of conducting Beethoven's Choral Symphony and of meeting Wagner. In 1854 two very different works of a religious character were performed: his *Te Deum*, a ceremonial piece in the manner of the *Grande messe des morts*, full of grand effects (some derived from the use of a children's choir of 600), and the gentle and charming oratorio *The Childhood of Christ*.

As Berlioz grew older, the travels diminished. He continued to write about music – memoirs, travel tales, and anecdotes as well as criticism and textbooks. Opera remained important to him, as a world he had never conquered yet vital to him because of his veneration of Gluck. His greatest work is his operatic epic *The Trojans*,

Berlioz: *Symphonie fantastique* ('Fantastic Symphony') (1830), first movement

In 1827, Berlioz went to the theater to see Shakespeare's *Hamlet*. He later called that evening 'the supreme drama of his life'. Shakespeare, he wrote, struck him like a thunderbolt; he recognized 'the meaning of grandeur, beauty, dramatic truth'. He did not even understand English, in which the play was given. But he did understand the acting of Harriet Smithson, playing Ophelia, and shedding real tears in the mad scene. He fell in love not only with Shakespeare but also with her.

His 'overwhelming passion' for the Irish actress continued, and reached fever point in 1829, when she was again in Paris – although she refused to respond to his letters. Early in 1830 he decided to write a 'fantasy' symphony which would embody his passionate feelings, expressing them and allowing them wider imaginative scope by setting the 'program' of the work within a series of visions or dreams induced by opium. He wrote notes on the work, to be distributed to the audience at performances: a young musician of high sensibility and rich imagination – Berlioz himself, of course – in despair because of hopeless love, had drugged himself; his sensations, feelings, and memories are transformed into musical ideas, and the beloved herself appears as a recurring melody, a 'fixed idea' (*idée fixe*), which haunts him. The melody appears in many different forms according to the character of his vision.

In the first of the five movements, called 'Reveries, Passions', he recalls the weariness of the soul, the dark melancholy, and the aimless joys of the time before he met his beloved; the volcanic love with which she inspired him, his delirious suffering, his return to tenderness, his religious consolations.

In the second movement he finds his beloved at a ball; in the third he is in the countryside when thoughts of her fill him with premonitions. In the fourth, a March to the Scaffold, he dreams that he has killed her and is executed; and in the last he is at a witches' sabbath, a grotesque black celebration with monsters and specters – to which the beloved now comes, her melody trivial and distorted, to join the diabolic orgy.

In a Romantic, programmatic work, one should not expect to find the standard forms used in orthodox fashion; the first movement here follows a sonata-form outline, but with unusual features.

 Listening Outline . . . .

First movement (Largo), 4/4, c – **(Allegro)**, 4/4, C; free sonata form
2 flutes, 2 oboes, 2 clarinets, 2 bassoons
2 horns, 2 trumpets, 2 trombones; timpani
1st and 2nd violins, violas, cellos, double basses

Time		
0.00	**introduction,** c	2 mm. on winds introduce an idea on violins, its hesitant character suggesting the 'weariness of soul' of Berlioz's description, while the faster violin music suggests the aimless joys; the slower music returns with added figuration for flute and clarinet (2.22), and then a horn melody is heard (4.14)
5.23 [6.57]	**exposition** first group, C	the music explodes in C (5.15), and soon the beloved's theme (ex. 1) is heard, on violins and flute. A passage marked 'con fuoco' (with fire) (6.03 [7.37]), with violins swooping up and down – his 'volcanic love' – as the music rapidly modulates

6.41 [8.14]	second group, G	the main theme here, ex. 2, begins similarly to ex. 1 but is interrupted (fig. *b*)
6.57	**exposition repeat**	(5.23–6.57 = 6.57–8.28)
8.28	**development**	ex. 1 opening (fig. *a*) in the bass strings; the four-note fig. *a* persists. Fig. *b* introduces a new section (8.51) with chromatic scales, leading to a climax and a 3 mm. silence (9.23); then the opening two notes of ex. 1 are repeatedly heard, introducing ex. 1 (flute, clarinet, bassoon) in G. A brief stormy section follows; fig. *b* is briefly treated in counterpoint (10.44); and a quieter, slower section heralds a long crescendo, with the opening of ex. 1 many times repeated in the strings against an oboe melody (11.42)
12.34	**recapitulation,** C	ex. 1 at last reappears in the home key, *fortissimo*; at the end of this exultant tutti it is heard more gently on woodwinds (13.11). There is no return of ex. 2; the music slows – 'return to tenderness' – and the series of soft chords ending the movement represent the 'religious consolation'
15.15		(end)

ex. 1

ex. 2

written in 1856–8. It was intended for the Paris Lyric Theater (where he conducted Gluck's *Orfeo* in 1859); that theater refused it, and the Opéra took it on; then the Opéra changed their minds and it was restored to the Lyric. Next it was found too long, and only the last three acts ("The Trojans at Carthage") were given; the first part ("The Fall of Troy") was never staged in Berlioz's lifetime. The two parts were, astonishingly, given simultaneously in two different halls in 1879, then on successive evenings in 1890. The work was not staged whole until 1957, in London.

In the 1860s Berlioz suffered from illness and was much depressed by deaths in his family – Harriet had died in 1854, Marie in 1862. He struck up a curious friendship at this time with a woman, by then an elderly widow, with whom he had been infatuated as a boy of 12. His Romantic quest for the unattainable was in a sense satisfied. In 1866–67 he undertook some final tours – to Vienna and (too arduous for him) Russia; he came home weakened, and in 1869 he died. No one did more than this most visionary of the Romantics to widen the scope of musical expression, equally in its means and in its wider objectives.

Berlioz was an arch-Romantic. Much of his inspiration was literary, from Shake-speare, Goethe, and Virgil in particular. He took little notice of the conventional musical forms of his day, creating his own to accommodate his ideas. For example, his treatment of *Romeo and Juliet* is in the form of a symphony, or symphonic poem, with chorus, made up of selected episodes from the play, interspersed with instrumental pieces to represent its atmosphere. His handling of *Faust*, too, is unconventional. *La damnation de Faust* has been given as an opera, but the setting is episodic as Berlioz provided music only for the parts of the story that specially inspired him. Among them are vivid crowd scenes, passionate love music for Marguerite, and a violent representation of Faust's Ride to the Abyss with Mephistopheles – we hear the pounding of horses' hooves, the prayers of peasants, monsters wailing and shrieking, and finally a "pandemonium scene" for the inhabitants of hell. His music is filled with images of Nature, of the macabre and the supernatural, of death and redemption, and of love, both idealized and intensely erotic.

Berlioz was not a pianist, and he never acquired the habits of mind that some of his contemporaries, such as Chopin and Schumann, developed from thinking at the piano; his harmonic style is less orderly, less conventional than theirs. He had an astonishing ear for the orchestra and tried all kinds of instrumental combinations in his overtures and his symphonies, to original, sometimes highly refined, and often intensely exciting effect. His sacred works too show this desire for experiment. The *Grande messe des morts* is on a huge scale. The French, at the time of the Revolution, had encouraged massive musical events to appeal to large audiences. Berlioz's work, in that tradition, calls for 16 drums and brass bands in the four corners of the church so that, in the movement dealing with the last trumpet, the listener hears music from all sides, sometimes in turn, sometimes all together. But the work is not mainly a noisy one; often it is stark and austere, with thin textures and plain, free-ranging counterpoint. In one movement the whole choir sings in unison on just two notes while around them the orchestra weaves an increasingly elaborate web.

Among Berlioz's orchestral works, the best known is the *Fantastic Symphony* (see **Listening Guide 32**), though his concert overtures, most of them inspired by literary works, are brilliant, short pieces, ideal to begin a symphony concert. He wrote three operas, of which *The Trojans* stands out for its classical grandeur and sense of tragic inevitability; it draws on the example of Gluck, but also on the newer tradition of French grand opera, with vast crowd scenes dealing with the fates of entire nations against which are set the loves and fears of individuals. Berlioz's opera, telling the story of Troy as related by Virgil, deals with the siege of the city and its fall to the Greeks, the escape of Aeneas to Carthage, and the doomed love between him and the Carthaginian queen, Dido. This noble work, which draws together many of the creative threads that run through Berlioz's life, embodies some of his grandest and noblest ideas, worked out on a huge scale; there is tragic irony in its failure to secure a performance in its creator's lifetime.

5 *Mendelssohn*

Felix Mendelssohn was born in 1809, in Hamburg, into a well-to-do upper-middle-class Jewish family (converted to Protestantism), with an established cultural and intellectual background. His grandfather, Moses Mendelssohn (1729–86), was an eminent philosopher and a literary man; his father was a banker. The family moved to Berlin, where he received a thorough education and his precocious musical gifts were encouraged. He wrote six "symphonies" for strings when he was 12 and a further seven over the next two years – works following the Classical style but with much spirit and individuality as well as great technical polish.

When Mendelssohn was only 12, he was introduced to Goethe, and a warm friendship developed. At 16 he was taken to Paris, where the senior Italian composer Luigi Cherubini (1760–1842), an opera composer much admired by Beethoven, encouraged him to follow a musical career. Few musicians up to this time had as full a grounding in literature and philosophy as did Mendelssohn. His father's house was the meeting-place of influential writers and thinkers. Lines from Goethe's *Faust* colored his Octet for strings, written when he was 17; the scherzo of this vividly and richly scored work, Mendelssohn's first to have a firm place in the repertory today and remarkable for its masterly construction, was inspired by a scene involving fairy spirits. More fairies, Shakespeare's from *A Midsummer Night's Dream*, affected another early work, his overture for the play (see **Listening Guide 33**).

Mendelssohn's chief teacher was the composer Carl Friedrich Zelter, director of the well-known Berlin choral society, the Singakademie. There Mendelssohn had come across choral music by J. S. Bach, which was unfamiliar – at this time performers preferred recent music and Bach's was largely forgotten. But Mendelssohn found a copy of the *St Matthew Passion* and, realizing its greatness, asked Zelter if he could perform it; Zelter agreed, and in 1829, just over a century after its première, the work was revived for the first time since Bach's own performances. This historic occasion initiated the long-term revival of Bach's choral works.

Mendelssohn's travels had been mainly in Germany. Now he went further afield; first to London, where he was particularly well received, and on to Scotland, where he carefully noted his impressions (and made many attractive and accomplished drawings); then, in 1830, to Italy, including Venice, Rome, and Naples, where again he stored his impressions. These journeys provided him with material for some of his finest works. The Scottish trip suggested to him musical ideas from which he composed a symphony and an overture.

In 1835 Mendelssohn became conductor of the orchestra of the Gewandhaus ("Cloth Hall") in Leipzig, a post he held for the rest of his life. He did much to raise the standard of the orchestra and improve its working conditions; he revived music by Bach and forgotten works by Mozart, he pressed the claims of Beethoven, still

Mendelssohn: Overture, *A Midsummer Night's Dream* (1826)

Mendelssohn was 17 when, in 1826, he wrote the overture *A Midsummer Night's Dream*; at the time, he was living in Berlin and a student at the university. It was not intended to serve as a preface to performances of the Shakespeare play; the word 'overture' means here simply a piece of music that the play had inspired. In fact, in some degree it represents Shakespeare's characters and his action. It is easy to suggest the significance attached to each of its themes: the opening chords surely stand for the evening in the wood, out of which the fairies – the more rapidly moving violin theme – so poetically emerge. The ceremonious tutti theme may seem to stand for Theseus's court, and the lyrical theme that ensues must be assigned to the young lovers. The one theme about which there can be no possible doubt is the next, which must represent the 'rustics' – its 'hee-haw'-like continuation unmistakably suggests Bottom in his 'translated' form, with an ass's head.

The music calls for the standard classical orchestra with the addition of an ophicleide, a bass instrument of the brass family with a raucous, rasping tone (at one point it seems to represent Bottom's intrusion into the fairy world when it appears against the tripping violin music). The ophicleide is now obsolete and a tuba is generally used for its music.

Much later in life, Mendelssohn was invited to write more music for *A Midsummer Night's Dream*. He responded with a group of pieces including an exquisite nocturne, a delicate scherzo, and a wedding march – the most famous of all wedding marches. These and the overture are occasionally used today with performances of the play.

 Listening Outline . . . .

Allegro di molto, 2/2, E; sonata form
2 flutes, 2 oboes, 2 clarinets, 2 bassoons
2 horns, 2 trumpets, 1 ophicleide; timpani
1st and 2nd violins, violas, cellos, double basses

Time		
	exposition	
0.00	first group, E	there are three main ideas: ex. 1, four chords on the winds; ex. 2, rapid, tripping violins (0.21); and ex. 3, a tutti theme (1.08). The continuation uses figures (*a*) from ex. 2
2.06	second group, B	first theme, begun by clarinet; ex. 4; taken over by violins and extended lyrically; second theme, tutti, ex. 5 (3.03) note the 'hee-haw', fig. *b*; the closing section (3.27) uses ex. 3
3.52	**development**	based on ex. 2 with interjections from winds; passes through many keys. A quiet, mysterious passage (4.51) leads to c♯ (5.24), with material from ex. 4
	recapitulation	
6.03	first group, E	exx. 1 and 2 only
7.07	second group, E	ex. 4 now begun by flute
9.34	**coda**	ex. 2; then wind chords, based on ex. 1, with softened version of ex. 3 (10.31); lastly the wind chords from the opening reappear
12.00		(end)

ex. 3

ex. 4

ex. 5

a "difficult" modern composer (he gave the Ninth Symphony, the Choral, six times), and he introduced music by Weber and Schubert, including the "Great C major" Symphony, of which he conducted the première in 1839. He gave new works by Schumann and directed "historical concerts", series which spanned from Bach to his own time.

In the early 1840s Mendelssohn spent some time in Berlin, at the request of the new Prussian king who wanted to reform the arts there; circumstances were difficult and he had mixed success, though it was for a Berlin performance that he supplemented his *Midsummer Night's Dream* overture with music for other scenes of the play, including the most famous wedding march ever written. Mendelssohn also made repeated journeys to England, where he was immensely popular – he was friendly with Queen Victoria and her German consort, Prince Albert, and much loved by the choral societies which had come to occupy a large place in English musical life. It was for one of these that he composed his oratorio *Elijah*, first performed in Birmingham in 1846.

In 1843 he founded in Leipzig what was to be the most famous of all the European music conservatories of the time; in the second half of the century it was the best place for musical study and attracted students from abroad, Britain, the USA, and northern Europe in particular.

246 THE ROMANTIC ERA

Felix Mendelssohn — Life and Works

1809	born in Hamburg, 3 February
1819	lessons with Carl Friedrich Zelter in Berlin
1820	prolific output of small-scale works
1821	taken by Zelter to Weimar to meet Goethe, with whom he developed a warm friendship
1822	Switzerland; began composing in larger forms, including string symphonies
1825	encouraged by Luigi Cherubini in Paris; Octet
1826	*A Midsummer Night's Dream* overture
1829	directed a performance in Berlin of Bach's *St Matthew Passion*, stimulating interest in Bach's music
1829	first of ten visits to London; toured Scotland, visiting Staffa and 'Fingal's Cave'
1830–31	Italy
1832	*Italian Symphony*
1833	inaugurated series of Handel oratorio performances in Düsseldorf, where he was appointed city music director
1835	conductor of the Leipzig Gewandhaus orchestra; introduced music by Weber and Schubert as well as 'historical concerts'
1836	*St Paul* performed at Lower Rhine Music festival, Düsseldorf
1837	married Cécile Jeanrenaud
1841	director of music section, Berlin Academy of Arts
1843	founded the Leipzig Conservatory
1844	Violin Concerto
1846	*Elijah*, first performed in Birmingham, England
1847	died in Leipzig, 4 November

Orchestral music symphonies – no. 3, 'Scottish' (1842), no. 4, 'Italian' (1833), no. 5, 'Reformation' (1832); overtures – A Midsummer Night's Dream (1826), Calm Sea and Prosperous Voyage (1828), The Hebrides [Fingal's Cave] (1830, rev. 1832), Ruy Blas (1839); piano concertos – no. 1, g (1831), no. 2, d (1837), Violin Concerto, e (1844); 12 string symphonies

Oratorios St Paul (1836), Elijah (1846)

Chamber music Octet (1825); 6 string quartets; 2 string quintets; piano quartets, cello sonatas, violin sonatas

Piano music Songs without Words, 8 vols. (1829–45); sonatas, variations

Vocal music cantatas, motets, anthems, psalms, songs, partsongs

Organ music preludes and fugues

Incidental music

In the mid-1840s Mendelssohn seemed to be at the highpoint of his career: in a secure and important post, admired and sought after by music-lovers across Europe, and happy in his family life (he had married, in 1837, and had five children). But the freshness of his youthful work had gone, and nothing had quite taken its place. In 1847 he heard of the death of his sister Fanny, who had always been particularly close to him. He was unwell that summer; in the fall he grew weak, and in November he died. It is tempting to offer a Romantic interpretation and see his death as an answer to the dilemma of a prodigious genius that never quite discovered the inner resources needed for its fulfillment.

Mendelssohn's musical talents developed early: possibly he excels even Mozart in his sheer inventiveness and technical command during his early years. Some of the works of his youth are among those with the most secure place in the repertory: the Octet for strings, exuberant and richly scored, and *A Midsummer Night's Dream* overture (see **Listening Guide 33**). His grasp of musical form is already clear in these early works; his approach was essentially classical and he never wrote an ill-proportioned piece of music.

Like many early Romantics, however, Mendelssohn responded to non-musical stimuli, especially literary or artistic, or geographical ones. Among these last are his two most admired symphonies, the "Italian", remarkable for its energy, its clarity, and its tunefulness, and the "Scottish", less immediately appealing but a highly-wrought work with an elegiac flavor. Also deriving from Scotland is the overture *The Hebrides*, suggestive of the swell of the waves on the rocky coastline; with a brilliant stroke of artistry, a storm is unleashed in the development section, when the figure depicting the waves is tossed among the orchestra — with the recapitulation providing a welcome calm.

Notable works by Mendelssohn include the *Songs without Words* for solo piano, pieces whose title speaks for itself, and the Violin Concerto in E minor, where his capacity for appealing, poetic writing found an ideal outlet in the sweet, refined tone of the violin as it draws lyrical and sometimes plaintive melodies above the orchestra.

6 *Chopin*

The greatest master of the Parisian salons in the early Romantic era was a Pole by birth and by sentiment. The father of Fryderyk (or Frédéric) Chopin was in fact a Frenchman who had left France in 1787 to avoid army service; he took a Polish wife and settled in Warsaw a few months after the birth of their only son in 1810. Frédéric had a natural gift for the keyboard, improvising readily at the piano and composing dances in the familiar Polish rhythms; when he was only seven one of his polonaises was published. As a child he often played in aristocratic homes, and he took part in a public concert before his eighth birthday. While he was at school he took music lessons with the head of the Warsaw Conservatory, where he became a student in theory and composition. He was soon celebrated for his treatment of national melodies and rhythms, and his absorption of Polish folk traditions into high art.

Frédéric Chopin — Life and works

1810	born near Warsaw, 1 March
1818	first public appearance
1822–7	music lessons with the director of the Warsaw Conservatory
1827–9	student at the Warsaw Conservatory
1829	encouraged by noble families in Warsaw
1830	acclaimed in Vienna; toured Germany
1831	Paris
1832	reputation established in Paris after first public concert; became fashionable teacher, member of salon society, popular with noble Polish families, friendly with leading composers, writers, and artists
1836	met George Sand; first signs of illness
1837	England
1838	Majorca with Sand and her children; worsening of illness; worked on 24 Preludes
1839	recovered at Sand's summer home at Nohant; B♭ minor Piano Sonata
1841–6	summers at Nohant
1847	liaison with Sand ended
1848	Paris Revolution; concert tour of England and Scotland; last public concert in London
1849	died in Paris, 17 October

Piano music 3 sonatas – c, op. 4 (1828), b♭, op. 35 (1839), b, op. 58 (1844); 4 ballades – g, op. 23 (1835), F, op. 38 (1839), A♭, op. 47 (1841), f, op. 42 (1842); 24 Preludes, op. 28 (1839); Fantasie-impromptu, c♯, op. 66 (1835); Barcarolle, F♯, op. 60 (1846); nocturnes, polonaises, rondos, scherzos, studies, waltzes, variations

Orchestral music (all with solo piano) piano concertos – no. 1, e (1830), no. 2, f (1830); Variations on Mozart's 'Là ci darem' (1827); Andante spianato and Grande polonaise (1831)

Chamber music Piano Trio (1829); Cello Sonata (1846)

Songs

But Warsaw was too small and too provincial, as Chopin must have realized. In 1829 he visited Berlin and Vienna; he returned to plan an extended concert tour, but there were delays, partly because of political unrest. Chopin left for Vienna in 1830 and stayed there some months without particular success. The next year he settled in Paris, where he was soon taken up by patrons, became a fashionable teacher, and – being as polished a person as he was a musician – moved with ease in the salon world. A concert he gave in February 1832 was well received, but he made it clear that he did not seek a virtuoso's career, which would not only have made heavy demands on him physically but would also have called for a more demonstrative, flamboyant approach to pianism. He gave fewer than 30 public performances in his entire career; his delicate, veiled, finely detailed playing was better heard among connoisseurs in a private drawing-room.

Chopin quickly became accepted into the élite artistic society of Paris. His musician friends included Berlioz, Liszt, Meyerbeer, and the Italian opera composer Bellini, whose graceful vocal style has its echoes in Chopin's music; he also came to know men like Alfred de Musset, Heine, Balzac, and Delacroix, who painted his portrait. He mixed in Polish émigré circles, and may there have met the Countess Delfina Potocka, a notorious beauty; it has been said that they were lovers, but it is doubtful whether Chopin had any sexual interest in women.

Among his music for these early Paris years are dances, studies, nocturnes, and a ballade. For the dances – not intended for actual dancing – Chopin usually chose either the waltz or one of the Polish national types, mazurka or polonaise. Some of the mazurkas, especially, even though transferred from countryside to salon, capture the flavor of the folk-dance rhythm (see **Listening Guide 34**).

In the 1830s Chopin had a famous liaison with the novelist George Sand (her real name was Aurore Dudevant). When, through Liszt, they met in 1836, she was 32, separated from her husband, author of two novels that questioned social institutions (notably marriage), striking rather than beautiful, respected in literary circles for

---

LISTENING GUIDE 34

CD 4 TRACK 28

Chopin: Mazurka in g, op. 67 no. 2 (1849)

The Mazurka in G minor is one of Chopin's latest works, written in Paris during his last months; he was suffering from tuberculosis, his career as pianist and teacher was over, and his financial position was precarious. The impulse to compose was only sporadic and little besides a couple of mazurkas was written at this time.

It is perhaps not surprising that at this stage Chopin should have chosen to write mazurkas. The mazurka was the most characteristic of Polish dances; it came from the Mazur people, who lived in the Warsaw region. It is in triple meter, usually with a stress on the second or third beat of the measure; Chopin's G minor Mazurka follows closely one of the standard patterns in which the stress alternates between the second beat and the third. The piece is in ternary form.

 Listening Outline

Time

0.00   first section: two phrases, each 8 mm. (the first is shown in ex. 1), the second providing a cadence in g

0.26   second section: in B♭, two phrases each of 8 mm., the first moving in a downward sequence B♭ – A♭ – G♭, the second following the same pattern but ending decisively in B♭; then follows a slightly mysterious linking passage for the right hand alone (0.50), leading to . . .

1.02   repeat of first section

1.32   (end)

ex. 1

her intelligence and her progressive thinking. In the winter of 1838–9 Chopin went with her and her two children to the Spanish Mediterranean island of Majorca. For much of their time they were living in primitive, damp conditions, and Chopin had bronchitis, which must have accelerated the tuberculosis that eventually was to kill him. They returned and went to Sand's country home, where she nursed the weak Chopin back to health. They went back to Paris in October 1839, living close to one another but not together; each summer from 1841 to 1846 they went to Sand's country home. This ambiguous relationship, which ended in 1847 when Chopin became involved in Sand's family quarrels, was a potent source of inspiration to him; much of his most deeply felt music dates from his years with her, and once they had parted he wrote scarcely another note.

Without Sand's nursing, Chopin's health began to fail. Circumstances were against him: the 1848 revolution in Paris left him without pupils or means of support. He accepted an invitation to London (he had been there in 1837), where he played at private concerts and was generously treated; he also went to Manchester and Scotland, staying near Edinburgh with his pupil and passionate admirer, Jane Stirling. He was back in Paris by the end of 1848, and grew steadily weaker. His sister came from Poland to care for him, and was with him when he died in October 1849.

MUSIC

Nearly all Chopin's music is for solo piano. There is a fine cello sonata from his late years and a handful of Polish songs; his orchestral works all have solo piano parts – the most important are the two concertos he wrote as a young man in Poland, though they are criticized, not unfairly, for weak orchestral writing.

Of the solo music, his studies (or *Etudes*, the familiar French title) show how real music can be made out of a technical piano-playing challenge; each piece deals with some specific issue, such as complex patterns of accentuation across the beat combined with sustaining particular left-hand notes. These are generally brief pieces. The ballades are more extended: there he used broader themes, sometimes assigning to each a particular keyboard texture; the themes are not "developed" in the Beethovenian sense, but their recurrences, in part or complete, in the home key or a related one, make the formal outlines clear. This is a natural method of constructing a piece for a composer who, like Chopin, worked by improvising at the piano. Further, Chopin usually added an increasing element of virtuosity in the course of a piece, so making each recurrence more of a dramatic event.

The works of Chopin's time with Sand include relatively small-scale dances, such as mazurkas and waltzes, and the nocturnes, in which he imaginatively exploited the textures available on the new piano (see **Listening Guide 35**), but also several larger items: three ballades, three scherzos, several polonaises (in which Chopin's feelings for his homeland drew from him some splendidly heroic music), and two sonatas. The scherzos include some of Chopin's most vivid and red-blooded music, fiery and fast-moving. The two sonatas of his maturity, each in four movements, demand a new view of what a sonata is: there is no Beethovenian unity, though the B♭ minor work acquires coherence from having been composed around its slow

Chopin: Nocturne in E♭, op. 9 no. 2 (1830–31)

'Nocturne', originally a French word meaning a piece of music having associations with night, or 'night-piece', was first used by the Irish composer John Field as a title for some piano pieces written in about 1813. He used a new delicacy of texture, making the right hand 'sing' while weaving a soft accompanying texture with the left, using the sustaining pedal to make important bass notes persist. Chopin carried this further, using a wide range of accompanying patterns, graceful and often richly ornamented melody (in this he was influenced by Italian opera composers, especially Vincenzo Bellini, 1801–35), and imaginative harmonic support.

The Nocturne in E♭, from the set of three published in 1832 as Chopin's op. 9, illustrates the graceful and florid melodic style and the way in which, on the new piano (as opposed to the harpsichord or the earliest types of piano) a left-hand tone could be held and a soft wash of accompanying harmony added in the middle register. The form is basically ternary, A–B–A, but the addition of repeats and an extended coda, as well as the increasing ornamentation of the melodic line, makes it best represented as A–A'–B–A"–B–A"–C.

 Listening Outline

Time		
0.00	1st section, E♭	a 4-m. melody, ex. 1
0.32	1st section, E♭	repeated with elaboration, ex. 2
1.02	2nd section, B♭	a 4-m. continuation
1.33	1st section, E♭	repeated with further elaboration, ex. 3
2.05	2nd section, B♭	repeated
2.35	1st section, E♭	repeat of ex. 3 elaboration
3.09	coda, E♭	a 4-m. phrase, repeated with much elaboration and a cadenza-like passage (4.10)
4.45		(end)

ex. 1

ex. 2

ex. 3

movement, the famous funeral march (written two years before the other movements) – its dark colors cast a pall on the composition of the remaining part. The later sonata has much invention and fantasy, and its outer movements show a true, sonata-like purposefulness. Chopin was above all a poet of the piano. But it would be wrong to underrate his range, which extends from the graceful to the grandiose, the tenderly poetic to the tempestuously passionate.

7 *Schumann*

LIFE

If just one composer had to be chosen to represent the features of Romanticism, probably Robert Schumann would be the best choice. He was almost as much literary man as musician, and images from literature pervade his music; he was preoccupied with self-expression; he was a miniaturist with a strong lyrical and harmonic gift. And his own life embodied Romantic events in abundance.

His father was a publisher, bookseller, and writer, working in the Saxon town of Zwickau when, in 1810, Schumann was born. As a boy he was an accomplished pianist, but also a writer of poems and articles. There are tales of his early love affairs and his enthusiasm for champagne. His literary enthusiasm was above all for the writings of Jean Paul, the novelist J. P. F. Richter (1763–1825), noted for his richly sentimental but humorous style. In 1828 he went to Leipzig University to study law, but he spent his time in musical, social, and literary activity and never attended a lecture. He also took piano lessons from an eminent teacher, Friedrich Wieck (1785–1873), who had a nine-year-old daughter, Clara.

The next spring Schumann moved to Heidelberg University, studying music rather than law. Eventually he persuaded his mother, with a letter from Wieck to say that he could be a fine pianist if he would work hard, to let him turn to a musical career. He came back to Leipzig, to live in Wieck's house and study theory as well as the piano. Nothing went according to plan. Wieck was often away; the theory lessons were slow to begin and quick to finish; and Schumann had trouble with his right hand – almost certainly the result of his contracting syphilis (in 1828 or 1829). His finger was weakened and a career as a virtuoso pianist was closed to him.

But composition could continue, and did. His first work to be published, a set of piano variations on the name of a girl acquaintance, Abegg (its theme uses the notes A, B, E, G, G), appeared in 1831. A similar idea runs through another, larger work, *Carnaval*. Here the "theme" is A, S, C, H (in German A, E♭ [Es], C, B, or A♭ [As], C, B, see **Listening Guide 37**). Asch was a Bohemian town from which Ernestine von Fricken, a 17-year-old pupil of Wieck's, came; Schumann and she had a love affair.

In 1835 his interest in Wieck's daughter took a new direction, when she was 16. By then, Schumann had embarked on a career in music journalism. In 1834 he had founded the *Neue Zeitschrift für Musik* ("The New Journal for Music"; it still exists); he was its editor and leading writer. He was not a balanced critic; his taste was very personal, but he was quick to spot the talent of such men as Chopin and Brahms, and to praise Schubert (on whose "Great C major" he wrote a detailed essay) and Berlioz (whose *Fantastic Symphony* he likewise lauded). His writing has great spirit and character, and he uttered many wise and penetrating remarks about the nature of music which, taken together, summarize the musical philosophy of Romanticism.

Robert Schumann   Life and Works

1810	born in Zwickau, Saxony, 8 June
1828	law student at Zwickau University; neglected studies in favor of music and literature
1829	piano lessons with Friedrich Wieck; Heidelberg University
1830	lodged with the Wiecks in Leipzig
1831	'Abegg' Variations published
1832	first trouble with hand, prejudicing his career as a concert pianist
1834	founded *Neue Zeitschrift für Musik* which he edited for ten years
1835	*Carnaval*; first serious interest in Clara Wieck, Friedrich's daughter
1837–9	relationship with Clara interrupted by her long absences on concert tours with her father, who strongly opposed their marriage
1840	married Clara after court case; nearly 150 songs including *A Woman's Love and Life, A Poet's Love*
1841	orchestral music
1842	chamber music
1843	choral music
1844	toured Russia with Clara; moved to Dresden
1846	Clara gave first performance of Piano Concerto
1850	*Genoveva* (Leipzig); appointed musical director in Düsseldorf
1852	health deteriorated
1853	met Brahms
1854	attempted suicide; committed to asylum
1856	died in Endenich, near Bonn, 29 July

Songs song cycles – Frauenliebe und -leben (A Woman's Love and Life, 1840), Dichterliebe (A Poet's Love, 1840), Liederkreis, op. 24 (1840), op. 39; *c*275 others; partsongs

Piano music 'Abegg' Variations, op. 1 (1830); Papillons, op. 2 (1831); Davidsbündlertänze, op. 6 (1837); Carnaval, op. 9 (1835); Phantasiestücke, op. 12 (1837); Scenes from Childhood, op. 15 (1838); Kreisleriana (1838); Faschingsschwank aus Wien (Carnival Jest in Vienna), op. 26 (1840); Album for the Young, op. 68 (1848); 3 sonatas (1835, 1838, 1853); character-pieces

Orchestral music symphonies – no. 1, 'Spring', B♭ (1841), no. 2, C (1846), no. 3, 'Rhenish', E♭ (1850), no. 4, d (1841, rev. 1851); Piano Concerto, a (1845); Konzertstück for 4 horns and orchestra (1849); Cello Concerto, 1850

Chamber music Piano Quintet, E♭ (1842); Piano Quartet, E♭ (1842); 3 string quartets (1842); piano trios, violin sonatas

Opera Genoveva (1850)

Choral music Das Paradies und die Peri (1843); Scenes from Faust (1853)

Incidental music Manfred (1849)

Organ music

Schumann continued composing for the piano; these next years produced sonatas as well as studies and character-pieces of different sorts. But affairs of the heart dominated his life. Clara, by now on her way to becoming well known as a pianist, and he wanted to marry, but Clara's father would not hear of it; he took her away and forbade contact between them. However, in the summer of 1837 Clara communicated with Schumann and formally agreed to their marriage, though her father continued to thwart it. Schumann was often deeply depressed and close to suicide. But in May 1839 they took legal steps to make Wieck's consent unnecessary; not until September 1840, after Wieck had disgraced himself with violent outbursts in court, did they marry.

In 1839 Schumann had composed little. But 1840, when his and Clara's love was realized, was wonderfully creative – and in a medium he had neglected for more than ten years. It was natural that he should turn to song. He wrote almost 150 songs in 1840, including several collections and two cycles: one, clearly provoked by his and Clara's situation, tells the story of "A Woman's Life and Love", through falling in love, marriage, motherhood, and widowhood; the other, like Schubert's two great cycles, tells of a love that fails. This is *Dichterliebe* ("A Poet's Love"), to words by Heinrich Heine (1797–1856), with whose subtle, often pained poetry with several layers of meaning he felt a natural sympathy (see **Listening Guide 36**).

LISTENING GUIDE 36

CD 4 TRACK 36;   CASS. 2 EX. 6

Schumann: *Dichterliebe* (1840), excerpt

Dichterliebe ('A Poet's Love'), to words by Heinrich Heine, is the greatest of Schumann's song cycles (a song cycle is a group of songs, unified either by an element of continuity or sometimes simply by mood or style). He composed it during his 'year of song', 1840–41. The work – which has its roots in his relationship with Clara, estrangement and pain, then renewal and lifelong love – treats the subject of love lost and regained, drawing symbols from Nature (the birds, the flowers, the sunshine, the seasons).

Such a song as the opening one of the cycle, 'Im wunderschönen Monat Mai', illustrates the extra depth that music can add. Heine's words are a simple and straightforward expression of the flowering of love in the springtime; but Schumann's minor key and his use of dissonance (at the opening, for example), and his ending, left hanging uncertainly in the air, harmonically and melodically, show that he is thinking rather of love lost and poignantly recalled. As so often with Schumann, the piano, in its prelude (ex. 1), interlude, and postlude, carries the main emotional message; but note too the pained appoggiaturas ('leaning notes', marked x in ex. 2) on even such a word as 'wunderschön', lending irony to the perception of beauty, and the parallel one on 'Herz'. The upward curve of the line, however, from 'da ist' to 'aufgefangen', is characteristic in treating the surging emotions of new love.

The second song, 'Aus meinen Tränen', begins with simple musical phrases, directly representing the idea of the poet's sighs and tears becoming flowers and songs; note that the voice remains uncertainly poised after each line and the piano rounds off the harmony. The fifth line – '*if* you love me', brings in uncertainty, and Schumann symbolizes that in the chromatic inflection; it resolves in the final line, yet the voice's stopping on an unresolved note, again, leaves a sense of the wistful, of doubt.

The third song is even more a miniature: a fleeting representation of the poet's images, now passed since they are eclipsed by the image of the beloved – who herself embodies them all more powerfully. The music parallels this by its change of motion, and rising line, at the crucial middle point, 'Sie selber', meaning 'she herself'.

Time

0.00 *piano prelude*

0.14 Im wunderschönen Monat Mai,   In the most beautiful month of May,
      als alle Knospen sprangen,   as all the buds were breaking,
      da ist in meinem Herzen   there was in my heart
      die Liebe aufgefangen.   the awakening of love.

0.38 *piano interlude*
0.49 Im wunderschönen Monat Mai,   In the most beautiful month of May,
      als alle Vögel sangen,   as all the birds were singing,
      da hab' ich ihr gestanden   then did I tell her
      mein Sehnen und Verlangen.   of my longings and desires.

1.12 *piano postlude*
1.28 (end)

0.00 Aus meinen Tränen spriessen   From my tears there will spring
      Viel blühende Blumen hervor   many blooming flowers;
      Und meinen Seufzer werden   and my sighs will become
      Ein Nachtigallenchor.   a choir of nightingales.

0.25 Und wenn du mich lieb hast, Kindchen,   And if you love me, little one,
      Schenk ich dir die Blumen all',   I shall give you all the flowers,
      Und vor deinem Fenster soll klingen   and at your window shall be heard
      Das Lied der Nachtigall.   the song of the nightingale.

0.52 (end)

0.00 Die Rose, die Lilie, die Taube, die Sonne,   The rose, the lily, the dove, the sun,
      Die liebt' ich einst alle in Liebeswonne.   I once loved them all in the joy of love.
      Ich lieb sie nicht mehr, ich liebe alleine   I love them no longer, I love only
      Die Kleine, die Feine, die Reine,   the little one, the exquisite one, the pure one,
        die Eine   the unique one;
0.10 Sie selber, alle Liebe Wonne   She herself is all the joy of love,
      Ist Rose und Lilie und Taube und Sonne.   she is rose and lily and dove and sun.

0.21 *piano postlude*
0.29 (end)

From song Schumann now moved to orchestral music, anxious to attempt the larger forms which so far had defeated him. Clara, perhaps unwisely, encouraged him. In the early days of 1841 he composed a symphony, which Mendelssohn conducted in March. More symphonic works followed, and, for Clara, a movement which later became the first of his Piano Concerto.

Married to a concert pianist, Schumann began to feel that he was living in her shadow, and he sometimes stayed at home rather than traveling with her. During such a spell in 1842 he turned to chamber music, and wrote, soon after her return, three string quartets and three works with piano, of which the Piano Quintet has always been a favorite for the freshness and the romantic warmth of its ideas and the vigor with which it is carried forward.

In the next year, Schumann turned to choral music. He went on a lengthy tour of Russia with Clara, during which he was again depressed, and he had some kind of breakdown that summer. He and Clara now moved to Dresden, where they spent five years. Schumann had given up the editorship of the *Neue Zeitschrift* and in 1849 he took up the post of town musical director of Düsseldorf. The early months there were prolific: he wrote his Cello Concerto, the noble *Rhenish Symphony*, with a movement inspired by the grandeur of Cologne Cathedral which it splendidly conveys, and revised an earlier symphony to form the one we know as no. 4 in D minor. But Schumann's indifferent conducting meant that the Düsseldorf orchestra

LISTENING GUIDE 37

CD 4 TRACK 39

Schumann: *Carnaval*, op. 9 (1835), excerpt

Carnaval, begun in 1834 and completed the next year, was the first work in which Schumann showed the scope of his imaginative gifts. The title is the same word as the English 'carnival' and the music represents a festive collection of people in various disguises. There are players from the traditional Italian *commedia dell'arte*, the standard stage comics throughout Europe (Harlequin, Columbine, Pantalon etc.); there are other musicians, Chopin and the famous violinist Paganini; there are Schumann's girlfriends; and there is Schumann himself. The work culminates in a march (not a real one – it is in triple time) for Schumann's friends, the League of David (in German, *Davidsbund*) against the Philistines, the anti-art people – taking his cue from the Bible, where David conquers Goliath and the Philistines.

The individual pieces that make up *Carnaval* are short and include some dances: at this time of his life, Schumann was at his best composing short, fanciful pieces, simple in form. The set begins with a 'Préambule', the music of which is more fully developed in the concluding movement. The other two movements we hear are the ones representing the two sides of Schumann's own character, as he saw them: the dreamy and reflective Eusebius and the virile, impassioned Florestan.

The work has a sub-title: 'Little scenes on four notes'. The four notes in question are the ones made up from the 'musical letters' in the name of the town, Asch, from which Schumann's girlfriend Ernestine von Fricken came – which happened to coincide with the musical letters of his own name. These letters can be read, by a German speaker, as A–Es (=E♭)–C–H (=B), or as As (=A♭)–C–H. These note patterns run through the work, except its outer movements; the appearance of the A–E♭–C–B motif is marked by asterisks in exx. 3 and 5 below.

Time

Préambule (Quasi maestoso, 'as if majestic'), 3/4, A♭

0.00	1st section, A♭	6-m. phrase, using dotted rhythms (ex. 1), with cadence in E♭; repeated (after 8 mm.) to end in A♭
0.50	2nd section	more brilliant in style, built on ex. 2, fig. *a*: a repeated 8-m. phrase, continuing with same material, pausing briefly for a theme on fig. *a*, in A♭ (1.11) and passing through several keys (in c for an *animato* passage in playful dotted rhythms, 1.29); brilliant treatment of fig. *a* resumes
1.52	coda, A♭	marked 'Presto', with syncopated rhythms
2.07		(end)

ex. 1

ex. 2

Eusebius (Adagio), 2/4, E♭

2.09	1st section (*A*)	4 mm., based on a dreamy septuplet figure (7 notes in the time of 4), repeated: ex. 3
2.20	2nd section (*B*)	4 mm., on a quintuplet and triplet rhythm, on the same shapes of phrase: ex. 4
2.44	*A*	simple repeat
2.56	*B*	now in octaves and marked 'Slower, very tenderly'
3.09	*A*	also in octaves
3.22	*B*	as originally
3.38	*A*	as originally
3.52		(end)

ex. 3

ex. 4

Florestan (Passionato), 3/4, g

3.53	1st section, g	main theme, 10 mm., ex. 5 (slowing at end), repeated with extension to 12 mm., then shortened to 7 mm
4.22	2nd section, B♭	similar theme but now in B♭ major, 8 mm., repeated; then 8 mm. development, treating four-note phrase (fig. *b*) in different harmonies
4.35	1st section, g	only 4 mm.; then music tails off to lead into the succeeding number . . .
4.45		(end)

ex. 5

75 *Robert and Clara Schumann: daguerreotype, 1850.*

and the chorus disliked performing under him. During 1852–3 his health and spirits deteriorated, and though he had another creative summer in 1853 and made a loyal new friend – a young man by the name of Brahms – it was becoming impossible for him to maintain his directorship.

At the beginning of 1854 Schumann, who all his life had dreaded going mad, began to have hallucinations. In February he attempted suicide by throwing himself in the Rhine; he was rescued and taken to an asylum. His disease finally killed him in July 1856.

MUSIC

Schumann's piano works represent, collectively, one of the most characteristic fruits of the Romantic movement. Some have a literary basis, for example the early collection called *Papillons* ("Butterflies"), inspired by the writings of his beloved Jean Paul. Others are evocative of an atmosphere, like the group entitled *Carnival Jest in Vienna* or the pieces for children such as *Scenes from Childhood*; some convey purely abstract ideas, for example the *Fantasy Pieces*, each one reflecting a mood. Several represent his own ideas about art and society – a good example is *Davidbündlertänze* ("Dances for the League of David"), an imaginary association who, for the sake of art, fought against the Philistines. One of his richest and most typical piano works is *Carnaval*, which depicts in music a colorful array of characters, among them the two embodiments of opposite aspects of his own personality, the impetuous

"Florestan" and the reflective "Eusebius" (see **Listening Guide 37**). Schumann's command of keyboard texture and color, his appealing melody, and his fresh and adventurous harmony combine to give his music a wide range of evocative effect.

In his songs, he was less spontaneous a Nature poet than Schubert. He concentrated more on a poem's emotional focal point than on details of the text. As a piano composer, he was used to conveying feeling through his writing for the instrument, and this he continued to do in his songs: many of the finest achieve their most powerful moments in a final piano solo (or "postlude") when the voice has stopped and the piano alone can give fullest expression to the emotion. Of his major instrumental works the Piano Concerto has a special place in the repertory; although a virtuoso piece, it appeals more for its delicate textures, its poetic feeling, and its graceful style than for its brilliance.

8 *Liszt*

The third of the great composer-pianists of the Romantic era was Franz Liszt. To his contemporaries he was not third but, as a pianist, comfortably the first. He was by far the greatest and the best-known pianist of the time.

Liszt was born in Hungary (as Ferenc Liszt, though his family were German speakers) in 1811. His father in fact worked for the Esterházy family, Haydn's employers. Liszt studied in Vienna – one of his teachers was Salieri, famous as Mozart's rival – and he gave his first concert when he was 11. The family soon moved to Paris, where he was a great success; he made his London début when he was 12 and he was a veteran touring virtuoso by the time he was 16, when he considered giving it up to teach and to become a priest. By now Liszt was a well-known figure in the literary society of Paris, the intellectual center of the world. Berlioz and Victor Hugo were among his friends, and so later was Chopin.

In 1831 Liszt heard the violinist Paganini, whose phenomenal skill had changed people's ideas of what the violin could do. Liszt resolved to do the same on the piano. He began by arranging other composers' music, convinced that anything could sound as well on the piano as in the medium for which it had been written. By the mid-1830s he was composing significant original music for his instrument.

Liszt was a glamorous figure, intensely appealing to women. In 1834 he met the Countess Marie d'Agoult; they went to live first in Switzerland (Liszt took a teaching post in Geneva), then they traveled, particularly in Italy. Their third child was born in Rome in 1839. Liszt gave numerous concerts and composed prolifically for the piano. Wherever he went, he found inspiration, and his music reflects his travels and his love of art and literature. Often he wrote pieces embodying the impressions made by the places he had visited; they are sometimes headed by a verse

LIFE

Franz Liszt   Life and Works

1811	born in Raiding, near Sopron, 22 October
1821	studied the piano with Carl Czerny and composition with Antonio Salieri in Vienna
1822	first public concert, in Vienna
1823	Paris; first tours as an acclaimed virtuoso pianist
1826	first important piano works
1827–30	contact with leading writers and artists in Paris; friendship with Berlioz
1831	deeply impressed by Paganini's violin playing and determined to emulate his virtuosity on the piano
1833	friendship with Chopin; first piano transcriptions
1835	teaching in Geneva; living with Countess Marie d'Agoult (they had three children)
1839	undertook to pay for Beethoven memorial in Bonn; beginning of years of travel throughout Europe and most brilliant period as a flamboyant virtuoso
1844	separated from the Countess
1847	beginning of relationship with Princess Carolyne Sayn-Wittgenstein
1848–57	music director to the Grand Duke of Weimar; made Weimar a leading musical center, conducting new orchestral works and operas, some by Wagner (now a close friend); many orchestral works
1858	resigned Weimar post
1861	Rome
1865	took minor holy orders; religious music
1869–85	divided time between Rome, Weimar, and Budapest
1886	died in Bayreuth, 31 July

Orchestral music Faust Symphony (1854); Dante Symphony (1856); symphonic poems – Tasso (1849, rev. 1854); Les préludes (1854); Hunnenschlacht (The Slaughter of the Huns, 1857); Hamlet (1858); piano concertos – no. 1, E♭ (1849), no. 2, A (1849), Totentanz for piano and orchestra (1849)

Piano music Transcendental Studies (1851); Album d'un voyageur (Traveler's Album), 3 books (1836); Années de Pèlerinage (Years of Pilgrimage), 3 books (1837–77); Six Consolations (1850); Sonata, b (1853); Mephisto Waltz no. 2 (1881); Hungarian Rhapsodies, ballades, studies; numerous transcriptions (music by Bach, Beethoven, Bellini, Berlioz, Schubert, Wagner etc.)

Choral music St Elizabeth (1862); Christus (1867); Masses, psalms

Songs   Organ music

of poetry (Byron, Schiller, Michelangelo, and others), and sometimes the poetry itself provided the inspiration. Later he collected some of these pieces as *Années de Pèlerinage* ("Years of Pilgrimage"). The music is often graphic, as in the one called "The Fountains of the Villa d'Este", where the torrents of water are represented by the sweeping torrents of arpeggios. But most represent Liszt's personal, emotional reactions to the worlds he encountered.

In the years 1839–47 Liszt's schedule looks like a guide to European travel – he played everywhere, from St Petersburg and Moscow to Spain and Portugal, from Scotland to Turkey. Everywhere he was fêted and loved. He and the Countess

76 *Liszt idolized by women after a concert: caricature from* Bolond Istók *(25 March 1876).*

separated in 1844 and he established a new relationship with Princess Carolyne Sayn-Wittgenstein. In 1847 she persuaded him to give up the traveling virtuoso life and he settled at Weimar, where the Grand Duke, eager to re-establish the city as the cultural center it had been in Goethe's day, had appointed him music director. There he had an orchestra and a theater at his disposal. He staged premières of several important operas; and he experimented with the orchestra, composing almost all his orchestral works, among them two piano concertos, 12 symphonic poems, and two programmatic symphonies. He soon became the figurehead of the "New German School".

Towards the end of the 1850s Liszt's position at Weimar grew more difficult: Princess Carolyne had been ignored there, as she was married to someone else; and the court, under a new Grand Duke, did not share Liszt's progressive attitudes to music, nor his support of Wagner (see p. 277), then in political disfavor.

In 1861 he went to Rome, tried unsuccessfully to secure a divorce for the Princess, and thought of entering the priesthood, taking minor orders. Not surprisingly, his music of this period reflects his increasing religious interests, but he also wrote piano pieces, many of them dark, austere, and harmonically bold. He gave piano lessons, in Weimar and Budapest as well as Rome.

For a time Liszt's friendship with Wagner cooled, because of Wagner's relationship with Cosima, Liszt's daughter, who was already married; but they were eventually reconciled. Liszt's travels continued; in 1886 he was in London, conducting an oratorio and being received by Queen Victoria. The next summer he was in Bayreuth, listening to Wagner's operas; it was there that he died.

Liszt was a strange mixture – would-be priest, yet with a diabolic streak, notorious for his love life, a musician who lived by his virtuosity yet a searching, adventurous thinker with new ideas about the future of music.

MUSIC

Liszt experimented with large-scale structures and with the process of thematic transformation: a single, short idea is subjected to changes of mode, rhythm, meter, tempo, or accompaniment to form the thematic basis of an entire work. He used this technique particularly in his symphonic poems (a term he invented). They are based on ideas from art or literature: *Hamlet* was inspired by Shakespeare, *Tasso* by a Goethe play, and *Hunnenschlacht* ("The Slaughter of the Huns") by a huge picture of a medieval battle. The music is less narrative or story-telling than expressive of the emotions aroused by the subject, though some themes represent aspects of the original (there is an Ophelia theme in *Hamlet*, for example).

These principles are carried further in the *Faust Symphony* of 1854, where the three movements are headed "Faust", "Gretchen", and "Mephistopheles", and the themes are treated along the lines of the Faust story – for example, the themes for Faust and Gretchen are intermingled, and the Faust ones are mocked and distorted in the Mephistopheles movement. This technique, similar to Berlioz's in the *Fantastic Symphony* (see p. 240), allows the movement to express character development and in some degree to tell a story.

Liszt did not regard this as solely a dramatic technique. He used it, for example, in his greatest piano work, the Sonata in B minor, composed in 1852–3 and dedicated to Schumann; its three movements, which are played continuously, are largely derived from a single main theme and its offshoots, so that the sonata has a powerful unity.

Piano works naturally make up the greater part of Liszt's output. They range from the brilliant, early studies and Nature pieces of the first and second books of the *Années de Pèlerinage* (see **Listening Guide 38**) to the more austere, impressionist pieces of the third. His harmony was adventurous and unconventional, several of his later pieces containing passages of advanced chromaticism.

Liszt's "transcendental" piano technique sprang from a desire to make the piano sound as rich as an orchestra. Throughout his life he made arrangements of other composers' works, including symphonic transcriptions (notably of Beethoven, Berlioz, and Schubert) and fantasies on themes from popular operas – brilliant reworkings that would thrill his adoring audiences. If more important, ultimately, for his contributions to the art of music than for the music he actually composed, he remains one of the most fascinating of the Romantics.

Liszt: *Petrarch Sonnet no. 104*, from *Années de Pèlerinage*, Book II, Italy (1838–58)

In 1837 Liszt went to Italy, and remained there during 1838 and part of 1839, partly living by Lake Como (with Countess Marie d'Agoult), but also traveling, playing, and above all taking in impressions of Italy, a country always appealing to artists from north of the Alps. There was much reading of Dante and Petrarch, and much contemplation of Italian Renaissance paintings and sculpture. His reactions found musical expression particularly in the second book of his *Années de Pèlerinage*, or 'Years of Pilgrimage' (the first year had been in Switzerland). Liszt said that he had written between four and five hundred pages of piano music in Italy, though he did not put the seven pieces in this collection into final form until much later; they were published only in 1858. Three of the pieces were inspired by the poetry of Petrarch. Liszt first composed them as songs, settings of the sonnets for voice and piano; he immediately rewrote them for piano alone, and later revised them in their present form. No. 104, the fifth item in the collection, is based on a sonnet about passionate love.

 · Listening Outline · . . . .

Time		
0.00	**introduction**	marked 'Agitato', then 'Adagio'; note the poignant phrase at the 'Adagio' (0.12)
0.34	**main theme**	a theme in E, the main key of the work, 'molto espressivo' ('very expressive'), declaimed by the piano, marked by the three repeated tones with which it begins (ex. 1, *a*; note also figs. *b* and *c*). The theme is in two 4-m. phrases, then (in the left hand, 1.18) three 2-m. phrases
1.18	**variation**	in effect a variation on the theme; it is played more loudly, 'singing, with passion', and with a flowing left-hand accompaniment – culminating in a flourish for the piano (2.42)
2.55	**further variation**	the theme is marked 'molto appassionato', 'fortissimo': an impassioned statement, with melodic line breaking off into rich elaboration – notice the three repeated tones (4.22) becoming nine accelerating ones, and the double trill (3.20); during this 'variation' the structure of the theme breaks down and the outline is changed, the first 2-m. phrase (starting at 3.28) becoming 4 mm., the second starting urgently higher in pitch (on B rather than G♯, 3.43): this sets the pattern for the freer section that follows (4.21), using figs. *b* and *c*; it ends with a flourish, descending and fading
5.05	**coda**	the music resumes at a slightly slower tempo, and leads to a cadence in E (5.44); the figure from the beginning of the Adagio is heard, and then a poetic ending, with use of fig. *b*
6.54		(end)

ex. 1

Adagio

₉Women Composers

From the Renaissance onwards, increasing numbers of women were undergoing professional training as performers and composers. In the seventeenth and eighteenth centuries, young women of the aristocracy were given instruction in playing instruments and were encouraged by distinguished musicians in their fathers' service to try their hand at composing. The women obliged by birth and circumstance to pursue careers usually came from musical dynasties; they often continued to work as musicians after they married, their children being cared for by their families.

In the wake of the Enlightenment and the French Revolution, traditional views of women altered, though in varying degrees in different places. Child prodigies, usually the offspring of professional musicians, were intensively trained as pianists and composers so that they might tour with their own compositions in hand. Such famous musicians and composers as Mozart, Mendelssohn, Liszt, and Dvořák took on talented female pupils. For many, audiences were confined to salons, but a remarkable number traveled widely and performed extensively in public. Among the best known was Maria Theresia von Paradis (1759–1824), a blind woman who studied with Salieri and knew more than 60 concertos by heart. There was also the Alsatian pianist Marie Bigot de Morogues (1786–1820), who is said to have been invited in 1805 to perform in the inaugural concert of the Vienna Augarten by Beethoven, who asked her to play his *Appassionata* Sonata at sight from his autograph manuscript (afterwards making her a present of it). The flamboyant Venezuelan Maria Teresa Carreño (1853–1917), at one time a pupil of Gottschalk, played for President Lincoln at the White House in 1863. Several virtuosos were appointed to court posts, most famous among them being Clara Schumann, who, in spite of being Protestant, foreign, and a woman, was appointed royal and imperial chamber virtuoso at the Viennese court.

FANNY MENDELSSOHN

The lives of Fanny Mendelssohn (1805–47), sister of a famous musician, and Clara Schumann (1819–96), wife of another, offer specific examples of how social circumstances and necessity affected exceptionally talented women musicians

LISTENING GUIDE 39

CD 5 TRACK 1

Fanny Mendelssohn: Piano Sonata in g (1843), first movement

In her lifetime Fanny Mendelssohn published almost nothing but small-scale music: five books of songs and five of piano pieces, and then one larger work, a trio for piano, violin, and cello. The notion that a woman should confine herself to miniatures was widely accepted, and there is reason to think that she was not encouraged to think in terms of larger-scale music.

Yet she did have musical ideas of a force and vitality that need expansive treatment, as the Piano Sonata in G minor that she composed in 1843 shows. It is part of her tragedy that, when she did conceive such ideas, she was not equipped by training or by the attitudes and expectations of society to give them the context they need for their full expression. The first movement of this sonata lasts just under four minutes, and one feels at the end of it that there is more to be said.

The movement, broadly speaking, is in sonata form, in that it has two recognizable thematic and tonal groups. Its scale is very modest and its manner is somewhat improvisatory – as if the composer-pianist were expressing a 'stream of consciousness' of a high order – with its sections flowing continuously into one another without the usual clear points of division. There are three further movements, a Scherzo, an Adagio, and a final Presto. The movements are played without any break and the entire sonata lasts some 18 minutes.

 Listening Outline . . . .

First movement: Allegro molto agitato, 4/4, g; sonata form

Time		
	exposition	
0.00	first group, g	a theme, richly harmonized, in g (ex. 1), whose first three tones (fig. *a*) and second three (fig. *b*) form the basis of much of the movement; it is repeated with a more vigorous accompaniment and reaches a decisive cadence
0.35	transition	a new, faster theme begins, still in g, but soon moves to the main key, d, of the second group
0.50	second group, d	the theme continues, with a moment of stability in the new key (ex. 2), with piano figuration of a Chopin-like character; but soon it begins a rapid and radical series of key changes (e♭ for an appearance in the piano's tenor register) (1.05) and the process of development is already under way
1.17	**development**	the development of themes continues; ex. 1 in b (1.19), ex. 2 in g♯ (1.30) and b♭, then the three-tone pattern of fig. *b* (its accent shifted) with the three-tone falling shape of fig. *a* (1.45) heralds ex.1, which returns in c (1.56), its intervals stretched, making it more dramatic and impassioned, leading to . . .
	recapitulation	
2.07	first group, g	the main theme reappears, very briefly, and with a change of harmony that makes it seem transitional
2.28	second group, G, g	ex. 2 returns, in G, a rare moment of tonal stability; then the minor mode returns for the darker ex. 1 material, beginning the coda
2.57	**coda**	further development of ex. 1, moving rapidly through a range of keys and leading to a cadence in G (3.29) for ex. 2 material, but there remains flickers of g in the figuration that ends the movement
3.56		(end)

ex. 1

Allegro molto agitato

a *b*

ex. 2

during the nineteenth century. The Mendelssohns, as we have seen (p. 243), were a prominent and cultured Berlin family. Fanny was four years older than her brother Felix and, some would say, inherently no less good a musician, though never encouraged to think of herself as such. Both children were intensively trained, but Fanny was permitted to perform in public only on one occasion, a charity concert in 1838 at which she played Felix's first piano concerto.

Before and after her marriage in 1829 to the Prussian court painter, Wilhelm Hensel, Sunday *musicales* (small, social musical gatherings) provided the sole occasions on which she could perform her music, which included songs, the remarkable Piano Trio op. 11, a string quartet, and quantities of piano pieces, including a Piano Sonata in G minor, composed in 1843 (see **Listening Guide 39**). Her diaries and voluminous correspondence reveal exceptionally knowledgeable opinions on music; more poignantly, they show the noble delicacy with which she struggled against the protectionism of her father and brother for a degree of independence and recognition. Felix's attitude towards the promotion of her music appears to have been bound up with promoting his own; he salved his conscience for not matching her selfless encouragement of him by allowing three of her songs to be included in each of his 1827 and 1830 collections. Though 11 sets of her chamber music were eventually published, they were issued only after her death from a stroke in 1847.

CLARA SCHUMANN

Clara Schumann, however, who counted Felix Mendelssohn among her closest friends, was very differently treated by her musician father, Friedrich Wieck. She was groomed from the cradle to be a concert artist and, at the age of 11, made her début at the Leipzig Gewandhaus. For the next 60 years she toured, taught, and, with the support of her husband Robert Schumann, composed – piano music and songs, but also some chamber music, including a Piano Trio in G minor (see **Listening Guide 40**). In spite of her evident gifts as a composer, she shrewdly

LISTENING GUIDE 40

CD 5 TRACK 6;   CASS. 2 EX. 7

Clara Schumann: Piano Trio in g, op. 17 (1846), first movement

Most of Clara Schumann's music is on a fairly modest scale, written to dimensions that must have seemed appropriate to someone for whom composition could never be regarded as a central activity, or, perhaps, one that she expected the world to take very seriously. Naturally, she wrote mainly songs and piano pieces: music she herself could play or participate in. But she made a few ventures into larger-scale works. Chief among these is the Piano Trio in G minor that she composed in 1846. It was published the next year.

In style, the music, not surprisingly, is close to that of her husband, with its warm harmonies, its freshness of melody, and its mainly piano-based style: the violin, however, is assigned some of the main themes and a certain amount of dialog throughout, and the comments and counterpoints of the strings greatly enrich the texture.

First movement (Allegro moderato), 4/4, g; sonata form

Time

0.00 [2.45]	**exposition** first group, g	opening theme (ex. 1), violin with piano accompaniment; repeated by piano, with strings accompanying, and extended (with chromatic passage) to lead to emphatic passage in g (0.37 [3.22]) heralding lyrical music for violin and change of key
0.52 [3.37]	second group, B♭	theme on the piano (ex. 2), a syncopated phrase (i.e. its stresses fall off the main accented beat), answered by a phrase in repeated notes; brief modulation to D (1.42 [4.28]), then the theme is repeated with elaboration from the strings
2.45	**exposition repeat**	(2.45−5.29 = 0.00−2.44)
5.29	**development**	begins softly, with continuation of the descending phrase heard in the piano at the end of the exposition; then comes (5.55) some vigorous development of ex. 1, the strings in dialog and imitation (based on the opening phrases of ex. 1) over busy piano figuration; it moves through g, c, and f, and becomes more lyrical, with the violin and cello in imitation above a light accompaniment (6.27), in c, moving back to g for . . .
	recapitulation	
7.24	first group, g	as before up to emphatic statement in g (8.02), after which it is modified to remain in g
8.45	second group, g, G	theme now in G, again repeated with string additions
9.56	**coda,** g	the music returns to g and a new idea is heard; then the start of ex. 1 leads into a vigorous coda with textures similar to those in the development, the piano in support of the strings
10.57		(end)

ex. 1

ex. 2

rejected that path, writing in her diary in 1839: "a woman must not desire to compose – not one has been able to do it, and why should I expect to?"

At the time of their marriage in 1840, Clara already enjoyed an international reputation as a piano virtuoso while Robert was not yet well known as a composer; when her father obstructed the marriage she demonstrated the courage of her convictions and successfully took legal action. Schumann was already afflicted with the syphilis that led to his death 14 years later, and, although Clara escaped its scourge, several of their eight children were also tragically affected.

Soon after the birth of their last child, in 1854, Clara Schumann returned to the concert platform, determined to support the family. Widely admired for her sublime musicianship and formidable keyboard technique, considered the equal of Liszt's, she departed from the convention of performing only her own works; she played her husband's music and championed that of such eighteenth-century composers as Bach and Domenico Scarlatti, as well as playing pieces by Beethoven, Schubert, Mendelssohn, Chopin, and the young Brahms. To the end of her life, she served as mentor and close confidant of Brahms. Between engagements, she found time to edit her husband's complete works and to prepare a teaching edition of his piano music. Her skill and humanity led her to be much in demand as a teacher and she inspired the careers of such pupils as Luise Adolfa Le Beau (1850–1927) and Ethel Mary Smyth (1858–1944).

10 *Verdi*

*77 Giuseppe Verdi:
photograph.*

LIFE

Giuseppe Verdi was born in October 1813, near Busseto in north Italy. He had the classical education normal for a middle-class child, and studied music under the church organist. At 18 he applied for admission to the Milan Conservatory, but was refused: he was past the proper admission age and inadequate as pianist and in counterpoint. He studied in Milan nevertheless, then returned to Busseto in 1835 as town music-master. On the strength of his new appointment he married Margherita Barezzi, daughter of his patron. During these years he composed some sacred works, choruses, and short orchestral pieces.

In 1839 Verdi moved to Milan; later in the year his first opera, *Oberto*, was staged at the famous opera house there, La Scala. It was successful enough to interest the leading Italian publisher, Ricordi, and to induce the Scala director to commission further operas from him. But his next, a comic work, was a failure and Verdi, whose two infant children and his wife had just died, went into a depression and resolved to give up composing. He was nursed through it by the Scala director, who found a libretto, on the biblical story of Nebuchadnezzar, to fire him. The result, *Nabucco*, was a triumph when, in 1842, it reached the stage; within a few years it had carried Verdi's name to every important musical center in Europe, and then beyond, to America, south as well as north.

Giuseppe Verdi — Life and Works

1813	born in Roncole, near Busseto, 9 or 10 October
1832	study in Milan
1835	town music-master in Busseto; married Margherita Barezzi
1839	Milan; *Oberto* given at La Scala; his wife and two children died; beginning of period of deep depression
1842	*Nabucco* (La Scala), established Verdi's international reputation; beginning of steady output of operas and travels throughout Europe to supervise productions
1847–9	Paris
1851	*Rigoletto* (Venice)
1853	*Il trovatore* (Rome), *La traviata* (Venice)
1859	married Giuseppina Strepponi, with whom he had already had a long relationship
1860	entered parliament
1867	*Don Carlos* (Paris)
1871	*Aida* (Cairo)
1874	*Requiem* performed in Milan
1887	*Otello* (Milan)
1893	*Falstaff* (Milan)
1901	died in Milan, 27 January

Operas Oberto (1839), Nabucco (1842), Macbeth (1847), Rigoletto (1851), Il trovatore (1853), La traviata (1853), Les vêpres siciliennes (The Sicilian Vespers, 1855), Simon Boccanegra (1857), Un ballo in maschera (A Masked Ball, 1859), La forza del destino (The Force of Destiny, 1862), Don Carlos (1867), Aida (1871), Otello (1887), Falstaff (1893)

Choral music Requiem (1874); Quattro pezzi sacri (1889–97); songs

Chamber music String Quartet (1873)

Now came what Verdi later called his years in the galleys: years of hard work and drudgery, when composing was a matter more of perspiration than inspiration. He wrote not only for Milan but for other Italian cities, London, and Paris. Eight further operas date from the 1840s; much the finest is *Macbeth*, after Shakespeare (1847). The somber grandeur of the play appealed profoundly to Verdi, and he matches it in his score.

One of the most moving scenes in *Macbeth* falls at the beginning of the last act, where a group of Scottish exiles, who have fled from Macbeth's oppression, are mourning their situation. There is a similar scene in *Nabucco*. When Verdi wrote music of this kind, with a patriotic message, he was really writing about the unhappy lot of the Italians, who had been under foreign – Austrian and Spanish – domination for centuries. Italy was at this time not a country but a geographical region, tied together by language and culture; the move towards union, the Risorgimento, grew stronger and Verdi was deeply committed to it. The meaning of his stirring music was well understood.

With the 1850s, Verdi reached a creative turning-point, producing three of his finest and most admired operas (*Rigoletto*, *Il trovatore*, and *La traviata*). By this time his personal life was more secure. In his early days in Milan he had been befriended by the soprano Giuseppina Strepponi; they met in Paris in 1847 and soon lived together, finally marrying in 1859. Verdi was a non-believer and strongly opposed to what he saw as the oppressive influence of the church; some of this feeling comes through in his operas.

Verdi lived, of course, in oppressive times. When *Rigoletto* was given in Venice, it had to have an anonymous duke as its central figure, not (as in the Victor Hugo original) the King of France; for Rome, the *Macbeth* witches had to be gypsies; and later an opera involving the assassination of a Swedish king, *Un ballo in maschera* ("A Masked Ball"), had to be shifted to Boston and the king turned into a colonial governor. The censor took a stern view of the politically subversive.

Rigoletto was a huge success on its first performance; so was *Il trovatore*. *La traviata* failed initially, but Verdi made changes and it soon established itself. Then he was invited to write an opera for Paris, and went to live there for more than three years before the production of the new work, *The Sicilian Vespers*. He had numerous difficulties with the Paris Opéra and legal actions against other houses where unauthorized performances of his works were given. He left early in 1857. The contact with the French grand opera tradition was fruitful, and the Italian operas of Verdi's next years are infused with grand opera elements. The personal dramas of his earlier Italian operas no longer gave him the scope he wanted. *Simon Boccanegra*, composed for Venice in 1857, is a grandly somber piece, concerned with political power in medieval Genoa, the rivalries of the nobles and the plebeians, and a love affair that crosses those barriers.

Next came *A Masked Ball*, written for Naples in 1858 and more Italian in its focus on personal drama and the incident surrounding it. Third is *The Force of Destiny* (St Petersburg, 1862), a fascinating but rambling opera, in which a tragic personal drama – an accidental killing and the vendetta that arises from it – is set against a rich pageant of military and monastic life.

Meanwhile, Verdi had become involved in real politics. In 1860 Italy had thrown off most of her foreign oppressors and achieved nationhood; Verdi deeply admired the chief architect of these developments, Cavour, and agreed to enter the new parliament. In 1874 he was honored by election to the Senate.

Verdi had regarded himself as retired from composing from about 1860. Each opera thereafter was composed simply because he wanted to undertake it – for *The Force of Destiny* the reason was a trip to Russia, but for most it was the challenge of the subject. One particularly exciting challenge was offered by *Don Carlos*, a grand opera written in French, after the play by Schiller. For his next opera Verdi chose a simpler, more direct plot: this was *Aida*, first given at Cairo in 1871, soon after the opening of the Suez Canal. His next major work was not an opera but a *Requiem*. This originated in a proposal he made in 1868, on Rossini's death, for a *Requiem* to commemorate him, to which several leading Italian composers would contribute movements. It never materialized, but in 1873 the Italian poet Alessandro Manzoni, whom Verdi revered, died: so Verdi used the movement he had written for a Rossini *Requiem* in a new, complete one for Manzoni. Verdi's *Requiem* has been criticized as operatic in style; but the kind of music he wrote for the expression of strong emotion was inevitably operatic and the style finds a proper use here. The *Requiem* had its first performance at a Milan church in 1874. It was repeated at La Scala, and the next year Verdi took it to London, Paris, and Vienna.

Verdi conducted occasional performances, like an acclaimed *Aida* in Paris in 1880, but he had apparently ceased composing. He was close on 70. His friends knew there was more music in him – none better than his publisher, Ricordi, who hinted to him at the possibility of a Shakespeare opera, on *Othello*. His friend the poet and composer Arrigo Boito (1842–1918) produced a libretto, and he was duly tempted. He composed the work slowly, during 1884–5, and it was given at La Scala in 1887. It is Verdi's tragic masterpiece.

This was still not the end. In 1889, when Verdi was 76, Boito again tempted him with a Shakespeare text, this time a comedy – a genre Verdi had not touched for more than 50 years, and in which his only previous effort had been a failure. Verdi took up the challenge, and *Falstaff* eventually came to the stage in 1893, the year he was 80. It was a triumph. Although he was a lifelong unbeliever, he then wrote a group of sacred choral pieces, partly experimental in nature, completing them in 1897. That year Giuseppina died; Verdi lived on, in Milan, where he died in 1901. At his burial there was national mourning.

Verdi's early operas follow the patterns established by his predecessors, with stirring melody and a vigorous, almost crude orchestral style, applied usually to strong, often tragic stories. He quickly established certain standard character types associated with particular voices – the ardent, courageous tenor hero, the masculine, determined baritone, the severe bass (usually a king, priest, or father).

The climax to this period comes first in *Macbeth*, which powerfully catches the atmosphere of the Shakespeare original, and in his three masterpieces of the early 1850s. *Rigoletto* is set in sixteenth-century Mantua: it concerns the daughter of the court jester who is abducted and presented to the libertine Duke, for whom she later sacrifices her life. Verdi's music not only conveys the atmosphere of a court ball and of the sinister night-time life on the streets and in the inns of the city but draws a telling picture of the Duke himself, singing of his delight in women, the professional assassin offering his services, the innocence of Rigoletto's daughter, and the furious desire of Rigoletto, the jester, for vengeance. *Il trovatore*, on a more traditional type of story about rivalry in love and war, carries the older style of opera to its ultimate point, with much forceful and strongly atmospheric writing. Of a rather different kind is *La traviata*, altogether more tender and intimate in tone (see **Listening Guide 41**).

These operas are to a large extent made up of individual "numbers": arias, duets, choruses, connected by dialog sections. As time moved on, Verdi began to work towards a more continuous, seamless style of composition, though he was always conscious of the central place in the Italian tradition of eloquent singing. His next

78 Below *Verdi's* La traviata: *Kiri Te Kanawa (Violetta) at the Royal Opera House, Covent Garden.*

MUSIC

Verdi: *La traviata* (1853), excerpt from Act 1

Verdi wrote *La traviata* for performance in Venice in 1853. Although now perhaps the best-loved of all his operas, it was at first a failure, probably because the singers were ill-suited to their roles. But Verdi made some changes, and a new cast was assembled, and when it was given again in Venice the next year it was received with enthusiasm. Among Verdi's operas it is unique for the warmth and the tenderness of its music, and in particular for its sympathetic portrayal of the heroine, Violetta, 'la traviata' herself.

'La traviata' means, literally, 'the woman gone astray'. The plot comes from a novel (which he later turned into a play) by the French writer Alexandre Dumas, called *La dame aux camélias*; it was loosely based on events in his own life. Violetta, who is suffering from the early stages of consumption (tuberculosis), is a courtesan in the *demi-monde* of Paris; she is not a prostitute, selling her favors indiscriminately, but a woman who is kept on a longer-term understanding by a man of substance, usually an aristocrat (at this time it was considered neither abnormal nor improper for such a man to have a mistress). At the start of the opera Violetta's 'protector' is Baron Douphol, but in the course of the first act she is greatly drawn to the young and ardent Alfredo, who dearly loves her. In the scene described below, she is struggling with herself – prompted by love to leave the rich and middle-aged Douphol to share her life with Alfredo, constrained by common sense to stay and not to give up security, comfort, and an easy life of pleasure for what might be a passing fancy. At the end of the scene, common sense seems to have prevailed; but in the opera she does in fact go to Alfredo – later to be parted from him for family reasons, but in the end to die, reconciled, in his arms.

The most usual form for a major aria in an Italian opera of this period is a slow section followed by a fast one; either or (as in this case) both may be preceded by a recitative. An unusual feature here is that the voice of Alfredo (a tenor) too is heard in the course of it, in the distance, echoing the words (and music) of Violetta (a soprano) about the force of love – which he had sung earlier in the opera – from below the balcony of the upstairs reception room where she has remained after a party (or perhaps just echoing in her mind).

🎧 Listening Outline

Time		VIOLETTA	
0.00	Recitative, punctuated by orchestra	È strano! è strano! in core scolpiti ho quegli accenti! Saria per me sventura un serio amore? Che risolvi, o turbata anima mia? Nell'uomo ancora t'accendava.	How strange! his words are engraved upon my heart! Would a serious love bring me ill fortune? What should I decide, oh my troubled spirit? No man before has so inflamed me; such a joy I have never known, to be loving and beloved! How can I disdain it for the empty follies of my present existence?
0.44	flourish on 'gioia' ('joy')	Oh gioia Ch'io non conobbi, esser amata amando! E sdegnarla poss'io per l'aride follie del viver mio?	
1.24	Aria (first part); Andantino, 3/8, f (ex.1)	Ah, fors' è lui che l'anima solinga ne' tumulti, godea sovente pingere de' suoi colori occulti. Lui, che modesto e vigile all'egre soglie ascese e nuove febbre accese destandomi all'amor!	Oh, perhaps this is the man who, while alone in the bustling crowds, I have often delighted in imagining in his secret colors; he who, gentle and watchful, came across my threshold, and turned my illness to a new fever, in awakening me to love!
2.47	music moves to F and broad, expressive phrases (ex. 2), fuller accompaniment; here she sings the music with which, earlier, Alfredo had wooed her	A quell'amor ch'è palpito dell'universo intero, misterioso, altero, croce e delizia al cor.	Oh, that love, heartbeat of the entire universe, mysterious, proud, torture and delight to the heart.
3.39	second verse of aria (music as at 1.24)	A me, fanciulla, un candido e trepido desire quest' effigio dolcissimo signor dell' avvenire, quando ne' cieli il raggio di sua beltà vedea e tutta me pascea di quel divino error.	To me, a young girl an innocent and timorous desire for this sweetest image lord of the future, when I see in the heavens the light of his beauty, and all nourishes me completely with that divine folly.

6.06	music moves to F (as at 2.47)	Sentia che amore, che amore è il palpito, *etc.*	I feel that it is love, love which quickens, *etc.*
6.12	miniature cadenza		
6.56	Recitative	Follie! delirio vano è questo! Povera donna, sola, abbandonata in questo popoloso deserto che appellano Parigi, che spero or più? che far degg'io? gioir! di voluttà ne'vortici perir! gioir!	Madness! all this is vain raving! Poor woman that I am, alone, abandoned, in this crowded desert that they call Paris, what more can I hope? what can I do? Pleasure! to perish in a whirlwind of delights! pleasure!
7.10	tone of alarm (more than two lines on the same tone, repeated)		
7.36	vocal flourishes as she contemplates endless delights		
8.00	Aria (second part): Allegro brillante, 6/8, A♭ in brilliant style and dance-like rhythm (ex. 3)	Sempre libera degg'io folleggiare di gioia in gioia, vo' che scorra il viver mio pei sentieri del piacer. Nasca il giorno, o il giorno muoia, sempre lieta ne' ritrovi, a diletti sempre nuovi dee volare il mio pensier.	Ever free, I shall frolic from one joy to the next, and run my life along the paths of pleasure. As each day dawns, and each day dies, ever happy, I shall turn to the new delights that give flight to my spirit.
8.52	flourishes at 'volare' (flight)		
		ALFREDO *(distant)* Amor è palpito dell' universo intero . . .	Love is the heartbeat of the entire universe . . .
8.58	He echoes the earlier music about the power of love, now in A♭		
		VIOLETTA Oh! Amore!	Oh! love!
		ALFREDO Misterioso, altero, croce e delizia al cor!	. . . mysterious, proud, torture and delight to the heart!
9.42 10.12	She dismisses the idea in ever more brilliant and showy vocal writing, emphasizing the superficiality of her view of life.	**VIOLETTA** Follie! gioir! Sempre libera, *etc.*	Madness! pleasures! Ever free, *etc.*
11.53	(end)		

ex. 1

dolciss.

Ah fors' è lui che l'an - ni - ma so - lin - ga ne' tu -

- mul - ti, so - lin - ga ne' tu - mul - ti

ex. 2

Ah, quell' a - mor, quell' a - mor ch'é pal - pi - to

ex. 3

Sem - pre li - be - ra degg' i - o fol - leg - gia - re di gio - ia in gio - ia,

operas move only slowly in that direction: they include one of the grandest of all of them, *Don Carlos*, a French grand opera written for the Paris opera house, and treating the personal drama of the Spanish prince, his friend, and his beloved, against the larger canvas of Spanish religious and political oppression of the Netherlands – there are scenes for the Spanish king and the Grand Inquisitor, and one where heretics are burned by the Inquisition. This work touches on all the themes that had appealed to Verdi, among them nationhood, the rival power of church and state, courage and comradeship, the conflict of generations, and above all love. Verdi's music speaks here not of the conventional characters of some of the earlier operas but of real people, coping with powerful internal conflicts. There is a place in this rich and wide-ranging work for every kind of music that Verdi could write, and in it he extended himself to new limits.

Aida, always one of Verdi's most popular operas, deals with similar themes, personal love and jealousy set against the fate of nations. In his next opera, *Otello*, he produced some of his most impassioned music, particularly in his portrayal of the malevolence of Iago and the gradual undermining of Otello's character by the ravages of jealousy. Though still firmly within the tradition of operas built up of arias, duets, and so on, *Otello* has more continuity than any of his earlier operas. Verdi wanted to move away from the traditional formality of arias sharply marked off from neighboring items, except where the dramatic context makes it natural. There are "set pieces" in *Otello*, but they arise from dramatic necessity, and the surrounding musical texture is fluid. The orchestration and harmony have a new subtlety and expressiveness.

Verdi's last opera was *Falstaff*. In method it is akin to *Otello*, but there are fewer formal arias or ensembles and more dialog – conversation, exclamation, interjection, laughter. The plot centers on a fat old man who likes to think he is still a dab hand at seduction, but all he achieves is a ducking in the river Thames and a drubbing from a troop of mock fairies in Windsor Forest. There are no real arias, except one for the "Fairy Queen", but the music bounds along at a great pace, little motifs flecking in and out of the gossamer orchestral texture, aria and recitative meeting at some middle point. This wonderfully benign, good-humored piece ends up with a fugue – a form Verdi abhorred and could use only as a joke – on an Italian version of Shakespeare's "All the world's a stage": an appropriate ending for the greatest master of Italian opera.

11 *Wagner*

Richard Wagner was the greatest German opera composer of his day, the German counterpart to Verdi. He was not merely that. As no one had done before, he changed opera – not just opera, but music itself. Nor just music, but indeed art: the impact of the man, his creations, and his thoughts, left the world a different place. He aroused people's passions, intellectual and emotional, as no artist had done before, nor any since. He has been hailed as a high priest of a thousand philosophies, many of them mutually exclusive, even contradictory. His music is hated as much as it is worshiped. The only issue beyond dispute is his greatness.

Wagner was born in Leipzig on 22 May 1813. The first of many questions surrounding him concerns his paternity: was he the son of the police actuary Friedrich Wagner, his mother's husband, who died six months after his birth, or of the painter, actor, and poet Ludwig Geyer, a close friend, whom she married soon after? Probably the former, but the evidence is ambiguous; all we know is that Wagner was affected by the doubts over his origins.

The family moved to Dresden, where Richard attended the leading church school; later he moved to Leipzig, going to St Thomas's School, where a century earlier Bach had taught. His interests were ancient Greek tragedy, the theater (especially Shakespeare and Goethe), and above all music. He had taken lessons in harmony, piano, and violin, and eagerly copied out music by Beethoven for study. He composed a number of pieces and had an overture played at a Leipzig concert. In 1831 he entered Leipzig University to study music, but his chief studies were under the Kantor at St Thomas's. The truth about these early years – and indeed about other parts of his life, too – is not always easy to establish. Wagner left a detailed autobiography, but when his information is checked against other sources it often proves to be wrong; he was inclined to angle the facts, or even alter them, to suit his purpose.

At the end of 1832, a symphony of Wagner's had performances in Prague and Leipzig. It was well received, but this was his last substantial instrumental work. That winter he wrote a libretto for an opera, started composing it, then scrapped it; he embarked on another, *The Fairies*, in 1833, and quickly completed it, but it remained unheard until after his death. His first opera to gain a hearing was his next, *The Ban on Love* (based on a Shakespeare comedy), which he conducted at Magdeburg in 1836. It had just one performance; then the company giving it, which Wagner had conducted since 1834, dissolved.

A soprano in this company was Minna Planer; Wagner fell in love with her and in 1836 they were married. She left him for another man for several months during 1837, but that summer, when he was appointed conductor at the theater in

Early years

79 *Richard Wagner: photograph.*

Richard Wagner — Life and Works

1813	born in Leipzig, 22 May
1830	St Thomas's School, Leipzig
1831	Leipzig University
1834	musical director of theater company in Magdeburg
1836	*The Ban on Love* given in Magdeburg; married Minna Planer
1837	music director of the theater in Riga
1839	Paris; contact with Meyerbeer
1842–3	*Rienzi* and *The Flying Dutchman* acclaimed in Dresden; appointed *Kapellmeister* to Saxon court in Dresden
1848	banned from Germany because of involvement in revolutionary politics; to Weimar (to see Liszt), Switzerland, Paris
1849	settled in Zürich
1850	*Lohengrin* (Weimar); *Opera and Drama*; *Ring* cycle started; began traveling widely as a conductor
1861	revised version of *Tannhäuser* given in Paris to hostile audience
1864	moved to Munich at the invitation of King Ludwig II of Bavaria; began affair with Liszt's daughter Cosima von Bülow
1865	*Tristan and Isolde* (Munich)
1866	set up house with Cosima at Tribschen, by Lake Lucerne
1868	*The Mastersingers of Nuremberg* (Munich)
1870	married Cosima; composed *Siegfried Idyll* for Cosima in gratitude for their son
1871	moved to Wahnfried, a house near Bayreuth
1874	*Ring* cycle completed
1876	first festival at Bayreuth where Wagner had designed an opera house for the *Ring*, which was given its first performance
1882	*Parsifal* (Bayreuth)
1883	died in Venice, 13 February

Operas Das Liebesverbot (The Ban on Love, 1836), Rienzi (1842), Der fliegende Holländer (The Flying Dutchman, 1843), Tannhäuser (1845, rev. 1861), Lohengrin (1850), Tristan und Isolde (1865), Die Meistersinger von Nürnberg (The Mastersingers of Nuremberg, 1868); Der Ring des Nibelungen (The Ring of the Nibelung, 1876): Das Rheingold (The Rhinegold, 1869), Die Walküre (The Valkyrie, 1870), Siegfried (1876), Götterdämmerung (Twilight of the Gods, 1876); Parsifal (1882)

Orchestral music Siegfried Idyll (1870); Kaisermarsch (1871); Grosser Festmarsch (1876)

Songs Wesendonk-Leider (1857–8)

Choral music   Piano music

Riga, on the Baltic, she rejoined him. In 1839 he was not re-employed; in any case, he wanted to go to Paris, for the opera on which he was now working, *Rienzi*, was in the grand opera tradition. He and Minna had to stow away on a ship to evade their creditors. After a stormy journey they reached England, and then went on to France.

In Paris, Wagner scraped a living with hack-work for publishers and theaters. He was befriended by Giacomo Meyerbeer and influenced by the music of Berlioz. *Rienzi* was soon finished and a *Faust* overture composed; he also drafted a libretto on the legend of *The Flying Dutchman* – it was accepted by the Opéra, but for setting by another composer. With a recommendation from Meyerbeer, he submitted *Rienzi* to the Dresden Court Opera; it was accepted, and in 1842 Wagner left for Dresden, where it had a triumphant première in October. Three months later his own setting of *The Flying Dutchman* followed. *Rienzi* is an enormously long, grandiose opera, dealing with the rise and fall of a hero of the people. *The Flying Dutchman* is much shorter and more intense; it treats a supernatural theme, the haunted Dutchman who sails the seas endlessly until redeemed by a woman's trusting love.

After the success of *Rienzi*, Wagner accepted the post of royal *Kapellmeister* at the Dresden court. It gave him security, a place where his music could gain a hearing, and opportunities to exercise his organizational genius. Yet it was perhaps a curious position for a man with revolutionary leanings. Wagner had for some time been associated with "Young Germany", a semi-revolutionary intellectual movement, and the reforms he wanted in the theater had broad social and political implications.

For the moment, he kept clear of active politics. During the 1840s he wrote two more operas, *Tannhäuser* (1845) and *Lohengrin* (1847). The former is concerned with the triumph of a woman's Christian love over pagan sensuality – the theme of redemption again, set in medieval Germany. *Lohengrin* is about a knight of the Holy Grail; again a woman's love and faith are central.

In 1848, Europe's year of revolution, Wagner was caught up in political activity. He was involved in revolutionary and anarchical propaganda, and although publicly he had supported the monarchy he sided with the rebels when in 1849 Dresden was the scene of turmoil. To escape arrest he fled to Weimar, where he sought Liszt's help, and then to Switzerland and safety. Germany was closed to him for 11 years. Soon he went to Paris, where he met and almost eloped with a young woman he had known from Dresden.

Meanwhile, *Lohengrin* had its première in Weimar, under Liszt; its limited success provoked Wagner into thinking more deeply about new forms of opera or musical theater. He wrote an important book on this topic, *Opera and Drama*, in 1850 – his basic statement about his view of the relationship of music and theater. Wagner was a prolific writer; over the years he had written numerous essays, criticisms, theoretical studies, and polemical articles. One is called *The Artwork of the Future*; another, notorious one is his bitterly anti-semitic *Judaism in Music*, some of it a merciless attack on Meyerbeer (who had generously helped him earlier).

Wagner spent most of the 1850s in Switzerland, active in Zürich musical life but expending most of his energies on a new, great conception. This started as an opera based on the mythological story, from the Nordic and Germanic sagas, of the hero Siegfried. He started with the idea of an opera treating the story of Siegfried's death, but then prefaced it with another, on the young Siegfried. These were to become *Götterdämmerung* ("Twilight of the Gods") and *Siegfried*. Then he planned a third opera to precede these, telling an earlier part of the story, *Die Walküre* ("The Valkyrie"), and finally another, prefatory work, *Das Rheingold* ("The Rhinegold"). Thus he wrote the text in reverse order, but he composed the music forwards, and more than 20 years elapsed between the first part of *Rheingold* (at the end of 1853) and the conclusion of *Twilight of the Gods* (at the end of 1874).

Two other works, of more normal dimensions, were composed while this four-opera cycle, called *The Ring of the Nibelung*, was in progress: *Tristan und Isolde* and *The Mastersingers of Nuremberg*. *Tristan*, written in 1857–9, was stimulated by a love affair he had with Mathilde Wesendonck, the wife of a silk merchant in Zürich who was one of Wagner's most generous patrons. Wagner set some of her poems to music, and clearly identified their illicit love with that of the lovers in this new work, the greatest of all love operas. He was part-way through the third of the *Ring* operas, *Siegfried*, when the need to write *Tristan* intervened. And before he had finished *Siegfried* he paused again, to write *The Mastersingers*. These pauses were not made purely for personal or artistic reasons: his publishers would not accept the *Ring* – its huge length made it commercially unattractive – but would pay him well for an opera of normal length. He was chronically in debt and needed the money.

There were other interruptions. In 1860 he was in Paris, revising *Tannhäuser* to suit French tastes. When the new version was performed, it was shouted down – not simply because of Wagner's music, but as a political protest against the Austrians who had supported the performance. Still, Wagner's prestige was enhanced by his having the work given at the Opéra, and that led to his being allowed back into Germany. In that year, 1862, Wagner and Minna parted. Wagner conducted concerts in London in the 1850s, Vienna and Russia in the early 1860s. But the crucial event of the early 1860s, the one that made possible the achievements of Wagner's late years, was the invitation from the notoriously eccentric young King Ludwig II of Bavaria. This inaugurated patronage from Ludwig on a scale that cleared Wagner's debts, provided him with a regular income, permitted him to compose the music he wanted to, and eventually to found a festival for its performance.

Munich, Tribschen, Bayreuth

Wagner moved to Munich in 1864, having slipped out of Vienna earlier in the year to avoid imprisonment for debt. He was generously treated by Ludwig, but the Bavarian politicians mistrusted his influence at court and his freedom with Bavarian money. Moreover, he became the center of scandal when he had an affair with Cosima von Bülow, daughter of Liszt and wife of the conductor Hans von Bülow – whom Ludwig, at Wagner's request, had appointed to a post as royal musician. The affair had Bülow's connivance. The next April, on the day Bülow conducted the first rehearsal of *Tristan und Isolde*, their first child was born; she was christened Isolde.

Tristan was produced in June, but the singer of Tristan died and it had only four performances. At the end of the year, Ludwig was obliged to ask Wagner to leave Munich. Early in 1866 Wagner and Cosima set up house at Tribschen, by Lake Lucerne in Switzerland, though it was not for another two years that she came to live with him. Meanwhile, he completed *The Mastersingers*, which had its première in Munich in June 1868, with Wagner seated beside Ludwig in the royal box. His once-progressive political stance had now taken a sharp turn to the Right and towards a ferocious German nationalism.

Wagner remained at Tribschen until 1872. In 1870 he had married Cosima, whom Bülow had now divorced (Minna Wagner had died in 1866). By then she had borne him two more children. He completed the third of the *Ring* operas, to which he had now returned, and the first two were given at Munich in 1869 and 1870. The fourth was drafted early in 1872. By then, Wagner was hard at work on his plans for a new opera house, designed for the *Ring*. This was to be at the small town of Bayreuth. Wagner and his friends devised numerous fund-raising schemes but had little success, and only through Ludwig's intervention in 1874 could the plans be carried through. At the end of that year the last of the *Ring* operas was completed.

The first Bayreuth Festival was in the summer of 1876. It was an artistic triumph, but a financial disaster, and again the Bavarian treasury bailed him out. Now Wagner started work on a new opera, a "sacred festival drama" to be called *Parsifal*; this occupied him up to the beginning of 1882 – he was working more slowly now, troubled by his health (he had heart trouble and other complaints), and had to devote some of his energies to money-raising. He also spent time traveling in Italy in the early 1880s. *Parsifal* had its first performances at the 1882 Bayreuth Festival. Wagner went back to Italy, to recuperate. He had decided to write no more operas but to return to the symphony. But in February 1883, in Venice, he had a heart attack and died. A few days before, his father-in-law, Liszt, had visited him and had been seized by the idea of composing a piano piece about a funeral procession with a gondola. Wagner's body was conveyed by gondola to the railway station, then by train to Bayreuth, where he was buried in the garden of his house.

MUSIC

In *The Flying Dutchman*, *Tannhäuser*, and *Lohengrin*, Wagner was beginning to move away from traditional conceptions of opera towards a new and powerful unity, mainly through the use of recurring themes with particular dramatic associations and a more continuous musical texture. These ideas are carried very much further in his mature operas – or music dramas, as he preferred to call them. The idea of recurring themes was not of course new. The seeds of it can even be found in Mozart; and several other composers used an already-heard theme later in an opera as a reminder of a person, an event, or a state of mind – as in *La traviata*, where Verdi's musical recall tells us that the dying Violetta is remembering her and Alfredo's early passion. The kind of thematic recurrence used by Berlioz and Liszt, in orchestral music, is similar.

Wagner drew all these ideas together, and combined with them a Beethovenian sense of the way in which developing themes can support a large symphonic structure. He made the *leitmotif* ("leading motif") his basic way of linking music and drama. In his mature works, some kind of brief theme is associated with every significant idea in the drama: people, objects, thoughts, places, states of emotion, and so on. These musical motifs are related in character to what they portray, as some examples – taken from the *Ring*, which has over its four evenings a huge corpus of

Wagner: *Das Rheingold* (1869), closing scene

Das Rheingold tells the first part of the story of *The Ring of the Nibelung*. In its opening scene, Alberich, the Nibelung (a dark, dwarf-like figure from a race who live in caverns beneath the earth), steals the Rhinegold, a piece of gold with magic properties, which had been carelessly guarded by the three Rheinmaidens. In the second scene, Wotan, head of the gods, and his wife Fricka contemplate the great fortress they have had built (to be called Valhalla); but the giants who built it, Fasolt and Fafner, require payment, and take as hostage Freia, Fricka's sister, goddess of youth and beauty – without whom the gods will lose their immortality. Wotan calls on the crafty spirit of fire, Loge, to help him; and Loge takes him to Nibelheim, where they find that Alberich has used the magic power of a ring made from the Rhinegold to enslave the Nibelungs and build up a hoard of wealth; they play on his vanity, trick him, tie him up, and take him to the mountain near Valhalla, where they commandeer his hoard and the ring – on which Alberich, in his rage, places a curse. Now they pay off the giants with the gold, but the giants demand even the ring – which Wotan, after long thought, yields. Its curse promptly works: the giants quarrel over the spoils and Fafner kills his brother.

In this last scene the gods enter Valhalla (where Wotan plans to set up an army, of men who have died heroically in battle, brought back to life, to protect the gods' power). The characters involved are Wotan himself (bass-baritone), his wife Fricka (mezzo), Freia (soprano), Donner, and Froh, as well as Loge (tenor), who although god of fire is somewhat detached from the other gods, and the three Rhinemaidens.

The orchestral fabric against which the drama is enacted is largely composed of *leitmotifs*, musical phrases associated with some person, object, or concept; they always allude in some way to the action or to the meaning behind it. In *Das Rheingold* they are generally presented quite simply, not as 'labels', but as allusions and statements; but as the plot develops over the cycle the musical texture becomes much richer and the developing relationships of the *leitmotifs* and what they stand for grow more complex.

 ## Listening Outline

	Time	DONNER	
The somber events of the preceding scene are symbolized in the gathering of oppressive clouds. Donner, god of thunder, resolves to clear the air; the motif of his hammer-swings (ex. 1) is heard passing through the orchestra. The music is in B♭, passing through g and b♭ and returning at the hammer-blow.	0.00	Schwüles Gedünst schwebt in der Luft; lästig ist mir der trübe Druck! Das bleiche Gewölk samml' ich zu blitzendem Wetter, das fegt den Himmel mir hell! *(he climbs on to a rock and swings his hammer; the mists collect around him)*	Heavy steams float in the air; its gloomy pressure is oppressive to me! I shall gather the pallid clouds into a thunderstorm, that will wipe the heavens clean again!
	0.38	Heda! Heda! Hedo! Zu mir, du Gedüft! Ihr Dünste, zu mir! Donner, der Herr, ruft euch zu Heer!	Heda! Heda! Hedo! To me, you winds! You mists, to me! Donner, your ruler, summons his armies!
	1.01	Auf des Hammers Schwung schwebet herbei! Dunstig Gedämpf! Schwebend Gedüft! Donner, der Herr, ruft euch zu Heer! Heda! Heda! Hedo!	At the swing of my hammer, float this way! Steamy vapors! Floating mists! Donner, your ruler, summons his armies! Heda! Heda! Hedo!
	2.01	*(Donner and Froh are covered by a thundercloud, thick and black; as his hammer strikes the rock, there is a flash of lightning, followed by a violent clap of thunder)*	
		Bruder, Zu mir! Weise der Brücke den Weg!	Brother, to me! show us the way over the bridge!
The music moves to G♭ and the texture softens, while the motif (ex. 2) associated with Froh's rainbow – an arc-like series of phrases – is heard (horns, clarinets, bassoons, cellos)	2.21	*(as the clouds lift, Donner and Froh are seen; a brilliant rainbow bridge stretches across the valley to the fortress, now gleaming in the evening sunlight)*	

At the end of it, as the music turns to D♭, a soft and majestic theme (ex. 3) is heard on the Wagner tubas (small tubas, akin to horns, invented by Wagner): this is the Valhalla motif, which rings out ever more nobly and strongly, with a trumpet fanfare rhythm in support, as the great fortress comes more clearly into our view and the gods' view. The Valhalla motif remains prominent in the orchestra as Wotan sings, modulating and leading to A♭.

But at 'Von Morgen', as he recalls the troubling events of the day, the texture darkens, the firm major-key harmony sours and the music moves to a♭; and in place of the confident Valhalla music the Ring motif (ex. 4) appears – but note the resemblance between them, hinting to the listener of the link between Valhalla and the Ring.

The music moves to C for a noble trumpet phrase, ex. 5. This motif will later stand for the magical sword that Wotan passes to his son – to regain the gods' dominion. (At a rehearsal at Bayreuth in 1876, Wagner told the Wotan to seize and brandish a sword from the pile of Nibelung treasure still on the stage.)

The Valhalla motif returns, back in D♭, as Wotan calls Fricka to enter.

A flickering phrase, associated with Loge (ex. 6), heralds his words, mixing with the Valhalla music and, as his expression of shame, with the Ring motif; the shimmering music (at 'statt mit der Blinden') is a further Loge theme. But as he rejoins the gods the music moves back to A♭ and the pendant to the Valhalla theme.

FROH

2.53
| Zur Burg führt die Brücke, leicht, doch fest eurem Fuss: beschreitet kühn ihren schrecklosen Pfad! | Leading to the fortress is the bridge; it is light but firm underfoot. Stride boldly on its danger-free path! |

3.17 *(Wotan and the other gods gaze speechless at the sight)*

WOTAN

4.05
| Abendlich strahlt der Sonne Auge; in prächtiger Glut prangt glänzend die Burg. In des Morgens Scheine mutig erschimmernd, lag sie herrenlos, hehr verlockend vor mir. | The evening rays stream from the eye of the sun; in the splendid glow the fortress proudly gleams. In the radiance of morning it bravely glittered, as it lay unoccupied, loftily inviting before me. |

5.06
| Von Morgen bis Abend, in Müh' und Angst, nicht wonnig ward sie gewonnen! Es naht die Nacht: vor ihrem Neid biete sie Bergung nun. | Between morning and evening, with trouble and anxiety, it was acquired, but not happily! The night draws on, from whose envy it now offers shelter. |

5.54 *(struck by a noble thought, he stands resolutely)*
| So grüss' ich die Burg, sicher vor Bang' und Grau'n! | Thus do I greet the fortress, safe from fear and horror. |

(he turns solemnly to Fricka)

6.32
| Folge mir, Frau: Im Walhall wohne mit mir! | Follow me, wife: dwell with me in Valhalla! |

FRICKA

6.56
| Was deutet der Name? Nie, dünkt mich, hört ich ihn nennen. | What does the name mean? I do not think I have heard it before. |

WOTAN

7.05
| Was, mächtig der Furcht, mein Mut mir erfand, Wenn siegend es lebt, leg' es den Sinn dir dar. | What power over my fear my courage inspired in me, if it lives victorious the sense will become clear. |

(taking Fricka by the hand, he slowly walks to the bridge: Froh, Freia, and Donner follow)

LOGE

7.34
| Ihrem Ende eilen sie zu, die so stark im Bestehen sich wahnen. | They are hurrying towards their end although they imagine themselves so strong and secure. |

7.42
| Fast schäm' ich mich, mit ihnen zu schaffen; zur leckenden Lohe mich wieder zu wandeln, spür' ich lockende Lust: sie aufzuzehren, die einst mich gezähmt, | I am almost ashamed to work with them; I am tempted to turn myself back into flickering fire – to consume those who once tamed me, and not foolishly to pass on with the blind ones (even if they are the most godlike of gods!), does not seem stupid to me. I shall think it over; who knows what I might do! |

7.55
| statt mit der Blinden blöd' zu vergeh'n, und wären es götlichste Götter! Nicht dumm dünkte mich das! Bedenken will ich's: wer weiss, was ich tu'! | |

8.08 *(he goes, as if unconcernedly, to join the gods)*

RHINEMAIDENS
(unseen, in the valley below)

The cry of the Rhinemaidens is heard (ex. 7 shows its original form and the version here, affected by their sorrow at having lost the gold).

8.20 Rheingold! Rheingold! | Rhinegold! Rhinegold! Pure gold!
Reines Gold! | How pure and brilliant you shone
wie lauter und hell | so beautifully for us!
leuchtetest hold du uns! |

WOTAN
(pausing with one foot on the bridge)

As Wotan responds, the original Rhinegold motif (ex. 8) is heard on the horn, in E♭.

8.38 Welch' Klagen klingt zu mir her? | What is that wailing sound I hear?

RHINEMAIDENS

Um dich, du klares, | For your gleam we now lament:
wir nun klagen: | give us the gold! oh give us back
gebt uns das Gold! | its purity!
O gebt uns das reine zurück! |

LOGE
(looking down into the valley)

Das Rheines Kinder | The children of the Rhine are
beklagen des Goldes Raub! | mourning the theft of the gold!

WOTAN

Verwünschte Nicker! | Wretched nymphs! Stop them
Wehre ihrem Geneck! | irritating us!

LOGE
(calling down into the valley)

Valhalla music accompanies Loge's words; at the end of his remarks a further motif for Loge, ex. 9 (related to ex. 6) is heard.

9.07 Ihr da im Wasser! | You there in the water! why are
was weint ihr herauf? | you crying to us? Hear what
Hört, was Wotan | Wotan wants for you! The gold
euch wünscht! | shall shine no more for you
Glänzt nicht mehr | maidens, but in future you
euch Mädchen das gold, | can happily sun yourselves in
in der Götter neuem Glanze | the gods' new brightness!
sonnt euch selig fortan! |

(the gods laugh and move in procession over the bridge)

RHINEMAIDENS

The Rhinemaidens' cry returns, with a marked minor inflection; the horn's Rhinegold motif too is in the minor, f.

9.41 Rheingold! Rheingold! | Rhinegold! Rhinegold! Purest
Reines Gold! | gold! If only your brilliant glitter
O leuchtete noch | still shone in the depths!
in der Tiefe dein laut'rer Tand! |

10.02 Traulich und treu | Tenderness and truth are only
ist's nur in der Tiefe: | in the depths; false and
falsch und feig | cowardly are those who rejoice
ist' was dort oben sich freut! | up there!

As the gods cross the bridge, the Valhalla motif, in D♭, becomes even more grand and imposing; and finally the Rainbow motif (ex. 2, 10.50) returns, now in D♭, the Valhalla key, symbolizing the link between the rainbow and Valhalla – as too does the resemblance between the rhythms and the melodic outlines of these two motifs.

10.50 *(the gods cross the rainbow bridge to the fortress; the curtain falls)*

11.43 (end)

ex. 1

He - da!   He - da! He-do!

ex. 2

ex. 3

ex. 4

ex. 5

ex. 6

ex. 7

(original)   (now)

80 *Wagner's
Götterdämmerung
("Twilight of the Gods")
in Harry Kupfer's
production of the Ring
cycle at the Bayreuth
Festival, 1991.*

ex. 8

ex. 9

leitmotif material – can readily show (**ex. a–d**): these ideas represent respectively the forging of metal, the idea of a sword powerful enough to redeem the world, the hero Siegfried's horn-call, and a love theme.

These *leitmotifs* are not simply "labels", designed to draw attention to something that is happening on the stage. Often they stand for much larger concepts. Thus the *leitmotif* used for the ring – forged from gold from the Rhine, and capable of bestowing power on its possessor – has also been described as standing for the purpose of the psyche or the self, and the one used for Loge, the god of fire, can be interpreted as representing libido or primal energy from the unconscious. Then, further, a *leitmotif* may develop and change to signify development and change in what it stands for. For example, the joyous cry of "Rhinegold!" heard from the Rhinemaidens, custodians of the gold (**ex. e**), acquires a dark flavor when the gold, stolen from them, is being forged (**ex. f**).

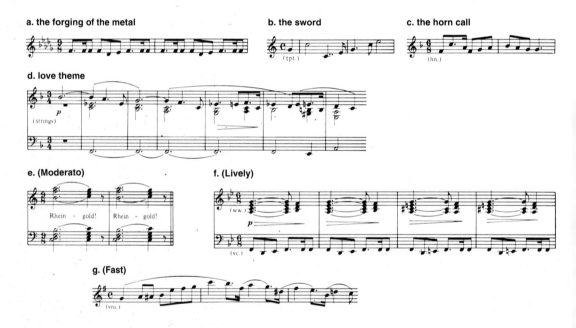

The *leitmotif*, as Wagner used it, offers the composer great opportunities for the subtle treatment of ideas. It may, for example, be heard in the orchestra to represent an unspoken thought of a character on the stage; or it may tell the audience something unknown to those on the stage, like the identity of a disguised character or the motives behind some action. It may establish a connection with some earlier event. A number of *leitmotifs* may be combined to show links between ideas. Many are in any case thematically related where the ideas they stand for are connected. Sometimes the relationships become clear only as the music and the drama progress – **ex. g**, for example, shows a motif associated with passion and agitation which is clearly linked with the love theme of **ex. d**.

Plate 13 Opposite
Fryderyk Chopin: *detail of portrait, 1838, by Eugène Delacroix. Musée du Louvre, Paris.*

There are no "songs" in the *Ring*. The musical texture is made up of an enriched narrative and dialog (there are virtually no instances of two characters singing simultaneously); the orchestra supplies a texture of commentary and explanation. It has been said, only half-jokingly, that the entire action of the *Ring* could be followed by listening to the orchestra alone, with the voices left out. The work is enormously long: *Rheingold* (see **Listening Guide 42**) plays continuously for about two and a half hours, *Walküre* and *Siegfried* each around five hours (including intervals), and *Twilight of the Gods* six. The network of *leitmotifs*, which multiplies as the work proceeds, holds this structure together, and Wagner supports it in two main ways: first, through his superb sense of theater, which enables him to give each act a powerful shape; and second, through his clever building-up of musical recapitulations. In *Walküre*, for example, Wotan, chief of the gods, tells his daughter the Valkyrie (warrior maiden) Brünnhilde of the events portrayed in *Rheingold*; in *Siegfried* there is a "riddle scene" in which earlier events are discussed: and in *Twilight of the Gods* there is a lengthy prolog in which the Norns (or Fates) discuss what has happened in the world above, and a Funeral March for Siegfried in which the events of his life are recalled. In all of these Wagner is able to draw together the musical material associated with what is being discussed. As the work proceeds – and particularly in the last part of *Siegfried* and *Twilight of the Gods*, written after the long break when Wagner composed other operas – the musical fabric becomes thicker, but that makes good dramatic sense as the plot does so too.

The *Ring* is Wagner's greatest achievement; it has even been claimed, not unreasonably, as the greatest achievement of Western culture, so huge is its scale, so wide-ranging the issues it deals with, so profoundly unified is it on so many planes. It is based on ancient sagas: Wagner believed, as others have done too, that the truths embodied in myth have meanings far beyond any literal interpretation. The story of the *Ring* is about gods, dwarves (Nibelungs), giants, and humans; it has been read (and performed) as a manifesto for socialism, as a plea for a Nazi-like racialism, as a study of the workings of the human psyche, as a forecast of the fate of the world and humankind, as a parable about the new industrial society of Wagner's time. It is all of these, and much more too. It touches at some point on every kind of human relationship and on numerous moral and philosophical issues. It is inevitably the focus of all debate on Wagner's greatness and the meaning of his works.

Plate 14 Opposite
Hector Berlioz: *portrait,
1830, by Emile Signol.
Villa Medici, Rome.*

The *Ring* does not, however, embody all of Wagner. The other three operas of his full maturity each go uniquely far in a particular direction. *Parsifal*, in which acts akin to Holy Communion are portrayed on the stage, treats in a Christian context the theme of redemption which runs through all Wagner's works (the *Ring* included, for there Brünnhilde redeems the world with her immolation on Siegfried's funeral pyre and her restoration to the Rhine of the stolen gold). The theme of *Tristan und Isolde* is sexual love, expressed with the full force of the language Wagner was devising in the 1850s: the same narrative style as he used in the *Ring*, though here warmer and more lyrical, and the same large orchestra, though here treated in a richer and more sensuous way than in the more austere mythological saga.

Above all, Wagner here extended the expressive capacity of music by developing a style more chromatic than anyone had attempted before. Chromaticism, since the times of Monteverdi, Bach, and Mozart, had been recognized as a means of heightening emotional expression. Then, it always operated within a clear sense of key, which it would contradict only momentarily; but with Wagner it was used so freely, and in so many simultaneous layers, that it loosened the sense of key or even broke it down altogether. This had long-term implications, as we shall see in later chapters; in *Tristan*, it led to a sense of instability for as soon as the listener feels that the music is moving in one direction, that direction is contradicted. There are similar procedures in the *Ring*, but they move more slowly and less restlessly. The particular melodic style of *Tristan* enhances the restlessness: the sense of passionate yearning that permeates the opera is conveyed partly through the chromatic dissonances and the way they demand to be resolved – the notes seem to press urgently onward, and often upward. Later, Wagner uses this device in different instruments at the same time, not merely to make the effect the more strongly but also to give a sense of harmonically shifting sands. This applies above all to the second act of the opera, which is virtually a continuous love scene, touching on every emotion from the gentlest and tenderest to the most fiercely passionate. At the end of the work, Tristan dies, at the instant of reunion with Isolde; she then dies too, a "Love-Death", by his body – the ultimate, transcendental act of love being union in death.

Tristan, Isolde, Wotan, Brünnhilde, Siegfried: these are not people you meet every day. They are not meant to be "real" people at all, but ideal embodiments of human qualities. Wagner did however write one opera about real people, or more nearly real ones: *The Mastersingers of Nuremberg*. Here he abandoned myth in favor of history – German history, of course – setting the opera in the sixteenth century and in a famous center of Germanic art, one of the homes of the Renaissance Mastersinger tradition. The characters in this work, a comic opera though in its way deeply serious, are worthy citizens of Nuremberg, including one historical figure, the cobbler-musician Hans Sachs; another of them is in effect Wagner himself. The hero of this opera is Walther von Stolzing, a noble poet-musician who loves the daughter of a rich Mastersinger and hopes to win her hand by victory in a song contest. At first he is derided for his strange song, which breaks all known rules, but ultimately he triumphs, helped by Sachs's explanation that art cannot be constrained by old rules and that true genius creates new ones; the analogy with Wagner's view of his role as extending through his genius the laws of music needs no emphasis.

The Mastersingers does not in fact follow Tristan into the world of harmonic complexity, nor does it follow the Ring into that of motivic elaboration. The work is distinguished by the constant warmth and good humor of its music, the expressiveness of its individual themes, and above all by the richness with which they are interwoven. Perhaps to some extent taking a cue from its setting in the sixteenth century, a great age of polyphony, The Mastersingers contains some of the most fluent and sumptuous polyphonic writing of the nineteenth century; and in it Wagner created some memorable characters, like Sachs the benign and generous cobbler, Beckmesser the foolish and pedantic town clerk (whom Wagner identified with his critics and especially his chief opponent, the conservative Viennese writer Eduard Hanslick), and the lovers Walther and Eva. It may not be Wagner's greatest or most important work, but it shows his humor and humanity as no other does.

12 *Brahms*

Johannes Brahms was born in Hamburg in 1833, the son of a double-bass player; his mother was older than his father by 17 years. At seven he started piano lessons, made rapid progress, and in his early teens was sent to a leading Hamburg pianist and composer. He was soon playing in taverns around the Hamburg dock area and making arrangements of music for his father's group. At 15 he gave his first solo recital. On concert tours in the 1850s he met the eminent violinist Joseph Joachim (1831–1907), Liszt (with whom he felt out of sympathy), and Robert and Clara Schumann. Schumann drew attention to him in an enthusiastic article. Soon after his return to Hamburg, Brahms heard of Schumann's breakdown and went to be near him – and near Clara, for whom he developed a romantic passion which lasted, at a calmer level, all his life.

Brahms's main compositions in these years were principally for the piano. They include three substantial sonatas, of which the last, in F minor, shows, in its mixture of the passionate and the contemplative, and in its rich, often dark-toned textures, the direction his genius was taking. He also wrote songs. In the late 1850s he spent some months each year at the small court at Detmold, where he could work with an orchestra. For this group he composed two more relaxed orchestral works, which he called serenades: he did not yet feel ready to write anything as ambitious as a symphony. He tried embarking on one, but decided to use the music instead in a concerto for his own instrument – the Piano Concerto in D minor, a work of extraordinary fire and originality.

Johannes Brahms — Life and Works

1833	born in Hamburg, 7 May
1848	first piano recital; earned living playing in taverns etc.
1850	concert tour with the violinist Reményi during which he met the violinist Joachim, who became a close friend, and Liszt
1853	met Schumann, who proclaimed his genius in a periodical article
1854	to Bonn to see Clara Schumann, to whom he became passionately devoted; first piano works
1857	Hamburg; piano teacher and conductor of the court orchestra at Detmold
1860	signed a manifesto opposing the 'new music' of Liszt
1863	conductor of the Vienna Singakademie
1864–71	freelance teacher in Vienna; piano and chamber works, *German Requiem*
1872–5	conductor of Vienna Philharmonic concerts; *St Antony Variations*
1876	completed First Symphony, started in 1855
1877–9	Second Symphony, Violin Concerto
1879	awarded many honors; *Academic Festival Overture*
1881	rift in friendship with Joachim; offered Meiningen court orchestra to try out works
1883	Third Symphony
1885	Fourth Symphony
1891	met the clarinetist Richard Mühlfeld who inspired four works
1897	died in Vienna, 3 April

Orchestral music symphonies – no. 1, c (1876), no. 2, D (1877), no. 3, F (1883), no. 4, e (1885); piano concertos – no. 1, d (1858), no. 2, B♭ (1881); Violin Concerto (1878); Concerto for violin and cello (1887); Academic Festival Overture (1880); Tragic Overture (1881); St Antony Variations (1873); serenades

Chamber music 2 string sextets (1860, 1865); 2 string quintets (1882, 1890); 3 string quartets – c, a (1873), B♭ (1876); Piano Quintet, f (1864); 3 piano quartets (1861, 1862, 1875); 3 piano trios (1854, 1882, 1886); Clarinet Quintet (1891); violin sonatas

Piano music sonatas – no. 1, C (1853), no. 2, f♯ (1852), no. 3, f (1853); rhapsodies, intermezzos, ballades, capriccios, variations; piano duets – Liebeslieder Waltzes (1874, 1877); Hungarian Dances (1852–69)

Choral music A German Requiem (1868); Alto Rhapsody (1869); partsongs

Songs Four Serious Songs (1896); over 180 others

Organ music

Original it may have been, but still firmly in a tradition of purely musical expression: Brahms had no interest in changing the nature of expression in music, or lending it non-musical implications, as did Liszt, Berlioz, and Wagner. Indeed he said so, in a famous, outspoken manifesto that he and some friends published in 1860. He was now living in Hamburg, where he held a post as conductor of a ladies' choir, but he was also active as a pianist-composer and traveled frequently to play. Some important piano works belong to this period.

Brahms had published a good deal of music by this date, but, coming up to the age of 30, looked for wider recognition. He hoped for a position as conductor of the Hamburg Philharmonic concerts, but was passed over. He had in fact left Hamburg shortly before, to make himself known in Vienna; now he decided to stay there, accepting a post as director of the Singakademie in 1863. This was a choral society which often sang unaccompanied, and Brahms was accordingly drawn to study earlier music. He remained only one season there, however; he could make a living by playing, and he also did some teaching.

Brahms: Symphony no. 1 in c, op. 68 (1876), first movement

Brahms began work on his First Symphony in 1855, when he was 22. The first movement, though without its slow introduction, was fully completed by 1862, but it was another 12 years before he resumed work – he had in the meantime acquired more experience of writing for orchestra, and now felt more secure about it – and it was not until 1876 that the whole symphony was ready for performance. The musical world had come to see Brahms as Beethoven's successor in the field of instrumental music, and this had made him all the more reluctant to present a new work in an older mold – for many recent orchestral works by other composers had embodied a programmatic element – until he was sure that the music was well worthy of him. Even when the symphony was in rehearsal, he made cuts in the inner movements. The first performance was not in Vienna but in Karlsruhe, though at the end of 1876 he let the Viennese hear it and it was warmly received: they had expected a work following up Beethoven's symphonies, and when the finale of Brahms's work turned out to have a theme with an obvious resemblance to that of Beethoven's Ninth a few people dubbed the new work 'Beethoven's Tenth'.

The symphony is in four movements: the first is followed by an Andante in E major, an Allegretto in A♭ major (not a lively scherzo in the Beethoven tradition but rather a gentle, wistful intermezzo), and a large-scale sonata-form finale with a slow introduction, in which the C minor tonality gives way to a brighter, triumphant C major, with much the same implications as in Beethoven's no. 5 (Listening Guide 28).

 Listening Outline

First movement (Un poco sostenuto – Allegro), 6/8, c; sonata form
2 flutes, 2 oboes, 2 clarinets, 2 bassoons, double bassoon
2 horns, 2 trumpets; timpani
1st and 2nd violins, violas, cellos, double basses

Time		
0.00	**introduction**	ex. 1: note the violin theme, striving upwards, against the woodwind theme, moving down, and figs. a^1 and a^2, b and c, all later to be important – and used both as they are and upside-down. Another idea, ex. 2, is heard on woodwinds and pizzicato strings. Ex. 1 returns, in g (1.48); an oboe solo follows (2.06)
	exposition	
2.46	first group, c	ex. 3: based on a^1 and a^2, continued with b; ex. 4 follows (compare ex. 2)
3.21	transition	ex. 5: note combination of a^1 (inverted) and b, and later the rising semitone of a^1 in pizzicato strings
4.17	second group, E♭	ex. 6, oboe and cellos, followed by a new oboe theme and dialog with clarinet, then horn–clarinet dialog; a tutti ensues, built on c and b (both inverted)
5.45	**development**	a short, turbulent tutti on b; then a quiet, sustained passage for flute and oboe and a development (in f) of c (inverted; 6.26) leading to emphatic dialogs between wind and strings in distant keys. Back in c, a quiet, reflective passage begins (7.18) based on a^1, then taken up by bass instruments; a combination of c and a^2 (8.14) brings the music to a powerful climax
	recapitulation	
8.39	first group, c	as before, slightly shortened at end
9.18	transition	shortened, leading to c/C
9.37	second group, c/C	partly in c, partly C
10.58	**coda**	violent dialog on two-note figure between winds and strings; then a quieter passage (similar to 7.18), and the music slows down (notably at 11.45), using a^1
12.35		(end)

For a three-year period, in the early 1870s, Brahms conducted the Vienna Philharmonic Society concerts. But all he really wanted to do was compose. He was a slow and intensely self-critical composer; he consulted his friends, especially Joachim and Clara Schumann, about new works, and was always ready to revise – he destroyed much that he wrote, held pieces back from publication, and was often indecisive (as with the D minor Piano Concerto) over the form a piece should take. In 1864, for example, he completed a piano quintet which he had started as a string quintet and then converted into a two-piano sonata before he settled on its final form. But he still did not feel ready to undertake a symphony.

Brahms did produce a major choral piece, the *German Requiem*, in the late 1860s. He had begun work on it many years earlier (again unsure of just what form it should take), and took it up soon after his mother's death in 1865. It came before the public in piecemeal fashion – three movements in 1867, six the next year, and the complete seven in 1869. It is not a traditional Roman Catholic *Requiem* for the dead but a series of settings of biblical texts, in German, that speak of death, mourning, and comfort (he was not in fact a believer, and composed no church music).

In 1876 Brahms at last felt ready to give his first symphony to the impatient world. He had begun its composition as far back as 1855, but had moved even more slowly than usual, conscious of the role that he had come to occupy in people's minds as heir to the Beethoven symphony tradition and anxious to be worthy of so weighty a responsibility. He did not fail (see **Listening Guide 43**).

The completion and successful early performances of his symphony seem to have released something in Brahms. Now he felt ready to fulfill his destiny as an orchestral composer. His Second Symphony, gentler and more relaxed than his First, was written the following year, and first performed by the Vienna Philharmonic. The next year he wrote his Violin Concerto, for his friend Joachim: another extended and spacious work, it taxes the soloist severely (a "concerto *against* the violin", said Joachim), and in doing so it surpasses even the Beethoven concerto in its heroic effect as the solo voice of the violin struggles against the orchestra.

One of the few surviving private orchestras in Europe at this time was at the court of the Duke of Saxe-Meiningen. Its director was Hans von Bülow, who, since hearing Brahms's First Symphony – and since the time of his break with Wagner on personal grounds – had come to see Brahms as the true custodian of the Beethoven symphonic tradition. He offered Brahms the use of the Meiningen orchestra to try out his works in progress; Brahms eagerly accepted. This encouraged him to pursue orchestral composition. In 1883 he completed his Third Symphony, in 1885 his Fourth (and last), working at them chiefly during the summers and usually by a lake or some other rural setting.

Meanwhile, chamber music and songs had flowed steadily from Brahms's pen. His third and last violin sonata dates from 1888 and a string quintet – Brahms loved the richer textures that could be obtained from a group larger than the traditional quartet – from 1890. About that time he heard the clarinetist Richard Mühlfeld play at Meiningen and he wrote a series of works for him, including a Clarinet Quintet (1891) in which Brahms revels in the variety of soft and rich colors in the ensemble of clarinet and strings.

Now Brahms returned, after more than ten years, to piano music. He wrote four sets of short, independent pieces with titles like "intermezzo" or "capriccio", some of them fiery and brilliant but mostly reflective, subtle, and fanciful, and all written with the serene mastery of the mature composer. Virtually all his life Brahms had composed songs; at the very end, in 1896, he wrote a set called *Four Serious Songs* – to biblical texts, concerned, as in the *German Requiem*, with death and consolation. These are somber music, dark-toned and powerful, written when he knew that death was close.

The *Four Serious Songs* were Brahms's last composition. He was only in his early 60s; but in spite of the universal recognition accorded to him in his late years – he had received many honors, and was offered the freedom of his native Hamburg, for example – he had suffered from the deaths of many friends. In 1896 he developed cancer of the liver; a cure at a spa did not help him, and next spring he died.

MUSIC

Brahms was regarded in his day as a musical conservative – indeed *the* musical conservative. This was because he rejected the outlook of the "progressives" of his day – Wagner and Liszt above all – in their wish to give music meanings outside itself, relating it to literature or the visual arts. Brahms's musical forms, accordingly, are governed not, as Liszt's are, by a narrative or a philosophical idea, or, as Wagner's are, by dramatic considerations. He followed the same formal principles as Beethoven did, in his works for orchestra, his chamber music, and in most of his piano music; sometimes he looked even further back – it was his interest in early music (unusual for composers of his time) that led him, in his Fourth Symphony, to use a Bach-style ground-bass scheme, and he used Bachian forms and techniques too in the organ music he composed late in his life.

But it would be a mistake to regard Brahms as backward-looking. A leading twentieth-century composer, Arnold Schoenberg (see p. 342), once called him "Brahms the progressive". Writing extended instrumental works, he had to find ways of giving them formal coherence and unity, and he found that the ways used by Haydn and Beethoven did not always work in the richer harmonic and textural style he wanted (Brahms always favored full, sumptuous textures, as his preference for such types as the string quintet and string sextet, and his full, chordal writing for piano and orchestra, shows). So he developed a way of weaving into his music motifs or entire themes, working them into the texture, often as accompaniment to something else that was going on, often transformed in some way – for example by inverting them, or turning them upside-down. This gives the music a powerful sense of holding together, especially when he used these ideas across several movements of a long work.

Brahms was original in other ways too. He developed a melodic style of his own, influenced, especially in his songs, by German folksong. He tried writing a new kind of scherzo movement, sometimes called the "intermezzo" type: he used this kind of gentle, contemplative, graceful piece, in a moderate tempo, in most of his symphonies. He pursued Beethoven's manner of writing variations, particularly in his piano music – his early works include several fine sets, notably one on a theme by Handel – and this technique runs through all his music, helping to give it unity. It was above all his grasp of large-scale form, in which all these techniques played a part, that established Brahms's mastery. He was no revolutionary, and his innovations are all of an unobtrusive kind (though they were later to have a profound influence). His principles were classical, yet in his music a warm and truly Romantic spirit is unmistakable beneath a surface that may be gruff and even austere.

Part VII The Turn of the Century

1 *Nationalism and Decadence*

The Romantic era is usually seen as continuing up to those critical years around 1910–13, just before the outbreak of World War I. But we do well to distinguish between its beginnings, in the hands of such composers as Chopin, Schumann, and Berlioz, and the post-Wagnerian period. The break is not, of course, sharp and clear; history does not usually fall conveniently for historians who want to draw lines. In the last chapter, however, we dealt principally with composers who preceded Wagner or stood apart from him (like Verdi and Brahms) because they had already found their own musical language before they felt Wagner's impact. Of the composers considered in the present chapter, virtually all were affected by Wagner, even those who consciously rejected him. These are men who were active chiefly between the 1870s and World War I, though some lived longer (Richard Strauss even beyond the end of World War II).

Composers of the Turn of the Century

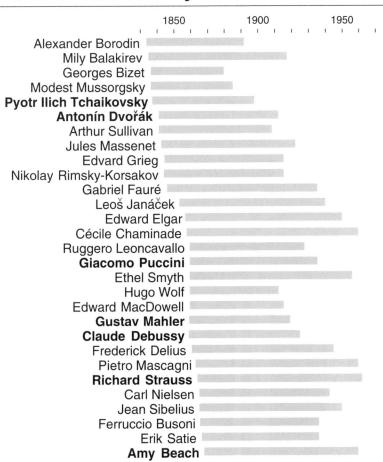

Essentially, this is the era when composers sought new ways of developing the language of music. It was not, however, mainly because of Wagner that the composers of Russia and eastern Europe chose the directions they did. The middle of the nineteenth century was a time when the peoples of many European countries became increasingly aware of their national identity. Partly this was because of the growing interest in the past and in the meaning of national traditions. But it was also closely linked with current political developments, as the traditional rulers, princely and ecclesiastical, were forced to give way to more democratic forms of government and as groups bound by language and tradition threw off foreign domination. Belgium and the Netherlands (or Holland) became kingdoms in 1830, Italy in 1861, Germany an empire in 1871.

Others, while remaining under foreign dominion, found a new awareness of their traditions: the Czechs and Hungarians, for example, began to cherish their folksong and literature although German was the language, generally speaking, of the ruling

Nationalism

classes. In these countries and in Poland and Russia, the traditions of cultivated music were largely Italian and German, but new composers began to set words in the tongue spoken by the large majority of the people. It was natural that in doing so they should make efforts to incorporate features of their national folksong traditions – not only did such melodies fit with the rhythms and the rise and fall of the words, but they also had a familiarity that was bound to be appealing. Economic factors played a part: with the advance of industrialization, larger population centers were beginning to develop, and from what had once been a rural peasant class a middle class was forming, ready to go to concerts and opera houses.

The composers of Russia – not all of them, for the greatest, Tchaikovsky, stood somewhat apart from this development – formed the most prominent and most deliberate group of nationalists, using folksong liberally in their music. This was a period when other arts flowered in Russia, with the poet Pushkin at the beginning of the century and the writers Tolstoy, Chekhov, and Dostoyevsky later.

82 *Čapek's design for the lawyer's office in Janáček's opera* The Makropoulos Case, *first performed 18 December 1926. Moravské Muzeum, Brno. The opera was based on a play by the artist's brother.*

Russian music, which for social and religious reasons had hardly escaped its medieval roots until the middle of the eighteenth century, was a later growth. Under the eighteenth-century rulers, the Russian court had sought to place itself abreast of developments elsewhere in Europe by inviting leading Italian composers to work there and sending Russian composers to study abroad. Russian music had begun, only with the work of the eccentric genius Mikhail Glinka (1804–57), to acquire a character of its own; part of that character – a part widely admired in the rest of Europe – came from the incorporation of Russian folk elements. The ideals of Glinka, who was regarded by the next generation as the "father of Russian music", were taken up by such men as Modest Mussorgsky (1839–81) and Nikolay Rimsky-Korsakov (1844–1908), the most important members of the group of so-called nationalist composers known as "The Five" or "Mighty Handful". These men drew extensively on Russian history, Russian legend, and the colorful and appealing fund of Russian folksong in their operas and their orchestral works.

Another important center of Slavic nationalism was Prague, capital of the Czech lands. Here, however, nationalism had an additional political element as the Czech peoples tried to assert their national identity while still under the dominion of the Austrian Empire. Although the Czech language – an important symbol in a land where the ruling classes chiefly spoke German – had occasionally been used in opera since the eighteenth century, the first important operas in Czech were by Bedřich Smetana (1824–84), who also wrote six symphonic poems about the countryside, the history, and the legends of his native land. His two best-known works are his opera *The Bartered Bride* (1870), an entertaining tale of Czech village life, and his symphonic poem *Vltava*, which traces in music the course of the national river as it flows through the Bohemian countryside and reaches its full majesty in the capital city of Prague. Smetana's younger contemporary, Dvořák (see p. 307), achieved greater international fame. But perhaps the most enterprising and original of the Czech operatic composers was Leoš Janáček (1854–1928), whose operas, deeply influenced in their musical style by the rhythms and inflections of the Czech language, cover a wide range of topics, from family conflict (involving the oppression of womenfolk) to journeys to the moon, animal life in the Czech forests, and the tale of a woman who stayed young for more than three centuries.

Outside central Europe, musical nationalism took rather different forms. The links between northern Europe and Germany had long been strong, and such composers as Edvard Grieg (1843–1907), from Norway, and Jean Sibelius (1865–1957), from Finland, had as a matter of course studied at the Leipzig Conservatory. However, Grieg went back to Norway to compose his most characteristic works in a distinctively Nordic manner ("pink bon-bons stuffed with snow", the Frenchman Debussy described them), while Sibelius – whose thinking, unlike Grieg's, was on an extended scale – carried in his seven symphonies the motivic manner of the Beethoven-Brahms tradition to its logical conclusion. Their scale is epic, yet their argument is often dense and compressed. The Dane Carl Nielsen (1865–1931) also wrote extended symphonies but of a more quirky and fanciful character.

The rise of Sibelius and Nielsen in the Nordic countries is paralleled by that of

Edward Elgar (1857–1934) in England: he too was a symphonist, essentially in the Brahmsian tradition, but is best remembered for his *Enigma Variations* for orchestra (dedicated to his "friends pictured within", each variation being a portrait of someone from his circle) and for his nostalgic and deeply poetic Cello Concerto. Elgar, however, was less nationalist in his music – in the sense of drawing on a national pool of folksong, or on the long traditions of English music – than Ralph Vaughan Williams (1872–1958), an avid collector of English folksong who used his knowledge of both the folk and art traditions of English music to impart to his symphonies, his songs, and his other works a distinctive English flavor.

Spanish composers at the end of the century, such as Albéniz and Granados, also drew strongly on colorful local tradition and especially dance rhythms in their music, which is mostly limited in scale.

The increase in national consciousness was not confined to the periphery of Europe. Brahms, as we have seen, used German folksong, and Wagner was deeply aware of his identity as a German; Verdi was equally alive to his as an Italian. But in these countries, and in France, the traditions of art music were strong and individual enough for the use of folksong to be neither necessary nor manageable: composers' language was already marked by national taste, while folksong did not readily fit into the well-formed style that composers of these countries used. In Britain, the predominant taste was Germanic, though eventually a powerful folksong movement was to assert itself. In the United States, art music traditions, which essentially were imported from Europe, were very diverse though again mainly

83 Symposium: *group portrait, 1894, by Akseli Gallén-Kallela, with* (right to left) Sibelius, *the conductor Robert Kajanus, Oskar Merikanto, and the artist. Private collection.*

German. Louis Moreau Gottschalk (1829–69) drew on Afro-American and Hispanic elements, but the best-known American composer of the century, Edward MacDowell (1860–1908), was fully cosmopolitan in his musical language.

The use of national features could be something more than national assertion. The Russian composer Rimsky-Korsakov wrote a *Spanish Caprice*, using the colors and the rhythms of Spain, and a work called *Sheherazade* hinting at the music of the Middle East. This was part of a fairly widespread movement towards the mysterious and the exotic. Other composers looked beyond Europe: Debussy, for example, sought inspiration in the gamelan music and gongs of Indonesia, which he heard at the Paris Exhibition of 1889, and wrote an Egyptian ballet (he also composed Spanish-colored music, like many Frenchmen, including Bizet before him and Ravel after), while Puccini looked still further afield – to Japan, China, and the American West – in search of new colors and ideas.

There are parallels in the visual arts, for example in the inspiration sought by Paul Gauguin (1848–1903) in the South Pacific. Here there was also a clear element of escape from the sophistication and artificiality of Western society in favor of a "return to Nature", to which there could be no exact analogy in music although the composers who used folksong certainly had similar feelings. A close parallel at this period between music and painting, however, may be drawn between Debussy and the French Impressionists, such as Claude Monet (1840–1926) and Camille Pissarro (1830–1903), in his use of washes of color and vague, suggestive harmony in place of clear-cut themes, and in his reliance on dreaminess and sensory impression. Arguably he is even closer to the Symbolist school, including such painters as Gustave Moreau (1826–98), and the poet Stéphane Mallarmé (1842–98), the author of the poem that gave rise to his most famous work, *Prélude à "L'après-midi d'un faune"*, but to see precise parallels between them is difficult.

2 *Tchaikovsky*

Pyotr Ilyich Tchaikovsky was born in 1840 in the Vyatka province, where his father was a mining engineer and factory manager. His mother had a French grandfather, but his attraction to things French has normally been connected not so much with this blood tie as with his having been taught by a French governess. In 1848 the Tchaikovskys moved to St Petersburg, where the future composer was educated at the School of Jurisprudence (1850–59). During this time, and particularly after his mother's death in 1854, he began to compose seriously, but on leaving the school he was obliged to take a post in the Ministry of Justice. In 1863 he became a full-time student again, at the St Petersburg Conservatory, where his composition teacher was the young and energetic director Anton Rubinstein.

Pyotr Ilyich Tchaikovsky — Life and Works

1840	born in Kamsko-Votkinsk, Vyatka province, 7 May
1850–59	student at the School of Jurisprudence, St Petersburg
1859–63	clerk at the Ministry of Justice
1863–5	studied with Anton Rubinstein at the St Petersburg Conservatory
1866	professor of harmony at the Moscow Conservatory; First Symphony
1868	met Balakirev and his group of nationalist composers ('The Five') but did not join their circle
1870–74	nationalist compositions, especially operas, attract attention
1875	Piano Concerto no. 1
1876	began correspondence with Nadezhda von Meck, a wealthy widow who helped him financially
1877	married Antonina Milyukova but separated after a few weeks; emotional breakdown
1878	Fourth Symphony, *Eugene Onegin*, Violin Concerto; resigned from Moscow Conservatory; beginning of period of creative sterility but increasing popularity in Russia
1885	*Manfred* Symphony
1890	Nadezhda von Meck ends correspondence and allowance; beginning of deep depression
1891	USA
1893	Sixth ('Pathétique') Symphony; died in St Petersburg, 6 November

Operas The Voyevoda (1869), The Snow Maiden (1873), The Oprichnik (1874), Vakula the Smith (1876), Eugene Onegin (1879), Mazeppa (1884), The Queen of Spades (1890)

Ballets Swan Lake (1877), The Sleeping Beauty (1890), Nutcracker (1892)

Orchestral music symphonies – no. 1, 'Winter Daydreams', g (1866), no. 2, 'Little Russian', c (1872), no. 3, 'Polish', D (1875), no. 4, f (1878), no. 5, e (1888), no. 6, 'Pathétique', b (1893), Manfred (1885); piano concertos – no. 1, b♭ (1875); Violin Concerto (1878); Francesca da Rimini (1876); Hamlet (1888); overtures – Romeo and Juliet (1869), 1812 (1880); Italian Capriccio (1880); suites, variations

Instrumental music Souvenir de Florence, string sextet (1890); string quartets, piano trio; piano music

Songs

Rubinstein was cosmopolitan, concerned for the standard genres of European music and conservative in his musical tastes. The young Tchaikovsky, naturally influenced by his views, wrote a symphony in 1866 (sub-titled "Winter Daydreams"). But in the winter of 1867–8 he came into contact with Mily Balakirev, who was a guiding light among the group of composers known as "The Five" (see p. 299). Balakirev's views were directly opposite to Rubinstein's: he was adamantly Russian nationalist and attracted to folk traditions.

Recognizing Tchaikovsky's talent, Balakirev was eager to make him a sixth member of the circle. But two things prevented that. The first was distance: the Five were based in St Petersburg, whereas Tchaikovsky was now teaching at the new conservatory in Moscow. The second was a natural solitariness on the part of Tchaikovsky himself, who seems already to have sensed that his homosexuality set him apart. Nevertheless, Balakirev had considerable sway in encouraging nationalism in Tchaikovsky. That nationalist streak found expression in his now rarely heard operas.

However, the other early work written under Balakirev's influence was one of the most popular of concert pieces and Tchaikovsky's first mature achievement: the "fantasy overture" *Romeo and Juliet* (1869). The theme of doomed love had an obvious significance to Tchaikovsky and he returned to it in his later illustrative pieces with a literary basis: *Francesca da Rimini* (after Dante, 1876), *Manfred* (after Byron, 1885) and *Hamlet* (after Shakespeare, 1888). In *Romeo and Juliet*, with its vivid orchestration and emotional themes, Tchaikovsky adapted sonata form, preparing the way for integrating the techniques of the symphonic poem into the four-movement symphony. He attempted this in his Second Symphony (1872), whose Ukrainian folksongs earned it the nickname "Little Russian", and again in his Third (1875), called the "Polish". But both these works suggest he was suppressing his dramatic instincts, and his best orchestral piece of this period was one where drama could play a central part: his much admired Piano Concerto no. 1 (1875).

In his first ballet, *Swan Lake* (1877), Tchaikovsky delighted in the opportunity to write exquisitely illustrative music without thought of large-scale musical form. It was a fairy-tale musical world to which he was to return much later in two full-length ballets, the magnificent *Sleeping Beauty* (1890) and his masterpiece of orchestral brilliance, *Nutcracker* (1892).

Meanwhile, in the real world Tchaikovsky's state was not so happy. He became convinced that marriage could release him from the homosexual inclinations about which he felt so guilty. When a certain Antonina Milyukova wrote to him in the spring of 1877 with a confession of love, he was prepared to see where it might lead – especially when he thus found himself in much the same position as the hero of the opera he was just beginning, *Eugene Onegin*. Onegin repulsed his admirer and came to regret his folly; Tchaikovsky accepted the attentions of his Antonina, but the outcome was the same. The two were married less than three months after that first letter; by October they were permanently separated, after a summer which the composer had largely spent escaping from his new wife.

Tchaikovsky's emotional perturbation during this period of crisis is documented in the letters he wrote to his brother Modest and to his distant patron Nadezhda von Meck, who gave him financial and (by correspondence) moral support on condition they never meet. But the intensity of his feelings comes out as well in the music he was writing, above all in his Fourth Symphony (1878), in F minor (see **Listening Guide 44**).

Tchaikovsky completed it during a long stay in western Europe, where he had gone to get over his marriage. It was a productive holiday, for he also finished *Eugene Onegin* and saw the ballet *Sylvia*, of which the music by Léo Delibes (1836–91) greatly impressed him and left its mark on his own *Sleeping Beauty*. Towards the end

84 *Pyotr Ilyich Tchaikovsky: photograph.*

Tchaikovsky: Symphony no. 4 in f (1878), first movement

Tchaikovsky began work on his Fourth Symphony in 1877, the year of his disastrous marriage; he completed it in the early days of 1878, in Italy away from the traumas connected with his marriage (which had driven him to attempt suicide). This was also the time during which he established a relationship, by letter, with his patron Nadezhda von Meck, who did much to encourage him and help him over the crisis in his personal life. The symphony is dedicated to her.

It is in the usual four movements. The first is discussed below, but it should be mentioned here that Tchaikovsky, interested as were many composers of his time in program music, sketched out for Mme von Meck a 'program' for this movement (something he was usually unwilling to do): the motif heard at the beginning he called 'Fate' (the 'germ of the whole symphony', he called it, likening it to the mythological sword of Damocles that 'hangs over our heads'); the main theme stood for depression and hopelessness, the second group as 'escape from reality'. The program is not continued into the other movements. The second is a gentle, tuneful, but pathetic piece using a folksong-like melody, played by the oboe at the start. The scherzo is a remarkable movement, in that the strings play pizzicato throughout; there are sections for the woodwinds as a group and also the brass (heard as if distantly, like a passing band). The last movement is a vigorous and noisy piece incorporating a well-known Russian folksong.

 Listening Outline

First movement (Andante sostenuto – Moderato), 3/4–9/8, f; introduction, sonata form
2 flutes, 2 oboes, 2 clarinets, 2 bassoons
4 horns, 2 trumpets, 3 trombones, tuba; timpani
1st violins, 2nd violins, violas, cellos, double basses

Time		
0.00	**introduction**	motto theme, ex. 1, first on horns and bassoons, then on trumpets and woodwinds
	exposition	
1.19	first group, f	ex. 2, violins and cellos; it is developed and heard in dialog and in the bass, and presented in a fierce tutti
4.40	transition	clarinet and bassoon solo
5.20	second group, a♭	main theme (ex. 3), clarinet, then flute and oboe, then bassoons; the counter-theme (lower line in ex. 3) is heard first on cellos, then flute and bassoon
6.30	closing section	lower line of ex. 3 is taken up by violins, while woodwinds use rhythms of ex. 2 (ex. 4); the music, in B, builds up to a powerful climax
9.03	**development**	ex. 1 bursts in on trumpets, echoed by horns and woodwinds; an extended development of ex. 2 material follows, beginning hesitantly, gradually filling out and taking the form of a very long crescendo, and at its climax the motto theme on trumpets cuts through the texture, twice, heralding the . . .
	recapitulation	
12.24	first group, a	only a perfunctory statement, and not in the expected key (f)
12.53	second group, d	started by bassoon, with counter-theme on horns
14.06	closing section, F	as before but slightly shortened
16.04	**coda**	as before, the motto theme interrupts; soon the music moves to a quicker tempo (17.01) and greater urgency, bringing the movement to an end
18.29		(end)

ex. 1

Andante Sostenuto
horns, bassoons

ex. 2

violins

p espr.

ex. 3

clarinet

ex. 4

woodwinds

violins

pp

of this period he enjoyed the companionship of the handsome young violinist Josif Kotek (1855–85) in Switzerland, and wrote for him his Violin Concerto in D.

Tchaikovsky returned to Russia in April 1878 and in October resigned from the Moscow Conservatory, since he could now live on his allowance from Mme von Meck. His marriage was over (divorce followed in 1881) and outwardly his life was peaceable. These were not, however, the conditions under which he worked best, and for the next few years he produced relaxed suites instead of symphonies, grand epics instead of strong, intimate dramas like *Onegin*.

The ending of this period was announced by *Manfred* (1885), where Tchaikovsky again followed a plan of Balakirev's, this time for a four-movement symphony based on Byron's verse drama. No doubt he recognized himself in the hero, doomed to roam the mountains in a hopeless attempt to expiate nameless sins, and the symphony bears comparison, both in its structure and in its expressive character, with its F minor predecessor. So too, still more so, does the Fifth Symphony in E minor (1888). The opera *The Queen of Spades* (1890) is also about a man accursed by fate and cut off by his obsessional nature from normal social life.

The suggestion in all these works – though not directly in his sumptuously escapist ballet *The Sleeping Beauty* – is that Tchaikovsky was not able to live at peace with himself in the way suggested by the works of the early 1880s. His Sixth Symphony in B minor (1893), for which his brother Modest suggested the descriptive title "Pathétique", makes this quite clear. Again his urge to ruthless self-disclosure produced a new kind of musical structure, for this was the first great symphony of the nineteenth century to end with a slow movement. Within a few days of its first performance, on 28 October 1893, Tchaikovsky died, possibly because he caught cholera from drinking untreated water.

MUSIC

Tchaikovsky's music represents a coming together of nationalism and Europeanism. His most important works are cast in the standard genres of his day – symphony, concerto, opera – but his Russianness is unmistakable: in the cut of many of his themes, which echo the folksong of his country, but even more in the note of melancholy, of yearning, of emotional intensity that runs through so many of them.

His music is not tightly organized. Its appeal lies more in its emotional force, its colorful orchestral style (his use of the woodwind instruments is especially novel and enterprising), and its drama: the climaxes often have a cataclysmic quality, sometimes built up by a long growth of tension and volume, sometimes through a dramatic interruption by a motto theme. Dance is ever-present, as an undercurrent, even in his symphonic music; Tchaikovsky was the first composer to create large-scale ballets in which the music is of high artistic value. He made much use of it in his operas, too: the greatest of them, *Eugene Onegin*, has two splendid ball scenes, depicting aspects of Russian rural and aristocratic life, against which the drama of the young Tatyana's love for the aloof Onegin is set – and Tchaikovsky's portrait of her, as love-stricken girl and as young married woman true to her elderly husband, is one of the most acute and perceptive characterizations of a woman in the operatic repertory.

But Tchaikovsky is valued most for his orchestral music: the First Piano Concerto, with its famous rhetorical opening theme; the brilliant Violin Concerto; the illustrative music, such as the *Romeo and Juliet* overture with its expressive representation of Shakespeare's characters; and the last three symphonies, of which the *Pathétique* represents his most poignant statement about himself – he refuses the lures of peasant jollity that resolve the Fourth, or the triumphal march of the Fifth, and provides instead an ultimate statement of despair in the great Adagio that ends the work – and indeed ends his entire output.

85 *Characters from the first production of Tchaikovsky's ballet* Nutcracker *at the Mariinsky Theater, St Petersburg, 1892: photograph.*

3 *Dvořák*

Antonín Dvořák was born in 1841 in the village of Nelahozeves, where his father was a butcher. He studied at the organ school in Prague (organ schools were centers of general musical education in Bohemia: Janáček attended the same institution 20 years later). Then he worked as a viola player, in one of the Prague theater orchestras under the direction of Bedřich Smetana, the leading Czech composer; there he played in the first performance of Smetana's popular opera about Czech rural life, *The Bartered Bride*, and in a concert conducted by Wagner.

Smetana and Wagner were the main influences on Dvořák's early music, though from the first he was intent on writing in the conventional genres of symphony and string quartet. His Third Symphony (1873) won an Austrian national prize and brought him to the notice of Brahms, whose encouragement may well have contributed to his rapid creative development at this relatively late stage. It was when he wrote a series of *Slavonic Dances* (1878 and 1886), which sounded a new note, that his reputation spread.

The proof that a Bohemian style could appeal outside central Europe came in 1884 when Dvořák conducted his music in London to immense acclaim. Commissions came for an oratorio for the Leeds Festival (*St Ludmilla*), a cantata for the Birmingham Festival (*The Specter's Bride*), and a new symphony for the Philharmonic Society of London (no. 7 in D minor). During the next few years he paid several visits to England and visited Russia. In 1891 he began teaching at the Prague Conservatory. That year there came a request from Jeannette Thurber to direct the National Conservatory of Music in New York. He accepted the post, and, apart from one holiday at home, spent 1892–5 in the USA. There he took an interest in the music of black Americans and Indians and did much to encourage the development of an American national tradition. Some of his American research went into the works he wrote, including his Ninth Symphony in E minor, "From the New World" (see **Listening Guide 45**), and his F major quartet, "American" (both 1893).

But for family and financial reasons he returned to Bohemia. Dvořák wrote two more quartets in 1895, his last chamber works; they were followed by a group of five symphonic poems. His final years were mostly devoted to opera, ranging from Bohemian folktale comedy to high Wagnerian tragedy by way of the fairytale fantasy of his dramatic masterpiece, *Rusalka* (1900). Though a truly international figure, who had received many honors and awards, he remained a loyal Czech. He died in Prague in 1904.

Dvořák took a long time to find his individual creative voice. He began, like most composers of his generation, influenced by Wagner; then, being a Bohemian, he was inevitably affected by his contact with Smetana – although Dvořák did not quite

Dvořák: Symphony no. 9 in e, op. 95 ('From the New World') (1893), first movement

Dvořák arrived in New York, to teach at the National Conservatory there, in September 1892. It was in January 1893 that he began serious work on a new symphony – his ninth and last – sketching out the first three movements; he worked on it later in the year, in New York and in Spillville, Iowa, where many Czech immigrants lived. In Spillville he heard American Indian singing and dancing, and in New York his pupils included several blacks: so he had opportunities to hear the music of ethnic minorities, to which he had drawn attention in his writings.

Dvořák was happy to embrace such new influences as these, and they colored his music, but the 'folkish' tendencies in the New World Symphony are not new to his music – he had always shown an awareness of his native Bohemian folk music and there are many ideas in the symphony similar to those of earlier works. One critic, writing of the first performance, in the Carnegie Hall in New York at the end of 1893, felt that the symphony embodied a Czech composer's impressions of America; and Dvořák himself said to one of his former pupils, who was later conducting a performance, that he had not used American melodies so much as 'composed in the spirit of . . . American national melodies', and that his music remained 'genuine Bohemian music'. Bohemian, American, or a blend of the two, the symphony is truly 'From the New World', and has remained the most appealing and loved of his works either side of the Atlantic.

The symphony is in four movements. The second (slow) one opens with an eloquent melody that has become Dvořák's most famous. A vigorous scherzo follows, and the work ends with a finale that recalls earlier thematic material.

Listening Outline

First movement (Adagio–Allegro molto), 4/8–2/4, e; introduction and sonata form
2 flutes, 2 oboes, 2 clarinets, 2 bassoons
2 trumpets, 4 horns, 3 trombones; timpani
1st and 2nd violins, violas, cellos, double basses

Time		
0.00	**introduction**	made up of two figures, one gentle, one more aggressive (ex. 1, *a* and *b*); note the phrase, in horns and lower strings, that anticipates the main theme of the Allegro (1.34)
	exposition	
2.07 [4.41]	first group, e	main theme, ex. 2, in two phrases: horns answered by clarinets and bassoons, repeated by oboes answered by flutes and others; a tutti takes up its rhythms (fig. *c*) and restates it (2.39 [5.14]), continuing with fig. *d*
3.10 [5.44]	second group, g–G	first theme, flute and oboe (ex. 3), repeated on violins; continuation based on fig. *e* and by violins in G with version of ex. 3 (3.48 [6.25])
4.08 [6.44]		second theme, ex. 4, flute (note rhythm of fig. *c*), then violins
	exposition repeat	(2.02–4.40 = 4.41–7.12)
7.13	**development**	mainly based on ex. 4 (horn, piccolo, and trumpet [7.23]), then in quicker rhythm (note the interrupting tuttis, recalling the introduction) and passing through various keys including E, A, F, and f♯; further development of fig. *d* follows; hints of ex. 2 on winds introduces the recapitulation

ex. 1

ex. 2

ex. 3

ex. 4

share his colleague's feelings about the Czechs and their political domination by the Austrians. He was eager to make his mark less as a Bohemian composer than simply as a composer.

So it is not surprising that he found much in common with Brahms. Ironically, the work that most aroused the interest of Brahms, and of the rest of the musical world, was the set of *Slavonic Dances* he wrote in the mid-1870s. Here he used the rhythms of Bohemian folk music, and some of its actual melodies. Thereafter the style of Slavic music increasingly became a part of his music; it can be heard in his Sixth Symphony (which again much impressed Brahms) in the rhythm of its scherzo, related to the dance known as the *furiant*; and in several works he used slow movements based on the *dumka*, a melancholy Slavic dance (not specifically Czech).

Both of these appear in his Piano Quintet op. 81; and the Piano Trio op. 90 is called the *Dumky Trio* because each of its movements is a *dumka*, with rapid, exultant music alternating with the slow passages. In the works of his full maturity, such as the *New World* Symphony and the late string quartets, the inflections of Czech music are so much a part of his idiom that they blend in with those of the black and Indian music that he met during his time in the USA. Dvořák's nationalism, then, was less

DR. DVORAK'S GREAT SYMPHONY.

"From the New World" Heard for the First Time at the Philharmonic Rehearsal.

ABOUT THE SALIENT BEAUTIES.

First Movement the Most Tragic, Second the Most Beautiful, Third the Most Sprightly.

INSPIRED BY INDIAN MUSIC.

The Director of the National Conservatory Adds a Masterpiece to Musical Literature.

Dr. Antonin Dvorak, the famous Bohemian composer and director of the National Conservatory of Music, dowered American art with a great work yesterday, when his new symphony in E minor, "From the New World," was played at the second Philharmonic rehearsal in Carnegie Music Hall.

The day was an important one in the musical history of America. It witnessed the first public performance of a noble composition.

It saw a large audience of usually tranquil Americans enthusiastic to the point of frenzy over a musical work and applauding like the most excitable "Italianissimi" in the world.

The work was one of heroic proportions. And it was one cast in the art form which such poet-musicians as Beethoven, Schubert, Schumann, Mendelssohn, Brahms and many another "glorious one of the earth" has enriched with the most precious outwellings of his musical imagination.

And this new symphony by Dr. Antonin Dvorak is worthy to rank with the best creations of those musicians whom I have just mentioned.

Small wonder that the listeners were enthusiastic. The work appealed to the æsthetically beautiful by its wealth of tender, pathetic, fiery melody; by its rich harmonic clothing; by its delicate, sonorous, gorgeous, ever varying instrumentation.

And it appealed to the patriotic side of them.

For had not Dr. Dvorak been inspired by the impressions which this country had made upon him? Had he not translated these impressions into sounds, into music? Had they not been assured by the composer himself that the work was written under the direct influence of a serious study of the national music of the North American Indians? Therefore were they not justified in regarding this composition, the first fruits of

HERR ANTONIN DVORAK.

Antonin Dvořák	Life and Works
1841	born in Nelahozeves, 8 September
1857	Prague Organ School
1863	viola player in Prague Provisional Theater orchestra, from 1866 under Smetana
1873	married Anna Cermáková; organist of St Adalbert, Prague
1874	Third Symphony won Austrian national prize
1878	*Slavonic Dances* published; encouragement from Brahms and first international recognition
1884	first of nine visits to England, where he became extremely popular and where several works (e.g. Eighth Symphony, *Requiem*) were first performed
1891	professor of composition at the Prague Conservatory; many honors
1892–5	director of the National Conservatory of Music, New York; 'New World' Symphony, 'American' String Quartet, Cello Concerto
1895	director of the Prague Conservatory
1898	beginning of concentration on opera
1904	died in Prague, 1 May

Orchestral music symphonies – no. 1, c (1865), no. 2, B♭ (1865), no. 3, E♭ (1873), no. 4, d (1874), no. 5, F (1875), no. 6, D (1880), no. 7, d (1885), no. 8, G (1889), no. 9, 'From the New World', e (1893); Slavonic Dances (1878, 1887); Slavonic Rhapsodies (1878); Symphonic Variations (1887); Nature, Life, and Love (1892); Violin Concerto (1880); Cello Concerto (1895); symphonic poems

Operas The Jacobin (1897), Rusalka (1900)

Chamber music 14 string quartets – no. 12, 'American', F (1893), no. 13, G (1895), no. 14, A♭ (1895); Piano Quintet, A (1887); piano trios – Dumky, op. 90 (1891); 3 string quintets; string sextet, 2 piano quartets

Choral music Stabat mater (1877); St Ludmilla (1886); Mass (1887); Requiem (1890); Te Deum (1892); choral songs

Piano music Dumka (1876); Humoresques, op. 101 (1894); piano duets – Slavonic Dances (1878, 1886)

Songs

self-conscious than Smetana's, and its gradual absorption into his music symbolizes the naturalness of the man's approach to his art: the result is an idiom of unusual freshness and openness of spirit. His greatest achievements were – as well as the last three symphonies (a sturdy one in D minor, a more lyrical one in G, and the *New World*; see **Listening Guide 45**) – his chamber music, and also his Cello Concerto, perhaps the finest of all concertos for that eloquent instrument.

4 *Mahler*

Gustav Mahler was born in 1860 in the Bohemian village of Kalischt. The family soon moved to Iglau, where Mahler came into contact with various kinds of music – military bands, folksongs, café music, and salon pieces – storing up childhood memories that were to be revived in his symphonies. He learned the piano and even started an opera, displaying enough talent to gain admission to the Vienna Conservatory, where he studied from 1875 to 1878. He remained in Vienna, attending lectures at the university, working as a music teacher, and writing a cantata, *Das klagende Lied* (1880).

When he was 20, Mahler began a career as a conductor that led him to important posts in Prague, Leipzig, Budapest, Hamburg, Vienna, and New York. He became one of the outstanding conductors of his day, unstinting in his demands on players and singers, but unstinting too in his demands on himself. He strove to achieve the most persuasive rendering of a work, even if that meant making alterations to its text.

Mahler took very much the same line with his own works. His First Symphony may have been begun as early as 1884 but was not completed until the mid-1890s, when it had been reduced from five movements to four and changed from a symphonic poem into a work in the more traditional form. That it was first a symphonic poem suggests the importance of Richard Strauss to the young Mahler, less as an influence than as a champion, though very soon the two men were to be forced into the position of rivals as torch-bearer of the great tradition.

The second, third, and fourth symphonies followed, all involving voices as well as instruments. While no. 4 was in progress, Mahler was baptized into the Catholic church, though apparently for practical rather than religious reasons: his Jewishness was an obstacle to his gaining an appointment in Vienna, where he became director of the Court Opera later the same year.

In 1902 he married Alma Schindler (1879–1964), the daughter of a painter and later, after Mahler's death, the wife successively of an architect (Walter Gropius) and a novelist (Franz Werfel). He embarked on a period of intense creativity, and though his conducting duties left him only the summers in which to compose, by 1905 he had completed three new symphonies, nos. 5–7. Again there were associated volumes of songs including the *Kindertotenlieder*, setting five of the 400 or so poems that Friedrich Rückert wrote on the deaths of his two children.

Much of this music – the symphonies as well as the songs – seems to convey Mahler's feeling of being pursued by fate, represented in the immense finale of the Sixth Symphony by the crushing blows of a hammer. In his own life the doom was prophetic rather than actual. At the Vienna Opera he was staging radically new productions, and he became the proud father of two daughters. It was in 1907

86 Opposite *Part of an article on Dvořák's Symphony no. 9 in E minor ("From the New World") from the* New York Herald *(16 December 1893) after its first performance in the Carnegie Hall a few days earlier.*

Gustav Mahler — Life and Works

1860	born in Kalischt (now Kaliště), 7 July
1875–8	Vienna Conservatory
1880	*The Song of Sorrow*, conductor at Bad Hall summer theater
1881–3	conductor at Laibach and Olmütz
1883–5	opera conductor at Kassel; composed *Songs of a Wayfarer* after unhappy love affair
1885–6	conductor of German Opera, Prague
1886	conductor of New State Theater, Leipzig
1888	met Richard Strauss, who became a lifelong friend; conductor of the Budapest Royal Opera
1891–7	conductor at the Hamburg State Theater; Second, Third, and Fourth Symphonies
1897	baptized Roman Catholic; conductor of the Vienna Court Opera and, with gifted colleagues, was responsible for one of its most brilliant decades
1902	married Alma Schindler; beginning of period of intense composition
1907	elder daughter died; Mahler diagnosed to have heart disease
1908	conductor of the Metropolitan Opera, New York, spending summers in Europe composing
1909	conductor of New York Philharmonic Orchestra; *The Song of the Earth*
1911	died in Vienna, 18 May

Symphonies no. 1, D (1888); no. 2, 'Resurrection', c (1894), no. 3, d (1896); no. 4, G (1900), no. 5, c♯ (1902), no. 6, a (1904), no. 7, e (1905), no. 8, E♭ (1907), no. 9, D (1909), no. 10, f♯ (1910, unfinished)

Songs (with orchestra) song cycles – Lieder eines fahrenden Gesellen (Songs of a Wayfarer, 1885), Kindertotenlieder (Songs for the Death of Children, 1904); Des Knaben Wunderhorn (Youth's Magic Horn, 1893–8); Das Lied von der Erde (The Song of the Earth, 1909)

Choral music Das klagende Lied (The Song of Sorrow, 1880)

that life caught up with his art. His elder daughter, like Rückert's children, died, and he himself was diagnosed as having a heart condition. That year saw the completion of his massive Eighth Symphony, sometimes known as the "Symphony of a Thousand".

In the fall of 1907 Mahler conducted his last operas in Vienna. Although his years at the Court Opera had been among the most distinguished in its history, they were not untroubled and his ideas often met with resistance. But he became a great champion of younger, radical composers, among them Schoenberg, Berg, and Webern (see pp. 342–9).

Meanwhile he had been invited to conduct at the Metropolitan Opera in New York, which he did for two seasons, beginning in 1908 – though the outlook of the company, with its emphases on Italian opera and star singers, was alien to him. In 1909 he accepted the conductorship of the New York Philharmonic, resigning from the Metropolitan. He was to conduct only one complete season, for it was during

87 Opposite *Mahler conducting: silhouettes by Otto Böhler.*

Mahler: *Das Lied von der Erde* ('The Song of the Earth') (1908), excerpt

In the summer of 1908, Mahler was trying to come to terms with the life that his heart condition imposed upon him. It was, he said, not simply a matter of fearing death, but of now not being able to achieve the inner calm he needed to compose. Eventually, however, he found that his state of mind and body led him to become particularly involved in the world of a set of 83 Chinese poems, translated by Hans Bethge in a collection called *The Chinese Flute*.

Mahler finally chose seven of them to form the text of a work he might have called a symphony but preferred to consider a symphonic song cycle. Setting Chinese poems in translation, he used some supposedly Chinese color in the orchestra (notably the use of metal percussion) and in the musical ideas (with patterns based on the pentatonic, five-note scale favored in much folk music, Chinese included). But *The Song of the Earth* is much more a work of European than oriental sensibility, not least in the long final song of farewell. The six songs are alternately for tenor and contralto. The orchestra Mahler calls for is large, but nevertheless the score has an almost chamber-music-like refinement. 'Der Trunkene im Frühling' is the fifth song, occupying a place analogous to that of a scherzo in a symphony.

 Listening Outline . . . .

Der Trunkene im Frühling ('The Springtime Drunkard')
tenor solo
piccolo, 2 flutes, 2 oboes, E♭ clarinet, 2 B♭ clarinets, 2 bassoons, double bassoon
4 horns, trumpet; harp
1st violins, 2nd violins, violas, cellos, double basses

Time
0.00   verse 1: the winds open the song on the dominant of A, then swerving up drunkenly as the tenor enters in B♭. An important rhythmic motif (ex. 1) appears in his second line, which ends in A, but the orchestra shifts to F (ex. 2) and ex. 1 is developed; then the music returns to A with a filling-out of the music from the opening
0.43   verse 2: varied repeat of verse 1
1.23   verse 3: slower tempo, also a harmonic uncertainty (conveying the drunkard's awakening); note the questioning tone at 'sinnend' ('pensively')
2.15   verse 4: original tempo returns, but the music, as implied by the 'dream', is unfamiliar; note the violin as the 'twittering bird' and at mention of spring a shift to the warmth of D♭
3.17   verse 5: in C, as the drunkard refills his glass, then moving up to A
3.58   verse 6: a varied repeat of verse 1
4.30   (end)

Wenn nur ein Traum das Leben ist	If life's only a dream
warum denn Müh' und Plag'!?	why all this fuss and bother!?
Ich trinke, bis ich nicht mehr kann,	I drink till I'm full
den ganzen, lieben Tag!	the livelong day!
Und wenn ich nicht mehr trinken kann,	And when I can't take any more,
weil Kehl' und Seele voll,	when body and soul are full,
so taund' ich bis zu meiner Tür	I stagger back home
und schlafe wundervoll!	and sleep like a top!
Was hör' ich beim Erwachen? Horch!	What do I hear when I wake up? Hist!
Ein Vogel singt im Baum.	A bird sings from a tree.
Ich frag' ihn, ob schon Frühling sei.	I ask him if it's springtime yet.
Mir ist als wie im Traum.	To me it's like a dream.
Der Vogel zwitschert: Ja! Ja!	The bird twitters: yes, yes!
Der Lenz ist da, sei kommen über Nacht!	Spring's here: it came overnight!
Aus tiefstem Schauen lauscht' ich auf,	I listened for it closely,
der Vogel singt und lacht!	the bird sings and laughs!

Ich fülle mir den Becher neu	I fill my glass again
und leer' ihm bis zum Grund	and drink it to the dregs,
und singe, bis der Mond erglänzt	and sing till the moon comes up
am schwarzen Firmament!	in the black heavens!
Und wenn ich nicht mehr singen kann,	And when I can't sing any more,
so schlaf' ich wieder ein. –	I go to sleep again.
Was geht mich denn der Frühling an!?	So what's the point of spring!?
Lasst mich betrunken sein!	Just let me be drunk!

ex. 1

ex. 2

his second that he contracted his last illness. Mahler introduced many new works to New York in the concerts he conducted with the orchestra (86 in all), but neither his programs nor his manner were popular with the orchestra or the public, and his departure was little regretted.

Mahler had spent the summers of his New York years back in Europe, where he continued to compose. Fearing to embark on a Ninth Symphony, which had been the last for Beethoven and the recent famous Austrian symphonist Anton Bruckner, Mahler wrote a symphony in the disguise of an orchestral song cycle and called it *Das Lied von der Erde* (1909; **Listening Guide 46**). Its atmosphere of melancholy departure then provided a similar emotional character for the whole of the Ninth Symphony (1909), though the unfinished Tenth (1910) would appear to have been working towards a much more positive close. Judgements have to be cautious, because Mahler left this work at quite an early stage of composition when he died, in Vienna, in the spring of 1911.

Symphonies and songs – and hybrid combinations of the two – make up virtually the whole of Mahler's output. His early *Lieder eines fahrenden Gesellen* ("Songs of a Wayfarer") have a key scheme that breaks away from the tradition of beginning and ending in the same key, symbolizing the changing fortunes of the traveling hero; this idea recurs in many of his symphonies. Mahler's First Symphony uses themes from this song cycle. This was something that Schubert had done in several of his later chamber works, but in Mahler's case the introduction of a song theme hints at a psychological program underlying the music. In his next three symphonies such programs become explicit, since songs are included. They use texts from *Des Knaben Wunderhorn* ("The Boy's Magic Horn"), a collection of folk poetry (and imitations of folk poetry) of the early nineteenth century. Mahler also made a number of independent settings of the *Wunderhorn* poems, whose naivety was a perfect vehicle for his music, so much more ironic, complex, and questioning.

The Second and Third Symphonies use other verse too. The grand choral finale to no. 2 sets an ode on resurrection by Klopstock: a work that begins with a movement filled with doubt ends in gigantic optimism. The Third Symphony, according to its original program, is an ascent through the realms of existence. Its huge first movement, lasting for half an hour, is followed by five movements in which the composer listens in turn to meadow flowers (a delicate minuet), forest animals (a scherzo), the night (the contralto song, with words by Nietzsche), bells (with angel choirs of women and boys), and love (Adagio). The Fourth, of more normal dimensions, may be considered to make a similar climb, since it ends with the soprano singing of the delights of heaven.

Nos. 5, 6, and 7 however are wholly instrumental: no. 5 moves from a funeral march, in C sharp minor, to a triumphant conclusion in D major; no. 6, a tragic work in which there is no escaping destiny, begins and ends in the same key (A minor). As narratives, Mahler's symphonies are filled with picturesque detail: the music of café and barracks, the sound of cowbells in the Alps (nos. 4 and 5), the serenades of guitar and mandolin (no. 7). The largest of them all is no. 8, whose second part – a setting of words from the second part of Goethe's *Faust*, and philosophically highly complex – is a combination of cantata, oratorio, song cycle, and choral symphony.

In contrast to this public pronouncement is the more private one of *Das Lied von der Erde* (see **Listening Guide 46**). Setting Chinese poems in translation, the music has some naive Chinese color in its use of metal percussion and pentatonic motifs, but it is much more a work of European than oriental sensibility, not least in the long song of farewell with which it ends. Mahler's Ninth Symphony is another deeply pessimistic work (it moves from D major to D flat major). It is possible to see Mahler's extension of the symphony's expressive scope, and his individual use of the orchestra (characterized by the pained sound of instruments, especially the winds, at the top of their compass and often required to play sharply angular lines), as an agonized farewell to the world of Romanticism.

5 *Strauss*

Four years younger than Mahler, Richard Strauss also composed early. Unlike Mahler, however, whose genius was not fully recognized until the 1960s, he enjoyed public acclaim almost from the first, so that for more than 60 years he was regarded as the outstanding German composer.

Richard Strauss was born in Munich in 1864, son of the principal horn player in the Court Orchestra. He never attended a conservatory, though he spent two terms at Munich University before the growing success of his music emboldened him to devote himself to composition.

At this time he veered towards the more classical stream in nineteenth-century music, represented by Mendelssohn and Brahms. But then, while embarking on his career as a conductor at Meiningen (1885–6) and Munich (1886–9 and 1894–8), he became a follower much more of Wagner and of Liszt. Symphonies and quartets were replaced in his output by symphonic poems, eight in all during the next dozen years. There was also a first opera, the Wagnerian *Guntram* (1893), but this was not a success, and Strauss's early reputation was as a composer of symphonic poems and of songs.

The symphonic poems, including *Till Eulenspiegel* (see **Listening Guide 47**), were played all over Europe and in the USA almost as soon as they were composed. It was not a large step from these "theatrical" symphonic poems into opera, and Strauss's main efforts went into this form. *Salome* (1905) and *Elektra* (1909) are each in a long single act and each projects a world of emotions at high pitch, backed by music of corresponding harmonic extremity. The first sets Oscar Wilde's play on the biblical story of John the Baptist at the court of Herod, the latter uses Hugo von Hofmannsthal's drama on the Greek myth of Electra.

Strauss's next opera was *Der Rosenkavalier* ("The Cavalier of the Rose", 1911), a highly polished and humane comedy on a much larger scale. It initiated one of the most fruitful partnerships in the history of opera, for now Strauss was fully collaborating with Hofmannsthal, not simply setting an existing play of his. The combination of the highly cultivated Austrian poet and the practical, theater-bred Bavarian musician worked well. Though the two men irked each other at times, they went on from *Der Rosenkavalier* to create four more operas over the next two decades.

Strauss had intended that the opera *Capriccio* should be his last work: he was 78 when it was first performed, in Munich in 1942, at the turning-point in World War II. Unlike many of his colleagues, he remained in Germany after 1933, and even naively allowed his name to be used to add some spurious prestige to the Third Reich, though for most of the Hitler years he lived in retirement at his Bavarian home.

Richard Strauss   Life and Works

1864	born in Munich, 11 June
1882	Munich University; Serenade for 13 wind instruments performed; beginning of period of prolific output
1885	assistant conductor of the Meiningen Orchestra; international recognition as a composer
1886–9	conductor at the Munich Court Opera
1889	Weimar; *Don Juan* established him as the most important young composer in Germany
1894	married Pauline de Ahna; conductor at Munich Court Opera
1895–8	prolific years, especially of orchestral music (including *Till Eulenspiegel, Thus spake Zarathustra, Don Quixote, A Hero's Life*)
1898	conductor of the Royal Court Opera, Berlin; turned to opera composition
1904	conducted first performance of *Symphonia domestica* in New York
1905	*Salome* (Dresden) causes scandal
1909	*Elektra* (Dresden), the first of many successful collaborations with the librettist Hugo von Hofmannsthal (*d*1929)
1911	*Der Rosenkavalier* (Dresden)
1919–24	joint director of the Vienna State Opera; output diminishing
1933–5	appointed (without consultation) president of the Nazi state music bureau but removed for collaborating with a Jewish librettist
1942	*Capriccio* (Munich); beginning of period of concentration on instrumental works
1945	voluntary exile in Switzerland
1948	*Four Last Songs*
1949	died in Garmisch-Partenkirchen, 8 September

Operas Salome (1905), Elektra (1909), Der Rosenkavalier (The Cavalier of the Rose, 1911), Ariadne auf Naxos (1912), Die Frau ohne Schatten (The Woman without a Shadow, 1919), Intermezzo (1924), Arabella (1933), Capriccio (1942)

Orchestral music symphonic poems – Aus Italien (1886), Don Juan (1889), Till Eulenspiegels lustige Streiche (Till Eulenspiegel's Merry Pranks, 1895), Also sprach Zarathustra (Thus spake Zarathustra, 1896), Don Quixote (1897), Ein Heldenleben (A Hero's Life, 1898); Symphonia domestica (1903); Eine Alpensinfonie (1915); Metamorphosen for 23 strings (1945); horn concertos – no. 1, E♭ (1883), no. 2, E♭ (1942); Oboe Concerto (1945)

Choral music Deutsche Motette (1913)

Songs Four Last Songs, with orchestra (1948); *c*200 others

Chamber music

Piano music

Retirement from composition, however, was not so easy. He wrote no more operas, but returned to the forms and genres of his youth: a Second Horn Concerto (1942) joined the one he had written for his father in 1883, and in the same key of E♭. There were other instrumental pieces, including *Metamorphosen* (1945), an elegy for the Germany that was being destroyed in the bombing raids on Dresden, Berlin,

Plate 15 *Puccini's* Tosca: *scene by Hohenstein from Act 1 in the original production at the Teatro Costanzi, Rome, 1900 (see p. 330). Commemorative postcard.*

Н. РИМСКІЙ-КОРСАКОВЪ

ЗОЛОТОЙ ПѢТУШОКЪ

НЕБЫЛИЦА ВЪ ЛИЦАХЪ

ОПЕРА ВЪ 3 ДѢЙСТВІАХЪ

ШЕМАХАНСКАЯ ЦРЦА

ЦРЧИ ГВИДОНЪ И АФРОНЪ

ЦАРЬ ДОДОНЪ

ВОЕВОДА ПОЛКАНЪ

ЗВѢЗДОЧЕТЪ

ИЗДАНІЕ П. ЮРГЕНСОНА ВЪ МОСКВѢ

И. БИЛИБИНЪ. 1908

Электропечатня нотъ П. Юргенсона въ Москвѣ.
SOLE AGENTS FOR THE
BRITISH EMPIRE:
BREITKOPF & HARTEL

and other cities. As if these works were somehow unofficial, coming after the main body of his music, Strauss gave them no opus numbers. He ended the sequence with the conscious farewell of the *Four Last Songs* (1948) and died at his home in Garmisch in September 1949, before those songs had been heard.

Strauss composed music in almost every form, but his main contributions were in two genres: the tone poem and opera. Most of his tone poems were written around the turn of the century. They are sometimes illustrative, sometimes narrative, sometimes literary, sometimes philosophical – on topics as varied as the scenery of Italy (*Aus Italien*), the Don Juan story, works by Shakespeare and Cervantes (*Macbeth* and *Don Quixote*), and life in the Strauss household (*Symphonia domestica*) and Strauss's attitudes to his critics (*Ein Heldenleben* – "A Hero's Life"). In these, and in *Till Eulenspiegel* (see **Listening Guide 47**), he used something akin to a Wagnerian *leitmotif* technique, with themes representing people or ideas and changing as the story of the work dictated, within a brilliant, elaborate, and colorful orchestral style; but he often kept to the classical forms – *Don Juan* uses sonata form, *Till Eulenspiegel* rondo, *Don Quixote* a variation scheme.

Strauss's first opera dates from 1894, but his first important one, *Salome*, was not heard until 1905. Based on Oscar Wilde's play, it is a harsh and intensely complex score and, with its elaborate layers of motifs, probes deeply into the psychology of the main characters, especially Salome herself; the biblical theme, however, led to its being regarded as blasphemous and even salacious. *Elektra* followed, in 1909: again an exploration into abnormal female psychology, this time of the Greek

MUSIC

Plate 16 Opposite The Golden Cockerel *by Rimsky-Korsakov: title page of the first edition of the vocal score (Moscow, 1908). See p. 299.*

88 *Richard Strauss's* Der Rosenkavalier: *stage design by Alfred Roller for Act 1 of the first performance. Dresden Court Opera, 26 January 1911.*

Strauss: *Till Eulenspiegels lustige Streiche* ('Till Eulenspiegel's Merry Pranks') (1895)

In 1894, Richard Strauss decided to write an opera, to see if he could improve on the very modest success of his *Guntram*. He chose as the subject the rogue of German medieval folk legend, Till Eulenspiegel. He soon abandoned an attempt to write a libretto; his literary gifts were limited, and he was anyway discouraged about opera. But he was taken with the subject and decided instead to write an orchestral piece on it; he already had several successful tone poems behind him (*Don Juan*, for example) and saw that the tale offered attractive opportunities for colorful illustrative music.

Till Eulenspiegel is in fact one of Strauss's wittiest and orchestrally most brilliant pieces. He called it a rondo, but it is that only in a loose, general sense – in that the main theme constantly recurs. It also has elements of sonata form and, in the transformation of themes, of variation form too.

 Listening Outline

piccolo, 3 flutes, 3 oboes, english horn, clarinet in D, 2 clarinets in B♭, bass clarinet in B♭, 3 bassoons, double bassoon
4 horns in F (4 horns in D ad lib), 3 trumpets in f (3 trumpets in D ad lib), 3 trombones, tuba; timpani, triangle, cymbals, bass drum, side drum, large ratchet
16 1st violins, 16 2nd violins, 12 violas, 12 cellos, 8 double basses

Time	
0.00	the opening phrase (ex. 1) seems to say 'Once upon a time . . .'; later it will represent Till
0.17	the main Till motif (ex. 2) is heard on the horn, then taken up by other instruments
0.59	the Till motif, ex. 3 (based on ex. 1) appears on high clarinet; possibly it stands for Till's witty, subversive nature; it is developed at some length
2.20	quiet passage (note ex. 3 on the bass strings; then flute): this introduces an episode where Till rides into the market place and upsets the stalls (theme on trombones)
3.48	now the rhythm is altered and Till, disguised as a priest, marches in a procession (bassoons, violas) – but mocking derivations of ex. 3 intervene followed by muted brass and a violin slide as he reveals himself
5.09	Till in amorous mood: ex. 2 and ex. 3 are smoother and sweeter than before; but when he is rejected he is angry: ex. 3 appears in a forceful, heavy-footed version (6.13)
6.44	solemn people, probably professors, approach: Till mocks them (ex. 4); fragments of Till themes mix with and overcome those for the professors
8.12	Till sings a street song; then the music becomes mysteriously shadowy
9.28	ex. 2 (akin to recapitulation), but development continues with increasing high spirits, reaching a climax of outrageous defiance
11.45	the noise is halted; a drum roll represents Till's being brought to trial. Dark chords in the orchestra are answered by Till's perky phrase, now faintly pathetic; he is sentenced and executed
13.26	epilogue; music recalls opening – then a reminder of ex. 3 ends the work positively
14.35	(end)

ex. 1

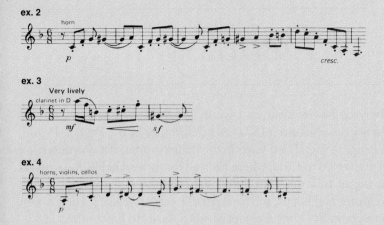

ex. 2

ex. 3

ex. 4

princess preoccupied with vengeance on her mother, her father's murderess. In both, the soprano voice is pressed to dramatic extremes.

Strauss did not pursue this course. In *Der Rosenkavalier* (1911), set in eighteenth-century Vienna, he applied the same methods to the treatment of social comedy; in a score full of tenderness and nostalgia, and colored by the presence of sentimental Viennese waltzes, the exploration of female psychology is concerned with love and the passing of youth. Strauss's special feeling for the high female voice is very clear in this beautiful score, in which the music for the three sopranos is lovingly written. Next followed *Ariadne auf Naxos* (1912–16), a mythological opera, treated as if the stage is part of an eighteenth-century opera house: we see the characters both as people and in their stage roles. Comedy is liberally mixed in. But the work has a new refinement of detail, apt to the setting.

In his operas of the 1920s and 30s, Strauss tried, with limited success, to recapture the world of *Der Rosenkavalier*; but the only fully successful opera of this later period is *Capriccio*, written in 1942, a "conversation piece" in one act, again set in the elegant eighteenth century and dealing with a topic beloved of every opera composer: the rivalries of poet and musician, symbolized in the rivalry of two men for the love of their patron, a Countess (soprano). The music is suffused with a golden, nostalgic warmth, and this is to be felt, too, in the instrumental works that Strauss produced in his 80s, including several concertos, and *Metamorphosen*, sumptuously scored for 23 solo strings, and in his *Four Last Songs* – for soprano, of course.

6 *Debussy*

Claude Debussy, born at St Germain-en-Laye in 1862, studied as a pianist and composer at the Paris Conservatoire (1872–84). As winner of the Prix de Rome, he left the Conservatoire to spend two years in the Italian capital, but was unsettled there and returned with relief to Paris, where he lived for the rest of his life. Around this time his music began to acquire an individual character, for example in the cantata for soprano, women's chorus, and orchestra *La damoiselle élue* ("The Chosen Maiden", 1888), on a poem by Dante Gabriel Rossetti. Visits to Bayreuth in 1888–9 and an encounter with Javanese music quickened his artistic progress. First-hand experience of Wagner convinced him of the need to approach music differently. Eastern influence, particularly oriental art, pervades a good deal of his output.

Equally strong is Debussy's appeal to Greek culture. The search for a new esthetic freedom in an imaginative re-creation of the Orient or of ancient Greece was important to artists of all kinds in Paris in the 1890s and 1900s. It may be seen in the Symbolist poetry of Mallarmé and his imitators, in the novels of Debussy's friend Pierre Louÿs, and in the paintings of Gustave Moreau and others; and it was this strand in French culture, rather than that represented by the Impressionist painters, to which Debussy most belonged. His friendships were all with literary men and his works – particularly the many uncompleted stage projects and the smaller body of songs – testify to the importance of literature in his creative mind. It was a poem that released his *Prélude à "L'après-midi d'un faune"* (see **Listening Guide 48**).

In 1893 Debussy went to a performance of Maeterlinck's play *Pelléas et Mélisande* and began to sketch an opera on the subject; it was not staged until 1902 but was quickly acclaimed as a masterpiece. After its success, he composed prolifically – mostly piano works and songs. But his life was stormy; he was prosecuted for debt, and in 1904 he left his wife to live with Emma Bardac, and another scandal ensued when his wife attempted suicide.

Debussy's best-known orchestral scores, *La mer* ("The Sea") and the orchestral *Images*, followed. But early in 1909 he began to be troubled by the cancer that was to kill him. He wrote several works for the theater, including *Jeux* ("Games", 1913) for the Diaghilev ballet company's season that also included Stravinsky's sensational *The Rite of Spring*, and he continued sketching an opera on a story by Edgar Allan Poe.

Illness and the outbreak of war depressed Debussy's creativity, so that little was achieved in 1914, but the next year his compositional spirits were revived by a commission to edit Chopin's piano works, and he added to his own a set of 12 remarkable studies. Prompted by wartime patriotism, he became increasingly conscious of his heritage as a French artist, and his final project was a set of six sonatas for different ensembles, looking back to Couperin and Rameau, and proudly signed "Claude Debussy, musicien français". Only three were composed.

Claude Debussy — Life and Works

1862	born in St Germain-en-Laye, 22 August
1872	entered the Paris Conservatoire to study the piano and (from 1880) composition
1880–81	summers in Russia as pianist to the family of Madame von Meck, Tchaikovsky's patron, with whom he toured Europe
1885	to Rome after winning the Prix de Rome at the Conservatoire
1887	Paris
1888	heard Wagner's music at Bayreuth
1889	impressed by Javanese music, heard at the World Exhibition in Paris
1890	beginning of 'Bohemian' years and friendships with literary figures
1894	*Prélude à 'L'après-midi d'un faune'*
1897	married Rosalie (Lily) Texier
1901	music critic of *La revue blanche*
1902	*Pelléas et Mélisande*; reputation as a composer established
1904	beginning of prolific period; left wife to live with Emma Bardac; Lily's attempted suicide caused scandal
1905	*La mer*, daughter born; growing international acclaim
1908	married Emma Bardac
1909	first signs of illness
1913	concentration on stage works and projects; *Jeux*
1914	depressed by illness and outbreak of war
1915	Studies for piano, *En blanc et noir*, two sonatas
1918	died in Paris, 25 March

Orchestral music Prélude à 'L'après-midi d'un faune' (Prelude to 'The Afternoon of a Faun', 1894); Nocturnes (1899); La mer (The Sea, 1905); Images (1912)

Operas Pelléas et Mélisande (1902)

Ballets Jeux (Games, 1913)

Piano music Suite, pour le piano (1901); Suite bergamasque (1905); Estampes (1903); Images (1905, 1907); Children's Corner (1908); Preludes, 2 books (1910, 1913); Studies (1915); two pianos – En blanc et noir (In white and black, 1915)

Chamber music String Quartet (1893); Cello Sonata (1915); Sonata for flute, viola, and harp (1915); Violin Sonata (1917)

Incidental music Le martyre de St Sébastien (1911)

Songs Fêtes galantes (1891, 1904); Chansons de Bilitis (1898); c60 others

Choral music La damoiselle élue (The Chosen Maiden, 1888)

MUSIC

Debussy was one of the great innovators, and his influence on the music of the twentieth century was profound. The Javanese music he heard in Paris as a young man – the strange scales, the fluid rhythms, and the jangle of the gong-chimes – opened up to him a variety of possibilities. He became interested in the idea of modes (scale systems different from the standard major and minor), and he experimented with the whole-tone scale, which could break down the normal sense

Debussy: *Prélude à 'L'après-midi d'un faune'* ('Prelude to "The Afternoon of a Faun"') (1894)

It was, characteristically, a work of literature that provoked Debussy's first orchestral masterpiece – a poem by Stéphane Mallarmé. It concerns the erotic reverie of a faun on a hot afternoon. On some levels, there are close links between music and poem – for example, Debussy wrote exactly as many measures as Mallarmé did lines – but in other respects the relationship is more one of evocation. Debussy's work, however, does also adopt the general form of the poem, with lazily contemplative outer sections and a more active middle.

An essential feature is the use of instrumental color. The opening melody is unmistakably a theme specifically for the flute; it will work effectively on other instruments (oboe and horns in the last part of the work) only if its rhythm and key are altered. Its harmony is constantly changing, too. The initial flute phrase falls through an augmented 4th – an interval that at once creates vagueness of key – and returns, marking out the whole-tone scale G–A–B–C♯. Throughout Debussy's music the whole-tone scale is a prominent feature, melodically and harmonically, permitting through its symmetry a rapid movement among distantly related keys.

 Listening Outline

3 flutes, 2 oboes, english horn, 2 clarinets in A, 2 bassoons
4 horns, 2 harps, antique cymbals in E and B
1st violins, violas, cellos, double basses

Time		
0.00	**main section**	*Très modéré* ('very moderate'): unaccompanied solo flute sounds the main theme (ex. 1), in or near E, echoed by horns
0.59		repeat of ex. 1 with orchestral support; its latter part involves oboe and then tutti before dying away on clarinets
2.07		two short developments of ex. 1, still for solo flute, both with harp arpeggios
3.30		variant of ex. 1 (clarinet) initiating move towards the middle section
4.01	**middle section**	*En animant* ('becoming animated'). Diatonic variant of ex. 1, oboe, leads to clearer harmony and forward movement; the oboe phrases appear in alternation, violins and woodwinds
4.32		*Toujours en animant* ('more animated'): above process comes to a climax and then grows still
5.03		*1er mouvement* ('original speed'): activity begun again by clarinet
5.26		*Même mouvement et très soutenu* ('the same speed, very sustained'): new theme in D♭ (ex. 2), only distantly related to what has gone before, heard in quiet but full orchestration and briefly developed
7.25	**main section**	*Mouvement du début* ('speed of the opening'): ex. 1, flute, supported by string chord and harp arpeggios; oboe leads commentary (*un peu plus animé*: 'a little livelier')
8.02		repeat of previous section, theme now on solo oboe and at first in E♭; the harmony turns to E again, led this time by english horn
8.43		*Dans le 1er mouvement avec plus de langueur* ('at the original speed with more languor'): ex. 1 on two flutes, leading to trails of triplets and a further statement on flute, then oboe

10.32	*Très lent et très retenu* ('very slow and held back'): final appearance of ex. 1, horns and 2nd violins, followed by last appearance of the work's characteristic cadence, c♯ to E
11.06	(end)

of key and create a "floating" harmony analogous to the use of words and ideas in contemporary literature, or to the use of paint in the Symbolist and Impressionist art of the time.

A critical work in this is the *Prélude à "L'après-midi d'un faune"* (see **Listening Guide 48**). His one completed opera, *Pelléas et Mélisande*, is also highly individual: the music speaks softly and reticently, hinting at the mental processes of his characters in their mysterious world (the kingdom of Allemonde – implying "all the world"). Their hopes, fears, and motivations are only glancingly expressed, and only faintly hinted at in the orchestral music.

From soon after *Pelléas*, first given in 1902, come several orchestral works, strong in atmosphere, though always by suggestion rather than statement – there is *La mer*, and a group of *Nocturnes* (after paintings by Whistler), music that depicts waves, clouds, and other such fleeting images with its gentle, shifting textures, its fluid forms, and its often vague rhythms. In his piano music, which includes atmosphere pieces with titles like *Reflets dans l'eau* ("Reflections in the Water") and *La cathédrale engloutie* ("The Submerged Cathedral"), both from his two-volume collection of Preludes, he favored washes of sound, using the piano's special ability to resonate and produce dream-like textures, almost always avoiding the Germanic tradition of a developing musical form in favor of a static one. There are other types of music, too, including piano studies (designed to exploit different keyboard techniques) and ballets, as well as the late set of instrumental sonatas. But Debussy's central contribution lies in his freeing of music from the domination of the central European tradition of musical "argument" in favor of something more delicate and suggestive.

7 *Puccini*

LIFE

Giacomo Puccini was born in 1858 in Lucca, where his father was of the fourth generation of Puccinis to have served the republic and the church as composers. Giacomo, five when his father died, studied with local teachers with a view to taking on the family responsibilities, but when he was 17 he saw *Aida* and determined to be an opera composer instead. He therefore went to the Milan Conservatory. In 1883 he finished his studies and wrote his first opera, *Le villi*, on a tale of supernatural enchantment. It had some success when given in Milan in 1884, and on the strength of it the astute publisher Giulio Ricordi initiated an association that was to continue throughout Puccini's life. He then tried his hand, rather less successfully, at a tragic opera after an Alfred de Musset book.

Puccini found the way forward pointed by his junior, Pietro Mascagni, whose one-act *Cavalleria rusticana* (1889) introduced a new kind of opera, *verismo* opera: it

Giacomo Puccini   Life and Works

1858	born in Lucca, 23 December
1872	organist in Lucca
1876	heard Verdi's *Aida* in Pisa and decided to become an opera composer
1880–83	Milan Conservatory
1884	*Le villi* performed in Milan; beginning of long association with the publishers Ricordi
1889	*Edgar*
1893	*Manon Lescaut* performed in Turin; international recognition
1896	*La bohème* (Turin)
1900	*Tosca* (Rome)
1904	*Madama Butterfly* (Milan); married Elvira Geminiani who had had his son in 1886
1905–9	silent years; period of domestic crisis culminating in highly publicized court case
1910	*The Girl of the Golden West* acclaimed in New York
1911–12	criticized in European musical press
1918	*Il trittico* (New York)
1921	worked on *Turandot*; moved from Torre del Lago to Viarreggio
1924	died in Brussels, 29 November

Operas Le villi (1884), Edgar (1889), Manon Lescaut (1893), La bohème (1896), Tosca (1900), Madama Butterfly (1904), La fanciulla del West (The Girl of the Golden West, 1910), Il trittico (1918) [three one-act operas: Il tabarro (The Cloak), Suor Angelica, Gianni Schicchi], Turandot (posthumous, 1926)

Choral music   Instrumental music   Songs

89 *Puccini (seated) with the librettist Luigi Illica, a few months before the composer's death: photograph.*

deals with contemporary life, including its more sordid side, in a naturalistic and full-bloodedly emotional way. The first of his operas that shows the influence of the *verismo* school is *Manon Lescaut* (1893), the story of tragic love that Massenet had set nine years before. Here Puccini proves himself a superior musician to any of his Italian contemporaries (and to Massenet) through his command of musical-dramatic resource. It was a great success.

Puccini did well, however, not to attempt to repeat it. He now turned to something different, *La bohème* (1896), a tale of aspiring artists and their loves in the "bohemian" world of Paris in the 1830s. It is Puccini's most popular opera – indeed one of the most popular of all time – but his next two, *Tosca* (see **Listening Guide 49**) and *Madama Butterfly*, run it close.

Puccini then was at the center of a scandal. His wife, whom he had married in 1904, accused one of their servants of having an intimate relationship with Puccini; the servant committed suicide, but a court later found her innocent. Even so, the resulting publicity had a profound effect on Puccini, and he was unable to compose for several years.

Puccini: *Tosca* (1900), excerpt from Act 3

The basis for Puccini's *Tosca* was a play by the French dramatist Victorien Sardou, famous for his cleverly crafted plays, effective in the theater though despised by serious critics (Bernard Shaw coined the term 'Sardoodledom' to describe the kind of play he wrote). Puccini had been interested in setting his *La Tosca* since 1889, and contracted to do so in 1895 while he was finishing *La bohème*. The opera is set in Rome in the summer of 1800, when Napoleon's armies were trying to free Italy from oppressive monarchic rule; it was natural that Puccini should have chosen Rome for its première, which took place in 1900. One of Puccini's librettists said that, while *La bohème* was all poetry and no plot, *Tosca* was all plot and no poetry. In it Puccini moved from a delicate and lyrical manner to a more full-blooded, 'veristic' one (that is, a style dealing with ordinary, sometimes sordid, events and emotions); to cope with the eventful plot and strong characterization he went some way towards a Wagnerian, *leitmotif*-like method. He did not use it with the psychological depth of Wagner and he retained the essentially Italian approach of 'numbers' (arias, duets, and so forth) in which the characters express their feelings and their reactions to the dramatic situation.

In Act 3 of the opera Mario Cavaradossi, a painter, who is in sympathy with the forces of progress, is held in the Roman prison, the castle of Sant' Angelo: he is under sentence of death for helping conceal a political prisoner. His aria 'E lucevan le stelle' is sung shortly before the sentence is to be carried out (he had been given a pen and paper, to write his last letter, but could not write, and he had refused a priest – the Church being on the side of the royalist oppressors). Here he remembers a loving encounter with Tosca.

 Listening Outline . . . .

Time			
0.00	Cavaradossi (a tenor) puts down his pen; as he recalls his love for Tosca, the orchestra – an intensely expressive piece of writing for two violas and four cellos – recalls the music of their love duet, heard earlier		
1.10	the clarinet plays a melody, also heard earlier (on Cavaradossi's entry shortly before)		
1.34	the voice enters: Cavaradossi, as if trying to hold back emotion, sings each of the first few phrases to a repeated single note while the clarinet continues to express his passion (it is marked 'longingly')	E lucevan le stelle . . . e olezzava la terra . . . stridea l'uscio dell'orto . . . a un passo sfiorava la rena.	And the stars were shining . . . and the earth smelt sweetly . . . there was a creak at the garden gate . . . and a step brushed the gravel.
2.33	as if he can hold back no longer, he takes up the clarinet melody and gives full rein to his feelings	Entrava ella, fragrante, mia cadea fra le braccia. Oh! dolci baci, o languide carezze, mentr'io fremente le belle forme disciogliea dei veli!	She entered, fragrant, and fell into my arms. Oh, soft kisses, languid caresses, as I, trembling, drew the clothes from her beautiful body!
3.06	the same melody, now more forcefully expressed, and with fuller, darker orchestral accompaniment as Cavaradossi expresses his despair	Svani per sempre il sogno mio d'amore . . . L'ora è fuggita e muoio disperato! E non ha amato mai tanto la vita!	My dream of love is vanished for ever . . . The hour has flown, and in despair I die! And never have I loved life so much!
4.17	(end)		

However, in 1910 came the première of his *La fanciulla del West* ("The Girl of the Golden West"), set in California in the gold rush: to Puccini the Far West was just as exotic as the Far East. He then wrote a "triptych", three operas for the Metropolitan in New York (containing his only comedy, *Gianni Schicchi*, a slightly macabre piece set in medieval Florence).

In his 60s Puccini wanted to write an opera that would sound a new note: he started work on *Turandot*, a savage drama set in China. But in 1923 he developed cancer of the throat and in 1924 he died – he had struggled with the final scenes but left them incomplete, and the opera is now given with an ending by the composer Franco Alfano.

Puccini was not truly a *verismo* composer: his operas are not set in the (then) present; many have exotic locations; only a few have elements of the "realistic" world of feeling. But the heightened emotional condition of *verismo* opera is very much a feature. *La bohème* (1896) is a sentimental piece, much of it in a light-hearted, conversational style, but with a deeply touching final scene where – as in Verdi's *La traviata* – a girl dies of tuberculosis, reconciled with her lover. Here Puccini used the

90 Above *Puccini's opera* Tosca: *Plácido Domingo (Cavaradossi), Royal Opera House, Covent Garden, 1981.*

pentatonic scale as a source of strikingly memorable orchestral ideas, and as a means for penetrating beneath the civilized surface of the major-minor system to a more raw, coarser musical and expressive world.

Madama Butterfly (1904), set in Japan, incorporates some real Japanese melodies, but also has a good deal of pentatonic music to convey its oriental exoticism. Most of Puccini's heroines are "little women", who suffer and die for their true, limitless love. One such is Madam Butterfly, the Japanese girl duped by an American naval officer into marriage, then deserted; Puccini's capacity to compel the audience's emotions in sympathy with his heroines is particularly striking here. It happens again in his next opera, *La fanciulla del West*. *Turandot* shows him enlarging his harmonic and orchestral style, influenced by Strauss and especially Debussy. But none of these has ever challenged in appeal the three operas — *La bohème*, *Tosca*, and *Madama Butterfly* — that he composed around the turn of the century.

8 *Beach*

The New Englander Amy Marcy Cheney, born in New Hampshire in 1867, was precocious by any standard. Her mother, an amateur singer and pianist, encouraged her musical gifts and by the age of one Amy could sing 40 tunes; within a year she could improvise alto lines while her mother sang the tunes. She developed perfect pitch and associated keys with colors. She learned to read at three, and at four could play the piano by ear; at seven she performed in public pieces by Handel, Beethoven, Chopin, and her own compositions. Her family moved to Boston so that she could study the piano and composition but, unlike many young European women musicians of her generation, she was never encouraged to go abroad for training. Nevertheless, she developed a superb keyboard technique, greatly enhanced by a prodigious memory. She published her first work at the age of 13 and made her début with the Boston Symphony Orchestra five years later.

Her professional career was much affected by her marriage that same year (1885) to Henry Harris Aubrey Beach, a prominent physician and lecturer at Harvard University. During their 25-year marriage, Mrs. H. H. A. Beach, as she was always known, performed only at charity events; they had no children and so she put her considerable energy into composition. After her husband's death in 1910, she toured as a pianist in pre-war Germany (she spoke German fluently), where both she and her music were well received. She later returned to Europe; but meanwhile, at home in America, she continued to give concerts and compose. She also found time to take an active role in national musical organizations and in 1926 co-founded and served as the first president of the Association of American Women Composers. She died in 1944.

LISTENING GUIDE 50

CD 6 TRACK 35

Beach: Violin Sonata in a, op. 34 (1896), second movement

Amy Beach was a disciplined and fast-working composer and she wrote this violin sonata within a period of six weeks in 1896, after she had finished her *Gaelic Symphony*. An accomplished pianist, she gave its first performance, with the violinist Franz Kneisel, in Boston in 1899, and in 1912 played it in several German cities. The work demonstrates well many of Beach's compositional characteristics: lyricism and eloquence (somewhat in the manner of Brahms), chromaticism and swift modulations, idiomatic piano writing, rich textures, and strong contrasts – all within a well-controlled conventional structural framework.

The sonata has four movements: an Allegro moderato, in triple time, in which a stately opening theme is followed by a large-scale sonata-form movement of great vigor; a scherzo (see below); an intense, chromatic largo, in 9/8 in E minor; and a dashing, fiery finale in the home key of A minor.

 Listening Outline ·

Scherzo (Molto vivace), 2/4, a; ternary form

Time	main section	
0.00	first part, a	main theme (ex. 1); note the opening rhythmic figure (*a*) and the rising arpeggio figure (*b*); repeated an octave higher; the music leads to the dominant, D (0.23)
0.29	first part repeated	
0.56	second part	ideas from the main theme are closely worked, swiftly modulating via C (1.09) to E♭, G♭ and back, ending with secondary material in G (1.18)
1.35	**middle section**	slower music centering on g: a sustained tone (G) on the violin is held for the opening 8 mm. while the piano plays full, soft chords; the piano introduces a new theme, ex. 2 (1.55), taken up by the violin (2.27) while the piano left hand has a sustained G; the music hints at the main section textures and rhythms to herald . . .
3.17	**main section**	the music begins as before, but moves straight on to the second part, following the earlier key scheme, and leading to a short coda (3.57)
4.09		(end)

ex. 1

ex. 2

Amy Beach was a prolific composer of piano and vocal music. She also composed an opera, a symphony, a piano concerto, a Mass, chamber music, and a violin sonata, for which she is best known today (see **Listening Guide 50**). Her music is in a late Romantic idiom, richly chromatic with long melodic lines sometimes tinged with folk music.

MUSIC

Part VIII The Modern Age

1 *New Languages of Music*

The story of modern music begins, essentially, in the years leading up to World War I. These years saw the composition of numerous works firmly rooted in the past, such as the symphonies of Mahler, Sibelius, and Elgar, or the operas of Strauss and Puccini (discussed in the previous section). But they saw, too, a number of works, by younger men, that struck a new – and harsher – note. The most famous, or notorious, of them was Igor Stravinsky's *Rite of Spring*, which caused a riot on its first performance. There are also several by Arnold Schoenberg (piano pieces, chamber works, above all the pieces for speaker and chamber group called *Pierrot lunaire*) and his students Alban Berg and Anton Webern, and by Béla Bartók (the opera *Bluebeard's Castle*, the *Allegro barbaro* for piano).

These works – and there are many more by other composers – did not merely carry further the continuing processes of the breakdown of tonality and an increase

Composers of the Modern Age

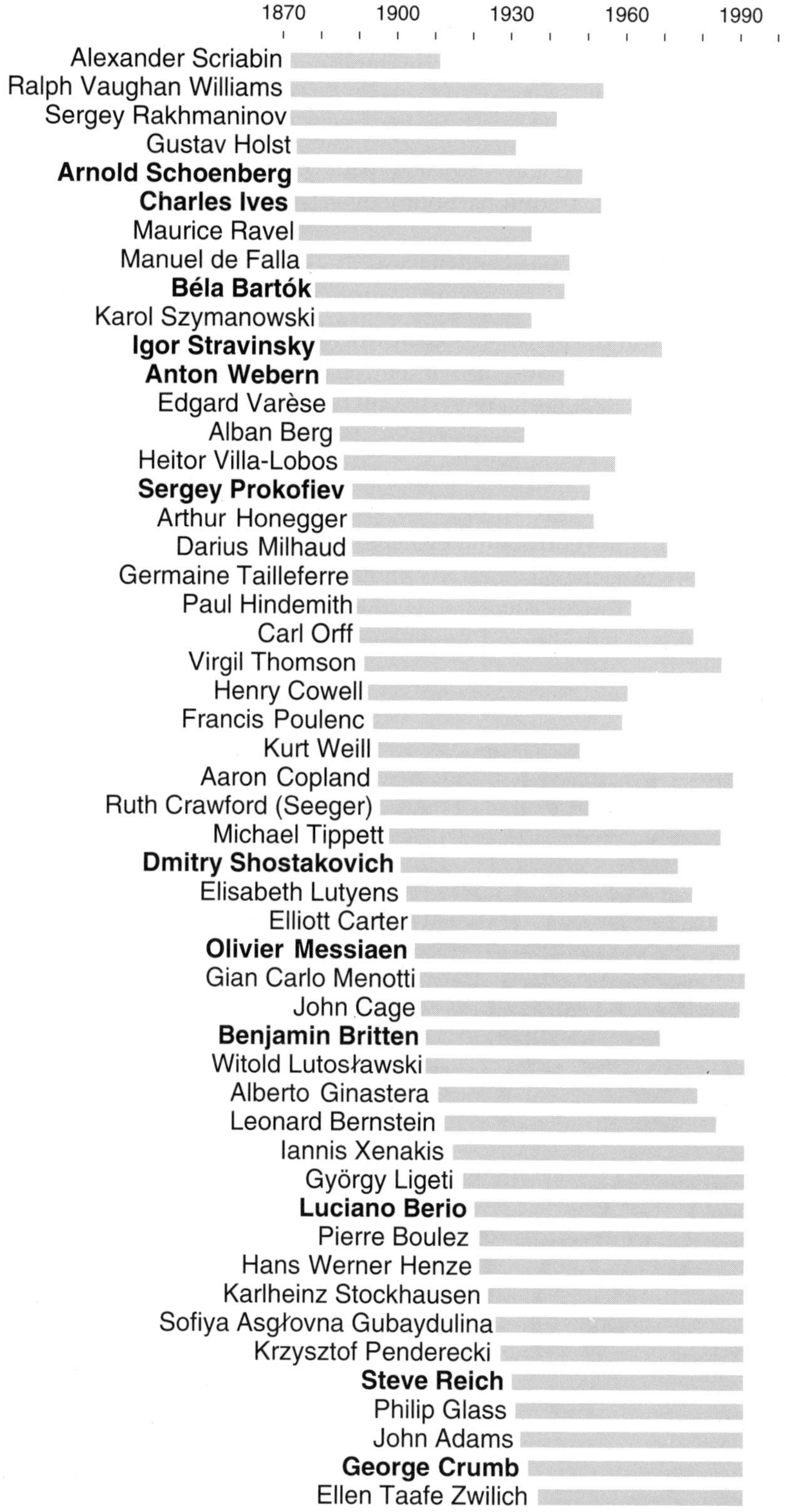

	1870	1900	1930	1960	1990

Alexander Scriabin

Ralph Vaughan Williams

Sergey Rakhmaninov

Gustav Holst

Arnold Schoenberg

Charles Ives

Maurice Ravel

Manuel de Falla

Béla Bartók

Karol Szymanowski

Igor Stravinsky

Anton Webern

Edgard Varèse

Alban Berg

Heitor Villa-Lobos

Sergey Prokofiev

Arthur Honegger

Darius Milhaud

Germaine Tailleferre

Paul Hindemith

Carl Orff

Virgil Thomson

Henry Cowell

Francis Poulenc

Kurt Weill

Aaron Copland

Ruth Crawford (Seeger)

Michael Tippett

Dmitry Shostakovich

Elisabeth Lutyens

Elliott Carter

Olivier Messiaen

Gian Carlo Menotti

John Cage

Benjamin Britten

Witold Lutosławski

Alberto Ginastera

Leonard Bernstein

Iannis Xenakis

György Ligeti

Luciano Berio

Pierre Boulez

Hans Werner Henze

Karlheinz Stockhausen

Sofiya Asgłovna Gubaydulina

Krzysztof Penderecki

Steve Reich

Philip Glass

John Adams

George Crumb

Ellen Taafe Zwilich

Violence

in dissonance. There is in them a conscious, deliberate element of violence and distortion, a renunciation of traditional ideas of the beautiful and the expressive. Bartók's "barbaric" Allegro involves ferocious pounding of the keyboard. Stravinsky's ballet sets new levels in dissonance and rhythmic energy, of a "primitive", disorienting kind. Schoenberg's *Pierrot lunaire* inhabits a world of nightmare fantasy, macabre and absurd, with hints of cabaret music. The traditional bourgeois concert-goers were meant to be offended and disturbed from complacency by such works; and they duly were, just as the traditional bourgeois art-lovers were infuriated by the art of the time.

Expressionism

This was a period when artists of all kinds were seeking to find a more truthful, more expressive way than a photographic realism could offer of treating the realities of human existence in the harsh, dissonant world of the twentieth century. Vincent van Gogh, back in the 1880s, had intentionally represented an altered, even distorted reality to reflect his feelings. His methods were pursued by such Expressionist painters as Oskar Kokoschka (1886–1980) and Wassily Kandinsky (1866–1944) – Kandinsky's move towards abstraction invites analogy with Schoenberg's towards atonality. Equally an analogy may be drawn between Stravinsky and early Cubism, particularly as represented by Pablo Picasso (1881–1973), an artist with whom Stravinsky in fact collaborated. Another fascinating parallel with musical developments of the time is suggested by the prose of James Joyce (1882–1941), which relinquishes the traditional priority of meaning in favor of various kinds of patterning and allusion.

91 *The Kolisch Quartet rehearsing Berg's* Lyric Suite *in the presence of Schoenberg (*right, standing*) and the composer (*center back*) before its first performance in Vienna, 8 January 1927: drawing by Benedict Dolbin. Meyer Collection, Paris.*

France – with Paris still the artistic capital of Europe, and the natural home for an expatriate Russian such as Stravinsky – and the German-speaking countries, with their weight of tradition from the previous century, led in most of these new developments. But the wind of change was felt everywhere. In America, Charles Ives was composing pieces with irrational juxtapositions of musical ideas and deliberately distorted harmonies. Soon Edgard Varèse (1883–1965) was to arrive in the country with his revolutionary ideas about musical sounds, partly based on the noise-world of an industrial, urbanized society. In Italy, the Futurists – a movement including visual and literary artists as well as musicians – were thinking along similar lines; one of this group of machine-age artists. Luigi Russolo (1885–1947), spent years devising an ingenious series of *intonarumori* (noise-intoners) – musically a dead end, but a symptom of the times nonetheless, comparable perhaps with Dadaism.

Atonality

With the total abandonment of tonality, as is found in the work of Schoenberg and his disciples during the first decade of the twentieth century, it became necessary to devise new methods of musical structure. In these "atonal" works, Schoenberg, Berg, and Webern found themselves drawn – at a subconscious, creative level – to use complex forms of imitation between voices or instruments. It is out of this necessity and their reaction to it that Schoenberg's 12-tone system began to be devised. It was codified in the mid-1920s, but not widely used outside the circle of Schoenberg's direct influence for more than 20 years. Even then its use was not long sustained. It did however give rise to more complex forms of serialism: Schoenberg's method applies serial processes to pitch, but others later carried the principle further and applied it to such elements of music as rhythm, dynamics, and tone-color. Pierre Boulez was among these "total serialists".

At the end of his life even Stravinsky, attracted by Webern's use of serialism, adopted it; but his earlier work, once past his strongly Russian phase (to which *The Rite of Spring* belongs), is primarily neo-classical. The term "neo-classicism" is used in music to describe those works of the first half of the twentieth century that look back beyond the Romantic era to the Classical, the Baroque, or even earlier for inspiration or simply for technical procedures. Others besides Stravinsky, notably Prokofiev, have drawn on classical forms in their instrumental music; in opera Stravinsky's *The Rake's Progress*, with its strong Mozart echoes, is outstanding among neo-classical works. Paul Hindemith (1895–1963), whose music is notably tidy in its forms and techniques, and unromantic in feeling, has also often been called a neo-classicist. Another, of a rather different kind, was the Italian composer and pianist Ferruccio Busoni (1866–1924), who particularly sought inspiration in Bach, as his *Fantasia contrappuntistica* testifies.

Neo-classicism

There were other significant and widespread influences on music in the years around and after World War I. The folksong interests of the previous generation persisted but had changed in focus. Composers like Ralph Vaughan Williams (see p. 300) in England and Béla Bartók in Hungary were collecting folksong on a methodical, scientific basis, using recording machines as well as pencil and paper.

92 *Bartók transcribing folksongs from an Edison phonograph, c1910.*

Bartók researched not only in his native country but in neighboring regions and even in Turkey and the Middle East. These men used folksong in their music, Bartók in particular in such a way as to reinvigorate it rhythmically after the sterile, sluggish, mechanical rhythms of some late Romantic music.

There was a social, or political, element in this too, aimed at bringing music out of the drawing-room, the salon, and even the concert hall into a wider realm and giving it contact with and meaning to a broader and perhaps less sophisticated public. One way of doing this was to introduce elements from the folk or traditional music of the people. In the USA, where folk-music traditions were relatively recent, composers like Aaron Copland and George Gershwin also drew on native jazz traditions. These traditions influenced Europeans too, notably Stravinsky and, in France, Maurice Ravel (1875–1937).

The political events of the first half of the twentieth century had a good deal of influence on music. They always have, of course: composers in the employ of royal or noble patrons have naturally been expected to compose music to the greater glory – and the perpetuation in power – of their masters, and we should not expect a state to exercise any lesser rights over those it pays to provide its music. States can, however, change their attitudes, as Soviet Russia did in her early days. After the revolution in 1917, Stravinsky left Russia for good (apart from a brief visit as an honored guest at the end of his life). Prokofiev, also out of sympathy with the new regime – and fairly certain that it would be out of sympathy with his music – left, though the pull of his native land later proved irresistible. Initially, the Soviet regime encouraged many sorts of experimental music; but later, with Stalin in charge and intellectuals increasingly under pressure, experimentation was strongly discouraged, the experimental composers were removed and their works banned. Music was required to be optimistic in spirit and readily appealing to large audiences, as well as encouraging self-sacrifice and effort on behalf of the community. Prokofiev and Shostakovich were, broadly, ready to accept these principles without regarding them as attacks on artistic freedom (which is always a relative concept); but they were often troubled by official disapproval of particular works.

At the opposite end of the political spectrum lies the music of Nazi Germany and Austria in the 1930s and 40s. Here, in another kind of totalitarian society, other (and no less ruthless) forms of censorship were applied. Music that challenged the existing order, like Kurt Weill's settings of texts by Bertolt Brecht, was not permitted, and here too experimentation of almost any kind was regarded as degenerate. Forward-looking composers, and not only such Jewish ones as Schoenberg or Weill, fled the country; most of those who remained and were approved have faded into a proper obscurity, and with them their music.

The dust has now settled on the first half of the twentieth century, and it is growing easier, in spite of the very great diversity of musical style and idiom, to see what lies in common between composers of the time. Doubtless it will be easier still a hundred years from now. But it is too soon for us to establish much of a perspective on music since 1950. Many composers pressed further the movements of the preceding years, like the "total serialists" and the Soviet bloc composers who developed a popular, patriotic vein that often drew on folksong. But after World War II, as after World War I, the younger generation strove to find fresh means of expressing in their music the ethos of their times, dominated by new and alarming technologies and the uncertainties to which they gave rise.

93 *Prokofiev's* The Love for Three Oranges: *scene from the Glyndebourne production, designed by Maurice Sendak, 1983.*

Electronics

One technological development of the war years particularly important to musicians was, of course, tape recording: not only for performance but also for composition. A composer could now conceive and execute a piece without depending on performers to play and interpret it. In the early days, this was chiefly done (by a group based in Paris) by the manipulation of sounds from everyday life, like traffic noise or leaves rustling in the wind. With tape recording, the sounds could be speeded up, slowed down, superimposed, played backwards, given an echo, and so on. The term *musique concrète* was used for "compositions" of this kind. Later, these techniques were applied to musical sounds, for example by Stockhausen in *Gesang der Jünglinge* ("Song of the Youths"), and in America by composers at the influential Columbia-Princeton Center. With the advent of the synthesizer a large range of sounds could be generated and processed electronically, giving the composer a new degree of control over the sound of his or her music.

Not all composers, in fact, wanted that kind of control. Some preferred exactly the opposite. Even in the electronic world, a device called the ring modulator was sometimes used which would distort the sound in ways that could not always be calculated in advance. And some composers combined a pre-existing tape with live music-making, while others used electronic devices like amplifiers or throat microphones to introduce deliberately random elements.

Random and chance music

In this area the most influential and revolutionary figure was the American composer John Cage (see p. 377), who systematically questioned all the assumptions on which our musical culture is based: he proposed the elevation of noise and silence to the level at which we hold music, opposed the idea of the formal concert in favor of the musical "happening", and used in his own compositions such elements as radio receivers randomly tuned to produce crackles and snatches of haphazard speech or music. Some composers have used chance (or "aleatory") elements in other ways, for example by using the toss of a coin (as in Cage's *Music of Changes*) or the throw of dice to determine the order in which sections are played.

Many of Cage's suggestions have been followed up by younger composers. In the turbulent late 1960s and early 70s, especially, audiences earnestly (though sometimes impatiently) listened to such events as a player on an amplified cello sounding one note continuously for two hours, perhaps with occasional accompaniment from others using instruments or noise-makers. In terms of traditional artistic values such events meant little, but they did serve to sharpen the listener's awareness of the nature and the effects of sound.

Other composers of this period – not necessarily disciples of Cage – moved along similar lines. Some, recognizing and wishing to extend the role of the performer, abandoned traditional notation in favor of symbolic graphic patterns which the player could interpret as he or she felt inclined; nothing is "wrong", and anything that reflects the player's feelings, on seeing the music, is "right". A piece of music might even be presented as a piece of prose, to which the performer would react by playing something. Many other composers, however, were attracted to the idea of random elements in a much less extreme form – in a string quartet by the Polish composer Witold Lutosławski, for example, the players are asked to improvise on given phrases until the first violinist gives a signal to move on; and in a Stockhausen piano piece the player is required to make decisions, while performing, on which sections to include and in what sequence.

There are limited analogies for such ideas in the other arts. Some modern poets have had their works printed in such a way as to leave the reader free to choose the sequence of sections. The graphic arts do not embody the time element that is central to such procedures, but there are obvious parallels between the art of Jackson Pollock (1912–56), who let paint fall at random on canvases lying on the floor, and the music of Cage.

One of the trends among the post-Cage generation, eager to escape the intellectu- **Minimalism** alism (as they saw it) of much twentieth-century music in the West, was to seek new types of simplicity. Some European composers experimented with music made up almost entirely of textural effect. But the clearest indications of this new simplicity are to be found in the music of certain American composers sometimes classified as "minimalists": they include LaMonte Young (b. 1935), Terry Riley (b. 1935), Philip Glass (b. 1937), Steve Reich (b. 1936), and John Adams (b. 1947).

Minimalism involves static harmony, patterned rhythms, and continuing repetition, sometimes with slowly shifting relationships so that the repetitions move out of phase. In Reich's music of the late 1960s, for example, the aim is the projection of a simple process of change with repeated patterns of pure tonal harmony.

There are evident signs, however, that for Reich and his colleagues such simplicity is only a stepping-stone to complexity of another sort, for in works such as *Drumming* (1971; see p. 381) Reich created much more ambitious and complicated processes while retaining the mesmeric intensity of his repetitive rhythm and glowing harmony. Glass (*Einstein on the Beach*, 1976) and Adams (*Nixon in China*, 1987) have even applied these procedures to full-length music drama. The style of such music brings some of these pieces closer to the world of pop music, and in fact some minimalist composers have also worked in pop and rock.

There has, understandably, been a substantial reaction among composers against the experimentalist generation. Several have found what might be called a neo-Romantic idiom in which, without denying the more recent past, traditional values are affirmed. Other composers have looked, in these times of rapid world communications and ethnic mixing, to non-Western cultures for fresh inspiration – to the ragas of Indian music, for example, with their quality of timeless meditation, or to the strangely mystical clangor of gongs in the gamelan music of Indonesia. Still others have sought a coming-together with rock music, a notion that is particularly attractive because it implies an ending to the social and intellectual divisiveness hinted at by the existence of different music systems and the different publics that support them. Certainly it seems that music is at a crossroads; but then, looking back over the entire scope of this book, it is hard to escape the conclusion that it nearly always has been.

2 *The Second Viennese School*

94 Arnold Schoenberg: self-portrait, 1910. Arnold Schoenberg Institute, Los Angeles.

One area in which music has most conspicuously changed since 1900 is that of harmony. The change, once it came, came fast. In the nineteenth century, composers had introduced an ever greater variety of chords and an ever faster rate of harmonic change. The major–minor system had been threatened in Wagner's *Tristan und Isolde* (see p. 288). In the music of composers otherwise as different as Richard Strauss, Debussy, and Mahler, there began to be times when the pull of the tonic was so weak as hardly to be felt at all. To keep their music going, composers had to use larger orchestras and bigger forms, as in Mahler's symphonies; the alternative was the almost *atonal* miniature, such as Schoenberg's *Pierrot lunaire*.

In 1908, the decisive break to atonality was made by a slightly younger composer, who was thereby to establish himself as one of the dominant influences on the music of the twentieth century: Arnold Schoenberg (1874–1951). Schoenberg was the creator and father-figure of what has come to be called the Second Viennese School – the "First" being Haydn, Mozart, Beethoven, and perhaps Schubert. This group consists essentially of three composers, Schoenberg, Webern, and Alban Berg (1885–1935), remembered in particular for his creation of two of the monuments of twentieth-century opera (*Wozzeck*, 1925; *Lulu*, 1937) and a deeply expressive Violin Concerto.

SCHOENBERG

Life

Schoenberg was a reluctant revolutionary. He was born in Vienna in 1874, when Brahms was working there, and remained devoted to the Viennese tradition as expressed in the music of Haydn, Mozart, Beethoven, Schubert, and Brahms. He saw himself not as overturning that tradition but as perpetuating it, continuing a natural process of development. Just as Brahms's harmonies were more complex then Haydn's, Schoenberg's had to be more complex than Brahms's. But the aims stayed the same. Music must unfold with logic, stating its themes, developing them, and then recalling them. And the vehicle for the most profound musical thinking would have to be chamber music.

Schoenberg started violin lessons when he was eight and was soon composing little duets and trios to play with friends. Because the family was not well off, there was no opportunity for him to study as a composer. He had to leave school and work in a bank. So he developed the enthusiasm and the offbeat attitudes of one who has learned his art for himself: there would be no betrayal of the ideals of the great Viennese tradition, but nor would there be any compromising of the new musical ideas that came rushing into the young composer's mind.

Only at the end of the decade did he start writing music he considered worthy. *Verklärte Nacht* ("Transfigured Night"), a symphonic poem for string sextet, was the first instrumental score he acknowledged. It was also the first of his works to create a scandal. The work combined program music with orthodox form, so bringing together the Wagner–Strauss tradition and that of Brahms. It brought *Tristan*-style harmonies into chamber music. For Schoenberg's contemporaries that was unacceptable: the Composers' Union in Vienna declined to perform it.

By this time Schoenberg had left the bank and was earning his living by conducting choirs and orchestrating operettas. In 1901 he moved to Berlin, where he had a job as musician at a literary cabaret. He returned to Vienna in 1903 and soon began giving composition lessons. Among his first pupils were Alban Berg and Anton Webern. Both were to stay close to him, musically and personally, for the rest of their lives.

To earn money Schoenberg undertook a heavy program of teaching; the conservative Viennese public failed to take to his music and on the rare occasions that his works were performed they met with incomprehension or worse. About this time he turned seriously to painting (see **fig. 94**), becoming a friend of Kandinsky's. With slender hopes of success in Vienna, he moved back to Berlin in 1911. But there too his ideas and his music were coldly received, though in 1912 his *Pierrot lunaire* met with some success in Germany, Austria, and further afield.

Schoenberg's high moral seriousness and his restless search for the indefinable are linked with religious searching in the work that should have crowned this period but was never completed, the oratorio *Jacob's Ladder* (1917–22). Schoenberg had been brought up an orthodox Jew, but he was no longer practicing his religion (he made a formal return in 1933, soon after he had been ejected from Berlin on Hitler's rise to power). A Jewish sense of the divinity, urging mankind to a perpetual search after truth, underlies *Jacob's Ladder*. The same feeling pervades the opera *Moses and Aaron* (1932), again concerned with the thorny road to God, and again significantly unfinished. For though *Jacob's Ladder* was interrupted because of the war (Schoenberg had spent almost a year in the army), the real reason for its incompleteness is the impossibility of adequately describing the soul's eventual union with God.

The 1920s were a period of preparation for *Moses and Aaron*. Its biblical theme was close to Schoenberg's heart: it is the insoluble problem of communicating the most important truths. Moses's tragedy is to be a prophet who perceives divine truth but lacks the means to tell it; Aaron's curse is to be articulate but blind, so that he distorts and even destroys his brother's vision. It is plain that Schoenberg felt himself to be more a Moses (a prophet) than an Aaron (a communicator – though he was able to admire such Aarons of the musical world as George Gershwin). An attempt to create a sympathetic, semi-private environment for the performance of new music in Vienna had had some success in 1919–21, but it foundered; and in Berlin, where Schoenberg moved in 1926 to teach composition at the Prussian Academy of Arts, racial intolerance was mixed with musical. When he left in 1933, he went first to France and thence to the USA.

Arnold Schoenberg   Life and Works

1874	born in Vienna, 13 September
1890	began working in a bank; contact with musicians including Alexander von Zemlinsky who became a lifelong friend and musical influence
1899	*Transfigured Night*
1900	conducted choirs, orchestrated operettas; began work on *Gurrelieder*
1902	composition teacher at the Stern Conservatory, Berlin
1903	Vienna; began giving private composition lessons, Alban Berg and Anton Webern being among his pupils; met Mahler
1908	composed first atonal pieces; Piano Pieces op. 11, *The Book of the Hanging Garden*
1910	his latest works greeted with incomprehension; mounted exhibition of his Expressionist paintings
1911	Berlin; published harmony treatise
1912	*Pierrot lunaire*
1913	*Gurrelieder* first performed in Vienna
1915	Vienna; joined army as volunteer
1918	founded the Society for Private Musical Performances
1923	first serial works: Piano Pieces op. 23
1926	composition teacher at the Prussian Academy of Arts, Berlin; period of prolific composition
1933	left Germany because of Nazi anti-semitism; emigrated to the USA, to Boston
1934	moved to Hollywood because of health; took private pupils
1936	professor at the University of California at Los Angeles; Violin Concerto, Fourth String Quartet
1944	health began to deteriorate; left professorship
1951	died in Los Angeles, 13 July

Operas Erwartung (Expectation, 1909), Die glückliche Hand (The Blessed Hand, 1913), Von heute auf morgen (From One Day to the Next, 1929), Moses und Aron (1932, unfinished) [dates are of composition]

Choral music Gurrelieder (1900–01); A Survivor from Warsaw (1947); Die Jakobsleiter (Jacob's Ladder, 1922, unfinished); Kol nidre (1938)

Orchestral music Pelleas und Melisande (1903); 5 Pieces, op. 16 (1909); Variations (1928); Violin Concerto (1936); Piano Concerto (1942); 2 chamber symphonies

Chamber music Verklärte Nacht (Transfigured Night, 1899) for string sextet; 4 string quartets; string trio; wind quintet

Vocal music Das Buch der Hängenden Gärten (The Book of the Hanging Garden; 15 songs, 1909); Pierrot lunaire (1912); cabaret songs; c75 others; choruses

Piano music 3 Pieces, op. 11 (1909); 6 Little Pieces, op. 19 (1911); 5 Pieces, op. 23 (1920, 1923); Suite, op. 25 (1923)

In 1934 he settled in California, his home for the rest of his life. This late period was one of continued teaching, both of private pupils (among them John Cage) and at the University of Southern California.

The religious nature of his quest also became fully apparent during his American years. There was a liturgical piece, *Kol nidre*, for rabbi, chorus, and orchestra (1938), and at the end a set of "modern psalms", setting his own words. But these too, like all his most profoundly spiritual works, were not to be finished: at his death in 1951 he had left the first of them in mid-air, on the words "and still I pray".

Music

Transfigured Night set the pattern of Schoenberg's music in its heavy emotional load and its density of feelings in conflict, achieved through a web of polyphonic lines that strain out of the harmony. In effect a one-movement symphony, it was soon followed by a string quartet where the thematic development is pursued through music embracing the conventional four movement-types; the absence of a justifying program helps make the expressive contortions still more intense.

The same style is continued in the First Chamber Symphony (1906), which again plays continuously through sections that correspond to the normal symphonic movements. Again, the music is made tonal only with severe strain; this contributes to the sense of turmoil in so much of Schoenberg's music. It is scored for 15 soloists, a crack team who can tackle the dynamism and complex counterpoint more effectively than larger forces could. Significantly, he wrote no "normal" symphonies but preferred to bring the genre within the sphere of chamber music.

His next chamber work, String Quartet no. 2, completes the move into atonality. After two tonal movements, the third has little feeling of key and the finale is wholly atonal until it finally settles in the work's home key of F♯. The revolution was momentous – as momentous as that of Sigmund Freud (1856–1939) in psychology, and for similar reasons. Schoenberg and Freud both pull the carpet out from under our feet, showing that accepted certainties (the major–minor system, moral categories) may be artificial. Freudian, too, is the analysis of extreme emotional states of Schoenberg's first fully atonal works. Among these are the short opera *Erwartung* (1909), a monologue for a woman seeking her lost lover in a wood, and *Pierrot lunaire* (1912; see **Listening Guide 51**). The use of a key had always given music a feeling of direction. Without it, the creation of satisfactory instrumental forms was harder: that is one reason why Schoenberg at this time preferred to use words to give him structural backbone.

Gradually he evolved the basic principles of 12-tone serialism, which was intended not so much as a system as an aid to extended composition without tonality. We have already seen (pp. 33 and 337) something of how it works and the possibilities it offers. For Schoenberg, serialism made it possible again to compose in the large instrumental forms, and so the appearance of the new method came with a certain neo-classicism typical of the 1920s. A notable early example is the Piano Suite (1923), Schoenberg's first wholly serial work. As he insisted, "one uses the series and then one composes as before". His largest serial work was *Moses and Aaron*: the whole opera, nearly two hours of music, is based on a single series. Serialism was

Schoenberg: *Pierrot lunaire* (1912), excerpt

Pierrot lunaire is one of Schoenberg's earliest atonal works and, typical of his music of the time, is shaped by a text, in this case settings of poems from Albert Giraud's collection *Pierrot lunaire* in the German translations of Otto Erich Hartleben. The 21 brief poems speak in fractured terms of madness, alienation, uncertainty, and disquiet, and they draw from Schoenberg music of ambiguity and individuality. The words are delivered in what the composer's preface calls a *Sprechmelodie* ('speech-melody', also referred to as *Sprechgesang*, or 'speech-song'): the notated pitches should be sung but the voice should immediately change to a speaking character. Such a manner of delivery is the stock-in-trade of the popular singer, and perhaps in this and in the small accompanying instrumental group Schoenberg was recalling his cabaret experiences in Berlin a decade earlier. Cabaret, too, provides the background for what Schoenberg called the 'light, ironic, satirical tone' of the work, for its savagery, macabre humor, isolation, and nostalgia. The harmony is ambiguous, hovering round keys or other stable points. The poems are all rondeaus, i.e. the first two lines of the first stanza become the last two lines of the second, and the final line of all repeats the first. Usually Schoenberg draws on this to create a two-part musical form, the first part closed by the internal repetition at the end of the second stanza, and the second part, often more violent, closed by the further repetition at the very end of the poem.

· · · · · · · · Listening Outline · · · · · · · · · · · ·

Mondestrunken ('Moondrunk')
reciter, flute, violin, cello, piano

Time
0.00   movement begins, ex. 1, quiet piano ostinato; note the pizzicato violin, an image of the cascades from the moon
0.03   voice enters; ostinato is expanded
0.19   'stillen Horizont'; note the pure sung tone and the soft 3rd
0.22   flute begins ostinato
0.31   ostinato alternated between flute and piano
0.39   voice enters for second verse; violin melody comes to forefront; flute and piano share ostinato music
1.03   final verse opens with sudden *forte* and cello has impassioned melody doubled and accompanied by piano; climax at 'Haupt'; piano and flute ostinato return for last line
1.37   (end)

Den Wein, den man mit Augen trinkt,	The wine one drinks through opened eyes
giesst nachts der Mond in Wogen nieder,	pours down from the moon at night in waves,
und eine Springflut überschwemmt	and a spring tide overflows
den stillen Horizont.	the still horizon.
Gelüste, schauerlich und süss,	Desires, terrible and sweet,
durchschwimmen ohne Zahl die Fluten!	arrive countless in those floods!
Den Wein, den man mit Augen trinkt,	The wine one drinks through opened eyes
giesst nachts der Mond in Wogen nieder.	pours down from the moon at night in waves.
Der Dichter, den die Andacht triebt,	The poet, lost in his devotions
berauscht sich an dem heilgen Tranke,	grows dizzy on the holy drink,
gen Himmel wendet er verzückt das Haupt	and heavenwards turns in ecstasy
und taumelnd saugt und schlürft er	and staggering sucks and sips
den Wein, den man mit Augen trinkt.	the wine one drinks through opened eyes.

ex. 1

the most appropriate technique for the work, since its possible forms are infinite, just as Jehovah is infinite: the voice in the burning bush, heard at the start of the work, is only one representation. The late 1930s and early 40s were the years, in California, of Schoenberg's most complex and coherent instrumental serial works. He extended his serial practice to take command of large spans, even feeling confident enough to go back to his earlier technique of combining several movements into one.

Anton Webern came from a middle-class family. He had studied musicology at the University of Vienna, his native city, and took from it a liking for strict canon and thorough motivic working along the lines of such Renaissance composers as Josquin and Palestrina. After leaving Schoenberg's class, in 1908, he took a variety of short-lived and unsatisfactory conducting jobs, while closely following his teacher's compositional development.

In 1918 Webern settled near Schoenberg in Vienna, where he lived for the rest of his life. During the 1920s and early 1930s he held conducting appointments, notably with the Workers' Symphony Concerts, but gradually he lost his posts as the Nazis gained control of Austria. Meanwhile he was writing his refined serial compositions, including not only the instrumental pieces but also a series of settings of verses by Hildegard Jone; the nature symbolism and tremulous mysticism of her work obviously struck a chord in him. There were two sets of songs and three little choral works, all responding to her imagery with eagerness disciplined by the mechanics of serialism. He was working on a further Jone cantata in 1945 when he was shot in error by an American soldier.

Webern's training gave him a natural disposition towards serialism, which he brought to an extreme of concentration and calculation in such works as his Symphony (1928), Concerto for nine instruments (1934), and String Quartet (1938). The symphony, scored for a small orchestra of clarinets, horns, harp, and strings, has only two movements – the first in sonata form but characteristically also a four-part canon, the second a set of variations that pivots at its halfway point (after which the music goes backwards and ends as it began).

Webern's music is an architecture of polyphonic lines, playing constantly on the tiniest motifs (six notes in the case of the symphony) and closely organized in instrumentation, in rhythm, and dynamic level. But since Webern's expressiveness is retained even in the tiny gestures of his music, the impression is not so much one of engineering in sound as of created equivalents to the things he liked to bring home from his walks in the Austrian Alps: bright mountain flowers and mineral crystals.

It had taken Webern a while to achieve this purity. A clear step in this direction is to be seen in the miniatures he produced soon after leaving Schoenberg's class, such as his Six Bagatelles for string quartet (1913), each occupying only a small page of score (see **Listening Guide 52**).

LISTENING GUIDE 52

Webern: *Six Bagatelles*, op. 9 (1913): no. 4

After Webern left Schoenberg's composition class, he produced a group of works of extraordinary concision, among them these bagatelles. This new, extreme brevity caused Webern great anguish, and he recalled that while working on the bagatelles he 'had the feeling that once the 12 notes had run out, the piece was finished . . . It sounds grotesque, incomprehensible, and it was immensely difficult'. The bagatelles are not literally serial compositions, but are, of course, atonal. The six make up a miniature string quartet, with an *A–B–A* first movement, two scherzos, two slow movements (the first of which is discussed below), and a quick finale. Each movement is compact (occupying only a page of score), and each is constructed of tiny phrases, ostinatos, and single chords.

 Listening Outline . . . .

no. 4, very slow, *pianissimo* throughout
string quartet

Time

0.00 first phrase (ex. 1) played by 2nd violin, surrounded by soft phrases in other instruments, presenting each of the 12 tones once; note the variegation of color: all play with mutes, but the 1st violin plays *sul ponticello* (by the bridge), the viola *pizzicato* (plucking), and the cello by the fingerboard

0.16 1st violin plays repeated E

0.25 accompaniments precede melody in harmonics on 1st violin; all 12 tones are completed for the second time

0.44 (end)

ex. 1

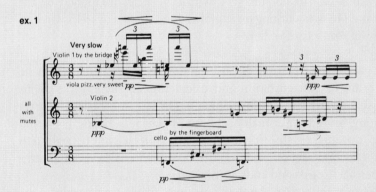

95 *Anton Webern: black chalk drawing, 1918, by Egon Schiele. Private collection.*

3 *Stravinsky*

LIFE

In terms of both creative achievement and influence, there can be no doubt that Igor Stravinsky (1882–1971) stands with Schoenberg as one of the dominant figures in twentieth-century music. His influence, indeed, has probably been the greater, for where Schoenberg's principal effort was towards continuing the Austro-German symphonic tradition, Stravinsky interested himself in radical alternatives to that tradition.

The difference in musical temperament is partly to be explained by a difference in cultural background. Though Stravinsky spent much of his life in France, Switzerland, and the USA, he was very much a Russian composer, with a Russian's uncertainty over western European values. His father was a well-known opera singer. He studied law at university, but was more interested in his music studies, working under the father-figure among Russian composers, Rimsky-Korsakov, in the years 1905–8. In 1908 his work took off, when two of his short orchestral pieces, *Scherzo fantastique* and *Fireworks*, were given at a concert in St Petersburg. Their youthful brilliance, and perhaps their echoes of recent French music, caught the ear of one member of the audience in particular – the ballet impresario Sergei Diaghilev, who at once commissioned him to orchestrate pieces by Grieg and Chopin for his 1909 ballet season in Paris. This was the beginning of a long and richly fruitful association: between 1910 and 1913 Stravinsky wrote for Diaghilev three ballet scores that have remained at the center of the repertory.

The outbreak of World War I severed Stravinsky from Russia. He and his family set up home in Switzerland, and in exile his thoughts turned towards Russian folk traditions. His next ballet for Diaghilev, *The Wedding*, was based on the rituals of a Russian peasant marriage ceremony. Other Russian-flavored works followed, among them *The Soldier's Tale*. After the war he went to live in France – the revolution in Russia made it impossible for him to return – but he traveled widely, to make recordings and to work with Diaghilev's ballet company. His works of this period include several ballets and an "opera-oratorio" *Oedipus rex*, written in collaboration with Jean Cocteau and designed for a formal, monumental staging, with the cast standing like statues, a narrator in evening dress, and a narration in the audience's language but the singing in Latin.

By the 1930s Stravinsky had developed connections with the USA; and with the darkening political situation in Europe it was natural for him to decide to move there. In 1940 he settled in Hollywood. His compositions of this period include more ballets but also some purely orchestral works, notably two symphonies. Soon after his return to the Russian Orthodox Church he had written a Symphony of Psalms, and there are other religious works from his late years, including a setting of the Roman Catholic Mass (1948). In 1951 Stravinsky returned to Europe, where

Igor Stravinsky — Life and Works

1882	born in Oranienbaum (now Lomonosov), 17 June
1901	law student at St Petersburg University but chiefly interested in music
1902	met Rimsky-Korsakov, who became his mentor
1908–9	*Scherzo fantastique* and *Fireworks* acclaimed in St Petersburg; Diaghilev commissioned music from him, starting a long association with the Ballets Russes
1910	*The Firebird* (Paris) secured him an international reputation
1911	*Petrushka* (Paris)
1913	*The Rite of Spring* – riot in Paris theater
1914	settled in Switzerland
1917	revolution made it impossible for him to return to Russia; *The Wedding* completed
1920	France; *Pulcinella*, the first of his "neo-classical" works, performed
1921	first European tour with Ballets Russes
1925	first American tour as conductor and pianist
1927	*Oedipus rex*
1935	second American tour
1937	*The Card Party* (New York) led to several American commissions, including the 'Dumbarton Oaks' Concerto
1939	professor at Harvard University
1940	settled in Hollywood
1945	naturalized American
1946	Symphony in Three Movements first performed in New York
1951	*The Rake's Progress* (Venice)
1957	*Agon* (New York)
1958	began international conducting tours
1962	well received in Russia
1966	*Requiem Canticles*
1971	died in New York, 6 April; buried in Venice

Operas Oedipus rex (1927), The Rake's Progress (1951)

Ballets The Firebird (1910), Petrushka (1911), The Rite of Spring (1913), Pulcinella (1920), The Wedding (1923), Apollon musagète (1928), The Fairy's Kiss (1928), Jeu de cartes (The Card Party, 1937), Orpheus (1947), Agon (1957)

Music theater The Soldier's Tale (1918)

Orchestral music Symphonies of Wind Instruments (1920); Concerto 'Dumbarton Oaks' (1938); Symphony in C (1940); Symphony in Three Movements (1945); Violin Concerto (1931); Ebony Concerto for clarinet (1945); Concerto for Strings (1946)

Choral music Symphony of Psalms (1930); Mass (1948); Cantata (1952); Threni (1958); A Sermon, a Narrative, and a Prayer (1961); Requiem Canticles (1966)

Vocal music (with ensemble) Pribaoutki (1914); Abraham and Isaac (1963); songs

Chamber music Duo concertante for violin and piano

Piano music Sonata (1924); two pianos – Concerto (1935); Sonata (1944)

Stravinsky: *The Rite of Spring* (1913), excerpt

If there is any single work that symbolizes the rejection of an old order, it is Stravinsky's ballet *The Rite of Spring*. It was written for the Diaghilev Ballets Russes to perform in Paris, the third of Stravinsky's major ballets for this famous, brilliant, and adventurous company. In his previous ballets Stravinsky had continued the tradition he had inherited of colorful, pungent, and picturesque scoring; here he went very much further.

The scoring (as you will see from the huge orchestra list below) is on a new scale, giving him opportunities for all kinds of new combinations of instruments and a wide range of effects. More original still are the rhythms. Although this is music for dancing, its rhythms rarely have any regular pulse. The time-signature is constantly changing, and when it does stay the same there are many sharp accents written into the score in irregular patterns; the effect, to anyone used to normally regular patterns, is unnerving. Then the harmony is as dissonant as that of any music that had yet been composed, with crashing discords and lines swerving into collisions. And the melodic idiom, drawing on Russian and oriental folk music, with its repetitive figures, its fragmentary little phrases, treated with nagging persistence, has a character all its own. It is no wonder that the fashionable Paris audience in 1913 rioted: this music assaulted them and contradicted all the values in which they believed.

They objected, too, to the subject matter and the suggestive choreography. Stravinsky said that the idea of the work had first occurred to him as a fleeting vision in 1910: 'I saw in imagination a solemn pagan rite: wise elders, seated in a circle, watching a young girl dance herself to death' – a sacrifice to propitiate the spring god. Primitive cultures were attracting many scholars and artists at this time. Nature was important too; he later recalled in association with the work the violence of the Russian spring, that 'was like the whole earth cracking'.

The work divides into two parts, 'The Adoration of the Earth' and 'The Sacrifice'.

 Listening Outline

'The Adoration of the Earth'
3 flutes, 1 piccolo, 1 alto flute; 4 oboes, 1 english horn; 3 clarinets, 1 E♭ clarinet, 1 bass clarinet; 4 bassoons, 1 double bassoon
1 trumpet in D, 4 trumpets; 8 horns; 3 trombones; 2 tubas
timpani (2 players), bass drum, tam-tam, triangle, guero, tambour de Basque, antique cymbals
1st and 2nd violins, violas, cellos, double basses

Time		
0.00	**Introduction**	the opening theme (ex. 1), on a high bassoon, derives from a Lithuanian folk melody; the english horn takes up a continuation of it (0.45), the clarinet (1.15) and the oboe and flute (1.25) when the texture becomes more elaborate; then a repetitive figure is heard on the english horn and flutes (1.38), and there are increasingly florid lines for the woodwinds (note the small clarinet at 2.08, the oboe at 2.18) shortly before the strings enter with soft chords, leading to a climax of elaboration, when (2.52) the bassoon is heard again, followed by a pizzicato violin figure (ex. 2, 3.04)

3.27	**Omens of Spring: Dance of the Adolescents**	repeated string chords, irregularly accented (ex. 3), the horns reinforcing the accents, as the texture grows fuller; the repeated chords return (4.06) and soon a theme on the bassoons is added (4.16), taken up by trombones and oboes; after a dramatic pause a shrill woodwind gesture (4.53), fragments based on ex. 2 are heard, also a horn theme (ex. 4, 5.12) answered by flute; the agitation increases, the ex. 2 figure pounding away, while ex. 4 and other rhythms (notably ex. 5, a trumpet theme, 5.48, fig. *a* from the horn theme, 6.23) are set against it: a crescendo leads to . . .
6.52	**Abduction Games**	rapid music, with orchestration of glittering brilliance; note the horn calls (7.07, 7.37), then at the climax the music breaks off for passages of uneven rhythms (7.50; see ex. 6), leading to flute trills and . . .

ex. 1

ex. 2

ex. 3

ex. 4

ex. 5

ex. 6

8.15	**Spring Round Dances**	a mysterious line for clarinets, then slow, ponderous music (8.46), with ex. 6 begun on horns (9.22), then violas and flutes, leading to full orchestra (10.38 – note the trombone snarls, the first at 10.56); a rapid passage (11.30) and the music from the opening of the movement (11.52) brings it to an end
12.21	**Games of the Rival Clans**	short passages from different orchestral groups, with a persistent theme (ex. 7), for a time yielding to another (ex. 8, 12.55), and these remain in contest; then a slow theme enters on the tubas (ex. 9, 13.51), leading into . . .
14.12	**Procession of the Sage**	the heavy, brutish tuba theme, the processional march, becomes more insistent, and activity increases around it
14.51	**Adoration of the Sage**	an instant of quiet leads to . . .
15.14	**Dance of the Earth**	the music explodes into violent action, with orchestral writing of a fierce brilliance; it briefly quietens as scurrying strings and horns take over (15.41) and builds up into a climax
16.23		(end)

96 Stravinsky's ballet The Rite of Spring, *Metropolitan Opera Ballet, New York, 1984.*

his opera *The Rake's Progress* was given in Venice. With the American musician Robert Craft acting as his assistant, he traveled to other European centers and, in 1962, visited Moscow – his first time in Russia since before World War I. He also made many recordings of his works. His own music, now more austere in style, includes several memorial pieces, for Dylan Thomas, J. F. Kennedy, and others.

MUSIC

The first music with which Stravinsky made a mark was the group of ballets he wrote for Diaghilev: *The Firebird* (1910), *Petrushka* (1911), and *The Rite of Spring* (1913). Of these, *Petrushka* is his first wholly individual creation. Interestingly, the central character is a Russian equivalent of the Western Pierrot, who was the subject, at the same time, of a work by Schoenberg (see p. 346). It might be supposed that both composers were looking for a puppet figure who could display human emotions more intensely than any real human being; Stravinsky found his in the tale of a doll brought to wretched life just as Schoenberg found his in poems for spoken song. But the comparison points up the differences between the composers as well as the similarities. Stravinsky's orchestral score is flamboyant in gesture, brilliant in color, and crisp in outline. It has no pretensions to Schoenberg's constant development. Instead, Stravinsky cuts from one idea to another and back again, to give his music a kaleidoscopic quality. Lacking long-term growth, the score can accommodate a great variety of materials. It includes Russian peasant-style dances and more intimate mime sequences in which Petrushka's dual nature is expressed in the superimposition of opposed keys.

The Rite of Spring takes all the novelties of *Petrushka* suddenly to a giant extreme. Scored for a very large orchestra, it is a dance-play of spring festivities in pagan Russia, ending with the sacrifice of a virgin in a tearingly self-destructive dance. This also completes a musical revolution as profound as Schoenberg's at the same time. Just as Western music had hitherto been dependent on concepts of mode or key, so its rhythmic foundation had depended on meter, an underlying stable pattern of beats. Stravinsky dispenses with that in the most overwhelming sections of *The Rite of Spring*; its new, "barbaric" rhythm was immediately admired or detested by Stravinsky's contemporaries (see **Listening Guide 53**).

Stravinsky took six years to find the right orchestration for his next ballet, *The Wedding*, a Russian peasant ballet: a small percussion orchestra, led by four pianos, to join the chorus – an efficient, quick-moving, machine-like ensemble for music that jumps freely among different repeating patterns geared to an unchanging pulse. In this respect *The Wedding* is a prolonged development of one rhythmic principle from *The Rite*, and shares its ritual solemnity, heightened at the end by a characteristic reference to the sound of bells.

The Soldier's Tale, a short play with musical interludes and dances, departs from the established genres. This was just one expression of Stravinsky's breaking with tradition. He soon began, however, to find his own ways of re-using the past. Diaghilev's next project for him, *Pulcinella*, was an arrangement of pieces attributed to the early eighteenth-century composer Pergolesi. The music is newly imagined for a modern chamber orchestra, the harmony changed to add piquancy, the scoring thought out to heighten contrast and character. The ballet sounds more like real Stravinsky than an eighteenth-century retrieval. It was, he said later, a confrontation with himself "in the mirror of the past".

It helped open the way to neo-classicism. There is hardly a major work of his after 1920 that does not refer to the music of other composers. Yet in his hands neo-classicism is not an appeal to timeless precepts of form, but rather a way of showing how much things have changed. A characteristic of these works is that the strings have very little importance: he was eager to avoid their warmth and expressiveness. Stravinsky preferred the mechanical exactness of the piano and the harder outlines of wind instruments.

The Symphony of Psalms for choir and orchestra (1930), in three movements, each a setting of a Latin psalm, is solemn in tone – and excludes violins lest they introduce too expressive an effect. It marks a stage on Stravinsky's path back towards the Austro-German tradition, against which everything he had written in his maturity had been a decisive reaction. A "real" symphony duly emerged a decade later in the Symphony in C (1940), where the presence of four movements serves only to exhibit, in typical neo-classical fashion, how very unconventional the music is. This is not a symphony in C like those of Haydn, Mozart, Beethoven, or Schubert. This piece goes through the "proper" motions, but this is only the outline, and its skeleton nature is made clear by the unsuitable nature of the material used to fill it. Stravinsky does not develop his ideas but rather alters them: traditional symphonic continuity is not an aim.

Stravinsky's neo-classical works tend to be harmonically static, and this focuses attention on rhythm. They give the feeling of running on the spot: a pulsating "motor rhythm" persists, often with dislocations. This makes his neo-classical scores highly suitable for dancing. Having reached maturity as a ballet composer, he seems to have found strongly marked rhythm indispensable to his musical thinking.

In the 1950s Stravinsky suddenly began to move in two new directions at the same time. He developed an interest in medieval and Renaissance music. He also began to investigate serialism, to which his own style, with its great dependence on tonality, had seemed utterly opposed. Possibly he felt freer to do this after Schoenberg's death. His gradual adoption of serialism is charted in his works of the 1950s, for example the Canticum sacrum written as a ceremonial honoring of St Mark in his own basilica in Venice; yet he remained very much himself despite the great change in manner. Serialism also did nothing to curb his exact, always imaginative instrumentation or his rhythmic vitality. Indeed, since he was not above learning from composers two generations his junior – Pierre Boulez and Karlheinz Stockhausen – he found the stimulus for highly elaborate polyphonies of complex rhythms.

Stravinsky's last memorial, however, was to himself, and it took the form of a typically compact and austere Mass for the Dead, the Requiem Canticles (1966). This was sung at his funeral, which he directed was to take place in Venice, scene of the first performances of The Rake's Progress as well as the Canticum sacrum, and last resting place too of Diaghilev.

4 *Bartók*

Schoenberg and Stravinsky, like Brahms and Wagner in an earlier age, seemed to offer clear alternatives to their contemporaries: either to ground their music in the past, or to make a clean break. In art, however, no alternative can ever be clear-cut, and it is notable that several of the greatest composers of the first half of the twentieth century found a way to steer some kind of middle course. The composer next considered, a Hungarian, belongs to this group.

Béla Bartók (1881–1945) followed a career loosely matched by the history of his country. During his youth, Hungary was a part of the Habsburg Empire, ruled from Vienna, and Bartók was much influenced as a young composer by the Austro-German tradition stretching from Haydn to Strauss, with a Hungarian nationalist dash of Liszt. But in 1904 he discovered that the real peasant music of Hungary had little to do with the gypsy fiddle-playing that Brahms and Liszt heard in Hungarian restaurants and put into their "Hungarian" dances and rhapsodies. As one who had set himself the task of becoming above all a Hungarian composer – he had studied at the conservatory in Budapest rather than go to Vienna for his training, as was normal – Bartók set about using true folk music in his creative work. But because he had first to collect and study this music, he became at the same time one of the founders of modern ethnomusicology (the study of the music of different ethnic groups).

His works of this period include two string quartets, a ballet (*The Wooden Prince*) and an opera (*Duke Bluebeard's Castle*). But the years after World War I were years of stocktaking. He abandoned his field trips to collect folksongs, which had brought him great happiness: he had enough material in his sketchbooks and on phonograph cylinders. He devoted himself to organizing what he and other collectors had gathered, analyzing the styles of folksong within any one culture, the influences between different cultures, and the ways in which a tune would be varied as it passed from village to village. Through this he gained a formidable understanding of musical variation, always one of his favorite techniques. His music of the 1920s and 30s – which includes four more string quartets, the Music for Strings, Percussion, and Celesta, and the Sonata for Two Pianos and Percussion – is ever more coherently based on the variation of small motifs.

In addition to his studies as an ethnomusicologist, Bartók was one of the most eminent concert pianists of his day, and a piano teacher, first at the conservatory in Budapest. This is one reason why he produced so much educational music, including six volumes of *Mikrokosmos* (1926–39) for piano, which range from the most elementary exercises to big pieces suitable for concert performance by virtuosos.

Béla Bartók   Life and Works

1881	born in Nagyszentmiklós, Hungary (now Sînnicolau Mare, Romania), 25 March
1899	Budapest Royal Academy of Music; began career as concert pianist and started composing
1902–3	influenced by hearing Richard Strauss's music; *Kossuth*
1905	met Zoltán Kodály, with whom he began collecting Hungarian folk music
1906	first folk-music collection published
1907	professor of the piano at the Budapest Royal Academy
1909	married Márta Ziegler
1917	*The Wooden Prince* produced in Budapest, the first of his works to be received favorably
1918	*Duke Bluebeard's Castle*; established as an international figure
1920	toured Europe as a pianist
1923	*Dance Suite* composed to mark the union of Buda and Pest; divorced; married Ditta Pásztory
1926	*The Miraculous Mandarin* causes stir; First Piano Concerto
1934	commissioned by the Hungarian Academy of Sciences to publish folksongs
1940	emigrated to the USA
1942	health deteriorated
1943	Concerto for Orchestra
1945	died in New York, 26 September

Opera Duke Bluebeard's Castle (1918)

Ballets The Wooden Prince (1917), The Miraculous Mandarin (1926)

Orchestral music Kossuth (1903); Dance Suite (1923); Music for Strings, Percussion, and Celesta (1936); Divertimento for strings (1939); Concerto for Orchestra (1943); piano concertos – no. 1 (1926), no. 2 (1931), no. 3 (1945); violin concertos – no. 1 (1908), no. 2 (1938); Viola Concerto (1945)

Chamber music string quartets – no. 1 (1908), no. 2 (1917), no. 3 (1927), no. 4 (1928), no. 5 (1934), no. 6 (1939); Sonata for two pianos and percussion (1937); Contrasts for violin, clarinet, and piano (1938); Sonata for solo violin (1944); rhapsodies for violin and piano; duos for two violins

Piano music 14 Bagatelles (1908); Allegro barbaro (1911); Suite (1916); Sonata (1926); Out of Doors (1926); Mikrokosmos vols. 1–6 (1926–39)

Vocal music Cantata profana (1930); unaccompanied choruses; songs; folksong arrangements

A virtuoso technique is required for Bartók's other piano works, mostly written for his own recitals and concerto appearances internationally during the 1920s and 30s.

Like Stravinsky, and like Schoenberg, Bartók left Nazi Europe for the USA, though he waited until October 1940 before he went, with his second wife, Ditta Pásztory (he had divorced his first wife and married another young pupil in 1923). His American years were overshadowed by leukemia and financial hardship, as well as a longing for his homeland. The money problem was partly alleviated by a grant from Columbia University enabling him to study a huge archive there of Yugoslav folk music. Despite the difficulties, his American works display a great deal of

exuberance and a new simplicity of harmony and construction. Bartók died, in a
New York hospital, in 1945.

It was the purity and naturalness of folk music that gave it a special legitimacy for
Bartók; he based his own music on it in almost every particular of melody, rhythm,
ornamentation, variation technique, and so on. But he almost never quoted a
folktune direct. Bartók was ready to learn not only from his fellow Hungarians but
also from Romanians, Slovaks, Turks, and north African Arabs. These, with their
different modalities and rhythmic styles, contribute to the richness of such a work
as String Quartet no. 2 (1917), one of the first in which almost everything seems
to spring from folksong. Bartók had learned, too, from his great contemporaries:
from Debussy in his liking for ancient and newly invented modes, from Stravinsky
in the rhythmic force and brilliance of the central scherzo, and perhaps from
Schoenberg in the wandering harmony of the first movement.

MUSIC

    This quartet came in the middle of a group of theater pieces: *Duke Bluebeard's
Castle*, *The Wooden Prince*, and a mime drama, *The Miraculous Mandarin*. All show the
same awareness of folk music and of current developments in Paris and Vienna. All
are somewhat self-revealing for a composer who – whatever the explosive fury at
times of his music – was unusually reserved. The opera, dedicated to his young wife,
is almost too blatantly a warning: in it Bluebeard's young wife Judith demands to
know all the secrets of his heart – symbolized as a row of seven doors – and thereby
loses all chance of happiness with him, for what she discovers appals her. The music
is in effect a sequence of vivid tone poems, depicting Bluebeard's bloodstained
jewels, or his procession of former wives, or his other secrets, linked by dialog
which finds a Hungarian operatic style by way of folksong.

    Another folksong-linked aspect of Bartók's style is found in his motivic variation
technique. A fine example is his Music for Strings, Percussion, and Celesta (1936),
a four-movement piece for two chamber orchestras of strings and percussion, one
including piano and celesta, the other xylophone and harp. This grouping provides
typically varied and precise sounds. Though his own instrument was the piano,
Bartók was a challenging but thoroughly knowledgeable writer for strings, introducing new effects in his quartets and orchestral works; he also gave unusual
attention to percussion. Equally characteristic is the form of the Music for Strings
and its dependence on variation. For instance, the principal idea of the canonic first
movement reappears at the climax of the dance-like finale, taken from four solo
violas to full strings and from unharmonized, chromatic austerity into full-toned
diatonic richness. This theme also turns up in disguise in the other two movements,
an Allegro in sonata form and an Adagio; the whole work is bound by similarity of
material into a tight slow–fast–slow–fast structure.

    That kind of form, alternating slow music with quick rhythmic dancing, is to be
found also in String Quartet no. 3. Still more typical of Bartók, as of Berg and
Webern, are palindromic structures. String Quartet no. 4 (1928), for instance, has
the pattern Allegro–scherzo–slow movement–scherzo–Allegro. The two outer
movements share themes and the two scherzos are distinguished not only by

Bartók: Concerto for Orchestra (1943), first movement

After Bartók settled in the USA, he wrote some large-scale pieces which confirm the more exuberant, diatonic, relaxed style that had already become a feature of his works. He was commissioned by Serge Koussevitzky, conductor of the Boston Symphony Orchestra, to write this concerto, but hesitated to accept the commission because of his ill-health. However, a temporary improvement enabled him to complete the concerto in less than two months, and it remains one of Bartók's most popular compositions, with its brilliant, colorful orchestral writing and free references to music of other composers.

The concerto, typically, is meticulously worked out in matters of form, and is a symmetrical, five-movement structure. The opening sonata-form movement is followed by an Allegretto scherzando, sub-titled 'Giuoco delle coppie' ('Game of the couples'), in which instruments are presented in pairs. The work's formal and expressive core is an elegy, using material from the first movement, in three episodes, framed, according to Bartók, by 'a misty texture of rudimentary motifs'. In the fourth movement, an 'interrupted intermezzo', a lilting oboe melody in 5/8 is interrupted by a raucous episode reminiscent of Shostakovich. The brilliant, virtuoso finale is again based on sonata form, and ends with a flourishing coda.

· · · · · · · · · · · **Listening Outline** · · · · · · · · · · · · · · · ·

First movement (Andante, Allegro vivace): sonata form with slow introduction
3 flutes/piccolo, 3 oboes/english horn, 3 clarinets in B♭, bass clarinet, 3 bassoons
4 horns, 3 trumpets in C, 2 tenor trombones, bass trombone, tuba; timpani, cymbal, harp
1st violins, 2nd violins, violas, cellos, double basses

Time		
0.00	**introduction**	a pentatonic arch, ex. 1, cellos and basses; solo flute plays brief melody; accompaniment figure in low strings is speeded up to lead into the . . .
3.05	**exposition**	first theme, ex. 2
3.20		second theme, a variation of the first
3.48		third theme, ex. 3, related to the first, trombone
4.04		*Tranquillo*, second subject, ex. 4, oboe, clarinets, etc.
5.18	**development**	develops ex. 2
5.48		lyrical version: clarinet, then english horn
6.25		ex. 2, interrupted by ex. 3, trombones; ex. 3 then treated in canon
7.12	**recapitulation**	ex. 2, heard briefly
7.24		ex. 4, solo clarinet, flutes, etc.
8.38	**coda**	ex. 2, tutti
8.54		ex. 3, brass
9.00		(end)

ex. 4

character but also by their unusual sound – the first is muted, the second all plucked.

Along with Stravinsky, Bartók was one of the great pioneers of the percussive piano, his music suggesting hammered precision rather than a smooth, singing style: the piano was numbered among the percussion in the Music for Strings. This concept was fully developed by the time of the stamping *Allegro barbaro* (1911) and remains vital in all the later solo works and concertos, as well as in the electric tension of the Sonata for Two Pianos and Percussion (1937).

By the early 1920s, Bartók was a composer of world renown whose works were performed throughout Europe and the USA. He must have been aware that his complex native language would be an obstacle to the wider appreciation of vocal pieces, and he concentrated on instrumental music. Nevertheless, his preference seems also to answer deeper needs in Bartók's personality: his secretiveness, his irony, his liking for strict creative rules and his wish to balance interior reflection with vigorous activity. He found instrumental forms better fitted to his structural thinking; and he preserved harmonic centers with only a hint of traditional tonality. There is a similarity here with the Stravinsky of the 1930s, also a composer mostly of instrumental music.

It would be possible to see Bartók's music as becoming steadily more inward-looking and chromatic, reaching an extreme around the time of String Quartets nos. 3 and 4. Thereafter there is a more diatonic feel and a more relaxed style, this change being marked already by the time of Piano Concerto no. 2. In America the process continued, with a further piano concerto and especially the boisterous Concerto for Orchestra (1943). This work, with its brilliant orchestral style, is another example of mirror symmetry grounded in a structure of five movements (see **Listening Guide 54**).

5 *Soviet Russia*

In the early days of the Soviet regime, many of the leading composers, including Stravinsky and Prokofiev, left the country, expecting that the kinds of music they wrote would not be acceptable to the new rulers. They were probably right. A number of older composers, linked to the Russian nationalist tradition, remained, and composed in the way they always had. The new government at first encouraged younger composers to experiment, but soon, particularly when Stalin took charge, experiment came to be regarded as decadent and Western, and composers were expected to produce music with a tone of optimism, suitable for a regime that wanted to be seen as improving the lot of working people, and to write in a style that would appeal to a wide audience rather than an elite. Music had to have a social purpose and – just as court composers had in the past – Soviet composers were required to adhere to it. The "Soviet cantata" became an accepted type, a choral composition to words that exhorted the worker to greater efforts for his country, in the factories or the fields (or in wartime to greater sacrifices); it would be composed to rousing tunes, sometimes drawing on a folk-music idiom, and would express faith in the Soviet future.

PROKOFIEV

Life

Sergey Prokofiev (1891–1953) began his career before the 1917 revolution. He showed precocious talent as a pianist and composer and in 1904 entered the St Petersburg Conservatory. He made his début as a pianist in 1908, quickly gaining a reputation as an *enfant terrible* – an image he was happy to cultivate. By the time he left the conservatory he had several published works to his credit, including his First Piano Concerto. Critics found his music modern and incomprehensible (one wrote that his Second Piano Concerto, given in Moscow in 1913, left him "frozen with alarm, his hair standing on end"). Not surprisingly Prokofiev attracted Diaghilev's attention.

Political developments now upset Prokofiev's plans. An opera, *The Gambler*, had been in rehearsal in St Petersburg when the first 1917 revolution began; but it might anyway not have been given as the director had resigned, the orchestra had walked out, and the singers had refused to sing their roles. From that year dates Prokofiev's First Symphony, called the "Classical", because it takes the procedures of Haydn – in four movements, using a modest-sized orchestra – and reinterprets them in a modern style. Prokofiev left Russia in 1918 and went to the USA, first to New York, then to Chicago, where his fairy-tale opera *The Love of Three Oranges* was given. He returned to Europe, married a Spanish singer, and in 1923 settled in Paris. Like Stravinsky, he wrote music for the Ballets Russes. Unlike Stravinsky, he did not sever his links with his own country; he visited it first in 1927 and eventually, in 1936, he returned to live there.

Sergey Prokofiev   Works

born Sontsovka, Ukraine, 1891; *died* Moscow, 1953

Operas The Love for Three Oranges (1921), The Fiery Angel (1928), The Gambler (1929), War and Peace (1944)

Ballets The Prodigal Son (1929), Romeo and Juliet (1938), Cinderella (1945)

Orchestral music symphonies – no. 1, 'Classical', D (1917), no. 2, d (1925), no. 3, c (1928), no. 4, C (1940), no. 5, B♭ (1944), no. 6, E♭ (1947), no. 7, c♯ (1952); Peter and the Wolf (1936); piano concertos – no. 1, D♭ (1912), no. 2, g (1913), no. 3, C (1921), no. 4, B♭ (1931), no. 5, G (1932); violin concertos – no. 1, D (1917), no. 2, g (1935); Cello Concerto, e (1938)

Choral music Alexander Nevsky (1939)

Chamber music string quartets – no. 1, b (1930), no. 2, F (1941); Flute Sonata (1943); Violin Sonata (1946); Cello Sonata (1949)

Piano music sonatas – no. 1, f (1909), no. 2, d (1912), no. 3, a (1917), no. 4, c (1917), no. 5, C (1923), no. 6, A (1940), no. 7, B♭ (1942), no. 8, B♭ (1944), no. 9, C (1947)

Songs   Incidental music   Film scores

Up to this time, his music had varied greatly in style. Now, in the Soviet context, his options were reduced, but he was anyway in his mid-40s, back in his native country, and more ready to settle into a more regular way of composing. In these early Soviet years he composed some of his most appealing music. A turning-point came with his four-act ballet *Romeo and Juliet*, written for the Bolshoy Theater in Moscow. From the same year, 1936, comes his children's piece *Peter and the Wolf*, and two years later he produced his powerful music for *Alexander Nevsky*, a film on a Russian traditional heroic story.

During the war years Prokofiev, like most other Soviet artists, was sent out of Moscow to the provinces. He had made several attempts to compose operas, but none had been acceptable to the Soviet authorities. Now he worked, topically, on Tolstoy's *War and Peace*, producing an epic score on a scale worthy of the great novel. It was to occupy him off and on for the rest of his life. Again it ran foul of the Soviet authorities; some of it was performed at a concert in 1944, and parts were given on other occasions, but it had no complete or near-complete performance in the Soviet Union until well after the war. The year 1945 saw the completion of a second full-length ballet, *Cinderella*.

The war inevitably heightened the demand from government quarters for music to be cheerful, inspiring, and direct. After it came extreme suppression. Prokofiev was one of the outstanding composers to be attacked in a notorious speech in 1948 by Andrey Zhdanov, speaking for the Central Committee of the Communist Party; they were charged with "formalism", a term applied to anything the government disliked, but really used to condemn any link between a composer's music and the newest music in the West. Prokofiev, as a loyal Soviet citizen, went on trying, adopting a blander style; but even a new opera about the heroism of a Russian World War II pilot proved unacceptable. When he died, in 1953 (ironically, on the

Prokofiev: *Romeo and Juliet* (1935), op. 64, excerpt

Prokofiev's ballet on the story of *Romeo and Juliet* was among the first of his works written in the Soviet Union around the time of his return. He was an experienced ballet composer, and the invitation he received from the Kirov Theatre in Leningrad (now St Petersburg) must have been welcome in giving him an opportunity to compose for the Russian public in a genre in which he was confident.

But there were difficulties. First, the project had to be taken over by the Bolshoy Theatre in Moscow; then it ran into political trouble – when he played it over to the theater staff they rejected it as unsuitable for dancing. He revised it, but it had its first performance in Czechoslovakia in 1938, before being seen in Leningrad in 1940. Before then, the music had been arranged in a series of orchestral suites, for concert performance; Suite no. 2, which begins with 'The Montagues and the Capulets', was given in Leningrad in 1937.

Romeo and Juliet is Prokofiev's finest ballet. He wrote of it: 'People sometimes urge me to put more feeling, emotion, and melody into my music. I believe there is plenty of that in it . . . I have always tried to create melody, but a new type of melody, which some listeners may not understand as melody because it is different from what they are used to. In *Romeo and Juliet* I have taken particular trouble to achieve a simplicity which will, I hope, reach the hearts of all listeners'.

 Listening Outline . . . .

The Montagues and the Capulets: Dances of the Knights and of Juliet (Andante–Allegro pesante), 4/4, e, ternary form
2 flutes and piccolo, 2 oboes and english horn, 2 clarinets and bass clarinet; saxophone; 2 bassoons and double bassoon
2 trumpets, cornet, 4 horns, 3 trombones, tuba
timpani, cymbals, side and bass drums
1st and 2nd violins, violas, cellos, double basses

Time		
0.00	**introduction**	loud, ominous chords on the brasses and then full winds; when they break off, soft string chords are heard; this happens twice
1.22	**first section**	the march-like theme (ex. 1) in e, marked 'pesante' ('heavily'), represents the pompous and menacing old men of the warring families of Verona; it consists of 2 mm. of preparation, then an 8-m. phrase, partly repeated and extended, incorporating a new idea on the horns; the music moves to f (1.44), with the horn theme more prominent, in the bass and then (2.55) on trumpets, and then (3.06) the 2 plus 8 mm. return, adjusted for a full close in e
3.34	**second section**	a flute theme in e, ex. 2, is heard four times: twice with harps and pizzicato string accompaniment, then with a shimmering violin line in the background and finally with celesta
4.55	**first section**	the music of the opening returns, first on a saxophone and clarinet, then with strings; it is repeated by full orchestra (5.25)
5.49		(end)

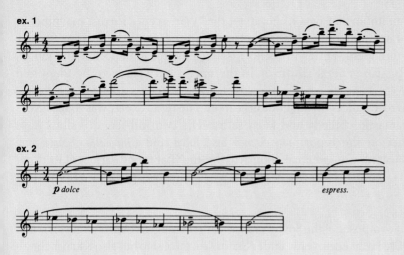

ex. 1

ex. 2

p dolce

espress.

same day as Stalin), he had still not in practice come to terms with the needs, as they were then seen, of his own country.

Prokofiev was inevitably affected by the turbulent political age in which he lived, but by an early stage he had established a musical personality that could flourish whatever the surrounding circumstances. His music was often tinged with a vein of bitter irony and, particularly in his stage works, satirical humour.

His early piano music from the revolutionary years (concertos, sonatas, the adventurous set of pieces *Visions fugitifs*) is violent and extravagant – and formidable technically: Prokofiev, like his fellow-countryman Sergey Rachmaninov, was a renowned virtuoso pianist. In his cycle of three sonatas (nos. 6–8) from the war years, however, he implicitly responded to the call for patriotism, though still with a characteristic grimness. His seven symphonies, which span his creative career, similarly reflect the political situation. From the refined neo-classicism of the First (1917), Prokofiev in the Second (1925) followed a fashion for mechanistic music with massive sonorities and chugging motor rhythms. The Third, which includes material from his opera *The Fiery Angel*, is intense and passionate. But the Fifth, a wartime work, is effectively a return to the abstract design of the First, though on a grander scale and with a triumphant, affirmative conclusion apt for the patriotic climate.

Prokofiev's operas embrace a similar diversity. After the powerful *Gambler* came *The Love for Three Oranges* (1921). Its plot is complicated and nonsensical, serving merely to stimulate Prokofiev to create a variety of brilliant musical-dramatic situations; emotions are exaggerated to the point of absurdity. Typically, Prokofiev then launched himself into a very different kind of opera: *The Fiery Angel*, a tale of sex, obsession, and religious hysteria (it was not heard complete until after his death). His *War and Peace* is on a huge scale. He focused the "Peace" sections on the heroine, Natasha, which gave him opportunities for the lyrical, expressive music that was now an important part of his style; the "War" scenes form a magnificent patriotic panorama, depicting Russian heroism in the face of the foreign invader (Napoleon in the opera, Hitler in reality), set against the sound, humane judgement of the Russian general (Kutuzov in the opera, but clearly to be identified with Stalin).

Prokofiev wrote ballets throughout his career. The first, *Chout*, was in his favorite mode of fantastic comedy and keen satire. His two full-length ballets have retained a place in the repertory: *Romeo and Juliet* and *Cinderella*. *Romeo and Juliet*, at first rejected, won eventual popularity for the vitality and variety of its dancing rhythms, its skillful orchestration, and its passionate love music (see **Listening Guide 55**).

SHOSTAKOVICH

Life, Music

The other great composer of the Soviet era was rather younger. Dmitry Shostakovich was born in 1906. He lived not only under Stalin's dictatorship but also Khrushchev's and Brezhnev's, and so had to deal with subtler forms of intervention than the crude censorship of the 1930s, 40s, and early 50s. It is not, however, helpful to speculate on what Shostakovich's music would have been like had he lived in a different society; the requirements of officialdom became a part of his musical personality, as did the irony and the growing cynicism with which he extricated himself from them.

Shostakovich studied at the conservatory in Leningrad (now St Petersburg), and in the year he finished, 1925, he wrote his First Symphony, which at once placed him among the leading creative figures in the country. He soon associated himself with the movement that saw artistic revolution as a necessary companion of political revolution, and he was eager to know what the leading figures in the West (Stravinsky, Bartók, Schoenberg) were doing. But this curiosity had to be set aside when, in the 1930s, Stalinism reached arts. Shostakovich's next two symphonies

---

Dmitry Shostakovich　　　　　　　　　　　　　　　　　　　　Works

born St Petersburg, 1906; *died* Moscow, 1975

Orchestral music symphonies – no. 1, f (1925), no. 2, 'To October', B (1927), no. 3, 'The First of May', E♭ (1929), no. 4, c (1936), no. 5, d (1937), no. 6, b (1939), no. 7, 'Leningrad', C (1941), no. 8, c (1943), no. 9, E♭ (1945), no. 9, E♭ (1945), no. 10, e (1953), no. 11, 'The Year 1905', g (1957), no. 12, 'The Year 1917', d (1961), no. 13, 'Babi-Yar', b♭ (1962), no. 14 (1969), no. 15, A (1971); October (1967); piano concertos – no. 1, c (1933), no. 2, F (1957); violin concertos – no. 1, a (1948), no. 2, c♯ (1967); cello concertos – no. 1, E♭ (1959), no. 2 (1966)

Operas The Nose (1930), Katerina Izmaylova (1963) [revision of Lady Macbeth of the Mtsensk District, 1932]

Chamber music 15 string quartets; Piano Quintet (1940); 2 piano trios

Piano music sonatas – no. 1 (1926), no. 2 (1942); 24 Preludes (1933); 24 Preludes and Fugues (1951)

Songs　Choral music　Incidental music　Film scores

draw on the "industrial music" tradition encouraged by the new developments in the country and carried orthodox messages in their finales, with choral episodes "To October" and "The First of May". Between them came his opera *The Nose*, after a story by Nikolay Gogol, similar in its "fantastic" style to Prokofiev's *The Love for Three Oranges*. He then composed another, *Lady Macbeth of the Mtsensk District*, which also has typically Russian satirical elements within a bourgeois setting – the central character, the "Lady Macbeth", is stifled by the world she lives in, takes a lover, and has her husband killed. It was at first a great success, but then Stalin saw it: his prudish attitudes led him to disapprove and the opera was fiercely attacked in the official newspaper, *Pravda*.

Shostakovich's troubles with Soviet authority did not stop there. His Fourth Symphony was hastily withdrawn, because of its pessimistic tone; the Fifth was composed and interpreted as his coming to terms with the demands of society (see **Listening Guide 56**). If the tone of this work now seems ambiguous, or at least partly ironic, there is no doubt that some of the ensuing works, of the war years, are totally sincere and deeply felt. No. 7, the "Leningrad" Symphony, deals with the long siege by the Nazis of that city (Shostakovich was there throughout) and the heroism of the resistance. No. 8 can be interpreted only as a contemplation of the tragedy of war. No. 9, a celebration of victory, turned out too light and perhaps ironic to please the authorities. But after Stalin's death Shostakovich went on composing works in the approved mold, with every sign of sincerity: after Symphony no. 10, a personal and grandly tragic work which aroused debate in Russia, no. 11 keeps within the "socialist realism" limits with its basis in the abortive 1905 revolution, while no. 12 was dedicated to Lenin's memory and is concerned with the events of 1917, the year of the revolutions. But no. 13 (1962) includes settings of Yevtushenko's anti-Stalinist poetry, critical of government, of the murder of Jews at Babi-Yar, of rulers and their hypocrisy, and of the harsh lot of Soviet women; it aroused strong reactions. No. 14 (1969) was a pessimistic work, concerned with death, while the last, two years later, quotes enigmatically from earlier composers. Shostakovich died in 1975.

There were of course many works other than symphonies from Shostakovich, notably a series of 15 string quartets of much originality and spiritual power, and as varied in their more subdued way as the symphonies. Shostakovich's symphonies, however, stand as one of the monuments of the twentieth century, and their wider meaning – in a society where music was expected to convey some message, political and social – cannot be separated from the great events during which they were created, while remaining, as no doubt he intended, full of enigmas and ambiguities.

Shostakovich: Symphony no. 5, op. 47 (1937), first movement

Shostakovich was the greatest symphony composer of the central part of the twentieth century. He wrote his First Symphony in 1925, when he was 19 and still a student; it created a sensation with its originality and its angry brilliance. His somber last, no. 15, was written in 1971, two years before his death.

Like all art in what was then the Soviet Union, purely orchestral music was required to have some social purpose. Shostakovich had been in some trouble with his symphonies in the difficult times of the 1930s, when Stalin's arbitrary taste and ruthless censorship prevailed. His Fifth Symphony appeared in 1937 and was judged a success. The phrase 'a Soviet artist's answer to just criticism' has often been applied to it; the phrase was not his own, but the work certainly seems to embody some response to what had been said – though we have no idea whether he thought the criticisms 'just'. Listeners to the symphony have often thought that it was more optimistic in tone, especially the rather tub-thumping, martial music with which the fourth movement ends. But there is much pathos in it, too, and a typically Russian tone of satire. We do not, in fact, know precisely how Shostakovich related to the authorities; nor can we be sure what the symphony was intended to express. It remains, by any standard, a great piece of music.

The symphony has four movements: the Moderato is followed by a Scherzo (an Allegretto), then a slow, contemplative Largo, and finally a fast and brilliant Allegro with a slow central section.

 Listening Outline . . . .

First movement (Moderato), 4/4, d; free sonata form
2 flutes and piccolo, 2 oboes, 3 clarinets, 2 bassoons and double bassoon
4 horns, 3 trumpets, 3 trombones, tuba
2 harps, piano, timpani, bass and side drums, triangle, cymbals, tam-tam, xylophone, celesta, bells
1st and 2nd violins, violas, cellos, double basses

Time		
	exposition	
0.00	first section	opening theme, stated by violins (at first following cellos and basses), ex. 1; with quieter continuation, ex. 2 (0.35: above rhythm of ex. 1 in lower instruments); often the rhythms are softened (see ex. 3). These thematic ideas are continued, by violins, with flute (2.33), then taken over by woodwinds (3.06: ex. 4 – note fig. *d*), horns (3.32), and full orchestra (note fig. *c*)
4.45	second section	against rhythms of fig. *c*, new theme on violins, e♭, ex. 5 (related in general shape and rhythm to ex. 1); it appears on high violas (5.48) accompanied by a new figure in rhythms of fig. *c*, ex. 6; ex. 6 is the starting-point for phrases on flute (6.24) and clarinet (7.07); ex. 5 returns, violas, in b
8.01	**development**	faster section, ex. 6 on piano and pizzicato basses, against ex. 2 on low horns, later trumpets; woodwinds have ex. 2 and ex. 4. Ex. 4 and 'softened' version of fig. *b* become main development material; fast version of ex. 5 (low strings, then woodwinds), 9.04, entry of fig. *a*, 9.18; a striding figure based on ex. 5 is heard (9.22), then ex. 2 (woodwinds followed by lower strings), 9.34, as speed continues to increase; then, slightly slower, ex. 2 as a military march on trumpets, in a, joined by woodwinds (9.54); most of the themes appear – ex. 4 on woodwinds and violins (10.21), a version of ex. 1 on low strings, tuba, and bassoons (10.26), ex. 2 on brasses (10.31); at the climax comes the . . .

recapitulation

10.46	first section	strings and woodwinds take up ex. 1 in a frenzied manner while brass and double basses enter with ex. 5, leading to the music slowing (fig. *b*) for a grand rhetorical statement; fig. *c* and inverted fig. *a* leads to . . .
12.51	second section	ex. 5, in D, on flute and horn; ex. 6 returns on woodwinds (13.56)
14.53	**coda**	above 'softened' fig. *a*, ex. 2 is heard inverted on flute, then ex. 4 on piccolo, taken up by solo violin, then ex. 1 in low strings (15.46); fig. *a* on trumpet and timpani (16.11) accompanies the dying phrases on celesta (end)

6 *America*

A remarkable number of great composers from Europe were driven by Nazism and war to seek a better life in the Americas – Schoenberg, Stravinsky, and Bartók among them. Their presence did much to stimulate the development of music in the New World: several were teachers, and apart from anything else the presence of such names, like the earlier presence of Dvořák (see p. 307), was a boost to the morale of American composers. However, American music was in fact quite strong enough to take care of itself: decades before it had produced its first genius in Charles Ives.

IVES

Life

Ives, born in 1874, was a contemporary of Schoenberg. His father had been a young bandmaster in the Civil War. Living in the small Connecticut town of Danbury, he was a musician of extraordinary open-mindedness who encouraged his son to sing in a key different from that of the accompaniment, and in other ways to take nothing for granted. This urge to experiment was pursued by the young Ives in psalm settings he composed around the age of 20, some of them in several keys at the same time or vaguely dissonant. Ives also had the benefit of a more normal musical education at Yale, where he was a pupil of Horatio Parker (1863–1919), one of a group of gifted but unadventurous composers in New England. The result was a creative splitting. While at Yale, between 1894 and 1898, he continued his experiments, but he also composed works of a more conventional kind, such as his First Symphony (1898). Academic training gave Ives the technique to improve and enlarge his experiments, and the orthodox background provides a frame against which his departures seem all the more extraordinary.

On leaving Yale, Ives went into the insurance business. Most American composers would have gone to Europe for further training, but Ives felt no such need. He would probably have found it limited to take up either of the two professional courses open to a composer: teaching or serving as a church musician. Insurance gave him the livelihood which made it possible for him to compose in his spare time, and he had a firm belief in the moral virtue of insurance as a way of safeguarding a family's future. He prospered, and his music silently prospered with him. Most of his output dates from the two decades up to 1918, when he suffered a heart attack, but almost nothing of it was known outside a small circle of musicians whom Ives invited occasionally to play pieces through.

Ives's Second Piano Sonata, sub-titled "Concord" and picturing the personalities of four writers associated with that Massachusetts town – Ralph Waldo Emerson, the far-seeing thinker, Nathaniel Hawthorne, the Alcotts (the slow movement, a picture of domestic tranquillity), and finally Henry Thoreau, the plain man's seer – had a prominent place in the belated discovery of Ives and his music. In 1920 Ives published it, privately, following it in 1922 with a volume of 114 songs. In both cases

Charles Ives	Life and Works

1874	born in Danbury, Connecticut, 20 October
1894–8	studied with Horatio Parker at Yale
1898	First Symphony; composed songs; took first of several posts as a church organist; began working for an insurance company in New York, composing at night and weekends
1906	*The Unanswered Question; Central Park in the Dark*
1908	married Harmony Twichell
1911	moved to Hartsdale; finished *Three Places in New England*
1912	began studying at West Redding
1920	*Concord* Sonata
1925	period of international recognition began
1932–3	toured Europe
1947	won Pulitzer Prize
1954	died in New York, 19 May

Orchestral music symphonies – no. 1 (1898), no. 2 (1902), no. 3 (1904), no. 4 (1916); First Orchestral Set (Three Places in New England) (1914); Second Orchestral Set (1915); The Unanswered Question (1906); Central Park in the Dark (1906); Emerson Overture (1907); Washington's Birthday (1909); Robert Browning Overture (1912); Decoration Day (1912); The Fourth of July (1913)

Choral music Psalm 67 (?1894); The Celestial Country (1899)

Chamber music From the Steeples and the Mountains (1902); string quartets – no. 1 (1896), no. 2 (1913); violin sonatas – no. 1 (1908), no. 2 (1910), no. 3 (1914), no. 4 (1916)

Piano music sonatas – no. 1 (1909), no. 2, 'Concord' (1915); Studies (1908)

Organ music Variations on 'America' (?1891)

Songs The Circus Band (?1894); General William Booth Enters into Heaven (1914); *c*180 others

he sent his music off to anyone who might be interested, and asked for no financial recompense. It was only gradually that performances began to take place, and it was not until the 1940s that Ives began to be recognized as the first great American composer, who, in the great mix of styles and materials he cultivated, created musical images that could have come only from America. But by then he had long stopped composing: his poor health caused him to abandon composition in 1926 and insurance in 1930, even if he continued to dream of a *Universe Symphony* which would have been a still more comprehensive undertaking than any of his achievements.

At the center of Ives's work stands a body of around 180 songs, ranging from gentle hymn-like pieces (*At the River*) to robust philosophical meditations (*Paracelsus*), from student imitations of German *Lieder* (*Feldeinsamkeit*) to exuberant pictures of an America that had disappeared with Ives's boyhood (*The Circus Band*). In responding to a text, he was willing to use any materials that seemed suitable, and his enthusiastic identification with such a great range of poems was responsible for the

Music

vast range of his musical technique. The more nostalgic pieces may be filled with quotations from hymns, parlor songs, marches, and dances, whereas the more strenuous mental exertions tend naturally to go with dissonant chords and complex rhythms that are awkward and difficult to grasp. These sometimes suggest the atonal Schoenberg, though Ives worked in ignorance of what was happening in Europe during the years of his most hectic compositional activity.

Because he was not building up a professional body of work, he had the freedom to make different versions of the same piece, often for very different forces. This sprang in part from his conviction that what mattered in music was, in his own words, the "substance" and not the "manner". He could even be impatient of the physical practicalities of music-making: "Why can't music go out in the same way it comes into a man", he wrote, "without having to crawl over a fence of sounds, thoraxes, catguts, wire, wood and brass? . . . Is it the composer's fault that man has only ten fingers?" For him, therefore, there was an ideal beyond the notation: hence his continued revision of his score.

A key work, typical in its marriage of personal vision and national destiny, is the set *Three Places in New England* (see **Listening Guide 57**). Many of Ives's other orchestral works, especially those for small ensembles, are similarly memories of place and time: *Central Park in the Dark*, with the darkness presented in the atonal strings which circle unperturbed while the other instruments enter in mounting clamor, or *All the Way Around and Back*, a musical skit on a baseball maneuver.

There are also the symphonies, in which illustration plays only a secondary role. The first two, by Ives's standards, are mild and academic: the third is more individual; the fourth is one of his greatest and most demanding works, and also one of his most all-embracing. Its third movement is a fugue, originally composed to open a string quartet and here serving as a resting-place between much more ambitious movements. The second movement is the most complex of those jumbles of quotations that represent Ives in most vital spirits, like "Putnam's Camp" from the *Three Places* and "The Fourth of July" from the *Holidays* symphony, though in the Fourth Symphony the raucous enjoyment of these pieces is modified by the density of marches, hymns, and dances woven together, to symbolize a vast panorama of mundane life. Ives himself suggested that the symphony was asking the reason for human existence; its second movement might well give as its answer earthly pleasure, whereas the third, the fugue, responds only with formal correctness. The finale then returns to the slower, quieter, more distanced manner of the brief first movement. But where that opening had appeared to ask the questions, with its hymn fragments (the symphony requires a chorus as well as a huge orchestra), the finale is a departure into higher realms of transcendent vision, with muted percussion and far-off voices. A similar sort of music is present in other works where contemplation comes at the end of strenuous questioning or in answer to abundantly physical music with quotations strewn throughout.

Another, more condensed product of the philosophical Ives is the orchestral piece *The Unanswered Question*, where, as the title indicates, there is no meditative finale. The "question" is posed several times by a solo trumpet, while offstage strings

Ives: *Three Places in New England* (1914, rev. 1929), excerpt

Ives's *Three Places in New England*, also known as the First Orchestral Set or *A New England Symphony*, was composed between 1912 and 1914, from material dating back to 1903. Ives revised it in 1929 for small orchestra; his original scoring, for a much larger one, was reconstructed by James B. Sinclair in his edition of 1976. The history of this work is typical of Ives: he often gathered material and ideas, revised and altered them, and arranged his music for different forces. *Three Places in New England* was first performed in Boston in 1930; after hearing the work in 1931 Ives commented: 'Just like a town meeting – every man for himself'. And that is exactly how much of this hectic, descriptive, multi-layered music sounds.

The first movement, 'Boston Common', is a slow march in which quotations of marching tunes and songs capture the impression made by a monument to a heroic black regiment in the Civil War. 'Putnam's Camp' is a scherzo between two slow movements. According to Ives's own program note, it is an impression of a Fourth of July picnic at the place near Redding Center, Connecticut, where General Israel Putnam had his winter quarters in 1778–9. It is a fine example of Ives's technique of superimposing tunes on a complex orchestral texture, creating several metrically independent lines which are heard simultaneously. The third movement, 'The Housatonic at Stockbridge', is more autobiographical: Ives recalls a riverside walk with his wife in music that ripples statically round a steadily moving melody in the middle of the texture.

 Listening Outline . . . .

Putnam's Camp
flute/piccolo, oboe/english horn, clarinet/bassoon
2 or more horns, 2 or more trumpets, 2 trombones, tuba
piano, timpani, drums, cymbals
1st violins, 2nd violins, violas, cellos, double bass

Time
0.00   orchestral flourish in quick-step time
0.10   dance tune, ex. 1, first violins
0.51   five metrically independent lines played simultaneously
2.16   nine-note chord: 'Goddess of Liberty'
2.28   'cause' theme, ex. 2, oboe
2.38   *The British Grenadiers*, ex. 3
3.26   arrival of Putnam, ex. 4
3.31   *The British Grenadiers*, flute
4.14   dance tune emerges out of collage of many marches
4.37   music returns to the complexity of 0.51
4.52   *The British Grenadiers*, added in trumpet
5.05   episode, for brass and drums
5.38   dense chords
5.55   (end)

proceed through slow-motion diatonic chords, as if ignorant that any question needs an answer, and a quartet of flutes rushes about in vain panic. Composed in 1906, this work antedates Schoenberg's properly atonal compositions. It provides an extraordinary instance of Ives's prefiguring of many of the techniques and interests that have guided the course of music in this century.

Ives's position as a precursor, as has already been suggested, is borne out by many other features. His use of recognizable musical quotations – found in most of his larger orchestral, chamber, and piano pieces – looks forward as far as the 1960s. He experimented too with tuning a piano in quarter-tones and with the close calculation of pitch, interval, and rhythm structures. He seems to have felt that his musical "substance" should not be compromised by convention or technique. Ives is the model of the truly American composer: unfettered by European norms, ready to go his own way, unashamed of the incongruous.

Ives was one of those who represented the strand of what was called "ultra-modern" music in the USA between the wars. But there was much else to be heard. This was, for instance, a golden age for popular song and musical comedy in New York. This repertory is discussed in a broader context in **Part IX** – including the music of its greatest exponent, George Gershwin (see p. 394).

COPLAND

The divide between popular and art music is crossed in the music of Aaron Copland (1900–90). Born in Brooklyn, he came from a prosperous family and had the benefit of formal musical training from early boyhood. He studied in Paris and in 1924 returned to New York with the intention of becoming a specifically American composer. From jazz he borrowed syncopated rhythms and certain harmonic features in his Piano Concerto (1926). He also set the words of various American poets in choral pieces and songs.

Copland was active in support of his fellow composers, sponsoring concerts of new music in New York between 1928 and 1931. He also took an interest in the

---

Aaron Copland   Works

born Brooklyn, 1900; *died* North Tarrytown, New York, 1990

Ballets Billy the Kid (1938), Rodeo (1942), Appalachian Spring (1944)

Operas The Tender Land (1955)

Orchestral music symphonies – no. 1 (1928), no. 2 (1933), no. 4 (1946); El salón México (1936); Lincoln Portrait (1942); Fanfare for the Common Man (1942); Orchestral Variations (1957); Music for a Great City (1964); Inscape (1967); 3 Latin American Sketches (1972); Piano Concerto (1926); Clarinet Concerto (1948)

Chamber music Vitebsk, Study on a Jewish Theme (1928); Violin Sonata (1943); Piano Quartet (1950); Nonet for strings (1960); Threnody I: Igor Stravinsky, in memoriam (1971)

Piano music Variations (1930); Sonata (1941); Fantasy (1957); Night Thoughts (1972)

Songs 12 Poems of Emily Dickinson (1950)

Choral music   *Film scores*

development of music within the southern neighbors of the USA. A visit to a nightclub in Mexico City gave him the stimulus for his first essay in light music, *El salón México* (1936), catching the exuberance of the dance music he heard there. The opportunity soon came for a similar hybrid of popular material and serious setting on an American theme in a ballet, *Billy the Kid*. This was followed by another, rowdy cowboy ballet, *Rodeo*, and then by a treatment of the theme of Stravinsky's *Wedding* in pioneer New England: *Appalachian Spring* (1944). Like Ives, Copland used folksong, traditional dance, and hymn, joined by modern notions of rhythm, harmony, and orchestration. The difference is that Copland, welding all these together, created a musical style in which he could move freely from quotation into original music and back again.

Its success led him to contemplate more ambitious works in the same style, notably his Third Symphony (1946) – encouraged too by Stravinsky's Symphony in C, for the neo-classical Stravinsky had been a central influence on Copland. His energy is similarly owed to interruptions and displacements of a marked meter; both, of course, had learned from jazz.

97 *Aaron Copland conducting in the Henry Wood Hall, London, 1980.*

Copland went beyond Stravinsky in the range of levels at which he composed, especially in the late 1930s and 1940s. At one extreme are some searching and rarefied chamber and instrumental pieces; at the other are the *Lincoln Portrait* for speaker and orchestra and the *Fanfare for the Common Man* (both 1942), representing the public composer, addressing the nation at a time of crisis and using a language that presents no difficulties, even though it is definitely his own. He died in 1990.

BERNSTEIN

An American composer who embraced a multiplicity of traditions is Leonard Bernstein (1918–90). His music looks to the symphonic tradition of Mahler and Shostakovich, to American jazz, to Jewish sacred music, to the rhythmic verve and clear scoring of Copland and Stravinsky, to the snappy melody of the Broadway musical. Usually these strands are moderated according to the nature of the work, and Bernstein showed an unusual ability to compose in different genres almost at the same time. Moreover, he combined his career as a composer with that of one of the outstanding conductors of his generation, though most of his works date from before or after the period of his musical directorship of the New York Philharmonic (1958–68). He was also uniquely distinguished as a popularizer of music through his brilliant television programs.

His earlier works include two symphonies, sub-titled *Jeremiah* (1943) and *The Age of Anxiety* (1949). The latter has a solo piano and a program derived from W. H. Auden's long poem: it was the first evidence of Bernstein's willingness, like Copland, to address the great issues of the day, in this case the conflicts and tensions of the Cold War. Both are in the Mahler–Berg–Shostakovich line of Bernstein's music; his Broadway style is more in evidence in a ballet, *Fancy Free*, in the musical *On the Town*, and most successfully of all in the musical *West Side Story* (1957). This is discussed more fully on p. 396.

Bernstein's more serious works of the 1950s and 60s are broadly of two kinds, reflective and declamatory. The *Chichester Psalms* are melodious settings in Hebrew

---

Leonard Bernstein   Works

born Lawrence, Massachusetts, 1918; *died* New York, 1990

Stage music On the Town (1944), Candide (1956), West Side Story (1957), Mass (1971)

Ballet Fancy Free (1944)

Orchestral music The Age of Anxiety [Symphony no. 2] (1949); On the Waterfront (1955)

Choral music Jeremiah Symphony [no. 1] (1943); Symphony no. 3, 'Kaddish' (1963); Chichester Psalms (1965)

Piano music Seven Anniversaries (1943); Four Anniversaries (1948)

Chamber music Clarinet Sonata (1942)

Songs

for choir and orchestra. But another Hebrew work, the *Kaddish* Symphony (1963), belongs in style and manner with its two predecessors, though benefiting from the heightened grasp of different idioms that Bernstein had now achieved.

His *Mass* (1971) is a more startling mix of styles. Using the words of the Roman Catholic Mass and enacting the ritual on stage, Bernstein attempted to explore the meaning of the ceremony for a contemporary audience: this brings the world of the *Chichester Psalms* into contact with that of *West Side Story*. In later works, however, Bernstein was more selective in his style and chose to compose only to mark special occasions: his *Songfest*, for example, is an anthology of American poetry set to celebrate the Bicentennial.

CAGE

In quite a different part of the American tradition lay the radical pioneer composer, John Cage (1912–92; see p. 340). He studied with Henry Cowell, an experimental composer very much in the Ives tradition, and also briefly with Schoenberg, in 1934, when he wrote some serial compositions. Serialism even contributed, along with his awareness of Balinese and other exotic music, to the repetitious style Cage developed in works for percussion such as his *First Construction (in Metal)*. He discovered the possibilities of the piano as a one-man percussion ensemble if miscellaneous objects are placed between the strings: he used the result, the "prepared piano", in various works of the 1940s.

By then Cage had settled in New York, where he was active as a teacher and ballet musician. Partly through his association with other New York composers, partly through his contacts with painters, and partly through his studies of Eastern thought, he wanted to remove from music every trade of personal intention. This led him into a laborious process of coin-tossing to decide the nature and layout of events in his *Music of Changes* for piano (1951). He made *Imaginary Landscape no. 4* (also 1951) still more arbitrary by scoring it for 12 radio sets. Then, in *4′ 33″* (1952), he realized a long-cherished ideal in creating a piece that has no sounds at all: the performer sits or stands as if to play, but nothing is heard except the environmental sounds and any audience reaction. These, in Cage's view, have as much value as anything else: the artist's function becomes that of pointing people towards the potential art surrounding them.

Cage was a pioneer in the involvement of electronics in music-making. His earliest experiments go back to 1939. A mature successor is *Cartridge Music* (1960), for performers amplifying the "small sounds" they can make with objects to hand, using phonograph cartridges to pick them up. Later works use seashells and plant materials.

Another main thrust of Cage's activity was in the direction of freeing music from the concert. In the 1960s he was responsible for stimulating jamborees bringing together musical performers, video, and light shows, and so on. Cage produced few works in the later 1950s and 60s, but in the 1970s he became prolific again, partly in response to a reactivated conscience about the orchestra. As a body of skilled professionals, the orchestra might seem unsympathetic for Cage's music of non-

98 *John Cage's prepared piano.*

intention and freedom: indeed, a performance by the New York Philharmonic of his *Atlas eclipticalis* (1961), where the parts consist of star maps from which the musicians play as the spirit moves them, had proved disastrous. In *Cheap Imitation* (1972), he tried to provide a model of what an orchestra might be in an age of musical democracy: not ruled by the composer, not swayed by the conductor, but working harmoniously at a common task. In later works for orchestra he returned to looser forms of notation.

CRUMB

George Crumb (b. 1929) has evolved a style which, though it draws on the music of others, is outside any "school" but has an unmistakable identity. He is unconcerned with experimentation, his method of composition is direct, and many of his works reflect his preoccupation with world issues.

Crumb studied both in the USA and in Berlin. His first mature works, the Five Pieces for Piano (1962) and *Night Music I*, show the influence of Debussy, of Bartók's "night" music, and of Webern's delicacy and brevity. During the 1960s Crumb identified his artistic intentions with those of the great Spanish poet Federico García Lorca (1898–1936), whose words he set or alluded to in numerous works. It was to Lorca that he turned in his *Ancient Voices of Children* (1970); in the introduction to it he wrote: "I have sought musical images that enhance and reinforce the powerful yet strangely haunting imagery of Lorca's poetry. I feel that the essential meaning of this poetry is concerned with the most primary things: life, death, love, the smell of the earth, the sounds of the wind and the sea". And these are topics on which many of Crumb's works focus. His *Madrigals* are among those that draw directly on Lorca (see **Listening Guide 58**).

LISTENING GUIDE 58

CD 7 TRACK 25

Crumb: *Madrigals*, Book 2 (1965), excerpt

Crumb's *Madrigals* are settings of fragments from poems by the Spanish poet Federico García Lorca. To reinforce the poems' imagery, Crumb conceived a world of sound that is very much his own. He makes much use of percussion instruments, small cymbals, marimbaphone, and vibraphone, in particular, for their soft and subtle shimmering sounds; there are drums, too, used not for rhythmic or dynamic effects but for gentle, sometimes faintly sinister rolling ones. To these he adds other sounds, typically that of the flute: the three madrigals of Book 2 use different sizes of flute, in turn the large alto flute with its mysterious, shaded lower notes, the ordinary flute, and the small, shrill piccolo.

His handling of the voice too is unconventional. Almost nothing is sung in a traditional way; some words are whispered, some are exclaimed to dramatic flourishes, some are sung on slides from one pitch to another, some are separated into syllables and set to abrupt high notes or, at one point, declaimed to a series of staccato notes.

 . Listening Outline . . . .

Three Madrigals: *Bebe el agua*; *La muerte entra*; *Caballito negro*

Time			
0.00	tinkling percussion, flourish on the alto flute, and the voice enters	Bebe el agua tranquila de la canción añeja.	Drink the tranquil water of the ancient song.
0.27	Lorca's words begin		
1.18	jagged lines on alto flute		
1.47	(end)		
0.00	faint, ghostly percussion and single flute notes	La muerta entra y sale de la taberna.	Death goes in and out of the tavern.
0.40	voice enters		
1.16	tinkling percussion and flute, then heavier percussion		
1.49	voice re-enters		
2.11	flute and percussion, whistling effects		
2.47	voice staccato, then florid melisma		
3.18	(end)		
0.00	brilliant writing for piccolo and vibraphone (heard at several points)	Caballito negro. ¿Dónde llevas tu jinete muerto?	Black little horse. Where are you taking your dead rider?
0.26	voice entry	Caballito frío. ¡Que perfume de flor cuchillo!	Cold little horse. What a scent of blossom.
0.44	'Caballito frío', 'clucking' effects		
1.24	(end)		

Like many Americans of his generation, Crumb has been attracted by primitive and Asiatic music. In several of his pieces, oriental qualities dominate not only melody, rhythm, and instrumentation but the whole esthetic and manner of performance. In *Lux aeterna* (1971), for example, the performers are instructed to be robed and masked and to sit in a circle; the music, which has a timeless air, includes parts for sitar, tabla, and bells (bells and gongs are prominent in Crumb's works). The theatrical and visual are important factors and Crumb often adopts a collage technique that enables him to bring together disparate fragments and to quote from other composers. He has an ability to create haunting timbres through unusual combinations of instruments and unconventional playing techniques, for example requiring a violinist to play wearing thimbles. His scores are teeming with detail and visually arresting.

REICH

One of the leading composers of minimalist music is Steve Reich (b. 1936). Central to his musical language is rhythm: his early minimalist works eliminate dynamics, melody, and harmony, and concentrate on simple, ostinato rhythms which are subjected to cyclic variation during the course of a piece. This technique usually features parts that at first play in unison then change their relationship as one part plays the same material at a given time delay, creating the illusion of an echo. (This is known as "phasing".) The effect of Reich's music is calm and static, almost orientally meditative, in spite of a profusion of movement.

Reich studied drumming from the age of 14 and in the 1970s went to Ghana to investigate African drumming and to Bali to hear gamelan music. His stylistic development culminated in *Drumming*, a 90-minute elaboration of a single rhythmic cell and the work that brought him international renown (see **Listening Guide 59**). Subsequently he introduced harmony into his works, for example in *Music for Mallet Instruments, Voices, and Organ* (1973). His later works are on a larger scale. *The Desert Music* (1983), for example, is more expansive and sets words by William Carlos Williams; harmony and melody are sustained and slow-moving, with varied ostinatos and changes in orchestral color that combine to give the music emotive power.

Reich: *Drumming* (1970–71), excerpt

Steve Reich's *Drumming* is the classic of minimalism. It is a large-scale work, in four sections, lasting one and a half hours, designed to be played without a break; its impact is to a large extent dependant on the near-hypnotic effect that this very repetitive music has over a long time. The first part is for three pairs of small drums ('bongo drums'), of a kind that have definite pitch, and male voice; the second part is for marimbas, with female voice, the third for glockenspiels with whistling and piccolo, and the fourth for all these together.

Repeating rhythmic patterns very gradually fade in and out of phase with one another, producing a surface to the music that changes with great subtlety and almost imperceptibly. The excerpt we hear is from the opening of the work: it starts with what sound like single drum strokes and at the moment we leave it there seem to be several interweaving patterns.

This extraordinary music demands from the listener a patience and concentration that may seem more oriental than Western in philosophical approach. The listener is compelled to a kind of sensitivity and awareness to refined changes of pattern quite unlike those of the normal Western tradition.

The notes below draw attention to what seem to be 'landmarks', such as the entry of a new element or the arrival at a notable musical pattern. But the music must be understood less as a series of events than as a continuous and constantly shifting stream, in which the formation and de-formation of apparent patterns is almost accidental and incidental.

 Listening Outline . . . .

Drumming, Part 1: opening

Time

0.00	regular single beats
0.13	the beats become double
0.24	the beats are more separated, and a third, at higher pitch, joins
0.38	the third beat becomes double
0.48	an extra beat joins and soon (0.59) the final one becomes double
1.18	a lower-pitched beat follows the main group
1.46	the lower beat becomes double
2.09	a new beat follows the lower pair
2.35	an additional higher beat enters
2.51	a new beat enters, gradually forming a pattern of a more melodic character
3.25	the group seems to have coalesced into two distinct elements, a central 'crackling' and a pattern that for the moment (around 3.30) is more melodic
4.08	a new pattern has by now emerged, two beats at medium pitch, two low; this becomes dominant (4.25) and gradually seems to refine
5.00	(fade out)

7 *Post-war Europe*

Though the careers of many composers extend across the end of World War II – Stravinsky, Shostakovich, and Copland are among those already mentioned – 1945 is still a useful boundary. Bartók and Webern died in that year, Schoenberg soon afterwards, and the next few years saw the first acknowledged works of the Frenchman Pierre Boulez, the German Karlheinz Stockhausen and many others who were to play leading roles in the development of music. Even composers active before the war – including the six mentioned above – went through periods of stylistic change in the postwar years, when serialism, hitherto a specialty of the Schoenberg circle, began to gain the enthusiastic attention of all.

99 Below *Olivier Messiaen collecting birdsong, 1951.*

MESSIAEN

One of the central radical figures in European music was Olivier Messiaen (1908–92). He studied at the Paris Conservatoire (1919–30), where he taught from 1941, at the same time serving as organist of a leading Paris church, La Trinité. In the 1940s his Conservatoire class included Boulez and Yvonne Loriod (a brilliant pianist whom he was later to marry).

Messiaen's works may seem to indicate a profound fixation on the mysteries of the Catholic faith and an intense modality rather than a concern with new techniques. However, Messiaen's career proved his readiness to bring into his music the fruits of his constant inquisitiveness. From stable foundations in the "church modes", he went on to incorporate serialism, rhythms calculated according to the patterns of ancient Indian music or Greek verse, dense harmonies chosen with his eye for the "color" of sounds, birdsongs collected in the field and imaginatively transcribed, representations of the marvels of Nature, even sacred messages coded in musical notation. All these elements are applied, ultimately, to the celebration of the mysteries of the Roman Catholic Church, the central force behind Messiaen's music. They come into play in his hugely extended, virtuoso meditation on the Christ child, *Vingt regards sur l'enfant-Jésus* ("Twenty Glimpses of the Infant Jesus", 1944).

Such a wealth of material could not be accommodated in smooth, continuous forms. Messiaen's structures typically are made up of distinct blocks, often in alternation or other symmetrical arrangements. This is especially true of his *Turangalîla-symphonie* (1948). The title is made up of Sanskrit words connoting "rhythm" and "play" (or "love"). Messiaen described this ten-movement work also as a *Tristan* symphony, and in certain of the movements, notably the sixth, "Jardin du sommeil d'amour" ("Garden of the Sleep of Love"), he was not afraid to wallow in lush, sensuous string music. The mathematical and the erotic are often found side by side in Messiaen: he praised God both as architect of the universe and as creator of the human body as his choicest work.

The *Turangalîla-symphonie* summarizes Messiaen's early manner. But the symphony also looks forward to the serial constructions in which Messiaen was soon to interest himself, following up the interest of Boulez and others among his pupils. Beginning here, he applied serialism to rhythm by making successions of durations chosen from an arithmetical series (e.g. from one to 12 thirty-second notes), and then performing serial operations of reversing and so on. The furthest he went in this direction was in his *Mode de valeurs et d'intensités* ("Mode of Durations and Volume") for piano, a crystalline mixture of three lines passing through series of pitches, rhythmic values, and dynamic levels.

This had an enormous influence on Boulez and Stockhausen. For Messiaen himself it was an isolated event and his least characteristic work. He then withdrew to his personal world of the organ, bringing together the old modality and the new constructivism in his *Livre d'orgue* ("Organ book", 1951). After this he turned to birdsong for his material, used almost exclusively in the *Catalogue d'oiseaux* (1956–8), a collection of impressions of different birds in their habitats around France, worked into substantial pieces each representing 24 hours of activity. Religion, color, birdsong, and complex rhythms come together in *Couleurs de la cité céleste* ("The Colors of the Heavenly City"; **Listening Guide 60**).

Messiaen saw himself as a musician-theologian who expounded the truths already revealed to the church. In his immense *La Transfiguration* (1969), for example, each of the 14 movements is an illustration of a text from the New Testament or St Thomas Aquinas. Though the range of reference is intensely personal – including birdsong along with the complex rhythmic apparatus, percussion ensemble, color chords, evocations of nature, and modality – the usual building-block forms convey a sense of inevitability and objectivity.

Olivier Messiaen   Works

born Avignon, 1908; *died* Paris, 1992

Orchestral music L'ascension (1933); Turangalîla-symphonie (1948); Oiseaux exotiques (Exotic Birds, 1956); Chronochromie (1960); Couleurs de la cité céleste (Colors of the Heavenly City, 1963); Et exspecto resurrectionem mortuorum (I Look to the Resurrection of the Dead, 1964); Des canyons aux étoiles (From the Canyons to the Stars, 1974)

Choral music Trois petites liturgies de la Présence Divine (1944); La Transfiguration de Notre Seigneur Jésus-Christ (1969)

Vocal music Poèmes pour Mi (1936, later orchestrated); Harawi, chant d'amour et de mort (1945)

Piano music Vingt regards sur l'enfant-Jésus (Twenty Glimpses of the Infant Jesus, 1944); Catalogue d'oiseaux (Catalogue of Birds, 1956–8); two pianos – Visions de l'Amen (1943)

Organ music Le banquet céleste (1928); L'ascension (1934, version of orch. work); Le nativité du Seigneur (1935); Les corps glorieux (The Glorious Hosts, 1939); Livre d'orgue (Organ Book, 1951); Méditations sur le mystère de la Sainte Trinité (1969)

Instrumental music Quatuor pour le fin du temps (Quartet for the End of Time, 1940)

Opera St François d'Assise (1983)

Messiaen: *Couleurs de la cité céleste* (1963), excerpt

Several of Messiaen's preoccupations come together in his *Couleurs de la cité céleste* ('Colors of the Heavenly City'). First, it is a deeply religious work, concerned with the celestial city and descriptions of the Apocalypse: a rainbow encircling the throne, seven angels playing seven trumpets, the star with the key to the abyss, the crystalline clarity of the holy city, the ornaments of precious stones. Second, there are the precious stones themselves, whose colors are paralleled in the colors of the music. Third, Messiaen's love of birds, whose cries, in his imaginative transcriptions, are heard throughout the work; those whose song he draws on here come from South America, New Zealand, and Canada. Fourth, the rhythms, which derive from those of Indian and ancient Greek traditions. Last, there are plainsong Alleluias, cries of praise to God. Messiaen compares the display of colors to a cathedral rose window.

All these images are heard in the music, lending it hard, sharp timbres, darting lines, apocalyptic effects. In his score Messiaen often labeled the names of birds or precious stones at the points where they were sources of inspiration; some are noted below. The orchestra is used in a special way; the piano has a solo role (composed for Messiaen's wife, Yvonne Loriod) and the groups of instruments are almost always heard together.

 Listening Outline

3 clarinets; 2 horns; 4 trumpets; 4 trombones
piano; marimba; xylorimba; xylophone; cowbells and bells; gongs and tam-tams

Time

0.00 bird calls (from New Zealand and Argentina) are heard from the piano, clarinets and wooden percussion (ex. 1); then the piano begins a solo (0.20); these ideas are repeated and interchanged

0.38 brass – marked 'the seven angels with seven trumpets' – enter, against a plainsong Alleluia heard on the highest trumpet (ex. 2); then the earlier music (with scraps of birdsong) returns, with piano, clarinets, and wooden percussion; the music pauses

1.06 it resumes slowly, with soft chords on brass and clarinets, each echoed on piano, metal percussion, and horns: 'yellow topaz, clear green chrysoprase, crystal'; then the Alleluia is heard on wooden percussion (1.19, upper line of ex. 2, transposed); after more 'topaz' chords, new, dense high-pitched ones are heard, 'emerald green, amethyst violet' (1.35) and then 'red, orange, gold', before the original texture resumes

2.00 the Alleluia again, on wooden percussion, briefly interrupted (2.09) by the soft chords

2.40 the music slows for a sustained passage (emerald, violet; at 2.56, 'pink, mauve, and grey') followed by the Alleluia on wooden and metal percussion (2.58), then soft chords, with a piano flourish ('the star with the key to the abyss')

3.14 clarinet trills herald a more dramatic moment, with a clarinet phrase 'like a flash of lightning that cuts through the sky', and then a slow series of deepening strokes on the gongs and tam-tams (3.26) and a deep trombone and horn note (3.49)

4.02 piano solo passage (the cry of the Canadian stournelle)

4.24 all the winds, with bells, Alleluia of the Holy Sacrament (ex. 3); this ends with the shriek of the Brazilian araponga (4.53), answered by clarinets and repeated (5.03), with clarinets and piano in the cry of the toucan; then sustained, rasping notes on the trombones, followed by gongs, represent the abyss (5.27, 5.36)

5.40 (fade)

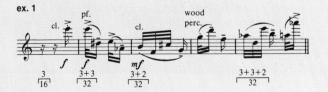

ex. 1

ex. 2

Alleluia   tpts.

7 angels   f

ex. 3   brass: Alleluia of the Holy Sacrament

Karlheinz Stockhausen (b. 1928) studied in Cologne. His encounter in 1951, at the Darmstadt summer school for advanced music, with Messiaen's *Mode de valeurs* was crucial. The next year he went to study with Messiaen in Paris, where he also became involved with electronic music at the studio run in Paris by Pierre Schaeffer (b. 1910). Schaeffer was the first to create effective electronic music from recordings in 1948, and his studio became a center of *musique concrète* (music made out of recorded natural sounds; see p. 340). Like his French colleague Pierre Boulez (b. 1925), he found the techniques of *musique concrète* too primitive. Stockhausen's response to Messiaen's *Mode de valeurs* was the equally difficult *Kreuzspiel* ("Crossplay") for piano, percussion, and two woodwinds.

Stockhausen found a more congenial studio in his native Cologne, where in 1953–4 he composed two studies – among the first music realized entirely by electronic means (that is, the sounds are electronically synthesized, not recorded from nature). No less significant, though, was his *Kontra-Punkte* for ten players (1953), in which he established a flexible style of writing for mixed instrumental ensemble that influenced all his European contemporaries. His pre-eminence was secured by three works, produced almost simultaneously, of the mid-1950s: *Gesang*

100 *Karlheinz Stockhausen at his electronic control panel.*

der Jünglinge ("Song of the Youths"), a brilliant tape piece merging a treble soloist into textures of synthetic sound; *Gruppen* ("Groups"), which divides an orchestra into three ensembles situated around the audience, their streams of music sometimes separate, sometimes joined; and *Piano Piece XI*, in which the soloist has to decide the order of the provided fragments.

The culmination of this period of parallel electronic and instrumental exploration came in *Kontakte* ("Contacts") for piano, percussion, and tape (1960), where, as Stockhausen said: "The known sounds . . . function as traffic signs in the unbounded space of the newly discovered electronic sound-world." Stockhausen's distrust of prescribed, outer form led him to develop the notion of "moment form", in which "moments" were to succeed each other without anyone worrying about their succession. But in the work entitled *Momente* (1964), the moments are arranged according to a pattern of resemblance and change.

During the later 1960s Stockhausen's methods became increasingly free, particularly in the works he was writing for his own performing ensemble of players on conventional instruments and electronic appliances. This process culminated in *Aus den sieben Tagen* ("From the Seven Days", 1968), in which the players are provided only with short texts as guides to their musical intuition. The only conceivable next step could have been silence, but in fact Stockhausen drew back and suddenly wrote an hour-long, fully notated score for two pianos and electronics: *Mantra* (1970). This was the first of his works created around a melodic theme or formula. The technique is somewhat akin to that of serialism in the way the whole composition is built out of this material by means of transposition, inversion, and other transformations.

Most of Stockhausen's later works offer a mix of music and drama, ritualized and selfconsciously portentous. *Licht* ("Light"), a large-scale project on which Stockhausen expects to be working until the end of the century, is a cycle of seven stage works devised to be presented operatically on consecutive evenings. It is concerned with a personal mythology centered on the figures of the Archangel Michael, Eve, and Lucifer.

BERIO

The Italian composer Luciano Berio (b. 1925), from a musical family, met Stockhausen in 1954 and soon became a central member of the group of composers associated with Darmstadt. From 1955 to 1961 he directed an electronic music studio at the Milan station of Italian Radio, and in 1958 he wrote *Sequenza I* for flute, the first of a series of ten "sequences" for soloists. These pieces are not merely essays in virtuosity but dramatic "scenes", each with its own special character or ambience: comic in *Sequenza V* for trombone, frantic in *Sequenza VII* for oboe, trapped in *Sequenza IX* for clarinet. *Sequenza III* is one of several works Berio wrote for his wife, the American soprano Cathy Berberian (1925–83) (see **Listening Guide 61**), and it demonstrates Berio's highly distinctive use of the voice, which was to influence many of his contemporaries.

One of Berio's finest pieces is *Circles* (1960), for soprano, harpist, and two percussionists, in which the sounds and sense of poems by e. e. cummings "circle" out of the voice and into the instruments. A characteristic feature of the work is

Berio: *Sequenza III* (1965)

Sequenza III, for solo soprano, is one of a series of ten 'sequences' for soloists that Berio composed between 1958 and 1984. It was written for his wife, Cathy Berberian, whose extraordinary vocal technique, vivid imagination, and strong stage personality inspired several composers to write for her (among them Cage and Boulez).

Berio described *Sequenza III* as a 'dramatic scena' in which he 'tried to assimilate many aspects of everyday vocal life, including trivial things like coughing, without losing intermediate levels – laughter becoming coloratura virtuosity, for instance – or indeed normal singing'. His starting-point was a 'modular text' supplied by Markus Ketter in response to Berio's request to 'give me a few words for a woman to sing'. The 'few words' are never heard in their original order and Berio uses them merely as a source of phonetic materials, from out of which a coherent phrase occasionally crystallizes. There are rapid switches from one type of voice production to another. Berio uses 44 different directions to the singer, most specifying a psychological state – 'frantic', 'joyful', and so on – but some using Berio's own symbols denoting the required mode of delivery: 'hands over mouth', 'breathy tone, almost whispered', 'mouth click', 'cough', etc. The piece is constantly interrupted by laughter and only about a fifth of it contains sounds of exact pitch. The following are some of the landmarks in this exuberant display of vocal acrobatics.

 Listening Outline

solo soprano

Time

0.00	rapid, quiet, speech-like sounds, accelerating to a click
0.12	first tone
0.42	'woman'
1.11	sigh, then pause
1.16	'Give me my few words'; more lyrical section punctuated by vocal and finger clicks and coughs, calming down towards a pause
2.45	'forcing me . . .'; cadenza-like section
3.15	more agitated, with laughs and clicks
4.09	slower and more lyrical, building to
4.53	'few words . . .': loud sung passage
5.14	increasingly agitated
5.41	'to me . . .': lyrical section
6.24	more extended sung phrases, gradually winding down to
6.55	(end)

Berio's dramatization of the concert platform: each percussionist is surrounded by a circle of instruments divided between the three families of wood, skin, and metal, and the soprano is required to move nearer the ensembles as the singer and players come closer in the musical landscape. Indeed, Berio's dramatic sense has been more often exercised in concert works than in his music for the stage. *Circles* and *Epifanie* (1961), an aleatory set of orchestral and vocal movements designed to exhibit different kinds of vocal behaviour, established Berio's main concerns: exploring the connections between vocal and non-vocal sounds and expanding the means of musical communication. Part of the latter process resulted in Berio making arrangements of folksongs.

For most of the 1960s Berio was in the USA, teaching and composing. From this period come *Laborintus II* and *Sinfonia*, both (typically) for voices and orchestra. *Opera* (1970) is a work that sets three very different texts about death, as a metaphor for the demise of the genre of opera – and of Western civilization itself. This inaugurated a spell of experimentation, but in the late 1970s Berio turned again to the stage. He collaborated with the writer Italo Calvino on two operas, *La vera storia* ("The True Story") and *Un re in ascolto* ("The King Listens"), both of which reflect Berio's concern to create in the hearer an interplay between losing oneself in the spectacle of the production and being conscious of oneself as a spectator. *Un re in ascolto*, for example, concerns a theater impresario who is auditioning ("listening") for a woman capable of portraying the female protagonist he has imagined for his opera. Characteristically, Berio has created a theater within a theater.

Part IX Popular Music Traditions

1 *Introduction*

The types and styles of popular music that have developed in the last hundred years are so diverse and so significant that they need to be discussed separately from the art music of the period.

Folk and popular traditions have always existed alongside the art music of the aristocratic court, opera house, concert hall, or church. These traditions were mostly transmitted from performer to performer, and from one generation to the next, without being written down. For many centuries there was give and take between folk and art music, just as there was between a rural society and an urban one.

The creation of a popular music that aimed simply at entertaining large numbers of people is a product of industrialization, in which music becomes a kind of commodity. It is in the rapidly industrialized nations, particularly Britain and the USA, that we first encounter composers who have devoted themselves to fulfilling a demand for popular, entertainment music. In the early nineteenth century, some wrote pieces for a specific social purpose: for the chapel, the bar, the eating-house, the music hall. In America, where the production of parlor pianos increased prodigiously during the nineteenth century, the creation of music for these instruments – transcriptions, pot-pourris, arrangements – became an industry in itself. Of the American composers of popular music, three figures stand out: Stephen Foster (1826–64), who wrote numerous songs and ballads; John Philip Sousa (1854–1932), whose extraordinarily popular marches include *The Stars and Stripes Forever* (1896); and Louis Moreau Gottschalk (1829–69), a brilliant virtuoso pianist who wrote for his instrument.

By this time, of course, live performance was no longer the means by which most popular music was disseminated. During the nineteenth century, popular pieces were cheaply printed and distributed, and the sheet music industry flourished. But the greatest factor in the spread of popular styles was the development of means of reproducing performance, first mechanical (player pianos, gramophones), then electrical (phonographs, discs, tapes, compact discs, film, video recordings), and of broadcasting. As the technology of recording has become more elaborate, synthesizers and computer-generated "special effects" have become an essential element of rock music and increasingly determine its context.

In the first part of this section we shall look at musical theater and trace the development of the musical from its origins in operetta. The next section explores *ragtime*, *jazz*, and *blues*. These genres grew out of the music of black America at the beginning of the twentieth century, as did *gospel* and *soul*. From them grew *rhythm and blues*. The final section discusses rock and pop music.

2 *The Musical Theater*

In the nineteenth century, in Europe and in Britain, the tradition of operetta, or light opera, was established. There were two styles: the romantic, frothy operettas of France and Germany, in which well-composed popular songs adorned the plots of such plays as *Orpheus in the Underworld* (1858, Jacques Offenbach) and *Die Fledermaus* (1871; Johann Strauss jr); and the witty and satirical operas of W. S. Gilbert and Arthur Sullivan, which provided British and American audiences with lighthearted social commentary in such works as *The Mikado* (1885) and *The Gondoliers* (1889). In different ways, both these styles were absorbed into a distinctive and characteristic twentieth-century genre: the *musical*.

Gilbert and Sullivan

The popularity of operettas was remarkable. The Gilbert and Sullivan shows, unprotected at that time by American copyright laws, were widely "pirated" – produced in unofficial, unauthorized versions. The songs of the "Savoyards" (as Gilbert and Sullivan became known, after their works were produced at the Savoy Theatre in London) were available as sheet music. But they were so distinctive that they were also widely spread aurally, by people singing or whistling the tunes and recalling their witty words. Some are "patter" songs, in which the words are sung at great speed. They were well suited to amateur performance, and an important factor in the spread and popularization of the musical was that amateur groups could perform them effectively to a wide, provincial audience. These operettas, and the works of Franz Lehár (1870–1948), Johann Strauss jr (1825–99), and Jacques Offenbach (1819–80), with their distinctive songs and choruses, had universal appeal.

Friml, Romberg

A transitional stage between operetta and "musical" is represented by the works of the American composers Rudolf Friml (1879–1972), Sigmund Romberg (1887–1951), and Jerome Kern (1885–1945). The first two were European by birth and brought to the USA the traditions of European operetta. In many ways their plays, for example Friml's *Rose Marie* (1924) and *Vagabond King* (1925), and Romberg's *Student Prince* (1924) and *Desert Song* (1926), were strong, romantic works with pauses for well-crafted and memorable songs that did not advance the plot or the audience's understanding of the characters. When, in the following decade, these shows were filmed, their relative lack of integration of plot and music allowed Hollywood film-makers to substitute whatever pieces of light musical whimsy took their fancy to transform them into vehicles for stars.

Kern

Jerome Kern, however, used song to develop the narrative of his shows and to give extra depth to his principal characters. The book and lyrics of his *Show Boat* (1927)

102 *A scene from Jerome Kern's* Show Boat *(1927), the first great Broadway musical.*

were by Oscar Hammerstein II, who had already written shows with Friml and Romberg. Its plot was based on a novel by Edna Ferber which tackles themes of mixed-race marriage and prejudice within a love story that spans 40 years. The work is set on the floating theater "Cotton Blossom", and its two most famous songs, "Ol' Man River" and "Can't Help Lovin' Dat Man", are central to the plot: the slow-rolling river is a metaphor for life, and the love between the young actress Magnolia and the itinerant Gaylord Ravenal is strong enough to withstand separation and the passage of time. *Show Boat* is the first great Broadway musical. Its subject matter and dramatic weight place it on the fringe of opera (it has been performed by many opera companies), but it includes self-contained, memorable songs born out of the European tradition and heavily influenced by the conventions of *Tin Pan Alley*.

> ### Tin Pan Alley
>
> The nickname given to the American popular song publishing industry from the late 19th century: the publishers were based in the district of New York City at 28th Street and 6th Avenue, known as Tin Pan Alley.

Berlin

In the following decade, the musical came into its own as a genre, with the works of Irving Berlin (1888–1989) and Cole Porter (1891–1964). Berlin achieved wide fame as a songwriter as early as 1911, with *Alexander's Ragtime Band*, but although he contributed songs to many revues and plays in the following years, he did not write a full-length musical until *The Cocoanuts* (1925, filmed in 1929, written for the Marx Brothers). It was rumored that Berlin could not read music. He based his piano playing in one key, using mainly the black notes, and had a special piano built that used a complex mechanism to transpose his unorthodox playing to other keys. He continued to write musicals in the 1940s and 1950s, notably *Annie Get Your Gun* and *Call Me Madam*, both conceived for the singer Ethel Merman. None of these plays has as well-integrated a plot and lyrics as *Show Boat*, and Berlin's strength remained his talent as a writer of individual songs.

103 *Irving Berlin plays the piano as Fred Astaire and Ginger Rogers dance, 1935.*

Porter

Berlin had little or no formal musical education. He shows that within twentieth-century popular music one could become an immensely successful composer without a conventional training. Porter, by contrast, taught harmony and composition. After studying at Harvard and Yale, he moved to Paris and even spent time in the Foreign Legion. He wrote many songs and ballet scores before his first London show, *Wake up and Dream* (1929). Porter went on to compose distinguished musicals, including *The Gay Divorce* (1932) and *Anything Goes* (1934) – the former (like many of Berlin's plays) for Fred Astaire, the latter for Ethel Merman.

A riding accident in 1939 left Porter severely crippled. It was nearly ten years before he regained his former command of the musical theater and produced the remarkably popular *Kiss Me, Kate* (1948), loosely based on Shakespeare's *The Taming of the Shrew*, after which he continued to write successfully for both stage and screen. If Berlin had achieved a style of songwriting that was original for its lack of adherence to the "rules" of composition, Porter showed that a complex and sophisticated style was possible by mastering those same rules. Even so, few of his stage shows give the impression of belonging to the mainstream of American art music. Rather, his urbane lyrics and well-crafted songs are supreme examples of Tin Pan Alley.

Gershwin

The pre-World War II period of the American musical theater was dominated, however, by a composer who had emerged from Tin Pan Alley and the Broadway stage, but who, by 1930, had also shown his mastery of several types of concert music. George Gershwin (1898–1937) began his musical career as a song-plugger (playing songs on behalf of their publisher to promote them to potential performers and producers). His talent as a pianist led him to Broadway rehearsal rooms and on to the concert stage, and by 1930 he had contributed to (or completely written) 21 musical plays or revues for New York and London. Gershwin's *Rhapsody in Blue* (1924) for piano and orchestra was a successful union of classical orchestration with clear melodies and some of the rhythm and harmony of jazz, and it made him famous and wealthy. More than any other Tin Pan Alley composer before him, Gershwin wrote songs that were admirable vehicles for jazz improvisation. "Lady Be Good", "S'Wonderful", and, above all, "I Got Rhythm" were not just successful songs which drew on the conventions of jazz: they were reabsorbed into the jazz tradition and adopted as "standards" of the repertory.

Gershwin's greatest stage work, *Porgy and Bess* (1935), styled as an American folk opera, shows his fascination with jazz and the fascination of the jazz world with Gershwin's work. At one level this cross-fertilization is purely musical. Gershwin uses the flattened 3rds and 5ths of the blues scale (see p. 399) to underline aspects of his characters. Sportin' Life (who lures away the heroine Bess from her crippled love Porgy) sings songs full of the resonances of the jazz idiom. The role of Sportin' Life was played for some time by the bandleader and singer Cab Calloway, himself a symbol of a particularly flamboyant element of the jazz culture. The songs from *Porgy and Bess* include the remarkable ballad "Summertime", which became a staple

of the jazz repertory, as did "I Got Rhythm". The story of *Porgy and Bess* concerns life in a black community in Charleston, South Carolina. It is now always performed with an all-black cast.

104 *Gershwin's* Porgy and Bess, *Metropolitan Opera, New York, 1985.*

Black musical theater

There was a strong, independent Broadway theater tradition in Harlem. This was part of African-American musical culture, and it produced shows that were riotously successful, not only in New York but all over the world. Sissle and Blake's *Shuffle Along* (1921) pioneered a genre of black musical revue which culminated in Fats Waller's *Hot Chocolates* (1929), a play that included the songs "Ain't Misbehavin'" and "Black and Blue" and that was responsible for the transition of Louis Armstrong from jazz trumpeter to popular singer and entertainer. Similar shows, such as *Blackbirds of 1926*, traveled to Europe and made international stars of Florence Mills and Josephine Baker.

105 *A scene from the musical* West Side Story *(1957).*

Lerner and Loewe, Rodgers and Hammerstein

In the 1940s and 1950s mainstream Broadway shows were dominated by the output of the composer-lyricist teams of Lerner and Loewe and Rodgers and Hammerstein. The former pair produced *Brigadoon* (1947) and *My Fair Lady* (1956); the latter produced a string of shows, almost all successful as films and on records. These included *Oklahoma!* (1943), *South Pacific* (1949), *The King and I* (1951), and *The Sound of Music* (1959). They furthered the integration of plot, songs, and movement; *Oklahoma!*, for example, contained a ballet sequence modeled on American square dancing.

Bernstein

If these musicals consolidated the genre, they were outshone by a work composed by Leonard Bernstein and written by Arthur Laurents, with lyrics by Stephen Sondheim: *West Side Story* (1957). Bernstein's life and music were discussed in Part VIII (see p. 376). The quality that sets *West Side Story* apart from all previous Broadway musicals is its depth and texture of composition. Bernstein assimilates enough of the language of Latin American music to identify the Puerto Rican community from which Maria, the heroine, comes. The "American" community of the hero, Tony, is represented by an assimilation of the language of American art music and jazz rhythms. The effect is eclectic, but unified, rather like the New York environment in which the story is set; even if the tale, based on Shakespeare's *Romeo and Juliet*, is of warring factions, the central theme is a love story, just as the backdrop of the city is bigger than the factions that occupy it. *West Side Story* contains love songs ("Maria", "Tonight"), big "production" song-and-dance numbers ("America"), and patter songs ("Gee, Officer Krupke"). Bernstein became principal conductor of the New York Philharmonic Orchestra the year after it was first produced.

Stephen Sondheim (b. 1930) went on to write lyrics (and compose music) for several further musicals, most of which (including *Follies*, 1971, and *A Little Night Music*, 1972) were very successful. He has been a tireless innovator in developing the musical, from using thematic clues to advance the plot of his "whodunnit" *Sweeney Todd* (1979) to incorporating Japanese musical ideas into *Pacific Overtures* (1976).

Sondheim

Throughout the 1960s, Broadway shows and musical films continued unabated. In 1970 a record was released that significantly changed the way in which musicals were written and their music disseminated. *Jesus Christ Superstar*, composed by Andrew Lloyd Webber (b. 1948) to a book and lyrics by Tim Rice, was first issued on disc. By the time the show was produced, the album was a best-seller and had established a hit song ("I don't know how to love him"). The same writers were responsible for *Evita* (1979), which contained the song "Don't Cry for me Argentina" and which was produced and pre-sold in the same way, as was Rice's *Chess* and Lloyd Webber's *Phantom of the Opera*.

Lloyd Webber

These shows led the British revival of stage musicals during the 1970s and 1980s. Lloyd Webber's *Starlight Express*, *Cats*, and *Phantom of the Opera* have made much of elaborate and highly complex stage productions. Spectacular staging is also a feature of two shows written by Alain Boublil with music by Claude-Michel Schönberg: *Les Misérables* and *Miss Saigon* are among the most widely performed musicals. A recording of *Les Misérables* was made between 1978 and 1980 in its original French version, before the work was staged in Paris. Translated and adapted by Herbert Kretzmer, the English version has been performed in more than 13 different countries, preceded or accompanied by cast recordings. By using the stage show to follow, rather than precede, a recording, impresarios and producers can go a long way to secure their audience before taking the risk of expensive staging.

3 *Jazz and Blues*

There is an increasingly accepted view that gospel, *spiritual*, blues, ragtime, and jazz, once seen as separate styles, are all parts of a complex matrix of black American music. Whether sacred or secular, there are broad similarities between these five types. In some cases, this is a matter of structure. The form of gospel and spiritual songs, for instance, like that of the blues, is dictated by the lyrics. Ragtime obeys the strict conventions of formal, notated compositions, and jazz has absorbed elements from all these styles, as well as from the 32-measure patterns of most Tin Pan Alley songs.

Of all the genres discussed here, the blues is the most significant. It has had the widest impact on the broad current of twentieth-century popular music and has shaped a number of derivative forms, including rhythm-and-blues (R&B) and soul music. Even jazz has drawn on and been shaped by the blues.

EARLY BLUES

As in many cultures in which music is not written down, the blues can only be assessed in terms of its recorded history. The first generation of blues players to record were all born towards the end of the nineteenth century, and there is a common core of thematic ideas in both their lyrics and musical approach that suggests a well-established and broadly based tradition. The blues has connections with the songsters who sang the black equivalents of Tin Pan Alley songs, with vaudeville variety entertainment, and with sources as varied as the English music-hall song, as well as with the tradition of improvised sermons and preaching.

The blues takes its name from the term applied to a melancholy state of mind. It is a secular style of song that adapted wholesale the lyric patterns, and some of the melodies, of African-American gospel and church music, and applied them to themes of sadness, love, the black person's lot, and various aspects of "low life". The music had its origins in the cotton culture of the Mississippi delta, but, as a result of the great diaspora in the early part of the twentieth century, by the time it came to be recorded in the 1920s it could be found in a broad swathe across the southern USA and as far north as Chicago.

The structure of the blues relies on underlying chord sequences of eight, 12, and 16 measures. The lyrics generally correspond to a three-line stanza. The first line of each stanza is usually repeated, balanced by a third line which may or may not rhyme.

Accomplished singers would have numerous stanzas at their disposal and, apart from singing songs with complete lyrics which, for instance, related a folk legend like *Frankie and Johnnie*, many would create songs simply by running together formulaic stanzas in a new or unusual order. A common characteristic is the "blue note", a microtonal flattening of the third, seventh, and (occasionally) the fifth degrees of the scale, which lends the music a special poignant quality.

Blues

A style of black American popular music that takes its name from the term applied to a melancholy state of mind. The lyrics, which usually express feelings of loneliness and depression, are crucial to the structure of blues, which relies on underlying chord sequences of eight, 12, and 16 bars (measures). The most widely adopted form is the 12-bar sequence, or '12-bar blues' (ex. 1).

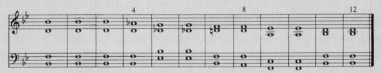

Further listening Bessie Smith: *Complete recordings*; Robert Johnson: *King of the Delta Blues Singers*; Blind Lemon Jefferson: *King of the Country Blues*; Albert Ammons, Jimmy Yancey, Pete Johnson: *Complete recordings*; Louis Jordan: *Five Guys Named Moe*; Roy Milton: *Big Fat Mama*.

The first generation of important blues artists included Papa Charlie Jackson (1885–1935), who was effectively a songster himself. His songs, such as *Shave 'em Dry* and *Shake That Thing*, became blues (and later, jazz) standards. Other important early singers were Charlie Patton (*c*1887–1934) and Blind Lemon Jefferson (*c*1897–*c*1930). The song *Long Lonesome Blues* by Jefferson is a good example of early "country" blues, so-called after its rural origins and typified by the extremely simple harmonic structure.

These male singers, and such others as Son House, Bukka White, and Leadbelly, represent only one branch of early blues singing. A number of talented female singers, many of whom worked on the vaudeville or Theater Owners' Booking Agency (TOBA) stages, were recorded singing what has come to be known as the "classic" blues since their performances and records preserved in fixed form a substantial body of aural tradition. All of them sang songs written and composed to emulate traditional blues, and collectively they established a corpus of material on which much of the subsequent development of blues was based. Most significant among these singers were Mamie Smith (1883–1946), Gertrude "Ma" Rainey (1886–1939), and Bessie Smith (1894–1937), who became known as the "Empress of the Blues". Bessie Smith brought great passion and emotion to her performances, and made even the most trite material sound sincere. She made over 200 recordings, and her artistry is best represented in the 1929 film *St. Louis Blues*. Her robust voice sailed through faster jazz standards but was at its best in measured performances that allowed her to plumb the emotional depths of songs like *Back Water Blues* (1927).

The early country singers had accompanied themselves on guitars, banjos, or sometimes homemade instruments such as jugs and washboards; but the female classic blues singers were often accompanied on record by full bands, just as they would be in the theater. Many of these bands included leading jazz musicians at the start of their careers; having sought work in touring vaudeville bands, they became the first "session" musicians, lending their skills to a variety of recording styles in the studios of Chicago and New York (this was before the microphones of recording "field units" searched out musical talent in the highways and byways of the USA). Bessie Smith recorded with many such jazzmen, including Louis Armstrong, who appeared on her recordings of *Careless Love Blues* and *St. Louis Blues*.

In the period leading up to World War II, blues artists were widely recorded all over the USA and a number of regional centers grew up. These included Memphis, Dallas, and various parts of Alabama, Georgia, and Mississippi. From the mid-1920s, there was a general black migration northward, principally to Detroit and Chicago, and to a lesser extent to the West Coast. In the 1920s, as "boogie-woogie" took hold, Chicago became the center for this further development of the blues styles. "Boogie-woogie" is a loud, fast piano blues, so called because the left hand plays in a driving repetitive rhythm.

Country blues artists from all over the south also migrated to Chicago and by 1940 they had begun to consolidate a tougher, "urban" blues style. The increasing use of amplification and electric guitars gave a hard, incisive edge to this music, and simpler accompaniments replaced the intricacies of the old country players.

RAGTIME

Ragtime was another popular style, again of African-American origin, that flourished principally in the Mid-West but with centers in Kansas City and St Louis, between 1890 and about 1920. It has had numerous revivals but is more important for the effect it had on other styles of music than as a genre in its own right. Principally a type of piano music, it drew on the multi-strain or multi-thematic type of composition popular in all fields, from marches to dances like quadrilles and *schottisches*, and absorbed them into a highly syncopated, virtuoso keyboard music. The "ragged time" of the right-hand piano lines, with their characteristic jerky contours, gave the genre its name. The pianist's left hand carries the rhythm, alternating bass notes with chords, the bass notes falling on the first and third beats of a 4/4 measure. The relentless, even movement of the left hand is usually in sharp contrast to the jagged rhythms of the right, and it is in this combination of regularity and syncopation that ragtime made its great contribution to the African-American mainstream. Most ragtime compositions are made up of several themes (or strains) of 16 or 32 measures, linked by elaborate "bridge" passages which sometimes also embody a key change.

Ragtime

A style of popular music that flourished in the USA between 1890 and 1920. The term was applied to piano music, instrumental ensembles, and to a style of popular song. It is characterized by "ragged time", a syncopation of treble parts against duple or quadruple meter accompaniments.

Further listening Scott Joplin: Complete piano roll recordings; Arr. Gunther Schuller: *The Red Back Book of Rags*.

Ragtime found its way into early jazz, as an inherent part of most players' approach to playing jazz on the piano; and the basic instruments of the jazz band came from the instrumentation of the "society" orchestras that played ragtime as an ensemble. Ragtime orchestras usually had cellos and violins, but otherwise generally consisted of trumpet (or cornet), clarinet, trombone, piano, double bass, and drums. This combination (occasionally with a guitar or banjo in place of the piano) may be divided into melody instruments (often called "horns" by jazz players) and a "rhythm section" (piano, bass, and drums) which underpins the harmony and rhythm. If this is thought of as equivalent to the roles of the ragtime pianist's right and left hands, then the contribution of ragtime to the thinking and practice that underpinned jazz (and large blues) bands becomes clear.

Before sound recording was established, ragtime was widely disseminated by sheet music and rolls for player pianos. The dominant figure in ragtime, Scott Joplin (1868–1917), sold over a million copies of the sheet music for his *Maple Leaf Rag* (1899), and made the fortune of his publisher through this and other successful compositions (including *Elite Syncopations*, 1902, *The Entertainer*, 1902, and *Chrysanthemum*, 1904). Other ragtime composers, including Arthur Marshall, Scott Haydon, and Louis Chauvin, enjoyed varying degrees of success, but their work, largely focused on Joplin's, is an identifiable Missouri school of composition. Since its revival in the 1970s it has been considered by some performers to be a contribution to twentieth-century serious piano music – a link between Western art music and the popular or folk traditions of African-Americans.

One significant characteristic of ragtime is that it was a style in which women quickly found a role and a voice, both as performers and composers. The Indiana composer May Aufderheide is the supreme female composer of rags (including *Dusty Rag*, 1908 and *Thriller Rag*, 1909), and some of her pieces found their way into the jazz repertory as the basis for piano or group improvisation.

JAZZ

So far in this chapter, jazz has been mentioned as an underlying force in popular music. It comprehends virtually all the developments discussed, from the musical theater to ragtime, from the harmonies and measure structures of blues to the use of electric amplification, and it has drawn on all the developing styles of African-American music. It has a well-documented development, a literature, and a discography of considerable size, and can claim to be as old as the century itself.

The origins of jazz are hard to define. It has often been said that it developed in New Orleans as a musical hybrid of blues, ragtime, marches, and creole hispanic music, that it traveled up-river to Chicago after the closure of Storyville (the red-light district of New Orleans) in 1917. But it is now clear that jazz grew up in many parts of the USA in the early years of the century. It is also clear that centers like Charleston, S.C., Los Angeles, St Louis, Kansas City – not to mention New York City and Chicago – played a major part in the development of jazz. Defining the music itself is no easier. However, among its distinctive features are improvisation (both collective and solo), "swinging" rhythms, and "bent" or "blue" notes.

Dixieland

The earliest traditional jazz. A rhythm section of piano, guitar or banjo, bass, and drums is contrasted with a 'front line' of trumpet, clarinet, and trombone. As the rhythm instruments underpin the harmonic changes and rhythmic pulse, the melody instruments play contrapuntal roles round the trumpet's lead.

Further listening King Oliver: Complete recordings; Louis Armstrong: The Hot Five and Hot Seven recordings; Original Dixieland Jazz Band: Complete recordings; Jelly Roll Morton: The Red Hot Peppers recordings; Sidney Bechet: Complete Bluebird recordings

---

DIXIELAND

106 *King Oliver's Creole Jazz Band, with whom Armstrong played in the early 1920s.*

The earliest style of traditional jazz, sometimes called "Dixieland", developed from the society or ragtime orchestra. Its essential ingredient is the combination of a "rhythm section" of piano, guitar or banjo, bass, and drums, and a "front line" of trumpet, clarinet, and trombone. As the rhythm instruments underpin the harmonic changes and rhythmic pulse, the melody instruments play contrapuntal roles around the trumpet's lead. The clarinet plays a treble obbligato, and the trombone

107 *Louis Armstrong.*

plays a low "tailgate" part (so named because when early players toured New Orleans on carts, the trombone slide protruded over the tailgate).

Although the term "Dixieland" is used for many styles of early jazz, it is particularly applied to white bands modeled on the Original Dixieland Jazz Band (ODJB) from New Orleans, who made the first jazz recordings in 1917. Instrumental solos are relatively rare and there are long passages of ensemble playing which are either collectively improvised or which follow pre-set patterns in the manner of instrumental ragtime. Instrumentalists sometimes produce comic effects, such as the animal sounds in the ODJB's *Barnyard Blues*.

Early jazz is dominated by two figures, Louis Armstrong (1900–71) and Duke Ellington (1899–1974). Armstrong developed a remarkable virtuoso style of solo trumpet improvisation, breaking free from the confines of the traditional Dixieland jazz ensemble (normally of six to eight players). Ellington led and developed the most consistently innovative large ensemble, for which he also composed.

In the early 1920s, Armstrong worked in Chicago with his mentor, "King" Oliver. Oliver's Creole Jazz Band captured something of the spirit of New Orleans's open-air street parades in the vitality of the cornet interplay between Oliver and Armstrong. In the mid-1920s Armstrong made an important series of solo recordings with a studio band in Chicago which he called his Hot Five – or Hot Seven,

Armstrong

108 *Duke Ellington at the Royal Albert Hall, London, 1967.*

depending on its personnel. These recordings include remarkable trumpet (or, in the earlier pieces, cornet) contributions by Armstrong, notably on *Potato Head Blues*, *Hotter Than That*, and *West End Blues*. Armstrong moved to New York to play with the big band of Fletcher Henderson, bringing the spontaneity of his improvisations to a much larger group than Oliver's. In the 1930s and 1940s, Armstrong led a big band of his own, playing arrangements that showed off his formidable talent as a trumpet soloist. For the last 20 years of his life Armstrong (who was nicknamed "Satchmo" or "Pops") returned to small-group Dixieland jazz, leading a band of fellow "All Stars" that included Earl Hines (piano) and Jack Teagarden (trombone).

Ellington Ellington recorded prolifically, and his orchestra played arrangements designed to show off the talents of his players, such as the clarinetist Barney Bigard or the saxophonists Johnny Hodges and Ben Webster. He pioneered a style known as "jungle music" in which his trumpeters Bubber Miley, and later Cootie Williams, and the trombonist "Tricky Sam" Nanton used mutes and vocal tones on their instruments to create wild and unusual effects. Ellington's skillful integration of these effects into conventional big-band music of the type pioneered by the white musicians Ferde Grofé and Paul Whiteman was a major achievement, exemplified by such recordings as *East St Louis Toodle-oo*. He also worked to create pieces that were not limited to the playing time of the 78 rpm disc, and often wrote works that extended over several sides or discs, such as *Reminiscing in Tempo*.

Ellington used his band to test new compositions and to experiment, having the opportunity denied to many composers of hearing his new works played almost as soon as they were written. In partnership with Billy Strayhorn (1915–67) he wrote and arranged more than 200 items for the band. In the later years of his life, Ellington turned to writing liturgical works, producing three *Sacred Concerts* in addition to such extended compositions as the *Far East Suite*.

Jelly Roll Morton (*c*1890–1941), who was most successful at tailoring jazz composition to the confines of the single 78 rpm disc, also played an important part in jazz history. As a pianist he bridged the gap between ragtime and jazz. As a bandleader he conjured coherent performances from random collections of musicians assembled to make records. As a composer he produced some of the standards of early jazz, including *The Pearls*, *Grandpa's Spells,* and *Black Bottom Stomp.*

Among other leading figures are Sidney Bechet (1897–1959), who did for the clarinet and soprano saxophone much as Armstrong did for the trumpet, and Coleman Hawkins (1901–69), who developed the tenor saxophone as the pre-eminent solo instrument in many styles of jazz.

From 1930 until the late 1940s, "big bands" dominated popular music. Their instrumentation retained the rhythm section of the Dixieland band, but included an expanded section of brass and woodwind. The biggest innovation was the gradual development of the saxophone section. Most bands used an alto saxophone (for the melody line), one or two tenor saxophones, and a baritone. Following the example of Fletcher Henderson and other big-band leaders of the 1920s, there were two or three trumpets and two or more trombones. The big bands played "swing", a style characterized by greater emphasis on solo rather than collective improvisation.

They often played arrangements, including those of Tin Pan Alley songs. Such arrangements included fast passages scored for the entire saxophone section (pioneered by the arranger Don Redman, among others); harmonic backgrounds to allow a single melody instrument to improvise a solo over an accompaniment by the whole band; and "riffs" in which short phrases are repeated in harmony by all the melody instruments. The most successful swing bandleaders were both black and white – Count Basie, Chick Webb, Fletcher Henderson, Artie Shaw, Glenn Miller, and Benny Goodman. Large orchestras of 12 players or more cost a great deal to maintain, however, and in the recession after World War II, most of the swing bands disbanded. In terms of jazz, they had already been left behind.

Swing

By the early 1940s, younger black musicians who (in many cases) played within the swing style of the time began to develop a far more complex kind of jazz – "bebop", or simply "bop"; this was built on a more intricate harmonic structure and broke down rhythmic conventions in fast and rapidly moving solo lines that appeared to ignore the measure structures on which they were based.

Bebop

Bebop was mainly associated with the trumpeter Dizzy Gillespie (b. 1917) and the alto saxophonist Charlie Parker (1920–55). Instead of basing their improvisations on the simple chord progressions of a Tin Pan Alley song, they would extend the chords in the progression by augmenting them, or adding 9ths, 13ths, and so on, using these extended chords as a basis for constructing their solos. Nevertheless, they did not stray far from conventional structure in the pieces on which they improvised. Their quintet recordings show this, and the bop style is well repre-sented by *Bloomdido*, built on the clear structure of a 12-bar blues which acts as a

Gillespie, Parker

Charlie Parker *Bloomdido*: (recorded New York, 6 June 1950)

This piece is typical of a small-group bop recording. The players repeat the same 12-measure cycle of harmonies 15 times. On the first and second repetitions, and on the 14th and 15th, Parker's melody is played in unison by himself and Gillespie. For the rest of the performance, the players improvise over the underlying harmonic pattern, without referring to the ideas of the melody for more than the odd phrase. Instead, each successive soloist picks up and develops melodic ideas introduced in the creative improvisation of the previous player. At one point a nursery jingle is paraphrased: the practice of quoting snatches of well-known melodies was favored by bop musicians.

. . . . 🎧 . Listening Outline . . . .

Charlie Parker (alto saxophone); Dizzy Gillespie (trumpet); Thelonious Monk (piano); Curly Russell (bass); Buddy Rich (drums)

Time	
0.00	Rich begins with 2 mm. on the hi-hat cymbal, setting the tempo in the manner of a big-band swing drummer. For 2 mm. Monk introduces a short, upward-moving figure like a bugle call, indicating the key and prefiguring the first phrase of the melody
0.05	Rich follows Monk's phrase with a 4-m. 'break' on the snare drum
0.09	first run through the melody over the 12-m. chord sequence, Monk's sparse piano chords emphasize the sequence which will be used for improvising (note that it differs from the traditional blues progression mainly in the chromatic descent of mm. 8 and 9)
0.22	repeat of melody and chord sequence
0.35	Parker's first solo: he quickly abandons the first phrase for his own free-ranging ideas forming a melodic line not dependent on three equal 4-m. phrases for its relationship to the underlying chords
0.48	Parker's second chorus: he returns to the opening phrase of his solo but uses it to steer his ideas in a different direction. Gradually he extends the phrase length so that by the beginning of his third and fourth choruses (1.01, 1.14) these are much longer. Paraphrase of a nursery jingle over mm. 1 and 2 (1.14)
1.27	Gillespie, muted, crosses Parker's final phrase with his own, picking up the contour of an earlier part of Parker's solo. Note that he explores the trumpet's full range and introduces fluent and rapid figures. These are mainly a series of 'fall-off' phrases (mm. 9–12 of his second chorus and mm. 9–12 of his third)
2.06	Monk's solo: he enters at the beginning of the tenth full chorus, playing very little with his left hand and developing an angular right-hand solo in the manner of a trumpeter or saxophonist. In mm. 10 and 11 he repeats Gillespie's falling phrase (2.16). Complex new melodic phrase, a quotation of another of his compositions (2.23)
2.32	Rich: solo keeping a metronomic beat on the bass drum. Solo divided into 4-m. phrases throughout choruses 12 and 13
2.50	final two choruses repeat original melody in unison
3.26	(end)

vehicle for long and fluent improvisations by Gillespie, Parker, and Thelonious Monk (1917–82) (see **Listening Guide 62**).

In bop, collective improvisation round a melody is rare. Instead, before and after solos by the group's leading instrumentalists, the melody instruments tend to play the theme in unison. The more complex the theme, the more it is a test of the musicians' skill. From Parker and Gillespie onward, many of the innovations in jazz

> ### Swing
>
> The music played by large jazz orchestras in the 1930s and 1940s. Their instrumentation retained the rhythm section of the Dixieland band, but included an expanded section of brass and woodwind, notably expanding the saxophone section. Swing bands played written arrangements, so improvisation played a minor role.
>
> **Further listening** Duke Ellington: The Cotton Club Orchestra; Duke Ellington: The Blanton-Webster Band 1939–42; Count Basie: The complete Decca recordings 1937. Benny Goodman: Big band, trio and quartet recordings; Artie Shaw: Big band and Gramercy Five recordings.

have been those of an art music with a relatively small dedicated audience and only a very few of the many hundreds of important and pioneering jazz musicians have broken through to a wider public.

Coltrane, Davis

The key innovators who have enjoyed wide popular success are John Coltrane (1926–67), who developed saxophone technique far beyond Parker to an intensity only possible through remarkable facility and control, and Miles Davis (1926–91). Davis began his career as a bop trumpeter (playing with Parker, among others) but developed into a remarkable, original musician who worked tirelessly to take his music (which he was reluctant to label "jazz") ahead of the tide of popular music. From his experiments with the arranger Gil Evans in playing with a large ensemble (including instruments not generally associated with jazz, such as French horns and tubas, on the recordings *Miles Ahead* and *Sketches of Spain*), to his pioneering works in jazz-rock (such as the recording *Bitches Brew*, 1969) and his 1980s "fusion" band (which produced recordings such as *Decoy* and *Tutu* that "fuse" elements of jazz with a rock rhythm section), Davis brought his music to an enormous public, through appearances at the open-air pop festivals of the 1970s and world tours in the 1980s (which emulated those of rock bands).

Few other postwar jazz innovators have played such a part in the development of popular music. Herbie Hancock (b. 1940) has recorded disco and rock music in addition to jazz, and Quincy Jones (b. 1933) has written widely for films and television as well as arranging for Aretha Franklin and Michael Jackson. Within the more limited horizons of jazz itself, significant contributions have been made by Charles Mingus, Ornette Coleman, and Sun Ra. Jazz-rock fusion was developed by the ensemble Weather Report. The Art Ensemble of Chicago developed a style of improvisation unfettered by adherence to harmonic or time structures; known as "free jazz", it was pioneered initially by Coleman.

The language of post-war jazz has followed the bop innovations of Parker and Gillespie. Art Blakey (1919–90) played with both men in the 1940s. He went on to lead his own bands for nearly half a century; they were a constant source of new ideas and provided platforms for talented young musicians. Among Blakey's sidemen was

109 *Billie Holiday.*

Wynton Marsalis, who developed into an outstanding jazz and classical trumpet soloist.

Some jazz musicians became part of popular music in other ways. The pianist Dave Brubeck, for instance, recorded many lightweight popular jazz pieces, including the well-known *Take Five,* in 5/4 time. The "cool" saxophonist Stan Getz, who had played with the swing orchestra of Woody Herman, became famous for his lightly swinging performances using Latin American "bossa nova" rhythms. Oscar Peterson took up the jazz piano style developed by musicians like Fats Waller, Art Tatum, and Teddy Wilson, and recorded numerous popular tunes incorporating remarkable, virtuoso jazz improvisation.

Another group of jazz performers to have made an impression on popular music are vocalists. Nat King Cole (1917–65) originally led a piano trio but became an immensely popular singer. Other male singers include Billy Eckstine and Mel Torme. But this area of jazz is dominated by a number of women who have taken the art of jazz singing to a high level of artistic expression. In the 1930s Billie Holiday (1915–59) made a series of recordings under Teddy Wilson's leadership, in which her anguished vocals on themes of tortured love and racial discrimination are perfectly counterbalanced by the saxophone improvisations of Lester Young. Holiday also sang straightforward swing performances, but here she was eclipsed by Ella Fitzgerald (b. 1918), a vocal improviser of unparalleled technique and imagination. Sarah Vaughan (1924–91) began her career as a pianist but became a close rival to Fitzgerald as a jazz singer. Her voice, though less technically perfect, encompassed a broader stylistic range, including jazz-rock, ballads to her own piano accompaniment, and music-theater recordings such as *South Pacific.*

In the late 1980s, jazz musicians began to incorporate into their work ideas from a range of other music. New York based collectives like M-Base explored links between jazz and other black music such as funk (a polyrhythmic call and response derivative of the blues) and rap (see p. 424). Saxophonists like the Norwegian Jan Garbarek and the Scot Tommy Smith experimented in combining the improvisational language of John Coltrane with repetitive accompaniment.

POST-WAR BLUES, RHYTHM-AND-BLUES, SOUL

R&B

The ambition of many blues musicians in the mid-1940s was to lead a big band. Such singers as Billy Eckstine and Big Joe Turner successfully sang in front of their own ten- or 12-piece bands. The underlying economic changes that made it increasingly difficult to maintain big bands were to have a major effect on the way blues was recorded and disseminated. The large record companies, Victor, Columbia, and Decca gradually withdrew their interest in what had been known as the "race" market. Instead, African-American interest was catered for by smaller, specialist record companies, including such labels as Atlantic, Chess, and King. These companies sought out the new currents in rhythm-and-blues and recorded them, selling the records to the black community. Unable to afford the big bands of the 1940s, they were prepared to accept an average-sized "R&B" band of singer, piano, bass, guitar, and drums. A couple of "horns" (saxophones or trumpets) might occasionally be added, but the groups dispensed with the melody instruments of the jazz band and concentrated on the "rhythm section" – hence (in part, at least) the style's name.

Performers who influenced the development of R&B include Louis Jordan (*Caldonia*, 1945), T-Bone Walker (*Stormy Monday*, 1943), Joe Liggins (*I've got a right to cry*, 1946), and Roy Milton (*R M Blues*, 1946). Gradually, as record companies aiming at the more affluent white market produced rock-and-roll versions of the more popular R&B songs, enthusiasm for the style increased. Singers who first became popular with the black audience as R&B performers began to appear in the rock-and-roll "charts" – the league table of weekly record sales used to measure the commercial success and popularity of singers. Such appearances indicated acceptance by a larger (predominantly white) public, and the careers of such singers as Ray Charles, James Brown, Fats Domino, Little Richard, and Chuck Berry have all involved success in the national best-seller charts.

We can see in their work the most significant shift in emphasis in public consciousness from the values attached to art music. The composer and writer of songs are irrelevant in most cases. It is the singer and the song – or rather, a particular singer's recording of a song – that is important. Success is measured in purely commercial terms: the weekly sales. As recording studio techniques have developed, responsibility for the sound on a recording is as much to do with arrangers, recording engineers, and tape editors as with the artist whose work is being recorded.

110   *Ella Fitzgerald.*

Soul, like many of the styles of music discussed so far, was predominantly a regional development, fostered in two centers. Soul was effectively rhythm-and-blues overlaid with some of the characteristics of black gospel music. A heavy backbeat (emphasis on the second and fourth beats of a 4/4 measure), harmonies redolent of a gospel choir, and the use of the electronic or Hammond organ all came into soul music from the black church. In Detroit (known as Motown because of its tradition of automobile manufacture) and Memphis, recording companies began to record and promote the style. Important performers included Ray Charles, the Supremes, Smokey Robinson, Stevie Wonder, the Temptations, Otis Redding, Booker T and the MGs, Nina Simone, and Roberta Flack.

One performer whose success in this sphere was rooted in R&B, and in the black audience, is James Brown (b. 1933). From a background of the black ghetto and juvenile delinquency, he became one of the most well-known R&B singers. Such hit songs as *Papa's Got a Brand New Bag* (1965) demonstrate his mastery of R&B and soul (see **Listening Guide 63**). His 1980s rock videos show an awareness of urban crazes like hip hop (a derivative disco-based type of funk), and the replacement of his earlier strong backbeat R&B accompaniments with the repetitive mesmeric disco beat, or "scratch" sounds, in which a small segment of an existing disc is played over and over again and re-recorded into the backing track, reflects trends in African-American music.

Soul

LISTENING GUIDE 63

CD 7 TRACK 48

James Brown: *Papa's Got a Brand New Bag* (1965)

This rhythm-and-blues record broadly follows a 12-bar blues chord sequence, in E (many blues are in the 'sharp' keys of E, A, and B since the guitar open strings easily accommodate them). Between the second and the third choruses, however, Brown inserts an eight-measure bridge passage that runs through the first four measures of the sequence twice (i.e. eight measures in E). The sequence is the simplest blues progression: E–E–E–E–A–A–E–E–B–B–E–E. In the bridge passage and the final chorus Brown sings about popular dances – the new bag or style which Papa (Brown himself) has taken up. On the tenth measure of each verse, the accompaniment stops for a one-measure 'break', and Brown sings: 'Papa's got a brand new bag'. In the 11th measure is a guitar chord, strummed repeatedly, before the band picks up the tempo again on the 12th. This style of break dates from the earlier country blues songs and survives intact here.

 . Listening Outline . . . .

Time	
0.00	introductory chord; Brown starts to sing
0.02	first 12-m. sequence begins; behind vocal line is a repeated bass pattern, and a brass 'riff' or unison phrase (ex. 1) played 'across' the timing of the vocal
0.24	second chorus
0.41	title line of the song unaccompanied, in a 1-m. 'break'
0.47	8 mm. bridge passage; 'Doin the Monkey, Mashed Potato . . . See Ya later, Alligator'
1.12	third full chorus
1.35	fourth (final) full chorus: 'He's doin' the twist – jus' like this'
1.57	further chorus: 'Come on, hey, hey' under which the brass riff is speeded up before the performance fades out
	(end)

ex. 1

Another leading singer is Diana Ross; after her career with the Supremes (which she led until 1969), she broadened the scope of her work from Motown and soul to encompass most of the main genres of black music. Following her successful appearance in the film *Lady Sings the Blues* (1972), in which she played the part of Billie Holiday, she produced several singles and albums during the 1970s and early 1980s, including a collaboration with Michael Jackson (*Muscles*, 1982).

Numerous Latin rhythms and styles have found their way into American popular music, and from the time of the big-band era, when groups such as that led by Machito enjoyed as great a commercial success as conventional jazz and blues orchestra, there has been a useful cross-fertilization with African-American styles. Among important Caribbean styles is *reggae*, which originated in Jamaica; it is characterized by short, ostinato-like figures emphasizing offbeats in quadruple meter. Its best-known exponent is Bob Marley, who first brought reggae to international attention. Many rock musicians experimented with reggae, including the British guitarist Eric Clapton.

111 *Bob Marley.*

4 *Rock and Pop Music*

Rock has been the most successful musical style of the second half of the twentieth century. It represents a synthesis of two independent musical traditions – country and western (C&W) and rhythm-and-blues (R&B). R&B was largely a black, urban music derived from the blues, and very often built upon the harmonic sequence of the 12-bar blues. C&W grew out of the music of the rural, conservative white community and had its roots in the folk music of the southern USA. In the early 1950s, however, elements of the two began to be combined; "crossover" versions of R&B songs were recorded by white singers and made into popular hits, while singers who grew up in the C&W tradition began to borrow elements from R&B.

By the early 1960s the basic sound of rock had been established, using a formula that has remained fundamental to the music ever since. The "classic" rock band consists of two guitars, bass guitar, and drums, though other instruments, particularly keyboards, are frequently added to the basic mix. Electric amplification of voices and instruments became increasingly important and an insistent rhythmic pulse defined by drums characterized much mainstream rock.

The first singer to achieve major commercial success with this recipe was Bill Haley (1926–81). With his backing group the Comets, whose instrumentation combined the guitars, piano, and double bass of C&W with the drums and saxophone of the R&B tradition, he recorded versions of the R&B songs *Shake, Rattle, and Roll* and *Rock Around the Clock*. The appearance of these records signaled the beginning of the rock-and-roll era. In 1955 Haley was established as the first "rock star". But it was the emergence of Elvis Presley in the same year that made rock-and-roll immensely popular.

Presley's background typified the cultural mix out of which rock-and-roll developed. Born in 1935, he grew up in Memphis, Tennessee, where he encountered blues singers such as B.B. King and Big Bill Broonzy. His first recordings in 1953 used a band of C&W musicians in a style that was labeled "rockabilly": country music was combined with R&B and overlaid with an emotional intensity derived from gospel music. His success grew rapidly, fuelled by the exciting, slightly suggestive impression of his stage act. With his first national hit, *Heartbreak Hotel* (1956), Presley established himself as a rock-and-roll singer who had successfully crossed the boundaries between genres. His version of *Heartbreak Hotel* added backing singers and drums to the C&W line-up of his early recordings, while the vocal delivery, full of unpredictable phrasing and emotional nuances, cut across the four-square melodic and rhythmic outlines of the song.

THE BEGINNINGS OF ROCK-AND-ROLL

Bill Haley

Elvis Presley

112 *Elvis Presley in the film* Jailhouse Rock, *1957.*

Presley's fame was increased by television appearances and a career in films. Although he remained hugely popular until his death in 1977, his subsequent career was increasingly peripheral to the development of rock. But his early work and performances were of crucial importance in establishing rock-and-roll as the dominant mode of popular music in the second half of the twentieth century.

While Presley's achievement had been to break away from the "rockabilly" style, others continued to use a C&W sound, grafting on to it carefully selected elements from R&B. The songs of the Everly Brothers, such as *Bye Bye Love* (1957) and *All I have to do is dream* (1958), used close harmony in the vocals and an instrumental sound based upon the acoustic guitar which clearly revealed their country-music roots.

Buddy Holly, Little Richard, and Chuck Berry

The most influential of this group of singers was Buddy Holly (1936–59). His songs, such as his first number-one hit *That'll be the Day* (1957), owed little to R&B and were obviously rooted in country music. They used carefully colored vocals and melismas to disrupt the smooth contours of the melodies. With the personal element in many of his lyrics, Holly's songs opened up to rock music new areas of expression that were to be exploited in the next decade.

The instrumentation of his band, the Crickets, with two guitars (lead and rhythm), bass guitar, and drums, anticipated the standard rock-band line-up of the next 30 years. Holly's appearance – bespectacled, quiet, self-effacing – was the very antithesis of the larger-than-life sexuality of Presley, yet Holly's death in a plane crash in 1959, coupled with the recordings released posthumously, established him as one of the early legends of rock-and-roll.

Another strand of rock in the late 1950s emphasized the contribution of rhythm-and-blues. Some of Presley's songs (*Hound Dog, Jailhouse Rock*) had used the formula of the 12-bar blues, and singers such as Little Richard (b. 1932) and Chuck Berry (b. 1926) developed their own brands of rock-and-roll directly out of the R&B tradition. Both were to be of great significance to the prime movers of rock in the following decade.

Richard's wild, egocentric performances drew upon black gospel singing as well as R&B. The qualities were all present in his first hit, *Tutti Frutti* (1955), with a 12-bar blues for its chorus, a modified 12-bar sequence for the verse, and a boogie-woogie piano bass, and were exploited further in *Long Tall Sally* (1956), *Lucille* (1957), and *Good Golly Miss Molly* (1958). Little Richard temporarily abandoned rock-and-roll for evangelism in 1958, but his influence remained potent; many white singers produced cover versions of his early hits, and his influence (as a performer rather than songwriter) can be detected in such 1960s performers as Paul McCartney and Jimi Hendrix.

Berry's influence has been similarly widespread. He started his career in the early 1950s in a blues trio, and developed his own highly distinctive style of guitar playing, favoring single string improvisations rather than chords and using them to propel the music with an insistent rhythm. His first great success was *Roll Over Beethoven* (1956), followed by *Sweet Little Sixteen* (1957) and *Johnny B. Goode* (1958). His songs were widely studied and their style imitated; performers such as the Beatles, Bob Dylan, and the Beach Boys all absorbed elements of his technique.

THE 1960s

By the end of the 1950s rock had become established as the most significant strand in popular music. It was an essentially American phenomenon with cross-cultural roots and a commercial base that linked success in the record charts with innovation and novelty. Yet its forms, rhythms, and melodic shapes were still entirely conventional, tied to the blues sequence and the popular ballad.

In the early 1960s American popular music was dominated by the sentimental ballads of singers such as Pat Boone, and by the rise of black close-harmony groups such as the Drifters and the Crystals. The emergence of the Beatles in 1962 switched attention to innovations in Britain, where rock music had previously imitated its American models, finding its own equivalents to Presley and Holly but largely favoring the softer-edged elements of the style.

The Beatles

The Beatles were Paul McCartney (b. 1942), John Lennon (1940–80), George Harrison (b. 1943), and Ringo Starr (b. 1940). Their first commercial recording was *Love Me Do* (1962), written by Lennon and McCartney. It was heavily influenced by the sound of the Everly Brothers, though a harmonica solo suggested a debt to R&B. In a series of singles released during the next year (*Please Please Me, She Loves*

You, etc.), the Beatles established a distinctive sound and gained unprecedented popularity in Europe and the USA. The wide-ranging roots of their music were revealed in the selection of songs on their first two albums: alongside Lennon and McCartney's own songs there were rock-and-roll and R&B standards (Chuck Berry's *Roll Over Beethoven*), as well as sentimental ballads (*Till There Was You*). The Beatles' success was partly the result of their synthesis of such influences.

In their early songs the Beatles had been content to compose within the framework of styles they had inherited. But their music soon became far more sophisticated, both in the imagery of its lyrics and the shapes of its melodies. The studio productions of their recordings, overseen by George Martin, also became more and more intricate, with new colors and textures in the accompaniments. The scoring of the ballad *Yesterday* included a string quartet, while the song *Norwegian Wood* introduced the sound of an Indian sitar, played by Harrison.

With *Sgt Pepper's Lonely Hearts Club Band* (1967) the Beatles, considerably helped by George Martin, produced a radical new kind of rock album. For the first time a series of songs was conceived as a self-contained cycle. Using audience noises, a brass band, a fairground organ, even a crowing rooster, the recording conjured up the atmosphere of a show, while the songs themselves ranged from straightforward, lively "pop" tunes to the dreamlike, hallucinatory effects in *Lucy in the Sky with Diamonds*. *Sgt Pepper* represented the peak of the achievement of the Beatles. The band broke up in 1969. Lennon, McCartney, and Harrison all went on to pursue solo careers during the 1970s but none of their later work came close to recapturing the same freshness and musical ingenuity. It was the scope and overall concept of *Sgt Pepper*, as much as the style of its individual songs, that proved most influential on subsequent rock performers.

The Beatles' worldwide success brought a boom to British popular music. Rock-and-roll ceased to be exclusively an American phenomenon, and during the mid-1960s a number of other British groups, such as the Animals, the Kinks, the Hollies, and later the Who, enjoyed great, if usually shortlived, popularity in the USA.

The Rolling Stones

The success of the Rolling Stones proved to be more enduring: of all the rock bands that became prominent during the 1960s, they alone have remained at the forefront of rock into the 1990s. Led by the vocalist Mick Jagger (b. 1943) and the guitarist Keith Richard (b. 1943), the Rolling Stones' aggressive brand of rock offered an alternative to the Beatles. Their music was more obviously grounded in blues and R&B, with Chuck Berry one of their main influences.

Although their first successful single in Britain was a Lennon and McCartney song (*I Wanna be Your Man*, 1964), songs such as *Little Red Rooster*, *Satisfaction*, and *Get off My Cloud* established a raw, menacing edge to their music. Over the next four years the Rolling Stones gained a reputation for being rebellious and non-conformist, while their blend of R&B, rock-and-roll, and country music was refined in songs like *Jumping Jack Flash* and *Sympathy for the Devil* (1968).

113 Opposite *Album cover of the Beatles'* Sgt Pepper's Lonely Hearts Club Band *(1967).*

The Beach Boys

The only American group to rival the popularity of the British bands during this period was the Beach Boys. The middle-class Californian society in which the members of the group grew up was celebrated in their name, and in the lyrics of many of their early songs; they were led by Brian Wilson (b. 1942). Their first hit single was *Surfin' USA* (1963) in which they created an unlikely mixture of the styles of Chuck Berry and early 1950s American close-harmony popular songs.

With their album *Pet Sounds* (1965), and especially the single *Good Vibrations* (1966), the Beach Boys' music became much more ambitious and complex. While retaining the basic bright, open sound of their earlier music and the high vocal lines, *Good Vibrations* incorporated abrupt changes of tempo and meter, used a wider variety of instrumental accompaniment (including the strange, unearthly timbre of an early electronic instrument, the Theremin). The main melody was surrounded with vocal counterpoints, ending with a section built around canonic entries for the voices.

FOLK AND FOLK ROCK

Another strand of popular music that complemented and ultimately reinforced American rock-and-roll in the 1960s derived from folk music. A revival of interest in the folk tradition had begun in the USA in the 1940s, led by a group of musicians that included Woody Guthrie, Alan Lomax, and Pete Seeger. By the beginning of the 1960s, singers such as the Kingston Trio and especially Peter Paul and Mary had attracted a predominantly young audience which rejected rock-and-roll as too commercialized and followed Seeger's example in identifying the folk movement as a force for protest and political change.

Folk rock

A style that became popular in the USA in the mid-1960s. It combined the melodic lines and harmonies of traditional folksong and blues with the drums-based rhythms and electric instrumentation of rock. Bob Dylan was the first to make the synthesis, with his song *Like a Rolling Stone* (1965). By the end of the 1960s folk rock had declined in importance, though elements of the genre persisted in the work of Neil Young and Joni Mitchell.

Further listening Bob Dylan: *Bringing It All Back Home* (1965); The Byrds: *Mr Tambourine Man* (1965); The Band: *Music from the Big Pink* (1968); Neil Young: *After the Gold Rush* (1970)

Bob Dylan

Bob Dylan (b. 1941; real name Robert Zimmerman) established himself in the New York folk scene in 1961. His first recordings, performing with acoustic guitar and harmonica, consisted mainly of traditional folk songs, spirituals, and blues. His second album, *The Freewheelin' Bob Dylan* (1963), was devoted almost exclusively to his own songs and included *Blowin' in the Wind*, which became a hit single for Peter Paul and Mary, and was taken up by the youth protest movement. Dylan became the leading voice of the protest movement, reinforcing his reputation with *The Times They Are A-Changing* (1964). On that album the numbers ranged from protests against war, racism, and social injustice to love songs of an ironic, detached tone. In all of them Dylan displayed a verbal imagination which set his songs apart from the stereotyped verses of most popular songs of the time.

In 1965 Dylan signaled a decisive break with the folk tradition, which was based firmly upon acoustic-guitar accompaniments, when he began to use electric guitars and drums. The move alienated him from the folk purists, but it brought him increasing influence in the world of rock-and-roll. The release of the single *Like a Rolling Stone* (1965), in which Dylan's hard-edged, aggressive vocal lines were surrounded by electric guitars, organ, and drums, marked the beginning of what became known as "electric folk" or, more commonly, "folk rock".

Following Dylan's example, other American bands began to mix elements of lyric-based songs with the grittier sounds of rock-and-roll. The Byrds, a five-man group led by Jim McGuinn (b. 1942), recorded Dylan's *Mr Tambourine Man* and established folk rock as a commercially successful sound in Britain and the USA.

In 1966 Dylan began to rehearse with a group of musicians who eventually became known simply as the Band. Through the late 1960s and early 1970s they appeared regularly with Dylan, as well as reinforcing their own position as the most influential American rock group of the period. Dylan's influence was added to the rich mixture of styles the Band had already absorbed. When they began making recordings in their own right – the albums *Music from the Big Pink* (1968) and *The Band* (1969) – their songs offered a fresh synthesis of American popular music centered on rock-and-roll, but with a sound dominated by piano and organ rather than guitars, and with blues, gospel music, and Cajun influences (from New Orleans) all playing a part.

The Band's years of greatest influence (1968–71) coincided with a period in which rock music seemed much more concerned with effect than with musical substance. "Acid" or "psychedelic rock" (represented by such groups as the Grateful Dead, Jefferson Airplane, and the Doors) developed in San Francisco in the late 1960s. Performances were designed to create trancelike states, using elaborate light shows and exotic instruments to mimic the effects of hallucinatory drugs like LSD. In such a context the Band's emphasis on purely musical innovations became even more distinctive.

Although folk rock proved to be a relatively short-lived phenomenon (it was effectively finished by the end of the 1960s), Dylan's influence on the lyrics of popular songs, first by demonstrating that they could deal with and comment upon serious issues, and later that they could be considered as sufficiently poetic and suggestive to be discussed in their own right, was a major factor in establishing rock as an enduring musical genre. Musically, too, his example paved the way for successive waves of solo singers who performed their own songs. They generally worked within the folk tradition but also brought together elements of blues, rock-and-roll, and country music, as Dylan himself did consistently.

Joni Mitchell

Joni Mitchell (b. 1943) was one of the foremost solo performers of the 1970s and has steadily expanded the range of her songs. Her early music established her distinctive style: she delivered elaborate, often melismatic vocal lines over simple guitar or piano chords, for example in *Big Yellow Taxi* (1970) and *A Case of You* (1971). Later she incorporated elements of other rock and jazz styles (including a proposed collaboration with the jazz bass-player Charles Mingus). However, the subject matter of her songs has largely remained the mixture of social and personal commentary inherited from Dylan; one of her later albums, *Chalk Mark in a Rain Storm*, for example, includes her version of the folksong *Corinne, Corinna*.

Bruce Springsteen

Other performers who have been prominent since the 1980s, such as Elvis Costello (b. 1954), Bruce Springsteen (b. 1949), and the band R.E.M., have all in different ways extended elements of Dylan's style. Though Springsteen's music, for instance,

114 *Bruce Springsteen singing "Born to Run" in New Jersey during his promotional tour in 1974.*

has been mainly indebted to the mainstream of rock-and-roll deriving from Presley and Chuck Berry, the subject matter of many of his songs, as on the album *Born in the USA* (1984), shows a concern with the American underprivileged which was a constant feature of Dylan's own music. Springsteen's emphasis on the importance of the lyrics of his songs also echoed Dylan. The musical substance of many of his best-known compositions is often strikingly straightforward, using simple chord progressions broken by expressive saxophone and keyboard solos. In concert this raw material is dramatically transformed by the intensity of Springsteen's stage act.

THE 1970s & 1980s

The basic elements of rock music laid down in the 1950s and 60s continued to define the music of the following two decades. But the commercial emphasis gradually shifted away from the "single" 45 rpm record, through which all the rock stars of the early years had made their mark, to the long-playing album (LP). The advent of the compact disc (CD) in the 1980s reinforced that change. With the main musical ingredients established, together with a standard instrumentation – two guitars, bass guitar, drums, and sometimes keyboard – rock music began to split into parallel lines of development. Each has tended to explore different aspects of performance. As studio technology and electronic instruments became more sophisticated the new possibilities they offered were quickly exploited, and in some areas came to determine the character of the music itself.

Art rock, glam rock

The term art rock, or "progressive" rock, came into use in the late 1960s and described different kinds of music in Britain and the USA.

In Britain, groups such as the Moody Blues and King Crimson extended the idea of the "concept album" in which songs were grouped round a common theme. The structures they built were elaborate and grandiose, involving resources, such as symphony orchestras, well beyond the usual range of rock-and-roll. King Crimson, led by Robert Fripp (b. 1946), had similar "symphonic" aspirations in their earlier albums, but Fripp's wider interests led him to studio collaborations with jazz musicians and minimalist composers in which improvisation played an important part.

Art rock

In Britain, "art rock" denoted the mainstream rock bands of the late 1960s and early 1970s who built their albums around a concept or theme. The musical treatments became increasingly elaborate, sometimes including full orchestral forces, and individual songs were less important in their own right.

In the USA, art rock described the music of groups such as the Velvet Underground, who developed a style close to that of the art music avant-garde of the period. Complex lyrics were delivered over simple, repetitive chordal accompaniments or instrumental drones.

Further listening Moody Blues: *Days of Future Passed* (1967); King Crimson: *In the Court of the Crimson King* (1969); Velvet Underground: *The Velvet Underground and Nico* (1967)

Pink Floyd proved one of the most durable and ambitious of all the British art rock bands. The sweep of their music, in which electronics and synthesizers were increasingly incorporated, was matched by the complex sets and lighting design of their stage shows. Pink Floyd began the vogue for "stadium rock", using massive levels of sound amplification to fill huge arenas.

Though some American bands attempted to copy the extravagances of their British counterparts, art rock music in the USA was very different in scale and intent. It was epitomized by the Velvet Underground, formed in New York in 1965 by the guitarist and singer Lou Reed (b. 1944) and the classically trained keyboard and viola player John Cale (b. 1942). Velvet Underground's music was much closer to the art music avant-garde of the period than to their rock contemporaries. In the 1960s, for instance, they collaborated with the painter and film maker Andy Warhol, the principal exponent of "pop art". Reed's intricate lyrics, delving into the darker corners of New York life, were delivered in a barely inflected monotone over an electronic drone and repetitive chord sequences, often driven by an insistent, primitive drum pulse. The Velvet Underground's music was never commercially successful. Yet, together with Reed's subsequent solo work, it was to prove of crucial importance to many *new wave* bands of the mid-1970s.

Glam rock

Glam rock, or "glitter" rock, described a vogue in the early 1970s for highly elaborate stage acts in which theatrical trappings and elements of mime became at least as important as the music itself. The performances of David Bowie in Britain and Lou Reed in the USA epitomized the style.

Further listening David Bowie: *The Rise and Fall of Ziggy Stardust and the Spiders from Mars* (1972); Lou Reed: *Transformer* (1972); Roxy Music: *Roxy Music* (1972)

In the early part of his solo career Reed worked with the British singer and composer David Bowie (b. 1947). Bowie was one of the most accomplished practitioners of *glam rock*, a style in which elaborate stage acts became at least as important as the music. He had trained as an actor and mime artist, and his stage shows emphasized the theatrical aspects of his music and the creation of a fictional persona, the alien Ziggy Stardust. Bowie had his first hit single in 1969 with *Space Oddity*, a typical song of its period, the style of which he was soon to replace with a harder-edged form of rock (see **Listening Guide 64**). Glam rock was also used to describe the music of many diverse performers, from singer-songwriters such as Elton John to sophisticated bands like Roxy Music and T. Rex, and performers like Gary Glitter.

Heavy metal   "Heavy metal" evolved out of the music of some of the most accomplished rock performers of the 1960s, among them the British blues-based group Cream (led by the guitarist Eric Clapton), the rock band the Who, and the virtuoso guitarist Jimi Hendrix. Heavy metal became immensely successful in Britain and the USA as a

David Bowie: *Space Oddity* (1969)

Space Oddity was released as a single shortly before the first Apollo moon landing in July 1969. It was Bowie's first hit record; soon afterwards his music changed dramatically, becoming much harder edged and acquiring the 'glam rock' packaging that proved so influential on rock musicians in the 1970s. But its sentiments and soundworld are typical of rock music at the end of the 1960s: the sound effects and elements of collage were indebted to The Beatles, in particular to the songs of the *Sgt Pepper* album.

The structure of *Space Oddity* consists essentially of two verses (*A*), each shared between the characters of 'ground control' and the astronaut, with a refrain (*B*); there is an extended introduction, a central instrumental episode, and a coda. The pattern is thus Introduction–*AB*–Episode–*AB*–Coda. The song's detached, disembodied character is enhanced by modal melodic lines and the verse structure, which falls into 14-measure units. Multi-tracking of Bowie's voice gives different timbres to the two characters. The basic instrumentation of the song is electric organ, rhythm guitar, and percussion, with an amplified flute added for the instrumental episode.

 Listening Outline . . . .

Time

0.00	Introduction: electric bass and tomtoms begin a 4-m. pattern that underpins much of the song, reinforced by cymbals, and in the coda (4.10) by hand-clapping
0.13	rhythm guitar joins accompaniment at beginning of third 4-m. pattern
0.17	voice enters with repeated phrase of 'Ground control to Major Tom'
0.34	as Bowie makes varied repeat of introductory phrases, a female voice begins 'count down', synchronized with the first beat of each measure
0.54	introduction ends with electronic sounds of 'lift-off'
1.07	*A* (ground control)
1.28	*A* (astronaut)
1.49	*B*
2.08	episode, guitars and solo flute
2.31	*A* (astronaut)
2.52	*A* (ground control), shortened and beginning to accelerate
3.06	refrain; last phrase interrupted by reprise of first four measures of instrumental episode and merging into
3.26	coda, built from final phrase of refrain and adding further instrumental lines and sound effects until fade out
4.29	(end)

> **Heavy metal**
>
> A style of rock music which has remained popular since the early 1970s, characterized by a heavily amplified guitar sound – "power chords" – and an insistent, uncomplicated beat. The vocal lines are shouted between the guitar chords. The effectiveness of heavy metal depends a great deal upon live performance, the use of garish lighting and dress, and ritualized gestures.
>
> **Further listening** Led Zeppelin: *Untitled* (1972); Aerosmith: *Toys in the Attic* (1975); Van Halen: *1984* (1984); Bon Jovi: *Slippery When Wet* (1986)

primitive, direct form of rock which attracted a predominantly male following.

In its essentials it has remained largely unchanged for almost 20 years, characterized by simple vocal lines shouted over hugely amplified guitar "power chords" and uncomplicated, persistent drum patterns, interspersed with guitar solos that use the extreme registers of the instrument. In live performance it is presented in an almost ritualistic manner, with much use of dramatic lighting and smoke machines.

The development of British heavy metal was triggered by the success in the 1970s of Led Zeppelin (led by the singer Robert Plant, b. 1948, and the lead guitarist Jimmy Page, b. 1944). In the USA, Aerosmith – formed by Steve Tyler (b. 1948) and clearly influenced in the early 1970s by the Rolling Stones – was the first heavy metal band to achieve a major impact, although in the 1980s Van Halen and Kiss both attracted enormous followings.

Punk and New Wave

By the mid-1970s the slick and glossy presentation of rock had often come to seem more important than the music itself. With the paraphernalia of art rock, the fancy-dress of glam rock, and the increasing desire of the record industry to control and exploit every aspect of their artists' public image, rock was in danger of losing its direction and its vitality.

The rise of "punk" in 1975 provided the sharp change of direction and emphasis urgently needed. The music which emerged under the punk banner was of relatively little intrinsic interest, but the whole punk movement, first in Britain, and then in the USA, led those musicians interested in innovation to reassess the basics of their music and to strip away all the unnecessary theatrical trappings. Punk provided the clean break that allowed the performers who followed – the singers and bands of the New Wave – to explore a leaner, more direct, and vital sound.

The Sex Pistols, the prototype for many of the British punk bands, was created in 1975 as a purely commercial enterprise by their manager Malcolm McLaren. He designed the Sex Pistols to be a contrast to the blandness of most current rock music: the vocalist Johnny Rotten (b. John Lydon, 1956) delivered his aggressive lyrics in a snarling monotone, while the other members of the band kept up a simple, deliberately harsh, chordal accompaniment. Though the Sex Pistols lacked a specific political dimension to their music, other leading punk bands became identified with

---

Punk

A term applied in the USA and especially Britain to a wave of rock bands in the mid-1970s that reacted against the elaborate, over-sophisticated, and heavily commercial rock styles of the early 1970s. Punk songs were deliberately primitive in their musical construction, harsh and aggressive in their sound, and often expressed violent sentiments in their lyrics. In the USA in particular punk bands were heavily influenced by the Velvet Underground.

Further listening The Sex Pistols: *Anarchy in the UK* (1976); The Clash: *The Clash* (1977); Patti Smith: *Horses* (1975); The Ramones: *Ramones Leave Home* (1976)

---

left-wing causes. The Clash were formed in 1975 yet remained active into the 1980s, becoming one of the most influential British bands of the period, not so much because of their music but through their ability to use it to address social and political issues.

In Britain, New Wave bands such as The Fall and Elvis Costello and the Attractions followed up the Clash's concerns, though Costello in particular had a much more varied musical pedigree. His songs have consistently shown his ability to use lyrics in an inventive way, while his melodies have acquired a subtlety and sophistication far removed from the incantations of punk.

New Wave

A development from punk in the late 1970s that played down its aggressive primitivism, introducing greater complexity and subtlety into its harmonies, lyrics, and melodic lines. However, the thin, lean textures of punk were preserved and New Wave became regarded as an alternative to the heavily amplified sound of many of the most commercially successful bands of the period.

Further listening Elvis Costello: *This Year's Model* (1978); The Jam: *All Mod Cons* (1978); Blondie: *Parallel Lines* (1978); Talking Heads: *Remain in Light* (1980)

In the USA, punk could trace its own ready-made pedigree back to Lou Reed and the Velvet Underground. However, American punk was never to gain the popularity or the notoriety of its British counterpart. It was soon overtaken by the varied collection of performers who were described as New Wave. They ranged from the group Blondie, fronted by Debbie Harry, who used the formulas of punk vocals and backings to create an entirely commercial sound, to the witty irreverence of the B-52s, and the conscious art rock constructions of the groups Television and Talking Heads.

Talking Heads were formed in 1974 by the vocalist and guitarist David Byrne (b. 1952) and the drummer Chris Frantz (b. 1951). Their early songs combined the simple, declamatory vocal lines of New Wave and a driving rhythmic impulse taken from the rock-and-roll mainstream, together with elements derived from the New

Talking Heads

York avant-garde and rhythmic patterns derived from African and Middle Eastern music.

It was the collaborations of David Byrne that did most to shape the music of Talking Heads and establish their importance. His interest in the visual arts introduced a new sophistication to rock videos in the early 1980s, and led the way towards the highly expensive and elaborate videos that now accompany the recordings of solo singers such as Madonna and Michael Jackson. Byrne also worked with minimalist art music composers, for example Philip Glass.

Disco

In the mid-1970s discotheques began to create their own brand of dance music. Disco was derived in part from soul and Tamla Motown (see p. 409) but the vocals were far less important than the unflagging, fast-tempo instrumental sections, usually in 4/4 time. The most popular of the disco singers was Donna Summer (b. 1948). The Bee Gees, a mainstream rock band of the 1960s, successfully turned to disco ten years later when they recorded the soundtrack to the definitive movie of the disco culture, *Saturday Night Fever* (1977).

Disco records went on to use electronic synthesizers to create the regular, mechanical beat considered essential to the music, but the genre began to lose popularity in the early 1980s. By then the discotheque culture had already begun to create music of its own in which the disc jockeys, who originally introduced and played the records, took an important part. In "scratching", for example, the disc jockey moved records backwards and forwards on the turntables under the stylus to create an insistent, rhythmic noise.

Rap

Rap also developed in discotheques and clubs, and grew in part out of the patter of disc jockeys. But its rhyming chant over a rhythmic accompaniment also had roots in the blues tradition and in the spoken narratives frequent in soul and it has mainly been the province of black performers. Rap has increased steadily in importance through the 1980s to become one of the most popular and pervasive of rock styles, and one that allowed the expression of protest and politics. The minimal resources required to perform a rap – essentially just a pre-recorded backing track to generate the accompaniment – has encouraged large numbers of performers.

Rap

A style that emerged in New York discotheques in the mid-1970s and which has remained largely associated with black performers. Rhymed verses are chanted over an insistent rhythmic accompaniment, sometimes with a choral refrain. Early raps used the instrumental sections of disco songs as backing, but the style now uses pre-recorded percussive tapes, and has gone on to emphasize vocal virtuosity and, often, expresses political views.

Video

The increasing capabilities of video recordings offered rock performers a new range of opportunities for promoting and expanding their music. Singers such as Madonna, Michael Jackson, and Prince began to conceive their albums and the associated video productions as integrated products, and they became the most widely popular rock performers of the late 1980s. Each represented a different strand of the rich stylistic mix of rock.

Madonna (b. 1958) expanded the traditional role of the solo female singer by exploiting her sexuality with songs such as *Like a Virgin* (1985). Her early songs were rooted in disco and dance music, but the increasing sophistication of her videos, and the correspondingly elaborate stagings of her live performances, brought a much wider stylistic range into her music.

Michael Jackson (b. 1958) was the lead singer in the Tamla Motown group the Jackson Five. He began his solo career at the age of 13, but it was the highly crafted form of dance music on his 1982 album *Thriller*, together with the cinematic ambitions of the associated video, that brought him enormous popularity.

Prince (b. Prince Rogers Nelson, 1960) has preserved his musical vitality whatever the theatricality of his videos, films, and stage acts. His success is derived in part from the breadth of musical styles synthesized in his songs, ranging from sentimental ballads at one extreme, through disco and dance material to hard rock numbers at the other, and in part from the high technical standard of their performances. Prince's own guitar playing derives very clearly from that of Jimi Hendrix; he is the outstanding representative of that tradition in 1990s rock.

World music

The commercial spread of the record industry has meant that pop music is now heard in almost every corner of the globe. At the same time, a range of indigenous musical cultures has become accessible to rock audiences in the 1980s. In some cases *world music* is heard in Europe and the USA in unadulterated form, using traditional instruments, melodies, and structures. More often elements of Western popular music, for example electronics, are added to the sound.

Some world music performers have launched successful careers in the USA and Europe in their own right. Rubén Blades (b. 1948), a Panamanian, used the South American dance music known as *salsa* as the basis for songs in which he protested the social injustices of his native country. In Europe, Salif Keïta from

---

World music

A term used to describe the work of performers who have incorporated music and instrumentalists from outside the Western tradition into their songs. World music also includes the music of non-Western performers available on record in Europe and North America.

Further listening Paul Simon: *Graceland* (1986); Talking Heads: *Naked* (1988); Rubén Blades: *Nothing But the Truth* (1988); Youssou N'Dour: *The Lion* (1985); Salif Keïta: *Soro* (1986)

Mali and Youssou N'Dour from Senegal, have developed substantial followings, with albums in which rock elements are discreetly added to fundamentally African styles.

World music was brought to the forefront of rock when Paul Simon's hugely successful album *Graceland* (1986) used musicians from South Africa and Zimbabwe to provide instrumental and vocal accompaniments. Other rock musicians have gone on to spread the net still wider and to introduce yet more musical traditions into their compositions; Simon's *Rhythm of the Saints* (1990), for instance, used South American instrumentalists.

CONCLUSION: THE 1990s

The story of rock music since the mid-1950s has been one of assimilation and adaptation, with a constantly broadening range of influences. The development of new technology has accelerated its progress by making available new styles and disseminating new ideas more quickly than ever before. Rock music in the 1990s contains a rich and strange mixture of ingredients and styles, ranging from elements taken from ethnic cultures to aspects of the art music avant-garde. Yet the elements that have defined rock-and-roll for 40 years have remained a constant feature of these cross-cultural experiments and have provided them with their energy and dynamism. They belong to the same tradition as Bruce Springsteen, Madonna, and Bon Jovi, whatever the superficial differences in their music.

Further Listening

The Listening Guides throughout this book (listed in the contents pages) treat in detail a carefully selected series of representative works or movements; listening to these works is the first priority. Next should come the remaining movements of works of which we have included only one or two in this book. Working outwards from that, music related to that already heard can then usefully be approached (for example another chanson by Josquin, another quartet by Haydn, another song by Schubert, more madrigals by Crumb).

The list below, drawn up in correspondence with the historical sections of the book, itemizes music that might suitably be used for following up such listening, naming some "landmark" works, or specially appealing ones, or ones that might help develop an understanding of or enthusiasm for a particular composer. Most are already referred to, if often only in passing, in the text; all are relevant to points made in the text and virtually all are readily available in good, modern recordings. And all should give pleasure to the listener and extend his or her musical horizons.

Part III
Any examples of plainsong
MACHAUT *Douce dame jolie* (virelai)
DUFAY *Ave regina coelorum* (motet); *Se la face ay pale* (chanson)
JOSQUIN *Ave Maria . . . virgo serena* (motet); *Mille regrets* (chanson)
LASSUS *Salve, regina, mater misericordiae* (motet); Lamentations
PALESTRINA *Tu es Petrus* (motet); *Missa Papae Marcelli*
GIOVANNI GABRIELI *In ecclesiis* (motet)
BYRD Mass in Four Voices: *Sing joyfully* (anthem); *This sweet and merry month of May* (madrigal); *The Carman's Whistle* for virginals

Part IV
MONTEVERDI Vespers (1610); *Lamento d'Arianna*; *Chiome d'oro* and *Zefiro torna* (madrigals)
PURCELL *Come, ye sons of art* (ode); *My heart is inditing* (anthem)
VIVALDI *Gloria* in D; Violin Concertos, *The Four Seasons* op. 8 nos. 1–4
BACH Toccata and Fugue in d for organ; Brandenburg Concertos nos. 3 in G, 5 in D; Partita no. 1 in Bb; Cantata no. 80, *Ein feste Burg*; *St Matthew Passion* [excerpts]
HANDEL *Water Music*; Concerto Grosso (e.g. op. 6); *Giulio Cesare* ("Julius Caesar") [excerpts], *Jephtha* [excerpts]

Part V
GLUCK *Orfeo ed Euridice* [excerpts]
HAYDN String Quartet in f op. 20 no. 5; Symphony no. 44 in e; *The Creation* [excerpts]
MOZART String Quartet in G K387; String Quintet in g K516; Symphony no. 41 in C K551; *Die Zauberflöte* ("The Magic Flute") [excerpts]
BEETHOVEN Piano Sonata in c op. 13, "Pathétique"; String Quartet in F op. 59 no. 1; Symphony no. 3 in Eb, "Eroica"; Symphony no. 9 in d, "Choral" (finale); String Quartet in a op. 132; *Fidelio* [excerpts]

Part VI
SCHUBERT Songs, e.g. *An die Musik* ("To Music"), *Der Erlkönig* ("The Erlking"), *Die Forelle* ("The Trout"), *Tod und das Mädchen* ("Death and the Maiden"); *Wanderer* Fantasia for piano; Symphony no. 9 in C, "Great C major"; String Quintet in C
MENDELSSOHN Violin Concerto; Symphony no. 4 in A, "Italian"
SCHUMANN Piano Concerto in a
CHOPIN Ballade no. 1 in g op. 23; Waltz in Db op. 64 no. 1
BERLIOZ *Les nuits d'été* ("Summer Nights"), songs, Overture, Roman Carnival
LISZT Piano concerto no. 1 in Eb
VERDI *Rigoletto* [excerpts]

WAGNER *Die Meistersinger von Nürnberg* ("The Mastersingers of Nuremberg") [excerpts]
BRAHMS Violin Concerto; Clarinet Quintet

Part VII
TCHAIKOVSKY *Romeo and Juliet* (overture)
DVOŘÁK Symphony no. 8 in G; String Quartet in F op. 96, "American"
MAHLER Symphony no. 4 in G
STRAUSS *Der Rosenkavalier* [excerpts]
DEBUSSY *La cathédrale engloutie* ("The Submerged Cathedral") (Préludes, i)
PUCCINI *La bohème* [excerpts]

Part VIII
SCHOENBERG *Verklärte Nacht* ("Transfigured Night")
BERG Violin Concerto
WEBERN Symphony op. 21
STRAVINSKY *Petrushka*; Symphony in C
BARTÓK Music for Strings, Percussion, and Celesta; String Quartet no. 4
IVES *The Unanswered Question*
COPLAND *Appalachian Spring*
SHOSTAKOVICH Piano Quintet; Symphony no. 8
BRITTEN *Peter Grimes* [excerpts]; Serenade for tenor, horn, and strings
MESSIAEN *Turangalîla-symphonie*
STOCKHAUSEN *Gesang der Junglinge*
BERIO *Circles*
ADAMS *Nixon in China* [excerpts]
BERNSTEIN *West Side Story* [excerpts]
KERN *Show Boat*

Further Reading

Below is listed a selection of books which should help the reader who wants to look more deeply into any particular topic. The reference books contain fuller bibliographies which may usefully be followed up. Publication dates are normally those of the most recent edition.

For a fuller picture of the context in which music has flourished at particular periods – the social, economic, political, intellectual, and religious background – the "Music and Society" series, so far five volumes, may profitably be consulted. In these volumes, developments in different cities and countries are discussed by individual authorities.

There exist numerous biographies and other studies of individual composers. Here we confine ourselves mainly to the rather factual biographies in the *New Grove* series (largely reprinted from *The New Grove Dictionary*), which have comprehensive lists of works and full bibliographies. Other composer studies are cited only when they have something rather different to offer on a major figure; similarly, a number of non-biographical books are listed where they afford particular insights.

In the "Composers" section below, studies treating groups of composers are listed first, then books on individual composers in chronological order by composer.

Reference
The New Grove Dictionary of Music and Musicians, ed. Stanley Sadie (New York: Grove's Dictionaries: London: Macmillan, 1980)
The New Harvard Dictionary of Music, ed. Don Randel (Cambridge, Mass.: Harvard UP, 1986)
Baker's Biographical Dictionary of Musicians, ed. Nicolas Slonimsky (New York: Schirmer, 1985)
The New Oxford Companion to Music, ed. Denis Arnold (New York: Oxford UP, 1983)
The Norton-Grove Concise Encyclopedia of Music, ed. Stanley Sadie (New York: Norton, 1988)

Special topics
INSTRUMENTS
Anthony Baines, ed.: *Musical Instruments through the Ages* (Baltimore: Penguin, 1966)
Robert Donington: *Music and its Instruments* (New York: Methuen, 1982)
Sybil Marcuse: *A Survey of Musical Instruments* (New York: Harper & Row, 1975)
Mary Remnant: *Musical Instruments of the West* (New York: St Martin's Press, 1978)

ELEMENTS, FORM
See individual subject articles in *The New Grove Dictionary of Music and Musicians* and the *New Harvard Dictionary of Music*

AMERICAN MUSIC
Charles Hamm: *Music in the New World* (New York: Norton, 1983)
H. Wiley Hitchcock: *Music in the United States: a Historical Introduction* (Englewood Cliffs, NJ: Prentice Hall, 1974)

JAZZ
James Lincoln Collier: *The Making of Jazz* (New York: Houghton, Mifflin, 1978)
Donald D. Megill and Richard S. Demory: *Introduction to Jazz History* (Englewood Cliffs, NJ: Prentice Hall, 1984)
Paul Oliver, Max Harrison, and William D. Bolcom: *Ragtime, Blues and Jazz* [The New Grove] (New York: Norton, 1986)

OPERA

Donald Jay Grout: *A Short History of Opera* (New York: Columbia UP, 1965)
Earl of Harewood, ed.: *Kobbé's Complete Opera Book* (New York: Putnam, 1986)
Joseph Kerman: *Opera as Drama* (New York: Vintage, 1988)
Stanley Sadie, ed.: *History of Opera* [The New Grove Handbooks] (New York: Norton, 1986)

NON-WESTERN

William P. Malm: *Music Cultures of the Pacific, the Near East, and Asia* (Englewood Cliffs, NJ: Prentice Hall, 1977)
Bruno Nettl: *Folk and Traditional Music of the Western Continents* (Englewood Cliffs, NJ: Prentice Hall, 1973)
Helen Myers, ed.: *Ethnomusicology: an Introduction* (New York: Norton, 1992)
Helen Myers, ed.: *Ethnomusicology: Area Studies* (New York: Norton, 1992)

History

GENERAL

Gerald Abraham: *The Concise Oxford History of Music* (New York: Oxford UP, 1980)
Edith Borroff: *Music in Europe and the United States: a History* (Englewood Cliffs, NJ: Prentice Hall, 1971)
Donald Jay Grout, rev. Claude Palisca: *A History of Western Music* (New York: Norton, 1988)
Paul Henry Lang: *Music in Western Civilization* (New York: Norton, 1941)
Karin Pendle, ed.: *Women and Music: a History* (Bloomington and Indianapolis: Indiana UP, 1991)

PERIODS

James McKinnon, ed.: *Antiquity and the Middle Ages* [Music and Society] (Englewood Cliffs, NJ: Prentice Hall, 1990)
Richard H. Hoppin: *Medieval Music* (New York: Norton, 1978)
Howard Mayer Brown: *Music in the Renaissance* (Englewood Cliffs, NJ: Prentice Hall, 1976)
Iain Fenlon, ed.: *The Renaissance* [Man and Music/Music and Society] (Englewood Cliffs, NJ: Prentice Hall, 1989)
Claude V. Palisca: *Baroque Music* (Englewood Cliffs, NJ: Prentice Hall, 1981)
Julie Anne Sadie, ed.: *Companion to Baroque Music* (New York: Schirmer, 1991)
Charles Rosen: *The Classical Style: Haydn, Mozart, Beethoven* (New York: Norton, 1972)
Neal Zaslaw, ed.: *The Classical Era* [Man and Music/Music and Society] (Englewood Cliffs, NJ: Prentice Hall, 1989)
Julian Rushton: *Classical Music: a Concise History from Gluck to Beethoven* (New York: Thames & Hudson, 1986)
Leon Plantinga: *Romantic Music* (New York: Norton, 1985)
Alexander Ringer, ed.: *The Early Romantic Era* [Music and Society] (Englewood Cliffs, NJ: Prentice Hall, 1990)
Jim Samson, ed.: *The Late Romantic Era* [Music and Society] (Englewood Cliffs, NJ: Prentice Hall, 1991)
Gerald Abraham: *A Hundred Years of Music* (Chicago: Aldine, 1974)
William W. Austin: *Music in the Twentieth Century* (New York: Norton, 1966)
Nicolas Slonimsky: *Music since 1900* (New York: Scribner, 1971)
Eric Salzman: *Twentieth-Century Music: an Introduction* (Englewood Cliffs, NJ: Prentice Hall, 1974)
Jim Samson: *Music in Transition . . . 1900–1920* (New York: St Martin's Press, 1977)
Paul Griffiths: *A Concise History of Modern Music from Debussy to Boulez* (New York: Thames & Hudson, 1978)
Arnold Whittall: *Music since the First World War* (New York: St Martin's Press, 1977)
Robert J. Morgan, ed.: *Modern Times* [Music and Society] (Englewood Cliffs, NJ: Prentice Hall, 1993)

Composers

MIDDLE AGES, RENAISSANCE, BAROQUE

David Fallows: *Dufay* [Master Musicians] (New York: Vintage, 1983)
Joseph Kerman and others: *High Renaissance Masters* [Byrd, Josquin, Lassus, Palestrina, Victoria; The New Grove] (New York: Norton, 1984)
Denis Arnold and others: *Italian Baroque Masters* [Monteverdi, Cavalli, Frescobaldi, A. and D. Scarlatti, Corelli, Vivaldi; The New Grove] (New York: Norton, 1984)
Joshua Rifkin and others: *North European Baroque Masters* [Schütz, Froberger, Buxtehude, Purcell, Telemann; The New Grove] (New York: Norton, 1985)

James R. Anthony and others: *French Baroque Masters* [Lully, Charpentier, Lalande, Couperin, Rameau; The New Grove] (New York: Norton, 1986)
Malcolm Boyd: *Bach* [Master Musicians] (New York: Vintage, 1984)
Christoph Wolff and others: *The Bach Family* [The New Grove] (New York: Norton, 1983)
Winton Dean: *Handel* [The New Grove] (New York: Norton, 1982)
Christopher Hogwood: *Handel* (New York: Thames & Hudson, 1984)

CLASSICAL
Jens Peter Larsen: *Haydn* [The New Grove] (New York: Norton, 1982)
Stanley Sadie: *Mozart* [The New Grove] (New York: Norton, 1982)
Emily Anderson, ed.: *The Letters of Mozart and his Family* (New York: Norton, 1985)
H. C. Robbins Landon: *The Mozart Compendium* (New York: Schirmer, 1990)
Maynard Solomon: *Beethoven* (New York: Schirmer, 1977)
Alan Tyson and Joseph Kerman: *Beethoven* [The New Grove] (New York: Norton, 1983)

ROMANTIC
Nicholas Temperley and others: *Early Romantic Masters I* [Chopin, Schumann, Liszt; The New Grove] (New York: Norton, 1985)
John Warrack and others: *Early Romantic Masters II* [Weber, Berlioz, Mendelssohn; The New Grove] (New York: Norton, 1985)
Philip Gossett, Andrew Porter and others: *Masters of Italian Opera* [Rossini, Bellini, Donizetti, Verdi, Puccini; The New Grove] (New York: Norton, 1983)
Deryck Cooke and others: *Late Romantic Masters* [Bruckner, Brahms, Wolf, Dvořák; The New Grove] (New York: Norton, 1985)
Michael Kennedy and others: *Turn of the Century Masters* [Strauss, Sibelius, Mahler, Janáček; The New Grove] (New York: Norton, 1984)
Gerald Abraham and others: *Russian Masters I* [Glinka, Borodin, Balakirev, Musorgsky, Tchaikovsky; The New Grove] (New York: Norton, 1986)
Gerald Abraham and others: *Russian Masters II* [Rimsky-Korsakov, Rakhmaninov, Skryabin, Prokofiev, Shostakovich; The New Grove] (New York: Norton, 1986)
John Reed: *Schubert* [Master Musicians] (New York: Vintage, 1987)
D. Kern Holoman: *Berlioz* (Cambridge, Mass.: Harvard UP, 1989)
John Deathridge and Carl Dahlhaus: *Wagner* [The New Grove] (New York: Norton, 1983)
Barry Millington: *Wagner* [Master Musicians] (New York: Vintage, 1984)
Julian Budden: *Verdi* [Master Musicians] (New York: Vintage, 1985)
John Warrack: *Tchaikovsky* (New York: Scribner, 1973)

TWENTIETH CENTURY
Oliver Neighbour and others: *Second Viennese School* [Schoenberg, Berg, Webern; The New Grove] (New York: Norton, 1983)
László Somfai and others: *Modern Masters* [Bartók, Stravinsky, Hindemith; The New Grove] (New York: Norton, 1984)
John Kirkpatrick and others: *Twentieth-Century American Masters* [Ives, Thomson, Sessions, Cowell, Gershwin, Copland, Carter, Barber, Cage, Bernstein; The New Grove] (New York: Norton, 1988)
Jean-Michel Nectoux and others: *Twentieth-Century French Masters* [Fauré, Debussy, Satie, Ravel, Poulenc, Messiaen, Boulez; The New Grove] (New York: Norton, 1986)
Diana McVeagh and others: *Twentieth-Century English Masters* [Elgar, Delius, Vaughan Williams, Holst, Walton, Tippett, Britten] (New York: Norton, 1986)
Edward Lockspeiser: *Debussy: his Life and Mind* (London: Cassell, 1962)
Charles Rosen: *Arnold Schoenberg* (New York: Viking; London: Boyars, 1975)
Arnold Schoenberg: *Style and Idea*, ed. Leonard Stein (New York: St Martin's Press; London: Faber, 1984)
J. P. Burkholder: *Charles Ives: the Ideas behind the Music* (New Haven, CT: Yale UP, 1985)
Paul Griffiths: *Stravinsky* [Master Musicians] (New York: Schirmer, 1992)
John Cage: *Silence: Lectures and Writings* (Middletown, CT: Wesleyan UP, 1961)
Robert S. Johnson: *Messiaen* (Berkeley and Los Angeles: U. of California Press, 1989)

POPULAR MUSIC TRADITIONS
G. Bordman: *The American Musical Theater* (New York: Oxford University Press)
Robert Palmer: *Deep Blues* (New York: Viking Press, 1981)
James Lincoln Collier: *The Making of Jazz* (New York: Houghton Mifflin, 1978)
Mark Gridley: *Jazz Styles* (Englewood Cliffs, NJ: Prentice Hall, 1985)
Charles Hamm: *Music in the New World* (New York: Norton, 1983)
G. Hirshey: *Nowhere To Run: The Story of Soul Music* (New York: Times Books, 1984)
Greil Marcus: *Mystery Train* (New York: Dutton, 1975)

Glossary of Musical Terms

Words given in capitals refer to other glossary entries. Page references are given for terms discussed more fully in the main text of the book. Terms used to describe styles and genres of jazz and rock music are defined in special "boxes" in Part IX.

absolute music Music with no extra-musical association or PROGRAM.

a cappella A Latin term, meaning choral music without accompaniment.

accent The emphasizing of a note in performance.

acciaccatura A "crushed" note, sounded just before the main one, used as a musical ornament.

accidental A sharp, flat, or natural sign occurring during a piece, temporarily altering the pitch of a note.

adagio Slow; a slow movement.

aerophone A generic term for a wind instrument.

air A simple tune for voice or instrument; also AYRE.

aleatory music Music in which chance or randomness is an element (p. 340).

allegretto Less quick than allegro; a movement in moderately quick tempo.

allegro Quick; a movement in lively tempo.

allemande A moderately slow Baroque dance in quadruple meter, often the opening movement of a SUITE; also *almain, almand,* etc.

alto **1** A female voice with a range lower than a soprano, or a high male voice (p. 63). **2** A term used for an instrument whose range is analogous to the alto voice, e.g. alto saxophone; hence *alto clef,* used by the viola.

andante At a moderately slow pace; a movement in moderately slow tempo.

andantino A little faster than andante.

answer A musical phrase that responds to one previously heard, particularly in a FUGUE.

anthem A choral work in English for performance in church services; a *national anthem* is a patriotic hymn.

antiphony Music in which two or more groups of performers are separated to create special effects of echo, contrast, etc; hence *antiphonal.*

appoggiatura A "leaning" note, usually a step above (or below) the main note, creating a DISSONANCE with the harmony, used as an expressive device and musical ornament.

arco A direction to bow rather than pluck the strings of a string instrument.

aria An air or song for solo voice with orchestra, usually part of an opera, cantata, or oratorio (p. 117).

arioso A style of composition or singing between RECITATIVE and ARIA.

arpeggio The notes of a chord sounded in succession rather than simultaneously.

Ars Nova A Latin term, meaning "new art", used for the new style of fourteenth-century French and Italian music (p. 76).

art music Music written with a seriousness of purpose consistent with the Western classical tradition, as opposed to popular or folk music.

art song A composed, written-down song (as opposed to a folksong).

atonality Without TONALITY or KEY; hence *atonal.*

augmentation The lengthening of time values of the notes of a melody (often by doubling them), particularly of a medieval *cantus firmus* or a fugue subject.

augmented interval An interval that has been increased by a semitone (p. 20).

avant-garde A French term used to describe composers (also artists and writers) whose work is radical and advanced.

ayre An English song (or air) for solo voice with lute or viols (p. 87).

bagatelle A short, light piece, usually for piano.

ballad A traditional song, often with a narrative; hence *ballad opera,* which has spoken dialogue and uses popular tunes.

ballade **1** An instrumental piece in narrative style, usually for piano. **2** A medieval polyphonic song form (p. 72).

ballata A late thirteenth- and fourteenth-century Italian poetic and musical form.

ballett A Renaissance partsong with a dance-like rhythm and a "fa-la" refrain; also *balletto.*

bar MEASURE.

baritone A male voice with a range between a tenor and a bass (p. 63).

barline Vertical line marking off one MEASURE from the next.

bass **1** A male voice with the lowest range (p. 63). **2** An instrument of bass range, or the lowest of a group of instruments, e.g. bass clarinet; hence *bass clef,* used by bass instruments and a pianist's left hand. **3** The lowest-pitched part in a piece of music, the basis of the harmony.

basse danse A medieval and Renaissance court dance, usually in slow triple meter.

basso continuo The term for which the more commonly used CONTINUO is an abbreviation.

beat The basic pulse underlying most music (p. 15).

bel canto A style of singing, particularly in Italian opera, that allows the voice to display its agile and sensuous qualities; hence *bel canto opera*.

binary form The form of a piece of music with two sections, *AB* (p. 34).

blues A type of black American folk or popular music (p. 399).

bourrée A fast Baroque dance in duple meter with a quarter-note upbeat.

break In jazz, a short solo passage (usually an IMPROVISATION) between passages for ensemble.

bridge 1 A linking passage in a piece of music. **2** The part of a string instrument over which the strings pass.

cadence A progression of notes or chords that gives the effect of closing a passage of music (p. 24).

cadenza A virtuoso passage (sometimes an IMPROVISATION) towards the end of a concerto movement or aria.

canon A type of polyphony in which a melody is repeated by each voice or part as it enters (p. 31).

cantata A work for one or more voices with instrumental accompaniment (p. 117); hence *church cantata*, with a sacred text.

cantus firmus A Latin term, meaning "fixed song", used for a borrowed melody on which composers from the late Middle Ages onwards based polyphonic compositions (p. 33).

canzona A short 16th- or 17th-century instrumental piece.

capriccio A short instrumental piece; also *caprice*.

chaconne A moderate or slow dance in triple meter, usually with a GROUND BASS.

chamber music Music for a chamber (or small room) rather than a hall; hence music played by small groups – duos, trios, quartets, etc. (p. 62).

chance music ALEATORY MUSIC.

chanson The French word for "song", used specifically for French medieval and Renaissance polyphonic songs (p. 85).

chant PLAINSONG.

characteristic piece A short piece, usually for piano, representing a mood or other extra-musical idea; also *character piece*.

chorale A traditional German (Lutheran) hymn-tune.

chorale prelude An organ piece based on a chorale.

chord The simultaneous sounding of two or more tones (p. 28).

chordophone A generic term for a string instrument (p. 43).

chorus 1 A choir. **2** The music a choir sings. **3** The REFRAIN of a song.

chromatic Based on an octave of 12 semitones rather than a DIATONIC scale; hence *chromaticism, chromatic scale, chromatic progression* (p. 21).

clef The sign at the beginning of the STAFF that indicates the pitch of one of its lines and therefore determines all of them; hence *treble clef, alto clef, tenor clef, bass clef* (p. 19).

coda An Italian term, meaning "tail", used for a movement's closing section added as a rounding-off rather than an essential part of the form.

coloratura A rapid, decorated style of singing, often high-pitched.

common time 4/4 time, i.e. four quarter-notes in a measure (p. 17).

compound meter A meter in which the unit beats are divisible by three (e.g. 6/8), unlike SIMPLE METER (p. 17).

con brio With spirit.

concertino 1 The small group of soloists in a CONCERTO GROSSO. **2** A small-scale concerto.

concerto Originally, a work (vocal or instrumental) with effects of contrast, but now a work in which a solo instrument (or occasionally two or three solo instruments) is contrasted with a large ensemble or orchestra; hence *solo concerto* (p. 224).

concert overture An overture written as a self-contained concert piece, not as the opening of a larger work.

consonance An interval or chord that sounds smooth and harmonious, as opposed to a dissonance; also *concord* (p. 29).

continuo 1 A term (abbreviated from *basso continuo*) for a type of accompaniment played, usually on a keyboard or a plucked instrument with or without a sustaining instrument, from a notated bass line to which figures may have been added to indicate the required harmony (p. 111). **2** The group of instrumentalists playing a continuo part.

contralto A female voice with a range lower than a soprano (p. 63).

counterpoint The simultaneous combination of two or more melodies, or POLYPHONY; hence *contrapuntal* (p. 30).

countersubject A subsidiary theme played simultaneously with the subject of a fugue (pp. 154–5).

countertenor A male voice with the highest range, similar to that of an alto (p. 64).

courante A moderately fast Baroque dance in triple meter, often the second movement of a SUITE; also *corrente*.

crescendo Getting louder.

cyclic form A form in which themes recur in more than one movement of the same work.

da capo An Italian term, meaning "from the head", placed at the end of a piece as an instruction to the performer to repeat the first part of the music up to a given point; hence *da capo aria* (p. 117).

development The process of developing (expanding, modifying, transforming, etc.) themes and motifs; the section of a movement in which development takes place (p. 35).

diatonic Based on a major or minor scale rather than a CHROMATIC one; hence *diatonic scale* (p. 21).

diminished interval An interval that has been reduced by a semitone (p. 20).

diminuendo Getting quieter.

diminution The shortening of time values of the notes of a melody (usually by halving them).

dissonance An interval or chord that sounds rough, not harmonious like a consonance; also *discord* (p. 29).

dominant The fifth step or degree of the scale; its key is the main complementary one to the tonic in, for example, sonata form (p. 26).

dotted note In notation, a note after which a dot has been placed to increase its time value by half (p. 16).

double 1 Lower in pitch by an octave; hence *double bass*. 2 A VARIATION.

double bar A pair of vertical lines to mark the end of a piece or a substantial section of it.

downbeat The accented beat at the beginning of a measure, indicated by a downward stroke of a conductor's stick, and sometimes anticipated by an UPBEAT.

duo A work for two performers (or a group who play such a work); also *duet*.

duple meter A meter in which there are two beats in each measure (p. 17).

duplet A pair of notes occupying the time normally taken by three of the same note value.

dynamics The gradations of loudness in music (p. 31).

electronic music Music in which electronic equipment plays a part.

electrophone A generic term for instruments that produce their sound by electric or electronic means (p. 43).

ensemble 1 A small group of performers. 2 A number in an opera or large choral work for two or more solo singers. 3 The quality of coordination in a performance by a group.

episode An intermediate passage, e.g. a section of a fugue or a rondo between entries of the subject.

étude The French term for a STUDY.

exposition The first section of a work, particularly of a movement in sonata form, in which the main themes are stated (p. 35).

expressionism A term borrowed from painting and literature for music designed to express a state of mind.

fanfare A ceremonial flourish for trumpets or other brass instruments.

fantasia In the Renaissance, a contrapuntal instrumental piece; later, a piece in free, improvisatory style; also *fantasy, phantasia, fancy*.

fermata The sign (⌒) indicating that a note or rest should be prolonged; also *pause*.

figured bass A system of notating the harmonies in a CONTINUO part.

finale The last movement of a work or the closing ensemble of an act of an opera.

flat In notation, the sign (♭) indicating that the pitch of a note should be lowered by a semitone; also *double flat* (♭♭) (p. 21).

florid A term used to describe a melody that is highly ornamented; also *fioritura*.

form The organization or structure of a piece of music (p. 34).

forte, fortissimo (f, ff) Loud, very loud.

French overture A piece in two sections (a pompous, jerky introduction followed by a fugue) that originated in the late seventeenth century as an introduction to an opera or ballet.

fugal In the style of a FUGUE.

fugato A passage in fugal style.

fugue A type of composition (or a technique) in which imitative polyphony is used systematically (p. 37).

galant A term for light, elegant, tuneful eighteenth-century music of no great emotional weight (p. 164).

galliard A lively sixteenth- and early seventeenth-century court dance in triple meter, often paired with a PAVAN.

gavotte A fast Baroque dance in quadruple meter, beginning on the third beat of the measure, often a movement of a SUITE.

Gebrauchsmusik A German term, meaning "functional music", used in the 1920s for music with a social or educational purpose.

Gesamtkunstwerk A German term, meaning "total art work", which Wagner used for his later music-dramas, in which music, poetry, drama, and the visual arts were all part of his concept.

gigue A fast Baroque dance usually in compound meter, often the last movement of a SUITE; also *jig*.

glissando A rapid instrumental slide up or down the scale.

Gregorian chant A repertory of PLAINSONG associated with Pope Gregory I (p. 69).

ground bass A bass melody repeated several times while upper parts have varying music (p. 37).

group A group of themes in a sonata form exposition; hence *first group*, *second group* (p. 36).

harmony The combination of tones to produce chords, and the relationship of successive chords; hence *harmonic*, *harmonize* (p. 27).

harmonics The sounds heard together when a tone is produced by a vibrating string or air column, through its vibrations in parts (two halves, then thirds, etc.); hence *harmonic series*.

heterophony A texture in which several different versions of the same melody are stated simultaneously; hence *heterophonic*.

hocket A medieval technique of staggering rests and short phrases between two or more voices to give a "hiccup" effect.

homophony A texture in which the parts generally move together – a melody with accompanying chords; hence *homophonic* (p. 30).

hymn A song of praise, usually in several stanzas, sung congregationally.

idée fixe A term used by Berlioz for a recurring theme in his symphonic works (p. 240).

idiophone A generic term for instruments that, when they are struck, produce the sound themselves (p. 43).

imitation A polyphonic technique in which the melodic shape of one voice is repeated by another, usually at a different pitch; hence *imitative counterpoint* (p. 30).

impressionism A term borrowed from painting to describe music that is intended to convey an impression rather than a dramatic or narrative idea (p. 301).

impromptu A short piece, usually for piano, that suggests improvisation.

improvisation Spontaneous performance without notated music but often with reference to a tune or chord progression.

incidental music Music composed as a background to, or interlude in, a stage production.

indeterminacy The compositional principle of leaving elements to chance (ALEATORY MUSIC) or at the discretion of the performer.

interval The distance between two notes (p. 20).

inversion 1 The rearrangement of the notes of a chord so that the lowest note is no longer the fundamental one. 2 The performance of a melody "upside-down", with the intervals from the starting note applied in the opposite direction.

isorhythm A fourteenth-century technique whereby a scheme of time-values is repeated, usually to a plainsong melody; hence *isorhythmic motet*.

Italian overture A piece in three sections (fast–slow–fast/dance) that originated in the early eighteenth century as an introduction to an opera or other vocal work.

jazz A style of popular music combining melodic improvisation with syncopated rhythms and harmonies involving microtonally altered or "bent" notes (pp. 401ff.).

jig GIGUE.

Kapellmeister The German term for the musical director of a prince's private chapel or other musical establishment.

key 1 The TONALITY and major or minor scale of a passage of music according to the note to which it is gravitating; hence *key note* (pp. 25, 26, 32). 2 The lever depressed by the player on a keyboard instrument.

key signature The group of sharp or flat signs at the beginning of each STAFF indicating the KEY (p. 26).

largo, larghetto Slow and grandly, slightly less slow; a slow movement.

lai A medieval song form (p. 72).

leading tone The seventh degree of the scale, a semitone below the tonic, to which it therefore gives a feeling of leading.

legato Smoothly, not STACCATO, indicated by a SLUR.

leger lines Small extra lines above or below the STAFF for notes too high or low to be accommodated on the staff itself; also *ledger lines* (p. 19).

leitmotif A German term, meaning "leading motif", used (chiefly by Wagner) for a recognizable theme or musical idea that symbolizes a person or a concept in a dramatic work.

lento Very slow.

libretto The text of an opera (or oratorio), or the book in which the text is printed.

lied The German word for "song", used specifically for nineteenth-century German songs for voice and piano; plural *lieder* (p. 226).

madrigal A Renaissance secular contrapuntal work for several voices that originated in Italy and later also flourished in England (p. 86).

maestro di cappella The Italian term for the music director of a prince's private chapel or other musical establishment.

Magnificat The hymn to the Virgin Mary, often set to music for liturgical use.

major The name given to a SCALE in which the distance from the first note to the third is four semitones, applied to keys, chords, intervals (pp. 20, 25).

manual A keyboard played with the hands, as opposed to a pedalboard, chiefly used with reference to the organ and harpsichord.

Mass The main service of the Roman Catholic church, frequently set to music for liturgical use (pp. 68ff, 74).

mazurka A Polish dance in triple meter.

measure A metrical division of music marked off by vertical lines (barlines); also *bar* (p. 17).

Meistersinger A member of a guild of German merchant musicians which flourished from the fourteenth century to the seventeenth.

melisma A group of notes sung to the same syllable; hence *melismatic*.

mélodie A French word for "song", used specifically for nineteenth- and twentieth-century French songs for voice and piano.

melody A succession of notes of varying pitch with a recognizable shape or tune; hence *melodic* (pp. 19–24).

membranophone A generic term for instruments that produce their sound from stretched skins or membranes (p. 43).

meter The grouping of beats into a regular pulse; hence *metrical* (p. 17).

metronome A device (mechanical or electrical) that sounds an adjustable number of beats per minute; hence *metronome mark*.

mezzo- Half, medium; hence *mezzo-forte* (*mf*), *mezzo-piano* (*mp*).

mezzo-soprano A female voice with a range halfway between a soprano and a contralto or alto (p. 63).

Minnesinger The German equivalent of a TROUBADOUR.

minor The name given to a SCALE in which the distance from the first to the third notes is three semitones, applied to keys, chords, intervals (pp. 20, 25).

minuet A moderate dance in triple meter, often a movement of a Baroque SUITE and later the third (occasionally second) movement of Classical forms like the symphony, string quartet, and sonata.

mode A term used to describe the pattern of tones and semitones within an octave, applied particularly to the eight church modes used in the Middle Ages; hence *modal*, *modality* (p. 27).

moderato At a moderate pace.

modulation The process of changing from one KEY to another in the course of a piece (p. 26).

monody A term for music consisting of a single line, applied to the type of accompanied song that flourished in Italy around 1600 (p. 111).

monophony A single line of melody without accompaniment, as opposed to polyphony; hence *monophonic* (pp. 30, 92).

motet A polyphonic choral work, usually with a Latin text, for use in the Roman Catholic church, that was one of the most important forms from the thirteenth century to the eighteenth (pp. 75–6).

motif A short, recognizable musical idea; also *motive* (p. 32).

motto A brief motif or phrase that recurs during a work.

movement A self-contained section of a larger composition.

musical An abbreviated term for musical comedy, a stage show that incorporates elements of opera and operetta with popular song.

music-drama Wagner's term for his later type of opera.

musique concrète Music in which real (or "concrete") sounds are electronically recorded (p. 340).

mute A device used on instruments to muffle the tone (Italian: *sordino*).

natural In notation, the sign (♮) indicating that a note is not to be sharp or flat (p. 21).

neo-classical A term describing the music of some twentieth-century composers whose techniques draw on those of the Baroque and Classical periods (p. 337).

neume A sign used in medieval notation showing the groups of notes to which a syllable should be sung.

nocturne A piece that evokes night, usually a short, lyrical piano piece (pp. 222, 251).

nonet A work for nine performers.

note The written symbol for a tone of definite pitch; also the tone itself.

obbligato A term for an instrumental part that is essential to a composition, second in importance only to the principal melody.

octave The interval between two notes of the same name, 12 semitones (an octave) apart (p. 20).

octet A work for eight performers.

ode 1 In ancient Greece a sung celebratory poem. **2** In the seventeenth and eighteenth centuries, a cantata-like work celebrating events, birthdays, etc.

Office The eight daily services (apart from Mass) of the Roman Catholic church.

opera A drama set to music (p. 113).

opera buffa Italian eighteenth-century comic opera.

opéra comique French opera, normally with spoken dialogue (not just "comic opera" and not necessarily comic at all).

opera seria Italian eighteenth-century opera on a heroic or tragic subject.

operetta Light opera with spoken dialogue, songs, and dances (p. 391).

opus The Latin word for "work", used with a number to identify a work in a composer's output.

oratorio An extended setting of a text on a religious topic for soloists, chorus, and orchestra (p. 115).

orchestration The art and technique of writing effectively for an orchestra or large group of instruments.

Ordinary The parts of the Mass with fixed texts that remain the same each day, as opposed to the Proper (table, p. 70).

organum A type of medieval polyphony in which one voice or more is added to a plainsong (p. 74).

ostinato A musical figure that is persistently repeated while the other elements are changing; hence *basso ostinato*, a GROUND BASS.

overture A piece of orchestral music introducing a larger work; also CONCERT OVERTURE, FRENCH OVERTURE, ITALIAN OVERTURE.

part **1** The written music for a performer or performing section in an ensemble, e.g. the violin part. **2** In polyphonic music a "strand", line, or voice, e.g. two-part harmony, four-part counterpoint; hence *part-writing*, *partsong*, a song for several parts.

passacaglia A GROUND BASS movement, in slow or moderate triple meter, in the Baroque period.

passing tone A tone, foreign to the harmony with which it sounds, linking by step two tones that are (normally) part of the harmony.

Passion An extended oratorio-like setting of the story of the crucifixion (p. 115).

pavan A slow, stately sixteenth- and early seventeenth-century court dance in duple meter, often paired with a GALLIARD: also *pavane*.

pedalboard A keyboard (e.g. on an organ) played by the feet.

pedal point A sustained tone, usually in the bass, round or above which the other parts proceed.

pentatonic A term used for a mode or scale consisting of only five tones (p. 21).

phrase A group of tones, often a unit of a melody, longer than a motif (p. 32).

piano, pianissimo (p, pp) Quiet, very quiet.

pitch The highness or lowness of a sound (p. 19).

pitch class A term for all notes of the same name, such as C or A♭.

pizzicato A direction to pluck rather than bow the strings of a string instrument.

plainsong Liturgical chant to Latin texts used since the Middle Ages, also known as GREGORIAN CHANT.

polonaise A stately Polish dance in triple meter.

polyphony A texture in which two or more independent melodic lines are combined, as opposed to heterophony, homophony, monophony; hence *polyphonic* (pp. 30, 74).

prelude A short instrumental work originally intended to precede another, but from the nineteenth century a short, self-contained piece usually for piano.

presto, prestissimo Very fast, very fast indeed.

program music Instrumental music that is narrative or descriptive of some non-musical idea, often literary or pictorial (p. 221).

progression A musically logical succession of chords; hence *harmonic progression*, *chord progression*.

Proper The parts of the Mass text that vary from day to day according to the church calendar, as opposed to the Ordinary (table, p. 70).

quadruple meter A meter in which there are four beats in each measure (p. 17).

quarter-tone An interval half the size of a semitone.

quartet A work for four performers (or a group that plays such a work).

quintet A work for five performers.

ragtime A type of American popular music characterized by syncopated melody, usually for piano (p. 400).

rallentando Slowing down.

recapitulation The third main section in a movement in sonata form, in which the thematic material stated in the exposition is repeated in the home key (p. 35).

recitative A type of writing for the voice with the rhythm and inflections of speech, used in opera, oratorio, and cantatas by the soloists (pp. 114–15).

refrain A verse of a song or vocal work that recurs after each new verse or stanza.

Requiem The Roman Catholic Mass for the dead, frequently set to music.

resolution The progression from dissonant, unstable harmony to consonant harmony.

rest In notation, one of several symbols corresponding to a given number of beats or bars, indicating a period of silence (p. 16).

rhythm The distribution of sounds into groups with a perceptible meter or pulse (p. 15).

ricercare A Renaissance instrumental work that usually displays skillful application of counterpoint; also *ricercar*.

ripieno The large group of instrumentalists in a CONCERTO GROSSO.

ritardando Becoming slower.

ritenuto Held back.

ritornello A passage that recurs, particularly the instrumental section of an aria or a passage for orchestra in a Baroque or Classical concerto; hence *ritornello form* (p. 36).

Rococo A term borrowed from art history to describe the decorative, elegant style of music between the Baroque and Classical periods (p. 164).

rondeau **1** A medieval polyphonic song form. **2** A seventeenth-century instrumental form, forerunner of the RONDO.

rondo A form in which a main section recurs between subsidiary sections (p. 35).

round A sung CANON in which the voices sing the same melody at the same pitch.

row SERIES.

rubato The Italian word for "robbed", used as an indication that the meter may be treated with some freedom by a performer for expressive effect.

sarabande A slow Baroque dance in triple meter often with a stress on the second beat of the measure, normally a movement of a SUITE.

scale A sequence of notes going upward or downward by step; hence *major scale*, *minor scale*, *chromatic scale* (p. 21).

scherzo 1 A lively movement in triple meter that came to replace the minuet as a symphony movement. 2 In the nineteenth century, a self-contained instrumental piece, usually for piano.

score The music-copy of a piece for several performers; hence *full score*, containing complete details of every participating voice and instrument, *short score*, a compressed version of a full score; *conducting score*, *miniature score*, *piano score*, *pocket score*, *vocal score*.

semitone Half tone, the smallest interval commonly used in Western music.

septet A work for seven performers.

sequence 1 The repetition of a phrase at a higher or lower pitch than the original. 2 A medieval and Renaissance polyphonic setting of a religious text.

serialism A method of composing using a series of tones (usually all 12 of the chromatic scale), or other musical elements, which are heard only in a particular order; hence *serial* (pp. 34, 345).

series A fixed set of tones used as the basis of a serial composition (p. 34).

sextet A work for six performers.

sforzato, sforzando (sf, sfz) Strongly accented.

sharp In notation, the sign (♯) indicating that the pitch of a note should be raised by a semitone; also *double sharp*, (p. 21).

simple meter A meter in which the main beats are grouped in twos (e.g. 2/4), unlike COMPOUND METER (p. 17).

sinfonia The Italian word for "symphony", used to designate a wide range of instrumental pieces; hence *sinfonia concertante*, a sinfonia with a concerto element; *sinfonietta*.

Singspiel A German eighteenth-century opera with spoken dialog (p. 115).

slur In notation, a curved line over a group of notes indicating that they should be smoothly joined in performance.

sonata A piece in several movements for small ensemble, soloist with accompaniment or solo keyboard; hence *sonata da camera* ("chamber sonata") and *sonata da chiesa* ("church sonata"), seventeenth- and eighteenth-century instrumental works in three or four movements; *sonatina* (pp. 168–9).

sonata form A form used from the Classical period onwards, chiefly for the first movements of large instrumental works (e.g. symphonies, string quartets, sonatas) (p. 35).

sonata-rondo form A form that combines elements of sonata form and rondo (p. 35).

song cycle A group of songs unified by their texts, a general idea, a narrative, or musical features.

soprano 1 The highest female voice (p. 63). 2 A term used for an instrument of high range, e.g. soprano saxophone.

spiritual A style of African-American folksong concerned with religious or devotional themes.

Sprechgesang A German term used to describe a vocal style between speech and song, used extensively by Schoenberg (p. 346); also *Sprechstimme*.

staccato Detached, not legato, indicated by a dot or a dash over a note.

staff The set of lines on and between which music is written; also *stave* (p. 19).

stretto 1 The overlapping of entries in the subject of a fugue. 2 A direction to the performer to increase the tempo, or a passage containing such an increase; also *stretta*.

strophic A term applied to songs in which each stanza (verse) of the text is sung to the same music.

study A piece, usually for solo instrument, intended to demonstrate or improve an aspect of performing technique; also *étude*.

Sturm und Drang A German expression, meaning "storm and stress", used for an eighteenth-century literary and artistic movement the ideals of which were to convey emotion and urgency.

subdominant The fourth step or degree of the scale.

subject A theme or a group of themes on which a work is based; hence *subject group*.

suite An instrumental work in several movements, usually a set of dances, which in the seventeenth and eighteenth centuries often took the form ALLEMANDE–COURANTE SARABANDE–optional dance movements–GIGUE (p. 119).

suspension A harmonic device whereby a tone or tones of one chord are held while the next, with which the prolonged tones are dissonant, is sounded; there is a resolution when the suspended tones fall to those of the new chord.

symphonic poem An orchestral piece based on a non-musical (literary, narrative, etc.) idea, or program (p. 223).

symphony An extended orchestral work usually in several (most often three or four) movements (p. 168).

syncopation The stressing of beats of a meter that are normally unstressed.

synthesizer A machine that produces and alters sounds electronically.

tablature A system of notation by symbols that represent the position of a performer's fingers (e.g. on a guitar) rather than the tone to be played (p. 14).

tempo The speed of a piece of music (pp. 15, 18).

tenor 1 The highest normal male voice (p. 63). 2 A term used for an instrument whose range is analogous to the tenor voice, e.g. tenor saxophone; hence *tenor clef* used by the cello.

tenuto A term telling the performer to hold a tone to its full length.

ternary form A form with three sections, the third a repetition of the first, *ABA* (p. 35).

texture The way in which the individual strands of a work are blended (p. 27).

thematic transformation A nineteenth-century process whereby themes are modified during a movement.

theme A musical idea on which a work is based, usually with a recognizable melody; hence *thematic*, *theme and variations* (p. 32).

thoroughbass CONTINUO.

through-composed A term applied to songs in which each stanza (or verse) is set to different music, as opposed to STROPHIC songs.

tie In notation, a curved line linking two notes of the same pitch, indicating that they should be one continuous sound.

timbre TONE-COLOR.

time signature The figures on the STAFF at the beginning of a piece indicating the meter and unit (p. 17).

toccata An instrumental piece in free form, usually for keyboard, intended to display the performer's technique.

tonality The feeling of gravitational pull towards a particular tone, determined by the KEY of the music (p. 25).

tone 1 A sound of definite pitch and duration. 2 The interval equal to two semitones. 3 The timbre or quality of a musical sound.

tone-color The quality of the sound of a particular instrument or voice, or a combination of them.

tone-poem SYMPHONIC POEM.

tonic The main note of a major or minor key (p. 25).

transition A subsidiary passage that leads from one more important section to another, e.g. a BRIDGE passage in sonata form.

transpose To write down or play music at a pitch other than the original one; hence *transposing instrument*, which plays a tone at a fixed interval from the written one, e.g. a clarinet in B♭ (p. 25).

treble 1 A high voice, usually a child's (p. 63). 2 A term used for an instrument of range similar to the treble voice, e.g. treble recorder; hence *treble clef* used by high instruments and a pianist's right hand.

tremolo A rapid reiteration usually of a single tone, e.g. by the trembling action of a bow of a string instrument; also *tremolando*.

triad A three-note "common" chord consisting of a fundamental tone with tones at the intervals of a 3rd and 5th above (p. 28).

trill The rapid alteration of two adjacent tones, used as a musical ornament; also *shake*.

trio 1 A work for three performers, or a group that plays such a work. 2 The middle section of a minuet, scherzo, march, etc.

trio sonata A Baroque sonata for two melody instruments and continuo (p. 119).

triple meter A meter in which there are three beats in each measure (p. 17).

triplet A group of three notes occupying the time normally taken by two of the same note value.

tritone The interval of three whole tones.

trope A passage, with or without a text, introducing or inserted into Gregorian chant.

troubadours, trouvères French poet-musicians who performed songs of courtly love at the feudal courts of Europe during the Middle Ages (p. 72).

tune A simple, singable melody.

tutti An Italian term, meaning "all the performers", used (e.g. in a concerto) to designate a passage for orchestra rather than soloist.

twelve-tone A term used to describe a technique of composition (SERIALISM) in which all 12 notes of the chromatic scale are treated equally (pp. 33, 345).

unison A united sounding of the same tone or melody; hence *unison singing*.

upbeat A weak or unaccented beat preceding the main beat (the DOWNBEAT), particularly the beat before a barline, indicated by an upward stroke of a conductor's stick.

variation A varied (elaborated, embellished, etc.) version of a given theme or tune; hence *theme and variations* (p. 37).

verismo An Italian term, meaning "realism", applied to some late nineteenth-century operas that feature violent emotions, local color, etc.

verse 1 A stanza of a song. 2 In Anglican church music, a term used for the passages for solo voice rather than choir; hence *verse anthem*.

vibrato A rapid fluctuation in pitch and/or volume, used for expressiveness and richness of sound, e.g. the "wobble" of a string player's left hand on the strings.

virelai A medieval polyphonic song form (p. 72).

vivace Vivacious.

vocalise A wordless solo vocal piece.

voice-leading The rules governing the progression of the voices in contrapuntal music; also *part-writing*.

waltz A nineteenth-century dance in triple meter.

whole tone The interval of two semitones; hence *whole-tone scale* a scale progressing in six equal tones (p. 325).

word-painting The musical illustration of the meaning of a word, or its connotation, in a vocal work.

Acknowledgements

The authors, the publisher, and Calmann & King Ltd wish to
thank the institutions and individuals who have kindly
provided photographic material for use in this book.
Museums, galleries, and some libraries are given in the
captions: other sources are listed below:

Alinari, Florence: 32
Archiv für Kunst und Geschichte: 59, pl.13
Archive Photos, New York: frontispiece, 109
Artothek, Munich: pl.9, pl.10
Clive Barda, London: 97
Imogen Barford, London: 5
Bartók Archive, Budapest: 92
Bayreuther Festspiele GmbH/Photo Bauch: 80
BBC Hulton Picture Library, London: 79
Bibliothèque Nationale, Paris: 41; 74
Bildarchiv Preussischer Kulturbesitz: 81
Trustees of the British Library, London: pl.2; 37; 42
Bureau Soviétique d'Information, Paris: 85
Chicago Symphony Orchestra/Jim Steere: 24
Giancarlo Costa, Milan: pl.15; 89
Brian Dear, Lavenham: 3, 18 (Oxford University Press): 23;
    25 (Macmillan Publishers Ltd, London)
Department of the Environment: pl.8 (reproduced by gracious
    permission of Her Majesty The Queen)
Dover Publications Inc., New York: 68
Editions Alphonse Leduc, Paris: 99
EMI Ltd, London: 113
Fotomas, London: 45; 61
Furstlich Oettingen-Wallersteinische Bibliothek und
    Kunstsammlung, Schloss Harburg: 55
Mrs Aivi Gallen-Kallela, Helsinki/Aksell Gallen-Kallelan
    Musesäätiö, Espoo: 83
Gemeentemuseum, The Hague: 17
Giraudon, Paris: pl.4
Glyndebourne Festival Opera/Guy Gravett: 93
Heritage of Music: 36; 72; 74; 82
Master and Fellows of St John's College, Cambridge: 27
Kerkelijk Bureau de Hervormde Gemeente, Haarlem: 21
Kobal Collection: 102; 105; 110
Collection H.C. Robbins Landon, Cardiff: 72
Mansell Collection, London: 51
Bildarchiv Foto Marburg: 29
Metropolitan Opera Association, New York/Photo Winnie
    Klotz: 64; 71; 96; 104
Museen der Stadt Wien: 54; 60; 73
Ampliaciones Y Reproducciones MAS, Barcelona: 48
National Library of Ireland, Dublin: 86
New York Public Library, Lincoln Center: 98

Österreichische Nationalbibliothek Bildarchiv, Vienna: 87;
    pl.11
Photo Service, Albuquerque: 22
Popperfoto: 103; 107
Redferns: 111; Redferns/Erica Echenberg: 114
Roger-Viollet, Paris: 84
Royal Collection (reproduced by gracious permission of Her
    Majesty The Queen): 58
Royal Opera House/Photo Clive Barda 78; Photo Houston
    Rogers 90
Scala, Florence: pl.1; 3; 5; 7; 12
Robert-Schumann-Haus, Zwickau: 75
Sotheby's, London: 7, 56
Mrs Sivvy Streli, Innsbruck: 95
University of Texas at Austin (Theater Arts Library, Harry
    Ransom Humanities Research Center): 112 (from the
    MGM release *Jailhouse Rock* © 1957, Loew's Incorporated
    and Avon Productions Inc.)
Courtesy of the Board of Trustees of the Victoria and Albert
    Museum, London: 50
Allan Dean Walker, Santa Monica (Cal.): 94
Val Wilmer, London: 108
Joseph P. Ziolo, Paris: 91

Examples of copyright music in Part VIII are reproduced by
    kind permission of the copyright-owners, as follows:

Bartók, *Concerto for Orchestra* (pp.360/61): copyright © 1946
    by Hawkes & Son (London) Ltd. Extract reprinted by
    permission of Boosey & Hawkes Music Publishers Ltd.
    Specifically excluded from any blanket photocopying
    arrangements.
Ives, *Three Places in New England* (p.373): Theodore Presser
    Company (Alfred A. Kalmus Ltd).
Schoenberg, *Pierrot lunaire* (p.346): Universal Edition
    (London) Ltd.
Strauss, *Till Eulenspiegel* (pp.322/323): © 1932 by C.F.
    Peters, reproduced by kind permission of Peters Edition
    Ltd, London.
Webern, *Six Bagatelles* op. 9 no. 4 (p.348): Universal Edition
    AG Vienna (Alfred A. Kalmus Ltd).

Index

Page numbers in **bold** indicate main references. Those in *italics* refer to illustration captions. Those with an asterisk (*) refer to Listening Guides.

1750–1875 Music	1750	Art and literature	History and philosophy
C. P. E. Bach: *Essay on the True Art of Playing Keyboard Instruments*			Diderot and others begin the *Encyclopédie*
			Rousseau: *Discourse on Inequality*
D. Scarlatti dies (71); J. Stamitz dies (39)		Voltaire: *Candide*	Johnson: *Dictionary*
Handel dies (74)			
Gluck: *Orfeo*; J. C. Bach moves Milan–London			
Haydn becomes *Kapellmeister* to Esterházys			
Boccherini settles as chamber composer in Madrid		Fragonard: *The Swing*	
	1775		
Mozart visit to Mannheim and on to Paris			America becomes independent
Haydn: String quartets op. 33; Mozart settles in Vienna			Kant: *The Critique of Pure Reason*
Mozart begins great series of piano concertos		Beaumarchais: *Le mariage de Figaro*	
Mozart: *Marriage of Figaro*			
Mozart: last three symphonies		Reynolds: *Master Hare*	French Revolution
Haydn's first London visit; Mozart: *The Magic Flute*, dies (35)		Blake: *Songs of Innocence*	
Haydn returns from second London visit (Symphonies 99–104); rejoins Esterházys (late Masses, 1796–1802)			
Paris Conservatory founded			
Haydn: *The Creation*	1800		
		Schiller: *William Tell*	Louisiana Purchase
Beethoven: Symphony no. 3			
Beethoven: *Fidelio*		Goethe: *Faust*, part 1; Friedrich: *Winter*	
Beethoven: Symphony no. 5		Byron: *Childe Harold*	Napoleon invades Russia
Haydn dies (77)		Austen: *Pride and Prejudice*	
Vienna Philharmonic Society founded		Goya: *The Third of May 1808*	Battle of Waterloo; Congress of Vienna
(Royal) Philharmonic Society, London, founded			
Schubert: *Erlking* (and about 150 other songs)			Schopenhauer: *The World as Will and Idea*
Rossini: *The Barber of Seville*		Constable: *The Haywain*	Hegel: *The Philosophy of Right*
Weber: *Der Freischütz*			Bolivar liberates South America
Beethoven: Choral Symphony			
Schubert: Great C major Symphony	1825		
Beethoven: late string quartets; Weber dies (39); Mendelssohn: Overture *Midsummer Night's Dream*			
Beethoven dies (56)		Delacroix: *Liberty leading the people*	Faraday discovers electrical induction
Schubert: String Quintet in C, *Winterreise*, dies (31)		Pushkin: *Eugene Onegin*	
Berlioz: *Fantastic Symphony*; Bellini: *Norma*			
Chopin: Nocturne in E♭			
Mendelssohn: *Italian Symphony*			
Schumann: *Carnaval*; Donizetti: *Lucia di Lammermoor*; Bellini dies (34)			
Schumann: *Dichterliebe*			
New York Philharmonic Symphony Society founded			
Leipzig Conservatory founded			
Berlioz: *The Damnation of Faust*			Marx: *The Communist Manifesto*; Revolutions sweep Europe; California Gold Rush
Mendelssohn dies (38)			
Chopin dies (39)	1850	Dickens: *David Copperfield*	
		Beecher: *Uncle Tom's Cabin*	
Verdi: *La traviata*; Liszt: Piano Sonata in b		Thoreau: *Walden*	
		Whitman: *Leaves of Grass*	
Schumann dies (46)		Baudelaire: *Fleurs du mal*; Flaubert, *Madame Bovary*	
Liszt: *Faust Symphony*			
Offenbach: *Orpheus in the Underworld*			Darwin: *Origin of Species*
Wagner: *Tristan und Isolde*; Gounod: *Faust*		Hugo: *Les misérables*	American Civil War begins; Unification of Italy
Brahms: Piano Concerto no. 1			Emancipation of slaves in USA
		Moreau: *Revelation*	
Smetana: *The Bartered Bride*		Dostoevsky: *Crime and Punishment*	Marx: *Das Kapital*
		Ibsen: *Peer Gynt*; Zola: *Thérèse Raquin*	
Brahms: *German Requiem*; Grieg: Piano Concerto; Wagner: *Mastersingers*		Tolstoy: *War and Peace*	
			Franco-Prussian War
			Unification of Germany
Mussorgsky: *Boris Godunov*; Smetana: *Vltava*; J. Strauss: *Fledermaus*; Verdi: *Requiem*		Degas: *Ballet Rehearsal*	
Bizet: *Carmen*, dies (36); Tchaikovsky: Piano Concerto no. 1	1875	Twain: *Tom Sawyer*	

1875–present Music	Art and literature	History and philosophy

Music

Wagner: *The Ring* performed at new Bayreuth theater; Brahms: Symphony no. 1
Tchaikovsky: Symphony no. 4, *Eugene Onegin*

Bruckner: Symphony no. 7; Wagner dies (69)

Sullivan: *The Mikado*

Verdi: *Otello*; Borodin dies (53), working on *Prince Igor*
Franck: Symphony; Wolf, great creative spell (songs) begins; Rimsky-Korsakov: *Sheherazade*
Fauré: *Requiem*

Dvořák: *New World Symphony*, String Quartet op. 96; Tchaikovsky dies (53)

Strauss: *Till Eulenspiegel*
Debussy: *L'après-midi d'un faune*

Elgar: *Enigma Variations*; Joplin: *Maple Leaf Rag*
Puccini: *Tosca*
Mahler: Symphony no. 4; Rachmaninov: Piano Concerto no. 2
Debussy: *Pelléas et Mélisande*

Ives: *The Unanswered Question*; Mahler: Symphony no. 8

Mahler: *Lied von der Erde*; Strauss: *Elektra*

Sibelius: Symphony no. 4; Strauss: *Rosenkavalier*
Ravel: *Daphnis et Chloé*; Schoenberg: *Pierrot lunaire*
Stravinsky: *Rite of Spring*; Webern: *Bagatelles*
Ives: *First Orchestral Set*
Ives: Symphony no. 4

Janàček: *Katya Kabanova*; Prokofiev: *Love for Three Oranges*; Varèse: *Amériques*

Schoenberg's first 12-tone works; Varèse: *Hyperprism*
Sibelius: Symphony no. 7; Fauré dies (79)
Berg: *Wozzeck*

Bartók: String Quartet no. 4; Webern: Symphony; Weill: *Threepenny Opera*; Louis Armstrong: *West End Blues*

Schoenberg leaves Germany for the USA
Berg: Violin Concerto; Gershwin: *Porgy and Bess*
Bartók: Music for Strings, Percussion and Celesta; Cowell: *United Quartet*;
Orff: *Carmina Burana*
Shostakovich: Symphony no. 5

Stravinsky: Symphony in C; Ellington: *Concerto for Cartie*
Copland: *Lincoln Portrait, Fanfare for the Common Man*
Bartók: Concerto for Orchestra; Britten: *Serenade*
Messiaen: *Vingt regards*; Prokofiev: *War and Peace*; Villa-Lobos: *Bachianas brasileiras*

Messiaen extends serialism in *Mode de valeurs et d'intensités*; Miles Davis: *Birth of the Cool*
Weill dies (50)
Electronic music studios, New York and Cologne
Cage: *4' 33"*; Tippett: *Midsummer Marriage*

Boulez: *Le marteau sans maître*
Stockhausen: *Gesang der Jünglinge*; Presley: *Heartbreak Hotel*
Bernstein: *West Side Story*

Britten: *War Requiem*; Cage: *Atlas eclipticalis*; Lutoslawski: *Venetian Games*
The Beatles: *Love me do*; Dylan: *Blowin' in the Wind*

Henze: *The Bassarids*; Penderecki: *St Luke Passion*; Stravinsky: *Requiem Canticles*

Stravinsky dies (81); Reich: *Drumming*

Stockhausen: *Inori*

IRCAM (Paris) opens

Art and literature

Renoir: *Boating Party*; James: *Portrait of a Lady*
Manet: *Bar at the Folies-Bergère*

Van Gogh: *Sunflowers*

Gauguin: *Two Women on the Beach*
Winslow Homer: *Coast in Winter*; Maeterlinck: *Pelléas et Mélisande*
Munch: *The Scream*

Chekhov: *The Seagull*

Cézanne: *The Bathers*
D'Annunzio: *Francesca da Rimini*

Matisse: *Red Room*

Shaw: *Pygmalion*

Braque: *Musical Forms*; Proust: *Swann's Way*;
Lawrence: *Sons and Lovers*

Monet: *Water Lilies*; Joyce: *Ulysses*; Mann: *The Magic Mountain*
Picasso: *Three Musicians*
Frost: *New Hampshire*; Pound: *Testament of François Villon*
Kandinsky: *Little Dream in Red*; Kafka: *The Trial*

Hemingway: *Farewell to Arms*

Faulkner: *Light in August*

Eliot: *Murder in the Cathedral*
Lloyd Wright: *Falling Water*, Bear Run, Pa.
Sartre: *La nausée*

Camus: *The Outsider*

Hesse: *The Glass Bead Game*

Mailer: *The Naked and the Dead*
Mies van der Rohe: Seagram Building, New York;
Wyeth: *Christina's World*; Orwell: *1984*
Pollock: *Blue Poles*

Le Corbusier: Chapel at Ronchamp; Beckett: *Waiting for Godot*

Johns: *False Start*

Warhol: *Marilyn Monroe*; Singer: *The Slave*

Moore: *Reclining Figure* (Lincoln Center, New York)

Solzhenitsyn: *The First Circle*

Utzon and others: Sydney Opera House; Bellow: *Humboldt's Gift*
Rogers and Piano: Pompidou Center, Paris

History and philosophy

Bell invents the telephone
Edison invents the phonograph

Nietzsche: *Beyond Good and Evil*

Marconi invents wireless telegraphy

Wright brothers make first powered flight
Freud: *Psychopathology of Everyday Life*
Einstein's first theory of relativity

Russell: *Our Knowledge of the External World*

World War I begins

Russian Revolution

Lindbergh makes first transatlantic flight

Wall Street crash, Depression begins

Hitler comes to power

Spanish Civil War begins

World War II begins

First atom bombs used

Russians put first Sputnik into space

Berlin Wall built
President Kennedy assassinated

America puts first men on moon

Timeline: 1875, 1900, 1925, 1950, 1975